Algebra 2

JM EDU

PREFACE

Joseph Pak was born and raised in South Korea and moved to the United States during his teenhood. Joseph graduated from high school in Texas, where he discovered his knack for studying mathematics. He received his Bachelor's degree in mathematics at the University of Texas at Austin. Subsequently, Joseph passed a content examination(135 Mathematics 8−12), which certified him to work as a mathematics instructor at Texas Public High School.

Joseph has been teaching U.S. mathematics to students in Seoul, South Korea, for over a decade, during which time he realized a desperate need for high−quality workbooks for his students. He has been researching and developing exquisite content for his workbooks to educate his students more effectively, and to mostly alleviate the hardships students often encounter when trying to tackle new concepts in mathematics.

After years of exhaustive research in math education methodology, Joseph has finally put out a series of comprehensive workbooks that include all of the following aspects:

1. 5−step systematic workbook.
    "Concept → Example → Check Point → Review Exercise → Chapter Test"

2. Detailed explanation for each topic and easy−to−understand problem−solving methods that provide a thorough understanding of the materials.

3. Step−by−step problem structure that enables students to study on their own.

4. Problems that foster creativity and thinking skills, based on a concrete understanding of the concepts.

5. A reliable and effective reference guide to preparing for standardized exams as well as school exams.

6. Detachable solution manual for ease and convenience for students.

Author's Words:

A well-structured workbook plays a critical role in students' learning experience. It serves as a very influential guide for students. I hope this book helps you realize all your inner-inquisitivity in learning mathematics, as well as contribute to the advancement of U.S. mathematics at large.

As a final note, I am thrilled that you've chosen this book to help you on this journey, and please do not hesitate to reach out to us to share your challenges, concerns, and successes. Wish you all the best of luck!

Joseph Pak
JM EDU
B.A. Mathematics —University of Texas at Austin, 2006

CONTENTS

Chapter 1. Working with Polynomials

1. Law of Exponents | 10
2. Calculating Monomials | 20
3. Calculating Polynomials: Addition and Subtraction | 28
4. Calculating Polynomials: Multiplication, Part 1 | 36
5. Calculating Polynomials: Multiplication, Part 2 | 48
6. Chapter Test | 58

Chapter 2. Factoring Polynomials

1. Factoring Binomials | 66
2. Factoring Trinomials | 74
3. Factoring by Grouping and Substitution | 84
4. Chapter Test | 94

Chapter 3. Rational Expression

1. Introduction to Rational Expression | 104
2. Addition, Subtraction and Complex Fraction | 114
3. Rational Equations | 126
4. Application of Rational Equations | 134
5. Chapter Test | 142

Chapter 4. Quadratic Equations

    1. Solving Basic Quadratic Equations | 150

    2. Complex Number | 160

    3. Completing the Square and the Quadratic Formula | 172

    4. More Complicated Quadratic Equations | 180

    5. Solutions and Coefficients of the Quadratic Equations | 184

    6. Word Problems | 196

    7. Chapter Test | 202

Chapter 5. Quadratic Functions, Part 1

    1. The Graph of $y=ax^2$ | 212

    2. Translation of the Graph | 219

    3. Application of Quadratic Functions | 228

    4. Chapter Test | 236

Chapter 6. Quadratic Functions, Part 2

    1. The Graph of $y=ax^2+bx+c$ | 246

    2. Writing Quadratic Functions | 258

    3. The Minimum and Maximum | 266

    4. Chapter Test | 274

Chapter 7. Roots and Radicals

1. The Square Roots | 284
2. Nth Roots and Rational Exponents | 292
3. Properties of Radicals, Part 1 | 302
4. Properties of Radicals, Part 2 | 308
5. Radical Equations | 316
6. Graphing Radical Functions | 322
7. Chapter Test | 336

Chapter 8. Special Functions

1. Absolute Value Functions | 346
2. Greatest Integer Functions and Piecewise Functions | 356
3. Operation of Functions | 368
4. Inverse Functions | 378
5. Chapter Test | 390

Chapter 9. Discrete Mathematics

1. Introduction to Sequences | 398
2. Introduction to Series | 408
3. Fundamental Counting Principles | 418
4. Probability | 430
5. Chapter Test | 438

Solutions Manual

Chapter 1
Working with Polynomials

1. Law of Exponents
2. Calculating Monomials
3. Calculating Polynomials: Addition and Subtraction
4. Calculating Polynomials: Multiplication, Part 1
5. Calculating Polynomials: Multiplication, Part 2
6. Chapter Test

Law of Exponents

01 Vocabulary

Definition	Examples
Constant: a number.	$3, -2, \frac{1}{3}$.
Monomial: a product of a constant and one or more variables, including a constant and a variable itself.	$5, x, 4xy^2, -4a^3b^2$.
Similar Monomial: monomials that are identical in their variables.	$2xy^2$ and $-4xy^2$ are similar. x^3y^2 and $5xy^3$ are not similar.
Degree of a monomial: the sum degrees of the variables.	Degree of x^3 is 3. Degree of $-4a^3b^2$ is $3+2=5$.
Polynomial: a monomial or a sum of monomials.	x^3-4x^2+1.
Term: each monomial in a polynomial.	The terms of x^3-4x^2+1 are $x^3, -4x^2$, and 1.
Degree of a polynomial: highest degree of its terms.	Degree of a polynomial $x^3-4x^2y^2+y^2$ is $2+2=4$.
Coefficient: the constant factor of each terms.	Coefficient of $-4x^2$ is -4.

02 Using Property of Exponents

The expression a^m where m is a positive integer represents the product that we obtain when base a is used as a factor m times.

$$\overbrace{a \times a \times a \times \cdots \times a \times a}^{m} = a^m$$

In this section, the law of exponents can be used to evaluate numerical expressions and to simplify algebraic expressions. A simplified algebraic expression contains only positive exponents.

03 Law of Exponent - Addition

Assume a is a real number and m and n are positive integers.

$a^m \times a^n = a^{m+n}$ → When the bases are identical, add the exponents.

Concept Check

1. $a^2 \times a^3 = (a \times a) \times (a \times a \times a) = a^5 = a^{2+3}$

Example 1

Simplify the expression.

① $a^3 \times a^4$ ② $b \times b^6 \times b^3 \times b^2$ ③ $a^4 \times a^5 \times b^4 \times b^7$

Solution

① $a^3 \times a^4 = a^{3+4} = a^7$
② $b \times b^6 \times b^3 \times b^2 = b^{1+6+3+2} = b^{12}$
③ $a^4 \times a^5 \times b^4 \times b^7 = (a^4 \times a^5) \times (b^4 \times b^7) = a^{4+5}b^{4+7} = a^9 b^{11}$

Check Point 1

Simplify the expression.

① $a^5 \times a^7$

② $a^3 \times b^4 \times a^5 \times b^2$

③ $2^3 \times 5^3 \times 5^4 \times 2^5 \times 5^2$

④ $a^4 \times b^2 \times a^x \times b^y$, x and y are positive integers.

04 Law of Exponent – Multiplication

Assume a is a real number and m, n, and r are positive integers.

1. $(a^m)^n = a^{mn}$ → When the bases are identical, multiply the exponents.
2. $((a^m)^n)^r = a^{mnr}$

Concept Check

1. $(a^2)^3 = a^2 \times a^2 \times a^2 = a^6 = a^{2+2+2} = a^{2\times 3}$
2. $((a^2)^3)^4 = (a^{2\times 3})^4 = a^{2\times 3 \times 4}$

Example 2

Simplify the expression.

① $(a^3)^4$
② $(b^3)^2 \times (b^2)^4$
③ $(a^2)^4 \times (b^5)^3$
④ $((b^2)^4)^3$

Solution

① $(a^3)^4 = a^{3\times 4} = a^{12}$
② $(b^3)^2 \times (b^2)^4 = b^{3\times 2} \times b^{2\times 4} = b^6 \times b^8 = b^{6+8} = b^{14}$
③ $(a^2)^4 \times (b^5)^3 = a^{2\times 4} \times b^{5\times 3} = a^8 b^{15}$
④ $((b^2)^4)^3 = b^{2\times 4 \times 3} = b^{24}$

Check Point 2 Solutions_Page 2

Simplify the expression.

① $(a^3)^7$
② $(b^5)^3 \times (b^2)^4$
③ $((a^2)^3)^2 \times (b^4)^2$
④ $(a^2)^x \times a^x \times (b^3)^y$, x and y are positive integers.

05 Law of Exponent – Subtraction

Assume a is a real number where $a \neq 0$ and m and n are positive integers.

$$a^m \div a^n = \begin{cases} a^{m-n}, & m > n \\ 1, & m = n \\ \dfrac{1}{a^{n-m}}, & m < n \end{cases} \rightarrow \text{When the bases are identical, subtract the exponents.}$$

Concept Check

1. $a^5 \div a^3 = \dfrac{a^5}{a^3} = \dfrac{a \times a \times a \times a \times a}{a \times a \times a} = a^2 = a^{5-3}$

2. $a^3 \div a^3 = \dfrac{a^3}{a^3} = \dfrac{a \times a \times a}{a \times a \times a} = 1$

3. $a^3 \div a^5 = \dfrac{a^3}{a^5} = \dfrac{a \times a \times a}{a \times a \times a \times a \times a} = \dfrac{1}{a^2} = \dfrac{1}{a^{5-3}}$

Example 3

Simplify the expression.

① $a^4 \div a^2$ ② $(a^3)^4 \div (a^6)^2$

③ $b^5 \div (b^2)^4$ ④ $b^4 \div b^2 \div b^5$

Solution

① $a^4 \div a^2 = a^{4-2} = a^2$ ② $(a^3)^4 \div (a^6)^2 = a^{12} \div a^{12} = 1$

③ $b^5 \div (b^2)^4 = b^5 \div b^8 = \dfrac{1}{b^{8-5}} = \dfrac{1}{b^3}$ ④ $b^4 \div b^2 \div b^5 = b^{4-2} \div b^5 = b^2 \div b^5 = \dfrac{1}{b^{5-2}} = \dfrac{1}{b^3}$

Check Point 3

Simplify the expression.

① $a^6 \div a^3$ ② $a^7 \div (a^2)^2$

③ $(b^6)^2 \div (b^4)^3$ ④ $b^5 \div (b^2)^2 \div (b^3)^4$

06 Law of Exponent – Distribution

Assume a and b are real numbers and m, n, and r are positive integers.

1. $(ab)^r = a^r b^r$
2. $(a^m b^n)^r = a^{mr} b^{nr}$
3. $\left(\dfrac{a}{b}\right)^r = \dfrac{a^r}{b^r}$, $b \neq 0$
4. $\left(\dfrac{a^m}{b^n}\right)^r = \dfrac{a^{mr}}{b^{nr}}$, $b \neq 0$

Concept Check

1. $(ab)^4 = ab \times ab \times ab \times ab = \overbrace{(a \times a \times a \times a)}^{4} \times \overbrace{(b \times b \times b \times b)}^{4} = a^4 b^4$

2. $(a^2 b^3)^3 = a^2 b^3 \times a^2 b^3 \times a^2 b^3$
$= (a^2 \times a^2 \times a^2) \times (b^3 \times b^3 \times b^3) = a^6 \times b^9 = a^{2 \cdot 3} \times b^{3 \cdot 3}$

3. $\left(\dfrac{a}{b}\right)^4 = \dfrac{\overbrace{a \times a \times a \times a}^{4}}{\underbrace{b \times b \times b \times b}_{4}} = \dfrac{a^4}{b^4}$

4. $\left(\dfrac{a^2}{b^3}\right)^3 = \dfrac{a^2}{b^3} \times \dfrac{a^2}{b^3} \times \dfrac{a^2}{b^3} = \dfrac{a^6}{b^9} = \dfrac{a^{2 \cdot 3}}{b^{3 \cdot 3}}$

Example 4

Simplify the expression.

① $(ab)^8$

② $(-2a^2)^4$

③ $\left(\dfrac{x^3}{y}\right)^5$

④ $\left(\dfrac{-3x^2}{y^3}\right)^3$

Solution

① $(ab)^8 = a^8 \times b^8 = a^8 b^8$

② $(-2a^2)^4 = (-2)^4 \times (a^2)^4 = 16a^8$

③ $\left(\dfrac{x^3}{y}\right)^5 = \dfrac{(x^3)^5}{y^5} = \dfrac{x^{15}}{y^5}$

④ $\left(\dfrac{-3x^2}{y^3}\right)^3 = \dfrac{(-3)^3(x^2)^3}{(y^3)^3} = \dfrac{-27x^6}{y^9} = -\dfrac{27x^6}{y^9}$

14 Chapter 1. Working with Polynomials

Check Point 4

Simplify the expression.

① $(2a^5)^3$

② $(a^3b^2)^4$

③ $\left(-\dfrac{2x^2}{y}\right)^5$

④ $\left(\dfrac{xy^3}{3z^2}\right)^2$

Review Exercise

01 Simplify the expression.

(1) $(x^4)^5 \times (y^3)^4 \times y^2$

(2) $a^4 \times (b^2)^5 \times (a^2)^3 \times (b^3)^2$

(3) $(-3)^2 \times (x^3)^5 \times x^2$

(4) $(-2)^3 \times a^6 \times (a^3)^4$

(5) $4^2 \times (x^2)^4 \times x^6 \times (y^4)^2 \times y^3$

(6) $(a^4)^x \times (b^2)^{3y} \times (a^{2x})^3 \times (b^4)^2$,

x and y are positive integers.

02 Simplify the expression.

(1) $(a^2)^3 \div a^4$

(2) $(x^4)^5 \div x^4 \div (x^5)^2$

(3) $2^{10} \div 2^5 \div (2^2)^4$

(4) $a^{25} \div (a^4)^2 \div (a^3)^5$

(5) $(x^6)^5 \div (x^4)^4 \div (x^2)^6$

(6) $a^{5x} \div a^x \div (a^{3x})^2$,

x is positive integer.

03 Simplify the expression.

(1) $(x^2y)^5$

(2) $(-2x^6y^3)^2$

(3) $(3x^4y^5z^2)^3$

(4) $\left(\dfrac{2a}{b^3}\right)^4$

(5) $\left(-\dfrac{3a^3c}{b^5}\right)^3$

(6) $\left(\dfrac{c^3}{ab^4}\right)^{4x}$, x is positive integer.

04 Find the value of a and b in the following equation.

(1) $x^5 \times (y^{2b})^5 \times (x^a)^3 = x^{17}y^{20}$

(2) $\left(\dfrac{2x^{2a}}{y^{3b+1}}\right)^3 = \dfrac{8x^{12}}{y^{12}}$

(3) $(x^5)^{2a} \times (y^3)^{2b} \times y^{2b} = x^{10}y^{24}$

(4) $\left(-\dfrac{3y^{b+1}}{x^{2a-1}}\right)^3 = -\dfrac{27y^{12}}{x^9}$

Chapter 1. Working with Polynomials

Review Exercise

05 Find x in the following equation.

(1) $2^x \times 16 = 4^x$

(2) $27^4 \div 9^x = 9$

(3) $9^x \times (3^x)^4 = 27^{x-1}$

(4) $32 \div 4^{x+1} \div 8 = \dfrac{1}{2}$

06 If $k = 2^3$, find each of the following in terms of k.

(1) 64

(2) 2^{12}

(3) 4^9

(4) 8^5

18 Chapter 1. Working with Polynomials

07 Using law of exponents, simplify each of the following

(1) $5^2+5^2+5^2+5^2+5^2$

(2) $7^4+7^4+7^4+7^4+7^4+7^4+7^4$

Challenging

08 If $m=3^{n+1}$, find 9^{n+2} in terms of m.

Challenging

09 If $a=2^{b-1}$, find 4^{2b} in terms of a.

Challenging

10 Solve the equation $2^{x+2}+2^x=40$.

Challenging

11 If $m=2^{a+2}$ and $n=3^{1-a}$, find 72^a in terms of m and n.

2 Calculating Monomials

01 Multiplication of Monomials

1. Multiply (constant × constant) and (variable × variable).
2. Use law of exponents.

Concept Check

1. $2a^3 \times 3ab^2 = (2 \times 3) \times (a^3 \times ab^2) = 6a^4b^2$

2. Geometric interpretation

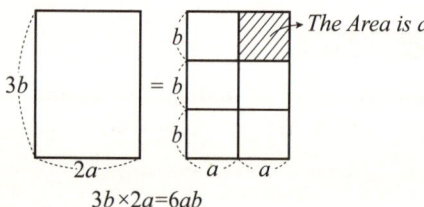

$3b \times 2a = 6ab$

The Area is ab.

Example 1

Simplify the expression.

① $4x^3 \times 5x^2$ ② $2a^2b^3 \times (-4ab^4)$

Solution

① $4x^3 \times 5x^2 = (4 \times 5) \times (x^3 \times x^2) = 20x^5$
② $2a^2b^3 \times (-4ab^4) = (2 \times (-4)) \times (a^2b^3 \times ab^4) = -8a^3b^7$

Check Point 1

Solutions_Page 4

Simplify the expression.

① $2x^3 \times 4x^6$ ② $-2xy^2 \times 5x^2y^3$ ③ $(-2a^3b^5) \times \dfrac{1}{2}ab^2$ ④ $(-3a^2b^3)^3 \times (2a^3b)^2$

20 Chapter 1. Working with Polynomials

02 Division of Monomials

1. Convert division to multiplication ⟹ $A \div B = A \times \dfrac{1}{B}$
2. Multiply (constant × constant) and (variable × variable).

Concept Check

1. $4a^5 \div 2a^3 = 4a^5 \times \dfrac{1}{2a^3} = \left(4 \times \dfrac{1}{2}\right) \times \left(a^5 \times \dfrac{1}{a^3}\right) = 2a^2$

2. $4a^2 \div \dfrac{8}{3} a^5 = 4a^2 \div \dfrac{8a^5}{3} = 4a^2 \times \dfrac{3}{8a^5}$
   $= \left(4 \times \dfrac{3}{8}\right) \times \left(a^2 \times \dfrac{1}{a^5}\right) = \dfrac{3}{2a^3}$

Example 2

Simplify the expression.

① $4x^3 \div 2x$

② $(3x^3)^2 \div \dfrac{9}{2} x^6$

③ $6a^2 b \div \left(\dfrac{1}{2ab^3}\right)^2$

④ $\left(-\dfrac{2a^2}{b}\right)^3 \div \dfrac{12a^4}{b^2}$

Solution

① $4x^3 \div 2x = 4x^3 \times \dfrac{1}{2x} = \left(4 \times \dfrac{1}{2}\right) \times \left(x^3 \times \dfrac{1}{x}\right) = 2x^2$

② $(3x^3)^2 \div \dfrac{9}{2} x^6 = 9x^6 \div \dfrac{9x^6}{2} = 9x^6 \times \dfrac{2}{9x^6} = \left(9 \times \dfrac{2}{9}\right) \times \left(x^6 \times \dfrac{1}{x^6}\right) = 2$

③ $6a^2 b \div \left(\dfrac{1}{2ab^3}\right)^2 = 6a^2 b \div \dfrac{1}{4a^2 b^6} = 6a^2 b \times 4a^2 b^6 = (6 \times 4) \times (a^2 b \times a^2 b^6) = 24 a^4 b^7$

④ $\left(-\dfrac{2a^2}{b}\right)^3 \div \dfrac{12a^4}{b^2} = -\dfrac{8a^6}{b^3} \div \dfrac{12a^4}{b^2} = -\dfrac{8a^6}{b^3} \times \dfrac{b^2}{12a^4}$
   $= -\left(8 \times \dfrac{1}{12}\right) \times \left(\dfrac{a^6}{b^3} \times \dfrac{b^2}{a^4}\right) = -\dfrac{2}{3} \times \dfrac{a^2}{b} = -\dfrac{2a^2}{3b}$

Check Point 2

Simplify the expression.

① $8x^5 \div 6x^3$

② $(2a^2)^3 \div 8a^6 b^2$

③ $\dfrac{2}{3} x^3 y^5 \div (2x^2 y^2)^2$

④ $\left(-\dfrac{b^2}{2a}\right)^5 \div \dfrac{4b^{10}}{a^2} \div \dfrac{1}{2b^2}$

03 Mixed Multiplication and Division

Follow the rules below.

1. If there are parentheses, first use the law of exponent to solve them.
2. Convert division to multiplication.
3. Multiply constants with constants and variables with variables.

Concept Check

$3a^4 \times (-2a)^2 \div (3a^2)^2$ → Given

$= 3a^4 \times 4a^2 \div 9a^4$ → Use the law of exponent to solve the parentheses

$= 3a^4 \times 4a^2 \times \dfrac{1}{9a^4}$ → Convert division to multiplication

$= \left(3 \times 4 \times \dfrac{1}{9}\right) \times \left(a^4 \times a^2 \times \dfrac{1}{a^4}\right)$ → Multiply constants with constants and variables with variables

$= \dfrac{4}{3}a^2$ → Simplify

Example 3

Simplify the expression.

① $4x^3y^4 \times (2xy^2)^2 \div x^2y^5$ ② $(-3a^2b^3)^2 \div (a^2b)^3 \times 5ab^2$

Solution

① $4x^3y^4 \times (2xy^2)^2 \div x^2y^5 = 4x^3y^4 \times 4x^2y^4 \times \dfrac{1}{x^2y^5}$

$= (4 \times 4) \times \left(x^3y^4 \times x^2y^4 \times \dfrac{1}{x^2y^5}\right) = 16 \times x^3y^3 = 16x^3y^3$

② $(-3a^2b^3)^2 \div (a^2b)^3 \times 5ab^2 = 9a^4b^6 \div a^6b^3 \times 5ab^2$
$= 9a^4b^6 \times \dfrac{1}{a^6b^3} \times 5ab^2 = (9 \times 5) \times \left(a^4b^6 \times \dfrac{1}{a^6b^3} \times ab^2\right)$
$= 45 \times \dfrac{b^5}{a} = \dfrac{45b^5}{a}$

Check Point 3

Simplify the expression.

① $5y^2 \times 2x^4y \div (x^3y)^2$

② $2x^3y \div (3xy^3)^2 \times 6y^5$

③ $(-2ab)^3 \times \left(\dfrac{3a}{b^2}\right)^2 \div \dfrac{4a^3}{3b^5}$

④ $8a^2 \div (-3a^3b)^2 \times \left(-\dfrac{3}{2}b^2\right)^3$

Review Exercise

01 Simplify the expression.

(1) $2x^3y \times 5x^2y^5$

(2) $ab^3 \times a^2b^4c^3$

(3) $4x^2 \times 2xy$

(4) $(2a^2)^2 \times 5a^2b^4$

(5) $(4x^3)^2 \times 3x^3y^2$

(6) $(-3x^4y)^2 \times (2x^2y^3)^3$

02 Simplify the expression.

(1) $(a^2b)^3 \times ab^4 \times (a^3)^5$

(2) $3ab^2 \times (2a^4)^2 \times (3a^3b)^2$

(3) $(-2a^2b)^3 \times (-ab^2)^4 \times \left(\dfrac{a^2b^3c}{2}\right)^2$

(4) $(a^2c)^2 \times \left(-\dfrac{b^3c^2}{4}\right)^3 \times (-4ab^2)^2$

04 Simplify the expression.

(1) $(-4x^3y)^3 \div (-2xy^2)^2$

03 Simplify the expression.

(1) $b^5 \div (ab^3)^2$

(2) $(4a^2bc^5)^3 \div (8b^3c^2)^2$

(2) $2x^3y^2 \div 8x^5y$

(3) $(ab^2)^2 \div \left(-\dfrac{3b}{2a^3}\right) \div \left(-\dfrac{a^2}{3b^2}\right)^2$

(4) $(4ab^2)^3 \div (8a^2b^3)^2 \div 24ab^4$

(3) $(-2x^2y^3)^3 \div (4x^3y^4)^2$

(4) $(x^2y^4)^2 \div (5x^3y)^2$

Review Exercise

05 Simplify the expression.

(1) $2^4 \times 5^3 \div (5^2)^3 \div (2^3)^4$

(2) $(3^2)^2 \times 15^4 \div 15^5 \times 9^2$

(3) $14^3 \div 49^2 \div (2^4)^2 \times (7^2)^2$

(4) $2a^2b \times 6ab^4 \div 8a^3b^7$

(5) $3x^2y^3 \times 2x^2y \div 9xy^5$

(6) $(-5x^3)^2 \div \dfrac{5y^2}{4x^5} \times (2x^2y^3)^2$

06 Simplify the expression.

(1) $(2x^2y^4)^3 \div (4xy^2)^2 \times (5x^4y^3)^2$

(2) $4abc \div (ab^2)^2 \div 6a^4bc^2 \times (2a^3bc)^3$

(3) $3xy^3 \times 4x^3y^2 \div 8x^3y^5 \div 6x^5$

(4) $12ab^2 \div (2b^3a^2)^3 \times (4a^3b^5) \div (6b^5)^2$

Challenging

07 Write the correct expression in □.

(1) $(-2x^2y)^4 \times \boxed{} \div (4x^3y^2)^3 = 8x^5y^4$

(2) $\boxed{} \div \dfrac{2a}{(b^2)^4} \times \dfrac{(a^3)^2}{6b^3} = \dfrac{a^4}{18b^5}$

08 If $x=2$ and $y=4$, what is the value of $x^2y^3 \times x^2y \div xy^5$?

Challenging

09 If $a=1$, $b=2$, and $c=4$, what is the value of $abc \div (ab^2)^2 \div a^4bc^2 \times (a^3bc)^3$?

3. Calculating Polynomials: Addition and Subtraction

01 Polynomials in Standard Form

To write any polynomial in standard from, look at the degree of each term and arrange the terms in order of decreasing degree. For example, the standard form of the polynomial $2+3x^2-4x$ can be written as $3x^2-4x+2$.

Example 1

Write the polynomial in standard form.

① $x^2-2x^3+x^4-x+1$ 　　　② $\frac{1}{2}y-y^2-y^3+2$

Solution

① $x^2-2x^3+x^4-x+1 = x^4-2x^3+x^2-x+1$

② $\frac{1}{2}y-y^2-y^3+2 = -y^3-y^2+\frac{1}{2}y+2$

Check Point 1

Write the polynomial in standard form.

① x^2-3x^4+2 　　　② $3x^4-5x-2x^3+1$

③ $10-2x-x^2+3x^3$ 　　　④ $2y+2+2y^3+y^4$

02 Simple Addition and Subtraction

1. Solving Parentheses

    (1) If there is a plus in front of the parentheses, leave the sign in parentheses.

    $+(A+B-C)=A+B-C$

    Example: $+(3x+2y-1)=3x+2y-1$

    (2) If there is a minus in front of the parentheses, reverse the sign in parentheses.

    $-(A+B-C)=-A-B+C$

    Example: $-(3x+2y-1)=-3x-2y+1$

2. Addition and Subtraction of Polynomials

    (1) Solve parentheses and collect similar terms.
    (2) Simplify similar terms.
    (3) Write polynomial in standard form.

Concept Check

$(7x-2)-(4x+1)$ → Given
$=7x-2-4x-1$ → Solve the parentheses
$=(7x-4x)+(-2-1)$ → Collect similar terms
$=3x-3$ → Write polynomial in standard form

Example 2

Simplify the expression.

① $(4x-2)+(3x+1)$ ② $(y-2x+3)-(3y+x-6)$
③ $(a^3-3a^2-4a-3)-(2-5a+6a^2)$ ④ $2(a-b+1)-4(5b-3a+2)$

Solution

① $(4x-2)+(3x+1)=4x-2+3x+1=(4x+3x)+(-2+1)=7x-1$
② $(y-2x+3)-(3y+x-6)=y-2x+3-3y-x+6$
$=(-2x-x)+(y-3y)+(3+6)=-3x-2y+9$
③ $(a^3-3a^2-4a-3)-(2-5a+6a^2)=a^3-3a^2-4a-3-2+5a-6a^2$
$=a^3+(-3a^2-6a^2)+(-4a+5a)+(-3-2)=a^3-9a^2+a-5$
④ $2(a-b+1)-4(5b-3a+2)=2a-2b+2-20b+12a-8$
$=(2a+12a)+(-2b-20b)+(2-8)=14a-22b-6$

Check Point 2

Solutions_Page 7

Simplify the expression.

① $(3x-4)-(7x-2)$ ② $(1-2x+x^2)+(4x^2-5x+1)$
③ $2(5a-3b)+3(1-4b+3a)$ ④ $3(2x+4y-5)-2(3x-5y+4)$

03 Addition and Subtraction in Fraction Form

1. Addition and Subtraction Methods

   (1) Find common denominator of each term.

   (2) The common denominator should be LCM(Least Common Multiple) of each denominator.

30 Chapter 1. Working with Polynomials

Concept Check

$$\frac{x-2}{2} - \frac{2x+1}{3}$$
$$= \frac{x-2}{2} \cdot \frac{3}{3} - \frac{2x+1}{3} \cdot \frac{2}{2} \quad \rightarrow \text{LCM of 2 and 3 is } 2\cdot 3$$
$$= \frac{3(x-2)-2(2x+1)}{6} \quad \rightarrow \text{Keep the denominator the same; add the numerator}$$
$$= \frac{3x-6-4x-2}{6} \quad \rightarrow \text{Multiply out the numerator}$$
$$= \frac{-x-8}{6} = -\frac{x+8}{6} \quad \rightarrow \text{Simplify the numerator}$$

2. Note the following:

   (1) If the numerator is a polynomial with two or more terms, enclose it in parentheses.

   Concept Check

   $$\frac{x-2}{2} - \frac{x+1}{4} = \frac{x-2}{2} \cdot \frac{2}{2} - \frac{x+1}{4} = \begin{cases} \dfrac{2(x-2)-x+1}{4} & \rightarrow \text{Incorrect} \\ \dfrac{2(x-2)-(x+1)}{4} & \rightarrow \text{Correct} \end{cases}$$

   (2) Numerator can be divisible when all the terms of the numerators are divisible by the denominator

   Concept Check

   $$\frac{2x-5}{4} = \frac{\cancel{2}x-5}{\cancel{4}} = \frac{x-5}{2} \quad \rightarrow \text{Incorrect}$$
   $$\frac{2x-6}{4} = \frac{\cancel{2}x-\cancel{6}}{\cancel{4}} = \frac{x-3}{2} \quad \rightarrow \text{Correct}$$

Example 3

Simplify the expression.

① $\dfrac{2x-1}{2} - \dfrac{x+3}{4}$ ② $\dfrac{3-a}{4} - \dfrac{3a-2}{5}$

③ $2x - \dfrac{3x}{4} + \dfrac{x-1}{2}$ ④ $\dfrac{1-3a+2b}{2} - \dfrac{a+2b-4}{3}$

Solution

① $\dfrac{2x-1}{2} - \dfrac{x+3}{4} = \dfrac{2x-1}{2} \cdot \dfrac{2}{2} - \dfrac{x+3}{4} = \dfrac{2(2x-1)-(x+3)}{4}$

$= \dfrac{4x-2-x-3}{4} = \dfrac{3x-5}{4}$

② $\dfrac{3-a}{4} - \dfrac{3a-2}{5} = \dfrac{3-a}{4} \cdot \dfrac{5}{5} - \dfrac{3a-2}{5} \cdot \dfrac{4}{4} = \dfrac{5(3-a)-4(3a-2)}{20}$

$= \dfrac{15-5a-12a+8}{20} = \dfrac{-17a+23}{20}$

③ $2x - \dfrac{3x}{4} + \dfrac{x-1}{2} = 2x \cdot \dfrac{4}{4} - \dfrac{3x}{4} + \dfrac{x-1}{2} \cdot \dfrac{2}{2}$

$= \dfrac{8x-3x+2(x-1)}{4} = \dfrac{8x-3x+2x-2}{4} = \dfrac{7x-2}{4}$

④ $\dfrac{1-3a+2b}{2} - \dfrac{a+2b-4}{3} = \dfrac{1-3a+2b}{2} \cdot \dfrac{3}{3} - \dfrac{a+2b-4}{3} \cdot \dfrac{2}{2}$

$= \dfrac{3(1-3a+2b)-2(a+2b-4)}{6}$

$= \dfrac{3-9a+6b-2a-4b+8}{6} = \dfrac{-11a+2b+11}{6}$

Check Point 3

Solutions_Page 7

Simplify the expression.

① $\dfrac{2-4x}{3} + \dfrac{2x-5}{2}$ ② $\dfrac{3y-1}{2} + 3 - 4y$

③ $\dfrac{a-b}{4} - \dfrac{b-a}{2}$ ④ $\dfrac{2a-b+1}{3} - \dfrac{b-3a}{4} + 1$

32 Chapter 1. Working with Polynomials

Review Exercise

01 Simplify the expression.

(1) $(2x-7)+(5-4x)$

(2) $(1-2x+x^2)-(4x^2-5x+1)$

(3) $(4x^2-2+5x)+2(3x^2+3x-7)$

(4) $(2a^3-3a^2-3a+5)$
$+(4a^3-6a^2+5a-1)$

(5) $6(2a^3-a^2+4)-3(4a^3-3a^2-4a+2)$

(6) $(a+2b-5)+(1-2a+3b)$

(7) $2(3x-y+2)-3(3y+2x+1)$

(8) $(4-y-5y^2+2x)$
$-2\left(-\dfrac{1}{2}x+y^2-5y-1\right)$

(9) $4(3a-b+1)-2(b+3)-\dfrac{1}{2}(4a-8)$

(10) $4(a^2-3a-2)+5(a^2-1)$
$-9(a^2-a+2)$

Review Exercise

02 Simplify the expression.

(1) $\dfrac{3x-1}{2}+\dfrac{x+2}{3}$

(2) $\dfrac{4x+5}{2}-\dfrac{x-1}{4}$

(3) $x+3-\dfrac{3(2-x)}{5}$

(4) $\dfrac{x+1}{4}-\dfrac{2(3-x)}{3}+\dfrac{3x-2}{2}$

(5) $\dfrac{2(3x-2y)}{5}+\dfrac{x-y+3}{4}$

(6) $\dfrac{3(2a+b-1)}{2}+\dfrac{3b-a+1}{6}$

03 Simplify the expression.

(1) $\dfrac{x-y}{2}-\dfrac{y-z}{3}-\dfrac{z-x}{6}$

(2) $\dfrac{a+b+c}{6}-\dfrac{a+b-c}{4}+\dfrac{a-b-c}{8}$

04 Write the correct expression in $\boxed{}$.

(1) $4(2x+y-3)+\boxed{}=4x-3y$

(2) $2(3a^2+a+4)-2(a^2-3a+1)-\boxed{}$
$=a^2-3$

(3) $\dfrac{3x-4y}{2}+\boxed{}=\dfrac{x+2y+8}{4}$

(4) $\dfrac{a+2b}{3}-\boxed{}-\dfrac{a-2b}{6}=\dfrac{a+b}{6}$

05 Simplify the expression.

(1) $3a-[4b-5a-\{4b+2(3b+3a)\}]$

(2) $4x-[2x^2+3x-2\{3x-(5x^2-x)+2\}]$

08 In some expression, a^2-3a-2 should be added to A, but subtracted from A by mistake. If the resulting expression is $4a^2+5a-4$,

(1) Find the expression A.

(2) Find the correct expression.

[Challenging]

06 If
$3b-2[4b-3\{b-2(5b-2a)-a\}+2a]$
$=ma+nb$,
what is the value of $m+n$?

09 If $\dfrac{x-2y}{3}-\dfrac{3x+2y}{4}=ax+by$,
what is the value of $a+b$?

[Challenging]

07 If
$3x+[x-\{2x-(4x-\boxed{})+y\}+3y]$
$=7x+8y$, find the correct expression in $\boxed{}$.

4 Calculating Polynomials: Multiplication, Part 1

To multiply two polynomials, distribute each term of the first polynomial to every term of the second polynomial. Then combine like terms if you can.

01 Monomial × Binomial

Expand the expression using distribution law.

$$a(b+c) = (a \times b) + (a \times c) = ab + ac$$

Concept Check

1. $a(3a+2) = (a \times 3a) + (a \times 2) = 3a^2 + 2a$

2. Geometric interpretation

$$a(3a+2) = 3a^2 + 2a$$

Example 1

Multiply the polynomials.

① $4(2a+3)$ ② $(y-4)2y$

③ $2x(3x^2-1)$ ④ $(2a-a^2)5a^3$

Solution

① $4(2a+3)=(4\times 2a)+(4\times 3)=8a+12$
② $(y-4)2y=(y\times 2y)+(-4\times 2y)=2y^2-8y$
③ $2x(3x^2-1)=(2x\times 3x^2)+(2x\times(-1))=6x^3-2x$
④ $(2a-a^2)5a^3=(2a\times 5a^3)+(-a^2\times 5a^3)=10a^4-5a^5$

Check Point 1

Solutions_Page 10

Multiply the polynomials.

① $2(4x+1)$ ② $4x(2x^2-5x+3)$

③ $5(3a-b)+4(2b-3a)$ ④ $\left(2a-\dfrac{1}{2}\right)(4b)-6b\left(-4+\dfrac{a}{3}\right)$

Chapter 1. Working with Polynomials

02 Binomial × Binomial

Expand the expression using the technique called FOIL (First, Outer, Inner, Last).

$$(a+b)(c+d) = (\overset{①}{a \times c}) + (\overset{②}{a \times d}) + (\overset{③}{b \times c}) + (\overset{④}{b \times d})$$
$$ \text{First} \quad \text{Outer} \quad \text{Inner} \quad \text{Last}$$
$$= ac + ad + bc + bd$$

Concept Check

1. $(a+2)(a+1) = (a \times a) + (a \times 1) + (2 \times a) + (2 \times 1)$
$$= a^2 + a + 2a + 2 = a^2 + 3a + 2$$

2. Geometric interpretation

3. Use the law of distribution
$$(a+2)(a+1) = a(a+1) + 2(a+1)$$
$$= a^2 + a + 2a + 2 = a^2 + 3a + 2$$

Example 2

Multiply the polynomials.

① $(x+2)(x+3)$

② $(2a+3)(a-4)$

③ $(x-1)(y+2)$

④ $(a-4b)(3a+2b)$

Solution

① $(x+2)(x+3) = (x \times x) + (x \times 3) + (2 \times x) + (2 \times 3)$
$ = x^2 + 3x + 2x + 6$
$ = x^2 + 5x + 6$

② $(2a+3)(a-4) = (2a \times a) + (2a \times -4) + (3 \times a) + (3 \times -4)$
$ = 2a^2 - 8a + 3a - 12$
$ = 2a^2 - 5a - 12$

③ $(x-1)(y+2) = (x \times y) + (x \times 2) + (-1 \times y) + (-1 \times 2)$
$ = xy + 2x - y - 2$

④ $(a-4b)(3a+2b) = (a \times 3a) + (a \times 2b) + (-4b \times 3a) + (-4b \times 2b)$
$ = 3a^2 + 2ab - 12ab - 8b^2$
$ = 3a^2 - 10ab - 8b^2$

Check Point 2

Solutions_Page 10

Multiply the polynomials.

① $(4a+1)(a-2)$ ② $(3x-y)(x+2)$

③ $(2x+y)(4x-3y)$ ④ $(a^2-2)(4a^2+1)$

03 Binomial × Trinomial

Expand the expression using distributive law.

$$(a+b)(c+d+e) = (a \times c) + (a \times d) + (a \times e) + (b \times c) + (b \times d) + (b \times e)$$

$$= ac + ad + ae + bc + bd + be$$

Concept Check

1. $(a+1)(a+b+2) = (a \times a) + (a \times b) + (a \times 2) + (1 \times a) + (1 \times b) + (1 \times 2)$
$ = a^2 + ab + 2a + a + b + 2$
$ = a^2 + ab + 3a + b + 2$

2. Geometric interpretation

3. Use the law of distribution

$(a+1)(a+b+2) = a(a+b+2) + 1(a+b+2)$

$\qquad = a^2 + ab + 2a + a + b + 2 = a^2 + ab + 3a + b + 2$

4. Trinomial × Binomial

$(a+b+c)(d+e) = \overset{①}{\overbrace{(a \times d)}} + \overset{②}{\overbrace{(a \times e)}} + \overset{③}{\overbrace{(b \times d)}} + \overset{④}{\overbrace{(b \times e)}} + \overset{⑤}{\overbrace{(c \times d)}} + \overset{⑥}{\overbrace{(c \times e)}}$

$\qquad = ad + ae + bd + be + cd + ce$

Example 3

Multiply the polynomials.

① $(a+2)(2a-b+4)$ ② $(x+1)(x^2-2x+3)$

Solution

① $(a+2)(2a-b+4) = (a \times 2a)+(a \times -b)+(a \times 4)+(2 \times 2a)+(2 \times -b)+(2 \times 4)$
$= 2a^2-ab+4a+4a-2b+8 = 2a^2-ab+8a-2b+8$

② $(x+1)(x^2-2x+3) = (x \times x^2)+(x \times -2x)+(x \times 3)+(1 \times x^2)+(1 \times -2x)+(1 \times 3)$
$= x^3-2x^2+3x+x^2-2x+3 = x^3-x^2+x+3$

Check Point 3

Solutions_Page 10

Multiply the polynomials.

① $(x-3)(x^2-x+1)$ ② $(2x-4y+1)(3x+y)$

③ $(2a^2-ab+b^2)(a-b)$

04 Expanding $(a+b)^2$ and $(a-b)^2$

1. $(a+b)^2 = a^2+2ab+b^2$ → $(\triangle+\bigcirc)^2 = \triangle^2+2\triangle\bigcirc+\bigcirc^2$
2. $(a-b)^2 = a^2-2ab+b^2$ → $(\triangle-\bigcirc)^2 = \triangle^2-2\triangle\bigcirc+\bigcirc^2$

Concept Check

1. Expand $(a+b)^2$ and $(a-b)^2$ by FOIL method.

   (1) $(a+b)^2 = (a+b)(a+b) = (a \times a)+(a \times b)+(b \times a)+(b \times b)$
   $= a^2+ab+ba+b^2 = a^2+2ab+b^2$

   $(a-b)^2 = (a-b)(a-b) = (a \times a)+(a \times -b)+(-b \times a)+(-b \times -b)$
   $= a^2-ab-ba+b^2 = a^2-2ab+b^2$

Chapter 1. Working with Polynomials

2. Geometric Interpretation

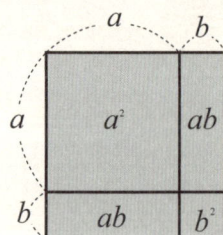 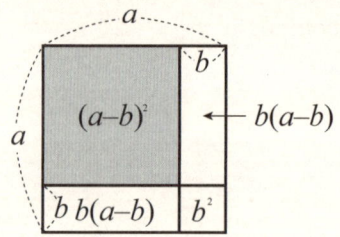

$(a+b)^2 =$ Area of the shaded square
$= a^2 + ab + ab + b^2$
$= a^2 + 2ab + b^2$

$(a-b)^2 =$ Area of the shaded square
$= a^2 - b(a-b) - b(a-b) - b^2$
$= a^2 - ba + b^2 - ba + b^2 - b^2$
$= a^2 - 2ab + b^2$

3. Note the following
   (1) $(-a-b)^2 = (a+b)^2$
      Because $(-a-b)^2 = (-a)^2 + 2(-a)(-b) + (-b)^2 = a^2 + 2ab + b^2 = (a+b)^2$.
   (2) $(-a+b)^2 = (a-b)^2$
      Because $(-a+b)^2 = (-a)^2 + 2(-a)b + b^2 = a^2 - 2ab + b^2 = (a-b)^2$.
   (3) $(a+b)^2 \neq a^2 + b^2$ and $(a-b)^2 \neq a^2 - b^2$.

Example 4

Multiply the polynomials.

① $(x+4)^2$ ② $(4a-1)^2$ ③ $(x-3y)^2$ ④ $(2a+3b)^2$

Solution

① $(x+4)^2 = x^2 + 2(x)(4) + 4^2 = x^2 + 8x + 16$
② $(4a-1)^2 = (4a)^2 - 2(4a)(1) + 1^2 = 16a^2 - 8a + 1$
③ $(x-3y)^2 = x^2 - 2(x)(3y) + (3y)^2 = x^2 - 6xy + 9y^2$
④ $(2a+3b)^2 = (2a)^2 + 2(2a)(3b) + (3b)^2 = 4a^2 + 12ab + 9b^2$

Check Point 4

Multiply the polynomials.

① $(x+2)^2$

② $(2x-5y)^2$

③ $\left(\dfrac{1}{4}+3b\right)^2$

④ $\left(-a-\dfrac{2b}{3}\right)^2$

05 Expanding $(a+b)(a-b)$

$(a+b)(a-b)=a^2-b^2 \quad \rightarrow \quad (\triangle-O)(\triangle+O)=\triangle^2-O^2$

Concept Check

1. Expand $(a+b)(a-b)$ by FOIL method.

$$(a+b)(a-b)=(a\times a)+(a\times -b)+(b\times a)+(b\times -b)$$
$$=a^2-ab+ba-b^2=a^2-b^2$$

2. Geometric Interpretation

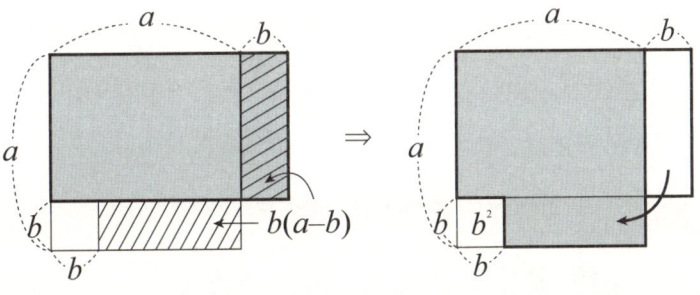

$$(a+b)(a-b)=a^2-b^2$$

3. Note the following

   (1) $(-a+b)(a+b)=(b-a)(b+a)=b^2-a^2$

   (2) $(-a-b)(a-b)=-(a+b)(a-b)=-(a^2-b^2)=b^2-a^2$

Example 5

Multiply the polynomials.

① $(a+2)(a-2)$ ② $(5x-3)(5x+3)$

③ $(x+4y)(-x+4y)$ ④ $(3a-2b)(3a+2b)$

Solution

① $(a+2)(a-2) = a^2 - 2^2 = a^2 - 4$
② $(5x-3)(5x+3) = (5x)^2 - 3^2 = 25x^2 - 9$
③ $(x+4y)(-x+4y) = (4y+x)(4y-x) = (4y)^2 - x^2 = 16y^2 - x^2$
④ $(3a-2b)(3a+2b) = (3a)^2 - (2b)^2 = 9a^2 - 4b^2$

Check Point 5

Solutions_Page 11

Multiply the polynomials.

① $(x-2y)(x+2y)$ ② $(2x-5y)(-2x-5y)$

③ $\left(\dfrac{3a}{4} - \dfrac{b}{3}\right)\left(\dfrac{3a}{4} + \dfrac{b}{3}\right)$ ④ $(a-3)(a+3)(a^2+9)$

Review Exercise

01 Multiply the polynomials.

(1) $3x(x^2-y)$

(2) $\dfrac{2x}{5}\left(25xy-\dfrac{25}{2}x^2\right)$

(3) $(a+4b^2)(-2a)$

(4) $-4a(3a-b+3)$

(5) $2a^2(2a-a^2)$

(6) $\dfrac{1}{3}(6x^2-9x+1)-\dfrac{2x}{5}(10x-15)$

(7) $-2(x^2+2x-5)-2x(x-1)$

(8) $5(x^2-1)+3(x^2+x-1)+4$

02 Multiply the polynomials.

(1) $(x-1)(2x+3)$

(2) $(3x-1)(2x-4)$

(3) $(-2y+3)(y-1)$

(4) $(1-y)(-1-3y)$

(5) $(x-y)(2x+3y)$

(6) $(a^2-2)(4a+1)$

(7) $(2a+a^2)\left(-5+\dfrac{1}{2}a\right)$

(8) $(2m^2-mn)(n^2+2mn)$

(9) $(-a+b+4)(3a+2b)$

(10) $(x+2y)(-2x-1+3y)$

Chapter 1. Working with Polynomials

Review Exercise

03 Multiply the polynomials.

(1) $(x+2)^2$

(2) $(2x-1)^2$

(3) $(x+5y)^2$

(4) $\left(\dfrac{2x}{3}-4y\right)^2$

(5) $(-3a+4b)^2$

(6) $\left(-\dfrac{2a}{3}-\dfrac{b}{2}\right)^2$

(7) $(x-3)(x+3)$

(8) $\left(x+\dfrac{1}{2}\right)\left(x-\dfrac{1}{2}\right)$

(9) $(2a-3b)(2a+3b)$

(10) $\left(\dfrac{2b}{3}-\dfrac{a}{3}\right)\left(\dfrac{2b}{3}+\dfrac{a}{3}\right)$

04 Find the correct positive integer in $\boxed{}$.

(1) $(4x+\boxed{})^2$
$=16x^2+16x+\boxed{}$

(2) $(\boxed{}x-4)^2=9x^2-\boxed{}x+16$

(3) $(4a^2+3)(\boxed{}a^2-3)$
$=16a^4-\boxed{}$

(4) $(2a-3)(2a+3)(4a^2+9)$
$=(\boxed{}a^2-9)(4a^2+9)$
$=\boxed{}a^4-\boxed{}$

46 Chapter 1. Working with Polynomials

05 Find the value of a and b in the equation given below.

(1) $(x-a)(2x+3)=2x^2+bx-12$

(2) $(x-3)(5x+a)=5x^2-11x+b$

[Challenging]

06 If $(2x+ay)(bx-5y)=cx^2-4xy-10y^2$, what is the value of $a+b+c$?

[Challenging]

07 Find the coefficient of the xy term in the expression given below.

(1) $(x-4y+3)(3x+y-2)$

(2) $(4-2x+3y)(5-2y+2x)$

08 If the coefficient of the xy of $(3x+2y-4)(ax-3y+b)$ is 8, what is the value of a?

09 If $x^2=32$ and $y^2=20$, what is the value of $\left(\dfrac{3x}{4}-\dfrac{5y}{2}\right)\left(\dfrac{3x}{4}+\dfrac{5y}{2}\right)$?

[Challenging]

10 Simplify each of the following.

(1) $(4-1)(4+1)(4^2+1)(4^4+1)$

(2) $(2^3-1)(2^3+1)(2^6+1)(2^{12}+1)$

5 Calculating Polynomials: Multiplication, Part 2

01 Special Products

1. $(a+b+c)^2 = a^2+b^2+c^2+2ab+2bc+2ca$
   $\rightarrow (\triangle^2+O^2+\nabla^2) = \triangle^2+O^2+\nabla^2+2\triangle O+2O\nabla+2\nabla\triangle$

2. $(a+b)^3 = a^3+3a^2b+3ab^2+b^3 \rightarrow (\triangle+O)^3 = \triangle^3+3\triangle^2 O+3\triangle O^2+O^3$
   $(a-b)^3 = a^3-3a^2b+3ab^2-b^3 \rightarrow (\triangle-O)^3 = \triangle^3-3\triangle^2 O+3\triangle O^2-O^3$

Concept Check

1. $(a+b+c)^2 = ((a+b)+c)^2 = (a+b)^2+2(a+b)c+c^2$
   $= a^2+b^2+c^2+2ab+2bc+2ca$

2. $(a+b)^3 = (a+b)^2(a+b) = (a^2+2ab+b^2)(a+b)$
   $= a^3+a^2b+2a^2b+2ab^2+ab^2+b^3$
   $= a^3+3a^2b+3ab^2+b^3$

3. $(a-b)^3 = (a-b)^2(a-b) = (a^2-2ab+b^2)(a-b)$
   $= a^3-a^2b-2a^2b+2ab^2+ab^2-b^3$
   $= a^3-3a^2b+3ab^2-b^3$

Example 1

Multiply the polynomials.

① $(a+2b-3)^2$ ② $(x+4)^3$ ③ $(a^2-2)^3$

Solution

① $(a+2b-3)^2 = a^2+(2b)^2+(-3)^2+2a(2b)+2(2b)(-3)+2(-3)a$
   $= a^2+4b^2+9+4ab-12b-6a$
   $= a^2+4b^2+4ab-6a-12b+9$

48 Chapter 1. Working with Polynomials

② $(x+4)^3 = x^3 + 3x^2(4) + 3x(4)^2 + 4^3 = x^3 + 12x^2 + 48x + 64$
③ $(a^2-2)^3 = (a^2)^3 - 3(a^2)^2(2) + 3a^2(2)^2 - 2^3$
   $= a^6 - 6a^4 + 12a^2 - 8$

Check Point 1

Multiply the polynomials.

① $(x+y-z)^2$ ② $(2a-3b-c)^2$

③ $(3a+2)^3$ ④ $\left(2b - \dfrac{1}{2}\right)^3$

02 Expand by Grouping

If the expression has a common part(usually a binomial), then use the substitution to multiply the polynomials.

Concept Check

$(x+y+2)(x+y-2)$ → Given
$= ((x+y)+2)((x+y)-2)$ → $x+y$ is the common part
$= (A+2)(A-2)$ → Let $x+y = A$
$= A^2 - 2^2$ → $(a+b)(a-b) = a^2 - b^2$
$= (x+y)^2 - 2^2$ → Replace $A = x+y$
$= x^2 + 2xy + y^2 - 4$ → Expand

Example 2

Multiply the polynomials by grouping.

① $(x-1+2y)(x-1-2y)$ ② $(2a-y+3)(2a+2y+3)$

Solution

① $(x-1+2y)(x-1-2y)$
$= ((x-1)+2y)((x-1)-2y)$
$= (A+2y)(A-2y) = A^2-(2y)^2$ → Let $x-1=A$
$= (x-1)^2 - 4y^2$ → Replace $A=x-1$
$= x^2 - 2x + 1 - 4y^2$

② $(2a-y+3)(2a+2y+3) = (2a+3-y)(2a+3+2y)$
$= ((2a+3)-y)((2a+3)+2y)$
$= (A-y)(A+2y) = A^2+yA-2y^2$ → Let $2a+3=A$
$= (2a+3)^2 + y(2a+3) - 2y^2$ → Replace $A=2a+3$
$= 4a^2 + 12a + 9 + 2ay + 3y - 2y^2$

Check Point 2   Solutions_Page 13

Multiply the polynomials by grouping.

① $(2x-y+4)(2x-y-4)$ ② $(a+3b-2)(3b+a+1)$

③ $(a^2-2a-1)(a^2+a-1)$ ④ $(a-1)(a+6)(a+2)(a+3)$

---

03 Numerical Calculation using Multiplication Formula

1. Calculation in square form

    $(a+b)^2 = a^2 + 2ab + b^2$

    $(a-b)^2 = a^2 - 2ab + b^2$

2. Calculation of product of two numbers

    $(a+b)(a-b) = a^2 - b^2$

Concept Check

1. $104^2 = (100+4)^2 = 100^2 + 2(100 \times 4) + 4^2 = 10{,}000 + 800 + 16 = 10{,}816$

    $99^2 = (100-1)^2 = 100^2 - 2(100 \times 1) + 1^2 = 10{,}000 - 200 + 1 = 9{,}801$

2. $101 \times 99 = (100+1)(100-1) = 100^2 - 1^2 = 10{,}000 - 1 = 9{,}999$

Example 3

Calculate the following using the multiplication formula.

① 102^2 ② 1003×997

Solution

① Use $(a+b)^2 = a^2 + 2ab + b^2$.
$102^2 = (100+2)^2 = 100^2 + 2(100 \times 2) + 2^2$
$= 10{,}000 + 400 + 4 = 10{,}404$

② Use $(a+b)(a-b) = a^2 - b^2$.
$1{,}003 \times 997 = (1{,}000+3)(1{,}000-3)$
$= 1{,}000^2 - 9 = 1{,}000{,}000 - 9 = 999{,}991$

Check Point 3

Solutions_Page 14

Calculate the following using the multiplication formula.

① 98^2 ② 9.8×10.2 ③ 101×103

---

04 Transformation of Multiplication Formula

1. $(a+b)^2 = a^2 + 2ab + b^2$ → $a^2 + b^2 = (a+b)^2 - 2ab$
   $(a-b)^2 = a^2 - 2ab + b^2$ → $a^2 + b^2 = (a-b)^2 + 2ab$
2. $(a+b)^2 = (a-b)^2 + 4ab$, $(a-b)^2 = (a+b)^2 - 4ab$
3. $a^2 + \dfrac{1}{a^2} = \left(a + \dfrac{1}{a}\right)^2 - 2 = \left(a - \dfrac{1}{a}\right)^2 + 2$
4. $\left(a + \dfrac{1}{a}\right)^2 = \left(a - \dfrac{1}{a}\right)^2 + 4$, $\left(a - \dfrac{1}{a}\right)^2 = \left(a + \dfrac{1}{a}\right)^2 - 4$

Example 4

Suppose $a+b=4$ and $ab=-2$. Find each of the following.

① a^2+b^2 ② $(a-b)^2$ ③ $\dfrac{1}{a}+\dfrac{1}{b}$

Solution

① $a^2+b^2=(a+b)^2-2ab=4^2-2(-2)=16+4=20$
② $(a-b)^2=(a+b)^2-4ab=4^2-4(-2)=16+8=24$
③ $\dfrac{1}{a}+\dfrac{1}{b}=\dfrac{1}{a}\cdot\dfrac{b}{b}+\dfrac{1}{b}\cdot\dfrac{a}{a}=\dfrac{b+a}{ab}=\dfrac{4}{-2}=-2$

Check Point 4

Solutions_Page 14

Suppose $x-y=-5$ and $xy=3$. Find each of the following.

① x^2+y^2 ② $(x+y)^2$ ③ $\dfrac{x}{y}+\dfrac{y}{x}$

Remember these as Formulas!

1. $(a\pm b)^2=a^2\pm 2ab+b^2$
2. $(a+b)(a-b)=a^2-b^2$
3. $(a+b+c)^2=a^2+b^2+c^2+2ab+2bc+2ca$
4. $(a\pm b)^3=a^3\pm 3a^2b+3ab^2\pm b^3$

Review Exercise

01 Multiply the polynomials.

(1) $(2x+y-1)^2$

(2) $\left(2-x+\dfrac{1}{2x}\right)^2$

(3) $\left(\dfrac{a}{4}-4b+2\right)^2$

(4) $\left(3a-5-\dfrac{3}{5a}\right)^2$

(5) $(x+2)^3$

(6) $(2x-1)^3$

(7) $\left(2ab+\dfrac{1}{2}\right)^3$

(8) $(3a^2-b)^3$

Review Exercise

02 Multiply the polynomials by grouping.

(1) $(a-b+1)(a-b-1)$

(2) $(a^2-a-2)(a^2-a+2)$

(3) $\left(a+2-\dfrac{1}{2b}\right)\left(a-3-\dfrac{1}{2b}\right)$

(4) $(x+2y+3z)(x+y+3z)$

(5) $(2x+1)(2x+1-4y)$

(6) $(x^2+x+1)(2x^2+2x-2)$

(7) $(a-b)^2(a+b)^2$

(8) $(a-2b+2)(a+2)^2$

03 Calculate the following using the multiplication formula.

(1) 10.2^2

(2) 299^2

(3) 50.2×49.8

(4) $101^2 \times 99^2$

04 Suppose $a+b=8$ and $ab=6$. Find the value of each of the following.

(1) a^2+b^2

(2) $(a-b)^2$

(3) $\dfrac{3}{a}+\dfrac{3}{b}$

Review Exercise

05 Suppose $x+\dfrac{1}{x}=4$. Find the value of each of the following.

(1) $x^2+\dfrac{1}{x^2}$

(2) $\left(x-\dfrac{1}{x}\right)^2$

(3) $x^4+\dfrac{1}{x^4}$

06 Suppose $x+y=3$ and $x^2+y^2=8$. Find the value of each of the following.

(1) xy

(2) $\dfrac{x}{y}+\dfrac{y}{x}$

Challenging

07 Calculate $2020 \times 2018 - 2019 \times 2017$ using the multiplication formula.

Challenging

09 If $x^2 - 7x + 1 = 0$, what is the value of $x^2 + \dfrac{1}{x^2}$?

08 In the expression of $(3x - 4y + 2)^2$, what is the sum of the coefficients of the xy term and the coefficient of the x^2 term?

Challenging

10 If $2x^2 - x + 2 = 0$, what is the value of $x^2 + 1 + \dfrac{1}{x^2}$?

Chapter Test — Level 1

01 Which of the following is different from the other four?

(A) $2^6+2^6+2^6+2^6$ (B) $2^2\times 2^2\times 2^2\times 2^2$ (C) $(4^2)^2$

(D) $\dfrac{8^4}{2^3+2^3}$ (E) $4^8\div 8^2$

02 Simplify $\dfrac{6^4+6^4+6^4+6^4+6^4+6^4}{6^4\times 6^4}$.

03 If $\left(-\dfrac{3x^{a+1}y^2}{z^{4b-2}}\right)^3=\dfrac{cx^9y^6}{z^6}$, what is the value of $a+b+c$?

04 If $m=3^4$, which of the following is equal to $\dfrac{27^4}{81^5}$?

(A) $\dfrac{1}{m}$ (B) m^2 (C) $\dfrac{1}{m^2}$ (D) m^3 (E) $\dfrac{1}{m^3}$

05 If $n=2^{x+1}$, which of the following is equal to 16^{x+1}?

(A) n^4 (B) n^6 (C) n^8 (D) n^{10} (E) n^{12}

06 Find x in the equation $\dfrac{4^{3x+1}\times 8^2}{16^{x-5}}=32^{x-3}$.

07 $(8a^3b^2)^2\times \boxed{}\div(-4b^3)^3=2a^4b$

Which of the following is the correct expression for $\boxed{}$ above?

(A) $-\dfrac{a^2}{2b^6}$ (B) $-\dfrac{b^6}{2a^2}$ (C) $-\dfrac{2a^2}{b^6}$

(D) $-\dfrac{2b^6}{a^2}$ (E) $-\dfrac{1}{2a^2b^6}$

08 Suppose that $A=x^2-2x+3$, $B=3x^2-2$, and $C=2x^2+x$.

If $3A-(B+2C)+4C=ax^2+bx+c$, what is the value of a, b, and c?

Chapter 1. Working with Polynomials 59

Chapter Test — Level 1

09 Simplify the expression $5-2\left[3x-4y+\dfrac{1}{2}\{5y-(4x-y)-6\}\right]$.

10 Which of the following is equal to $(4x-3)(4x+3)-4(2x-1)^2$?

(A) $16x-5$ (B) $16x-13$ (C) $8x^2+16x-9$
(D) $8x^2-16x-13$ (E) $8x^2-16x+9$

11 Which of the following is different from the other four for the values of A to E?

(A) $(x-1)^2=x^2-Ax+1$ (B) $(3x+By)^2=9x^2+12xy+4y^2$

(C) $\left(\dfrac{a}{2}+4\right)\left(\dfrac{a}{2}-4\right)=\dfrac{a^2}{C}-16$ (D) $(a-5)(2a+8)=2a^2-Da-40$

(E) $(x-y)(x-y-4)=x^2-Exy-4x+y^2+4y$

12 $5y-4[2y-2\{5y-(3x+\boxed{}-4)+3x-2\}]=x+2y+4$

Write the correct expression for $\boxed{}$ above.

13 Calculate $\dfrac{2020 \times 2022 + 1}{2021}$ using the multiplication formula.

14 If $x^2 - 4x + 1 = 0$, what is the value of $x^2 + x + \dfrac{1}{x} + \dfrac{1}{x^2}$?

15 Simplify $(5-1)(5+1)(5^2+1)(5^4+1)(5^8+1)$.

Chapter Test — Level 2

Solutions_Page 18

01 If $16^{x+3}=4^{3x+1}=\dfrac{8^4}{2^{y-2}}$, what is the value of $x+y$?

02 Suppose that $(4^x \times 5^y)^z = 2^{48} \times 5^{36}$, where x, y, and z are positive integers. When z is the largest possible positive integer, what is the value of $x+y+z$?

03 If $(x+m)(x+n)=x^2+kx+40$, where m, n, and k are positive integers and $n>m$, which of the following values cannot be k.

(A) 41   (B) 36   (C) 22   (D) 14   (E) 13

04 $\dfrac{2x^3y^2 - \boxed{} + 8xy^4}{2xy^2} = (x-2y)^2$

Which of the following is the correct expression for $\boxed{}$ above?

(A) $8x^2y^3$ (B) $4x^2y^3$ (C) $4x^2y^2$
(D) $4xy^2$ (E) $8xy^2$

05 In the expression $(x+2y^2)^3+2x(x-y^2)^2$, what is the coefficient of x^2y^2 term?

06 If $x+y=3$ and $xy=\dfrac{5}{2}$, what is the value of $\dfrac{1}{x^2}+\dfrac{1}{y^2}$?

07 If $a^2=16$, find the value of $(a-4)(a-2)a^2(a+2)(a+4)$.

08 If $(2+1)(2^2+1)(2^4+1)(2^8+1)=2^a-b$, where $0<b<10$, what is the value of ab?

Chapter 1. Working with Polynomials 63

Chapter 2
Factoring Polynomials

1. Factoring Binomials
2. Factoring Trinomials
3. Factoring by Grouping and Substitution
4. Chapter Test

1 Factoring Binomials

01 Definition of Factoring

Factoring is to decompose a polynomial into a product of two or more polynomials. In other words, it is finding what to multiply together to get the original polynomial expression.

$$a^2-a-12 \underset{\text{expanding}}{\overset{\text{factoring}}{\rightleftarrows}} (a-4)(a+3)$$

When a polynomial is expressed as the product of two or more polynomials, each of these expressions is called a factor.

Concept Check

1. $a^2-a-12=1\times(a^2-a-12)$ or $a^2-a-12=(a-4)\times(a+3)$

2. We say 1, a^2-a-12, $a-4$, and $a+3$ are the factors of a^2-a-12.

Example 1

Find all the factors of the expression $2(x-1)(3x+2)$.

Solution

$2(x-1)(3x+2)=1\times 2\times(x-1)\times(3x+2)$
The factors of the expression above are
1, 2, $(x-1)$, $(3x+2)$, $2(x-1)$, $2(3x+2)$, $(x-1)(3x+2)$, and $2(x-1)(3x+2)$.

Check Point 1 Solutions_Page 20

Find all the factors of the expression.

① $4a(a+4)$ ② $x(2x+1)(x-4)$

02 Factoring Binomials

1. If each term in the polynomial has a common factor, those factors can be grouped and then factored. Applies to the factorization of all polynomials.
2. Use the following rules.
   (1) $a^2-b^2=(a-b)(a+b)$
   (2) $a^3+b^3=(a+b)(a^2-ab+b^2)$
   (3) $a^3-b^3=(a-b)(a^2+ab+b^2)$

Concept Check

1. $x^2+5x=\underline{x}\cdot x+5\underline{x}=\underline{x}(x+5)$
2. $6a^3-4a^2b=\underline{2a^2}\cdot 3a-\underline{2a^2}\cdot 2b=\underline{2a^2}(3a-2b)$
3. $y^4-4y^2=\underline{y^2}\cdot y^2-4\underline{y^2}$
   $=y^2(y^2-4)=y^2(y^2-2^2)$
   $=y^2(y-2)(y+2)$ → $a^2-b^2=(a-b)(a+b)$
4. $x^3+8=x^3+2^3$
   $=(x+2)(x^2-x\cdot 2+2^2)$ → $a^3+b^3=(a+b)(a^2-ab+b^2)$
   $=(x+2)(x^2-2x+4)$

Example 2

Factor the polynomial.
① $2x^2-4x$ ② $6xy^3-54xy$ ③ $3(x+2)^2+48(x+2)$
④ $8a^3+b^3$ ⑤ $(a+b)^3-1$ ⑥ $x(3a-2b)+4y(2b-3a)$

Solution

① $2x^2-4x=2x(x-2)$
② $6xy^3-54xy=6xy(y^2-9)=6xy(y^2-3^2)$ → $x^2-y^2=(x-y)(x+y)$
   $=6xy(y-3)(y+3)$

③ $3(x+2)^2+48(x+2)=3A^2+48A$ → Let $x+2=A$
$\qquad\qquad\qquad\qquad=3A(A+16)=3(x+2)(x+2+16)$
$\qquad\qquad\qquad\qquad=3(x+2)(x+18)$

④ $8a^3+b^3=(2a)^3+b^3$
$\qquad\qquad=(2a+b)((2a)^2-2a\cdot b+b^2)$ → $a^3+b^3=(a+b)(a^2-ab+b^2)$
$\qquad\qquad=(2a+b)(4a^2-2ab+b^2)$

⑤ $(a+b)^3-1=A^3-1^3$ → Let $a+b=A$
$\qquad\qquad\quad=(A-1)(A^2+A\cdot 1+1^2)$ → $a^3-b^3=(a-b)(a^2+ab+b^2)$
$\qquad\qquad\quad=(a+b-1)((a+b)^2+(a+b)+1)$

⑥ $x(3a-2b)+4y(2b-3a)=x(3a-2b)-4y(3a-2b)$
$\qquad\qquad\qquad\qquad\quad=xA-4yA$ → Let $3a-2b=A$
$\qquad\qquad\qquad\qquad\quad=A(x-4y)=(3a-2b)(x-4y)$

Check Point 2

Factor the polynomial.

① $9x^2-36$

② $4x^2-\dfrac{y^2}{25}$

③ $32a^3b-8ab^3$

④ $(a^2-4)^2-5(a^2-4)$

⑤ x^3-27y^3

⑥ $\dfrac{x^3}{16}+\dfrac{125y^3}{2}$

⑦ $3ab^3-81a^4b^6$

⑧ a^4-b^4

Review Exercise

01 Factor the polynomial.

(1) $2ay+4ax$

(2) $10ab^2-15a^2b$

(3) xy^2+x^2-2xy

(4) $8ab^2+4ab-6a^2b^2$

(5) $x(a+b)-y(a+b)$

(6) $a(x-y)+b(y-x)$

(7) $2x(2a+b^2)-4y(2a+b^2)$

(8) $3a(4x-y)-2b(y-4x)$

Review Exercise

02 Factor the polynomial.

(1) x^2-4

(2) $4x^2-100$

(3) $16x^2-1$

(4) $4x^3-64x$

(5) $2x^2-8y^2$

(6) $(x-5)^2-9y^4$

(7) $(2x+1)^2-(3x-2)^2$

(8) $4(x^2+6)^2-25(x^2+6)$

Challenging

03 Factor the polynomial.

(1) $3(9a^2-4)+(9a^2-4)^2$

(2) $8a^3+1$

(3) $3a^3+81b^3$

(4) $16a^3-54b^6$

(5) $24a^3b+375b^4$

(6) $4a^6-\dfrac{b^3}{16}$

04 Which of the following is NOT a factor in polynomial $ab(a+b)(a-b)$?

(A) a
(B) ab
(C) a^2-b^2
(D) a^2+b^2
(E) $a(a+b)$

Review Exercise

05 $2y(x-y)(x-2y)$, x^2y-2xy^2

Which of the following is common factor to the two polynomials given above?

(A) $2xy$
(B) $(x-y)$
(C) $y(x-2y)$
(D) $y(x-y)$
(E) $xy(x-2y)$

06 If
$6ab^2(a-3)+4ab(3-a)=2ab(a-3)$
$(xb+y)$, what is the value of xy?

07 If $9y^2-16x^4=-8$ and $4x^2-3y=2$, what is the value of $3y+4x^2$?

08 If $x+y=4$ and $x-y=-3$, what is the value of $x^2(x-y)+y^2(y-x)$?

Challenging

09 Suppose that $a=\dfrac{\sqrt{5}+2}{\sqrt{5}-2}$ and $b=\dfrac{\sqrt{5}-2}{\sqrt{5}+2}$. Find the value of a^2-b^2.

Challenging

10 Suppose $a=200$ and $b=100$.
Find the value of $\dfrac{8a^3-27b^3}{4a^2+6ab+9b^2}$.

Challenging

11 Factor the polynomial.
(1) $2a^4-32b^4$

(2) a^6-b^6

2 Factoring Trinomials

01 Factoring Trinomials: Perfect Squares

1. The square of a polynomial is called the perfect square. A perfect square may be multiplied by a constant.

2. $a^2+2ab+b^2=(a+b)^2$ ⎤ perfect Squares
   $a^2-2ab+b^2=(a-b)^2$ ⎦

3. The middle term $(2ab)$ of the perfect square is twice the product of the square roots of the first and last terms.

Concept Check

1. For instance, $(x+1)^2$, $(y-2)^2$, and $(a+2b)^2$ are perfect squares.

2. $x^2+6x+9=x^2+2(x)(3)+3^2=(x+3)^2$
   $4a^2+20a+25=(2a)^2+2(2a)(5)+5^2=(2a+5)^2$

3. $9a^2-12a+4$ is a perfect square because $9a^2=(3a)^2$, $4=2^2$, and $12a=2\times 3a \times 2$.

Example 1

Factor the polynomial.

① a^2+4a+4 ② $2x^2-16x+32$
③ $9a^2-6a+1$ ④ $4x^2+20xy+25y^2$

Solution

① $a^2+4a+4=a^2+2(a)(2)+2^2=(a+2)^2$
② $2x^2-16x+32=2(x^2-8x+16)=2(x^2-2(x)(4)+4^2)=2(x-4)^2$
③ $9a^2-6a+1=(3a)^2-2(3a)(1)+1^2=(3a-1)^2$
④ $4x^2+20xy+25y^2=(2x)^2+2(2x)(5y)+(5y)^2=(2x+5y)^2$

Check Point 1

Factor the polynomial.

① $x^2+10x+25$

② $4x^2-12xy+9y^2$

③ $25a^3b^2-20a^2b^3+4ab^4$

④ $a^2+\dfrac{ab}{2}+\dfrac{b^2}{16}$

02 Factoring Trinomial: $x^2+(a+b)x+ab$

$x^2+(a+b)x+ab=(x+a)(x+b)$ → The coefficient of x^2 is 1.

1. Find a and b such that

   (1) Their product is equal to the constant term ab.

   (2) Their sum is equal to the coefficient of x.

Concept Check

x^2+x-6 → Find two integers with a product of -6 and a sum of 1.

Two integers with a product of -6		Sum of two integers
-1	6	5
1	-6	-5
-2	3	1
2	-3	-1

$x^2+x-6=(x-2)(x+3)$

Example 2

Factor the polynomial.

① $x^2-3x-10$

② $x^2+10x+24$

③ $2x^2-26x+84$

④ $4x^2-4xy-8y^2$

Solution

① Two integers whose product is -10 and whose sum is -3 are -5 and 2.
$x^2-3x-10=(x-5)(x+2)$

② Two integers whose product is 24 and whose sum is 10 are 4 and 6.
$x^2+10x+24=(x+4)(x+6)$

③ $2x^2-26x+84=2(x^2-13x+42)$
Two integers whose product is 42 and whose sum is -13 are -7 and -6.
$2(x^2-13x+42)=2(x-7)(x-6)$

④ $4x^2-4xy-8y^2=4(x^2-xy-2y^2)$
Two integers whose product is -2 and whose sum is -1 are -2 and 1.
$4(x^2-xy-2y^2)=4(x-2y)(x+y)$

Check Point 2

Solutions_Page 22

Factor the polynomial.

① x^2-x-12

② $x^2+3x-10$

③ $x^2-xy-30y^2$

④ $3x^2y+24xy^2+36y^3$

03 Factoring Trinomial: $acx^2+(ad+bc)x+bd$

$acx^2+(ad+bc)x+bd$ → The coefficient of x^2 is NOT 1.

$ax \quad\quad b \rightarrow \quad\quad bcx$
$cx \quad\quad d \rightarrow \quad (+)\ adx$
$\quad\quad\quad\quad\quad\quad\quad\quad (ad+bc)x$

$\Rightarrow (ax+b)(cx+d)$

1. If you multiply in the diagonal direction as shown above, the sum of the two terms is the same as the middle term.

2. Another way is,

   (1) Multiply the leading coefficient and the constant.

76 Chapter 2. Factoring Polynomials

(2) List all of the factors from step (1) and determine which two factors add up to the coefficient of x.

Concept Check

1. $3x^2 - 11x - 4 \rightarrow -12 = -12 \times 1 \Rightarrow -12 + 1 = -11$
   $\underbrace{}_{3 \times -4 = -12}$

   $3x 1 \rightarrow x$
   $x -4 \rightarrow (+) -12x$
   $ -11x$

   $3x^2 - 11x - 4 = (3x + 1)(x - 4)$

2. $3x^2 - 11x - 4$

Two integers with a product of -12. ($3 \times -4 = -12$)		Sum of two integers
-1	12	11
1	-12	-11
-2	6	4
2	-6	-4
-3	4	1
3	-4	-1

$\Rightarrow 3x^2 - 11x - 4 = (3x+1)(x-4)$
$ -12x$

Example 3

Factor the polynomial.

① $2x^2 + 3x - 2$ 　　　　　　　　② $6x^2 + 11x + 3$
③ $2x^4 - 5x^3 - 7x^2$ 　　　　　　④ $15x^2 - 7xy - 2y^2$

Solution

① $2x^2+3x-2$ → $-4=-1\times 4 \Rightarrow -1+4=3$
    $\underbrace{}_{2\times -2=-4}$

    $2x \quad\searrow\nearrow\quad -1 \quad\rightarrow\quad\quad\quad -x$
    $x \quad\nearrow\searrow\quad 2 \quad\rightarrow\quad \underline{(+)\ \ 4x}$
    $\quad\quad\quad\quad\quad\quad\quad\quad\quad\quad\quad 3x$

    $2x^2+3x-2=(2x-1)(x+2)$

② $6x^2+11x+3$ →$18=9\times 2 \Rightarrow 9+2=11$
    $\underbrace{}_{6\times 3=18}$

    $3x \quad\searrow\nearrow\quad 1 \quad\rightarrow\quad\quad\quad 2x$
    $2x \quad\nearrow\searrow\quad 3 \quad\rightarrow\quad \underline{(+)\ \ 9x}$
    $\quad\quad\quad\quad\quad\quad\quad\quad\quad\quad\quad 11x$

    $6x^2+11x+3=(3x+1)(2x+3)$

③ $2x^4-5x^3-7x^2=x^2(2x^2-5x-7)$
    $\underbrace{2x^2-5x-7}_{2\times -7=-14}$ → $-14=-7\times 2 \Rightarrow -7+2=-5$

    $2x \quad\searrow\nearrow\quad -7 \quad\rightarrow\quad\quad\quad -7x$
    $x \quad\nearrow\searrow\quad 1 \quad\rightarrow\quad \underline{(+)\ \ 2x}$
    $\quad\quad\quad\quad\quad\quad\quad\quad\quad\quad\quad -5x$

    $2x^4-5x^3-7x^2=x^2(2x-7)(x+1)$

④ $15x^2-7xy-2y^2$ → $-30=-10\times 3 \Rightarrow -10+3=-7$
    $\underbrace{}_{15\times -2=-30}$

    $5x \quad\searrow\nearrow\quad y \quad\rightarrow\quad\quad\quad 3xy$
    $3x \quad\nearrow\searrow\quad -2y \quad\rightarrow\quad \underline{(+)\ -10xy}$
    $\quad\quad\quad\quad\quad\quad\quad\quad\quad\quad\quad -7xy$

    $15x^2-7xy-2y^2=(5x+y)(3x-2y)$

Check Point 3   Solutions_Page 22

Factor the polynomial.

① $6x^2-x-2$ ② $3x^2-10x+8$

③ $12x^2-13x-35$ ④ $10x^2y+9xy^2-9y^3$

Review Exercise

01 Factor the polynomial.

(1) $x^2+8x+16$

(2) $x^2-12x+36$

(3) $4x^2+4x+1$

(4) $25x^2-30xy+9y^2$

(5) $9x^2+3x+\dfrac{1}{4}$

(6) $2x^2-12x+18$

(7) $27x^2-36xy+12y^2$

(8) $20x^2+\dfrac{20xy}{3}+\dfrac{5y^2}{9}$

Review Exercise

02 Factor the polynomial.

(1) x^2-8x+7

(2) $x^2+6x-16$

(3) $\dfrac{x^2}{2}+8x+24$

(4) $18+3x-3x^2$

(5) $3x^3y-9x^2y-30xy$

(6) $\dfrac{x^2}{4}-\dfrac{5xy}{2}+4y^2$

03 Factor the polynomial.

(1) $3x^2-7x-6$

(2) $4x^2+7xy+3y^2$

(3) $5x^3y+4x^2y-xy$

(4) $6x^3y-13x^2y^2+6xy^3$

(5) $2x^2-\dfrac{7xy}{3}-y^2$

(6) $2x^2-\dfrac{16xy}{3}+\dfrac{5y^2}{6}$

04 Find the value of x^2-x-12 if $x=\sqrt{3}+4$.

Challenging

05 Find the value of
$4a^2+4b^2-8ab$ if $a=\dfrac{\sqrt{5}+\sqrt{3}}{\sqrt{5}-\sqrt{3}}$ and $b=\dfrac{\sqrt{5}-\sqrt{3}}{\sqrt{5}+\sqrt{3}}$.

06 If $x-2$ is a factor of $4x^2-5x+a$, what is the value of a?

07 If $6x^2+ax-10$ is divisible by $3x-2$, what is the value of a?

Review Exercise

Challenging

08 $4x^2+11x+a$, $2x^2+bx+3$

If $x+3$ is common factor to the two polynomial given above, what is the value of $a+b$?

10 Find the value of a, where $a>0$, for the following trinomial to be perfect square.

(1) $(x+5)(x+3)+a$

(2) $5x^2+4x(x-a)+16$

Challenging

09 Suppose that $x^2+ax-12=(x+b)(x+c)$. If a, b, and c are all integers, which of the following cannot be the value of a?

(A) 11   (B) 5
(C) -4 (D) 4
(E) -1

Challenging

11 $16x^2+axy^2+\dfrac{9y^4}{4}$

Find the value of a, where $a>0$, so that the expression above is a perfect square.

12 If $x^4+4x^2y-12y^2=(x^2+ay)(x^2+by)$, what is the value of $a+b$?

Challenging

13 If $3x^2-\dfrac{9xy}{2}-\dfrac{27y^2}{2}=\dfrac{3}{2}(2x+ay)(x+by)$, what is the value of a and b?

3. Factoring by Grouping and Substitution

01 Factoring by Grouping

Polynomials with four terms can usually be factored by grouping terms. To factor such polynomials, follow the instructions below.

1. Group two terms, find common factors, and then factor.
2. Sometimes three terms and one term are grouped and factored.
3. Often use $a^2-b^2=(a-b)(a+b)$ and $a^2\pm 2ab+b^2=(a\pm b)^2$ in factoring.
4. Check each factor to see if they can be factored further.

Concept Check

1. a^3+2a^2-4a-8

   $=(a^3+2a^2)-(4a+8)$ → Group the first two and the last two terms

   $=a^2(\underline{a+2})-4(\underline{a+2})$ → Find the common factor

   $=(a+2)(a^2-4)$ → Factor out $(a+2)$

   $=(a+2)(a-2)(a+2)$ → $a^2-b^2=(a-b)(a+b)$

   $=(a+2)^2(a-2)$ → Simplify

   $a^3+2a^2-4a-8=(a+2)^2(a-2)$

2. x^2-y^2+2x+1

   $=(x^2+2x+1)-(y^2)$ → Group into three and one terms

   $=(x+1)^2-y^2$ → $a^2+2ab+b^2=(a+b)^2$

   $=(x+1-y)(x+1+y)$ → $a^2-b^2=(a-b)(a+b)$

   $x^2-y^2+2x+1=(x-y+1)(x+y+1)$

Example 1

Factor the polynomial.

① a^3-2a^2-a+2 ② $x^2-y^2+9x-9y$

③ a^2-4b^2-4a+4 ④ $1+4xy-x^2-4y^2$

Solution

① $a^3-2a^2-a+2 = (a^3-2a^2)-(a-2)$
$\qquad\qquad\qquad = a^2(a-2)-(a-2)$
$\qquad\qquad\qquad = (a-2)(a^2-1)$
$\qquad\qquad\qquad = (a-2)(a-1)(a+1)$

② $x^2-y^2+9x-9y = (x-y)(x+y)+9(x-y)$
$\qquad\qquad\qquad = (x-y)((x+y)+9)$
$\qquad\qquad\qquad = (x-y)(x+y+9)$

③ $a^2-4b^2-4a+4 = (a^2-4a+4)-(4b^2)$
$\qquad\qquad\qquad = (a-2)^2-(2b)^2$
$\qquad\qquad\qquad = ((a-2)-2b)((a-2)+2b)$
$\qquad\qquad\qquad = (a-2b-2)(a+2b-2)$

④ $1+4xy-x^2-4y^2 = 1-(x^2-4xy+4y^2)$
$\qquad\qquad\qquad = 1^2-(x-2y)^2$
$\qquad\qquad\qquad = (1-(x-2y))(1+(x-2y))$
$\qquad\qquad\qquad = (1-x+2y)(1+x-2y)$

Check Point 1

Factor the polynomial.

① $xy-x-y+1$ ② $xy-4x+3y-12$

③ $1-2a-4b^2+8ab^2$ ④ $a^2+4b^2-4ab-9$

02 Factoring using Substitution Method

Sometimes the substitution method is very useful for complicated polynomials.

Concept Check

$2(a+b)^2+3(a+b)-2$
$=2A^2+3A-2$ → Let $a+b=A$
$=(2A-1)(A+2)$ → Factor the trinomial
$=(2(a+b)-1)(a+b+2)$ → Replace $A=a+b$
$=(2a+2b-1)(a+b+2)$ → Simplify.
$2(a+b)^2+3(a+b)-2=(2a+2b-1)(a+b+2)$

Example 2

Factor the polynomial.

① $(a+b)(a+b-1)-6$ ② $2(2x-1)^2-3(2x-1)-2$

Solution

① $(a+b)(a+b-1)-6$ → Let $a+b=A$. Then we have
$(a+b)(a+b-1)-6=A(A-1)-6=A^2-A-6$
$=(A-3)(A+2)$
$=(a+b-3)(a+b+2)$

② $2(2x-1)^2-3(2x-1)-2$ → Let $2x-1=A$. Then we have
$2(2x-1)^2-3(2x-1)-2=2A^2-3A-2=(2A+1)(A-2)$
$=(2(2x-1)+1)(2x-1-2)$
$=(4x-1)(2x-3)$

Check Point 2

Solutions_Page 26

Factor the polynomial.

① $(2x+3)^2-(2x+3)-12$
② $(x^2-1)^2-6(x^2-1)+9$
③ $(a+b-2)(a+b+5)-8$
④ $2(a-2)^2+9(a-2)(a+1)+9(a+1)^2$

03 Numerical Calculation using Factoring

1. $ka+kb=k(a+b)$
2. $a^2+2ab+b^2=(a+b)^2$, $a^2-2ab+b^2=(a-b)^2$
3. $a^2-b^2=(a-b)(a+b)$

Concept Check

1. $36\times75+36\times25=36(75+25)=36\times100=3,600$
2. $36^2+2\times36\times14+14^2=(36+14)^2=(50)^2=2,500$
3. $84^2-16^2=(84-16)(84+16)=68\times100=6,800$

Example 3

Calculate the following using factoring.

① $56\times135-56\times35$
② $124^2-2\times124\times74+74^2$
③ 26^2-24^2

Solution

① $56\times135-56\times35=56(135-35)=56\times100=5,600$
② $124^2-2\times124\times74+74^2=(124-74)^2=50^2=2,500$
③ $26^2-24^2=(26-24)(26+24)=2\times50=100$

Check Point 3

Calculate the following using factoring.

① $12 \times 157 + 12 \times 43$
② $37^2 + 23^2 + 2 \times 37 \times 23$
③ $41^2 - 82 + 1$
④ $50 \times 54^2 - 50 \times 46^2$

Review Exercise

01 Factor the polynomial.

(1) x^3-x^2+x-1

(2) $ab-a-b+1$

(3) $2x^3+6x^2+5x+15$

(4) $3x^3y-x^2y+6x-2$

(5) $45-18a-5a^2+2a^3$

(6) $a^3+5a^2b-4ab^2-20b^3$

(7) $32+16x^2-2x^4-x^6$

(8) $x^2-2x-16y^2+1$

(9) $a^2+b^2-2ab-4$

(10) $8a-9b^2+a^2+16$

Review Exercise

02 Factor the polynomial.

(1) $(x-1)^2+9(x-1)+20$

(2) $7(2x+3)^2-54(2x+3)-16$

(3) $(a-2b)^2-3(a-2b)-4$

(4) $(a+1)^2+(a+1)(2b-1)-12(2b-1)^2$

(5) $(x+3y-2)(x+3y+4)-27$

(6) $(2a-5b)(2a-5b-3)-10$

(7) $5x^4-9x^2+4$

(8) $2x^4-5x^2y^4-12y^8$

(9) $20-25(b-1)+8(b-1)^2-10(b-1)^3$

(10) $3(a+1)^6-2(a+1)^4-8(a+1)^2$

Challenging

03 Factor the polynomial.

(1) $x^2+xy-2x-y+1$

(2) $x^2-y^2+4x+6y-5$

(3) $x^2+2xy+4y+x-2$

(4) $x^2-y^2+6x+2y+8$

04 Calculate the following using factoring.

(1) 98^2-4

(2) $25\times 77-25\times 75$

(3) $54^2-8\times 54+16$

(4) $5.5^2\times 24.5-4.5^2\times 24.5$

Review Exercise

(5) $9+6\times 27+27^2$

(6) $\sqrt{6.5^2\times 12-5.5^2\times 12}$

05 If $10(x+2)^2-(x+2)-2=(ax+b)(2x+c)$, what is the value of $a+b+c$?

06 $x^2-3xy+2x-6y,\ 2x^2-6xy-x+3y$

Which of the following is the common factor of two polynomials shown above?

(A) $(x+2)$
(B) $(2x+1)$
(C) $(x-3y)$
(D) $(x+2y)$
(E) $(2y+1)$

07 If $x+y=2+\sqrt{2}$ and $x-y=\sqrt{2}$, what is the value of x^2-y^2-4x+4?

Challenging

08 If $x+y=7$ and $xy=9$, where $x>y$, what is the value of x^2-y^2+x-y?

Challenging

09 Factor the polynomial.

(1) $x^2-y^2-2x+4y-3$

(2) $x^2-y^2+8x+2y+15$

(3) $(x-3)(x-2)(x+1)(x+2)+3$

(4) $(a+1)(a+2)^2(a+3)-6$

Chapter Test — Level 1

01 Which of the following is NOT a factor of $4xy - 12xy^2$?

(A) xy (B) $4xy^2$ (C) $1-3y$ (D) $4x(1-3y)$ (E) $y(1-3y)$

02 Which of the following is NOT correct?

(A) $3x^2y^2 - 6x^2y = 3x^2y(y-2)$
(B) $2x^2 - 5x - 12 = (2x+3)(x-4)$
(C) $9x^2 + 30x + 25 = (3x+5)^2$
(D) $(2x-y)(2x-y-3) - 4 = (2x-y-4)(2x-y+1)$
(E) $4xy - 2x + 10y - 5 = (2x-5)(2y-1)$

03 Find the value of k, where $k>0$, for the following trinomial to be perfect square.

(1) $4(x-1)(x+7) + k$ (2) $4x^2 - (4k-1)xy + y^2$

04 Given $x=1-\sqrt{2}$ and $y=1+\sqrt{2}$, evaluate each of the following.

(1) x^2-y^2 (2) x^2+y^2

(3) $x^2-2xy+y^2$ (4) x^3+y^3

05 Which of the following is NOT a perfect square?

(A) $x^2-6xy+9y^2$ (B) $4x^2-x+\dfrac{1}{16}$ (C) $1-2a+a^2$

(D) $9a^2+12ab+4b^2$ (E) $25y^2-\dfrac{10}{3}y+\dfrac{4}{9}$

06 If $ax^2+(2b-1)x-12=(3x+4)(5x+c)$, what is the value of $a+b+c$?

Chapter Test — Level 1

07 If $ax^2-c=(2x+a)(x+b)$, what is the value of $a+b+c$?

08 $6x^2y-8xy-8y,\ 12x^3y-4x^2y-8xy$

Which of the following is common factor to the two polynomials given above?

(A) $y(3x+2)$ (B) $x(3x+2)$ (C) $y(x-2)$
(E) $x(x-2)$ (E) $xy(x-1)$

09 If $2x-1$ is a factor of $4x^2+kx-5$, what is the value of k?

10 Find the value of $-a^2(2b-a)-4b^2(a-2b)$ if $a-2b=2$ and $a+2b=5$?

11 Calculate each of the following using factoring.

(1) $15.5^2-15.5+0.5^2$

(2) $\dfrac{92\times 184+92\times 16}{96^2-16}$

12 If $x+y=4$ and $x-y=-3$, what is the value of $2x^2-2y^2-4x+4y$?

Chapter Test — Level 2

01 Factor the polynomial.

(1) $(x+2y-1)^2-(3x-2y)^2$

(2) $24x^3y+1029y^4$

(3) $4x^3y-32x^2y^2+64xy^3$

(4) $64-\dfrac{81}{4}x^4$

(5) $(x+y)^3-(x-y)^3$

(6) $(2x^2+3x)^2-(2x^2+3x+3)-3$

(7) $2(x-2)^2-3(x-2)(x+3)-20(x+3)^2$

(8) $x^2+4y^2-4xy-2x+4y$

02 If $16a^3-2b^3=6$ and $2a-b=\dfrac{1}{2}$, what is the value of $4a^2+2ab+b^2$?

03 If $x+y=\sqrt{5}$ and $xy=2$, what is the value of $x^3+x^2y+xy^2+y^3$?

04 Find the value of k so that the polynomial $\dfrac{1}{16}x^2-\dfrac{1}{4}xy+ky^2$ is a perfect square.

Chapter Test — Level 2

05 If $3x+2$ is the common factor of two polynomials $3x^2-7x+a$ and $6x^2+bx-2$, what is the value of $a+b$?

06 Suppose that $x^2+ax+16=(x+b)(x+c)$. If a, b, and c are all integers, which of the following cannot be the value of a?

(A) -17 (B) -10 (C) 8 (D) 12 (E) 17

07 Calculate $98\times 98+98\times 101-98\times 99-102\times 102$ using factoring.

08 Which of the following is one of the factors of $x^2-y^2+9x+y+20$?

(A) $(x-y+5)$ (B) $(x+y+5)$ (C) $(x-y+4)$
(D) $(x-y-4)$ (E) $(y-x+4)$

Chapter **3**

Rational Expression

1. Introduction to Rational Expression
2. Addition, Subtraction, and Complex Fraction
3. Rational Equations
4. Application of Rational Equations
5. Chapter Test

Introduction to Rational Expression

01 Definition of Rational Number

We already know that a rational number is any number that can be expressed as the quotient of two integers given that the denominator is not equal to zero (every integer is a rational number since the denominator of any number can be considered as 1). Similarly, a rational expression is one that can be expressed as a quotient of polynomials. Also, notice that the rational expression $\frac{A}{B}$ with the constant B can also be a polynomial.

Rational Number: $\frac{2}{5}$, $\frac{4}{13}$

Rational Expression:

$\frac{A}{B}\begin{cases} \text{Polynomial } (B \text{ is a number}): \frac{3x}{2}, \frac{2x^2+1}{5}, \cdots \\ \text{Frational Expression } (B \text{ contains variables}): \frac{1}{x}, \frac{x+1}{x-2}, \cdots \end{cases}$

02 Simplifying Rational Expression

A rational expression is in the simplified form provided its numerator and denominator have no common factors. To simplify rational expressions, use the following property of fractions:

Let A, B, and $C (B \neq 0, C \neq 0)$ be nonzero real numbers or variable expressions.

$\frac{A\cancel{C}}{B\cancel{C}} = \frac{A}{B} \Rightarrow$ Divide out common factor C

Simplifying a rational expression usually requires the following steps.
1. Factor both the numerator and denominator of the fraction.
2. Divide out common factors in the expression.

3. Rewrite any remaining expression in the numerator and denominator.

Concept Check

$\dfrac{x^2-x-6}{x^2-4}$ → Given

$=\dfrac{(x-3)(x+2)}{(x-2)(x+2)}$ → Factor the numerator and denominator

$=\dfrac{(x-3)\cancel{(x+2)}}{(x-2)\cancel{(x+2)}}$ → Divide out common factors

$=\dfrac{x-3}{x-2}$ → Rewrite remaining expression in the numerator and denominator

Example 1

Simplify the rational expression.

① $\dfrac{150xy}{180x}$ ② $\dfrac{4x^3-12x^2}{16x^2}$

③ $\dfrac{x^2-x-6}{x^2-3x}$ ④ $\dfrac{a^2-b^2}{a^3+b^3}$

Solution

① $\dfrac{150xy}{180x}=\dfrac{5\cdot 30x\cdot y}{6\cdot 30x}=\dfrac{5y}{6}$ ② $\dfrac{4x^3-12x^2}{16x^2}=\dfrac{4x^2(x-3)}{4\cdot 4x^2}=\dfrac{x-3}{4}$

③ $\dfrac{x^2-x-6}{x^2-3x}=\dfrac{(x-3)(x+2)}{x(x-3)}=\dfrac{x+2}{x}$ ④ $\dfrac{a^2-b^2}{a^3+b^3}=\dfrac{(a-b)(a+b)}{(a+b)(a^2-ab+b^2)}=\dfrac{a-b}{a^2-ab+b^2}$

Check Point 1 Solutions_Page 32

Simplify the rational expression.

① $\dfrac{18ab^3}{72a^3b^2c}$ ② $\dfrac{x^2-x-2}{x^2+x-6}$ ③ $\dfrac{3x^2+x-4}{5x^2-3x-2}$

④ $\dfrac{2x^3+11x^2+12x}{3x^2+11x-4}$ ⑤ $\dfrac{(a^3+b^3)(a^2-b^2)}{a^4-b^4}$ ⑥ $\dfrac{(a^3-b^3)(a^4-b^4)}{(a-b)(a^6-b^6)}$

Chapter 3. Rational Expression 105

03 Multiplication of Rational Expressions

To **multiply rational expressions**, use the following property of fractions:

Let A, B, C and D ($B \neq 0$, $D \neq 0$) be nonzero real numbers or variable expressions. Then,

$$\frac{A}{B} \times \frac{C}{D} = \frac{AC}{BD} \Rightarrow (\text{Denominator} \times \text{Denominator}) \text{ and } (\text{Numerator} \times \text{Numerator})$$

Multiplying rational expressions usually requires the following steps.

1. Factor both the numerator and the denominator of each expression.
2. Divide out the common factors in the expression.
3. Multiply the numerators with each other and the denominators each other.

Concept Check

$$\frac{x^2-3x-4}{x^2+2x+1} \times \frac{x^2-3x+2}{x^2+x-6}$$

$$= \frac{(x-4)(x+1)}{(x+1)^2} \times \frac{(x-2)(x-1)}{(x+3)(x-2)} \quad \rightarrow \text{Factor the numerators and denominators}$$

$$= \frac{(x-4)\cancel{(x+1)}}{(x+1)\cancel{(x+1)}} \times \frac{\cancel{(x-2)}(x-1)}{(x+3)\cancel{(x-2)}} \quad \rightarrow \text{Divide out the common factors}$$

$$= \frac{(x-4)(x-1)}{(x+1)(x+3)} \quad \rightarrow \text{Multiply the numerators and denominators}$$

Example 2

Multiply the rational expression and then simplify.

① $\dfrac{3xy^3}{4x^3y^2} \times \dfrac{x^3y^5}{x^5}$

② $\dfrac{a^2-a-6}{a^2-3a+2} \times \dfrac{a^2-4}{a^2-9}$

Solution

① $\dfrac{3xy^3}{4x^3y^2} \times \dfrac{x^3y^5}{x^5} = \dfrac{xy^2 \cdot 3y}{xy^2 \cdot 4x^2} \times \dfrac{x^3 \cdot y^5}{x^3 \cdot x^2} = \dfrac{3y}{4x^2} \times \dfrac{y^5}{x^2} = \dfrac{3y^6}{4x^4}$

② $\dfrac{a^2-a-6}{a^2-3a+2} \times \dfrac{a^2-4}{a^2-9} = \dfrac{(a-3)(a+2)}{(a-2)(a-1)} \times \dfrac{(a-2)(a+2)}{(a-3)(a+3)}$

$= \dfrac{(a+2)(a+2)}{(a-1)(a+3)} = \dfrac{(a+2)^2}{(a-1)(a+3)}$

Check Point 2

Solutions_Page 32

Multiply the rational expression and then simplify.

① $\dfrac{2x^2y}{6xy^4} \times \dfrac{8x^3}{10x^2}$ ② $\dfrac{x-3}{x-4} \times \dfrac{x^2-16}{5x-15}$

③ $\dfrac{x^2+8x+16}{x+2} \times \dfrac{x^2-4}{x^2+6x+8}$ ④ $\dfrac{x^2-1}{2x^2+x-1} \times (8x^3-1)$

04 Division of Rational Expressions

To divide rational expressions, use the following property of fractions:

Let A, B, C, and $D(B \ne 0, D \ne 0)$ be nonzero real numbers or variable expressions.

$$\dfrac{A}{B} \div \dfrac{C}{D} = \dfrac{A}{B} \times \dfrac{D}{C} = \dfrac{AD}{BC} \Rightarrow \text{Convert division to multiplication}$$

Dividing rational expressions usually requires the following steps.

1. Multiply the first expression by the reciprocal of the second expression.
2. Factor both the numerator and the denominator of each expression.
3. Divide out the common factors in the expression.
4. Multiply the numerators with each other and the denominators each other.

Concept Check

$$\frac{x-1}{2x^2-x-3} \div \frac{x^2-1}{6x-9}$$

$$= \frac{x-1}{2x^2-x-3} \times \frac{6x-9}{x^2-1} \qquad \rightarrow \text{Multiply the reciprocal}$$

$$= \frac{x-1}{(2x-3)(x+1)} \times \frac{3(2x-3)}{(x-1)(x+1)} \qquad \rightarrow \text{Factor the numerators and denominators}$$

$$= \frac{\cancel{x-1}}{(\cancel{2x-3})(x+1)} \times \frac{3(\cancel{2x-3})}{(\cancel{x-1})(x+1)} \qquad \rightarrow \text{Divide out the common factors}$$

$$= \frac{3}{(x+1)^2} \qquad \rightarrow \text{Multiply the numerators and denominators}$$

Example 3

Divide the rational expression and simplify.

① $\dfrac{9xy^2}{4} \div \dfrac{27y}{8x}$ ② $\dfrac{a^3-b^3}{a+b} \div \dfrac{a^2-b^2}{a^2+2ab+b^2}$

Solution

① $\dfrac{9xy^2}{4} \div \dfrac{27y}{8x} = \dfrac{9xy^2}{4} \times \dfrac{8x}{27y} = \dfrac{9y \cdot xy}{4} \times \dfrac{4 \cdot 2x}{9y \cdot 3} = \dfrac{2x^2y}{3}$

② $\dfrac{a^3-b^3}{a+b} \div \dfrac{a^2-b^2}{a^2+2ab+b^2} = \dfrac{a^3-b^3}{a+b} \times \dfrac{a^2+2ab+b^2}{a^2-b^2}$

$= \dfrac{(a-b)(a^2+ab+b^2)}{a+b} \times \dfrac{(a+b)^2}{(a-b)(a+b)} = a^2+ab+b^2$

Remember that we dont need to find a common denominator to multiply or divide rational expressions.

Check Point 3 Solutions_Page 32

Divide the rational expression and then simplify.

① $\dfrac{9xy^2z}{x^3z^2} \div \dfrac{18x^2y^3}{x^3y^4}$ ② $\dfrac{x^2+6x-7}{3x^2} \div \dfrac{2x+14}{3x}$

③ $\dfrac{a^3-a^2-a+1}{(a+1)^2} \div \dfrac{a^2-1}{a^3+1}$ ④ $\dfrac{2x-12}{x^2-4} \div \dfrac{x^2-2x+4}{3x-6} \div \dfrac{1}{x^3+8}$

Review Exercise

01 Simplify the rational expression.

(1) $\dfrac{75x^3y^6}{(5y^5)^2}$

(2) $\dfrac{27a^2b^3c}{(3bc^2)^3}$

(3) $\dfrac{6y^4-15y}{9y^2}$

(4) $\dfrac{2y^3+4y^2}{y+y^2-2}$

(5) $\dfrac{(a-b)^2}{a^2-b^2}$

(6) $\dfrac{a^2-5a+6}{a^2-7a+12}$

(7) $\dfrac{6a^2-5a+1}{12a^2+2a-2}$

Review Exercise

Challenging

02 Simplify the rational expression.

(1) $\dfrac{x^3+27}{x^2-9}$

(2) $\dfrac{x^4-x^2}{x^4-1}$

(3) $\dfrac{a^3+a^2-a-1}{a^3-a^2-a+1}$

(4) $\dfrac{-b^3+2b^2-b+2}{8+2b-3b^2}$

(5) $\dfrac{b^3+2b^2-2b-4}{b^3+8}$

(6) $\dfrac{a^4-2a^2b^2+b^4}{a^4-b^4}$

(7) $\dfrac{a^4-b^4}{a^4+a^3b-ab^3-b^4}$

03 Simplify the rational expression.

(1) $\left(-\dfrac{4x^3}{12}\right) \times \left(-\dfrac{18}{x^2}\right)$

(2) $\left(\dfrac{1}{x}\right)^3 \times \left(\dfrac{x^2}{2}\right)^2$

(3) $\dfrac{(-2x^2y)^2}{x^2y^5} \times \dfrac{4xy^2}{(2y^3)^3}$

(4) $\left(\dfrac{a^2}{b}\right)^3 \times \left(\dfrac{a}{b^3}\right)^2 \times (ab^2)^{-2}$

(5) $\dfrac{x^2-9}{x^2+5x+6} \times \dfrac{3-x}{x+2}$

(6) $\dfrac{x^2-7x+12}{2x^2-32} \times (x^2-5x+6)$

Review Exercise

Challenging

04 Simplify the rational expression.

(1) $\dfrac{6a^2-a-2}{2a^2-5a-3} \times \dfrac{2a^2-18}{3a^2+7a-6}$

(2) $\dfrac{a^2b-b^3}{4ab-8b^2} \times \dfrac{a^2-ab-2b^2}{a^4-2a^3b+a^2b^2}$

(2) $(-2a^3b^{-1})^3 \div \left(-\dfrac{3ab^2}{2b^2a^3}\right)^2$

(3) $\dfrac{15y^2}{4x} \times \dfrac{7x^2}{9y} \div \dfrac{35}{6xy}$

(4) $\dfrac{x^2-5x-14}{x^2-3x+2} \div \dfrac{x^2-14x+49}{x^2-4}$

05 Simplify the rational expression.

(1) $\dfrac{4y^2}{y^3} \div \left(-\dfrac{6y^3}{y^4}\right)$

Challenging

06 Simplify the rational expression.

(1) $\dfrac{a^2-1}{a^2-4} \div \dfrac{2a-1}{a-2} \times \dfrac{a+2}{2a^2+a}$

(2) $\dfrac{4x^2-1}{2x^2-3x-2} \times \dfrac{2x-1}{x^2-4} \div \dfrac{2x-1}{x+2}$

(3) $\dfrac{x^2-4}{x+11} \times (3x^3+6x^2) \div \dfrac{2x-4}{x^2+11x}$

(4) $(2x-10) \div \dfrac{x^2-9x+20}{4x^2-9} \div \dfrac{6x^3-9x^2}{x^3-4x^2}$

(5) $(x-y) \div (x^4-y^4) \times (x^4+2x^2y^2+y^4)$

Chapter 3. Rational Expression

2. Addition, Subtraction, and Complex Fraction

01 Addition and Subtraction of Rational Expressions

To add or subtract rations expressions, use the following properties.

1. When the denominator is identical, simply add or subtract numerators.

$$\frac{A}{B}+\frac{C}{B}=\frac{A+C}{B}, \quad \frac{A}{B}-\frac{C}{B}=\frac{A-C}{B}$$

2. When the denominator is NOT identical, find the least common denominator(LCD) and then add or subtract numerators.

$$\frac{A}{B}+\frac{C}{D}=\frac{AD}{BD}+\frac{BC}{BD}=\frac{AD+BC}{BD}, \quad \frac{A}{B}-\frac{C}{D}=\frac{AD}{BD}-\frac{BC}{BD}=\frac{AD-BC}{BD}$$

Concept Check

$$\frac{4}{x}+\frac{3}{x-2}$$

$$=\frac{4(x-2)}{x(x-2)}+\frac{3x}{(x-2)x} \quad \rightarrow \text{LCD of } x \text{ and } x-2 \text{ is } x(x-2)$$

$$=\frac{4x-8}{x(x-2)}+\frac{3x}{x(x-2)} \quad \rightarrow \text{Simplify each numerator}$$

$$=\frac{4x-8+3x}{x(x-2)} \quad \rightarrow \text{Add the numerators}$$

$$=\frac{7x-8}{x(x-2)} \quad \rightarrow \text{Simplify}$$

Example 1

Perform the indicated operation and simplify.

① $\dfrac{4}{x}-\dfrac{3}{2x}$

② $\dfrac{2}{a-1}+\dfrac{a}{a^2-1}$

③ $\dfrac{x-1}{x+1}+\dfrac{3x}{2x+3}$

④ $\dfrac{1}{a^2-b^2}-\dfrac{ab}{a^3-b^3}$

> Solution

① $\dfrac{4}{x}-\dfrac{3}{2x}=\dfrac{4\cdot 2}{x\cdot 2}-\dfrac{3}{2x}=\dfrac{8-3}{2x}=\dfrac{5}{2x}$

② $\dfrac{2}{a-1}+\dfrac{a}{a^2-1}=\dfrac{2}{a-1}+\dfrac{a}{(a-1)(a+1)}$

$=\dfrac{2(a+1)}{(a-1)(a+1)}+\dfrac{a}{(a-1)(a+1)}=\dfrac{3a+2}{(a-1)(a+1)}$

③ $\dfrac{x-1}{x+1}+\dfrac{3x}{2x+3}=\dfrac{(x-1)(2x+3)}{(x+1)(2x+3)}+\dfrac{3x(x+1)}{(2x+3)(x+1)}$

$=\dfrac{2x^2+x-3}{(x+1)(2x+3)}+\dfrac{3x^2+3x}{(x+1)(2x+3)}=\dfrac{5x^2+4x-3}{(x+1)(2x+3)}$

④ $\dfrac{1}{a^2-b^2}-\dfrac{ab}{a^3-b^3}=\dfrac{1}{(a-b)(a+b)}-\dfrac{ab}{(a-b)(a^2+ab+b^2)}$

$=\dfrac{a^2+ab+b^2}{(a-b)(a+b)(a^2+ab+b^2)}-\dfrac{ab(a+b)}{(a-b)(a^2+ab+b^2)(a+b)}$

$=\dfrac{a^2+ab+b^2}{(a-b)(a+b)(a^2+ab+b^2)}-\dfrac{a^2b+ab^2}{(a-b)(a+b)(a^2+ab+b^2)}$

$=\dfrac{a^2+ab+b^2-a^2b-ab^2}{(a-b)(a+b)(a^2+ab+b^2)}$

> Check Point 1

Solutions_Page 35

Perform the indicated operation and simplify.

① $\dfrac{2x-4}{x+3}-\dfrac{x+1}{3x-1}$ ② $\dfrac{x-4}{x}+\dfrac{x+3}{x+2}$

③ $\dfrac{x+4}{x^2-x-2}-\dfrac{x+2}{x^2-1}$ ④ $\dfrac{2}{x}-\dfrac{x}{x+1}+\dfrac{x+1}{x+2}$

02 Complex Fractions

A complex fraction is a fraction in which the numerator, the denominator, or both are themselves fractional expressions. Here is how to simplify complex fractions.

1. $\dfrac{A}{\dfrac{B}{C}} = \dfrac{A \cdot C}{\dfrac{B}{C} \cdot C} = \dfrac{AC}{B}$

2. $\dfrac{\dfrac{A}{B}}{C} = \dfrac{\dfrac{A}{B} \cdot B}{C \cdot B} = \dfrac{A}{BC}$

3. $\dfrac{\dfrac{A}{B}}{\dfrac{C}{D}} = \dfrac{\dfrac{A}{B} \cdot BD}{\dfrac{C}{D} \cdot BD} = \dfrac{AD}{BC}$

There is another way to simplify complex fractions.

1. $\dfrac{A}{\dfrac{B}{C}} = A \div \dfrac{B}{C} = A \times \dfrac{C}{B} = \dfrac{AC}{B}$

2. $\dfrac{\dfrac{A}{B}}{C} = \dfrac{A}{B} \div C = \dfrac{A}{B} \times \dfrac{1}{C} = \dfrac{A}{BC}$

3. $\dfrac{\dfrac{A}{B}}{\dfrac{C}{D}} = \dfrac{A}{B} \div \dfrac{C}{D} = \dfrac{A}{B} \times \dfrac{D}{C} = \dfrac{AD}{BC}$

Concept Check

$\dfrac{\dfrac{x}{2x-4}}{2 + \dfrac{1}{x-2}}$

$= \dfrac{\dfrac{x}{2(x-2)}}{2 + \dfrac{1}{x-2}}$ → Factor the numerator or denominator, if possible

$= \dfrac{\dfrac{x}{x(x-2)} \cdot 2(x-2)}{\left(2 + \dfrac{1}{x-2}\right) \cdot 2(x-2)}$ → Multiply by $2(x-2)$

$= \dfrac{x}{4(x-2)+2} = \dfrac{x}{4x-6}$ → Simplify

Example 2

Simplify the complex fraction.

① $\dfrac{x}{\dfrac{x-1}{x+1}}$ ② $\dfrac{2x-1}{1-\dfrac{1}{x+1}}$ ③ $\dfrac{\dfrac{3x}{x-1}}{\dfrac{x^2+x}{x^2-1}}$

Solution

① $\dfrac{x}{\dfrac{x-1}{x+1}} = \dfrac{x(x+1)}{\dfrac{x-1}{x+1}(x+1)} = \dfrac{x(x+1)}{x-1}$

② $\dfrac{2x-1}{1-\dfrac{1}{x+1}} = \dfrac{(2x-1)(x+1)}{1-\dfrac{1}{x+1}(x+1)} = \dfrac{(2x-1)(x+1)}{(x+1)-1} = \dfrac{(2x-1)(x+1)}{x}$

③ $\dfrac{\dfrac{3x}{x-1}}{\dfrac{x^2+x}{x^2-1}} = \dfrac{\dfrac{3x}{x-1}\cdot(x-1)(x+1)}{\dfrac{x(x+1)}{(x-1)(x+1)}\cdot(x-1)(x+1)} = \dfrac{3x(x+1)}{x(x+1)} = 3$

Check Point 2

Solutions_Page 35

Simplify the complex fraction.

① $\dfrac{\dfrac{x}{3}-7}{9+\dfrac{1}{x}}$ ② $\dfrac{\dfrac{10}{x-1}}{\dfrac{1}{5}-\dfrac{2}{x-1}}$

③ $\dfrac{xy^{-1}-1}{x^2-y^{-2}}$ ④ $\dfrac{\dfrac{1}{1-a}-\dfrac{1}{1+a}}{\dfrac{1}{1-a}+\dfrac{1}{1+a}}$

03 Decomposition of Partial Fractions

The rational expression below can be written as the sum of two simple expressions.

$$\frac{C}{AB} = \frac{C}{B-A}\left(\frac{1}{A} - \frac{1}{B}\right)$$

Concept Check

1. $\dfrac{C}{B-A}\left(\dfrac{1}{A} - \dfrac{1}{B}\right) = \dfrac{C}{B-A}\left(\dfrac{1}{A}\cdot\dfrac{B}{B} - \dfrac{1}{B}\cdot\dfrac{A}{A}\right) = \dfrac{C}{B-A}\cdot\dfrac{B-A}{AB} = \dfrac{C}{AB}$

2. $\dfrac{2}{(x+1)(x+2)} = \dfrac{2}{(x+2)-(x+1)}\left(\dfrac{1}{(x+1)} - \dfrac{1}{(x+2)}\right) = \dfrac{2}{(x+1)} - \dfrac{2}{(x+2)}$

3. Each fraction $\dfrac{2}{x+1}$ and $-\dfrac{2}{x+1}$ is called a **partial fraction**

Example 3

$$\frac{1}{x(x+1)} + \frac{1}{(x+1)(x+2)} + \frac{1}{(x+2)(x+3)}$$

Simplify the expression above using partial fractions decomposition.

Solution

Write the partial fraction of each fraction first.

$\dfrac{1}{x(x+1)} = \dfrac{1}{(x+1)-x}\left(\dfrac{1}{x} - \dfrac{1}{x+1}\right) = \dfrac{1}{x} - \dfrac{1}{x+1}$

$\dfrac{1}{(x+1)(x+2)} = \dfrac{1}{(x+2)-(x+1)}\left(\dfrac{1}{x+1} - \dfrac{1}{x+2}\right) = \dfrac{1}{x+1} - \dfrac{1}{x+2}$

$\dfrac{1}{(x+2)(x+3)} = \dfrac{1}{(x+3)-(x+2)}\left(\dfrac{1}{x+2} - \dfrac{1}{x+3}\right) = \dfrac{1}{x+2} - \dfrac{1}{x+3}$

Using the partial fractions to simplify the given expression, we have

$\dfrac{1}{x(x+1)} + \dfrac{1}{(x+1)(x+2)} + \dfrac{1}{(x+2)(x+3)}$

$= \left(\dfrac{1}{x} - \dfrac{1}{x+1}\right) + \left(\dfrac{1}{x+1} - \dfrac{1}{x+2}\right) + \left(\dfrac{1}{x+2} - \dfrac{1}{x+3}\right)$

$$= \frac{1}{x} - \frac{1}{x+3} = \frac{x+3-x}{x(x+3)} = \frac{3}{x(x+3)}$$

Check Point 3

Simplify the expression using partial fractions decomposition.

① $\dfrac{2}{(x+1)(x+3)} + \dfrac{2}{(x+3)(x+5)}$

② $\dfrac{1}{x(x+2)} + \dfrac{1}{(x+2)(x+4)} + \dfrac{1}{(x+4)(x+6)}$

Review Exercise

01 Simplify the rational expression.

(1) $\dfrac{x+2}{3}+\dfrac{x-4}{6}$

(2) $\dfrac{5}{2x+2}+\dfrac{2x-3}{2x+2}$

(3) $1-\dfrac{x-4}{x^2-1}$

(4) $\dfrac{-1}{2x^2+2x}+\dfrac{1}{2}$

(5) $\dfrac{3}{x+5}+\dfrac{5x}{2x-1}$

(6) $\dfrac{x}{2x^2+8x}-\dfrac{7}{2x}$

(7) $\dfrac{3}{x-6}+\dfrac{1}{x+2}$

(8) $\dfrac{1}{(x-1)^2}-\dfrac{1}{x^2-1}$

Challenging

02 Simplify the rational expression.

(1) $\dfrac{x^2+2x}{x^2-2x} - \dfrac{x}{2x^2-8}$

(2) $\dfrac{3x-1}{x^2+4x+4} - \dfrac{2}{x^2-4}$

(3) $\dfrac{1}{4x^2-y^2} + \dfrac{1}{2x^2-3xy+y^2}$

(4) $\dfrac{1}{x-y} + \dfrac{x}{x+y} - \dfrac{y}{x^2-y^2}$

03 Simplify the complex fraction

(1) $\dfrac{\dfrac{1}{x}-x}{\dfrac{1}{x}-1}$

(2) $\dfrac{\dfrac{10}{x-1}}{\dfrac{1}{5}-\dfrac{2}{x-1}}$

(3) $\dfrac{\dfrac{1+x}{x^3}}{\dfrac{1}{x^2}-\dfrac{1}{x(x+1)}}$

Review Exercise

(4) $\dfrac{x-y}{\dfrac{1}{x}-\dfrac{1}{y^2}}$

(5) $\dfrac{1-\dfrac{1}{xy}}{\dfrac{1}{x}-\dfrac{1}{y}}$

(6) $\dfrac{\dfrac{1}{x-1}-\dfrac{1}{x+1}}{\dfrac{1}{x+1}+\dfrac{1}{x-1}}$

Challenging

04 Simplify the complex fraction.

(1) $\dfrac{\dfrac{1}{x}-\dfrac{1}{y}}{\dfrac{1}{x^2}-\dfrac{1}{xy}+\dfrac{1}{y^2}}$

(2) $\dfrac{1-\dfrac{1}{x-2}}{x+1-\dfrac{2}{x+1}}$

(3) $\dfrac{1+\dfrac{x}{x-y}}{\dfrac{y}{x+y}-2}$

(4) $\dfrac{\dfrac{x+y}{x-y}-\dfrac{x-y}{x+y}}{\dfrac{x+y}{x-y}+\dfrac{x-y}{x+y}}$

05 Given the equation, find the value of ab.

(1) $\dfrac{12}{x^2-4}=\dfrac{a}{x-2}+\dfrac{b}{x+2},\ x\neq\pm 2$

(2) $\dfrac{10}{(2x-1)(x+2)}=\dfrac{a}{2x-1}+\dfrac{b}{x+2}$,

$x\neq -2$ and $x\neq \dfrac{1}{2}$

06 Simplify $\dfrac{2}{1-x}+\dfrac{2}{1+x}+\dfrac{4}{1+x^2}+\dfrac{8}{1+x^4}$.

Challenging

07 Simplify the rational expression.

(1) $\dfrac{2}{x(x+2)}+\dfrac{2}{(x+2)(x+4)}-\dfrac{4}{x(x+4)}$

(2) $\dfrac{y}{x(x+y)}+\dfrac{z}{(x+y)(x+y+z)}$
$+\dfrac{1}{(x+y+z)(x+y+z+1)}$

Review Exercise

08 Evaluate $\dfrac{1}{2\times 4}+\dfrac{1}{4\times 6}+\dfrac{1}{6\times 8}+\dfrac{1}{8\times 10}$ using the partial fractions decomposition.

09 Given $x-4+\dfrac{1}{x}=0$, find the value of the following expression.

(1) $x^2+\dfrac{1}{x^2}$

(2) $x-\dfrac{1}{x}$

(3) $x^2-\dfrac{1}{x^2}$

(4) $x^3+\dfrac{1}{x^3}$

Challenging

10 Given the equation, find the value of a and b.

(1) $1 - \dfrac{1}{1 - \dfrac{1}{1 - \dfrac{1}{x}}} = ax + b, \ x \neq 0$

(2) $2 - \dfrac{2}{2 - \dfrac{2}{2 - \dfrac{2}{x-2}}} = -\dfrac{2}{ax+b}, \ x \neq 0$

11 If $x^2 + \dfrac{1}{x^2} = 14$, where $x > 0$, what is the value of $x + \dfrac{1}{x}$?

3 Rational Equations

01 Solving Rational Equations

Equations that contain rational expressions are called rational equations. To solve a rational equation, refer to the following steps.

1. Find the least common denominator(LCD).
2. Multiply both sides of the equation by LCD.
3. Solve the resulting polynomial equation.
4. Check the solution(s) to make sure there isn't an extraneous solution. In rational equations, the extraneous solution is the value that makes denominator equal to zero.

Concept Check

$\dfrac{1}{x-1}+\dfrac{4}{x+2}=2$

$\left(\dfrac{1}{x-1}+\dfrac{4}{x+2}\right)(x-1)(x+2)=2(x-1)(x+2)$ → Multiply by LCD $(x-1)(x+2)$

$(x+2)+4(x-1)=2x^2+2x-4$ → Expand each side

$5x-2=2x^2+2x-4$ → Simplify

$2x^2-3x-2=0$ → Subtract $5x-2$

$(2x+1)(x-2)=0$ → Factor

$2x+1=0$ or $x-2=0$ → Zero product property

$x=-\dfrac{1}{2}$ or $x=2$ → Solve for x

Check the solution

$\dfrac{1}{-\frac{1}{2}-1\neq 0}+\dfrac{4}{-\frac{1}{2}+2\neq 0}=2$ and $\dfrac{1}{2-1\neq 0}+\dfrac{4}{2+2\neq 0}=2$

When we substitute the solution back into the original equation, each denominator is not equal to zero. Therefore, both $x=-\dfrac{1}{2}$ and $x=2$ are solutions to the equation.

Example 1

Solve the rational equation.

① $\dfrac{2}{x} - 1 = \dfrac{1}{2x}$ ② $\dfrac{5}{x-3} - 2 = \dfrac{30}{x^2-9}$

Solution

① $\dfrac{2}{x} - 1 = \dfrac{1}{2x}$

$\left(\dfrac{2}{x} - 1\right) \cdot 2x = \left(\dfrac{1}{2x}\right) \cdot 2x$ → Multiply by LCD

$4 - 2x = 1$ → Expand

$-2x = -3,\ x = \dfrac{3}{2}$ → Solve for x

Check the solution

$\dfrac{2}{\underset{\ne 0}{\frac{3}{2}}} - 1 = \dfrac{1}{\underset{\ne 0}{2\left(\frac{3}{2}\right)}}$. Since $x = \dfrac{3}{2}$ does not make the denominator zero in the original equation, it is the solution to the equation.

$x = \dfrac{3}{2}$

② $\dfrac{5}{x-3} - 2 = \dfrac{30}{x^2-9}$

$\dfrac{5}{x-3} - 2 = \dfrac{30}{(x-3)(x+3)}$ → Factor the denominator

$\left(\dfrac{5}{x-3} - 2\right) \cdot (x-3)(x+3) = \dfrac{30}{(x-3)(x+3)} \cdot (x-3)(x+3)$ → Multiply by LCD

$5(x+3) - 2(x-3)(x+3) = 30$ → Expand each side
$2x^2 - 5x - 3 = 0$ → Simplify

$(2x+1)(x-3) = 0,\ x = -\dfrac{1}{2}$ or $x = 3$ → Factor and solve for x

Check the solution

$\dfrac{5}{\underset{\ne 0}{-\frac{1}{2}-3}} - 2 = \dfrac{30}{\underset{\ne 0}{\left(-\frac{1}{2}\right)^2 - 9}}$, but $\dfrac{5}{\underset{=0}{3-3}} - 2 \ne \dfrac{30}{\underset{=0}{3^2-9}}$

Since $x = -\dfrac{1}{2}$ does not make the denominator zero in the original equation, it is the solution to the equation. However $x = 3$ is an extraneous solution because it is the value that makes the denominator zero. So the only solution for this equation is $x = -\dfrac{1}{2}$.

$x = -\dfrac{1}{2}$

Check Point 1

Solve the equations.

① $2 + \dfrac{12}{5x} = \dfrac{2}{x}$

② $\dfrac{1}{x} + \dfrac{1}{x^2} = \dfrac{1}{2x^2}$

③ $\dfrac{5}{x^2-2x} + \dfrac{2}{x} = \dfrac{5}{x^2-2x}$

④ $\dfrac{30}{x+2} + \dfrac{x}{x-2} = 9$

02 Proportion

Proportion is the equation that two ratios are equal. When two ratios $a:b$ and $c:d$ are equal, we write

$$a : b = c : d \text{ or } \dfrac{a}{b} = \dfrac{c}{d}$$

and this equation is called proportion. The proportion has the following properties.

1. $a : b = c : d \Leftrightarrow \dfrac{a}{b} = \dfrac{c}{d} \Leftrightarrow ad = bc \Leftrightarrow \dfrac{a}{c} = \dfrac{b}{d}$

2. From $a : b = c : d$, if $\dfrac{a}{c} = \dfrac{b}{d} = k (k \neq 0)$, then $a = ck$ and $b = dk$

   From $a : b : c = d : e : f$, if $\dfrac{a}{d} = \dfrac{b}{e} = \dfrac{c}{f} = k (k \neq 0)$, then $a = dk$, $b = ek$, and $c = fk$

3. If $\dfrac{a}{b} = \dfrac{c}{d} = \dfrac{e}{f}$, then $\dfrac{a}{b} = \dfrac{c}{d} = \dfrac{e}{f} = \dfrac{a+c+e}{b+d+f} = \dfrac{ma+nc+pe}{mb+nd+pf}$

   ($b+d+f \neq 0$, $mb+nd+pf \neq 0$)

Proof of 3

Let $\dfrac{a}{b} = \dfrac{c}{d} = \dfrac{e}{f} = k$. Then, since $a = bk$, $c = dk$, and $e = fk$, we have

$a + c + e = bk + dk + fk = k(b+d+f) \Rightarrow k = \dfrac{a+c+e}{b+d+f}$.

Therefore, $\dfrac{a}{b} = \dfrac{c}{d} = \dfrac{e}{f} = k = \dfrac{a+c+e}{b+d+f}$ and also

$\dfrac{ma}{mb} = \dfrac{mc}{mf} = \dfrac{pe}{pf} = \dfrac{ma+nc+pe}{mb+nd+pf}$.

Concept Check

1. In proportion $\dfrac{6}{9}=\dfrac{2}{3} \Leftrightarrow 6\times 3 = 9\times 2 \Leftrightarrow \dfrac{6}{2}=\dfrac{9}{3}$

2. If $a:b=2:3$, the value of $\dfrac{a+b}{a-b}$ is obtained as follows.

Method 1

Let $\dfrac{a}{2}=\dfrac{b}{3}=k$. Then, $a=2k$ and $b=3k$. So we have

$$\dfrac{a+b}{a-b}=\dfrac{2k+3k}{2k-3k}=\dfrac{5k}{-k}=-5$$

Method 2

Since $a:b=2:3 \Leftrightarrow 3a=2b$, $a=\dfrac{2b}{3}$,

$$\dfrac{a+b}{a-b}=\dfrac{\frac{2b}{3}+b}{\frac{2b}{3}-b}=\dfrac{\frac{5b}{3}}{-\frac{b}{3}}=\dfrac{5b}{-b}=-5$$

3. If $\dfrac{1}{2}=\dfrac{2}{4}=\dfrac{3}{6}$, then

   (1) $\dfrac{1}{2}=\dfrac{2}{4}=\dfrac{3}{6}=\dfrac{1+2+3}{2+4+6}=\dfrac{1}{2}$

   (2) $\dfrac{1}{2}=\dfrac{2}{4}=\dfrac{3}{6}=\dfrac{11\cdot 1+12\cdot 2+13\cdot 3}{11\cdot 2+12\cdot 4+13\cdot 6}=\dfrac{1}{2}$

Example 2

Given $a : b = 3 : 4$, find the value of $\dfrac{a-3b}{3a-b}$.

Solution

If we let $a = 3k$ and $b = 4k$ from $a : b = 3 : 4$,

$$\dfrac{a-3b}{3a-b} = \dfrac{3k-3(4k)}{3(3k)-4k} = \dfrac{-9k}{5k} = -\dfrac{9}{5}.$$

$\dfrac{a-3b}{3a-b} = -\dfrac{9}{5}$

Check Point 2

Solutions_Page 40

Given $x : y = 2 : 5$, evaluate each of the following.

① $\dfrac{5x+y}{x-5y}$

② $\dfrac{x^2-y^2}{2x^2+xy}$

Example 3

Given $\dfrac{2a+b}{a+3c} = \dfrac{5b+3c}{c} = \dfrac{5c}{3b} = k$, find the value of k. ($abc \neq 0$, $k \neq 0$)

Solution

Using the property $\dfrac{a}{b} = \dfrac{c}{d} = \dfrac{e}{f} = \dfrac{a+c+e}{b+d+f}$,

$$k = \dfrac{2a+b}{a+3c} = \dfrac{5b+3c}{c} = \dfrac{5c}{3b} = \dfrac{2a+b+5b+3c+5c}{a+3c+c+3b}$$

$$= \dfrac{2a+6b+8c}{a+4c+3b} = \dfrac{2(a+3b+4c)}{a+3b+4c} = 2$$

$k = 2$

Check Point 3

Solutions_Page 40

Given $\dfrac{a-2b}{4} = \dfrac{a}{3} = \dfrac{4b+2c}{5} = \dfrac{3a+2b+2c}{k}$, find the value of k. ($abc \neq 0$, $k \neq 0$)

Review Exercise

01 Solve the rational equation.

(1) $\dfrac{6}{x^2} = \dfrac{1}{x^2} + \dfrac{1}{x}$

(2) $\dfrac{1}{x} - \dfrac{1}{3x^2} = -\dfrac{1}{6x^2}$

(3) $\dfrac{x-6}{3x} - 1 = \dfrac{x^2-5x-24}{3x}$

(4) $\dfrac{1}{x} + \dfrac{3x+12}{x^2-5x} = \dfrac{7x-56}{x^2-5x}$

(5) $\dfrac{1}{x-2} + \dfrac{1}{x^2-7x+10} = \dfrac{6}{x-2}$

(6) $1 - \dfrac{1}{x^2+2x} = \dfrac{x-1}{x}$

Challenging

02 Solve the rational equation.

(1) $\dfrac{x-2}{x+3} - \dfrac{3}{x+2} = 1$

(2) $\dfrac{4}{x+5} + \dfrac{1}{x^2} = \dfrac{5}{x^3+5x^2}$

(3) $\dfrac{x+5}{x^2+x} = \dfrac{1}{x^2+x} - \dfrac{x-6}{x+1}$

(4) $\dfrac{x}{x-1} - \dfrac{1}{x+2} = \dfrac{3}{x^2+x-2}$

Review Exercise

Challenging

03 Given the equation below, find the value of $a+b$.

(1) $\dfrac{2}{2x^2-7x-4}$
$=\dfrac{a}{x-4}-\dfrac{bx}{(x-4)(2x+1)}$

(2) $\dfrac{3x-5}{3x^2-11x+6}$
$=\dfrac{a}{x-3}-\dfrac{x}{(x-3)(3x-2)}+\dfrac{b}{3x-2}$

04 Given $a:b=4:5$, evaluate each of the following.

(1) $\dfrac{a^2+b^2}{2ab}$

(2) $\dfrac{ab+b^2}{a^2-ab}$

05 Given $x:y:z=1:2:3$, evaluate each of the following.

(1) $\dfrac{2x-y+2z}{x+y+z}$

(2) $\dfrac{xy-xz+yz}{x^2+z^2}$

Challenging

06 If $x=2y$ and $3y=4z$, and what is the value of $\dfrac{4x+2y+3z}{x+y+z}$?

07 Given

$$\frac{4a+3c}{7a+9b+10c}=\frac{b+3c}{5a-2c}=\frac{2a+5b}{3b+4c}=k,$$

find the value of k. ($abc \neq 0$, $k \neq 0$)

Challenging

09 If $\dfrac{a+b}{3}=\dfrac{b+c}{4}=\dfrac{a+c}{5}$,

what is the ratio $a:b:c$?

08 Given

$$\frac{2a+4b}{2}=\frac{b+3c}{3}=\frac{2c-a}{4}=\frac{5a+14b+8c}{k},$$

find the value of k. ($abc \neq 0$, $k \neq 0$)

4 Application of Rational Equations

Rational expressions and rational equations can be useful tools for representing real life situations and finding answers to real life problems. It is best to develop your skills by solving problems in various situations.

01 Number Problems

Some applications involve the reciprocals of numbers. The definition of the reciprocal of real number a is the number $\frac{1}{a}$. The product of a number and its reciprocal is always equal to 1:

$$a \times \frac{1}{a} = 1$$

Example 1

There are two positive integers. The first integer is 1 less than twice the second integer. If the sum of the reciprocals of the two integers is $\frac{8}{15}$, what are the two integers?

Solution

Let x be the second integer. Then the first integer is $2x-1$. The reciprocals of these two integers are $\frac{1}{x}$ and $\frac{1}{2x-1}$. Since the sum of the reciprocals of the two integers is $\frac{8}{15}$, we have $\frac{1}{x} + \frac{1}{2x-1} = \frac{8}{15}$.

$$\frac{1}{x} + \frac{1}{2x-1} = \frac{8}{15}$$

$$\left(\frac{1}{x} + \frac{1}{2x-1}\right)15x(2x-1) = \left(\frac{8}{15}\right)15x(2x-1)$$

$$15(2x-1) + 15x = 8x(2x-1)$$

$$30x-15+15x=16x^2-8x$$
$$0=16x^2-53x+15$$
$$0=(16x-5)(x-3), \quad x=\frac{5}{16} \text{ or } x=3$$

Since x is integer, $x=3$. The second integer $2x-1=2(3)-1=5$.

Two integers are 3 and 5

Check Point 1 Solutions_Page 43

① Find two positive numbers that differ by 8 and whose reciprocals differ by $\frac{1}{6}$.

② The difference between two integers is 5. If the reciprocal of the smaller number is added to twice the reciprocal of the larger number, the result is $\frac{23}{66}$. Find the two integers.

02 Distance-Rate-Time Problems

Many distance−rate(speed)−time problems lead to rational equations. Recall that the distance(d), rate(r), and time(t) are related by the following formula:

$$d=rt \Rightarrow r=\frac{d}{t} \Rightarrow t=\frac{d}{r}$$

Also, the average speed is equal to the total distance divided by total time.

Example 2

On his way home from work, Paul traveled 120 miles on local roads and 300 miles on the highways. He traveled 20 miles per hour faster on the highways than he did on local roads. If the trip took a total of 10 hours, what was Paul's speed on each part of the trip?

Solution

Let x be the rate on local roads.

	Local Road	High Way
Rate, r	x mi/hr	$x+20$ mi/hr
Distance, d	120 mi	300 mi
Time, t	$\dfrac{120}{x}$ hr	$\dfrac{300}{x+20}$ hr

Since the trip took a total of 10 hours, we have the equation $\dfrac{120}{x}+\dfrac{300}{x+20}=10$.

$$\dfrac{120}{x}+\dfrac{300}{x+20}=10$$
$$\left(\dfrac{120}{x}+\dfrac{300}{x+20}\right)x(x+20)=(10)x(x+20)$$
$$120(x+20)+300x=10x(x+20)$$
$$120x+2400+300x=10x^2+200x$$
$$0=10x^2-220x-2400,\ 0=x^2-22x-240$$
$$0=(x-30)(x+8),\ x=30 \text{ or } x=-8$$

Since the rate cannot be negative, the value of x must be 30.

Speed on local road: 30 miles per hour
Speed on high way: 50 miles per hour

Check Point 2

Solutions_Page 44

① When it was raining, Josh drove for 75 miles. When the rain stopped, he drove 10 mph faster than he did when it was raining. He drove for 30 miles after the rain stopped. If Josh drove for a total of 2 hours, how fast did he drive when it was raining?

② David rode his rollers skate 24 miles from his house to the park. On his way back, he borrowed a bicycle from his friend. Going twice as fast on the bicycle, the return trip took 2 hours less. What is his average speed for the entire trip?

03 Work Problems

Work problems are those that involve the speed of people or machines. Work problem involving the amount of work done(W), rate of work(r), and the time spent working(t) are simplified by using the following work principles:

$$W=rt \Rightarrow r=\frac{W}{t} \Rightarrow t=\frac{W}{r}$$

Example 3

James can paint his house in 14 hours less time than John, his younger brother, can. Together they can paint the house in 24 hours. How much time would it take for James to paint his house alone?

Solution

Let t be the number of hours for James to paint his house. Then $t+14$ is the number of hours for John to paint the house. Assuming that the total amount of work done(finishing painting) is W,

Part of house painted by James in one hour: $\frac{W}{t}$

Part of house painted by John in one hour: $\frac{W}{t+14}$

Since they can paint the house in 24 hours, we have $\left(\frac{W}{t}+\frac{W}{t+14}\right)\times 24=W$

$$\left(\frac{W}{t}+\frac{W}{t+14}\right)\times 24=W$$
$$\frac{24W}{t}+\frac{24W}{t+14}=W$$
$$\left(\frac{24W}{t}+\frac{24W}{t+14}=W\right)\times\frac{t(t+14)}{W}$$
$$24(t+14)+24t=t(t+14)$$
$$24t+336+24t=t^2+14t$$
$$0=t^2-34t-336$$
$$0=(t-42)(t+8),\ t=42\ \text{or}\ t=-8$$

Since the number of hours cannot be negative, the value of t must be 42.

James can paint his house in 42 hours by himself

Check Point 3

① Joseph and Nick can paint the room in 5 hours working together. If Joseph can paint twice as fast as Nick, how long would it take Nick to paint the room by himself?

② Pump A and B can fill an empty tank in 30 hours and 24 hours, respectively. If both pumps are used together, how long would it take to fill the same empty tank?

Review Exercise

Solutions_Page 45

01 A positive integer is 4 greater than another positive integer. The sum of the reciprocals of the two positive numbers is $\frac{14}{45}$. Find the two integers.

02 A positive integer is 5 more than the other. When the reciprocal of the larger number is subtracted from the reciprocal of the smaller one, the result is $\frac{5}{14}$. Find the two integers.

03 The difference between the reciprocals of two consecutive positive odd integers is $\frac{2}{15}$. Find the two integers.

04 On the Han river, a boat paddled upstream at 12 km per hour and descends back down the same distance(downstream) at 18 km per hour. How far upstream did the boat travel if the total time for the trip was 5 hours?

Chapter 3. Rational Expression 139

Review Exercise

05 Again on the Han river, a boat traveled 15 miles upstream and then traveled the same 15 miles downstream. If the total time for the trip was 4 hours and the boat traveled 8 miles per hour in still water, what is the speed of the current in the river?

06 Min's motorcycle can travel 30 miles against the wind in the same amount of time that it takes him to cover 60 miles with the wind. If the speed of the wind is 3 mph, what is the speed of Min's motorcycle when he is traveling with the wind?

07 Vincent rode a bicycle from city K to city L at a constant speed. For the return trip, he rode at 2 miles per hour faster. The distance between city K to city L is 12 miles. If it took him 5 hours for the entire round trip, what is the speed of the bicycle from city K to city L?

08 Tom's garden hose can fill the pool in 12 hours. His neighbor has a hose that can fill the pool in 15 hours. How long would it take to fill the pool using both hoses?

09 Eric can complete his backyard work in 3 hours. If his son works together, they will be able to finish the work in 2 hours. How long would the yard work take if his son was working alone?

10 On average, it takes Jason 80 minutes to mow the lawn, but his brother can mow the same lawn only in an hour. How long, in minutes, would it take them to mow the same lawn if they work together using two lawn mowers?

Chapter Test — Level 1

01 Simplify the rational expression.

(1) $\dfrac{16x^2-1}{8x-2}$

(2) $\dfrac{6x^2-5x-6}{3x^2+14x+8}$

02 Simplify the rational expression.

(1) $\dfrac{4a+8}{a^2+a-2} \times \dfrac{a^2-1}{4a^3+4a^2}$

(2) $\dfrac{x^2+2x+1}{x^2+3x+2} \div \dfrac{1}{x^2+2x}$

03 Simplify the rational expression.

(1) $\dfrac{1-4x}{2x+1}+\dfrac{2x}{x-4}$

(2) $\dfrac{x+2}{x^2-6x+8}-\dfrac{2}{x-2}$

04 Simplify the complex fraction.

(1) $\dfrac{2-\dfrac{2}{x+2}}{\dfrac{2}{x+2}+2}$

(2) $4-\dfrac{1}{3-\dfrac{1}{1-\dfrac{1}{x}}}$

05 Solve the rational equation.

(1) $\dfrac{6}{x+3}+\dfrac{2}{x-2}=3$

(2) $\dfrac{x-4}{x^2-x-12}+\dfrac{1}{x+3}=1$

06 Given the equation, find the value of $a+b+c$.

(1) $\dfrac{10x+1}{x^2-x-2}=\dfrac{ax+b}{x-2}-\dfrac{cx}{x+1}$

(2) $\dfrac{9x^2+2x-5}{3x^2-5x-2}=\dfrac{a}{3x+1}+\dfrac{bx+c}{x-2}$

07 Use the decomposition of partial fractions to simplify the following rational expression.

(1) $\dfrac{1}{x(x-1)}+\dfrac{1}{(x-1)(x-2)}$

(2) $\dfrac{1}{(x-2)x}+\dfrac{1}{x(x+2)}+\dfrac{1}{(x+2)(x+4)}$

08 Evaluate $\dfrac{1}{1\cdot 2}+\dfrac{1}{2\cdot 3}+\dfrac{1}{3\cdot 4}+\cdots+\dfrac{1}{9\cdot 10}$ using the partial fractions decomposition.

Chapter Test — Level 1

09 Given $x:y = 2:3$, find each of the following.

(1) $\dfrac{3x+2y}{4x-2y}$

(2) $\dfrac{x^2+y^2}{xy}$

10 Given $\dfrac{a+2b}{2a+3b} = \dfrac{b+2c}{3b+4c} = \dfrac{c+2a}{2c+4a} = k$, find the value of k. ($abc \neq 0$, $k \neq 0$)

11 A positive integer is 2 more than the other. When the reciprocal of the larger number is subtracted from the reciprocal of the smaller one, the result is $\dfrac{1}{4}$. Find the two integers.

12 One day, Andy drove 50 miles from home to work. When he returned home, he increased his average speed 10 miles per hour higher than the speed on the way to work. If this reduced his return time by 10 minutes, what was his average speed going to work?

Chapter Test — Level 2

01 Simplify the rational expression.

(1) $\dfrac{(a^3+b^3)(a^2+ab+b^2)}{a^6-b^6}$

(2) $\dfrac{(x^4-y^4)(x^2+xy+y^2)}{(x^3-y^3)(x+y)}$

02 Simplify the rational expression.

(1) $\dfrac{2x+y}{x^3-y^3} \times \dfrac{x^2-y^2}{2x^2+3xy+y^2}$

(2) $\dfrac{x+2}{x^2-x-2} \div \dfrac{x^2-1}{x^3-8} \div \dfrac{x^2+4x+4}{x-1}$

03 Simplify the rational expression.

(1) $\dfrac{x-2}{2x^2-5x-3} + \dfrac{2}{2x+1} - \dfrac{3}{x-3}$

(2) $\dfrac{3}{x^2-x-12} - \dfrac{2}{x^2-16} + \dfrac{1}{x+4}$

04 If $2 - \dfrac{1}{2-\dfrac{1}{2-\dfrac{1}{2-x}}} = \dfrac{ax-b}{cx-d}$, where a, b, c, and d are all positive integers, what is the value of $a+b+c+d$?

Chapter Test — Level 2

05 $A \div B = \dfrac{1}{\dfrac{B}{A}}$

For each of the following equations, where a, b, and c are all positive integers, use the above method to find the value of $a+b+c$.

(1) $\dfrac{43}{30} = 1 + \dfrac{1}{a + \dfrac{1}{b + \dfrac{1}{c}}}$

(2) $\dfrac{20}{69} = \dfrac{1}{a + \dfrac{1}{b + \dfrac{1}{c + \dfrac{1}{2}}}}$

06 $\dfrac{AB+C}{A} = \dfrac{AB}{A} + \dfrac{C}{A} = B + \dfrac{C}{A}$

Use the above method to simplify the following expression.

(1) $\dfrac{x+1}{x} + \dfrac{x+2}{x+1} - \dfrac{x+3}{x+2} - \dfrac{x+4}{x+3}$

(2) $\dfrac{x^2+2x+2}{x+2} - \dfrac{x^2-2x+2}{x-2}$

07 Use the decomposition of partial fractions to simplify the following rational expression.

(1) $\dfrac{1}{(x-4)(x-2)} + \dfrac{1}{(x-2)x} + \dfrac{1}{x(x+2)} + \dfrac{1}{(x+2)(x+4)}$

(2) $\dfrac{2}{x^2+2x} + \dfrac{1}{x^2+5x+6} + \dfrac{2}{x^2+8x+15} - \dfrac{5}{x^2+5x}$

08 Simplify $\dfrac{y}{x(x+y)}+\dfrac{z}{(x+y)(x+y+z)}+\dfrac{k}{(x+y+z)(x+y+z+k)}$ in terms of x, y, z, and k.

09 Given $x^2-3x+1=0$, find the value of the following expression.

(1) $x^3+\dfrac{1}{x^3}$

(2) $x^4+\dfrac{1}{x^4}$

(3) $x^5+\dfrac{1}{x^5}$

10 Given $\dfrac{3a}{4}=\dfrac{3a-b}{2}=\dfrac{2b-c}{3}=\dfrac{3a+b-2c}{k}$, find the value of k. ($abc\neq 0$, $k\neq 0$)

Chapter 4
Quadratic Equations

1. Solving Basic Quadratic Equations
2. Complex Number
3. Completing the Square and the Quadratic Formula
4. More Complicated Quadratic Equations
5. Solutions and Coefficients of the Quadratic Equations
6. Word Problems
7. Chapter Test

1 Solving Basic Quadratic Equations

01 Definition of Quadratic Equation

A Quadratic Equation is a polynomial equation of a second degree. For instance, $2x^2+4x+-5=0$ or $-3x^2+1=4x$ are typical examples of quadratic equations. A general quadratic equation can be written in the form:

$$ax^2+bx+c=0 \Rightarrow \begin{cases} ax^2 : \text{Quadratic term} \\ bx : \text{Linear term} \\ c : \text{Constant term} \end{cases}$$

where x represents a variable or an unknown and a, b, and c are constants with $a \neq 0$.

The solutions, roots, or zeros of a quadratic equation are the values of the variable, x, for which the equation is true. There are usually two solutions to the quadratic equation, although there sometimes is one or no solution to the equation.

Example 1

Which of the following is NOT a quadratic equation?

(A) $2x^2-5x+1=0$
(B) $2(x-1)(x+2)-x^2=1$
(C) $x^2(3x-2)-3x(x+1)=0$
(D) $3x^2-4x+1=4x(x-2)$
(E) $\frac{1}{2}(1-x)(1+x)-\frac{1}{2}=0$

Solution

(A) $2x^2-5x+1=0$ → Quadratic equation

(B) $2(x-1)(x+2)-x^2=1$
$2(x^2+x-2)-x^2=1$
$x^2+2x-5=0$ → Quadratic equation

(C) $x^2(3x-2)-3x(x+1)=0$
$3x^3-2x^2-3x^2-3x=0$
$3x^3-5x^2-3x=0$ → Cubic equation

(D) $3x^2-4x+1=4x(x-2)$
$3x^2-4x+1=4x^2-8x$
$x^2-4x-1=0$ → Quadratic equation

(E) $\frac{1}{2}(1-x)(1+x)-\frac{1}{2}=0$
$\frac{1}{2}(1-x^2)-\frac{1}{2}=0$
$\frac{1}{2}-\frac{1}{2}x^2-\frac{1}{2}=0$, $\frac{1}{2}x^2=0$ → Quadratic equation

The answer is (C)

Check Point 1 Solutions_Page 54

Which of the following is a quadratic equation?

(A) $3x+1=4(x-2)$
(B) $x^3-3x+1=2(x^2+1)$
(C) $(2x+1)^2-4x^2=0$
(D) $(x-2)(x+2)-(2x-1)(2x+1)+3=0$
(E) $(x-4)(4+x)+(x+1)(1-x)=x$

02 Solving by Finding Square Roots

This method can be used in the following two cases:

1. $ax^2=b$, where $\left(\frac{b}{a}\geq 0\right)$. The equation has no x term.
   $\Rightarrow x^2=\frac{b}{a}$, $x=\pm\sqrt{\frac{b}{a}}$

2. $(x+a)^2=b$, where $(b\geq 0)$.
   $\Rightarrow x+a=\pm\sqrt{b}$, $x=-a\pm\sqrt{b}$

Note that every positive number has two square roots: a positive square root and a negative square root.

Chapter 4. Quadratic Equations

Concept Check

$(x-4)^2 - 10 = 0$

$(x-4)^2 = 10$ → Add 10 to each side

$x-4 = \pm\sqrt{10}$ → Take the square root

$x = 4 \pm \sqrt{10}$ → Add 4 to each side

The solutions are $x = 4+\sqrt{10}$ and $x = 4-\sqrt{10}$

Example 2

Solve the equation by taking square roots.

① $4x^2 - 9 = 0$ ② $2(x+1)^2 + 3 = 15$

Solution

① $4x^2 - 9 = 0$

$4x^2 = 9$, $x^2 = \dfrac{9}{4}$

$x = \pm\sqrt{\dfrac{9}{4}} = \pm\dfrac{3}{2}$

The solutions are $x = \dfrac{3}{2}$ and $x = -\dfrac{3}{2}$

② $2(x+1)^2 + 3 = 15$

$2(x+1)^2 = 12$, $(x+1)^2 = 6$

$x+1 = \pm\sqrt{6}$, $x = -1 \pm \sqrt{6}$

The solutions are $x = -1+\sqrt{6}$ and $x = -1-\sqrt{6}$

Check Point 2   Solutions_Page 54

Solve the equation by taking square roots.

① $6x^2 + 5 = 59$ ② $4x^2 - 3 = 2 - x^2$

③ $(2x-1)^2 = 25$ ④ $2(2x-3)^2 - 4 = 10$

03 Solving by Factoring

Follow the instructions below.
1. Write the quadratic function in standard form. $\Rightarrow ax^2+bx+c=0$
2. Factor the left side of a quadratic equation. $\Rightarrow a(x-\alpha)(x-\beta)=0$
3. Use Zero-Product Property:

$a(x-\alpha)(x-\beta)=0$	$a(x-\alpha)^2=0$
$x-\alpha=0$ or $x-\beta=0$	$x-\alpha=0$
$x=\alpha$ or $x=\beta$	$x=\alpha$

Concept Check

$(x-2)(x+2)-1=4x$

$x^2-4-1=4x$ → Expand left side

$x^2-4x-5=0$ → Write in standard form

$(x-5)(x+1)=0$ → Factor

$x-5=0$ or $x+1=0$ → Zero product property

$x=5$ or $x=-1$ → Solve for x

The solutions are $x=5$ and $x=-1$

Example 3

Solve the equation by factoring.

① $x^2-x-2=0$ ② $2x^2+18x+36=0$

③ $x^2+8=2(4-3x)$ ④ $(x+2)^2=x+2$

Solution

① $x^2-x-2=0$
$(x-2)(x+1)=0$
$x-2=0$ or $x+1=0$
$x=2$ or $x=-1$

The solutions are $x=2$ and $x=-1$

② $2x^2+18x+36=0$, $x^2+9x+18=0$
$(x+3)(x+6)=0$
$x+3=0$ or $x+6=0$
$x=-3$ or $x=-6$

The solutions are $x=-3$ and $x=-6$

③ $x^2+8=2(4-3x)$, $x^2+8=8-6x$
$x^2+6x=0$, $x(x+6)=0$
$x=0$ or $x+6=0$
$x=0$ or $x=-6$

The solutions are $x=0$ and $x=-6$

④ $(x+2)^2=x+2$, $x^2+4x+4=x+2$
$x^2+3x+2=0$, $(x+1)(x+2)=0$
$x+1=0$ or $x+2=0$
$x=-1$ or $x=-2$

The solutions are $x=-1$ and $x=-2$

Check Point 3   Solutions_Page 54

Solve the equation by factoring.

① $2x^2+3x-2=0$ ② $3x^2-2x=2x^2+24$
③ $2(x-3)^2=8x$ ④ $(x+2)(x-2)=3x(x-1)-(x+2)$

Review Exercise

01 Solve each equation by taking square roots.

(1) $x^2+4=8$

(2) $x^2-4=32$

(3) $9x^2-12=60$

(4) $10+5x^2=330$

(5) $8x^2+8=31$

(6) $(2x-5)^2=81$

(7) $4(3x+1)^2=36$

(8) $\dfrac{5x^2}{2}-x^2=216$

Review Exercise

02 Solve each equation by factoring.

(1) $x^2+4x+4=0$

(2) $x^2-15x-100=0$

(3) $8x^2+4x=0$

(4) $3x^2-33x+72=0$

(5) $7x^2+35x-42=0$

(6) $6x^2+15x+9=0$

(7) $7x^2+32=7-40x$

(8) $x(x-2)=3(x-2)$

Challenging

03 Solve each equation by factoring.

(1) $(x+6)^2+x^2=3(x+12)$

(2) $\dfrac{(3x+1)(2x-3)}{2}=x^2-3$

(3) $2x^2+12=3(x-2)^2$

(4) $x^2-5x=\dfrac{3}{4}(x-4)(x+2)$

04 If the quadratic equation
$$4(x+3)(x-4)=\dfrac{1}{2}(2x+1)(x-2)+\dfrac{3}{2}x$$
is written as $ax^2+bx+c=0$, what is the value of $a+b+c$?

Challenging

05 Find the condition of the constant a such that $(x+3)^2+x^2=ax^2-4x+1$ is a quadratic equation.

Review Exercise

06 Which of the following quadratic equations has $x=3$ as the solution?

(A) $3x^2-x=0$

(B) $3x^2+8x-3=0$

(C) $(x-3)^2-1=0$

(D) $(x+3)(x-4)+2x=0$

(E) $\dfrac{(x+1)^2}{2}=2$

07 $\dfrac{1}{2}x^2+2kx-5=0$

If one of the solutions to the quadratic equation above is $x=4$, what is the value of k?

Challenging

08 Suppose that one of the solutions to the quadratic equation $2x^2-x+2=0$ is m. Evaluate each of the following.

(1) $2m^2-m+12$

(2) $m^2+\dfrac{1}{m^2}$

09 Solve the quadratic equation $(x-2)(x+3)=2(x-2)(2x+1)$.

10 If the larger of the two solutions of quadratic equation $x^2+5x-14=0$ is also the solution of quadratic equation $5x^2-2x-k=0$, what is the value of k?

2 Complex Number

01 Definition of Complex Number

A complex number is a number that can be written in the form $a+bi$, where a and b are real numbers and i is called the imaginary unit, where $i=\sqrt{-1}$. In this expression, a is called the real part and b the imaginary part of the complex number.

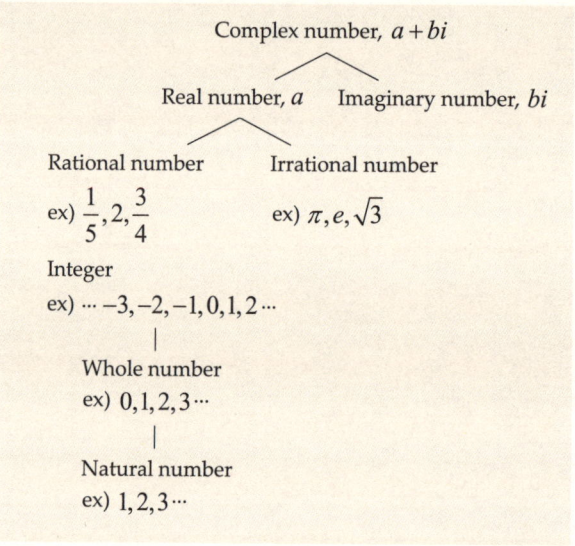

Property of imaginary unit, i

1. $i=\sqrt{-1}$
   $i^2=(\sqrt{-1})^2=-1$
   $i^3=i^1 \cdot i^2=i(-1)=-i$
   $i^4=i^2 \cdot i^2=(-1)(-1)=1$

   Concept Check

   $i^{27}=(i^4)^6 \cdot i^3=(1)^6(-i)=-i$
   $i^{1248}=(i^4)^{312}=(1)^{312}=1$
   $i+i^2+i^3+i^4=i-1-i+1=0$

2. For positive real number a
   (1) $\sqrt{-a}=\sqrt{a}i$
   (2) Square root of $-a$ is $\pm\sqrt{a}i$

   Concept Check

   $\sqrt{-16}=\sqrt{16}\cdot\sqrt{-1}=\sqrt{16}\,i=4i$
   Square root of -9 is $\pm\sqrt{9}i=\pm 3i$

02 Complex Conjugate

Complex conjugates are a pair of complex numbers with an identical real part and imaginary part of equal magnitude and opposite signs. The complex conjugate of the complex number $a+bi$ is defined to be $a-bi$.

Concept Check

1. The complex conjugate of $4+3i$ is $4-3i$.
2. The complex conjugate of $-2i$ is $2i$.

03 Identical Complex Number

Complex numbers are considered the same if the following conditions are satisfied.

For real number a, b, c, and d,
1. $a+bi=c+di$ ↔ $a=c$, $b=d$
2. $a+bi=0$ ↔ $a=0$, $b=0$

Concept Check

1. If $3+ai=b-4i$, then $a=-4$ and $b=3$
2. If $a+bi=2$, then $a=2$ and $b=0$

Example 1

Find a and b that satisfies the equations.

① $2ai+4b=4-3i$

② $a(1-2i)+b(3+i)=5+4i$

> Solution

① $2ai+4b=4-3i$
   $2a=-3$ and $4b=4$
   $a=-\frac{3}{2}$ and $b=1$

$a=-\frac{3}{2}, \ b=1$

② $a(1-2i)+b(3+i)=5+4i$
   $a-2ai+3b+bi=5+4i$
   $(a+3b)+(-2a+b)i=5+4i \Rightarrow \begin{cases} a+3b=5 \\ -2a+b=4 \end{cases}$
   Solving the system above, we have $a=-1$ and $b=2$.

$a=-1, \ b=2$

> Check Point 1   Solutions_Page 57

Find a and b that satisfies the equations.

① $3a-b(2-i)=4$ ② $a(1-i)+(1+2i)b=6+3i$

③ $(1+i)a-(1-i)b+2-3i=0$

04 Addition and Subtraction of Complex Numbers

Complex numbers are added or subtracted as follows.

For real number a, b, c, and d,

1. Addition: $(a+bi)+(c+di)=(a+c)+(b+d)i$
2. Subtraction: $(a+bi)-(c+di)=(a-c)+(b-d)i$

Concept Check

1. $(1+2i)+(2+3i)=1+2i+2+3i=(1+2)+(2+3)i=3+5i$

2. $(1+2i)-(2+3i)=1+2i-2-3i=(1-2)+(2-3)i=-1-i$

Chapter 4. Quadratic Equations ion

Example 2

Express the following in the form $a+bi$.

① $4-(3+5i)$
② $(2-3i)+(3-4i)$
③ $(7+\sqrt{-25})-(3-\sqrt{-36})$
④ $(2-\sqrt{-4})-(4+2\sqrt{-64})+4\sqrt{-16}$

Solution

① $4-(3+5i)=4-3-5i=(4-3)-5i=1-5i$

② $(2-3i)+(3-4i)=(2+3)+(-3-4)i=5-7i$

③ $(7+\sqrt{-25})-(3-\sqrt{-36})=(7+\sqrt{25}i)-(3-\sqrt{36}i)=(7+5i)-(3-6i)$
$=7+5i-3+6i=(7-3)+(5+6)i=4+11i$

④ $(2-\sqrt{-4})-(4+2\sqrt{-64})+4\sqrt{-16}=(2-\sqrt{4}i)-(4+2\sqrt{64}i)+4\sqrt{16}i$
$=(2-2i)-(4+2\cdot 8i)+4\cdot 4i=2-2i-4-16i+16i$
$=(2-4)+(-2-16+16)i=-2-2i$

Check Point 2

Express the following in the form $a+bi$.

① $(2-3i)+(5-i)$
② $(3-4i)-(4-9i)$
③ $2\sqrt{-121}+(4+\sqrt{-25})$
④ $(7+\sqrt{-16})+(2-\sqrt{-49})-2\sqrt{-9}$

05 Multiplication and Division of Complex Numbers

Complex numbers are multiplied or divided as follows.

For real number a, b, c, and d,

1. Multiplication: $(a+bi)(c+di)=(ac-bd)+(ad+bc)i$
2. Division
   (1) $\dfrac{a+bi}{ci}=\dfrac{a+bi}{ci}\cdot\dfrac{i}{i}=\dfrac{-b+ai}{-c}=\dfrac{b-ai}{c}$
   (2) $\dfrac{a+bi}{c+di}=\dfrac{(a+bi)(c-di)}{(c+di)(c-di)}=\dfrac{(ac+bd)+(bc-ad)i}{c^2+d^2}$, $(c+di\neq 0)$

Concept Check

1. $(1+2i)(2+3i)$
   $=2+3i+4i+6i^2$ → Expand the expression using FOIL
   $=2+3i+4i-6$ → $i^2=-1$
   $=-4+7i$ → Simphfy

2. $\dfrac{2+3i}{2i}$
   $=\dfrac{2+3i}{2i}\cdot\dfrac{i}{i}=\dfrac{2i+3i^2}{2i^2}$ → Multiply the denominator and the numerator by i
   $=\dfrac{2i-3}{-2}$ → $i^2=-1$
   $=\dfrac{3-2i}{2}$ → Simphfy

3. $\dfrac{2+3i}{1+2i}$
   $=\dfrac{(2+3i)(1-2i)}{(1+2i)(1-2i)}$ → The complex conjugate of the denominator multiplies the numerator and denominator
   $=\dfrac{2-i-6i^2}{1-4i^2}$ → Use FOIL to expand the numerator and $(a-b)(a+b)=a^2-b^2$ to expand the denominator

$$= \frac{2-i+6}{1+4} \quad \rightarrow\ i^2=-1$$

$$= \frac{8-i}{5} \quad \rightarrow\ \text{Simplify}$$

Example 3

Express the following in the form $a+bi$.

① $(3+4i)(-2i)$ ② $(1+2i)(3-5i)$

③ $\dfrac{3-5i}{3i}$ ④ $\dfrac{2+i}{1-2i}$

Solution

① $(3+4i)(-2i) = -6i-8i^2 = 8-6i$

② $(1+2i)(3-5i) = 3-5i+6i-10i^2$
$= 3+i+10 = 13+i$

③ $\dfrac{3-5i}{3i} = \dfrac{3-5i}{3i} \cdot \dfrac{i}{i} = \dfrac{3i-5i^2}{3i^2} = \dfrac{5+3i}{-3} = -\dfrac{5+3i}{3}$

④ $\dfrac{2+i}{1-2i} = \dfrac{(2+i)(1+2i)}{(1-2i)(1+2i)} = \dfrac{2+4i+i+2i^2}{1-4i^2} = \dfrac{2+5i-2}{1+4} = \dfrac{5i}{5} = i$

Check Point 3

Solutions_Page 58

Express the following in the form $a+bi$.

① $\sqrt{-4}(4-\sqrt{-9})$ ② $(-2-i)(4+i)$

③ $(2-\sqrt{-25})^2$ ④ $\dfrac{3-2i}{3+2i}$

Review Exercise

01 Find a and b that satisfies the equations.

(1) $a(2-i)+b(3+i)=10$

(2) $(i-4)a-(2+3i)b=-2(2i-1)$

(3) $(2a+1)(3+2i)+8=bi$

(4) $\dfrac{a}{1+i}+\dfrac{b}{1-i}=2-3i$

02 Express the following in the form $a+bi$.

(1) $(2+i)+6i$

(2) $\sqrt{-16}+\sqrt{-4}$

(3) $(2+3i)-(4-6i)$

(4) $(3+\sqrt{-1})-\sqrt{-27}$

(5) $-3\sqrt{-75}+\sqrt{-9}$

(6) $3(-1-\sqrt{-4})+(-\sqrt{-9}+7)$

(7) $(21-2i)-2(-3i+12)-(1+9i)$

(8) $\left(\dfrac{3}{2}+\dfrac{5}{8}i\right)+\left(-\dfrac{1}{4}+\dfrac{1}{4}i\right)$

03 Express the following in the form $a+bi$.

(1) $-i(2-i)$

(2) $(7-6i)(3i-8)$

(3) $(1+\sqrt{-1})(2-\sqrt{-4})$

(4) $(\sqrt{-36}-8)(4+\sqrt{-16})$

(5) $-i(3i+7)(-1-2i)$

(6) $(1+i)(4+3i)(7+8i)$

(7) $(1-i)^3$

(8) $(3+2i)^2(3-2i)^2$

04 Express the following in the form $a+bi$.

(1) $\dfrac{8i-1}{i}$

(2) $\dfrac{8}{1-i}$

(3) $\dfrac{\sqrt{-1}}{\sqrt{-9}-1}$

(4) $\dfrac{1+\sqrt{-1}}{1-\sqrt{-1}}$

(5) $\dfrac{3i+5}{10i-7}$

(6) $\dfrac{5i+10}{6-6i}$

05 Simplify each of the following.

(1) i^{18}

(2) $(1+i)^2$

(3) $(1-3i)^2$

(4) $(1+i)^4$

Review Exercise

06 Given $x=2-i$, evaluate each of the following

(1) x^2-5x+6

(2) x^3-x^2+1

Challenging

07 If $A=4-3i$, $B=4+3i$, and $A^2B+AB^2=a+bi$, what is the value of $a+b$?

Challenging

08 Simplify each of the following.

(1) $(1+i)^{10}$

(2) $\left(\dfrac{1+i}{1-i}\right)^{16}$

(3) $i+i^2+i^3+i^4+\cdots+i^{20}$

(4) $i+2i^2+3i^3+4i^4+\cdots+20i^{20}$

Challenging

09 If $0<k<1$, which of the following is equal to $\sqrt{-k}\times\sqrt{k}-\dfrac{\sqrt{k-1}}{\sqrt{1-k}}\times\sqrt{\dfrac{k-1}{1-k}}$?

(A) $k+i$

(B) $ki+1$

(C) $(k+1)i$

(D) $k+1$

(E) $k-1$

Challenging

10 Evaluete

$\dfrac{1}{i}+\dfrac{1}{i^2}+\dfrac{1}{i^3}+\dfrac{1}{i^4}+\cdots+\dfrac{1}{i^{100}}.$

3. Completing the Square and the Quadratic Formula

01 Completing the Square

Quadratic equations are best solved by factoring, but not all quadratic equations can be factored. Consider $x^2-x+1=0$, for example. However, we can solve any forms of quadratic equation by transforming

$$ax^2+bx+c=0 \Rightarrow (x-h)^2=d,$$

where h and d are constants. This process is called completing the square. This process is rather cumbersome, although it is very important in a variety of applications you may encounter in subsequent courses.

Concept Check

Given quadratic equation, $\qquad ax^2+bx+c=0$

1. Make the coefficient of the squared term 1. $\qquad x^2+\dfrac{bx}{a}+\dfrac{c}{a}=0$

2. Isolate the variable terms. $\qquad x^2+\dfrac{bx}{a}=-\dfrac{c}{a}$

3. Add the square of one-half the coefficient of the linear term to both sides. $\qquad x^2+\dfrac{bx}{a}+\left(\dfrac{b}{2a}\right)^2=-\dfrac{c}{a}+\left(\dfrac{b}{2a}\right)^2$

4. Factor the trinomial on the left side. $\qquad \left(x+\dfrac{b}{2a}\right)^2=\text{some constant } d$

5. Solve for x. $\qquad x=-\dfrac{b}{2a}\pm\sqrt{d}$

Example 1

Solve the equation by completing the square.

① $x^2-4x+2=0$ ② $2x^2+6x-5=0$

Solution

① $x^2-4x+2=0$
$x^2-4x=-2$ → Move constant term 2 to the right side
$x^2-4x+(2)^2=-2+(2)^2$ → Add square of half of 4, 2^2, to both sides
$(x-2)^2=2$ → Change to $(x-h)^2=d$ form
$x-2=\pm\sqrt{2}$ → Take square root for both sides
$x=2\pm\sqrt{2}$ → Solve for x

The solutions are $x=2+\sqrt{2}$ and $x=2-\sqrt{2}$

② $2x^2+6x-5=0$ → Given.
$x^2+3x-\frac{5}{2}=0$ → Divide all terms by 2
$2x^2+3x=\frac{5}{2}$ → Move constant term $-\frac{5}{2}$ to the right side
$x^2+3x+\left(\frac{3}{2}\right)^2=\frac{5}{2}+\left(\frac{3}{2}\right)^2$ → Add square of half of 3, $\left(\frac{3}{2}\right)^2$, to both sides
$\left(x+\frac{3}{2}\right)^2=\frac{5}{2}+\frac{9}{4}$ → Change to $(x-h)^2=d$ form
$\left(x+\frac{3}{2}\right)^2=\frac{19}{4}$ → Simplify the right side
$x+\frac{3}{2}=\pm\sqrt{\frac{19}{4}}$ → Take square root for both sides.
$x=-\frac{3}{2}\pm\frac{\sqrt{19}}{2}$ → Solve for x

The solutions are $x=\frac{-3+\sqrt{19}}{2}$ and $x=\frac{-3-\sqrt{19}}{2}$

Check Point 1

Solutions_Page 60

Solve the equation by completing the square.

① $x^2-8x+6=0$ ② $4x^2+12x-5=0$

③ $4x^2-1=(x+3)(x-2)$ ④ $\frac{1}{2}x^2+8x-\frac{3}{2}=0$

02 Quadratic Formula

The quadratic formula is developed through solving a quadratic equation by completing the square. It expresses the solutions to any quadratic equation.

The solutions to the equation $ax^2+bx+c=0$ $(a\neq 0)$ are $x=\dfrac{-b\pm\sqrt{b^2-4ac}}{2a}$.

Concept Check

$ax^2+bx+c=0\ (a\neq 0)$

$x^2+\dfrac{bx}{a}+\dfrac{c}{a}=0$ → Divide all terms by a

$x^2+\dfrac{bx}{a}=-\dfrac{c}{a}$ → Move constant term $\dfrac{c}{a}$ to the right side

$x^2+\dfrac{bx}{a}+\left(\dfrac{b}{2a}\right)^2=-\dfrac{c}{a}+\left(\dfrac{b}{2a}\right)^2$ → Add $\left(\dfrac{a}{2b}\right)^2$ to both sides

$\left(x+\dfrac{b}{2a}\right)^2=\dfrac{b^2-4ac}{4a^2}$ → Change to $(x-h)^2=d$ form

$x+\dfrac{b}{2a}=\pm\sqrt{\dfrac{b^2-4ac}{4a^2}}$ → Take square root for both sides

$x=-\dfrac{b}{2a}\pm\dfrac{\sqrt{b^2-4ac}}{2a}$ → Solve for x

The solutions to the equation $ax^2+bx+c=0(a\neq 0)$ are

$$x=\dfrac{-b+\sqrt{b^2-4ac}}{2a} \text{ and } x=\dfrac{-b-\sqrt{b^2-4ac}}{2a}.$$

Example 2

Solve the equation $x^2+3x-1=0$ by using quadratic formula.

> Solution

$x^2+3x-1=0$

The equation is in appropriate form $ax^2+bx+c=0$. Since the coefficients can be identified as $a=1$, $b=3$, and $c=-1$, substitute values into the formula
$x=\dfrac{-b\pm\sqrt{b^2-4ac}}{2a}$.

$x=\dfrac{-3\pm\sqrt{(3)^2-4(1)(-1)}}{2(1)}=\dfrac{-3\pm\sqrt{9+4}}{2}=\dfrac{-3\pm\sqrt{13}}{2}$

$x=\dfrac{-3+\sqrt{13}}{2}$ or $x=\dfrac{-3-\sqrt{13}}{2}$

The solutions are $x=\dfrac{-3+\sqrt{13}}{2}$ and $x=\dfrac{-3-\sqrt{13}}{2}$

> Check Point 2

Solve the equation by using quadratic formula.

① $x^2-4x-5=0$

② $2x^2-3x-3=0$

③ $0.3x^2+0.5x-1.1=0$

Review Exercise

01 Solve the equation by completing the square.

(1) $x^2 - 4x - 12 = 0$

(2) $x^2 - 2x - 35 = 0$

(3) $x^2 = -10x + 3$

(4) $9x^2 - 18x + 5 = 0$

(5) $4x^2 + 8x + 31 = 0$

(6) $5x^2 - 2x = 16$

Challenging

02 Solve the equation by completing the square.

(1) $\frac{1}{3}x^2 - 3x - \frac{1}{2} = 0$

(2) $\frac{1}{2}x^2 - 4x = -3$

(3) $0.5x^2 - x + 0.2 = 0$

(4) $(x+2)^2 = 3(x-4)$

(5) $(x-1)(x+1) - 4x$
    $= (2x-1)(2x+1)$

(6) $ax^2 + bx + c = 0$

03 Solve the equation by using quadratic formula.

(1) $x^2 - x - 12 = 0$

(2) $x^2 + 5x - 6 = 0$

(3) $2x^2 - x - 6 = 0$

(4) $x^2 - 3x + 1 = 0$

Review Exercise

(5) $-8x^2=6x+5$

(3) $x^2-\dfrac{5}{3}x=0.6$

(4) $(0.5x+2)\left(x-\dfrac{1}{2}\right)=x-1$

(6) $3x^2-x=-2$

Challenging

04 Solve the equation by using quadratic formula.

(1) $\dfrac{3}{4}x^2-\dfrac{1}{2}x-\dfrac{5}{6}=0$

05 If the quadratic equation $x^2-2x+a=0$ is solved by completing the square, the solution is $x=1\pm\sqrt{7}$. Find the value of a.

(2) $0.4x^2-x-0.1=0$

06 If the quadratic equation $\frac{1}{2}x^2 - x - \frac{1}{4} = 0$ is solved by using quadratic formula, the solution is $x = a \pm \frac{\sqrt{b}}{c}$, where a, b, and c are positive integers. Find the value of abc.

Challenging

08 If the quadratic equation $x^2 - 10x + 2m = 5$ has one real solution, what is the value of m?

07 If $2x^2 + \frac{1}{4}x + a = 2\left(x + \frac{1}{b}\right)^2$, what is the value of ab?

Challenging

09 If the quadratic equation $5x^2 + 4x + 1 = 0$ can be written in the form $(x+h)^2 = k$, what is the value of $\frac{h}{k}$?

4. More Complicated Quadratic Equations

01 More Complicated Quadratic Equations

Consider the following equations:

$$(x+1)^3-4(x+1)^2-5(x+1)=0, \quad x^4-9x^2+20=0, \quad \text{and} \quad 2\left(\frac{2y}{3}\right)^4-3\left(\frac{2y}{3}\right)^2-2=0.$$

None of these complicated equations are quadratic, yet each can be solved by using quadratic methods. Each equation can be rewritten in quadratic form using substitution method.

Concept Check

$(x+1)^3-4(x+1)^2-5(x+1)=0$

$k^3-4k^2-5k=0$ → Substitute k for $x+1$

$k(k-5)(k+1)=0$ → Factor

$k=0$, $k-5=0$ or $k+1=0$ → Zero product property

$x+1=0$, $(x+1)-5=0$ or $(x+1)+1=0$ → Substitute $x+1$ for k

$x=-1$, $x=4$ or $x=-2$ → Solve for x

The solutions are $x=-1$, $x=4$ and $x=-2$

Example 1

Solve the equations.

① $x^4-9x^2+20=0$

② $2\left(\frac{2y}{3}\right)^2-3\left(\frac{2y}{3}\right)-2=0$

Solution

① $x^4-9x^2+20=0$

$(x^2)^2-9(x^2)+20=0$ → Substitute k for x^2

$k^2-9k+20=0$
$(k-5)(k-4)=0$
$k-5=0$ or $k-4=0$
$x^2-5=0$ or $x^2-4=0$
$x=\pm\sqrt{5}$ or $x=\pm 2$

The solutions are $x=\pm\sqrt{5}$ and $x=\pm 2$

② $2\left(\dfrac{2y}{3}\right)^2-3\left(\dfrac{2y}{3}\right)-2=0$ → Substitute k for $\dfrac{2y}{3}$

$2k^2-3k-2=0$
$(2k+1)(k-2)=0$
$2k+1=0$ or $k-2=0$
$2\left(\dfrac{2y}{3}\right)+1=0$ or $\left(\dfrac{2y}{3}\right)-2=0$
$\dfrac{4y}{3}=-1$ or $\dfrac{2y}{3}=2$
$y=\dfrac{-3}{4}$ or $y=3$

The solutions are $y=\dfrac{-3}{4}$ and $y=3$

Check Point 1 Solutions_Page 64

Solve the equations.

① $(2a-5)^2-7(2a-5)+10=0$ ② $2x^4+5x^2-12=0$

③ $y^{-2}-y^{-1}-12=0$ ④ $5\left(\dfrac{3x-1}{2}\right)^2-3\left(\dfrac{3x-1}{2}\right)-2=0$

Review Exercise

01 Solve the equations.

(1) $(x+3)^2 - 5(x+3) + 4 = 0$

(2) $(2y-5)^2 - (2y-5) - 2 = 0$

(3) $(x^2-4)^2 - 2(x^2-4) - 15 = 0$

(4) $(2y^2-1)^2 - 10(2y^2-1) + 24 = 0$

(5) $\left(\dfrac{2x-5}{3}\right)^2 - 5\left(\dfrac{2x-5}{3}\right) + 6 = 0$

(6) $2\left(\dfrac{1}{x}\right)^2 + 5\left(\dfrac{1}{x}\right) - 3 = 0$

02 Solve the equations.

(1) $a^{-2} - a^{-1} = 20$

(2) $3a^{-2} - 8a^{-1} + 4 = 0$

(3) $x^4 - 6x^2 + 8 = 0$

(4) $2h^4 + 5h^2 - 12 = 0$

03 Solve the equations.

(1) $y^6 - 8y^3 + 15 = 0$

(2) $\dfrac{3}{2}(2x-3)^2 - 8(2x-3) = -\dfrac{5}{2}$

(3) $\dfrac{1}{4}(x-2)^2 - \dfrac{3}{20}(x-2) - \dfrac{1}{10} = 0$

(4) $\dfrac{3}{2}\left(\dfrac{1}{3x}+2\right)^2 - \left(\dfrac{1}{3x}+2\right) = \dfrac{1}{2}$

04 For the quadratic equation $(x-2y)(x-2y-4) = 5$, find all possible value of $4x - 8y$.

5. Solutions and Coefficients of the Quadratic Equations

01 Discriminant

Using the quadratic formula, we could find the solutions of the quadratic equation $ax^2+bx+c=0 (a \neq 0)$. In quadratic formula $x=\dfrac{-b \pm \sqrt{b^2-4ac}}{2a}$, the part b^2-4ac is called the discriminant D, and this is to determine the nature of the solutions of a quadratic equation.

Let $ax^2+bx+c=0(a \neq 0)$ be a quadratic equation with real coefficients.

1. $D=b^2-4ac>0$ → There are two real solutions.
2. $D=b^2-4ac=0$ → There is one real solution.
3. $D=b^2-4ac>0$ → There is no real solution, but two conjugate imaginary solutions, $a \pm bi$.

Concept Check

Without solving the equation, determine the nature of its solution.

$x^2+3x=-2$ → Given equation

$x^2+3x+2=0$ → Rewrite in the form of $ax^2+bx+c=0$

$D=b^2-4ac$ → Formula for discriminant

$D=3^2-4(1)(2)>0$ → $a=1$, $b=3$, and $c=2$

Since $D>0$, there are two real solutions to the equation $x^2+3x=-2$.

Example 1

Without solving the equation, determine the nature of its solutions.

① $x^2-x-6=0$ ② $2x^2=5x-4$

③ $3x^2-2\sqrt{3}x+1=0$

Solution

① $x^2-x-6=0$ → $a=1$, $b=-1$, and $c=-6$
$D=b^2-4ac=(-1)^2-4(1)(-6)=1+24=25>0$

There are two real solutions

② $2x^2=5x-4$
$2x^2-5x+4=0$ → $a=2$, $b=-5$, and $c=4$
$D=b^2-4ac=(-5)^2-4(2)(4)=25-32=-7<0$

There is no real solution, but two imaginary solutions

③ $3x^2-2\sqrt{3}x+1=0$ → $a=3$, $b=-2\sqrt{3}$, and $c=1$
$D=b^2-4ac=(-2\sqrt{3})^2-4(3)(1)=12-12=0$

There is one real solution

Check Point 1
Solutions_Page 66

Without solving the equation, determine the nature of its solutions.

① $3x^2+5x-1=0$ ② $\frac{1}{2}x^2-5x+\frac{25}{2}=0$

③ $2x^2-4x+6=0$ ④ $(x-4)^2-7=2x(x-4)$

Example 2

Find the values of k for which the equation $x^2-6x+k=0$ has

① Two real solutions

② One real solution

③ Two imaginary solutions

Chapter 4. Quadratic Equations

> **Solution**
>
> $x^2-6x+k=0 \rightarrow a=1, b=-6$ and $c=k$
>
> ① $D=(-6)^2-4(1)(k)>0$
> $36-4k>0, k<9$
>
> $k<9$
>
> ② $D=(-6)^2-4(1)(k)=0$
> $36-4k=0, k=9$
>
> $k=9$
>
> ③ $D=(-6)^2-4(1)(k)<0$
> $36-4k<0, k>9$
>
> $k>9$

Check Point 2   Solutions_Page 66

Find the values of k for which the equation $3x^2-6x-k=0$ has

① Two real solutions

② One real solution

③ Two imaginary solutions

02   The Sum and Product of the Solutions

We have found the solutions of the quadratic equation are $x=\dfrac{-b\pm\sqrt{b^2-4ac}}{2a}$.

Now let the solutions of the quadratic equation, $ax^2+bx+c=0 \, (a\neq 0)$, be α and β. Then

The sum of solutions is $\alpha+\beta=\dfrac{-b+\sqrt{b^2-4ac}}{2a}+\dfrac{-b-\sqrt{b^2-4ac}}{2a}=\dfrac{-2b}{2a}=-\dfrac{b}{a}$.

The product of solutions is $\alpha\cdot\beta=\dfrac{-b+\sqrt{b^2-4ac}}{2a}\cdot\dfrac{-b-\sqrt{b^2-4ac}}{2a}=\dfrac{(-b)^2-\sqrt{(b^2-4ac)^2}}{(2a)^2}$

$=\dfrac{b^2-(b^2-4ac)}{4a^2}=\dfrac{4ac}{4a^2}=\dfrac{c}{a}$.

186   Chapter 4. Quadratic Equations ion

1. The sum of solutions: $\alpha+\beta=-\dfrac{b}{a}$
2. The product of solutions: $\alpha\beta=\dfrac{c}{a}$

Concept Check

Solving quadratic equation $2x^2+4x-48=0$,

$2x^2+4x-48=0$, $x^2+2x-24=0$

$(x+6)(x-4)=0$ → -6 and 4 are solutions to the equation.

So, the sum of two solutions is $4+(-6)=-2$ and the product is $4(-6)=-24$.

However, we can simply use the formula to find the sum and product of two solutions of the quadratic equation.

$2x^2+4x-48=0$ → $a=2$, $b=4$, and $c=-48$

The sum of solutions is $-\dfrac{b}{a}=-\dfrac{4}{2}=-2$

The product of solutions is $\dfrac{c}{a}=-\dfrac{48}{2}=-24$

Example 3

Find the sum and product of solutions of the quadratic equation $3x^2-4x+5=0$.

Solution

$3x^2-4x+5=0$ → $a=3$, $b=-4$, and $c=5$

① Sum of the solutions: $-\dfrac{b}{a}=-\dfrac{-4}{3}=\dfrac{4}{3}$

② Product of the solutions: $\dfrac{c}{a}=\dfrac{5}{3}$

The sum is $\dfrac{4}{3}$ and the product is $\dfrac{5}{3}$

Check Point 3

Find the sum and product of solutions of the quadratic equations.

① $2x^2+5x-7=0$
② $\frac{1}{5}x^2-x=0.7$
③ $(x-4)^2=2x(x+3)$

Example 4

Let α and β be solutions of the quadratic equation $x^2-3x-4=0$. Find each of the following.

① $\frac{1}{\alpha}+\frac{1}{\beta}$
② $\alpha^2+\beta^2$

Solution

$x^2-3x-4=0 \rightarrow a=1, b=-3,$ and $c=-4$

The sum of the solutions: $\alpha+\beta=-\frac{b}{a}=-\frac{-3}{1}=3$

The product of the solutions: $\alpha\beta=\frac{c}{a}=\frac{-4}{1}=-4$

① $\frac{1}{\alpha}+\frac{1}{\beta}=\frac{\beta+\alpha}{\alpha\beta}=\frac{3}{-4}=-\frac{3}{4}$

② $\alpha^2+\beta^2=(\alpha+\beta)^2-2\alpha\beta=(3)^2-2(-4)=17$

Check Point 4

Let α and β be solutions of the quadratic equation $5x^2+4x-8=0$. Find each of the following.

① $\frac{1}{\alpha}+\frac{1}{\beta}$
② $\alpha^2+\beta^2$

03 Writing Quadratic Equations

Throughout this chapter, we have worked on finding solutions to quadratic equations. Now we will learn how to write a quadratic equation given information about the solutions. Consider the quadratic equation $2x^2+4x-48=0$.

$$2x^2+4x-48=0 \underset{\text{Writing Equation}}{\overset{\text{Solving Equation}}{\rightleftarrows}} x=-6 \text{ or } x=4$$

By reversing the steps we have been using to solve the quadratic equation, we can formulate the original quadratic equation when provided with solutions only.

Let α and β be solutions of quadratic equation.

1. If the coefficient of the quadratic term is 1, then

$$(x-\alpha)(x-\beta)=0 \longleftrightarrow x^2-\underbrace{(\alpha+\beta)}_{\text{Sum of 2 solutions}}x+\underbrace{\alpha\beta}_{\text{Product of 2 solutions}}=0$$

2. If the coefficient of the quadratic term is a, then

$$a(x-\alpha)(x-\beta)=0 \longleftrightarrow a(x^2-(\alpha+\beta)x+\alpha\beta)=0$$

3. If the coefficient of the quadratic term is a and there is only one solution α, then

$$a(x-\alpha)^2=0 \longleftrightarrow \begin{array}{l} a(x^2-2(\alpha+\alpha)x+\alpha\cdot\alpha)=0 \\ a(x^2-2\alpha x+\alpha^2)=0 \end{array}$$

Concept Check

If the solutions of quadratic equation are -6 and 4, and the coefficient of the quadratic term is 2, we have the following quadratic equation:

$$2(x+6)(x-4)=0$$
$$2(x^2-(-6+4)x+(-6)(4))=0$$
$$2(x^2+2x-24)=0$$
$$2x^2+4x-48=0$$

Example 5

Write a quadratic equation $ax^2+bx+c=0$ with coefficient a and following solution(s).

① Solutions 5 and -4; $a=1$ ② Solutions $\frac{1}{3}$ and 2; $a=3$

③ Solution -4; $a=2$ ④ Solutions $1+\sqrt{2}$ and $1-\sqrt{2}$; $a=\frac{1}{2}$

Solution

① $(x-5)(x+4)=0$
$x^2-(5+(-4))x+(5)(-4)=0$
$x^2-x-20=0$ $\quad x^2-x-20=0$

② $3\left(x-\frac{1}{3}\right)(x-2)=0$
$3\left(x^2-\left(\frac{1}{3}+2\right)x+\left(\frac{1}{3}\right)(2)\right)=0$
$3\left(x^2-\frac{7}{3}x+\frac{2}{3}\right)=0,\ 3x^2-7x+2=0$ $\quad 3x^2-7x+2=0$

③ $2(x+4)^2=0$
$2(x^2-2(-4)x+4^2)=0$
$2(x^2+8x+16)=0,\ 2x^2+16x+32=0$ $\quad 2x^2+16x+32=0$

④ $\frac{1}{2}(x-(1+\sqrt{2}))(x-(1-\sqrt{2}))=0$
$\frac{1}{2}(x^2-(1+\sqrt{2}+1-\sqrt{2})x+(1+\sqrt{2})(1-\sqrt{2}))=0$
$\frac{1}{2}(x^2-2x+(1-2))=0,\ \frac{1}{2}(x^2-2x-1)=0$
$\frac{1}{2}x^2-x-\frac{1}{2}=0$ $\quad \frac{1}{2}x^2-x-\frac{1}{2}=0$

Check Point 5

Solutions_Page 67

Write a quadratic equation $ax^2+bx+c=0$ with coefficient a and following solution(s).

① Solution 6; $a=2$ ② Solutions $-\frac{3}{2}$, 3; $a=4$

③ Solutions $1\pm2\sqrt{2}$; $a=1$ ④ Solutions $\frac{3\pm i}{2}$; $a=8$

Review Exercise

01 Find the discriminant of the quadratic equation and determine the nature of its solutions of the quadratic equation.

(1) $x^2-x+3=0$

(2) $2x^2+3x-1=0$

(3) $4x^2-8x+4=0$

(4) $10x^2+2x=x(x-2)$

(5) $2x^2+2x+3=0$

(6) $3x^2-5x-2=-8x$

02 Find the values of k for which each equation has (A) two real solutions, (B) one real solution, and (C) two imaginary solutions.

(1) $x^2-4x-2k=0$

(2) $k^2x^2-8x+4=0$

Review Exercise

03 Find the sum and product of solutions of the quadratic equations.

(1) $x^2+7x-9=0$

(2) $7x^2+2x-6=0$

(3) $2x^2+3x=1$

(4) $x^2-4x=4x^2+5$

(5) $\frac{1}{3}x^2-\frac{2}{5}x=4-x$

(6) $x(2-x)=5x-2(2x-1)$

04 Let α and β be solutions of the quadratic equation below.
Find (A) $\frac{1}{\alpha}+\frac{1}{\beta}$ and (B) $\alpha^2+\beta^2$ of each quadratic equation below.

(1) $4x^2-4x+3=0$

(2) $\frac{1}{2}x^2+2x+1=0$

05 Find a quadratic equation $ax^2+bx+c=0$ with given solution(s) and coefficient a.

(1) Solutions -2, 1; $a=1$

(2) Solution -4; $a=5$

(3) Solutions $\pm\sqrt{3}$; $a=1$

(4) Solutions $1\pm\sqrt{2}$; $a=3$

(5) Solutions $3\pm i$; $a=2$

(6) Solutions $\dfrac{1\pm 3i\sqrt{5}}{2}$; $a=4$

06 If the quadratic equation $6x^2+mx+n=0$ has two solutions $\dfrac{2}{3}$ and $-\dfrac{1}{2}$, what is the value of mn?

Review Exercise

Challenging

07 For the quadratic equation $4x^2-8x+3=0$, let m and n be the sum and product of solutions, respectively. Find the quadratic equation with coefficient 2, and solutions m and n.

08 If the sum of solutions of the quadratic equation $2x^2-6x+9=0$ is one of the solution to the quadratic equation $5x^2+(k-2)x-3=0$, what is the value of k?

Challenging

09 If the quadratic equation $a(3x+1)+2x^2=-\dfrac{1}{8}$ has only one real solution, find all possible values of a?

Challenging

10 If the difference of solutions of the quadratic equation $x^2-6x+m=0$ is 2, what is the value of m?

Challenging

11 If the ratio of solutions of the quadratic equation $x^2+10x+n+4=0$ is $2:3$, what is the value of n?

6 Word Problems

01 Solving Word Problems using Quadratic Equations

In this section, we will learn how to translate quadratic word problems. Solve the word problems using quadratic equations in the following order:

1. Let x be the unknown needed to be solved in the problem.
2. Write a quadratic equation.
3. Solve the equation to find the solution.
4. Make sure the solution you find fits the meaning of the problem.

Example 1

The product of two consecutive positive even integers is 6 more than three times their sum. Find the two integers.

Solution

Let x be the first even integer. Then next even integer is $x+2$.
The product of two consecutive positive even integers: $x(x+2)$
6 more than three times their sum: $3(x+(x+2))+6$

$$x(x+2)=3(x+(x+2))+6$$
$$x^2+2x=3(2x+2)+6$$
$$x^2+2x=6x+12$$
$$x^2-4x-12=0$$
$$(x+2)(x-6)=0, \; x=-2 \text{ or } x=6$$

Since we are looking for a positive integer, $x=6$. So two consecutive even integers are 6 and 8.

Two integers are 6 and 8

Check Point 1

① Find two consecutive positive odd integers whose product is 255.

② Find a number such that the sum of the number and its reciprocal is $\dfrac{10}{3}$.

Example 2

The length of a rectangular hockey field is 12 meters longer than its width. The area of the field is 640 square meters. Find the dimensions of the field.

Solution

Let x be the width of the hockey field. Then the length is $x+12$.

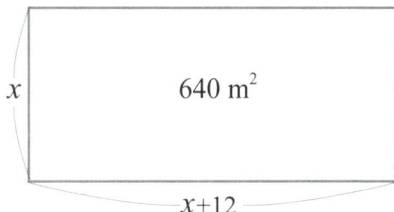

Area of rectangle is length times width. Therefore, we have

$x(x+12)=640$
$x^2+12x=640$
$x^2+12x-640=0$
$(x+32)(x-20)=0$, $x=-32$ or $x=20$

Since the length and width of the hockey field is positive number, $x=20$. So the width is $x=20$ meters and the length is $x+12=20+12=32$ meters.

The dimensions of the field are 20 meters by 32 meters

Check Point 2

① A rectangle has an area of 36 cm² and a perimeter of 30 cm. Find the dimensions of the rectangle.

② Suppose the length of a rectangle is twice its width. If the area of this rectangle is 450 square meters, what are the dimensions of the rectangle?

Example 3

At noon, John left school walking at 6 km per hour due south; an hour later, Chris left school walking at 5 km per hour due east. After how many hours will the boys be 13 km apart?

Solution

Let John left school x hours ago. Then, Chris left school $x-1$ hours ago.

	John	Chris
Rate	6	5
Time	x	$x-1$
Distance	$6x$	$5(x-1)$

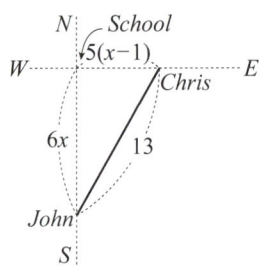

By the Pythagorean Theorem, we have

$$(6x)^2 + (5(x-1))^2 = 13^2$$
$$36x^2 + 25x^2 - 50x + 25 = 169$$
$$61x^2 - 50x - 144 = 0$$
$$(61x + 72)(x - 2) = 0$$
$$x = -\frac{72}{61} \text{ or } x = 2$$

Since the time must be positive, $x=2$.

The boys will be 13 km apart in 2 hours

Check Point 3

Solutions_Page 71

① Two buses A and B leave the same station at right angles at the same time. Bus B travels 1 mile per hour faster than bus A. If they are $2\sqrt{13}$ miles apart after 2 hours, what is the speed of each bus?

② Two bicycles leave the same intersection. One bicycle travels north and the other travels east. When the bicycle traveling north had gone 12 miles, the distance between the bicycles was 3 miles more than twice the distance traveled by bicycle heading east. Find the distance between the bicycles at this moment.

Review Exercise

01 Find the two consecutive positive even integers whose product is 80.

02 Find two consecutive negative integers such that the sum of their squares is 113.

03 The sum of the reciprocals of two consecutive odd integers is $\frac{8}{15}$. What are the two integers?

04 If the ratio of the length and width of the rectangle is 9 to 4 and the area of this rectangle is 144 square inches, what are the dimensions of the rectangle?

05 Find the lengths of the two legs of the right triangle if the hypotenuse is $\sqrt{13}$ inches and one leg is 1 inch longer than twice the other leg.

Review Exercise

06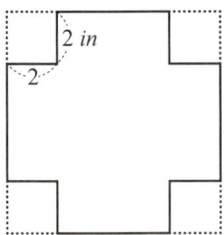

A square piece of cardboard was used to construct a box by cutting 2-inch squares out of each corner and turning up the flaps, as shown in Figure above. Find the length of one side of the square if the box has a volume of 128 cubic inches.

07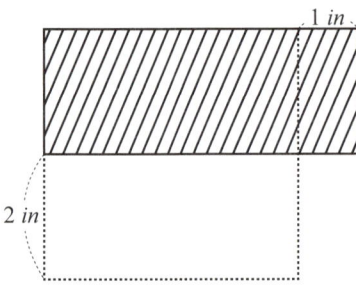

Suppose that one side of the square is increased by 1 inch, but the other side is decreased by 2 inches, as shown in Figure above. If the area of the resulting rectangle is 70 square inches, what is the length of one side of the original square?

08 A ball is thrown vertically upward from the ground. If height the ball at x seconds is given by $(-16x^2+28x)$ feet,

(1) After how many seconds does the ball hit the ground?

(2) After how many seconds does the ball reaches 12 feet above the ground?

09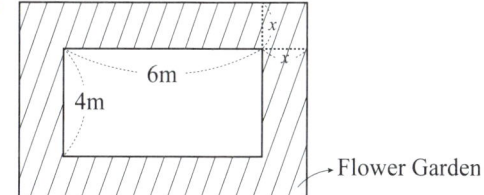
Flower Garden

A pond measuring 6 meters by 4 meters is surrounded by a flower garden of uniform width, as shown in Figure above. If the area of the flower garden is 144 square meters, what is the width of the flower garden?

10 David's family is traveling to Austin from Houston by car. It took a total of 6 hours to complete a round trip of 200 miles each way. If the car had a 4 miles per hour tailwind going and a 4 miles per hour headwind on the return trip, then what is the speed of the car in still air?

Chapter Test — Level 1

Solutions_Page 74

01 Which of the following is a quadratic equation? (There are 2 answers)

(A) $2x^3-5x^2+1=0$ 　　　　(B) $(x+1)(x+2)-(x+3)(x+4)=0$
(C) $x(2x^2+x-1)-2x(x^2-x+1)=0$ 　　(D) $4x^2+3x-2=4(1-x)(1+x)$
(E) $(1-2x)(1+2x)+4x^2=x$

02 Which of the following quadratic equations does NOT have $x=-2$ as the solution?

(A) $x^2+4x+4=0$ 　　(B) $x^2+2x=0$ 　　(C) $2x^2+5x+2=0$
(D) $2x^2-5x+2=0$ 　　(E) $3x^2+4x-4=0$

03 If $x=3$ is the solution of both $x^2-4x+m=0$ and $2x^2+nx-7=0$, what is the value of $m+n$?

04 If one of the solutions of $x^2+6x-4=0$ is $x=a$, what is the value of $2a^2+12a+7$?

05 The following is the process of solving quadratic equation by completing the square. Find the value of A, B, C, D and E. ($E>D$)

$$3x^2+4x-\frac{5}{3}=0, \left(3x^2+4x-\frac{5}{3}=0\right)\cdot\frac{1}{3}$$

$$x^2+\frac{4}{3}x-\frac{5}{9}=0, \; x^2+\frac{4}{3}x=\frac{5}{9}$$

$$x^2+\frac{4}{3}x+A=\frac{5}{9}+A$$

$$(x+B)^2=C, \; x=D \text{ or } x=E$$

06 If the quadratic equation $2x^2+12x-9=0$ can be written as $(x+h)^2=k$, what is the value of $h+k$?

07 If the solution to the quadratic equation $2x^2+mx-4=0$ is $x=\frac{1\pm\sqrt{n}}{2}$, where m and n are integers, what is the value of $m+n$?

08 Suppose that $x=2$ is one of the solutions of the quadratic equation $(k^2-4)x^2+(k+2)x=0$. Find all possible value of k.

Chapter Test — Level 1

09 If $(a+b)(a+b-3)=10$, what is the positive value of $a+b$?

10 If $m=1-2i$, $n=2+2i$, and $m^2n+mn^2=a+bi$, what is the value of $a+b$?

11 If $\dfrac{a}{1+i}+\dfrac{b}{1-i}=2+i$, what is the value of ab?

12 Suppose that the quadratic equation $2x^2-6x+1=0$ has two solutions, α and β. Evaluate each of the following.

(1) $\alpha^2+\beta^2$

(2) $(\alpha-\beta)^2$

(3) $\dfrac{1}{\alpha^2}+\dfrac{1}{\beta^2}$

(4) $\dfrac{1}{\alpha+1}+\dfrac{1}{\beta+1}$

13 $$x^2-(2k+1)x+24=0$$

In the quadratic equation above, one solution is 2 greater than the other. Find all possible values of k.

14 Josh tries to distribute 300 marbles equally to the students in his Algebra class. If the number of marbles each student receives is 5 less than the number of students, find the number students.

15 There are two different squares. The length of one side of the large square is 2 inches longer than the length of one side of the small square. If the sum of the areas of the two squares is 100 square inches, what is the length of one side of the small square?

Chapter Test — Level 2

Solutions_Page 77

01 If the quadratic equation $k(2x-1)+x^2=-2$, where $k<0$, has only one real solution, what is the value of k?

02
$$A : \frac{9}{4}x^2-3x+1=0$$
$$B : 6x^2-kx+2=0$$

Suppose the solution of the quadratic equation A is one of the solutions of the quadratic equation B. What is the other solution of the equation B?

03 If there is only one real solution in the quadratic equation $x^2-8x+m^2+3m+6=0$, where $m>0$, what is the value of m?

206 Chapter 4. Quadratic Equations ion

04 $2x^2-5x+m=0$

When one solution of the quadratic equation above is four times the other, what is the value of m?

05 $A : (2x-m)(x-3)=0$
$B : 2x^2+nx+3=0$

If two quadratic equations above are equal to each other for all x, what is the value of $m+n$?

06 Suppose that $25x^2-5x+1=a+bi$ when $x=\dfrac{2+i}{1+2i}$. Find the value of $a+b$.

07 Suppose that the quadratic equation $2x^2+x-4=0$ has two solutions, $α$ and $β$. Find a quadratic equation with coefficient of x^2 is 2, and solutions $α-2$ and $β-2$.

Chapter Test — Level 2

08 If $6x^2+7xy-3y^2=0$, where $xy>0$, what is the value of $\dfrac{3x^2+y^2}{4xy}$?

09 The product of two solutions of the equation $2x^2+(a-2)x+a(a+4)=0$, where $a<0$, is 6. What is the sum of two solutions of the equation?

10 Suppose that the quadratic equation $x^2-8x+9=0$ has two positive real solutions, α and β. Evaluate each of the following.

(1) $2\alpha^2-16\alpha$

(2) $\sqrt{\alpha}+\sqrt{\beta}$

11 When I opened the algebra book, the product of two pages was 210. Find the number of pages on each page.

12 There is a rectangle 16 cm long and 10 cm wide. If the length is reduced by 1 cm every second and the width is increased by 2 cm every second, how long does it take for the area of the new rectangle to be the same as the first one?

memo

Chapter 5
Quadratic Functions Part 1

1. The Graph of $y = ax^2$
2. Translation of the Graph
3. Application of Quadratic Functions
4. Chapter Test

1 The Graph of $y=ax^2$

01 Definition of Quadratic Function

A quadratic function is a polynomial function of the form $f(x)$ or $y=ax^2+bx+c$, where a, b, and c are constant and $a\neq 0$. For example, $y=-3x^2$, $y=2x^2+4x-2$, and $f(x)=2(x-3)^2$ are all quadratic functions. But $y=2x-4$, $f(x)=\dfrac{5}{x}-3$, and $y=6$ are not. The graph of a quadratic function is U−shaped and is called a parabola. The lowest or highest point of the graph of a quadratic function is called the vertex and vertical line through the vertex is called the axis of symmetry. The x−intercept(s) of the quadratic function is often called zero(s) or root(s). Refer to the graph below.

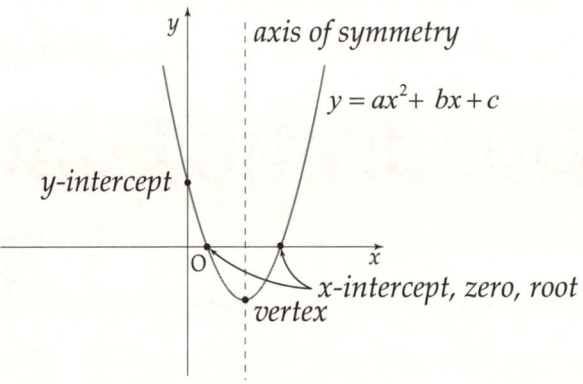

Concept Check

The most basic form of a quadratic function is $y=x^2$.

x	...	-3	-2	-1	0	1	2	3	...
y	...	9	4	1	0	1	4	9	...

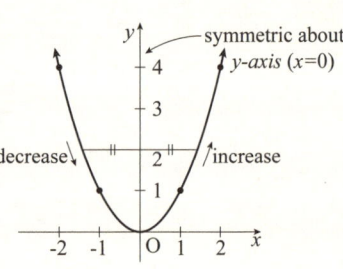

1. The vertex is $(0, 0)$.
2. The graph is symmetric about y−axis.
3. The equation of the y−axis is $x=0$.
4. For $x>0$, as x increases, y increases. For $x<0$, as x increases, y decreases.
5. The range is $\{y|y\geq 0\}$.

Example 1

Which of the following is a quadratic function?

(A) $y=2x+3$ (B) $y=(x-2)^2-x^2$ (C) $y=3x^2+4$

(D) $y=2x^3-2x^2+1$ (E) $y=x(2x+1)(2x-1)-4x^2$

Solution

The quadratic function has the form $y=ax^2+bx+c$, $a\neq 0$. It must have a squared term and the highest term must also be a squared term.

(A) $y=2x+3$ → Linear function
(B) $y=(x-2)^2-x^2$
$=x^2-4x+4-x^2=-4x+4$ → Linear function
(C) $y=3x^2+4$ → Quadratic function
(D) $y=2x^3-2x^2+1$ → If there is x^3 term, it is a cubic function
(E) $y=(2x+1)(2x-1)-4x^2$
$=4x^2-1-4x^2=-1$ → Constant function

The answer is (C)

Check Point 1

Solutions_Page 80

Which of the following is NOT a quadratic function?

(A) $y=-x(x+4)$ (B) $y=4+x-x^2$ (C) $y=2(x^2-1)-(1-2x^2)$

(D) $y=4x^2-2(2+x^2)$ (E) $y=3x(2+3x)-(3x+1)^2$

02 The Graph of $y=ax^2$

1. Vertex: Origin $(0, 0)$.
2. The graph is symmetric about y-axis.
3. Axis of symmetry: $x=0$
4. The graph opens upward if $a>0$ and opens downward if $a<0$.

$a>0$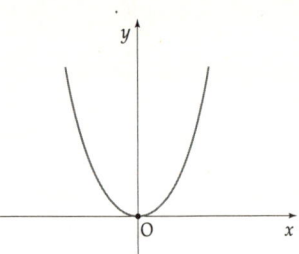

$a<0$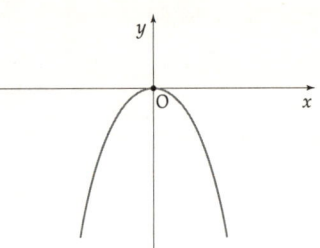

5. The larger $|a|$ is, the narrower the graph is.
   The smaller $|a|$ is, the wider the graph is.

6. $y=ax^2$ and $y=-ax^2$ are reflected across the x-axis each other.

214 Chapter 5. Quadratic Functions, Part 1

Example 2

Refer to the following quadratic functions.

A. $y=2x^2$
B. $y=4x^2$
C. $f(x)=-3x^2$
D. $f(x)=-\frac{1}{2}x^2$
E. $y=\frac{1}{3}x^2$
F. $y=-\frac{3}{5}x^2$

① Which of the quadratic function has narrowest parabola?
② Which of the quadratic function has widest parabola?
③ Which of the quadratic function opens upward?
④ Which of the quadratic function opens downward?

Solution

Since $\left|\frac{1}{3}\right|<\left|-\frac{1}{2}\right|<\left|-\frac{3}{5}\right|<|2|<|-3|<|4|$, $y=4x^2$ has narrowest parabola and $y=\frac{1}{3}x^2$ has widest parabola.

① B ② E

In $y=ax^2$, the graph opens upward if $a>0$ and downward if $a<0$. Thus, the graph of the quadratic function A, B, and E opens upward, whereas C, D, and F opens downward.

③ A, B, and E ④ C, D, and F

Check Point 2

Solutions_Page 80

Refer to the following quadratic functions.

A. $y=-4x^2$
B. $y=5x^2$
C. $f(x)=-x^2$
D. $y=\frac{1}{2}x^2$

① Which of the quadratic function has narrowest parabola?
② Which of the quadratic function has widest parabola?
③ Which of the quadratic function opens upward?
④ Which of the quadratic function opens downward?

Example 3

If the quadratic function $y=-2x^2$ passes through the point $(k, -18)$, find all values of k.

Solution

Substitute k for x and -18 for y.
$y=-2x^2$
$-18=-2k^2$, $k^2=9$, $k=\pm 3$

$$k=\pm 3$$

Check Point 3

Solutions_Page 80

If the quadratic function $y=\dfrac{3}{4}x^2$ passes through the point $(m, 6)$, find all values of m.

Review Exercise

01 Which of the following is a quadratic function? (There are 2 answers)

(A) $y=2x^2-2(x+1)^2$

(B) $y=x^2(x+2)-2x^2$

(C) $y=2x(x-1)-(2x+1)^2$

(D) $y=(2x-1)(2x+1)-(2x^2-1)$

(E) $y=x^2(x-2)-2x^2(x-2)$

02 Refer to the following quadratic functions.

A. $y=-\dfrac{1}{4}x^2$	B. $y=2x^2$
C. $f(x)=-4x^2$	D. $f(x)=-\dfrac{3}{2}x^2$
E. $y=\dfrac{1}{2}x^2$	F. $y=\dfrac{3}{2}x^2$

(1) Of the quadratic functions that open upward, which one has narrowest parabola?

(2) Of the quadratic functions that open downward, which one has widest parabola?

03 If the quadratic function $y=\dfrac{9}{2}x^2$ passes through the point $(a, 72)$, find all values of a.

04 If the quadratic function $y=ax^2$ passes through the point $(-2, 32)$ and $\left(\dfrac{1}{2}, b\right)$, what is the value of $a+b$?

Review Exercise

05 If the graph of quadratic function $y=ax^2$ opens downward and passes through the point $(3, -6)$, which of the following points is also on the graph of $y=ax^2$? (There are 2 answers)

(A) $\left(1, -\dfrac{2}{3}\right)$

(B) $\left(2, \dfrac{8}{3}\right)$

(C) $(-3, -8)$

(D) $(-4, 10)$

(E) $\left(-2, -\dfrac{8}{3}\right)$

06

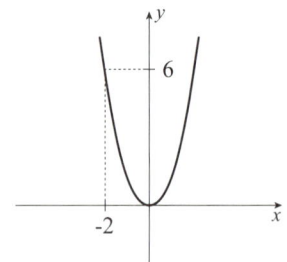

If the graph of quadratic function $y=ax^2$ above passes through the point $(4, m)$, what is the value of m?

2 Translation of the Graph

01 The Graph of $y=ax^2+k$

1. To graph $y=ax^2+k$, shift the graph of $y=ax^2$ vertically k units. If $k>0$, move it upward; If $k<0$, move it downward.
2. Vertex: $(0, k)$
3. The graph is symmetric about y-axis.
4. Axis of symmetry: $x=0$

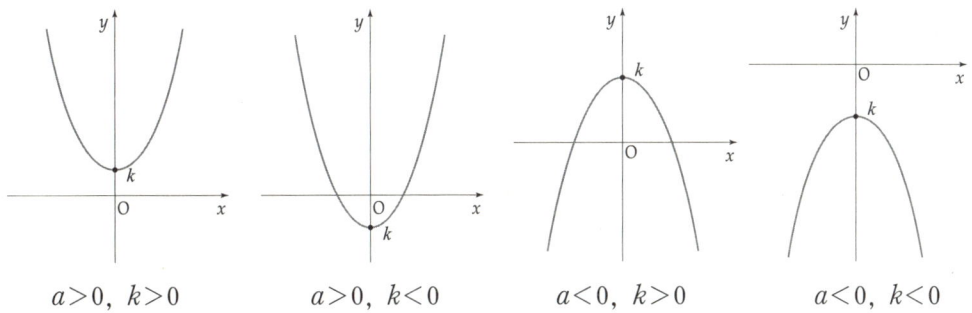

$a>0, k>0$ $a>0, k<0$ $a<0, k>0$ $a<0, k<0$

Concept Check

Graph $y=x^2+1$

x	...	-3	-2	-1	0	1	2	3	...
$y=x^2$	...	9 +1	4 +1	1 +1	0 +1	1 +1	4 +1	9 +1	...
$y=x^2+1$	...	10	5	2	1	2	5	10	...

1. $y=x^2 \xrightarrow{\text{Shift 1 unit up}} y=x^2+1$
2. Vertex: $(0, 1)$
3. y-intercept: $y=0^2+1=1$

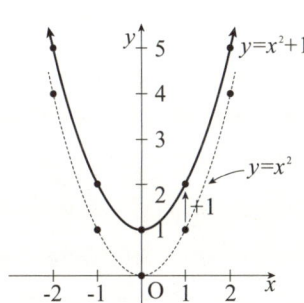

Example 1

Find the axis of symmetry, vertex, and y-intercept of the function. Then sketch the graph.

① $y = x^2 + 2$ ② $y = -2x^2 - 4$

Solution

① To graph $y = x^2 + 2$, sketch the graph of $y = x^2$ first and then shift 2 units up.
Axis of symmetry: $x = 0$
Vertex: $(0, 2)$
y-intercept: $y = 0^2 + 2 = 2$

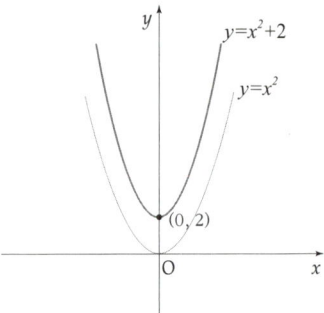

② To graph $y = -2x^2 - 4$, sketch the graph of $y = -2x^2$ first and then shift 4 units down.
Axis of symmetry: $x = 0$
Vertex: $(0, -4)$
y-intercept: $y = -2 \cdot 0^2 - 4 = -4$

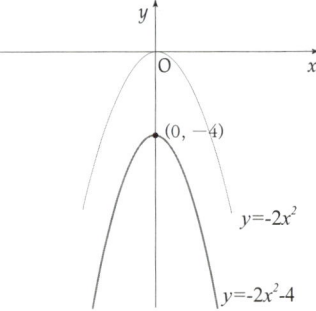

Check Point 1

Solutions_Page 81

Find the axis of symmetry, vertex, and y-intercepts. Then, sketch the graph.

① $y = x^2 - 2$ ② $y = -2x^2 + 3$

③ $y = \dfrac{1}{2}x^2 + 1$ ④ $y = -\dfrac{1}{3}x^2 - 2$

02 The Graph of $y=a(x-h)^2$

1. To graph $y=a(x-h)^2$, shift the graph of $y=ax^2$ horizontally h units.
   If $h>0$, move it to the right; If $h<0$, move it to the left.
2. Vertex: $(h, 0)$
3. The graph is symmetric about the line $x=h$.
4. Axis of symmetry: $x=h$

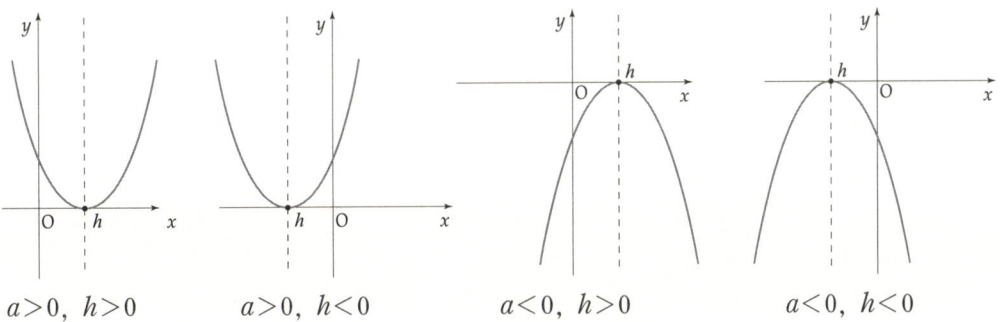

$a>0, h>0$ $a>0, h<0$ $a<0, h>0$ $a<0, h<0$

Concept Check

Graph $y=(x-1)^2$

x	$\cdots$	-3	-2	-1	0	1	2	3	$\cdots$
$y=x^2$	$\cdots$	9	4	1	0	1	4	9	$\cdots$
$y=(x-1)^2$	$\cdots$	16	9	4	1	0	1	4	$\cdots$

1. $y=x^2$ $\xrightarrow{\text{Shift 1 unit to the right}}$ $y=(x-1)^2$
2. Vertex: $(1, 0)$
3. y-intercept: $y=(0-1)^2=1$

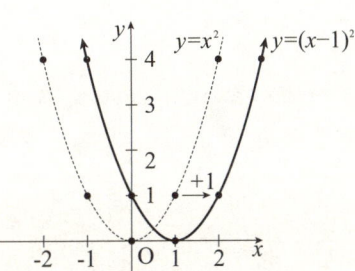

Example 2

Find the axis of symmetry, vertex, and y-intercept of the function. Then sketch the graph.

① $y=(x-2)^2$ ② $y=-2(x+1)^2$

Solution

① To graph $y=(x-2)^2$, sketch the graph of $y=x^2$ first and then shift 2 units to the right.
Axis of symmetry: $x=2$
Vertex: $(2, 0)$
y-intercept: $y=(0-2)^2=4$

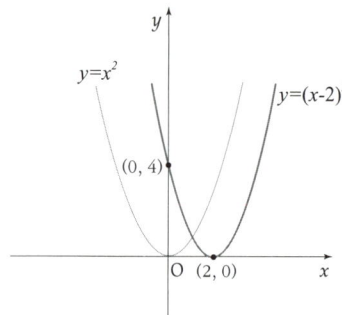

② To graph $y=-2(x+1)^2$ sketch the graph of $y=-2x^2$ first and then shift 1 units to the left.
Axis of symmetry: $x=-1$
Vertex: $(-1, 0)$
y-intercept: $y=-2(0+1)^2=-2$

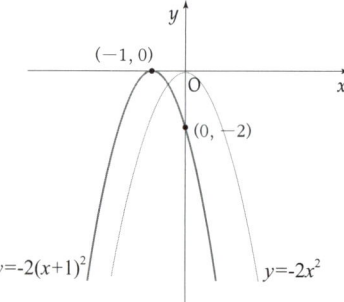

Check Point 2

Solutions_Page 82

Find the axis of symmetry, vertex, and y-intercepts. Then, sketch the graph.

① $y=(x+1)^2$ ② $y=-(x-2)^2$

③ $y=\frac{1}{2}(x-2)^2$ ④ $y=-2(x+3)^2$

03 The Graph of $y=a(x-h)^2+k$

1. To graph $y=a(x-h)^2+k$, shift the graph of $y=ax^2$ horizontally h units and vertically k units.
2. Vertex: (h, k)
3. The graph is symmetric about the line $x=h$.
4. Axis of symmetry: $x=h$

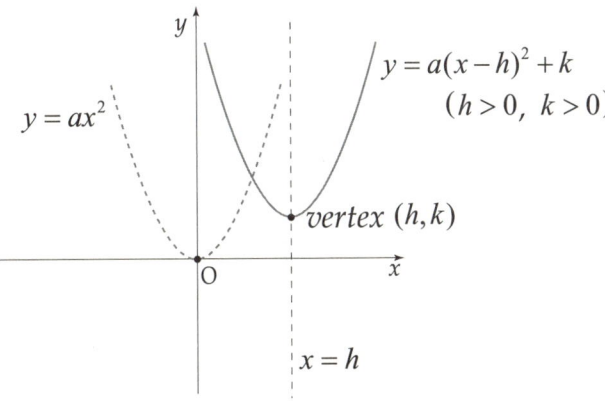

Example 3

Find the axis of symmetry, vertex, and y-intercept of the function. Then sketch the graph.

① $y=2(x-1)^2+1$

② $y=-\dfrac{1}{2}(x+1)^2-2$

Solution

① To graph $y=2(x-1)^2+1$, sketch the graph of $y=2x^2$ first and then shift 1 unit to the right and 1 unit up.

Axis of symmetry: $x=1$
Vertex: $(1, 1)$
y-intercept: $y=2(0-1)^2+1=3$

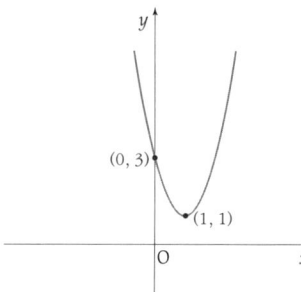

② To graph $y=-\dfrac{1}{2}(x+1)^2-2$, sketch the graph of $y=-\dfrac{1}{2}x^2$ first and then shift 1 unit to the left and 2 units down.

Axis of symmetry: $x=-1$
Vertex: $(-1, -2)$
y-intercept: $y=-\dfrac{1}{2}(0+1)^2-2=-\dfrac{5}{2}$

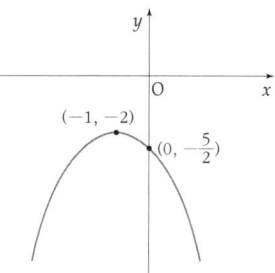

Check Point 3 Solutions_Page 83

Find the axis of symmetry, vertex, and y-intercepts. Then, sketch the graph.

① $y=(x-2)^2+1$ ② $y=2(x-1)^2-1$

③ $y=-\dfrac{1}{3}(x+3)^2+2$ ④ $y=-\dfrac{1}{2}(x-2)^2-3$

Review Exercise

Solutions_Page 84

01 Find the axis of symmetry, vertex, and y-intercepts. Then, sketch the graph.

(1) $y=x^2+3$

(2) $y=-2x^2-2$

(3) $y=(x-2)^2$

(4) $y=-\dfrac{1}{3}(x+3)^2$

02 Find the axis of symmetry, vertex, and y-intercepts. Then, sketch the graph.

(1) $y=(x-2)^2-2$

(2) $y=-2(x+1)^2+1$

(3) $y=4(x-1)^2+3$

(4) $y=-\dfrac{1}{2}(x+3)^2-2$

Review Exercise

03 If the graph of the quadratic function $y=2x^2$ is shifted 3 units to the right, then the graph passes through the point $(a, 8)$. Find all possible values of a.

04 If the graph of the quadratic function $y=-4x^2$ is shifted 1 unit to the left and 2 units up, then the graph passes through the point $(-2, b)$. Find the value of b.

05 If the graph of the quadratic function $y=-\frac{1}{2}(x-1)^2$ is shifted k units up, then the graph passes through the point $(3, 4)$. Find the value of k.

06 If the graph of the quadratic function $y=3x^2-2$ is shifted 4 units to the right and 2 units up, what is the coordinate of the vertex of the new function?

07 Which of the following is NOT true about the graph of $y=2(x-2)^2-5$?

(A) The graph opens upward

(B) The equation of the axis of symmetry is $x=2$

(C) The vertex of the graph is at $(2, -5)$.

(D) The graph is shifted 2 units to the left and 5 units down from the graph of $y=2x^2$

(E) The graph passes through the point $(1, -3)$.

08 Suppose that the graph of the function $y=2(x-h)^2+k$ has an axis of symmetry at $x=-2$ and passes through the point $(-1, 9)$. Find the value of $h+k$.

Challenging

09 Find the equation of the quadratic function shown below.

(1)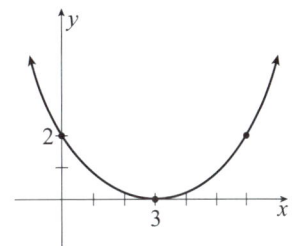

(2)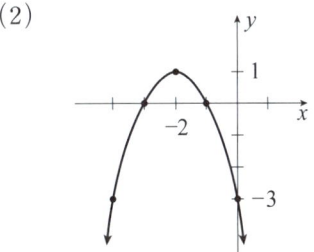

Challenging

10 Suppose that the vertex of the quadratic function is $\left(-2, \dfrac{3}{2}\right)$ and passes through the point $\left(1, \dfrac{9}{2}\right)$. What is the coordinate of the y-intercept?

3. Application of Quadratic Functions

01 Translation of the Graph $y=a(x-h)^2+k$

1. Suppose that $m>0$ and $n>0$. If we shift the graph of $y=a(x-h)^2+k$

   (1) m units to the right   → Substitute $x-m$ for x
   (2) m units to the left   → Substitute $x+m$ for x
   (3) n units up   → Substitute $y-n$ for y
   (4) n units down   → Substitute $y+n$ for y

2. $y=a(x-h)^2+k \longrightarrow y-n=a(x-m-h)^2+k$
   $$y=a(x-(m+h))^2+(k+n)$$

   Vertex: $(m+h, k+n)$

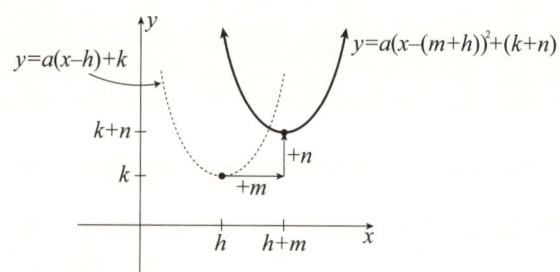

Concept Check

Given the graph of the function $y=2(x-3)^2+1$, shift

1. 2 units to the right   → $y=2(x-2-3)^2+1$, $y=2(x-5)^2+1$
2. 3 units to the left   → $y=2(x+3-3)^2+1$, $y=2x^2+1$
3. 2 units up   → $y-2=2(x-3)^2+1$, $y=2(x-3)^2+3$
4. 3 units down   → $y+3=2(x-3)^2+1$, $y=2(x-3)^2-2$

Example 1

Given the graph of the function $y=-3(x+1)^2-2$, find the function that shift 2 units to the left and 4 units up.

Solution

To shift 2 units to the left and 4 units up, substitute $x+2$ for x and $y-4$ for y.
$$y=-3(x+1)^2-2 \longrightarrow y-4=-3(x+2+1)^2-2$$
$$y=-3(x+3)^2-2+4$$
$$y=-3(x+3)^2+2$$

$$y=-3(x+3)^2+2$$

Check Point 1

Solutions_Page 87

Given the graph of the function $y=\frac{1}{2}(x-4)^2-1$, find the function that shift 4 units to the left and 2 units down.

02 Reflections of the Graphs

Vertical reflections reflect the graph vertically about the x-axis, and horizontal reflections reflect the graph horizontally about the y-axis.

1. Vertical Reflection (About x-axis):   → Substitute $-y$ for y

$$y=a(x-h)^2+k \longrightarrow -y=a(x-h)^2+k$$
$$y=-a(x-h)^2-k$$

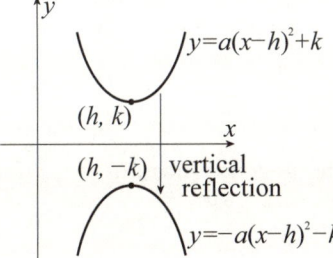

Chapter 5. Quadratic Functions, Part 1 229

2. Horizontal Reflection (About y-axis):   → Substitute $-x$ for x

$y=a(x-h)^2+k \longrightarrow y=a(-x-h)^2+k$
$y=a(x+h)^2+k$

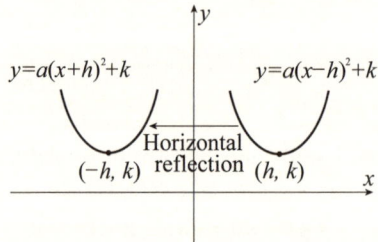

Concept Check

Given the graph of the function $y=2(x-3)^2+1$,

1. Reflect the graph about the x-axis: $-y=2(x-3)^2+1$, $y=-2(x-3)^2-1$
2. Reflect the graph about the y-axis: $y=2(-x-3)^2+1$, $y=2(x+3)^2+1$

Example 2

Given the graph of the function $y=-(x+2)^2-5$, find the function that

① Reflect the graph about the x-axis.

② Reflect the graph about the y-axis.

Solution

① To reflect the graph about the x-axis, substitute $-y$ for y.
$y=-(x+2)^2-5 \longrightarrow -y=-(x+2)^2-5$
$y=(x+2)^2+5$

$y=(x+2)^2+5$

② To reflect the graph about the y-axis, substitute $-x$ for x.
$y=-(x+2)^2-5 \longrightarrow y=-(-x+2)^2-5$
$y=-(x-2)^2-5$

$y=-(x-2)^2-5$

Check Point 2

Given the graph of the function $y=\frac{3}{2}x^2+2$, find the function that

① Reflect the graph about the x-axis.

② Reflect the graph about the y-axis.

03 The sign of a, h, and k from $y=a(x-h)^2+k$

1. The sign of a depends on the shape of the graph.

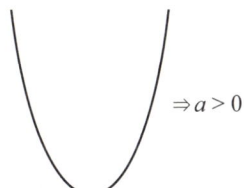 $\Rightarrow a>0$ 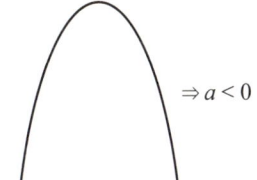 $\Rightarrow a<0$

The graph opens upward   The graph opens downward

2. The signs of h and k depend on the position of the vertex.

Quadrant	Signs
I	$h>0$, $k>0$
II	$h<0$, $k>0$
III	$h<0$, $k<0$
IV	$h>0$, $k<0$

```
         y
    II   |   I
  (−, +) | (+, +)
 ────────┼──────── x
   III   |   IV
  (−, −) | (+, −)
```

Concept Check

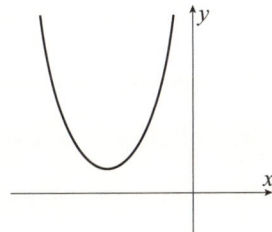

The graph in Figure above has

1. $a>0$ → because the graph opens upward
2. $h<0$, $k>0$ → because the vertex of the graph is in quadrant II

Example 3

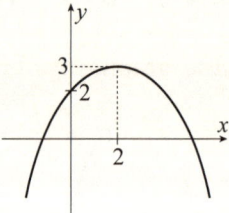

If the graph of the quadratic function $y=a(x-h)^2+k$ is shown above, specify the signs of a, h, and k.

Solution

The graph opens downward → $a<0$
The vertex of the graph is in quadrant I → $h>0$, $k>0$

$a<0$, $h>0$, and $k>0$

Check Point 3

Solutions_Page 87

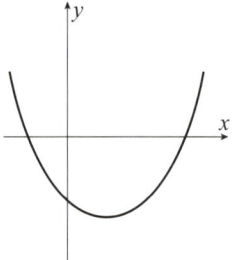

If the graph of the quadratic function $y=a(x-h)^2+k$ is shown above, specify the signs of a, h, and k.

Review Exercise

01 Given the graph of the function $y=\frac{2}{3}(x-3)^2-2$, find the function that

(1) Shift 3 units to the left and 2 units down.

(2) Shift 2 units to the right and 3 units up.

02 Given the graph of the function $y=\frac{2}{3}(x-3)^2-2$, find the function that

(1) Reflect the graph about the x-axis.

(2) Reflect the graph about the y-axis.

(3) Reflect the graph both about the x-axis and y-axis.

03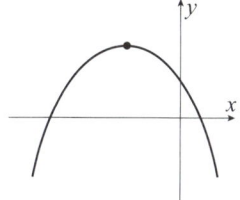

If the graph of the quadratic function $y=a(x-h)^2+k$ is shown above, which of the following must be true about the signs of a, h, and k?

(A) $a>0$, $h>0$, $k>0$

(B) $a>0$, $h<0$, $k>0$

(C) $a<0$, $h>0$, $k>0$

(D) $a<0$, $h<0$, $k>0$

(E) $a<0$, $h<0$, $k<0$

Review Exercise

04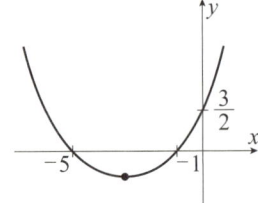

If the graph of the quadratic function $y=a(x-h)^2+k$ is shown above, which of the following must be true about the signs of a, h, and k? (There are 2 answers)

(A) $h>0$
(B) $k<0$
(C) $h \times k<0$
(D) $h+k>0$
(E) $a \times h \times k>0$

05 If $a<0$, $h>0$, $k<0$, which of the following could be the graph of $y=a(x-h)^2+k$?

(A)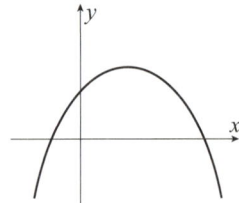

(B)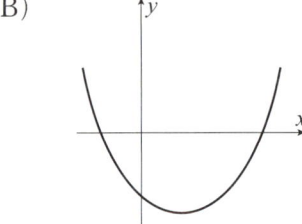

(C)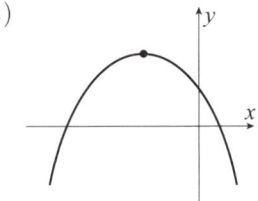

(D)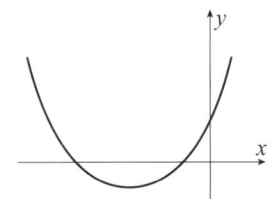

(E)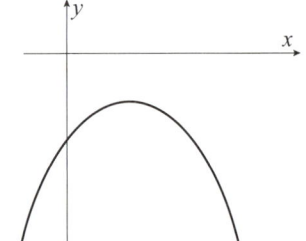

Challenging

06 If the graph of the function $y=5(x+2)^2-1$ shifts h units horizontally and k units vertically, then the function of the graph is $y=5(x-1)^2-4$. What is the value of $h+k$?

Challenging

08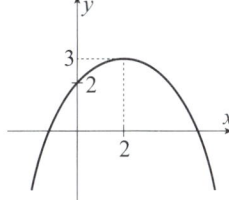

If the graph of the quadratic function above is shifted 3 units to the left, 1 unit up, and then reflected about the x-axis, what is the function of the new graph?

Challenging

07 If the graph of the function $y=-(x+2)^2+3$ is reflected both about the x-axis and y-axis, then it passes through the point $(a, 6)$. Find all possible values for a.

Chapter Test — Level 1

Solutions_Page 88

01 Which of the following is NOT a quadratic function? (There are 2 answers)

(A) $y=(2x-1)^2-4x^2$ (B) $y=x(2x+1)-x^2$
(C) $y=x(x-1)(x+1)-x^2+1$ (D) $y=2(3-x)(2x-1)$
(E) $y=4x^2(x+2)-2x^2(2x+1)$

02 Which of the following quadratic functions opens downward and has narrowest parabola?

(A) $y=\dfrac{1}{2}x^2$ (B) $f(x)=-3x^2$ (C) $y=\dfrac{5}{2}x^2$

(D) $y=-4x^2$ (E) $y=-\dfrac{1}{2}x^2$

03 Which of the following points is NOT on the graph of quadratic function $y=2x^2-3$?

(A) $(0, -3)$ (B) $(1, -1)$ (C) $(2, 5)$
(D) $(-1, 1)$ (E) $(-2, 5)$

236 Chapter 5. Quadratic Functions, Part 1

04 In quadratic function $f(x)=a(x+3)^2-4$, if $f(-1)=8$, what is the value of $f(-4)$?

05 Find the quadratic function that has vertex $(-3, -2)$ and y-intercept 2.

06 Which of the following quadratic functions can be shifted to be the graph of $y=-3(x+2)^2-1$?

(A) $y=3(x+1)^2$ (B) $y=-3x^2+4$ (C) $y=\frac{1}{3}(x+2)^2+1$

(D) $y=\frac{2}{3}x^2$ (E) $y=-\frac{3}{2}(x-2)^2-1$

07 If the graph of the quadratic function $y=\frac{1}{2}(x-2)^2$ is shifted 3 units to the right and 4 units down, then the graph passes through the point $(3, n)$. Find the value of n.

Chapter Test — Level 1

08 Which of the following is NOT true about the graph of $y=-\frac{1}{2}(x-1)^2-2$?

(A) The graph opens downward
(B) The equation of the axis of symmetry is $x=1$
(C) When $x>1$, y increases as x increases.
(D) The graph is shifted 1 unit to the right and 2 units down from the graph of $y=-\frac{1}{2}x^2$
(E) The y-intercept of the graph is -2.5

09 If the graph of the quadratic function $y=2-4x^2$ is shifted 1 unit to the left and 2 units down, then the graph passes through the point $(a, -6)$. Find all possible values of a.

10 Suppose that the graph of $y=a(x-h)^2+k$ has a vertex $\left(\frac{1}{2}, -2\right)$ and passes through the point $\left(-\frac{3}{2}, 6\right)$. Then, what is the value of a?

11 If the graph of the function $y=-2(x-4)^2+2$ shifts h units horizontally and k units vertically, then the function of the graph is $y=-2x^2-5$. What is the value of $h+k$?

12 Find the equation of the quadratic function shown below.

(1)
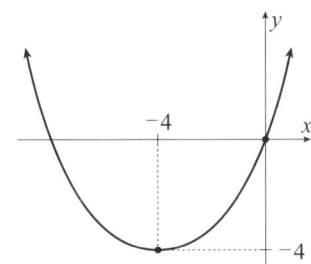

(2)
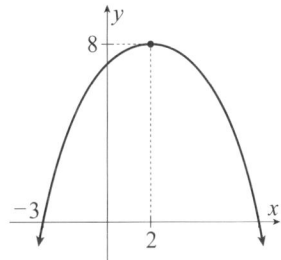

13
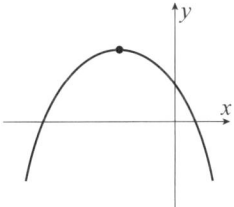

If the graph of the quadratic function $y=a(x-h)^2+k$ is shown above, which of the following must be true about the signs of a, h, and k?

(A) $a>0$, $h>0$, $k<0$
(B) $a>0$, $h<0$, $k>0$
(C) $a<0$, $h<0$, $k>0$
(D) $a<0$, $h>0$, $k<0$
(E) $a>0$, $h<0$, $k<0$

Chapter Test — Level 1

14 If $a>0$, $h<0$, $k<0$, which of the following could be the graph of $y=a(x-h)^2+k$?

(A)
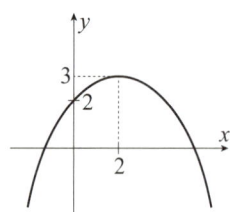

(B)
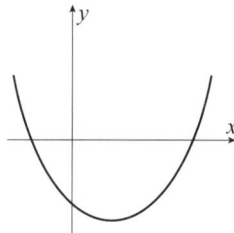

(C)
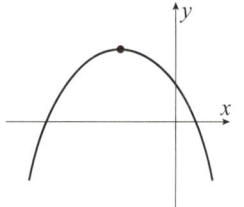

(D)
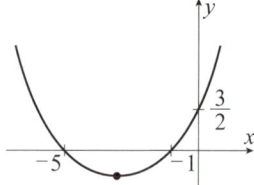

(E)
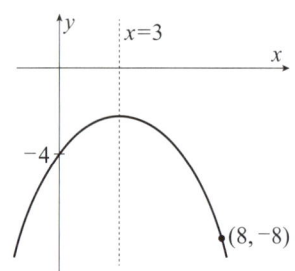

Chapter Test — Level 2

01 The graph of the quadratic function $y=a(x+3)^2-1$ is shifted 2 units to the left and then reflected about y-axis. If the graph passes through the point $(1, 4)$ now, what is the value of a?

02 The graph of the quadratic function $y=a(x-h)^2+k$ has an axis of symmetry $x=2$ and its y-coordinate of the vertex is 5. If the y-intercept of the graph is 2, what is the value of ahk?

03 Suppose that the graph of the quadratic function has an axis of symmetry at $x=-4$ and passes through two points $(-5, 3)$ and $(-1, 0)$. Write the equation of this quadratic function.

04 Which quadrant does the quadratic function $y=\dfrac{1}{3}(x+2)^2-1$ NOT pass through?

(A) I only (B) II only (C) IV only
(D) I and II only (E) I and IV only

Chapter Test — Level 2

05 Suppose that the graph of the function $y=3(x-1)^2-2$ is reflected about the x-axis and then shifted 2 units to the left and 4 units up. If this graph passes through the point $(-2, m)$, what is the value m?

06 If the graph of the function $y=-(x+2)^2$ is shifted m units horizontally and $m+2$ units vertically, then the vertex of the shifted graph is on the line $y=2x+1$. Find the value of m.

07

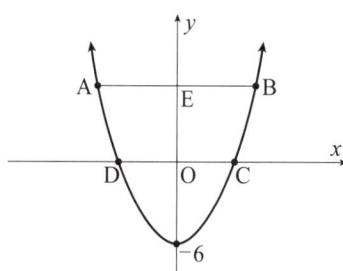

The graph above is the quadratic function $y=\dfrac{3}{4}x^2-6$. If the segment $\overline{AB}=8$ and $\overline{AB}$ is parallel to the x-axis, what is the area of trapezoid ABCD?

08

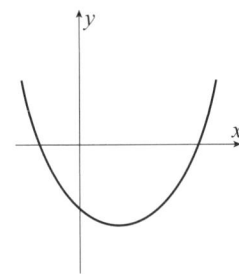

If the graph above is $y=a(x-h)^2+k$, which of the following could be a graph of $y=k(x-a)^2+h$?

(A)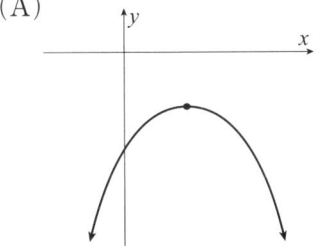

(B)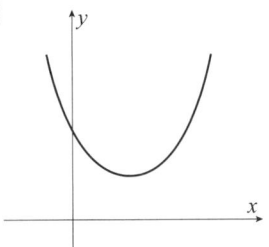

(C)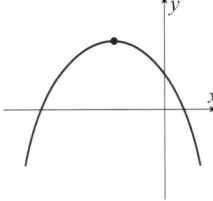

(D)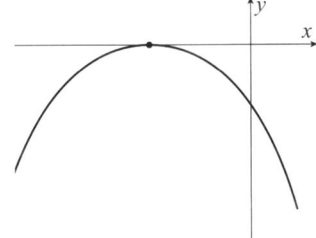

(E)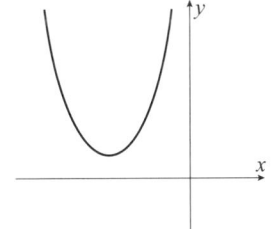

Chapter 6
Quadratic Functions Part 2

1. The Graph of $y=ax^2+bx+c$
2. Writing Quadratic Functions
3. The Minimum and Maximum
4. Chapter Test

1. The Graph of $y=ax^2+bx+c$

01   The Graph of $y=ax^2+bx+c$, $a\neq 0$

A quadratic function can be written in either of two forms.

> General Form: $\quad y=ax^2+bx+c$, $\ a\neq 0$
>
> Standard Form: $\quad y=a(x-h)^2+k$, $\ a\neq 0$

In this section, we will learn how to graph the quadratic function by transforming general form to standard form or by using the equation of axis of symmetry.

$y=ax^2+bx+c$ → General form

$y=a\left(x^2+\dfrac{b}{a}x\right)+c$ → Factor a from the first two terms

$y=a\left(x^2+\dfrac{b}{a}x+\left(\dfrac{b}{2a}\right)^2-\left(\dfrac{b}{2a}\right)^2\right)+c$ → Add and subtract $\left(\dfrac{b}{2a}\right)^2$

$y=a\left(x+\dfrac{b}{2a}\right)^2-\dfrac{b^2}{4a}+c$ → $a\times-\left(\dfrac{b}{2a}\right)^2=-\dfrac{b^2}{4a}$

$y=a\left(x-\left(-\dfrac{b}{2a}\right)\right)^2+\left(c-\dfrac{b^2}{4a}\right)$ → Rewrite in $y=a(x-h)^2+k$ form

$h=-\dfrac{b}{2a}$ and $k=c-\dfrac{b^2}{4a}$. So the vertex is $(h, k)=\left(-\dfrac{b}{2a},\ c-\dfrac{b^2}{4a}\right)$.

✔ You do not have to remember the expression for $k=c-\dfrac{b^2}{4a}$ because we can easily define it by substituting $-\dfrac{b}{2a}$ for x in the function.

✔ Since $y=c$ when $x=0$, y−intercept of $y=ax^2+bx+c$ is always $(0, c)$.

$$y=ax^2+bx+c \Leftrightarrow y=a\left(x-\left(-\frac{b}{2a}\right)\right)^2+\left(c-\frac{b^2}{4a}\right)$$

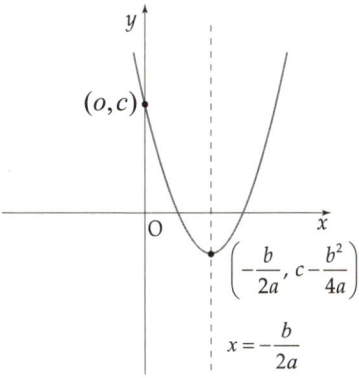

1. Vertex: $(h,\ k)=\left(-\dfrac{b}{2a},\ c-\dfrac{b^2}{4a}\right)$

2. Axis of symmetry: $x=h=-\dfrac{b}{2a}$

3. y−intercept: $(0,\ c)$

Example 1

For the quadratic function $y=2x^2-8x+5$,

① Rewrite the function in standard form.

② Use the axis of symmetry $x=-\dfrac{b}{2a}$ to sketch the graph.

Solution

① $y=2x^2-8x+5$
$y=2(x^2-4x)+5$
$y=2(x^2-4x+(2)^2-(2)^2)+5$
$y=2((x-2)^2-4)+5$
$y=2(x-2)^2-8+5$
$y=2(x-2)^2-3$
Vertex: $(2,\ -3)$
Axis of Symmetry: $x=2$
y−intercept: $(0,\ 5)$

② $y=2x^2-8x+5$

Axis of Symmetry: $x=-\dfrac{b}{2a}=-\dfrac{-8}{2(2)}=2$

Since $y(2)=2\cdot 2^2-8\cdot 2+5=-3$, its vertex is $(2, -3)$.

y-intercept: $(0, 5)$

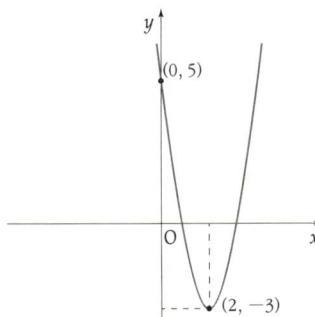

✔ In summary, we can find the vertex and graph the function $f(x)=ax^2+bx+c$ either by finding standard form or using formula for axis of symmetry.

Check Point 1-1

Solutions_Page 92

Rewrite the function in standard form.

① $y=3x^2-6x-1$ ② $y=\dfrac{1}{2}x^2+3x-\dfrac{3}{2}$

Check Point 1-2

Solutions_Page 92

Use the axis of symmetry $x=-\dfrac{b}{2a}$ to sketch the graph of the function.

① $y=3x^2-6x-1$ ② $y=\dfrac{1}{2}x^2+3x-\dfrac{3}{2}$

02 The Sign of $a, b,$ and c from $y=ax^2+bx+c$

1. The sign of a depends on the shape of the graph.

 (1) The graph opens upward   ⇒ $a>0$

 (2) The graph opens downward   ⇒ $a<0$

248 Chapter 6. Quadratic Functions, Part 2

2. The sign of b depends on the position of the axis of symmetry.

   (1) The axis is to the left of the y-axis $\Rightarrow$ a and b have the same signs $(ab>0)$

   (2) The axis is to the right of the y-axis $\Rightarrow$ a and b have the different sign $(ab<0)$

   (3) The axis is on the y-axis $\Rightarrow$ $b=0$

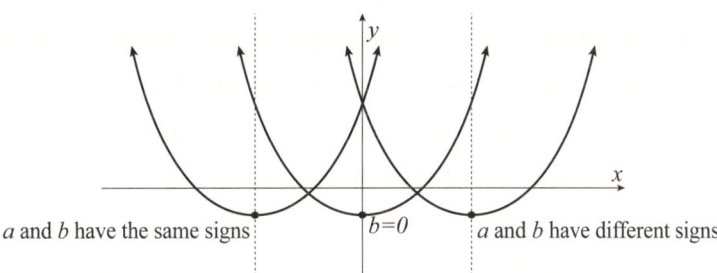

a and b have the same signs $\quad b=0 \quad a$ and b have different signs

Concept Check

The equation of the axis of symmetry is $x=-\dfrac{b}{2a}$.

(1) If the axis is to the left of the y-axis,

   $-\dfrac{b}{2a}<0$, $\dfrac{b}{2a}>0 \Rightarrow a$ and b have the same signs $(ab>0)$

(2) If the axis is to the right of the y-axis,

   $-\dfrac{b}{2a}>0$, $\dfrac{b}{2a}<0 \Rightarrow a$ and b have the different signs $(ab<0)$

(3) If the axis is on the y-axis, $-\dfrac{b}{2a}=0 \Rightarrow b=0$

3. The sign of c depends on the position of the y-intercept.

   (1) The y-intercept is above the x-axis $\Rightarrow c>0$

   (2) The y-intercept is below the x-axis $\Rightarrow c<0$

   (3) The y-intercept is on the x-axis $\Rightarrow c=0$

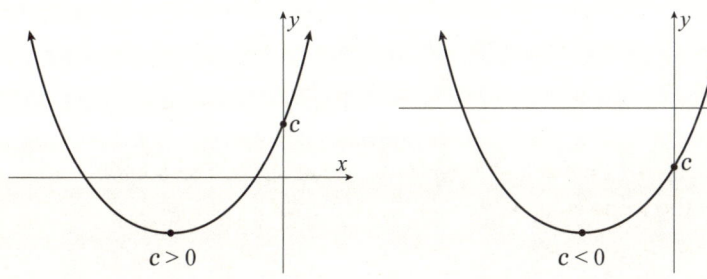

$c>0 \qquad\qquad c<0$

Concept Check

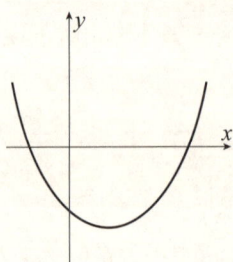

Suppose the graph of $y=ax^2+bx+c$ is shown above. Then,

(1) Since the graph opens upward, $a>0$

(2) Since the axis of symmetry is to the right of the y-axis, a and b have different signs. So, $b<0$

(3) Since the y-intercept is below the x-axis, $c<0$

Example 2

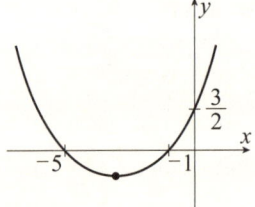

If the graph of the quadratic function $y=ax^2+bx+c$ is shown above, specify the signs of a, b, and c.

Solution

The graph opens upward: $a>0$
The axis is to the left of the y-axis: a and b have the same signs. So, $b>0$
The y-intercept is above the x-axis: $c>0$

Check Point 2

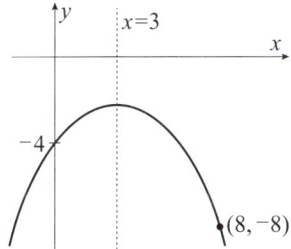

If the graph of the quadratic function $y=ax^2+bx+c$ is shown above, specify the signs of a, b, and c.

03 Zeros of the Quadratic Functions

A zero, also sometimes called a root or a x-intercept, of a function is a value of x such that $y=0$.

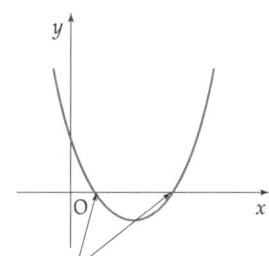

zeros, roots, x-intercepts

Concept Check

Find the zeros of $y=4x^2-3x-1$.

$y=4x^2-3x-1$

$0=4x^2-3x-1$ → Set $y=0$

$0=(4x+1)(x-1)$ → Factor. If it is not factorable, use quadratic formula.

$4x+1=0$ or $x-1=0$ → Zero product property

$x=-\dfrac{1}{4}$ or $x=1$ → Solve for x

The zeros are $-\dfrac{1}{4}$ and 1.

Chapter 6. Quadratic Functions, Part 2

✔ Note: The axis of symmetry is the midpoint of two zeros.

$$x = \frac{-\left(\frac{1}{4}\right)+1}{2} = \frac{3}{8}.$$

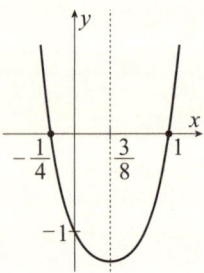

Example 3

Find the zeros of the quadratic function.

① $y = x^2 - 6x - 7$ ② $y = 2x^2 - 5x + 1$

Solution

① $y = x^2 - 6x - 7$
$0 = x^2 - 6x - 7$
$0 = (x-7)(x+1)$, $x = 7$ or $x = -1$

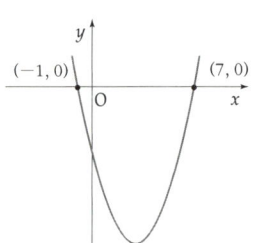

The zeros are 7 and -1

② $y = 2x^2 - 5x + 1$
$0 = 2x^2 - 5x + 1$
Using the quadratic formula, we have
$$x = \frac{-b \pm \sqrt{b^2 - 4ac}}{2a}$$
$$= \frac{-(-5) \pm \sqrt{(-5)^2 - 4 \cdot 2 \cdot 1}}{2 \cdot 2} = \frac{5 \pm \sqrt{17}}{4}$$

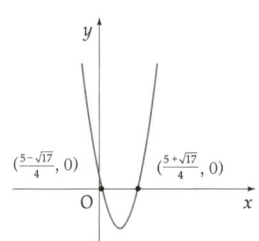

The zeros are $\frac{5+\sqrt{17}}{4}$ and $\frac{5-\sqrt{17}}{4}$

Check Point 3

Find the zeros of the quadratic function.

① $y = 2x^2 - 5x - 3$

② $y = -3x^2 + \dfrac{1}{2}x + \dfrac{5}{2}$

③ $y = x^2 - 5x - 1$

④ $y = -\dfrac{1}{4}x^2 + x - 2$

04 Quadratic Functions and Discriminant

By using discriminant $D = b^2 - 4ac$, we can determine the number of zeros of the quadratic function.

For the quadratic function $y = ax^2 + bx + c$,

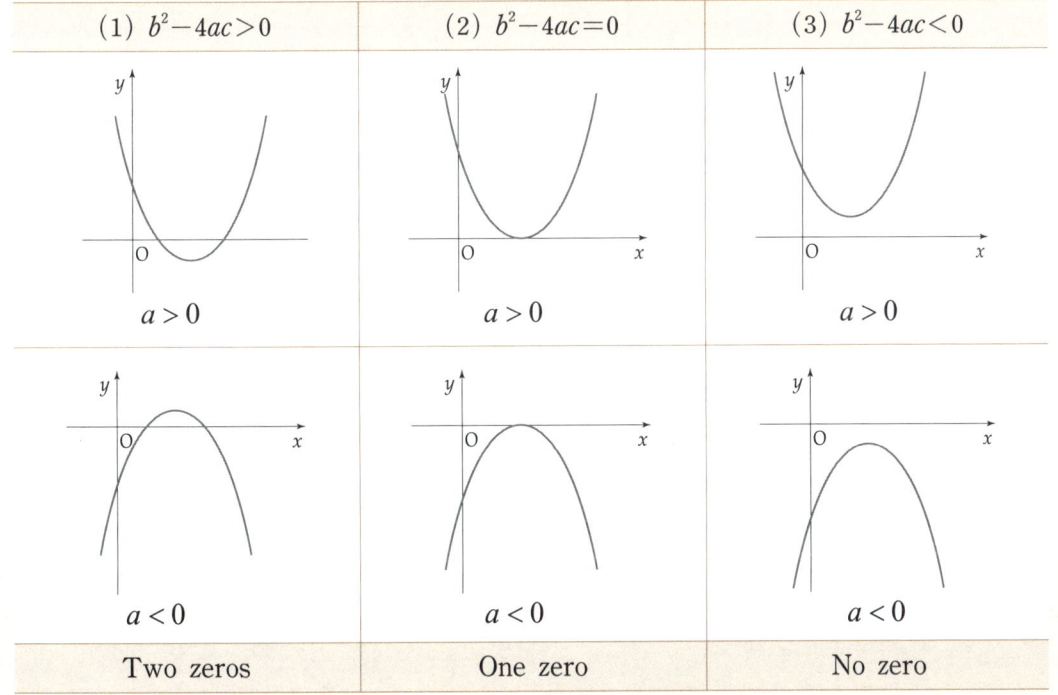

Example 4

Determine the number of zeros of the quadratic function.

① $y = x^2 - 4x + 4$ ② $y = -3x^2 + 7x - 1$

③ $y = \dfrac{1}{2}x^2 - 3x + 5$

Solution

① $y = x^2 - 4x + 4$
$D = b^2 - 4ac$
$= (-4)^2 - 4 \cdot 1 \cdot 4 = 16 - 16 = 0$
Since $D = 0$, there is one zero.

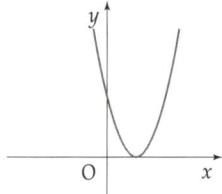

There is one zero

② $y = -3x^2 + 7x - 1$
$D = b^2 - 4ac$
$= 7^2 - 4(-3)(-1) = 49 - 12 = 37 > 0$
Since $D > 0$, there are two zeros.

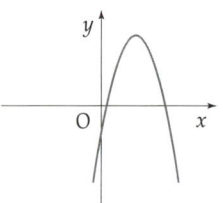

There are two zeros

③ $y = \dfrac{1}{2}x^2 - 3x + 5$
$D = b^2 - 4ac$
$= (-3)^2 - 4 \cdot \dfrac{1}{2} \cdot 5 = 9 - 10 = -1 < 0$
Since $D < 0$, there is no zero.

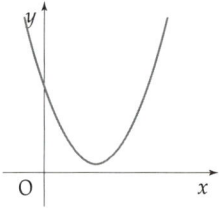

There is no zero

Check Point 4

Solutions_Page 93

Determine the number of zeros of the quadratic function.

① $y = x^2 + 4x + 3$ ② $y = -2x^2 + 5x - 7$

③ $y = -3x^2 + \dfrac{1}{2}x + 1$ ④ $y = \dfrac{1}{4}x^2 - \dfrac{3}{2}x + \dfrac{9}{4}$

Review Exercise

01 Rewrite the function in standard form and find the axis of symmetry, vertex, and y-intercept of the quadratic function.

(1) $y=x^2-4x-5$

(2) $y=-x^2-4x$

(3) $y=x^2-7x-10$

(4) $y=2x^2+12x-9$

(3) $y=-2x^2-7x-3$

(4) $y=\dfrac{1}{3}x^2-\dfrac{10}{3}x+\dfrac{13}{3}$

03 If the graph of $y=\dfrac{3}{2}x^2-2mx+3n$ has the axis of symmetry $x=4$ and y-intercept $(0,\ 9)$, what is the value of $m+n$?

02 Use $x=-\dfrac{b}{2a}$ to find the axis of symmetry, vertex, and y-intercept of the quadratic function.

(1) $y=\dfrac{1}{4}x^2+3x-4$

(2) $y=5x^2-8x+10$

04 If the graph of $y=ax^2+5x-2$ passes through the point $(-1,\ -3)$, what is the equation of the axis of symmetry?

Review Exercise

05 Which of the following is true about the graph of $y=2x^2+4x-\dfrac{3}{4}$?
(There are 2 answers)

(A) The graph opens downward
(B) The vertex is $\left(-1, -\dfrac{11}{4}\right)$
(C) The graph of $y=2x^2$ is shifted 1 unit to the left and 3 units up
(D) For $x>-1$, y increases as x increases.
(E) The y-intercept of the graph is $(0, 2)$

(3)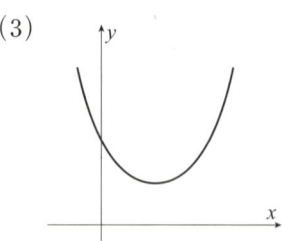

(4)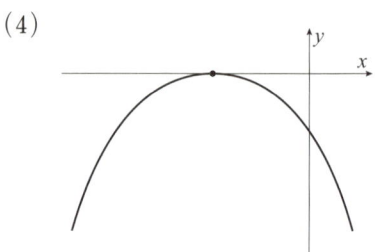

06 If the graph of the function $y=ax^2+bx+c$ is shown below, specify the sign of a, b, and c.

(1)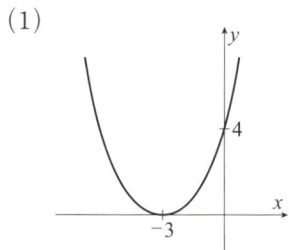

(2)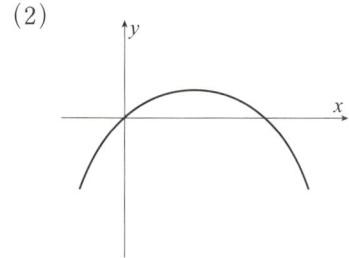

07 Find the zeros of the quadratic function.

(1) $y=3x^2-27$

(2) $y=x^2+4x+4$

(3) $y=\dfrac{1}{2}x^2+3x-\dfrac{7}{2}$

(4) $y=0.6x^2+1.1x-0.9$

Challenging

08 Suppose the quadratic function $y=4x^2+kx-15$ intersects the x-axis at two points. If one of the points is $\left(\dfrac{3}{2},\ 0\right)$, what is the coordinate of the other point?

09 Determine the number of zeros of the quadratic function

(1) $y=x^2-2x-10$

(2) $y=\dfrac{1}{2}x^2-2x-8$

(3) $y=5x^2-8x+10$

(4) $y=\dfrac{1}{4}x^2+\dfrac{3}{2}x-5$

10 If the graph of $y=4x^2-mx+3$ intersects the x-axis at one point, find all possible values of m.

11 If the graph of $y=ax^2-4x-5$ does not intersect the x-axis, find all possible values of a.

2. Writing Quadratic Functions

01 Using Vertex and a Point

Suppose the function has the vertex (h, k) and passes through a point.
(1) Start with the function $y = a(x-h)^2 + k$.
(2) Substitute a point into the function and solve for a.

Example 1

Find the equation of the quadratic function using given information.

① The graph has the vertex $(0, 0)$ and passes through the point $(1, 4)$.

② The graph has the vertex $(2, 5)$ and passes through the point $(3, 3)$.

Solution

① Start with the function $y = a(x-h)^2 + k$.
$y = a(x-0)^2 + 0$ → Write the function with given vertex $(0, 0)$
$4 = a(1-0)^2 + 0$ → Substitute a point $(1, 4)$ into the function
$a = 4$ → Solve for a
$y = 4(x-0)^2 + 0$ → Substitute $a=4$ into the function
$y = 4x^2$ → Simplify

② Start with the function $y = a(x-h)^2 + k$.
$y = a(x-2)^2 + 5$ → Write the function with given vertex $(2, 5)$
$3 = a(3-2)^2 + 5$ → Substitute a point $(3, 3)$ into the function.
$a = -2$ → Solve for a.
$y = -2(x-2)^2 + 5$ → Substitute $a=-2$ into the function.

Check Point 1

Find the quadratic function using given information.

① The graph has the vertex $(3, -3)$ and passes through the point $(5, 2)$.

② The graph has the vertex $\left(\dfrac{1}{2}, 0\right)$ and passes through the point $(1, -1)$.

02 Using Axis of Symmetry and Two Points

Suppose the graph has an axis of symmetry at $x=h$ and passes through two points.
(1) Start with the function $y=a(x-h)^2+k$.
(2) Substitute two points into the function and solve for a and k.

Example 2

If the graph has the axis of symmetry is $x=2$ and passes through two points $(1, 2)$, $(4, 8)$, what is the equation of the quadratic function?

Solution

Start with the function $y=a(x-h)^2+k$.
$y=a(x-2)^2+k$ → Substitute 2 for h.
$\begin{cases} 2=a(1-2)^2+k \\ 8=a(4-2)^2+k \end{cases} = \begin{cases} a+k=2 \\ 4a+k=8 \end{cases}$ → Substitute $(1, 2)$ and $(4, 8)$ into the function.
$a=2, \ k=0$ → Solve the system and find a and k.
$y=2(x-2)^2+0$ → Substitute $a=2$ and $k=0$ into the function.
$y=2(x-2)^2$ → Simplify

Check Point 2

Solutions_Page 96

① If the graph has the axis of symmetry is $x=-3$ and passes through two points $(-2, 4)$, $(0, -4)$, what is the equation of the quadratic function?

② If the graph has the axis of symmetry is $x=\frac{1}{2}$ and passes through two points $\left(\frac{3}{2}, 1\right)$, $\left(-\frac{3}{2}, 7\right)$, what is the equation of the quadratic function?

03 Using Three Points

Suppose the graph passes through three specific points.

(1) Start with the function $y = ax^2 + bx + c$.

(2) Substitute three points into the function and solve for a, b, and c.

Example 3

If the graph passes through three points $(0, -2)$, $(1, -3)$, and $(2, 2)$, what is the equation of the quadratic function?

Solution

Start with the function $y = ax^2 + bx + c$.

$$\begin{cases} -2 = a \cdot 0^2 + b \cdot 0 + c \\ -3 = a \cdot 1^2 + b \cdot 1 + c \\ 2 = a \cdot 2^2 + b \cdot 2 + c \end{cases}$$ → Substitute three points into the function

$$\begin{cases} c = -2 \\ a + b + (-2) = -3, \ a + b = -1 \\ 4a + 2b + (-2) = 2, \ 4a + 2b = 4 \end{cases}$$ → Simplify

$a = 3, \ b = -4, \ \text{and} \ c = 2$ → Solve for a, b, and c

$y = 3x^2 - 4x - 2$ → Rewrite the function with a, b, and c

Check Point 3

Solutions_Page 97

① If the graph passes through three points $(0, 6)$, $(-1, 4)$, and $(-2, -2)$, what is the equation of the quadratic function?

② If the graph passes through three points $(0, -4)$, $(2, 1)$, and $\left(\dfrac{1}{2}, \dfrac{5}{2}\right)$ what is the equation of the quadratic function?

04 Using x-intercepts and a Point

Suppose the graph has x-intercepts $(m, 0)$ and $(n, 0)$, and passes through a point.
(1) Start with the function $y=a(x-m)(x-n)$.
(2) Substitute a point into the function and solve for a.

Example 4

If the graph has the x-intercepts $(3, 0)$ and $(-2, 0)$ and passes through the point $(2, -8)$, what is the equation of the quadratic function?

Solution

Start with the function $y=a(x-m)(x-n)$.
$y=a(x-3)(x+2)$ → Write the function with given x intercepts
$-8=a(2-3)(2+2)$ → Substitute the point $(2, -8)$ into the function
$a=2$ → Solve for a
$y=2(x-3)(x+2)$ → Substitute $a=2$ into the function

Check Point 4

Solutions_Page 97

① If the graph has the x-intercepts $(2, 0)$ and $(5, 0)$ and passes through the point $(3, 4)$, what is the equation of the quadratic function?

② If the graph has the x-intercepts $\left(\frac{1}{4}, 0\right)$ and $(-1, 0)$ and passes through the point $\left(-\frac{1}{2}, -\frac{5}{2}\right)$, what is the equation of the quadratic function?

Review Exercise

01 Suppose that the quadratic function passes through the point with the following vertex. Find the equation of the quadratic function.

(1) Vertex $(0, 0)$ Point $(2, 3)$

(2) Vertex $(0, -2)$ Point $(2, 0)$

(3) Vertex $(-2, -5)$ Point $(3, 7)$

(4) Vertex $\left(\frac{1}{3}, 2\right)$ Point $\left(-\frac{2}{3}, 1\right)$

02 Suppose that the quadratic function passes through two points with the following axis of symmetry. Find the equation of the quadratic function.

(1) Axis of symmetry $x=0$
    Points $(-1, -2)$ and $(2, -4)$

(2) Axis of symmetry $x=3$
    Points $(1, 4)$ and $(4, 7)$

(3) Axis of symmetry $x=-1$
Points $(0, 2)$ and $(-3, 6)$

(3) Points $(0, 3)$, $(-2, -1)$, and $(1, -2)$

(4) Axis of symmetry $x=-\dfrac{3}{5}$
Points $(0, 0)$ and $(2, 3)$

(4) Points $\left(0, \dfrac{7}{2}\right)$, $\left(3, \dfrac{7}{2}\right)$, and $\left(\dfrac{1}{2}, -\dfrac{3}{2}\right)$

03 Suppose that the quadratic function passes through three points. Find the equation of the quadratic function.

(1) Points $(0, 0)$, $(-1, 1)$, and $(1, 1)$

04 Suppose that the quadratic function passes two x intercepts and a point. Find the equation of the quadratic function.

(1) $x-$intercepts $(1, 0)$, $(-1, 0)$
Point $(0, 1)$

(2) Points $(0, 4)$, $(2, 0)$, and $(3, 2)$

Review Exercise

(2) x-intercepts $(0, 0)$, $(6, 0)$
Point $(4, 2)$

(4) x-intercepts $\left(\dfrac{3}{4}, 0\right)$, $\left(-\dfrac{5}{4}, 0\right)$
Point $\left(1, -\dfrac{1}{2}\right)$

(3) x-intercepts $(-4, 0)$, $(2, 0)$
Point $(0, -6)$

05 Find the equation of the quadratic function shown in the graph below.

(1)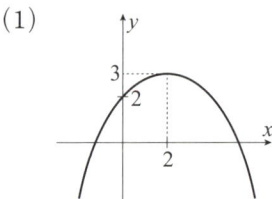

(2)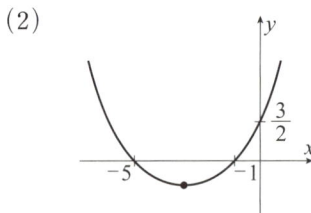

(3)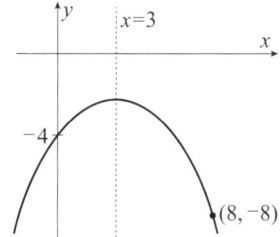

(4)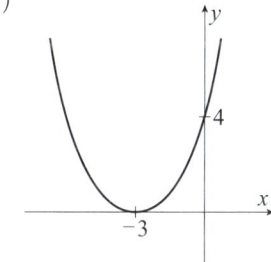

06 Find the equation of the quadratic function with vertex $\left(4, \dfrac{3}{2}\right)$ and y-intercept -2.

3. The Minimum and Maximum

01 Minimum and Maximum of the Quadratic Functions

The quadratic function has a minimum value at the vertex if its graph opens upward and a maximum value at the vertex if its graph opens downward. Since the quadratic function has an axis of symmetry at $x=-\frac{b}{2a}$, the maximum or minimum value of y occurs at $x=-\frac{b}{2a}$.

Let $y=ax^2+bx+c$, $a \neq 0$.
(1) If $a<0$, then $y\left(-\frac{b}{2a}\right)$ is a maximum value of y.
(2) If $a>0$, then $y\left(-\frac{b}{2a}\right)$ is a minimum value of y.

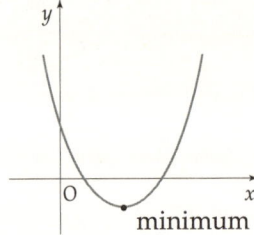
minimum

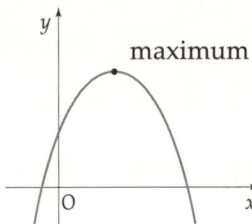
maximum

Example 1

Find the minimum or maximum of the quadratic function.

① $y=5x^2-10x+3$

② $y=-\frac{1}{2}x^2+2x-4$

Solution

① $y=5x^2-10x+3$
Since $a=5>0$, the function has the minimum value.

The axis of symmetry $x=-\dfrac{b}{2a}=-\dfrac{-10}{2\cdot 5}=1$.

So the minimum value is $y(1)=5(1)^2-10(1)+3=-2$.

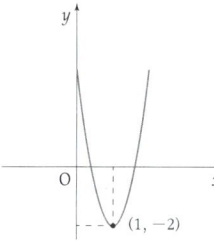

The minimum value is -2

② $y=-\dfrac{1}{2}x^2+2x-4$

Since $a=-\dfrac{1}{2}<0$, the function has the maximum value.

The axis of symmetry $x=-\dfrac{b}{2a}=-\dfrac{2}{2\left(-\dfrac{1}{2}\right)}=2$.

So the maximum value is $y(2)=-\dfrac{1}{2}(2)^2+2(2)-4=-2$.

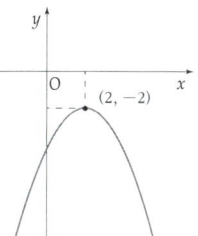

The maximum value is -2

Check Point 1

Solutions_Page 100

Find the minimum or maximum of the quadratic function.

① $y=x^2-6x+8$ ② $y=-2x^2-5x$ ③ $y=\dfrac{1}{3}x^2-3$

Example 2

If the maximum value of the function is 7 and the zeros are 0 and 6, what is the equation of the quadratic function?

Solution

The axis of symmetry is equal to the midpoint of the two zeros. So the axis of symmetry is $x=\dfrac{0+6}{2}=3$, as shown in Figure below.

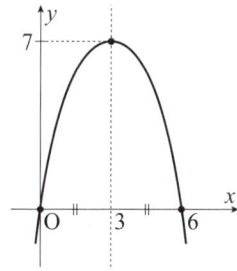

Chapter 6. Quadratic Functions, Part 2

Since the vertex of the function is (3, 7), we have $y=a(x-3)^2+7$. By substituting one of the zeros (0, 0), we have
$0=a(0-3)^2+7$, $a=-\dfrac{7}{9}$

Thus, the function is $y=-\dfrac{7}{9}(x-3)^2+7$.

$$y=-\dfrac{7}{9}(x-3)^2+7$$

Check Point 2

Solutions_Page 100

Find the quadratic function using given information.

① The minimum value is -4 and the zeros are -5 and 5.

② The minimum value is -8 when $x=-1$ and one of the zeros is -5.

02 Applications

There are many applications of quadratic functions. Many involve solving for the maximums or minimums of quadratic functions. Remember the maximum or minimum is the vertex of the quadratic function. The maximum or minimum value of the quadratic function can be found using the equation of the axis of symmetry or by method of completing the square.

Example 3

There are two numbers with a sum of 10. Find the two numbers when the product of these two numbers is maximized.

Solution

Let x be one of two numbers. Then, the other number is $10-x$. Also, let y be the product of these two numbers. Then, we have $y=x(10-x)$ and we need to find the vertex of this function.

Method 1
$$y = x(10-x) = -x^2 + 10x$$
$$= -(x^2 - 10x + 5^2 - 5^2)$$
$$= -(x-5)^2 + 25$$

Method 2
Since $y = x(10-x)$ has two zeros $x=0$ and $x=10$, the axis of symmetry is $x = \frac{0+10}{2} = 5$ and $y(5) = 5(10-5) = 25$.

So, y is maximum when $x=5$ and the maximum value is 25. Therefore, two numbers are $x=5$ and $10-x = 10-5 = 5$.

5 and 5

Check Point 3
Solutions_Page 101

There are two numbers with a difference of 6. Find the two numbers when the product of these two numbers is minimized.

Example 4

There is a string of 48 inches in length. What is the maximum area of a rectangle that can be made of this string?

Solution

Let x be the length of the rectangle. Then, the width of the rectangle is $24-x$, as shown in Figure below.

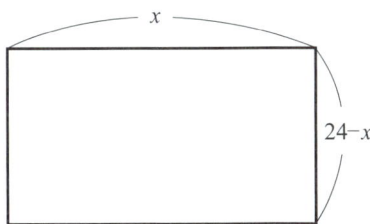

Also, let y be the area of the rectangle. Then, we have $y = x(24-x)$ and we need to find the vertex of this function.

Method 1
$$y = x(24-x) = -x^2 + 24x$$
$$= -(x^2 - 24x + 12^2 - 12^2)$$
$$= -(x-12)^2 + 144$$

Method 2

Since $y=x(24-x)$ has two zeros $x=0$ and $x=24$, the axis of symmetry is $x=\frac{0+24}{2}=12$ and $y(12)=12(24-12)=144$.

So, y is maximum when $x=12$ and the maximum value is 144.

The maximum area of the rectangle is 144 square inches

Check Point 4
Solutions_Page 101

Jason wants to make a rectangular garden. One side is his house wall. If he has 28 meters of fence that he will use to surround the other three sides, what is the maximum area of the garden that can be made of this fence?

Example 5

A ball is thrown vertically upward from the top of a 96-foot building. If the height h, in feet, of the ball from the ground after t seconds is given by $h=-16t^2+80t+96$, after how many second does the ball reaches the maximum height in the air? What is the maximum height of the ball?

Solution

Using the axis of symmetry $t=-\frac{b}{2a}=-\frac{80}{2(-16)}=\frac{5}{2}$, the maximum height of the ball is $h\left(\frac{5}{2}\right)=-16\left(\frac{5}{2}\right)^2+80\left(\frac{5}{2}\right)+96=196$

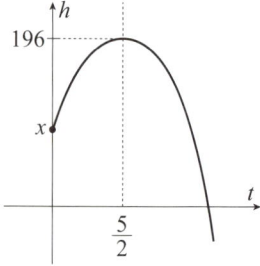

The ball reaches its maximum height of 196 feet after $\frac{5}{2}$ seconds

Check Point 5
Solutions_Page 101

A ball is thrown vertically upward from ground. If the height h, in meters, of the ball from the ground after t seconds is given by $h=-4.9t^2+19.6t$, what is the maximum height of the ball?

Review Exercise

01 Find the minimum or maximum of the function

(1) $y=-x^2+2x+8$

(2) $y=-2x^2-2x+4$

(3) $y=\dfrac{1}{2}x^2+3x-\dfrac{9}{2}$

(4) $y=x^2-\dfrac{5}{3}x$

(5) $y=4x^2-3x-1$

(6) $y=-2x^2+6x-\dfrac{3}{2}$

02 If the quadratic function $y=x^2-4x+3m-2$ has the minimum value of 4 when $x=n$, what is the value of $m+n$?

Review Exercise

03 If the quadratic function $y=-4x^2+mx-5n+1$ has the maximum value of 1 when $x=-\frac{1}{2}$, what is the value of mn?

Challenging

04 If the maximum value of $y=2mx^2-6x+3$ is equal to the minimum value of $y=\frac{1}{2}x^2+x-6$, what is the value of m?

05 Eugene wants to make a rectangular henhouse using 52-inch wire. Suppose that one side of the henhouse is the wall. If he uses all of the 52-inch wire to surround the other three sides, what is the maximum area of the henhouse that can be made?

06

There is a rectangle with length 10 and width 6. If we increase the width by x and decrease the length by x to create a new rectangle as shown in Figure above, what is the maximum area of the new rectangle?

07 A soccer ball is kicked vertically upward at a height of 12 feet from the ground. If the height h, in feet, of the soccer ball from the ground after t seconds is given by $h=-16t^2+16t+12$, after how many second does the ball reaches the maximum height in the air? What is the maximum height of the ball?

08 When a factory produces x products a day, the profit, in hundred dollars, is $-\dfrac{x^2}{2}+12x-40$. How many products must the factory produce to maximize profits per day? What is the maximum profit per day?

Challenging

10 Find the maximum area of the triangle whose sum of base and height is 16.

Challenging

09 If $x+2y=12$, what is the maximum value of xy?

Challenging

11 Suppose you have a cake that sells 30 pieces a day if you sell it for $5 per piece. If you raise the price of cake by $x per piece, you sell $2x$ pieces less. Then, how much should you sell a piece of cake to maximize profit?

Chapter Test — Level 1

Solutions_Page 104

01 Which quadrant does the quadratic function $y=2x^2-8x+11$ NOT pass through?

(A) I only (B) II only (C) III only
(D) I and II only (E) III and IV only

02 Which of the following is true about the graph of $y=-3x^2+6x-5$?

(A) The vertex is $(1, 2)$
(B) The equation of the axis of symmetry is $x=-1$
(C) When $x>1$, y increases as x increases.
(D) The graph is shifted 1 unit to the right and 2 units down from the graph of $y=-3x^2$
(E) The y-intercept of the graph is 5

03 If the graph of $y=2x^2+(5a+1)x+(3b-1)$ has the axis of symmetry $x=-3$ and y-intercept 4, what is the value of ab?

04 Suppose the quadratic function $y=3x^2-(2a+5)x-8$ intersects the x-axis at two points. If one of the points is $(4, 0)$, what is the coordinate of the other point?

05 If two quadratic functions $y=2x^2-6x+m$ and $y=-3x^2+9x-2m+1$ have the same vertex, what is the value of m?

06 If the graph of the quadratic function $y=3x^2-6x+5$ is shifted 2 units to the right and 3 units up, then the graph of the function is $y=ax^2+bx+c$. Find the value of $a+b+c$.

07

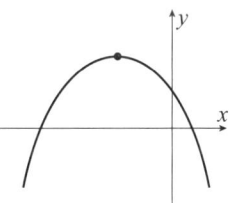

If the graph of the quadratic function $y=ax^2+bx+c$ is shown above, which of the following must be true?

(A) $a<0$, $b<0$, $c>0$ (B) $a<0$, $b>0$, $c<0$
(C) $a<0$, $b>0$, $c>0$ (D) $a>0$, $b>0$, $c<0$
(E) $a>0$, $b<0$, $c<0$

Chapter Test — Level 1

08

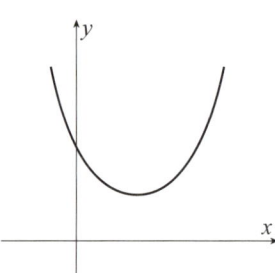

If the graph of the quadratic function $y=ax^2+bx+c$ is shown above, which of the following could be a graph of $y=cx^2+ax+b$?

(A)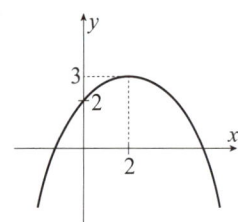

(B)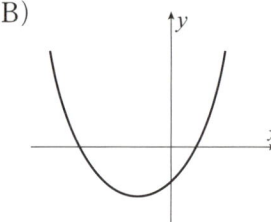

(C)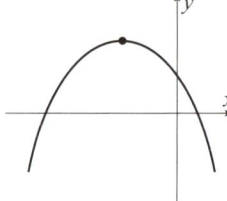

(D)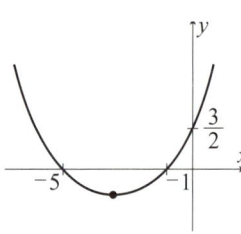

(E)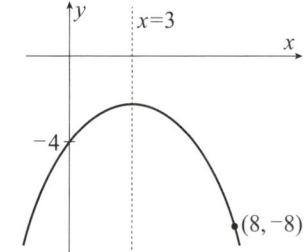

09 If the quadratic function $y=-3x^2-6x+m+1$ has the maximum value of 12, what is the value of m?

10 Find the quadratic function $y=ax^2+bx+c$ that satisfies the condition below.

(1) The maximum value of the function is 4 when $x=2$ and the graph passes through the point $(4, -1)$.

(2) The minimum value of the function is 0 when $x=-3$ and the graph passes through the point $(-6, 6)$.

(3) The graph of the function passes through two points $(-3, 0)$ and $(5, 0)$, and it has maximum value of 8.

11

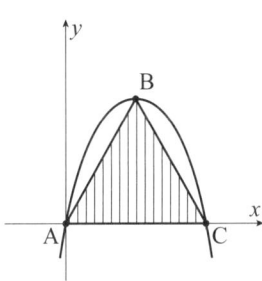

The graph of the quadratic function $y=4x-x^2$ is shown above. If the graph has the vertex at B and passes through two zeros A and C, what is the area of triangle ABC?

Chapter Test — Level 1

12 A baseball is thrown vertically upward at a height of 2 meter from the ground. If the height h, in meter, of the baseball from the ground after t seconds is given by $h = -5t^2 + 30t + 2$, answer the following question.

(1) After how many second does the baseball reaches the maximum height in the air?

(2) What is the maximum height of the baseball?

13

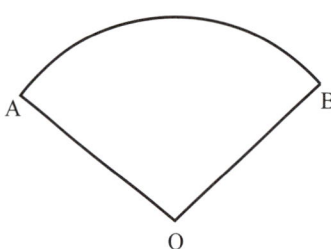

I want to make a sector by bending a wire of length 40 inches as shown above. What is the length of the radius to maximize the area of the sector?

$\left(\text{The area of the sector is } \dfrac{1}{2} \times \overline{\text{OB}} \times \overparen{\text{AB}}\right)$

Chapter Test — Level 2

01 If the graph of the quadratic function $y=4x^2-6x+b$ intersects the x-axis at one point, what is the value of b? ($b>0$)

02 Suppose that the graph of $y=ax^2+bx+c$ has the axis of symmetry at $x=1$ and passes through two points $(0,\ -2)$ and $(3,\ -4)$. If a, b, and c are all real numbers, what is the value of $a+b+c$?

03 If the vertex of the graph of $y=-x^2+kx-2k+2$ is on the line $y=2x-2$, what are all possible values of k?

04 If the quadratic function $y=-\dfrac{1}{2}x^2-6x+k$ intersects the x-axis at two points, the distance between two points is 8. What is the value of k?

Chapter Test — Level 2

05

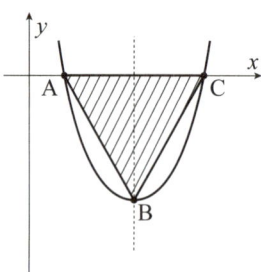

The graph of the quadratic function $y=2x^2-12x+b$ is shown above. If the graph has the vertex at B and $\overline{AC}=2$, what is the area of triangle ABC?

06 If the quadratic function $y=kx^2-5kx+2x-3$ has the vertex $(2, m)$, what is the value of $k+m$?

07 There are two numbers with a difference of 6. When the product of two numbers is minimum, what is the larger of the two numbers?

08 If $2x-y=4$, what is the minimum value of $2xy$?

09 Jason has a certain product that sells 12 products for $8 every day. If Jason drops the price by $x per product, he sells $2x$ products more. Then, how much should he sell a product to maximize profit?

Chapter **7**

Roots and Radicals

1. The Square Roots
2. n^{th} Roots and Rational Exponents
3. Properties of Radicals, Part 1
4. Properties of Radicals, Part 2
5. Radical Equations
6. Graphing Radical Functions
7. Chapter Test

1 The Square Roots

01 Definition of Square Root

A square root of a number $a(a>0)$ is a solution of the equation $x^2=a$. In other words, a number x whose square $(x \times x)$ is a. Every positive number a has two square roots, one positive and one negative.

$$x^2=a(a>0) \Rightarrow x=\left\{\begin{array}{c}\sqrt{a}\\-\sqrt{a}\end{array}\right\}=\pm\sqrt{a}$$

The positive square root, $\sqrt{a}$, is called the principal square root of a.

Example 1

Find the square roots of the number.

① 9 ② 2

Solution

① The square roots of 9 are $\sqrt{9}=3$ and $-\sqrt{9}=-3$, because $3^2=9$ and $(-3)^2=9$.

± 3

② The square roots of 2 are $\sqrt{2}$ and $-\sqrt{2}$, because $(\sqrt{2})^2=2$ and $(-\sqrt{2})^2=2$.

$\pm\sqrt{2}$

Check Point 1

Solutions_Page 110

Find the square roots of the number.

① 36 ② $\dfrac{9}{16}$

③ 0.81 ④ $(-5)^2$

284 Chapter 7. Roots and Radicals

02 Property of Square Root

1. For $a>0$,
   (1) $(\sqrt{a})^2 = a$
   (2) $(-\sqrt{a})^2 = a$
   (3) $\sqrt{a^2} = a$
   (4) $\sqrt{(-a)^2} = a$

Concept Check

(1) $(\sqrt{5})^2 = \sqrt{5} \times \sqrt{5} = 5$
(2) $(-\sqrt{5})^2 = (-\sqrt{5}) \times (-\sqrt{5}) = \sqrt{5} \times \sqrt{5} = 5$
(3) $\sqrt{5^2} = \sqrt{5 \times 5} = \sqrt{25} = 5$
(4) $\sqrt{(-5)^2} = \sqrt{(-5) \times (-5)} = \sqrt{25} = 5$

2. For all real number a, $\sqrt{a^2} = |a| = \begin{cases} a, & a \geq 0 \\ -a, & a < 0 \end{cases}$

Concept Check

(1) If $a=2$, $\sqrt{a^2} = \sqrt{2^2} = 2$

$$\sqrt{a^2} = \sqrt{2^2} = 2$$
The sign does not change

(2) If $a=-2$, $\sqrt{a^2} = \sqrt{(-2)^2} = -(-2) = 2$

$$\sqrt{a^2} = \sqrt{(-2)^2} = -(-2) = 2$$
The sign changes

Example 2

Simplify the following.

① $\sqrt{49}$

② $\sqrt{\dfrac{25}{4}}$

③ $\sqrt{4^2} - (-\sqrt{5})^2$

④ $(\sqrt{6})^2 - \sqrt{(-3)^2} + \sqrt{25}$

Solution

① $\sqrt{49} = \sqrt{(7)^2} = 7$

② $\sqrt{\dfrac{25}{4}} = \sqrt{\left(\dfrac{5}{2}\right)^2} = \dfrac{5}{2}$

③ $\sqrt{4^2} - (-\sqrt{5})^2 = 4 - 5 = -1$

④ $(\sqrt{6})^2 - \sqrt{(-3)^2} + \sqrt{25} = 6 - 3 + 5 = 8$

Check Point 2

Solutions_Page 110

Simplify the following.

① $\sqrt{0.04}$

② $-\sqrt{121}$

③ $\sqrt{\left(-\dfrac{1}{2}\right)^2} - \sqrt{\dfrac{1}{9}} + (-\sqrt{2})^2$

④ $\sqrt{25} - \sqrt{\left(\dfrac{5}{2}\right)^2} + \left(-\sqrt{\dfrac{1}{4}}\right)^2$

Example 3

Simplify the following.

① $\sqrt{(a-2)^2}$ if $a \geq 2$

② $\sqrt{(a-2)^2}$ if $a < 2$

Solution

① Since $a-2 \geq 0$ when $a \geq 2$, $\sqrt{(a-2)^2} = a-2$

② Since $a-2 < 0$ when $a < 2$, $\sqrt{(a-2)^2} = -(a-2) = -a+2$

Check Point 3

Simplify the following.

① $\sqrt{(x+3)^2}$ if $x \geq -3$
② $\sqrt{(x+3)^2}$ if $x < -3$
③ $\sqrt{(x-y)^2}$ if $x \geq y$
④ $\sqrt{(x-y)^2}$ if $x < y$

03 Inequality of Square Roots

For $a > 0$ and $b > 0$,

1. If $\sqrt{a} < \sqrt{b}$, $a < b$
2. If $a < b$, $\sqrt{a} < \sqrt{b}$
3. If $a < b$, $\sqrt{a} < \sqrt{b}$ and $-\sqrt{a} > -\sqrt{b}$
4. If $a < \sqrt{x} < b$, $\sqrt{a^2} < \sqrt{x} < \sqrt{b^2}$ and $a^2 < x < b^2$

Concept Check

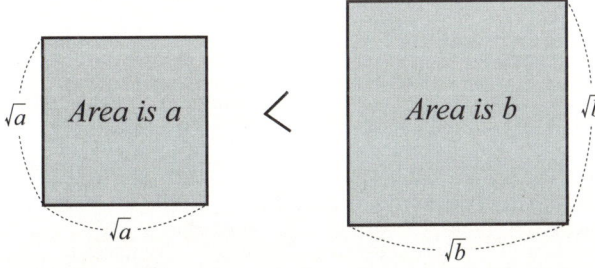

1. The longer the side of the square, the larger the area:
$$\sqrt{a} < \sqrt{b} \Rightarrow a < b$$

2. The larger the area of the square, the longer the side:
$$a < b \Rightarrow \sqrt{a} < \sqrt{b}$$

3. Since $2 < 3$, $\sqrt{2} < \sqrt{3}$ and $-\sqrt{2} > -\sqrt{3}$
4. Since $2 < \sqrt{6} < 3$, $\sqrt{2^2} < \sqrt{6} < \sqrt{3^2}$ and $2^2 < 6 < 3^2$

Example 4

$-\sqrt{11}$, 0, $\sqrt{6}$, -4, $-\sqrt{15}$, $\sqrt{3}$, 2

List the following numbers in order from least to greatest.

Solution

We have 3 positive numbers ($\sqrt{6}$, $\sqrt{3}$, 2), and 3 negative numbers ($-\sqrt{11}$, -4, $-\sqrt{15}$).
If we compare positive numbers,
$\sqrt{3} < 2(=\sqrt{4}) < \sqrt{6}$
If we compare negative numbers,
$-4(=-\sqrt{16}) < -\sqrt{15} < -\sqrt{11}$

So if we list following numbers in order from least to greatest, we have
$$-4, \ -\sqrt{15}, \ -\sqrt{11}, \ 0, \ \sqrt{3}, \ 2, \ \sqrt{6}$$

Check Point 4

Solutions_Page 110

$\sqrt{8}$, $-\sqrt{5}$, 0, -2, $-\sqrt{9}$, 3, $\sqrt{10}$

List the following numbers in order from least to greatest.

Example 5

Find all positive integers x that satisfy the following inequality.

① $2 < \sqrt{x} < 3$ ② $-2 < -\sqrt{x-3} < -1$

Solution

① $2 < \sqrt{x} < 3$
$2^2 < (\sqrt{x})^2 < 3^2$ → Square each side
$4 < x < 9$ → Simplify
So the solutions for x are 5, 6, 7, and 8.

5, 6, 7, and 8

288 Chapter 7. Roots and Radicals

② $-2<-\sqrt{x-3}<-1$
  $2>\sqrt{x-3}>1$ → $-\sqrt{a}<-\sqrt{b} \Rightarrow \sqrt{a}>\sqrt{b}$
  $1<\sqrt{x-3}<2$ → Rewrite the inequality
  $1^2<(\sqrt{x-3})^2<2^2$ → Square each side
  $1<x-3<4$ → Simplify
  $4<x<7$ → Add 3 to each side
  So the solutions for x are 5 and 6.

  5 and 6

Check Point 5

Solutions_Page 110

① Find all positive integers x that satisfy the inequality $3<\sqrt{x-1}<4$.

② Find the number of positive integer x that satisfy the inequality $-3<-\sqrt{2x-1}<-1$.

Review Exercise

01 Find the square roots of the number

(1) 25

(2) 144

(3) $\dfrac{1}{4}$

(4) 0.16

(5) $(-7)^2$

(6) $\left(-\dfrac{2}{3}\right)^2$

(3) $-\sqrt{\dfrac{9}{100}}$

(4) $\sqrt{36}-(\sqrt{5})^2$

(5) $(-\sqrt{6})^2+\sqrt{(-5)^2}-\sqrt{16}$

(6) $\sqrt{\left(\dfrac{1}{3}\right)^2}+\sqrt{\left(-\dfrac{1}{9}\right)^2}-\left(-\sqrt{\dfrac{1}{4}}\right)^2$

(7) $\sqrt{2.25}-\sqrt{(-5)^2}$

(8) $\sqrt{\left(-\dfrac{1}{2}\right)^2}-\sqrt{0.16}-\sqrt{25}$

02 Simplify the following.

(1) $\sqrt{196}$

(2) $\sqrt{0.25}$

03 If the positive square root of $\sqrt{81}$ is m and the negative square root of $(-3)^2$ is n, what is the value of $m+n$?

04 If the positive square root of $\left(-\sqrt{\dfrac{9}{4}}\right)^2$ is a and the negative square root of $\sqrt{(-4)^2}$ is b, what is the value of $2a-b$?

05 All values below are equal to each other EXCEPT

(A) $\sqrt{4^2}$
(B) $\sqrt{(-4)^2}$
(C) $(-\sqrt{4})^2$
(D) $-(-\sqrt{4^2})$
(E) $-\sqrt{(-4)^2}$

Challenging

06 Simplify the following.
(1) $\sqrt{a^2}-\sqrt{b^2}$ if $a>0$, $b<0$

(2) $\sqrt{(a-3)^2}+\sqrt{(a+1)^2}$ if $-1<a<3$

(3) $\sqrt{(x-2)^2}+\sqrt{(2y-1)^2}$ if $x<2$, $y>\dfrac{1}{2}$

(4) $\sqrt{x^2}+\sqrt{y^2}-2\sqrt{(y-x)^2}$ if $x>0$, $y<0$

07 Find the minimum value of x for $\sqrt{20x}$ to be a positive integer.

Challenging

08 Find the number of positive integer x that satisfy the inequality $4<\sqrt{3x+1}<5$.

2　n^{th} Roots and Rational Exponents

01　n^{th} Roots

A cube root of a number a, $\sqrt[3]{a}$, is a solution of the equation $x^3=a$. A fourth root of a number a, $\sqrt[4]{a}$, is a solution of the equation $x^4=a$ and so on. Here is a general definition of the nth root of a, where n is positive integer.

The symbol $\sqrt[n]{a}$ is called a radical.

$$\text{Index} \rightarrow \sqrt[n]{a} \leftarrow \text{radicand}, \quad \text{radical sign}$$

	Radicals	Radicand	Index	Root
①	$\sqrt{4a} \ (=\sqrt[2]{4a})$	$4a$	2	Square
②	$\sqrt[3]{2a-b}$	$2a-b$	3	Cube
③	$\sqrt[4]{4y^5}$	$4y^5$	4	Fourth
④	$\sqrt[5]{x^2y}$	x^2y	5	Fifth

1. An nth root of a, $\sqrt[n]{a}$, is a solution of the equation $x^n=a$.

2. (1) If n is even and $a>0$, there are two real n^{th} roots of a: $\pm\sqrt[n]{a}$.

   (2) If n is even and $a=0$, there is one real n^{th} root of a: $\sqrt[n]{0}=0$.

   (3) If n is even and $a<0$, there is no real n^{th} root of a.

3. If n is odd, there is exactly one real n^{th} root of a, whether a is positive, negative, or zero.

Concept Check

1. The cube root of 5 is $\sqrt[3]{5}$ and this is a solution of the equation $x^3=5$
2. (1) The fourth root($n=4$) of 5 are $\pm\sqrt[4]{5}$ $\Rightarrow$ $(\sqrt[4]{5})^4=(-\sqrt[4]{5})^4=5$
   (2) The fourth root($n=4$) of 0 is $\sqrt[4]{0}=0$ $\Rightarrow$ $0^4=0$
   (3) There is no fourth root($n=4$) of -5 $\Rightarrow$ NO solution that satisfy $x^4=-5$
3. The cube root($n=3$) of 5 is $\sqrt[3]{5}$
   The cube root($n=3$) of -5 is $-\sqrt[3]{5}$
   The cube root($n=3$) of 0 is 0

Example 1

① Find the cube root of -64

② Find fourth root of 81

Solution

① The cube root of -64 is $\sqrt[3]{-64}=-4$, because $(-4)^3=-64$.
② The fourth root of 81 is $\pm\sqrt[4]{81}=\pm 3$, because $3^4=81$ and $(-3)^4=81$.

Check Point 1   Solutions_Page 112

Find the indicated n^{th} root(s) of a.

① $n=2$, $a=36$ ② $n=3$, $a=-125$

③ $n=4$, $a=-16$ ④ $n=5$, $a=\dfrac{1}{32}$

Example 2

Simplify the following.

① $\sqrt[3]{27}$　　　　② $\sqrt[4]{16}$

③ $\sqrt[5]{-32}$　　　④ $\sqrt[3]{\dfrac{8}{27}}$

Solution

① Since $3^3=27$, $\sqrt[3]{27}=3$
② Since $2^4=16$, $\sqrt[4]{16}=2$
③ Since $(-2)^5=-32$, $\sqrt[5]{-32}=-2$
④ Since $\left(\dfrac{2}{3}\right)^3=\dfrac{8}{27}$, $\sqrt[3]{\dfrac{8}{27}}=\dfrac{2}{3}$

Check Point 2　　　　　　　　　　　　　　　　　　　　Solutions_Page 112

Simplify the following.

① $\sqrt[3]{-8}$　　　　② $\sqrt[4]{625}$

③ $\sqrt[4]{\dfrac{16}{81}}$　　　④ $\sqrt[3]{-0.001}$

02 Properties of nth Roots

	Examples
1. $(\sqrt[n]{a})^n = a$	$(\sqrt[4]{5})^4=5$, $(\sqrt[5]{-6})^5=-6$
2. $\sqrt[n]{a^n}=a$ if n is odd.	$\sqrt[3]{3^3}=3$, $\sqrt[7]{b^7}=b$
	$\sqrt[6]{(5)^6}=\|5\|=5$, $\sqrt[4]{(-4)^4}=\|-4\|=4$
3. $\sqrt[n]{a^n}=\|a\|$ if n is even.	$\sqrt[4]{(b+2)^4}=\|b+2\|=\begin{cases} b+2, & b \geq -2 \\ -(b+2), & b < -2 \end{cases}$

Chapter 7. Roots and Radicals

03 Rational Exponents

We can also write an nth roots of a as a power of a. For the particular case of a square root, suppose that $\sqrt{a}=a^h$. Then,

$\sqrt{a}\times\sqrt{a}=a$ → Definition of square root

$a^h\times a^h=a$ → Substitute a^h for $\sqrt{a}$

$a^{2h}=a^1$ → Exponent property

$2h=1$ → Exponents are equal when bases are equal

$h=\dfrac{1}{2}$ → Solve for h

Hence, we can write $\sqrt{a}=a^{\frac{1}{2}}$. In a similar way, $\sqrt[5]{x}=x^{\frac{1}{5}}$ and $\sqrt[4]{y^3}=y^{\frac{3}{4}}$ for instance. In general, $\sqrt[n]{a^m}=a^{\frac{m}{n}}$ for positive integer n.

Let $\sqrt[n]{a}$ be an nth roots of a and m be a positive integer.

(1) $\sqrt[n]{a^m}=(a^m)^{\frac{1}{n}}=a^{\frac{m}{n}}$

(2) $\dfrac{1}{\sqrt[n]{a^m}}=\dfrac{1}{(a^m)^{\frac{1}{n}}}=\dfrac{1}{a^{\frac{m}{n}}}=a^{-\frac{m}{n}}$, $a\neq 0$

When rewriting the radical expression using rational exponents, do prime factorization first if radicand is not prime.

Concept Check

1. $\sqrt[3]{5}=5^{\frac{1}{3}}$
2. $\sqrt{27}=\sqrt{3^3}=(3^3)^{\frac{1}{2}}=3^{\frac{3}{2}}$
3. $\sqrt[4]{18}=\sqrt[4]{2\cdot 3^2}=(2\cdot 3^2)^{\frac{1}{4}}=2^{\frac{1}{4}}\cdot 3^{\frac{2}{4}}=2^{\frac{1}{4}}\cdot 3^{\frac{1}{2}}$

Example 3

Rewrite the expression using rational exponents.

① $\sqrt{8}$
② $\sqrt[3]{50}$
③ $\sqrt[3]{-108}$
④ $\sqrt[5]{64}$

Solution

① $\sqrt{8} = \sqrt{2^3} = (2^3)^{\frac{1}{2}} = 2^{\frac{3}{2}}$

② $\sqrt[3]{50} = \sqrt[3]{2 \cdot 5^2} = (2 \cdot 5^2)^{\frac{1}{3}} = 2^{\frac{1}{3}} \cdot 5^{\frac{2}{3}}$

③ $\sqrt[3]{-108} = \sqrt[3]{-2^2 \cdot 3^3} = (-2^2 \cdot 3^3)^{\frac{1}{3}} = -2^{\frac{2}{3}} \cdot 3$

④ $\sqrt[5]{64} = \sqrt[5]{2^6} = (2^6)^{\frac{1}{5}} = 2^{\frac{6}{5}}$

Check Point 3

Solutions_Page 112

Rewrite the expression using rational exponents.

① $\sqrt[3]{4}$
② $\sqrt[4]{36}$
③ $-(\sqrt[4]{20})^7$
④ $\sqrt[3]{-\frac{4}{9}}$

Example 4

Rewrite the expression using radicals.

① $6^{\frac{1}{3}}$
② $2^{\frac{2}{5}}$
③ $3^{-\frac{3}{4}}$
④ $2^{\frac{3}{2}} \cdot 3$

Solution

① $6^{\frac{1}{3}} = \sqrt[3]{6}$

② $2^{\frac{2}{5}} = \sqrt[5]{2^2} = \sqrt[5]{4}$

③ $3^{-\frac{3}{4}} = \dfrac{1}{3^{\frac{3}{4}}} = \dfrac{1}{\sqrt[4]{3^3}} = \dfrac{1}{\sqrt[4]{27}}$

④ $2^{\frac{3}{2}} \cdot 3 = 2^{\frac{3}{2}} \cdot 3^{\frac{2}{2}} = \sqrt{2^3 \cdot 3^2} = \sqrt{72}$

Check Point 4

① $3^{\frac{4}{3}}$

② $2 \cdot 5^{\frac{1}{4}}$

③ $\left(\dfrac{1}{2}\right)^{-\frac{1}{3}}$

④ $\left(\dfrac{4}{25}\right)^{\frac{3}{2}}$

Review Exercise

01 Find the indicated n^{th} root(s) of a.

(1) $n=2$, $a=49$

(2) $n=3$, $a=-64$

(3) $n=3$, $a=-\dfrac{8}{27}$

(4) $n=4$, $a=0.0081$

02 Simplify the following.

(1) $\sqrt[3]{-27}$

(2) $\sqrt[4]{\dfrac{1}{16}}$

(3) $(\sqrt{9})^2$

(4) $(\sqrt[5]{-3})^5$

(5) $\sqrt[4]{0.0625}$

(6) $\sqrt[3]{-0.000001}$

(4) $\sqrt[5]{\left(\dfrac{1}{64}\right)^2}$

(5) $\sqrt{0.0025}$

03 Rewrite the expression using rational exponents.

(1) $\sqrt[3]{9}$

(6) $\sqrt[3]{(0.36)^2}$

(2) $\sqrt[4]{121}$

04 Rewrite the expression using radicals.

(3) $\sqrt{\dfrac{27}{4}}$

(1) $3^{\frac{2}{3}}$

(2) $2 \cdot 5^{\frac{1}{2}}$

Chapter 7. Roots and Radicals

Review Exercise

(3) $3^{\frac{3}{4}}$

(4) $27^{\frac{4}{5}}$

(5) $\left(\dfrac{3}{2}\right)^{\frac{3}{2}}$

(6) $(5)^{-\frac{1}{4}}$

05 If the positive fourth root of 16 is a and the cube root of $(-3)^3$ is b, what is the value of $a+b$?

06 Which of the following is equal to -3?

I. $\sqrt[3]{3^3}$	II. $-\sqrt[3]{3^3}$
III. $\sqrt[3]{(-3)^3}$	IV. $-\sqrt[3]{(-3)^3}$

(A) I and II only

(B) II and III only

(C) III and IV only

(D) II and IV only

(E) II, III, and IV only

07 All values below are equal to each other EXCEPT

(A) $\sqrt[4]{5^4}$

(B) $\sqrt[4]{(-5)^4}$

(C) $(-\sqrt[4]{5})^4$

(D) $-(-\sqrt[4]{5^4})$

(E) $-\sqrt[4]{(-5)^4}$

Challenging

08 Simplify the following.

(1) $\sqrt[3]{a^3}-\sqrt[3]{b^3}$ if $a>0$, $b<0$

(2) $\sqrt[4]{(a-2)^4}-\sqrt[4]{(a-4)^4}$ if $2<a<4$

(3) $\sqrt[4]{(2x+1)^4}+\sqrt[4]{(y-3)^4}$
if $x>-\dfrac{1}{2}$, $y<3$

3 Properties of Radicals, Part 1

01 Simplifying Radicals

Assume $\sqrt[n]{a}$ and $\sqrt[n]{b}$ are real numbers. Then,

1. $\sqrt[n]{a^n} = \begin{cases} a & \text{if } n \text{ is odd} \\ |a| & \text{if } n \text{ is even} \end{cases}$
2. $\sqrt[n]{a^n b} = a\sqrt[n]{b}$
3. $\sqrt[n]{\dfrac{b}{a^n}} = \dfrac{\sqrt[n]{b}}{a}$

✔ b in the radical is the number or variable in its simplest form.

Concept Check

1. $\sqrt[3]{2^3} = 2$, $\sqrt[4]{(-2)^4} = |-2| = 2$

   $\sqrt[3]{x^3} = x$, $\sqrt[4]{y^4} = |y|$

2. $\sqrt{12x^2} = \sqrt{2^2 \times 3 \times x^2} = 2|x|\sqrt{3}$

3. $\sqrt[3]{\dfrac{5y^4}{8}} = \sqrt[3]{\dfrac{5 \times y^3 \times y}{2^3}} = \dfrac{y\sqrt[3]{5y}}{2}$

Example 1

Simplify the expression.

① $\sqrt{45}$ ② $\sqrt[3]{72}$

③ $\sqrt[4]{16x^4}$ ④ $\sqrt{32a^2 b^4}$

⑤ $\sqrt{\dfrac{4x^2}{9}}$ ⑥ $\sqrt[3]{\dfrac{16x^5}{27y^6}}$

Solution

① $\sqrt{45} = \sqrt{3^2 \times 5} = 3\sqrt{5}$

② $\sqrt[3]{72} = \sqrt[3]{2^3 \times 3^2} = 2\sqrt[3]{3^2} = 2\sqrt[3]{9}$

③ $\sqrt[4]{16x^4} = \sqrt[4]{2^4 \times x^4} = 2|x|$

④ $\sqrt{32a^2b^4} = \sqrt{2 \times 4^2 \times a^2 \times (b^2)^2} = 4|a|b^2\sqrt{2}$

⑤ $\sqrt{\dfrac{4x^2}{9}} = \sqrt{\dfrac{2^2 \times x^2}{3^2}} = \dfrac{2|x|}{3}$

⑥ $\sqrt[3]{\dfrac{16x^5}{27y^6}} = \sqrt[3]{\dfrac{2^3 \times 2 \times x^3 \times x^2}{3^3 \times (y^2)^3}} = \dfrac{2x\sqrt[3]{2x^2}}{3y^2}$

Check Point 1

Solutions_Page 114

Simplify the expression.

① $3\sqrt[4]{162}$

② $\sqrt[3]{\dfrac{16}{27}}$

③ $\sqrt{4a^2b}$

④ $\sqrt[3]{54x^5y^3}$

⑤ $\dfrac{\sqrt[4]{48x^4y^6}}{2}$

⑥ $\sqrt[5]{\dfrac{64a^5b^{10}}{243}}$

02 Multiplication and Division of Radicals

Assume m and k are rational numbers, and $\sqrt[n]{a}$ and $\sqrt[n]{b}$ are real numbers. Then,

1. $\sqrt[n]{a} \times \sqrt[n]{b} = \sqrt[n]{a \times b} = \sqrt[n]{ab}$
2. $\sqrt[n]{a} \div \sqrt[n]{b} = \dfrac{\sqrt[n]{a}}{\sqrt[n]{b}} = \sqrt[n]{\dfrac{a}{b}}$
3. $m\sqrt[n]{a} \times k\sqrt[n]{b} = mk\sqrt[n]{ab}$
4. $m\sqrt[n]{a} \div k\sqrt[n]{b} = \dfrac{m\sqrt[n]{a}}{k\sqrt[n]{b}} = \dfrac{m}{k}\sqrt[n]{\dfrac{a}{b}}$

✔ Be careful that $\sqrt[n]{a+b} \neq \sqrt[n]{a} + \sqrt[n]{b}$ or $\sqrt[n]{a-b} \neq \sqrt[n]{a} - \sqrt[n]{b}$

Concept Check

1. $\sqrt{3} \times \sqrt{5} = \sqrt{3 \times 5} = \sqrt{15}$
2. $\sqrt[3]{3} \div \sqrt[3]{5} = \dfrac{\sqrt[3]{3}}{\sqrt[3]{5}} = \sqrt[3]{\dfrac{3}{5}}$
3. $2\sqrt{3} \times 3\sqrt{5} = (2 \times 3) \times \sqrt{3 \times 5} = 6\sqrt{15}$
4. $4\sqrt[3]{3} \div 2\sqrt[3]{5} = \dfrac{4}{2}\sqrt[3]{\dfrac{3}{5}} = 2\sqrt[3]{\dfrac{3}{5}}$

Example 2

Simplify the expression. Assume that all variables are positive real numbers.

① $\sqrt{3x} \times \sqrt{7x}$ ② $4\sqrt[3]{2a} \times 2\sqrt[3]{3a^2 b} \times \sqrt[3]{5b}$

③ $8\sqrt{6xy} \div 4\sqrt{2x}$ ④ $2\sqrt[4]{5a^2} \times 10\sqrt[4]{6a^3} \div 5\sqrt[4]{15a}$

Solution

① $\sqrt{3} \times \sqrt{7} = \sqrt{3x \times 7x} = \sqrt{21 \times x^2} = x\sqrt{21}$

② $4\sqrt[3]{2a} \times 2\sqrt[3]{3a^2 b} \times \sqrt[3]{5b} = 8\sqrt[3]{2a \times 3a^2 b \times 5b}$
$= 8\sqrt[3]{30 \times a^3 \times b^2} = 8a\sqrt[3]{30b^2}$

③ $8\sqrt{6xy} \div 4\sqrt{2x} = \dfrac{8\sqrt{6xy}}{4\sqrt{2x}} = 2\sqrt{\dfrac{6xy}{2x}} = 2\sqrt{3y}$

④ $2\sqrt[4]{5a^2} \times 10\sqrt[4]{6a^3} \div 5\sqrt[4]{15a} = \dfrac{2 \times 10}{5} \cdot \dfrac{\sqrt[4]{5a^2} \times \sqrt[4]{5a^2}}{\sqrt[4]{15a}} = 4\dfrac{\sqrt[4]{30a^5}}{\sqrt[4]{15a}}$
$= 4\sqrt[4]{\dfrac{30a^5}{15a}} = 4\sqrt[4]{2 \times a^4} = 4a\sqrt[4]{2}$

Check Point 2

Solutions_Page 114

Simplify the expression. Assume that all variables are positive real numbers.

① $\sqrt{2a} \times \sqrt{5a} \times \sqrt{10}$ ② $3\sqrt[3]{x^2 y} \times \sqrt[3]{4xy^2} \times \sqrt[3]{6x}$

③ $2\sqrt[4]{32x^5 y^2} \div 4\sqrt[4]{2xy^3}$ ④ $4\sqrt{9a} \div \sqrt{3b} \div 6\sqrt{b}$

Review Exercise

01 Simplify the expression.

(1) $\sqrt{125}$

(2) $\sqrt[3]{64}$

(3) $\sqrt[4]{162}$

(4) $\sqrt[3]{\dfrac{36}{1500}}$

(3) $\sqrt[3]{27x^{-7}y^{12}}$

(4) $\sqrt[3]{-16x^3y^8}$

(5) $\sqrt{\dfrac{9x^5}{8y^3}}$

(6) $\sqrt[3]{-\dfrac{5x^{13}y^4}{54z^6}}$

02 Simplify the expression.

(1) $\sqrt{512x^2}$

(2) $\sqrt[4]{x^7y^7}$

Review Exercise

03 Simplify the expression. Assume that all variables are positive real numbers.

(1) $\sqrt{12} \times \sqrt{24} \times \sqrt{6}$

(2) $\sqrt[3]{4} \times \sqrt[3]{40} \times \sqrt[3]{2}$

(3) $\sqrt{6x} \times \sqrt{3} \times \sqrt{8x^3}$

(4) $2\sqrt[3]{4x^5} \times 3\sqrt[3]{6xy^4}$

04 Simplify the expression. Assume that all variables are positive real numbers.

(1) $\sqrt[3]{48x^3y^4} \div \sqrt[3]{3y^2}$

(2) $3\sqrt[4]{54x^2y} \times 4\sqrt[4]{6x^7y^3}$

(3) $15\sqrt[4]{2x^5y} \div 30\sqrt[4]{32x^3} \times 4\sqrt[4]{x^2y^3}$

(4) $6\sqrt{y} \div 18\sqrt{4x^3} \div \sqrt{xy^3}$

05 If $2\sqrt{5}=\sqrt{a}$ and $\sqrt[3]{0.024}=b\sqrt[3]{c}$, what is the value of abc? (c is the smallest natural number)

06 If $\sqrt{2}=a$, $\sqrt{3}=b$, and $\sqrt{5}=c$, write $\sqrt{360}$ in terms of a, b, and c?

07 If $\sqrt[3]{2}=a$, $\sqrt[3]{3}=b$, and $\sqrt[3]{5}=c$, write $\sqrt[3]{720}$ in terms of a, b, and c?

[Challenging]

08 If $a=2m$ and $b=4m$, where $m>0$, write each of the following in terms of m.

(1) $\sqrt{ab^2}$

(2) $\sqrt{ab} \times \sqrt{2a^2b^3}$

(3) $\sqrt[3]{4a^2b}$

(4) $\sqrt[4]{6b} \times \sqrt[4]{9a^3b}$

4. Properties of Radicals, Part 2

01 Addition and Subtraction of Radicals

To add or subtract radicals, first convert each radical to its simplest form. Then simply add or subtract like radicals. Two radicals with the same index and radicand are called like radicals.

Assume m, h, and k are rational numbers, and $\sqrt[n]{a}$ is real number. Then,
1. $m\sqrt[n]{a} + k\sqrt[n]{a} = (m+k)\sqrt[n]{a}$
2. $m\sqrt[n]{a} - k\sqrt[n]{a} = (m-k)\sqrt[n]{a}$
3. $m\sqrt[n]{a} + h\sqrt[n]{a} - k\sqrt[n]{a} = (m+h-k)\sqrt[n]{a}$

Concept Check
1. $3\sqrt{2} + 4\sqrt{2} = (3+4)\sqrt{2} = 7\sqrt{2}$
2. $5\sqrt[3]{4} - 2\sqrt[3]{4} = (5-2)\sqrt[3]{4} = 3\sqrt[3]{4}$
3. $5\sqrt[4]{3} + 2\sqrt[4]{3} - 4\sqrt[4]{3} = (5+2-4)\sqrt[4]{3} = 3\sqrt[4]{3}$

Example 1

Simplify the expression. Assume that all variables are positive real numbers.

① $\sqrt{8} + 5\sqrt{2}$

② $5\sqrt{3} - \sqrt{27} + 2\sqrt{12}$

③ $\sqrt[3]{40a} + \sqrt{8b} - 5\sqrt[3]{5a} + 4\sqrt{2b}$

④ $\dfrac{\sqrt{8b}}{4} - \dfrac{\sqrt{32b}}{2} + \sqrt{18b}$

Solution

① $\sqrt{8}+5\sqrt{2}=2\sqrt{2}+5\sqrt{2}=(2+5)\sqrt{2}=7\sqrt{2}$

② $5\sqrt{3}-\sqrt{27}+2\sqrt{12}=5\sqrt{3}-3\sqrt{3}+4\sqrt{3}$
$\phantom{5\sqrt{3}-\sqrt{27}+2\sqrt{12}}=(5-3+4)\sqrt{3}=6\sqrt{3}$

③ $\sqrt[3]{40a}+\sqrt{8b}-5\sqrt[3]{5a}+4\sqrt{2b}=2\sqrt[3]{5a}+2\sqrt{2b}-5\sqrt[3]{5a}+4\sqrt{2b}$
$\phantom{\sqrt[3]{40a}+\sqrt{8b}-5\sqrt[3]{5a}+4\sqrt{2b}}=(2-5)\sqrt[3]{5a}+(2+4)\sqrt{2b}=-3\sqrt[3]{5a}+6\sqrt{2b}$

④ $\dfrac{\sqrt{8b}}{4}-\dfrac{\sqrt{32b}}{2}+\sqrt{18b}=\dfrac{2\sqrt{2b}}{4}-\dfrac{4\sqrt{2b}}{2}+3\sqrt{2b}=\dfrac{\sqrt{2b}}{2}-2\sqrt{2b}+3\sqrt{2b}$
$\phantom{\dfrac{\sqrt{8b}}{4}-\dfrac{\sqrt{32b}}{2}+\sqrt{18b}}=\left(\dfrac{1}{2}-2+3\right)\sqrt{2b}=\dfrac{3}{2}\sqrt{2b}$

Check Point 1   Solutions_Page 116

Simplify the expression. Assume that all variables are positive real numbers.

① $-4\sqrt{5}-3\sqrt{5}+5\sqrt{5}$
② $\sqrt[3]{81}-2\sqrt[3]{24}-2\sqrt[3]{3}$
③ $\sqrt{4ab^3}+3\sqrt{a^3b}$
④ $\sqrt[4]{32x^6y}-\sqrt[4]{2x^6y}$

Example 2

Simplify the expression.

① $(1+2\sqrt{2})(1-\sqrt{2})$
② $(2-\sqrt{5})(1+2\sqrt{5})$
③ $(\sqrt{3}-2\sqrt{7})^2$
④ $(\sqrt{x}-1)(2-\sqrt{x})$, where $x>0$

Solution

Use the FOIL method to multiply binomials that have radical expressions.

① $(1+2\sqrt{2})(1-\sqrt{2})=(1\times 1)-(1\times\sqrt{2})+(2\sqrt{2}\times 1)-(2\sqrt{2}\times\sqrt{2})$
$\phantom{(1+2\sqrt{2})(1-\sqrt{2})}=1-\sqrt{2}+2\sqrt{2}-4=-3+\sqrt{2}$

② $(2-\sqrt{5})(1+2\sqrt{5})=(2\times 1)+(2\times 2\sqrt{5})-(\sqrt{5}\times 1)-(\sqrt{5}\times 2\sqrt{5})$
$\phantom{(2-\sqrt{5})(1+2\sqrt{5})}=2+4\sqrt{5}-\sqrt{5}-10=-8+3\sqrt{5}$

③ $(\sqrt{3}-2\sqrt{7})^2=(\sqrt{3})^2-2(\sqrt{3}\times 2\sqrt{7})+(2\sqrt{7})^2$
$\phantom{(\sqrt{3}-2\sqrt{7})^2}=3-4\sqrt{21}+28=31-4\sqrt{21}$

④ $(\sqrt{x}-1)(2-\sqrt{x})=(\sqrt{x}\times 2)-(\sqrt{x}\times\sqrt{x})-(1\times 2)+(1\times\sqrt{x})$
$\phantom{(\sqrt{x}-1)(2-\sqrt{x})}=2\sqrt{x}-x-2+\sqrt{x}=3\sqrt{x}-x-2$

Check Point 2

Simplify the expression. Assume that all variables are positive real numbers.

① $(\sqrt{2}-\sqrt{3})(\sqrt{2}+\sqrt{3})$
② $(\sqrt{6}+x\sqrt{2})^2$
③ $\sqrt{x}(2\sqrt{x^2y}+4x\sqrt{9y})$
④ $(\sqrt{2a}+\sqrt{6b})(2\sqrt{3b}-3\sqrt{a})$

02 Rationalizing the Denominator

This is a process to remove radical in the denominator.

1. $\dfrac{b}{\sqrt{a}}=\dfrac{b}{\sqrt{a}}\cdot\dfrac{\sqrt{a}}{\sqrt{a}}=\dfrac{b\sqrt{a}}{a}$

   $\dfrac{b}{c\sqrt{a}}=\dfrac{b}{c\sqrt{a}}\cdot\dfrac{\sqrt{a}}{\sqrt{a}}=\dfrac{b\sqrt{a}}{ac}$

2. $\dfrac{c}{\sqrt{a}-\sqrt{b}}=\dfrac{c}{\sqrt{a}-\sqrt{b}}\cdot\dfrac{\sqrt{a}+\sqrt{b}}{\sqrt{a}+\sqrt{b}}=\dfrac{c(\sqrt{a}+\sqrt{b})}{a-b}$

   $\dfrac{c}{\sqrt{a}+\sqrt{b}}=\dfrac{c}{\sqrt{a}+\sqrt{b}}\cdot\dfrac{\sqrt{a}-\sqrt{b}}{\sqrt{a}-\sqrt{b}}=\dfrac{c(\sqrt{a}-\sqrt{b})}{a-b}$

Concept Check

1. Use the fact that $\sqrt{a}\times\sqrt{a}=(\sqrt{a})^2=a$.

2. Use the fact that $(\sqrt{a}-\sqrt{b})(\sqrt{a}+\sqrt{b})=(\sqrt{a})^2-(\sqrt{b})^2=a-b$.

Example 3

Rationalize the denominator.

① $\sqrt{\dfrac{6}{5}}$
② $\dfrac{1}{1+\sqrt{2}}$
③ $\dfrac{\sqrt{2}}{\sqrt{3}-\sqrt{2}}$

Solution

① $\sqrt{\dfrac{6}{5}}=\dfrac{\sqrt{6}}{\sqrt{5}}=\dfrac{\sqrt{6}}{\sqrt{5}}\cdot\dfrac{\sqrt{5}}{\sqrt{5}}=\dfrac{\sqrt{30}}{5}$

② $\dfrac{1}{1+\sqrt{2}}=\dfrac{1}{1+\sqrt{2}}\cdot\dfrac{1-\sqrt{2}}{1-\sqrt{2}}=\dfrac{1-\sqrt{2}}{1^2-(\sqrt{2})^2}=\dfrac{1-\sqrt{2}}{1-2}=-1+\sqrt{2}$

③ $\dfrac{\sqrt{2}}{\sqrt{3}-\sqrt{2}}=\dfrac{\sqrt{2}}{\sqrt{3}-\sqrt{2}}\cdot\dfrac{\sqrt{3}+\sqrt{2}}{\sqrt{3}+\sqrt{2}}=\dfrac{\sqrt{2}(\sqrt{3}+\sqrt{2})}{(\sqrt{3})^2-(\sqrt{2})^2}$

$=\dfrac{\sqrt{6}+2}{3-2}=2+\sqrt{6}$

Check Point 3

Solutions_Page 117

Rationalize the denominator.

① $5\sqrt{\dfrac{3}{5}}$ ② $\dfrac{\sqrt{2}}{\sqrt{3}-2}$ ③ $\dfrac{1}{\sqrt{2}+\sqrt{5}}$

Review Exercise

01 Simplify the expression. Assume that all variables are positive real numbers.

(1) $7\sqrt{7} - 2\sqrt{7} + 3\sqrt{7}$

(2) $\sqrt{98} + \sqrt{8} + \sqrt{18}$

(3) $2\sqrt[3]{16} - 3\sqrt[3]{54} + \sqrt[3]{40}$

(4) $2\sqrt[3]{135} + 2\sqrt[3]{16} - 4\sqrt[3]{5} - \sqrt[3]{320}$

(5) $2\sqrt[4]{48} + 3\sqrt[4]{3} + \sqrt[4]{80} - 4\sqrt[4]{5}$

(6) $5\sqrt{72x} - 4\sqrt{50x}$

(7) $3\sqrt{x^5 y} + 4\sqrt{xy^5}$

(8) $x\sqrt[3]{2x^3 y^6} + y\sqrt[3]{16x^6 y^3} - 2\sqrt[3]{2x^6 y^6}$

02 Simplify the expression. Assume that all variables are positive real numbers.

(1) $(\sqrt{5} - 1)(\sqrt{5} + 1)$

(2) $\sqrt{2}(4\sqrt{6} - \sqrt{10})$

(3) $(2\sqrt{5}-\sqrt{3})^2$

(4) $\sqrt{3x}(\sqrt{6x}+x\sqrt{2x})$

(5) $(4+\sqrt{3x})(\sqrt{3x}-7)$

(6) $(\sqrt{a}-\sqrt{b})(2\sqrt{a}-2\sqrt{b})$

(7) $(\sqrt{xy^3}+1)(\sqrt{x}-\sqrt{y})$

(8) $(\sqrt{x}-\sqrt{y})^2(\sqrt{x+y})^2$

03 Rationalize the denominator. Assume that all variables are positive real numbers.

(1) $\dfrac{2}{\sqrt{3}}$

(2) $\dfrac{15\sqrt{2}}{\sqrt{5}}$

(3) $\dfrac{1-\sqrt{3}}{1+\sqrt{3}}$

(4) $\dfrac{4+3\sqrt{2}}{3+\sqrt{2}}$

(5) $\dfrac{\sqrt{2}}{3-\sqrt{x}}$

Review Exercise

(6) $\dfrac{\sqrt{x}}{4-2\sqrt{x}}$

05 If $\dfrac{\sqrt{2}}{\sqrt{3}}+\dfrac{2}{\sqrt{6}}+\dfrac{\sqrt{3}}{\sqrt{2}}=a\sqrt{b}$, what is the value of ab? (b is the smallest positive integer)

04 If $a=\sqrt{5}+\sqrt{3}$ and $b=\sqrt{5}-\sqrt{3}$, find each of the following.

(1) ab

06 If the result of the expression below is rational number, what is the value of k?

(1) $2k\sqrt{3}-4k+3-4\sqrt{3}$

(2) $a\sqrt{3}+b\sqrt{5}$

(2) $(2-5\sqrt{2})(3k+2\sqrt{2})$

(3) $a\sqrt{5}-2b\sqrt{3}$

(3) $\sqrt{2}(\sqrt{2}-1)-\dfrac{k(3\sqrt{2}-1)}{3\sqrt{2}}$

(4) $ab\sqrt{3}+ab^2$

Challenging

07 If $x=\dfrac{2}{\sqrt{6}-2}$, find each of the following.

(1) x^2-4x+4

(2) x^3-6x^2+8x

Challenging

08 If $x=\dfrac{4}{3-\sqrt{5}}$ and $y=\dfrac{4}{3+\sqrt{5}}$, find each of the following.

(1) x^2-y^2

(2) $\dfrac{x}{y}-2+\dfrac{y}{x}$

5 Radical Equations

A radical equation is an equation that contains radical with a variable in the radicand. $x-3=\sqrt{2x-1}$ and $\sqrt[3]{x+1}-3=0$ are radical equations for instance. To solve radical equations, we need to eliminate the radicals and obtain a polynomial equation.

01 Square Root Equation

To solve a square root equation, the term with a square root must be eliminated. First, isolate the radical on one side of the equation, and then square the square root expression to get an equation without the radical. Sometimes solving the square root equation yields an extraneous solution. An extraneous solution is a solution that emerges from the process of solving the equation but is not a valid solution to the equation. When solving the square root equation, we always need to check for extraneous solution.

Concept Check

1. $\sqrt{x}=4$
   $(\sqrt{x})^2=(4)^2$
   $x=16$

   Check Substitute $x=16$ in the original equation.
   $\sqrt{16}=4$
   $4=4$
   $x=16$ is the solution to the equation $\sqrt{x}=4$.

2. $\sqrt{x}=-4$
   $(\sqrt{x})^2=(-4)^2$
   $x=16$

   Check Substitute $x=16$ in the original equation.
   $\sqrt{16}=-4$
   $4\neq-4$
   $x=16$ is the extraneous solution.
   Therefore, the equation $\sqrt{x}=-4$ has no solution.

Example 1

Solve the equation. Check for extraneous solutions.

① $\sqrt{x-1}-3=0$ ② $\sqrt{2x+9}-x=3$

③ $\sqrt{x-7}+\sqrt{x}=7$

Solution

① $\sqrt{x-1}-3=0$
$\sqrt{x-1}=3$ → Isolate the radical term
$(\sqrt{x-1})^2=(3)^2$ → Square both sides to eliminate the radical
$x-1=9$ → Simplify
$x=10$ → Solve for x

Check Substitute $x=10$ in the original equation.
$\sqrt{10-1}-3=0$
$3-3=0$
$0=0$ → Solution checks

The solution is $x=10$

② $\sqrt{2x+9}-x=3$
$\sqrt{2x+9}=x+3$ → Isolate the radical term
$(\sqrt{2x+9})^2=(x+3)^2$ → Square both sides to eliminate the radical
$2x+9=x^2+6x+9$ → Expand
$x^2+4x=0$ → Simplify
$x(x+4)=0$ → Factor
$x=0$ or $x=-4$ → Solve for x

Check Substitute $x=0$ in the original equation.
$\sqrt{2\cdot 0+9}-0=3$
$\sqrt{9}=3$
$3=3$ → Solution checks.

Check Substitute $x=-4$ in the original equation.
$\sqrt{2(-4)+9}-(-4)=3$
$\sqrt{1}+4=3$
$5 \neq 3$ → Extraneous solution

The solution is $x=0$

③ $\sqrt{x-7}+\sqrt{x}=7$

If two square roots are given, place one square root on each side and square each side to solve the equation.

$\sqrt{x-7}=7-\sqrt{x}$ → Place one square root on each side
$(\sqrt{x-7})^2=(7-\sqrt{x})^2$ → Square both sides to eliminate the radical
$x-7=49-14\sqrt{x}+x$ → Expand
$\sqrt{x}=4$ → Simplify
$(\sqrt{x})^2=(4)^2$ → Again, Square both sides to eliminate the radical
$x=16$ → Solve for x

Check Substitute $x=16$ in the original equation.
$\sqrt{16-7}+\sqrt{16}=7$
$3+4=7$
$7=7$ → Solution checks.

The solution is $x=16$

Check Point 1

Solutions_Page 119

Solve the equation. Check for extraneous solutions.

① $\sqrt{6x-5}-7=0$

② $2\sqrt{-3x+6}+1=5$

③ $\sqrt{x}-\sqrt{x-5}=2$

④ $3(\sqrt{x-3}-x)+15=0$

02 Cube Root Equation

Like the square root equation, the term with a cube root must be eliminated. First, isolate the radical on one side of the equation, and then cube the cube root expression to get an equation without the radical. In the cube root equation, there is no need to check the extraneous solution.

Example 2

Solve the equation.

① $\sqrt[3]{x} - 2 = 3$

② $2\sqrt[3]{2x-5} - 1 = 5$

Solution

① $\sqrt[3]{x} - 2 = 3$
   $\sqrt[3]{x} = 5$ → Isolate the radical term
   $(\sqrt[3]{x})^3 = (5)^3$ → Cube both sides to eliminate the radical
   $x = 125$ → Solve for x

The solution is $x = 125$

② $2\sqrt[3]{2x-5} - 1 = 5$
   $\sqrt[3]{2x-5} = 3$ → Isolate the radical term
   $(\sqrt[3]{2x-5})^3 = 3^3$ → Cube both sides to eliminate the radical
   $2x - 5 = 27$ → Simplify
   $x = 16$ → Solve for x

The solution is $x = 16$

Check Point 2

Solve the equation.

① $\sqrt[3]{4x-1} = 3$

② $\frac{1}{2}\sqrt[3]{(x-2)^2} - \frac{25}{2} = 0$

Review Exercise

Solutions_Page 120

01 Solve the equation. Check for extraneous solutions.

(1) $\sqrt{3x+1}=7$

(2) $8\sqrt{2x-5}-7=3$

(3) $\sqrt{x-2}+x=4$

(4) $\sqrt{3x+10}=4+x$

02 Solve the equation. Check for extraneous solutions.

(1) $\sqrt{3x-2}-\sqrt{10-x}=2$

(2) $\sqrt{x+3}-3=\sqrt{2-x}$

(3) $\sqrt{x}+\sqrt{x+5}=5$

03 Solve the equation.

(1) $\sqrt[3]{3x-1}=8$

(2) $2\sqrt[3]{2x-5}-1=5$

(3) $\dfrac{\sqrt[3]{x}}{4}=\dfrac{\sqrt[3]{x-7}}{2}$

(4) $2\sqrt[3]{(x-2)^2}-17=1$

Challenging

04 Solve the equation. Check for extraneous solutions.

(1) $\sqrt{1+\sqrt{x}}=\sqrt{x+1}$

(2) $\sqrt{4-\sqrt{x+4}}=\sqrt{x+6}$

6 Graphing Radical Functions

01 Definition of Radical Function

When $f(x)$ contains a radical in the function $y=f(x)$, it is called a radical function. In particular, in this section we will learn about graphs of the square root functions and the cube root functions.

Concept Check

1. $y=\sqrt{x+1}-2$ and $y=3\sqrt{2x-3}$ are typical examples of the square root functions.
2. $y=\sqrt[3]{x+1}$ and $y=2\sqrt[3]{x-2}+3$ are typical examples of the cube root functions.

02 Domain of the Radical Function

1. The Square Root Function: The domain is the set of all real number that the expression in the radical to be greater than or equal to zero.
2. The Cube Root Function: The domain is always the set of all real numbers.

Concept Check

1. In the square root function $y=3\sqrt{2x-3}$, the value of $\sqrt{2x-3}$ exists only if $2x-3\geq 0$, $x\geq \frac{3}{2}$

   So the domain of the above function is $\left\{x\mid x\geq \frac{3}{2}\right\}$.

2. In the cube root function $y=2\sqrt[3]{x-2}+3$, the domain is the set of all real numbers because the value of $\sqrt[3]{x-2}$ exists for all values of x.

03 The Graph of $y=a\sqrt{bx}$ $(a>0, b>0)$

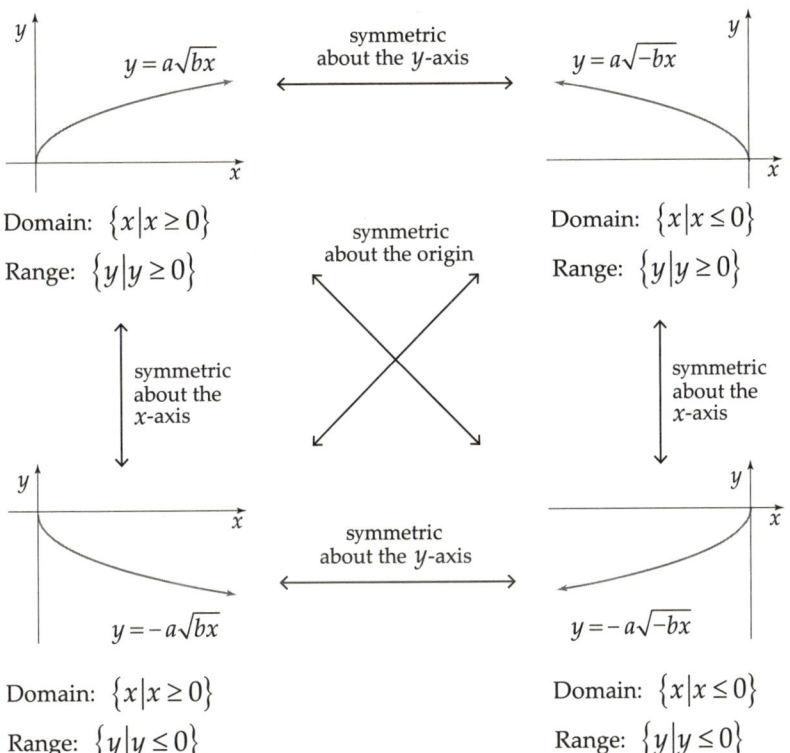

For the function $y=a\sqrt{bx}$, a and b indicates the degree of vertical stretch if $(a$ or $b)>1$ or shrink if $0<(a$ or $b)<1$.

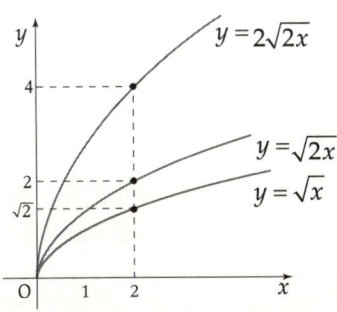

Example 1-1

Graph the function. State the domain and range.

① $y=2\sqrt{x}$ ② $y=2\sqrt{-x}$

③ $y=-2\sqrt{x}$ ④ $y=-2\sqrt{-x}$

Solution

① $y=2\sqrt{x}$

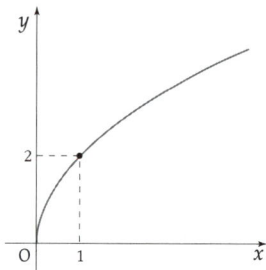

Domain: $\{x \mid x \geq 0\}$
Range: $\{y \mid y \geq 0\}$

② $y=2\sqrt{-x}$

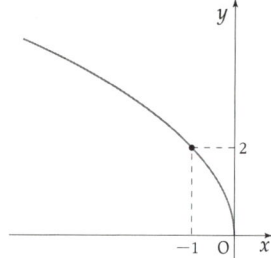

Domain: $\{x \mid x \leq 0\}$
Range: $\{y \mid y \geq 0\}$

③ $y=-2\sqrt{x}$

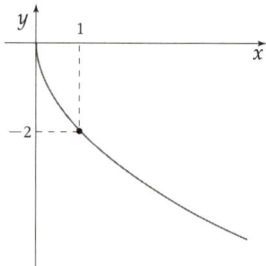

Domain: $\{x \mid x \geq 0\}$
Range: $\{y \mid y \leq 0\}$

④ $y=-2\sqrt{-x}$

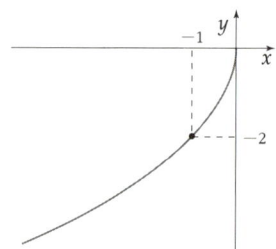

Domain: $\{x \mid x \leq 0\}$
Range: $\{y \mid y \leq 0\}$

Example 1-2

Graph the function $y=-\sqrt{x}$, $y=-\sqrt{2x}$, and $y=-\sqrt{4x}$ on the same coordinate plane.

Solution

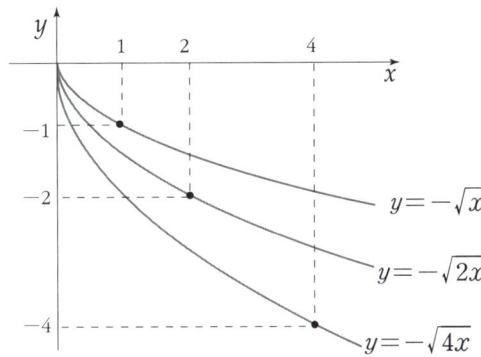

✔ From the graphs above, realize that the graph of $y=a\sqrt{bx}$ stretches vertically as b increases.

Check Point 1
Solutions_Page 122

Graph the functions on the same coordinate. Discuss the symmetry of the graphs.

① $y=2\sqrt{x}$, $y=2\sqrt{-x}$ 　　　　　② $y=\sqrt{4x}$, $y=-\sqrt{4x}$

③ $y=\dfrac{1}{2}\sqrt{3x}$, $y=-\dfrac{1}{2}\sqrt{-3x}$

04 The Graph of $y=a\sqrt{b(x-h)}+k$

1. To graph $y=a\sqrt{b(x-h)}+k$, follow these steps.

   (1) Sketch the graph of $y=a\sqrt{bx}$.
   (2) Shift the graph h units horizontally and k units vertically.
   (3) Domain: $\{x|x\geq h\}$
   (4) Range: $\{y|y\geq k\}$

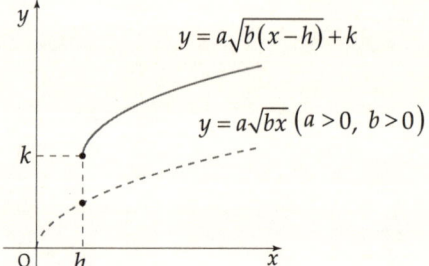

2. To graph $y=a\sqrt{bx+c}+d$, first transform the function
$$y=a\sqrt{bx+c}+d \Rightarrow y=a\sqrt{b\left(x+\frac{c}{b}\right)}+d$$
and then sketch the graph.

Example 2

Graph the function. State the domain and range.

① $y=\sqrt{x-1}+2$ ② $y=\sqrt{2(x+1)}-3$
③ $y=-\sqrt{3x+6}$ ④ $y=\sqrt{-2x+3}+2$

Solution

① $y=\sqrt{x-1}+2$

→ Graph $y=\sqrt{x}$
→ Shift 1 unit to the right and 2 units up
→ Domain: $\{x|x\geq 1\}$
→ Range: $\{y|y\geq 2\}$

② $y=\sqrt{2(x+1)}-3$

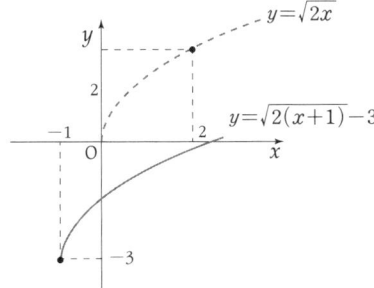

→ Graph $y=\sqrt{2x}$
→ Shift 1 unit to the left and 3 units down
→ Domain: $\{x|x\geq -1\}$
→ Range: $\{y|y\geq -3\}$

③ $y=-\sqrt{3x+6} \;\Rightarrow\; y=-\sqrt{3(x+2)}$

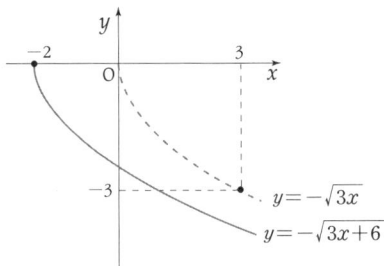

→ Graph $y=-\sqrt{3x}$
→ Shift 2 units to the left
→ Domain: $\{x|x\geq -2\}$
→ Range: $\{y|y\leq 0\}$

④ $y=\sqrt{-2x+3}+2 \;\Rightarrow\; y=\sqrt{-2\left(x-\dfrac{3}{2}\right)}+2$

→ Graph $y=\sqrt{-2x}$
→ Shift $\dfrac{3}{2}$ units to the right and 2 units up
→ Domain: $\left\{x|x\leq \dfrac{3}{2}\right\}$
→ Range: $\{y|y\geq 2\}$

Check Point 2

Solutions_Page 123

Graph the function. State the domain and range.

① $y=\sqrt{2x-4}$

② $y=\sqrt{-\dfrac{1}{2}x-1}$

③ $y=-\dfrac{1}{2}\sqrt{x+1}+2$

④ $y=-2\sqrt{-2x-5}-4$

05 The Graph of $y = a\sqrt[3]{bx}$ $(a>0, b>0)$

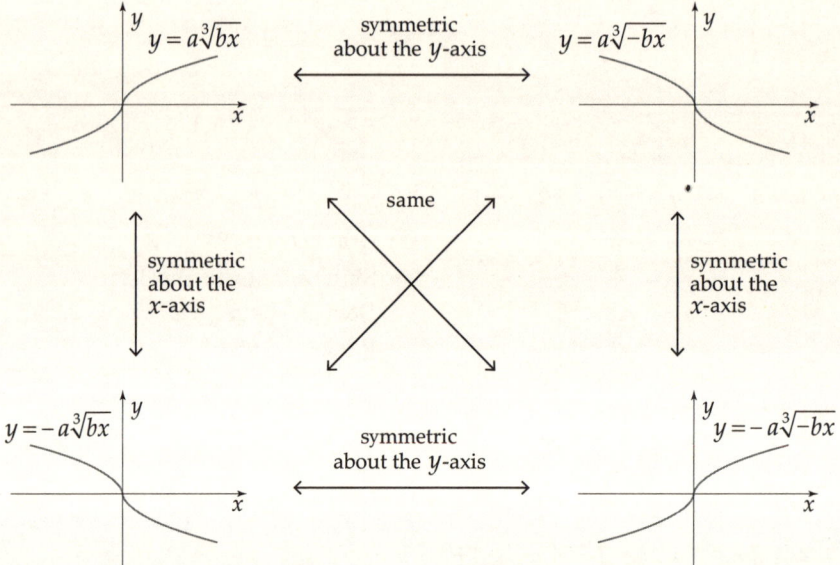

Notice that domain and range of cube root functions are always all real numbers. For the function $y=a\sqrt[3]{bx}$, just like the square root function, a and b indicates a vertical stretch if $(a \text{ or } b) > 1$ or shrink if $0 < (a \text{ or } b) < 1$.

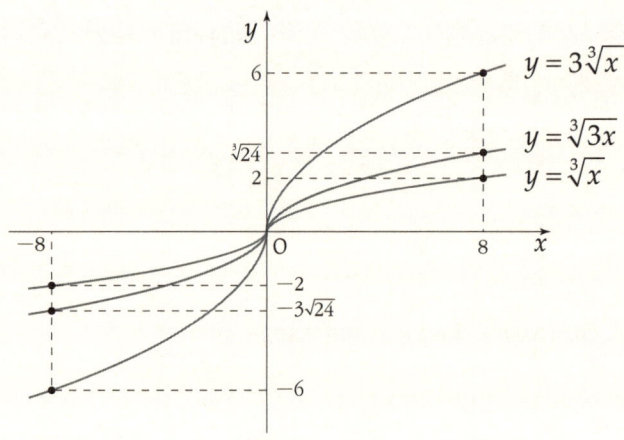

Example 3-1

Graph the function.

① $y=2\sqrt[3]{x}$ ② $y=2\sqrt[3]{-x}$

③ $y=-2\sqrt[3]{x}$ ④ $y=-2\sqrt[3]{-x}$

Solution

① $y=2\sqrt[3]{x}$

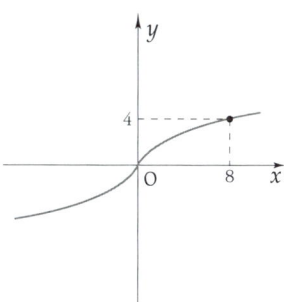

② $y=2\sqrt[3]{-x}$

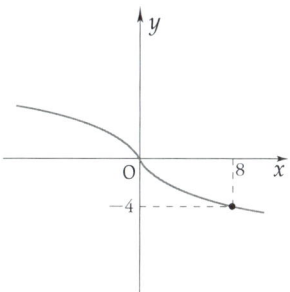

③ $y=-2\sqrt[3]{x}$

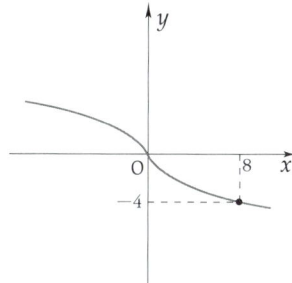

④ $y=-2\sqrt[3]{-x}$

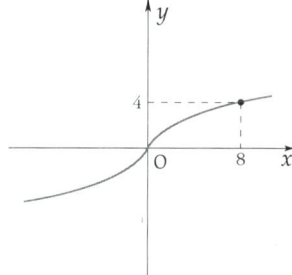

✔ **Remember** The domain and range of cube root functions are ALWAYS all real numbers.

Example 3-2

Graph the function $y=\sqrt[3]{x}$, $y=\sqrt[3]{4x}$, and $y=\sqrt[3]{8x}$ in the interval $-8 \leq x \leq 8$ on the same coordinate plane.

Solution

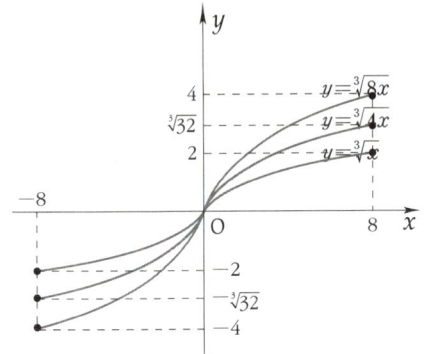

✔ From the graphs above, realize that the graph of $y=a\sqrt[3]{bx}$ stretches vertically as b increases.

Check Point 3   Solutions_Page 123

Graph the function $y=-2\sqrt[3]{x}$, $y=-2\sqrt[3]{2x}$, and $y=-2\sqrt[3]{4x}$ on the same coordinate plane.

06 The Graph of $y=a\sqrt[3]{b(x-h)}+k$

1. To graph $y=a\sqrt[3]{b(x-h)}+k$, follow these steps.

    (1) Sketch the graph of $y=a\sqrt[3]{bx}$.
    (2) Shift the graph h units horizontally and k units vertically.
    (3) Domain: All real numbers
    (4) Range: All real numbers

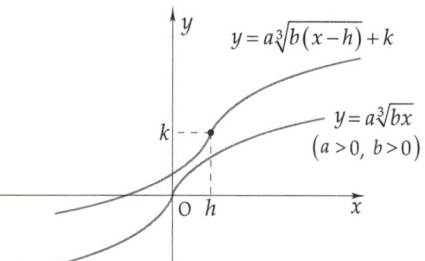

2. To graph $y=a\sqrt[3]{bx+c}+d$, first transform the function

$$y=a\sqrt[3]{bx+c}+d \Rightarrow y=a\sqrt[3]{b\left(x+\frac{c}{b}\right)}+d$$

and then sketch the graph.

Example 4

Graph the function.

① $y=\sqrt[3]{x}+1$ ② $y=\sqrt[3]{x-2}-2$
③ $y=\sqrt[3]{-2x-4}-1$ ④ $y=-\sqrt[3]{-3x+6}+3$

Solution

① $y=\sqrt[3]{x}+1$

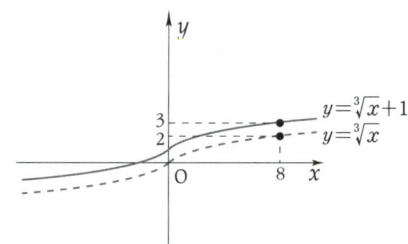

→ Graph $y=\sqrt[3]{x}$
→ Shift 1 unit up

② $y=\sqrt[3]{x-2}-2$

→ Graph $y=\sqrt[3]{x}$
→ Shift 2 units to the right and 2 units down

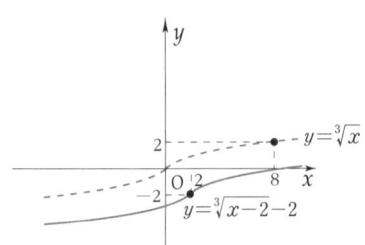

③ $y=\sqrt[3]{-2x-4}-1$ ⇒ $y=\sqrt[3]{-2(x+2)}-1$

→ Graph $y=\sqrt[3]{-2x}$
→ Shift 2 units to the left and 1 unit down

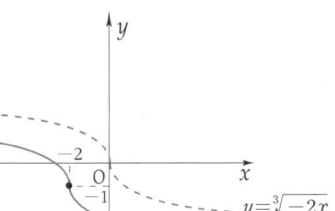

④ $y=-\sqrt[3]{-3x+6}+3$ ⇒ $y=-\sqrt[3]{-3(x-2)}+3$

→ Graph $y=-\sqrt[3]{-3x}$
→ Shift 2 units to the right and 3 units up

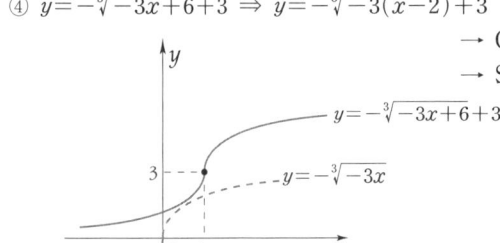

Check Point 4

Solutions_Page 123

Graph the function. State the domain and range.

① $y=\sqrt[3]{2x}-2$

② $y=2\sqrt[3]{\dfrac{1}{2}x+1}$

③ $y=\sqrt[3]{-x+3}-1$

④ $y=-3\sqrt[3]{\dfrac{1}{3}x-\dfrac{1}{2}}+2$

Review Exercise

01 Graph the functions on the same coordinate. Discuss the symmetry of the graphs.

(1) $y=\sqrt{x-2}$, $y=-\sqrt{x-2}$

(2) $y=\sqrt{2x+3}$, $y=\sqrt{-(2x+3)}$

(3) $y=\sqrt{\frac{1}{2}x-1}$, $y=-\sqrt{-\left(\frac{1}{2}x-1\right)}$

02 Graph the function. Then state the domain and range.

(1) $y=\sqrt{x-1}$

(2) $y=\sqrt{-x-2}$

(3) $y=\frac{1}{2}\sqrt{3x+4}$

(4) $y=-\sqrt{x+1}+1$

(5) $y=3\sqrt{2x-5}+3$

(6) $y=-\frac{1}{2}\sqrt{\frac{1}{3}x-\frac{1}{2}}-2$

03 The graph of the function $y=\sqrt{ax+b}+c$ or $y=-\sqrt{ax+b}+c$ is shown below. Find the equation of the function.

(1)
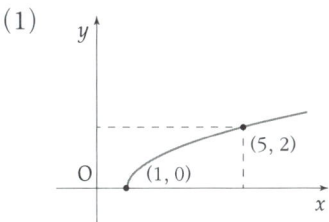

(2)
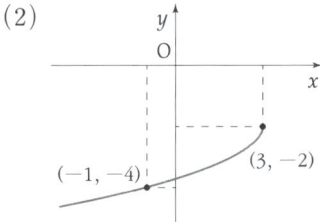

(3)
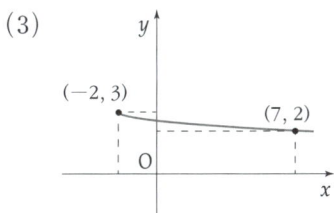

Review Exercise

04 Graph the function.

(1) $y=\sqrt[3]{x+2}$

(2) $y=-3+\sqrt[3]{x}$

(3) $y=\sqrt[3]{2x-3}+5$

(4) $y=-\sqrt[3]{x-1}+1$

05 The graph of the function $y=\sqrt[3]{ax+b}+c$ or $y=-\sqrt[3]{ax+b}+c$ is shown below. Find the equation of the function.

(1)

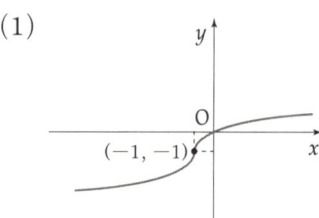

(2)

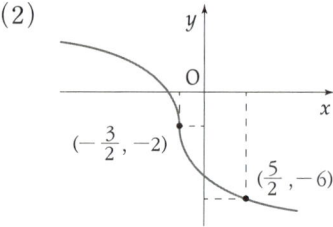

06 Given a function $y=\sqrt{ax-2}+b$, if the domain is $\{x|x\geq -1\}$ and the range is $\{y|y\geq 3\}$, what is the value of $a+b$?

Challenging

07 Suppose the graph of $y=\sqrt{-ax+b}+c$ passes through the point $(1, -2)$. If the domain and range of this function is $\{x|x\leq 4\}$ and $\{y|y\geq -4\}$ respectively, what is the value of $a+b+c$?

Challenging

08 Suppose that the graph of $y=\sqrt[3]{8x-1}+4$ is the result of the graph $y=2\sqrt[3]{x}$ by shifting m units to the right and n units up. Find the value of mn.

09

If the graph above is $y=-\sqrt{a(x-h)}+k$, what is the value of $a+h+k$?

10 Which of the following is NOT true about the graph of $y=-2\sqrt{-x-4}-1$?

(A) The domain is $\{x|x\leq -4\}$
(B) The range is $\{y|y\leq -1\}$
(C) The graph of $y=-2\sqrt{-x-4}-1$ is the result of the graph $y=-2\sqrt{-x}$ by shifting 4 units to the right and 1 unit down
(D) The graph passes through the points in quadrant III only
(E) The graph passes through the point $(-8, -5)$

Chapter 7. Roots and Radicals 335

Chapter Test — Level 1

Solutions_Page 128

01 If $a>0$, which of the following is NOT equal to a?

(A) $\sqrt{(-a)^2}$ (B) $(-\sqrt{a})^2$ (C) $\sqrt[3]{(-a)^3}$
(D) $-\sqrt[3]{(-a)^3}$ (E) $-(-\sqrt{a^2})$

02 If $a<0$ and $ab<0$, which of the following is equal to $\sqrt{(-b)^2}-\sqrt{4a^2}+\sqrt{16a^2b^2}$?

(A) $2a+b-4ab$ (B) $2a-b-4ab$ (C) $2a+b+4ab$
(D) $2a-b+4ab$ (E) $-2a-b-4ab$

03 Which of the following expression is equal to $\sqrt{(a+2)^2}-\sqrt{(-a-2)^2}-2\sqrt{(4-a)^2}$ if $-2<a<4$?

(A) $2a-12$ (B) $-8+2a$ (C) $2a-4$
(D) $-4a+8$ (E) $4a+4$

04 Which of the following expression is equal to $\sqrt[3]{(x-2)^3}+\sqrt[3]{(2-x)^3}-\sqrt[4]{(-2+x)^4}$ if $0<x<2$?

(A) $x-2$ (B) $-x+2$ (C) $3x-6$
(D) $6-3x$ (E) $-3x-6$

05 Find the number of positive integer x that satisfy the inequality $\sqrt{6}<x<\sqrt{40}$.

06 If $\dfrac{4xy}{\sqrt{75}}\times(-\sqrt{120x^3})\div\dfrac{\sqrt{80x}}{5y^2}=a\sqrt{2}$, where $x>0$ and $y>0$, which of the following expression is equal to a?

(A) $-4xy^2$ (B) $-4x^2y^2$ (C) $-2xy^2$
(D) $-2x^2y^3$ (E) $-2x^2y^2$

07 Simplify $(1+\sqrt{2}-\sqrt{3})(1-\sqrt{2}+\sqrt{3})$.

08 If $\dfrac{\sqrt{32}-4}{\sqrt{2}}-\dfrac{\sqrt{12}+\sqrt{48}}{\sqrt{3}}=a+b\sqrt{c}$, what is the value of abc?

(c is the smallest positive integer)

Chapter Test — Level 1

09 If the expression $(\sqrt{12}-2)(\sqrt{27}-a+2)$ is rational number, what is the value of a?

10 If $x=\dfrac{1}{3\sqrt{2}-4}$, what is the value of x^2+2x-8?

11 If $a=\dfrac{\sqrt{3}-\sqrt{2}}{4}$ and $b=\dfrac{\sqrt{3}+\sqrt{2}}{4}$, what is the value of $(a+b)^2(a-b)^2$?

12 Solve the equation. Check for extraneous solutions.

(1) $2\sqrt{2x+1}+4x=-2$

(2) $\sqrt{2x+9}-x=3$

(3) $\sqrt{x}-\sqrt{x+3}=\sqrt{3}$

13 Graph the function $y=-\frac{1}{2}\sqrt{4x+8}-2$. Then state the domain and range.

14 Graph the function $y=3\sqrt[3]{\frac{1}{2}x-1}+1$.

15 Given a function $y=\sqrt{-4x+3}+1-2b$, if the domain is $\{x|x\leq a\}$ and the range is $\{y|y\geq 7\}$, what is the value of $a+b$?

16

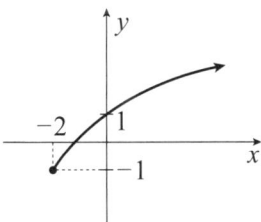

If the graph above is $y=a\sqrt{2(x-h)}+k$, what is the value of $a+h+k$?

Chapter Test — Level 2

Solutions_Page 131

01 Simplify each of the following.

(1) $\sqrt{(-4)^2}+(-3\sqrt{2})^2-\sqrt{125}\left(\sqrt{20}-\sqrt{\dfrac{1}{5}}\right)$

(2) $\dfrac{4\sqrt{12}}{\sqrt{3}}+\sqrt{6}(\sqrt{24}-2\sqrt{3})-\dfrac{4-2\sqrt{2}}{\sqrt{8}}$

02 If $a=\dfrac{1+\sqrt{2}}{1-\sqrt{2}}$ and $b=\dfrac{1-\sqrt{2}}{1+\sqrt{2}}$, what is the value of $\dfrac{\sqrt{a}-\sqrt{b}}{\sqrt{a}+\sqrt{b}}$?

03 If the expression $\dfrac{a}{2\sqrt{3}}(\sqrt{54}-4\sqrt{6})+2(2a\sqrt[3]{27}+2\sqrt{2})$ is rational number, what is the value of a?

340 Chapter 7. Roots and Radicals

04 If $\dfrac{a}{\sqrt{10}-3}-\dfrac{b}{\sqrt{10}+3}=6+4\sqrt{10}$, what is the value of a^2-b^2?

05 Find the value of $x\sqrt{\dfrac{2y}{x}}-\dfrac{4}{y}\sqrt{\dfrac{y}{2x}}+x\sqrt[3]{y^2}\times y\sqrt[3]{x^2}$ if $x>0$, $y>0$ and $xy=8$.

06 Simplify the expression $\dfrac{1}{\sqrt{2}+\sqrt{1}}+\dfrac{1}{\sqrt{3}+\sqrt{2}}+\cdots+\dfrac{1}{\sqrt{100}+\sqrt{99}}$.

Chapter Test — Level 2

07 Solve the equation. Check for extraneous solutions.

(1) $\sqrt{\sqrt{3x+1}} = \sqrt{2x-6}$

(2) $\sqrt{\sqrt{2x-1} - \sqrt{x-1}} = 1$

08

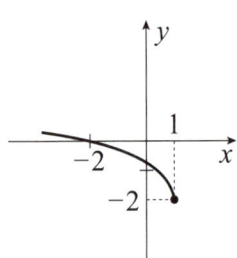

If the graph above is $y = \sqrt{ax+b} + c$, what is the value of abc?

09 Suppose the graph of $y=-\sqrt{ax+b}+c$ passes through the point $(2, -4)$. If the domain and range of this function is $\left\{x \mid x \geq -\frac{3}{2}\right\}$ and $\{y \mid y \leq 3\}$, respectively, what is the value of $a+b+c$?

10 Suppose that the graph of $y=\frac{1}{3}\sqrt{9x-18}-3$ is the result of the graph $y=\sqrt{x+1}+2$ by shifting h units to the right and k units down. Find the value of $h+k$?

memo

Chapter **8**

Special Functions

1. Absolute Value Functions
2. Greatest Integer Functions and Piecewise Functions
3. Operation of Functions
4. Inverse Functions
5. Chapter Test

Absolute Value Functions

01 Definition of Absolute Value Function

The simplest form of an absolute value function is $y=|x|$. The absolute value function is divided into two functions at the value x where the expression in the absolute value is zero. So the function $y=|x|$ can be written as $y=\begin{cases} x, & \text{if } x\geq 0 \\ -x, & \text{if } x<0 \end{cases}$, which is called a piecewise defined function and it has the following graph.

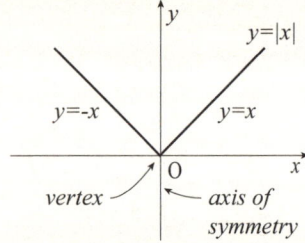

The graph is V-shaped and symmetric about a vertical line called the axis of symmetry. Just like a graph of quadratic function, a graph of an absolute value function has a maximum or minimum value, called the vertex, as shown above.

Concept Check

1. $y=|x-2| \Rightarrow y=\begin{cases} x-2, & \text{if } x\geq 2 \\ -(x-2), & \text{if } x<2 \end{cases} = \begin{cases} x-2, & \text{if } x\geq 2 \\ -x+2, & \text{if } x<2 \end{cases}$

2. $y=|x+3|-2 \Rightarrow y=\begin{cases} (x+3)-2, & \text{if } x\geq -3 \\ -(x+3)-2, & \text{if } x<-3 \end{cases} = \begin{cases} x+1, & \text{if } x\geq -3 \\ -x-5, & \text{if } x<-3 \end{cases}$

Example 1

Convert each absolute value function to a piecewise defined function and sketch the graph.

① $y=\dfrac{1}{2}|x|$ ② $y=|x-4|$ ③ $y=-2|x+1|+3$

Solution

① $y=\dfrac{1}{2}|x| \Rightarrow y=\begin{cases} \dfrac{1}{2}x, & \text{if } x\geq 0 \\ -\dfrac{1}{2}x, & \text{if } x<0 \end{cases}$

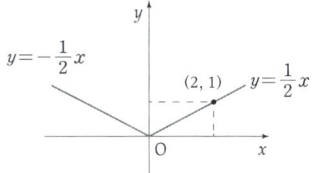

② $y=|x-4|$

$y=\begin{cases} x-4, & \text{if } x\geq 4 \\ -(x-4), & \text{if } x<4 \end{cases}$

$=\begin{cases} x-4, & \text{if } x\geq 4 \\ -x+4, & \text{if } x<4 \end{cases}$

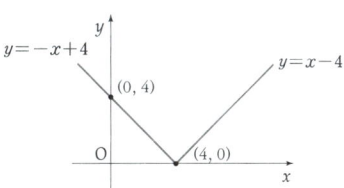

③ $y=-2|x+1|+3$

$y=\begin{cases} -2(x+1)+3, & \text{if } x\geq -1 \\ -2\cdot -(x+1)+3, & \text{if } x<-1 \end{cases}$

$=\begin{cases} -2x+1, & \text{if } x\geq -1 \\ 2x+5, & \text{if } x<-1 \end{cases}$

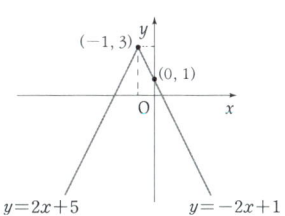

Check Point 1

Solutions_Page 134

Convert each absolute value function to a piecewise defined function and sketch the graph.

① $y=2|x|$ ② $y=2|x+5|$

③ $y=|3x+6|-2$

Chapter 8. Special Functions 347

02 The Graph of $y=a|x|$, $a>0$

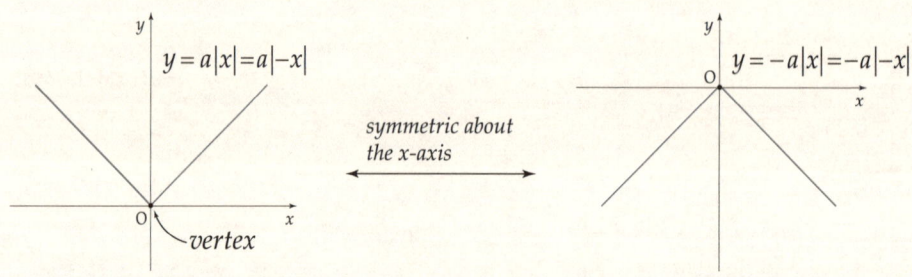

1. $a|x| = \begin{cases} ax, & \text{if } x \geq 0 \\ -ax, & \text{if } x < 0 \end{cases}$ $\xleftrightarrow{\text{Identical}}$ $a|-x| = a|x|$

2. $-a|x| = \begin{cases} -ax, & \text{if } x \geq 0 \\ ax, & \text{if } x < 0 \end{cases}$ $\xleftrightarrow{\text{Identical}}$ $-a|-x| = -a|x|$

Example 2-1

Sketch the graph of the function.

① $y=|x|$ 　　　　　　　② $y=|-x|$

③ $y=-|x|$ 　　　　　　　④ $y=-|-x|$

Solution

① $y=|x|$

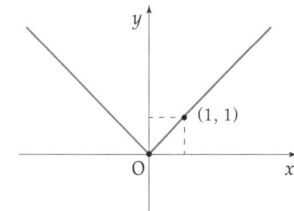

② $y=|-x|=|x|$

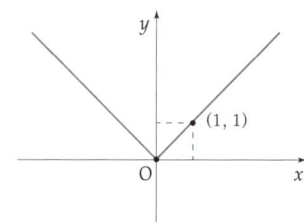

348 Chapter 8. Special Functions

③ $y=-|x|$

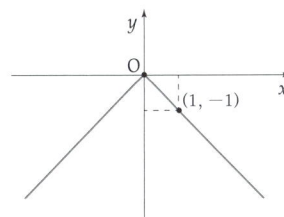

④ $y=-|-x|=-|x|$

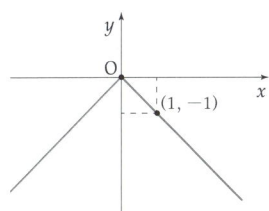

Example 2-2

Sketch the graph of the function $y=|x|$, $y=2|x|$, and $y=3|x|$ on the same coordinate plane.

Solution

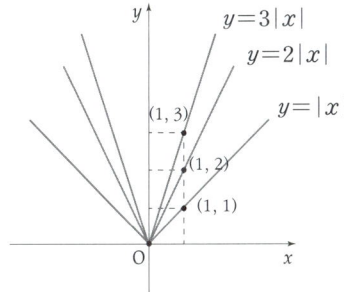

✔ Notice that, just like radical functions we have studied from previous chapter, a from the function $y=a|x|$ indicates a vertical stretch ($a>1$) or shrink ($0<a<1$).

Check Point 2 Solutions_Page 134

Sketch the graph of the function.

① $y=2|x|$

② $y=-4|x|$

③ $y=\dfrac{1}{4}|-2x|$

④ $y=-\dfrac{1}{2}|-4x|$

03 The Graph of $y=a|x-h|+k$, $a>0$

Like the quadratic and radical functions we learned earlier, absolute value functions can be graphed using the concept of translation.

To graph $y=a|x-h|+k$, follow these steps

(1) Sketch the graph of $y=a|x|$

(2) Shift the graph h units horizontally and k units vertically

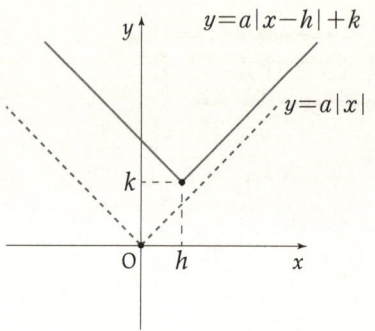

Example 3

Sketch the graph of the function $y=|x-2|+1$ using the concept of translation.

Solution

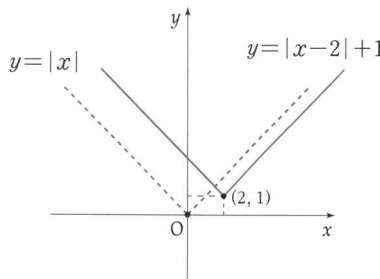

→ Graph $y=|x|$
→ Shift 2 units to the right and 1 unit up

Check Point 3 Solutions_Page 135

Sketch the graph of the function using the concept of translation.

① $y=2|x-1|$ ② $y=-|3x|+2$

③ $y=2|-x+3|+1$ ④ $y=-\left|-\dfrac{1}{2}x-2\right|-4$

04 Function with Two Absolute Values

If a function has two absolute values, the expression is divided by the value of x where the expression in each absolute value is zero.

Concept Check

$y=|x|+|x+2|$

$y=\begin{cases} x+(x+2), & \text{if } x\geq 0 \\ -x+(x+2), & \text{if } -2\leq x<0 \\ -x-(x+2), & \text{if } x<-2 \end{cases}$

$=\begin{cases} 2x+2, & \text{if } x\geq 0 \\ 2, & \text{if } -2\leq x<0 \\ -2x-2, & \text{if } x<-2 \end{cases}$

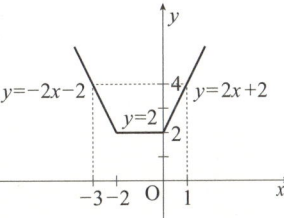

Example 4

Sketch the graph of the function $y=|x-2|+2|x|$.

Solution

$y=|x-2|+2|x|$

$y=\begin{cases} (x-2)+2x, & \text{if } x\geq 2 \\ -(x-2)+2x, & \text{if } 0\leq x<2 \\ -(x-2)-2x, & \text{if } x<0 \end{cases}$

$\begin{cases} 3x-2, & \text{if } x\geq 2 \\ x+2, & \text{if } 0\leq x<2 \\ -3x+2, & \text{if } x<0 \end{cases}$

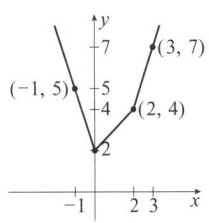

Check Point 4

Sketch the graph of the function.

① $y=2|x-1|+|x+1|$

② $y=\left|\dfrac{1}{2}x+1\right|-|x-2|$

Review Exercise

Solutions_Page 136

01 Convert each absolute value function to a piecewise defined function and sketch the graph.

(1) $y=-|3x|$

(2) $y=-\left|\dfrac{1}{2}x\right|-4$

(3) $y=|x-2|-1$

(4) $y=-\dfrac{1}{2}|4x+12|-3$

02 Sketch the graph of the function using the concept of translation.

(1) $y=-2\left|-\dfrac{3}{2}x\right|$

(2) $y=|x|+1$

(3) $y=2|-2x+2|-4$

(4) $y=-4\left|-\dfrac{2}{3}x+1\right|+1$

03 Write an equation for each translation of the graph of $y=2|x-4|+2$.

(1) Shifted 2 units to the right

(2) Shifted 3 units down

(3) Shifted 3 units to the left and 4 units up

(4) Shifted 1 unit to the right and $\frac{1}{2}$ unit down

(5) Shifted 5 units to the right and reflected over x-axis

(6) Shifted 2 units to the left and $\frac{5}{3}$ unit down. Then reflected over x-axis

Review Exercise

04 The graph of the function $y=a|x+b|+c$ is shown below. Find the value of $a+b+c$.

(1)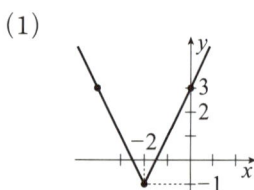

(2)

Challenging

05 Sketch the graph of the function.

(1) $y=|2x-3|-2|x+2|+x$

(2) $y=|x+1|+|x|-|x-1|$

Challenging

06 If $|x|\leq 3$, find the minimum and maximum value of the function $y=|x-2|+x$.

Challenging

07 Sketch the graph of the function $y=x^2-2|x|-8$.

2 Greatest Integer Functions and Piecewise Functions

01 Greatest Integer Function

The greatest integer function, well known as step function, is denoted by $y=[x]$ and defined as $[x]$ is equal to the greatest integer less than or equal to x.

If $[x]=n$, then $n\leq x<n+1$

Concept Check

1. $[2.4]=$ greatest integer $\leq 2.4=2$
2. $[4.999]=$ greatest integer $\leq 4.999=4$
3. $[-2.76]=$ greatest integer $\leq -2.76=-3$
4. $[1]=$ greatest integer $\leq 1=1$

Example 1

Evaluate each of the following.

① $[3.01]$

② $\frac{1}{2}[-0.009]$

③ $2[1.65]-[2]$

④ $\dfrac{4[2.001]}{[-3.001]}$

Solution

① $[3.01]=3$

② $\frac{1}{2}[-0.009]=\frac{1}{2}(-1)=-\frac{1}{2}$

③ $2[1.65]-[2]=2(1)-2=0$

④ $\frac{4[2.001]}{[-3.001]}=\frac{4(2)}{-4}=\frac{8}{-4}=-2$

Check Point 1

Solutions_Page 139

Evaluate each of the following.

① $2[-4.1]$

② $2[1.8]+[0.8]$

③ $3[-5.6]-\frac{1}{2}[1.98]$

④ $\frac{[-6.9998]\cdot[-1.0001]}{2[-0.001]}$

02 The Graph of $y=a[bx]$

The greatest integer functions make it easy to draw graphs using tables.
Let's sketch the graph of $y=[x]$.

x	$y=[x]$
$-3\leq x<-2$	-3
$-2\leq x<-1$	-2
$-1\leq x<0$	-1
$0\leq x<1$	0
$1\leq x<2$	1
$2\leq x<3$	2
$3\leq x<4$	3

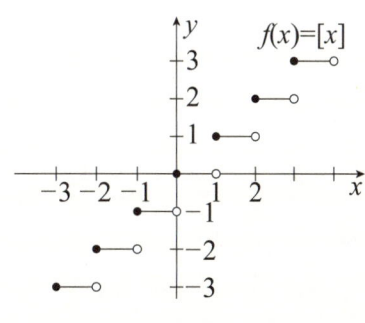

Properties of Greatest Integer Function $y=[x]$

1. The graph looks like stair steps.
2. The graph jumps vertically one unit at each integer value.
3. The domain is the set of all real numbers.
4. The range is the set of all integers.

Example 2

Sketch the graph of the function.

① $y=2[x]$　　　　　　　　　② $y=[2x]$

Solution

① $y=2[x]$

x	$y=2[x]$
$-2 \leq x < -1$	-4
$-1 \leq x < 0$	-2
$0 \leq x < 1$	0
$1 \leq x < 2$	2
$2 \leq x < 3$	4

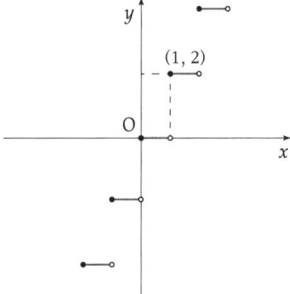

✔ As x increases by 1 unit, the graph jump 2 units vertically.

② $y=[2x]$

x	$y=[2x]$
$-1 \leq x < -0.5$	-2
$-0.5 \leq x < 0$	-1
$0 \leq x < 0.5$	0
$0.5 \leq x < 1$	1
$1 \leq x < 1.5$	2
$1.5 \leq x < 2$	3

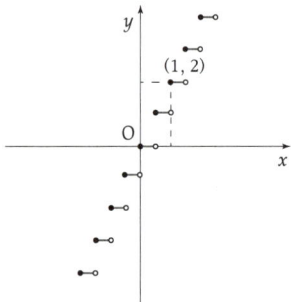

✔ As x increases by $\frac{1}{2}$ unit, the graph jump 1 unit vertically.

Check Point 2

Solutions_Page 139

Sketch the graph of the function.

① $y = \frac{1}{2}[x]$ 　　　　　　　　　② $y = \left[\frac{1}{2}x\right]$

03 The Graph of $y = a[b(x-h)] + k$

The greatest integer functions can also be graphed using the concept of translation.

To graph $y = a[b(x-h)] + k$, follow these steps

1. Create a table for the function $y = a[bx]$.
2. Create a table for the function $y = a[b(x-h)] + k$ by shifting each point h units horizontally and k units vertically.
3. Sketch the graph.

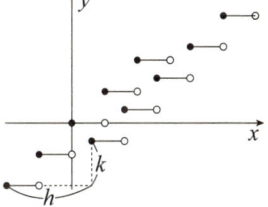

Example 3

Sketch the graph of the function $y = [x+1] - 2$.

> Solution

Create a table for the function $y=[x]$ and $y=[x+1]-2$.

		shift 2 units down	
x	$y=[x]$	x	$y=[x+1]-2$
$0 \leq x < 1$	0	$-1 \leq x < 0$	-2
$1 \leq x < 2$	1	$0 \leq x < 1$	-1
$2 \leq x < 3$	2	$1 \leq x < 2$	0
$3 \leq x < 4$	3	$2 \leq x < 3$	1
$4 \leq x < 5$	4	$3 \leq x < 4$	2
$5 \leq x < 6$	5	$4 \leq x < 5$	3

shift 1 unit to the left

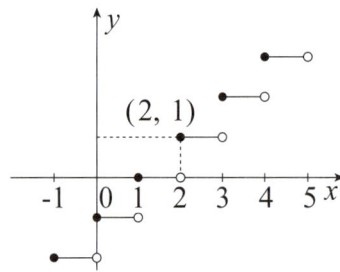

> Check Point 3

Solutions_Page 140

Sketch the graph of the function.

① $y=[x]+1$ ② $y=[x-2]-1$

04 Piecewise Defined Function

A **piecewise defined function** is a function defined by two or more equations over a specified domain.

$$y = \begin{cases} f(x), & \text{if } x \geq a \\ g(x), & \text{if } x < a \end{cases}$$

Concept Check

For the function $y = \begin{cases} x^2+1, & \text{if } x > 0 \\ 2x-3, & \text{if } x \leq 0 \end{cases}$,

1. $y(-2)$ → Since $-2 \leq 0$, $y(-2) = 2(-2) - 3 = -7$
2. $y(0)$ → Since $0 \leq 0$, $y(0) = 2(0) - 3 = -3$
3. $y(3)$ → Since $3 > 0$, $y(3) = (3)^2 + 1 = 10$

Example 4

Evaluate the function $y = \begin{cases} 2|x-1|-3, & \text{if } x \geq 1 \\ 3x^2-4, & \text{if } x < 1 \end{cases}$ for the indicated values.

① $y(0)$ ② $y(1)$

③ $y(2)$ ④ $y(a)$, where $a < 0$

Solution

① Since $0 < 1$, $y(0) = 3(0)^2 - 4 = -4$
② Since $1 \geq 1$, $y(1) = 2|(1)-1| - 3 = -3$
③ Since $2 \geq 1$, $y(2) = 2|(2)-1| - 3 = -1$
④ Since $a < 1$, $y(a) = 3(a)^2 - 4 = 3a^2 - 4$

Check Point 4   Solutions_Page 140

Evaluate the function $y = \begin{cases} \sqrt{x}+4, & \text{if } x \geq 1 \\ 2x^2-1, & \text{if } x < 1 \end{cases}$ for the indicated values.

① $y(4)$ ② $y(-1)$

③ $y(1)$ ④ $y(a+1)$, where $a < 0$

05 Graph of Piecewise Defined Function

For the graph of piecewise defined function, we simply graph given two or more functions over a specified domain. The range of the piecewise function is union of each functions.

Concept Check

For the function $y=\begin{cases} \sqrt{x}+1, & \text{if } x>0 \\ x, & \text{if } x\leq 0 \end{cases}$, graph $y=\sqrt{x}+1$ for $x>0$ and graph $y=x$ for $x\leq 0$.

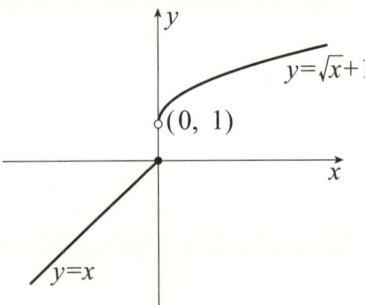

The range of $y=\sqrt{x}+1$, $x>0$ is $\{y|y>1\}$ and the range of $y=x$, $x\leq 0$ is $\{y|y\leq 0\}$. So, the union of the range of these two functions is $\{y|y\leq 0 \text{ or } y>1\}$.

Example 5

Sketch the graph of the function. State the range.

① $y=\begin{cases} -1-x, & \text{if } x>0 \\ 2x-3, & \text{if } x\leq 0 \end{cases}$

② $y=\begin{cases} -x^2-1, & \text{if } x\geq -2 \\ \sqrt{x+3}, & \text{if } x<-2 \end{cases}$

> Solution

① Graph $y=-1-x$ for $x>0$ and graph $y=2x-3$ for $x\leq 0$.

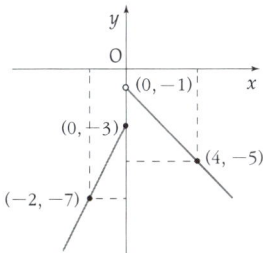

The range of $y=-1-x$, $x>0$ is $\{y|y<-1\}$ and the range of $y=2x-3$, $x\leq 0$ is $\{y|y\leq -3\}$. So, the union of the range of these two functions is $\{y|y<-1\}$.

② Graph $y=-x^2-1$ for $x\geq -2$ and graph $y=\sqrt{x+3}$ for $x<-2$. Remember that $\sqrt{x+3}$ is defined when $x\geq -3$.

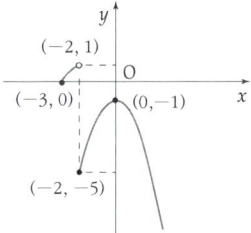

The range of $y=-x^2-1$, $x\geq -2$ is $\{y|y\leq -1\}$ and the range of $y=\sqrt{x+3}$, $-3\leq x<2$ is $\{y|0\leq y<1\}$. So, the union of the range of these two functions is $\{y|y\leq -1 \text{ or } 0\leq y<1\}$.

Check Point 5

Solutions_Page 140

Sketch the graph of the function. State the range.

① $f(x)=\begin{cases} 2x+1, & \text{if } x\geq 0 \\ -x, & \text{if } x<0 \end{cases}$

② $g(x)=\begin{cases} \sqrt{x}, & \text{if } x>0 \\ x-2, & \text{if } x\leq 0 \end{cases}$

③ $h(x)=\begin{cases} 2x+1, & \text{if } x>1 \\ x^2-1, & \text{if } x\leq 1 \end{cases}$

Review Exercise

01 Evaluate each of the following.

(1) $[3.91]$

(2) $[3(1.2)-4]$

(3) $4\left[\dfrac{1}{2}-\dfrac{1}{3}\right]$

(4) $\dfrac{2}{3}\left[-1-\dfrac{3}{2}\right]+3$

02 Sketch the graph of the function.

(1) $y=[x-2]$

(2) $y=[2x+3]$

(3) $y=-[x]+2$

(4) $y=[x+1]-1$

03 Evaluate the function
$$f(x) = \begin{cases} \frac{1}{2}x+3, & \text{if } x \geq 2 \\ 4\sqrt{x-1}, & \text{if } 0 \leq x < 2 \\ x^3 - 2, & \text{if } x < 0 \end{cases}$$
for the indicated values.

(1) $f(1)$

(2) $f(2)$

(3) $f(-2)$

(4) $f\left(\dfrac{5}{4}\right)$

(5) $f(a+2)$, where $a > 0$

(6) $f(2b-1)$, where $b < 0$

Review Exercise

04 Sketch the graph of the function. State the range.

(1) $y = \begin{cases} x-2, & \text{if } x>2 \\ \dfrac{1}{2}x, & \text{if } x\leq 2 \end{cases}$

(2) $y = \begin{cases} 3-2x, & \text{if } x\geq 1 \\ x^2+2, & \text{if } x<1 \end{cases}$

(3) $y = \begin{cases} (x-1)^2+1, & \text{if } x\geq 0 \\ |x+2|, & \text{if } x<0 \end{cases}$

05 Solve the equation.

(1) $[x-2]=5$

(2) $2[2x+1]+1=7$

(3) $[-x+1]=-2$

Challenging

06 Find the value of
$[\sqrt{1}]+[\sqrt{2}]+[\sqrt{3}]+\cdots+[\sqrt{9}]$.

Challenging

07 Sketch the graph of $y=x-[x]$.

3 Operation of Functions

01 Arithmetic Operation of Functions

We can always add, subtract, multiply, or divide functions as shown below.

1. Sum: $(f+g)(x)=f(x)+g(x)$
2. Difference: $(f-g)(x)=f(x)-g(x)$
3. Product: $(fg)(x)=f(x) \cdot g(x)$
4. Quotient: $\left(\dfrac{f}{g}\right)(x)=\dfrac{f(x)}{g(x)}, \ g(x) \neq 0$

However, one thing to note is the domain of each function. The domain of the function resulting from the operation consists of the x-values that are in the domains of both f and g.

Concept Check

Let $f(x)=\sqrt{x-1}+2$ and $g(x)=x-4$.

1. $(f+g)(x)=f(x)+g(x)=(\sqrt{x-1}+2)+(x-4)=x+\sqrt{x-1}-2$
2. $(f-g)(x)=f(x)-g(x)=(\sqrt{x-1}+2)-(x-4)=-x+\sqrt{x-1}+6$
3. $(fg)(x)=f(x) \cdot g(x)=(\sqrt{x-1}+2)(x-4)=x\sqrt{x-1}-4\sqrt{x-1}+2x-8$
4. $\left(\dfrac{f}{g}\right)(x)=\dfrac{f(x)}{g(x)}=\dfrac{\sqrt{x-1}+2}{x-4}$

The domain of f is $\{x \mid x \geq 1\}$ and the domain of g is the set of all real numbers.

The domain of f.   The domain of g.

The domain of $f+g$, $f-g$ and fg is the set of numbers common to the domain of both f and g, which is $\{x \mid x \geq 1\}$. The domain of $\dfrac{f}{g}$ is $\{x \mid x \geq 1, \text{ but } x \neq 4\}$ because $g(x)=0$ at $x=4$.

Chapter 8. Special Functions

Example 1

Given $f(x) = x-3$ and $g(x) = x^2 - x - 6$, find each of the following and their domains.

① $(f+g)(x)$ ② $(f-g)(x)$
③ $(fg)(x)$ ④ $\left(\dfrac{f}{g}\right)(x)$

Solution

① $(f+g)(x) = (x-3) + (x^2-x-6) = x^2 - 9$
② $(f-g)(x) = (x-3) - (x^2-x-6) = -x^2 + 2x + 3$
③ $(fg)(x) = (x-3) \cdot (x^2-x-6) = x^3 - 4x^2 - 3x + 18$
④ $\left(\dfrac{f}{g}\right)(x) = \dfrac{x-3}{x^2-x-6} = \dfrac{x-3}{(x-3)(x+2)} = \dfrac{1}{x+2}$

The domain of both f and g is the set of all real numbers. So the domain of $f+g$, $f-g$, and fg is the set of all real numbers. However, the domain of $\dfrac{f}{g}$ is the set of all real numbers except $x=3$ and $x=-2$, because $g(x)=0$ at these x values.

Check Point 1

Solutions_Page 144

Given $f(x) = 1 - \dfrac{1}{x+2}$ and $g(x) = x+1$, find each of the following and their domains.

① $(f+g)(x)$ ② $(f-g)(x)$
③ $(fg)(x)$ ④ $\left(\dfrac{f}{g}\right)(x)$

02 Composition of Functions

Given two functions $f: X \rightarrow Y$ and $g: Y \rightarrow Z$, we can define a new function where X is the domain and Z is the range by matching the element X to $g(f(x))$, as shown below.

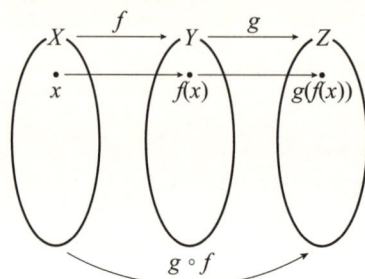

This function is called the composition of function g with function f and is defined as

$$g \circ f = (g \circ f)(x) = g(f(x))$$

In the same principle,

1. $f \circ g = (f \circ g)(x) = f(g(x))$
2. $f \circ f = (f \circ f)(x) = f(f(x))$
3. $f \circ g \circ h = (f \circ g \circ h)(x) = f(g(h(x)))$

Concept Check

Given $f(x) = \sqrt{x+1}$ and $g(x) = \dfrac{1}{x-1}$,

1. $g \circ f = (g \circ f)(x) = g(f(x)) = g(\sqrt{x+1}) = \dfrac{1}{\sqrt{x+1}-1}$
2. $f \circ g = (f \circ g)(x) = f(g(x)) = f\left(\dfrac{1}{x-1}\right) = \sqrt{\dfrac{1}{x-1}+1}$

   ✔ Notice that $f \circ g \neq g \circ f$.

3. $(g \circ f)(3)$

   Method 1: $(g \circ f)(x) = \dfrac{1}{\sqrt{x+1}-1}$, $(g \circ f)(3) = \dfrac{1}{\sqrt{3+1}-1} = \dfrac{1}{2-1} = 1$

   Method 2: $(g \circ f)(3) = g(f(3)) = g(\sqrt{3+1}) = g(2) = \dfrac{1}{2-1} = 1$

Example 2

Given $f(x)=3x-1$ and $g(x)=2x^2$, find each of the following.

① $g \circ f$ ② $f \circ g$ ③ $(g \circ f)\left(\dfrac{1}{3}\right)$

Solution

① $g \circ f = g(f(x)) = g(3x-1) = 2(3x-1)^2 = 2(9x^2-6x+1) = 18x^2-12x+2$
② $f \circ g = f(g(x)) = f(2x^2) = 3(2x^2)-1 = 6x^2-1$
③ **Method 1**: $g \circ f = 2(3x-1)^2$, $(g \circ f)\left(\dfrac{1}{3}\right) = 2\left(3\left(\dfrac{1}{3}\right)-1\right)^2 = 2(1-1)^2 = 0$

    Method 2: $(g \circ f)\left(\dfrac{1}{3}\right) = g\left(f\left(\dfrac{1}{3}\right)\right) = g\left(3\left(\dfrac{1}{3}\right)-1\right) = g(0) = 2(0)^2 = 0$

Check Point 2   Solutions_Page 144

Given $f(x)=\dfrac{1}{2}x^2-2$ and $g(x)=2x$, find each of the following.

① $f \circ g$ ② $g \circ f$
③ $(f \circ g)(2)$ ④ $(g \circ g \circ f)(-1)$

03   Composition of Functions and its Domain

The domain of $g \circ f$ is set of all x in the domain of f for which $f(x)$ is in the domain of g, as shown below.

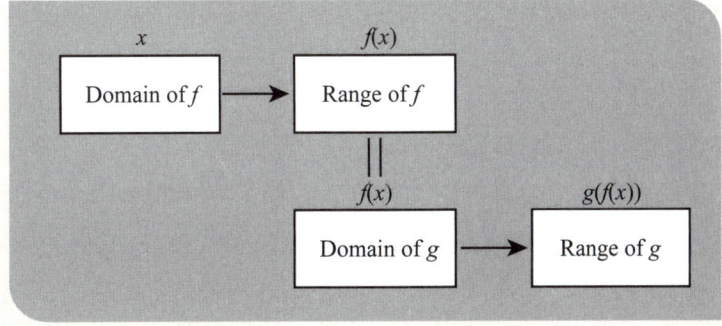

Finding the domain of the function $g \circ f = g(f(x))$ consists of three steps:

1. Find the domain of the function $f(x)$.

2. Construct the function $g(f(x))$ and find the domain of this new function.

3. The domain of the function $g(f(x))$ is the set of numbers common to the domain of both $f(x)$ and the new function constructed from $g(f(x))$.

Concept Check

Given $f(x) = \dfrac{1}{x+2}$ and $g(x) = \dfrac{1}{x-1}$, the domain of $g \circ f = g(f(x))$ can be found as follows:

1. The domain of $f(x) = \dfrac{1}{x+2}$ is all real numbers except $x = -2$.

2. $g \circ f = g(f(x)) = g\left(\dfrac{1}{x+2}\right) = \dfrac{1}{\dfrac{1}{x+2} - 1} = -\dfrac{x+2}{x+1}$

   and the domain of $g \circ f \Rightarrow y = -\dfrac{x+2}{x+1}$ is all real numbers except $x = -1$.

3. The domain of $g \circ f = g(f(x))$ is set of numbers common to the domain of both $f(x) = \dfrac{1}{x+2}$ and $y = -\dfrac{x+1}{x+2}$, which is all real numbers except $x = -2$ and $x = -1$.

Example 3

Given $f(x)=\sqrt{x-1}$ and $g(x)=2x$, find each of the following and their domains.

① $f \circ g$ ② $f \circ f$

Solution

① $f \circ g = f(g(x)) = f(2x) = \sqrt{2x-1}$

Domain of $g(x)=2x$: All real numbers.

Domain of $f \circ g \Rightarrow y=\sqrt{2x-1}$: $\left\{x \mid x \geq \dfrac{1}{2}\right\}$

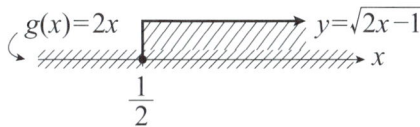

Domain of $f \circ g$: $\left\{x \mid x \geq \dfrac{1}{2}\right\}$

② $f \circ f = f(f(x)) = f(\sqrt{x-1}) = \sqrt{\sqrt{x-1}-1}$

Domain of $f(x)=\sqrt{x-1}$: $\{x \mid x \geq 1\}$

Domain of $f \circ f \Rightarrow y=\sqrt{\sqrt{x-1}-1}$:

For $\sqrt{\sqrt{x-1}-1}$ to be defined, we must have

$\sqrt{x-1}-1 \geq 0$, $\sqrt{x-1} \geq 1$

$x-1 \geq 1$, $x \geq 2$: $\{x \mid x \geq 2\}$

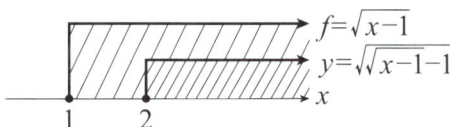

Domain of $f \circ f$: $\{x \mid x \geq 2\}$

Check Point 3

Solutions_Page 144

Given $f(x)=\dfrac{2}{x}$ and $g(x)=2x+5$, find each of the following and their domains.

① $f \circ g$ ② $g \circ f$ ③ $f \circ f$

Review Exercise

Solutions_Page 145

01 Given $f(x)=2x^2+x-2$ and $g(x)=\dfrac{x}{2}+3$, find each of the following and their domains.

(1) $(f+g)(x)$

(2) $(f-g)(x)$

(3) $(fg)(x)$

(4) $\left(\dfrac{f}{g}\right)(x)$

02 Given $f(x)=\dfrac{x}{x-2}$ and $g(x)=\dfrac{x-2}{x-1}$, find each of the following and their domains.

(1) $(f+g)(x)$

(2) $(f-g)(x)$

(3) $(fg)(x)$

(4) $\left(\dfrac{f}{g}\right)(x)$

03 Given $f(x)=2x-1$, $g(x)=\dfrac{1}{x-1}$, and $h(x)=\sqrt{3x+2}$, find each of the following.

(1) $(f \circ g)(-4)$

(2) $(g \circ h)\left(\dfrac{2}{3}\right)$

(3) $(f \circ g \circ h)(2)$

(4) $(g \circ g \circ g)(3)$

(5) $g \circ f$ and its domain

(6) $g \circ h$ and its domain

04 Given $f(x)=4x-a$ and $g(x)=-2x+5$, answer the following questions.

(1) If $(f \circ g)(2)=4$, what is the value of a?

(2) If $(g \circ g \circ g)(b)=-11$, what is the value of b?

Review Exercise

Challenging

05 Given $f(1-4x)=\dfrac{3x-2}{4}$, find each of the following.

(1) $f(x)$

(2) $f(4a-1)$

Challenging

06 Given $f\left(\dfrac{3x+1}{2}\right)=2x+5$, what is the value of $f(2)+f(5)$?

07 Let $f(x)=3x-2$ and $g(x)=kx+2$. If $f \circ g = g \circ f$, what is the value of k?

Challenging

08 Given $f(x)=-3x+4$ and $g(x)=4x-1$, find the function h that satisfies each of the following.

(1) $f \circ h = g$

(2) $h \circ g = f$

09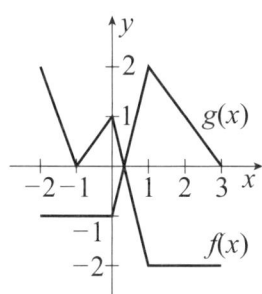

In the graphs of f and g shown above, find each of the following.

(1) $(f \circ g)(0)$

(2) $(g \circ f)(2)$

(3) $(f \circ f \circ f)(1)$

(4) $(g \circ f \circ g)(-1)$

4 Inverse Functions

01 The Definition of Inverse

The inverse of f, which is denoted by f^{-1}, can be formed by interchanging input (x-values) and output (y-values) of the function. As a result, the domain of f is equal to the range of f^{-1} and the range of f is equal to the domain of f^{-1}. The graph of f^{-1} is a reflection of the graph of f about the line $y=x$.

Concept Check

Let a set of ordered pairs of f be $\{(1, -3), (2, 0), (3, 1)\}$.

f: $\{(1, -3), (2, 0), (3, 1)\}$ f^{-1}: $\{(-3, 1), (0, 2), (1, 3)\}$
Domain of f: $\{1, 2, 3\}$ ⟶ Domain of f^{-1}: $\{-3, 0, 1\}$
Range of f: $\{-3, 0, 1\}$ ⟶ Range of f^{-1}: $\{1, 2, 3\}$

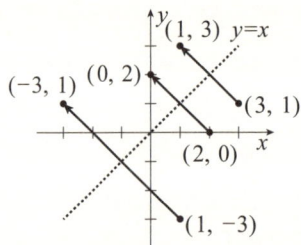

Given a function f, its inverse f^{-1} does not always become a function. f^{-1} is a function if and only if f is a one-to-one function. A function is one-to-one if each value of input corresponds to exactly one value of output. If the one-to-one function is continuous, it always either increases or decreases.

Concept Check

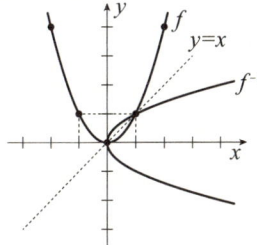

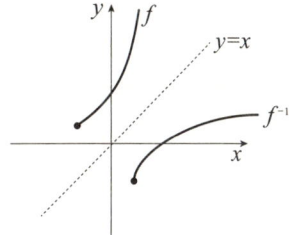

f is NOT one−to−one
→ f^{-1} is NOT a function.

f is one−to−one
→ f^{-1} is a function.

In summary, if the function $f: X \to Y$ is a one−to−one function,
1. Its inverse function $f^{-1}: Y \to X$ exists
2. $y = f(x) \Leftrightarrow x = f^{-1}(y)$

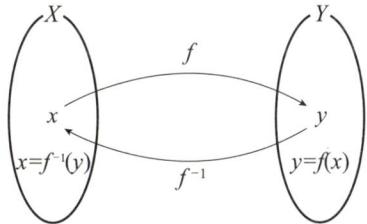

Concept Check

Given $f(x) = 3x - 2$, find $f(4)$ and $f^{-1}(4)$.
$y = f(x) \Leftrightarrow x = f^{-1}(y)$

1. Since $f(4)$ is the value of y when $x=4$,
   $3(4) - 2 = 10 \to f(4) = 10$

2. Since $f^{-1}(4)$ is the value of x when $y=4$,
   $4 = 3x - 2$, $x = 2 \to f^{-1}(4) = 2$

Example 1

Given $f(x)=5x+4$, find each of the following.

① $f(-1)$ ② $f^{-1}(3)$ ③ $f^{-1}(2b-1)$

Solution

① $f(-1)=5(-1)+4=-1$

② $3=5x+4$, $-1=5x$

$x=-\dfrac{1}{5}$, $f^{-1}(3)=-\dfrac{1}{5}$

③ $2b-1=5x+4$, $2b-5=5x$

$x=\dfrac{2b-5}{5}$, $f^{-1}(2b-1)=\dfrac{2b-5}{5}$

Check Point 1

Solutions_Page 147

Given $g(x)=2\sqrt{x-1}+1$, find each of the following.

① $g(5)$ ② $g^{-1}(5)$ ③ $g^{-1}(a)$

02 Properties of Inverse Function

If we have a one-to-one function $f: X \to Y$ and its inverse function $f^{-1}: Y \to X$, then

1. $(f^{-1})^{-1}=f$
2. $(f^{-1} \circ f)(x)=x$ and $(f \circ f^{-1})(x)=x$

Concept Check

1. Since $y=f(x) \Leftrightarrow x=f^{-1}(y) \Leftrightarrow y=(f^{-1})^{-1}(x)$, $(f^{-1})^{-1}=f$

2. $(f^{-1} \circ f)(x)=f^{-1}(f(x))=f^{-1}(y)=x$

   $(f \circ f^{-1})(y)=f(f^{-1}(y))=f(x)=y$. By replacing y with x, $(f \circ f^{-1})(x)=x$

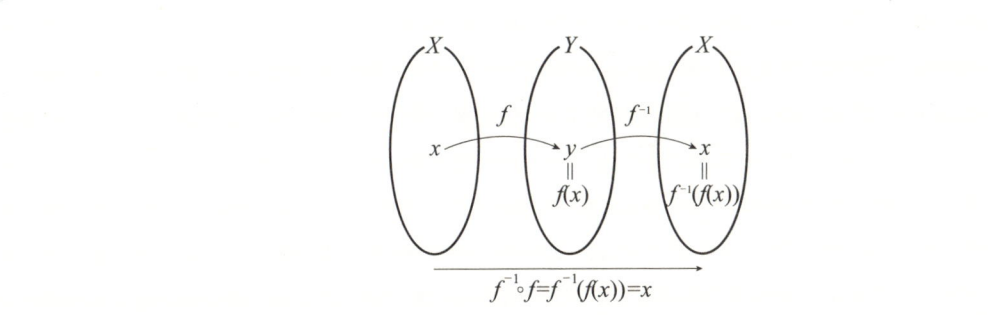

Example 2

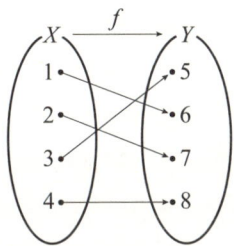

Given the function f as shown above, find each of the following.

① $f(2)$ ② $f^{-1}(5)$ ③ $(f^{-1} \circ f)(3)$

④ $(f \circ f^{-1})(8)$ ⑤ $(f^{-1})^{-1}(4)$

Solution

① $f(2)=7$ ② $f^{-1}(5)=3$

③ Since $(f^{-1} \circ f)(x)=x$, $(f^{-1} \circ f)(3)=3$ ④ Since $(f^{-1} \circ f)(x)=x$, $(f \circ f^{-1})(8)=8$

⑤ Since $(f^{-1})^{-1}=f$, $(f^{-1})^{-1}(4)=f(4)=8$

Check Point 2

Solutions_Page 147

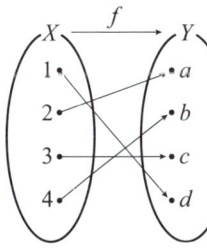

Given the function f as shown, find each of the following.

① $f(3)$ ② $f^{-1}(b)$

③ $f^{-1}(d)$ ④ $(f^{-1})^{-1}(4)$

⑤ $(f^{-1} \circ f)(4)$ ⑥ $(f \circ f^{-1})(a)$

Example 3

Show that $g(x) = \dfrac{x-1}{3}$ is inverse function of $f(x) = 3x+1$.

Solution

If g is inverse of f, $(f \circ g)(x) = x$ and $(g \circ f)(x) = x$.

$(f \circ g)(x) = f(g(x)) = f\left(\dfrac{x-1}{3}\right) = 3\left(\dfrac{x-1}{3}\right) + 1 = (x-1) + 1 = x$

$(g \circ f)(x) = g(f(x)) = g(3x+1) = \dfrac{(3x+1)-1}{3} = \dfrac{3x}{3} = x$

Therefore, g is inverse of f

Check Point 3 Solutions_Page 147

Show that $g(x) = \dfrac{1-2x}{4}$ is inverse function of $f(x) = -2x + \dfrac{1}{2}$.

03 Finding an Inverse of f

In general, when representing a function, we write the elements of the domain as x and the elements of the range as y. Therefore, in the inverse function $x = f^{-1}(y)$, x and y are interchanged and represented by $y = f^{-1}(x)$.
Use the following procedure to find the inverse function.

1. Check if the function f is a one−to−one function.
2. Replace f with y.
3. Interchange x and y.
4. Solve the resulting equation for y.
5. Replace y with f^{-1}.

Chapter 8. Special Functions

Concept Check

Find the inverse of $f(x)=2x-1$ and sketch the graph.

$f(x)=2x-1$ → f is a one-to-one function

$y=2x-1$ → Replace f with y

$x=2y-1$ → Interchange x and y

$y=\dfrac{x+1}{2}$ → Solve the resulting equation for y

$f^{-1}(x)=\dfrac{x+1}{2}$ → Replace y with f^{-1}

$f(x)=2x-1$	$f^{-1}(x)=\dfrac{x+1}{2}$
$(-1,\ -3)$	$(-3,\ -1)$
$(0,\ -1)$	$(-1,\ 0)$
$(1,\ 1)$	$(1,\ 1)$
$(2,\ 3)$	$(3,\ 2)$

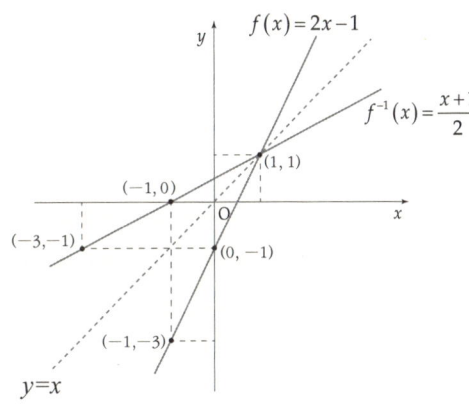

Example 4

Find the inverse of f and then determine whether the inverse is a function.

① $f(x)=\dfrac{x-2}{4}$ ② $f(x)=x^2+1$

Solution

① $f(x)=\dfrac{x-2}{4}$, $y=\dfrac{x-2}{4}$

$x=\dfrac{y-2}{4}$, $4x=y-2$

$4x+2=y$, $f^{-1}(x)=4x+2$

$f^{-1}(x)$ is a function because $f(x)$ is a one-to-one function.

② $f(x)=x^2+1,\ y=x^2+1$
$x=y^2+1,\ x-1=y^2$
$\pm\sqrt{x-1}=y,\ f^{-1}(x)=\pm\sqrt{x-1}$
$f^{-1}(x)$ is NOT a function because $f(x)$ is NOT a one-to-one function.

Check Point 4

Solutions_Page 148

Find the inverse of f and then determine whether the inverse is a function.

① $f(x)=\sqrt{x-3}+1$ ② $f(x)=\sqrt[3]{x}+1$

Example 5

Find the inverse function of f then sketch the graph.

① $f(x)=\dfrac{3x+1}{2}$ ② $f(x)=2\sqrt{x}+1$ ③ $f(x)=\sqrt[3]{x+1}$

Solution

① $f(x)=\dfrac{3x+1}{2},\ y=\dfrac{3x+1}{2}$

$x=\dfrac{3y+1}{2},\ 2x=3y+1$

$2x-1=3y,\ \dfrac{2x-1}{3}=y$

$f^{-1}(x)=\dfrac{2x-1}{3}$

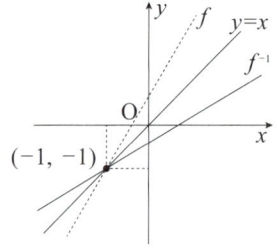

② $f(x)=2\sqrt{x}+1,\ y=2\sqrt{x}+1$
$x=2\sqrt{y}+1,\ x-1=2\sqrt{y}$

$\dfrac{x-1}{2}=\sqrt{y},\ \dfrac{(x-1)^2}{4}=y$

$f^{-1}(x)=\dfrac{(x-1)^2}{4}$ where $x\geq 1$

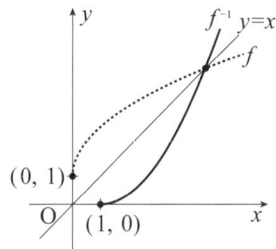

③ $f(x)=\sqrt[3]{x+1}$, $y=\sqrt[3]{x+1}$
$x=\sqrt[3]{y+1}$, $x^3=y+1$
$x^3-1=y$
$f^{-1}(x)=x^3-1$

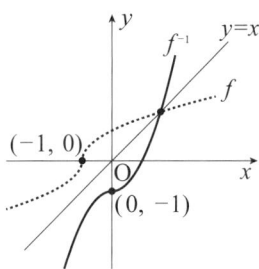

Check Point 5

Solutions_Page 148

Find the inverse function of f then sketch the graph.

① $f(x)=-4x-3$

② $f(x)=\dfrac{2-3x}{3}$

③ $f(x)=x^2-3$, $x\geq 0$

④ $f(x)=\sqrt{x-2}$

Review Exercise

01 Which of the following functions has the inverse function?

(A) $y=x^2+2$

(B) $y=|x-3|+1$

(C) $y=[x]+1$

(D) $y=-\frac{1}{2}\sqrt{x+1}+2$

(E) $y=\begin{cases} 2x+1, & \text{if } x>1 \\ x^2-1, & \text{if } x\leq 1 \end{cases}$

02 Given $f(x)=\dfrac{1+x}{x-2}$, find each of the following.

(1) $f(3)$

(2) $f^{-1}(3)$

(3) $f^{-1}(k)$ in terms of k

(4) $f^{-1}\left(\dfrac{m}{2}\right)$ in terms of m

03 Show that g is inverse function of f.

(1) $f(x)=2x-1$, $g(x)=\dfrac{x+1}{2}$

(2) $f(x)=\sqrt{x-4}$, $g(x)=x^2+4$ where $x\geq 0$

(3) $f(x)=\dfrac{x-1}{x+5}$, $g(x)=-\dfrac{5x+1}{x-1}$

(4) $f(x)=x^3-1$, $g(x)=\sqrt[3]{x+1}$

04 Find the inverse of f and then determine whether the inverse is a function.

(1) $f(x)=2x-4$

(2) $f(x)=\dfrac{2x+1}{x-2}$

(3) $f(x)=\dfrac{1}{2}x^2+2$

(4) $f(x)=\sqrt{x-2}+3$

05 Find the inverse function of f then sketch the graph.

(1) $f(x)=4-x^2,\ x\geq 0$

(2) $f(x)=\dfrac{2}{x}$

(3) $f(x)=2\sqrt[3]{x-2}-2$

Review Exercise

06 If $f(x)=5x+2$ and $f^{-1}(a)=4$, what is the value of a?

07 If $f(x)=3\sqrt{bx-2}+1$ and $f^{-1}(2)=1$, what is the value of b?

Challenging

08 Suppose that $f(x)=ax+b$. If the graph of f^{-1} passes through two points $(2, -3)$ and $(10, 1)$, what is the value of $a+b$?

Challenging

09 Given $f(x) = \frac{1}{4}x - 1$ and $g(x) = x^3$, find each of the following.

(1) $(f^{-1} \circ g)(2)$

(2) $(f \circ g^{-1})(8)$

(3) $(f^{-1} \circ g^{-1})(1)$

(4) $(g^{-1} \circ f^{-1})(-3)$

(5) $(f^{-1} \circ f^{-1})(0)$

(6) $(f^{-1} \circ g)(a)$ in terms of a

(7) $(g^{-1} \circ f^{-1})(a+3)$ in terms of a

(8) $(f \circ g)^{-1}(b)$ in terms of b

Chapter Test — Level 1

01 Write an equation for each translation of the graph of $y=\frac{1}{2}|x+1|-2$.

(1) Shifted 4 units to the left and 1 unit down

(2) Shifted 2 units up and reflected over y-axis

(3) Reflected over x-axis. Then, shifted 3 units to the right and $\frac{5}{2}$ units up.

02 Sketch the graph of the function $y=2\left|x+\frac{1}{2}\right|-4\left|x-\frac{1}{4}\right|$.

03 Evaluate each of the following.

(1) $-[2.78]+[-2.78]$

(2) $5\left[\frac{7}{2}\left(\frac{1}{2}-1\right)\right]-2[-3.25]$

04 Sketch the graph of the function.

(1) $y=[2x]-1$

(2) $y=-[x-1]-\frac{1}{2}$

05 Evaluate the function $f(x)=\begin{cases} 2x^2-3, & \text{if } x\geq 3 \\ |3x-2|-1, & \text{if } -1<x<3 \\ 5-4x, & \text{if } x\leq -1 \end{cases}$ for the indicated values.

(1) $f(-1)$ (2) $f(0)$

(3) $f(2)$ (4) $f(3)$

(5) $f(a)$, where $-1<a<0$ (5) $f(b+3)$, where $b>0$

06 Sketch the graph of the function $f(x)=\begin{cases} -x-1, & \text{if } x>2 \\ x, & \text{if } 0\leq x<2 \\ -x^2+2, & \text{if } x<0 \end{cases}$. State the range.

07 Given $f(x)=\dfrac{2}{x-2}$, $g(x)=4x-1$, and $h(x)=\sqrt{2x+1}+3$, find each of the following.

(1) $(f \circ g)(2)$ (2) $(g \circ h)(0)$

(3) $(f \circ g \circ h)(4)$ (4) $(f \circ f \circ f)(4)$

(5) $g \circ f$ and its domain (6) $h \circ f$ and its domain

Chapter Test — Level 1

08

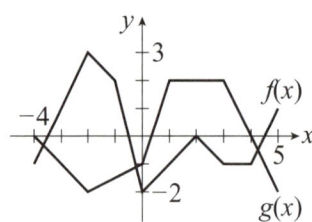

In the graphs of f and g shown above, find each of the following.

(1) $(f \circ g)(0)$

(2) $(g \circ f)(-1)$

(3) $(g \circ f \circ g)(4)$

(4) $(f \circ g \circ g)(-3)$

09 Given $f(x) = -\dfrac{1}{2}x + 3$ and $g(x) = 3x + k$, answer the following questions.

(1) If $(g \circ f)(-4) = -2$, what is the value of k?

(2) If $(f \circ g \circ g)(1) = 6$, what is the value of k?

10 If $g(x)=x+3k-1$ and $g=g^{-1}$, what is the value of k?

11 If the function $f(x)=\dfrac{ax+b}{x-c}$ has its inverse function $f^{-1}(x)=\dfrac{5x+1}{x-3}$, what is the value of $a+b+c$?

12 Suppose that $h(x)=ax+b$. If the graph of h^{-1} passes through two points $(-4,\ 6)$ and $(8,\ 3)$, what is the value of $a+b$?

13 Given $f(x)=2x+6$ and $g(x)=-x^2+4$ where $x\geq 0$, find each of the following

(1) $(f^{-1}\circ g)(2)$ (2) $(f\circ g^{-1})(-5)$

(3) $(f^{-1}\circ g^{-1})(2)$ (4) $(f^{-1}\circ f^{-1})(4)$

Chapter Test — Level 2

Solutions_Page 155

01 Sketch the graph of the function.

(1) $y=2|x|+3|x+2|+|x-1|$

(2) $y=|(|x+2|-|x-1|)|$

02 Given the function $y=2|x-1|+|x+1|$ where $|x|\leq 2$, find the difference between the maximum and minimum values of the function.

03 Solve the equation $[3x-4]-2=-7$.

04 Given $f\left(\dfrac{4-2x}{3}\right)=\dfrac{2x+1}{5}$, find $f(5x+4)$.

05 Given $f(x)=2x-3$ and $g(x)=3x+2$, find the function h that satisfies each of the following.

(1) $f \circ h = g$

(2) $h \circ g \circ f = f$

06   Let $f(x)=2-5x$ and $g(x)=bx-3$. If $f \circ g = g \circ f$, what is the value of b?

07

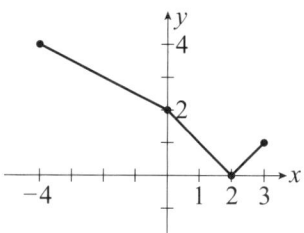

Given the graph of f above, if $(f \circ f \circ f)(m)=2$, what is the value of m?

08   If the graph of function $f(x)=5x+2$ and the graph of its inverse function f^{-1} intersects at (a, b), what is the value of a and b?

09   Given $f(x)=\dfrac{2}{x+k}-3$, if $f=f^{-1}$, what is the value of k?

Chapter **9**

Discrete Mathematics

1. Introduction to Sequences
2. Introduction to Series
3. Fundamental Counting Principles
4. Probability
5. Chapter Test

1 Introduction to Sequences

01 Definition of Sequence

A sequence is a list of ordered numbers where it has a first number, a second number, a third number and so on. A sequence is usually written as

$$a_1, a_2, a_3, \cdots, a_n.$$

and each number is called the term(also called a member or an element) of a sequence. For example, a_1 is first term, a_2 is second term, and a_n is n^{th} term. We say a sequence is finite if it has a limited number of terms($a_1, a_2, a_3, \cdots, a_n$) and infinite if it has an unlimited number of terms($a_1, a_2, a_3, \cdots, a_n, a_{n+1}, \cdots$). For instance, 1, 3, 5, 7 is a finite sequence and 1, 3, 5, 7, $\cdots$, 99, $\cdots$ is an infinite sequence.

Example 1

Write the first three terms and $(n+1)^{th}$ term of the sequence $a_n = 2n+1$.

Solution

$a_n = 2n+1$
1st term: $a_1 = 2(1)+1 = 3$ 2nd term: $a_2 = 2(2)+1 = 5$
3rd term: $a_3 = 2(3)+1 = 7$ $(n+1)^{th}$ term: $a_{n+1} = 2(n+1)+1 = 2n+3$

$$a_1 = 3, \ a_2 = 25, \ a_3 = 7, \ a_{n+1} = 2n+3$$

Check Point 1

Write the first three terms and $(n+1)^{th}$ term of the sequence.

① $a_n = n^2 - n + 3$ ② $a_n = \dfrac{n^3}{(2n-1)^2}$

02 Arithmetic Sequence

An arithmetic sequence is a sequence in which the difference between any two consecutive terms is constant. This constant is called the common difference and is denoted by d. Now, let's derive a formula for an arithmetic sequence.

2, 5, 8, 11, $\cdots$ → Each term after the first is found by adding 3 to the preceding term.

1st term:	$a_1=2=2+3(0)$	→ $a_1=a_1+d(0)$	$0d$ is added
2nd term:	$a_2=5=2+3(1)$	→ $a_2=a_1+d(1)$	$1d$ is added
3rd term:	$a_3=8=2+3(2)$	→ $a_3=a_1+d(2)$	$2d$ is added
4th term:	$a_4=11=2+3(3)$	→ $a_4=a_1+d(3)$	$3d$ is added
$\vdots$	$\vdots$	$\vdots$	
n^{th} term:	$a_n=2+3(n-1)$	→ $a_n=a_1+d(n-1)$	$(n-1)d$ is added

Notice that $d=5-2=8-5=11-8=3$. In other words, the common difference is $d=a_2-a_1=a_3-a_2=a_4-a_3=\cdots=a_n-a_{n-1}$.

There is also a formula for arithmetic sequence that can be an alternative. When a_k is given, the nth term is $a_n=a_k+(n-k)d$.

The nth Term of an Arithmetic Sequence:

1. Given $a_n=a_1+(n-1)d$
2. Given $a_n=a_k+(n-k)d$

Common Difference: $d=a_n-a_{n-1}$

> **Example 2**

Write a formula for the nth term and the 8th term of the sequence, 1, 5, 9, 13, $\cdots$.

> **Solution**

1, 5, 9, 13, $\cdots$ $\rightarrow$ $a_1=1$ and $d=4$.
$a_n=a_1+(n-1)d=1+(n-1)(4)=4n-3$
So $a_n=4n-3$ and $a_8=4(8)-3=29$.

$$a_n=4n-3,\ a_8=29$$

> **Check Point 2**

Solutions_Page 158

Write a formula for the nth term and the 10th term of the sequence.

① 2, 5, 8, 11, $\cdots$ ② 4, 1, -2, -5, $\cdots$

> **Example 3**

Find the first term and the formula for the nth term of the arithmetic sequences.

① $a_6=20,\ d=2$ ② $a_5=-6,\ a_{10}=-21$

> **Solution**

① $a_6=20,\ d=2,\ a_n=a_1+(n-1)d$
$a_6=a_1+(6-1)(2),\ 20=a_1+10,\ a_1=10$
$a_n=10+(n-1)(2)=2n+8,\ a_n=2n+8$

$$a_1=10,\ a_n=2n+8$$

② $a_5=-6,\ a_{10}=-21,\ a_n=a_1+(n-1)d$
$a_5=a_1+(5-1)d,\ -6=a_1+4d$ and $a_{10}=a_1+(10-1)d,\ -21=a_1+9d$

Now, solve the system.

$$\begin{array}{r} -6=a_1+4d \\ -\ -21=a_1+9d \\ \hline 15=-5d \end{array} \rightarrow d=-3 \quad \Rightarrow \text{Substitute } d=-3 \text{ into } -6=a_1+4d$$

$-6=a_1+4(-3)$, $a_1=6$
$a_n=6+(n-1)(-3)=-3n+9$, $a_n=-3n+9$

Alternative solution

$a_n=a_k+(n-k)d$
$a_{10}=a_5+(10-5)d$, $-21=-6+5d$, $d=-3$
Now, substitute $d=-3$ into $a_5=a_1+(5-1)d$.
$-6=a_1+(5-1)(-3)$
$-6=a_1-12$, $a_1=6$ and $a_n=6+(n-1)(-3)=-3n+9$, $a_n=-3n+9$

$a_1=6$, $a_n=-3n+9$

Check Point 3 Solutions_Page 158

Find the first term and a formula for the nth term of the arithmetic sequence.

① $a_{12}=38$, $d=4$　　　　　　　　② $a_{12}=10$, $a_4=-38$

03 Geometric Sequence

A geometric sequence is a sequence in which the ratio of any two consecutive terms is constant. This constant is called the common ratio and denoted by r.

3, 6, 12, 24, ⋯ → Each term after the first is found by multiplying 2 to the preceding term.

1st term:	$a_1=3=3\times(2)^0$	→ $a_1=a_1\times(r)^0$	r^0 is multiplied
2nd term:	$a_2=6=3\times(2)^1$	→ $a_2=a_1\times(r)^1$	r^1 is multiplied
3rd term:	$a_3=12=3\times(2)^2$	→ $a_3=a_1\times(r)^2$	r^2 is multiplied
4th term:	$a_4=24=3\times(2)^3$	→ $a_4=a_1\times(r)^3$	r^3 is multiplied
⋮	⋮	⋮	⋮
n^{th} term:	$a_n=3\times(2)^{n-1}$	→ $a_n=a_1\times r^{n-1}$	r^{n-1} is multiplied

Notice that $r=6\div3=12\div6=24\div12=2$. In other words, the common ratio is $r=a_2\div a_1=a_3\div a_2=a_4\div a_3=\cdots=a_n\div a_{n-1}$.
There is also a formula for geometric sequence that can be an alternative. When a_k is given, the nth term is $a_n=a_k r^{n-k}$.

The nth Term of a Geometric Sequence:
1. $a_n = a_1 r^{n-1}$
2. $a_n = a_k r^{n-k}$

Common Ratio: $r = \dfrac{a_n}{a_{n-1}}$

Example 4

Write a formula for the nth term and the 8th term of the sequence 2, 4, 8, 16, $\cdots$.

Solution

2, 4, 8, 16, $\cdots$ $\to$ $a_1 = 2$ and $r = 2$
$a_n = a_1 r^{n-1}$, $a_n = 2(2)^{n-1}$, $a_8 = 2(2)^{8-1} = 256$

$a_n = 2(2)^{n-1}$, $a_8 = 256$

Check Point 4

Solutions_Page 158

Write a formula for the nth term and the 10th term of the sequence.
① 3, 9, 27, 81, $\cdots$
② -5, 10, -20, 40, $\cdots$

Example 5

Find the first term and the formula for the nth term of the geometric sequence.

① $a_5 = 72$, $r = 3$
② $a_4 = 1$, $a_7 = \dfrac{1}{8}$

Solution

① $a_5=72$, $r=3$, $a_n=a_1r^{n-1}$

$a_5=a_1(3)^{5-1}$, $72=a_1(3)^4$, $a_1=\dfrac{8}{9}$

$a_n=\dfrac{8}{9}(3)^{n-1}$

$a_1=\dfrac{8}{9}$, $a_n=\dfrac{8}{9}(3)^{n-1}$

② $a_4=1$, $a_7=\dfrac{1}{8}$, $a_n=a_1r^{n-1}$

$a_4=a_1r^{4-1}$, $1=a_1r^3$ and $a_7=a_1r^{7-1}$, $\dfrac{1}{8}=a_1r^6$

Now, solve the system: $\dfrac{a_1r^6}{a_1r^3}=\dfrac{\frac{1}{8}}{1}=\dfrac{1}{8}$, $r^3=\dfrac{1}{8}$, $r=\dfrac{1}{2}$. So we have

$a_n=a_1r^{n-1}$

$a_4=a_1r^{4-1}$, $1=a_1\left(\dfrac{1}{2}\right)^3$, $a_1=8$. Therefore, $a_n=8\left(\dfrac{1}{2}\right)^{n-1}$.

Alternative solution

$a_n=a_kr^{n-k}$, $a_7=a_4r^{7-4}$, $\dfrac{1}{8}=1\cdot r^3$, $r=\dfrac{1}{2}$

Now, substitute $r=\dfrac{1}{2}$ into $a_4=a_1r^3$.

$1=a_1\left(\dfrac{1}{2}\right)^3$, $1=\dfrac{1}{8}a_1$, $a_1=8$. Therefore, $a_n=8\left(\dfrac{1}{2}\right)^{n-1}$.

$a_1=8$, $a_n=8\left(\dfrac{1}{2}\right)^{n-1}$

Check Point 5

Find the first term and a formula for the nth term of the geometric sequence.

① $a_2=3$, $r=-2$ ② $a_3=10$, $a_6=1250$

04 Recursive Sequence

Sometimes, sequences are defined recursively. This type of sequence always comes with the first few terms and a formula.

Example 6

Let $a_1=1$, $a_2=2$, $a_n=a_{n-2}+2a_{n-1}$, where $n\geq 3$. Find the first 5 terms of the sequence.

Solution

$a_1=1$ and $a_2=2$
$n=3$; $a_3=a_{3-2}+2a_{3-1}=a_1+2a_2=1+2(2)=5 \rightarrow a_3=5$
$n=4$; $a_4=a_{4-2}+2a_{4-1}=a_2+2a_3=2+2(5)=12 \rightarrow a_4=12$
$n=5$; $a_5=a_{5-2}+2a_{5-1}=a_3+2a_4=5+2(12)=29 \rightarrow a_5=29$

So the first 5 terms are 1, 2, 5, 12, 29

Check Point 6

Solutions_Page 159

Where $n\geq 3$, find the first 5 terms of the sequence.

① $a_1=6$, $a_2=-2$, $a_n=a_{n-1}-a_{n-2}$

② $a_1=6$, $a_2=4$, $a_n=\dfrac{a_{n-1}-n}{2}+\dfrac{3a_{n-2}}{4}$

Review Exercise

Solutions_Page 159

01 Find the 10th term of the sequence 15, 9, 3, −3, ⋯.

03 Find the 8th term of each sequence 200, 100, 50, 25, ⋯.

02 The fourth term of an arithmetic sequence is 24, and the eighth term is 8. What is the first term of this sequence?

04 The third term of a geometric sequence is 5, and the sixth term is 625. What is the first term of this sequence?

Review Exercise

05 If $a_1=10$ and $a_n=a_{n-1}-4n-1$, what is the value of a_4?

06 For set $\{-1, 1, 7, 25\}$, which of the following number should be added to each of the terms so that the resulting numbers form consecutive terms of a geometric sequence?

(A) 0
(B) 1
(C) 2
(D) 3
(E) 4

07 If the first term of an arithmetic sequence is 2 and fifth terms of sequence 14, what is the value of the first term of the sequence to exceed 600?

08

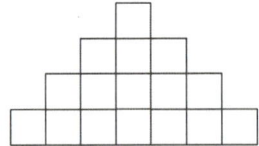

In Figure above, the first row has 1 square. If 2 additional squares are added to each new row after the first, how many squares will be in the 100th row?

09 A sequence is recursively defined as follows

$a_1=2$, $a_{n+1}=\begin{cases}2a_n-2, & \text{if } a_n \text{ is odd}\\ a_n+3, & \text{if } a_n \text{ is even}\end{cases}$

for $n\geq 1$. What is the sum of the first five terms?

10 A ball is dropped from a height of 243 ft above the ground. If the ball rebounds two-thirds of the distance it has fallen, how high does the ball rebound on the fifth bounce?

2 Introduction to Series

01 Definition of Series

A series is the sum of the terms of a sequence, and there is a notation for the series called the sigma notation (also called the summation notation).

> The sum of first n terms (also called the nth partial sum) of a sequences is written as
> $$\sum_{k=1}^{n} a_k = a_1 + a_2 + a_3 + \cdots + a_n = S_n, \text{ where}$$
> Σ: Sigma
> k: index
> 1: Lower limit
> n: Upper limit
> S_n: Sum of first n terms

Example 1

Find $\sum_{k=1}^{5} k^2$.

Solution

$\sum_{k=1}^{5} k^2 = (1)^2 + (2)^2 + (3)^2 + (4)^2 + (5)^2 = 1 + 4 + 9 + 16 + 25 = 55$

$\sum_{k=1}^{5} k^2 = 55$

Check Point 1   Solutions_Page 161

Find each of the following.

① $\sum_{k=1}^{4} (5k-1)$ ② $\sum_{k=1}^{3} \frac{1}{2} \cdot (-3)^k$

02 Finite and Infinite Series

There are two types of series, a finite and an infinite series.

1. Finite series
$$a_1+a_2+a_3+\cdots+a_n=\sum_{k=1}^{n} a_k$$

2. Infinite series
$$a_1+a_2+a_3+\cdots+a_n+a^{n+1}+\cdots=\sum_{k=1}^{\infty} a_k$$

Example 2

Write the series $2+4+6+8+10+12$ using the summation notation.

Solution

Since each term after the first is increased by 2, use $a_n=a_1+(n-1)d$ to find the sum.
$a_1=2$ and $d=2$. Thus, $a_n=2+(n-1)(2)=2n$, $a_n=2n$.

$$2+4+6+8+10+12=\sum_{k=1}^{6} 2k$$

Check Point 2

Solutions_Page 161

Write given series using the summation notation.

① $1+3+5+7+\cdots+179$

② $8-4+2-1+\cdots+\dfrac{1}{32}$

Chapter 9. Discrete Mathematics

03 Arithmetic Series

The sum of the terms of a finite arithmetic sequence is called an **arithmetic series**. There are two important formulas to remember. Let us derive the formula for the arithmetic series.

Let S_n be the sum of a finite arithmetic sequence with n terms and common difference d. The sum can be written as
$$S_n = a_1 + a_2 + a_3 + \cdots + a_n = a_1 + (a_1 + d) + (a_1 + 2d) + \cdots + a_n.$$

$$+ \begin{array}{l} S_n = a_1 + (a_1 + d) + (a_1 + 2d) + (a_1 + 3d) + \cdots + (a_n - d) + a_n \\ S_n = a_n + (a_n - d) + (a_n - 2d) + (a_n - 3d) + \cdots + (a_1 + d) + a_1 \end{array}$$

$$2S_n = \underbrace{(a_1 + a_n) + (a_1 + a_n) + (a_1 + a_n) + \cdots + (a_1 + a_n)}_{n \text{ terms}}$$

$2S_n = n(a_1 + a_n)$ → There are n terms of $(a_1 + a_n)$

$S_n = \dfrac{n}{2}(a_1 + a_n)$ → Divide both sides by 2

In addition, the sum can be written as

$S_n = \dfrac{n}{2}(a_1 + a_n)$ → We know that $a_n = a_1 + (n-1)d$

$S_n = \dfrac{n}{2}(a_1 + (a_1 + (n-1)d))$ → Substitute $a_1 + (n-1)d$ into a_n

$S_n = \dfrac{n}{2}(2a_1 + (n-1)d)$ → Simplify

Arithmetic Series

> The sum of the first n terms (n^{th} partial sum) of an arithmetic sequence is
> 1. $S_n = \dfrac{n}{2}(a_1 + a_n)$
> 2. $S_n = \dfrac{n}{2}(2a_1 + (n-1)d)$

Example 3

Find the sum of $1+2+3+4+\cdots+20$.

Solution

$a_1=1$, $a_{20}=20$, and there are twenty terms ($n=20$).
$S_n=\frac{n}{2}(a_1+a_n)$, $S_{20}=\frac{20}{2}(1+20)=210$

$$S_{20}=210$$

Check Point 3 Solutions_Page 161

Find the sum.

① $5+7+9+11+\cdots+135$
② $10+4-2-8-\cdots-110$

Example 4

Find the nth partial sum of the arithmetic sequence if
① $a_1=6$, $a_{10}=42$; $n=10$
② $a_8=20$, $a_{20}=-52$; $n=28$

Solution

① $S_n=\frac{n}{2}(a_1+a_n)$, $S_{10}=\frac{10}{2}(6+42)=240$

$$S_{10}=240$$

② We first need to find the difference d and first term a_1.
$a_n=a_k+(n-k)d$
$a_{20}=a_8+(20-8)d$, $-52=20+12d$, $d=-6$
$a_n=a_1+(n-1)d$
$a_8=a_1+(8-1)(-6)$, $20=a_1-42$, $a_1=62$
So the sum of 28 terms is
$S_n=\frac{n}{2}(2a_1+(n-1)d)$, $S_{28}=\frac{28}{2}(2(62)+(28-1)(-6))=-532$

$$S_{28}=-532$$

> **Check Point 4**   Solutions_Page 161
>
> Find the nth partial sum of the arithmetic sequence.
>
> ① $a_1=3$, $a_{15}=59$; $n=34$
>
> ② $a_8=9$, $a_{29}=-33$; $n=29$

04 Geometric Series

The sum of the terms of a finite or infinite geometric sequence is called a geometric series. There are two important formulas to remember in this section. Let us derive the formula for the geometric series.

1. Finite Geometric Series

    Let S_n be the sum of a finite geometric sequence with n terms and common ratio r, where $r \neq 1$. The sum can be written as
    $S_n = a_1 + a_2 + a_3 + \cdots + a_n = a_1 + a_1r + a_1r^2 + \cdots + a_1r^{n-1}$.

    $$\begin{aligned}
    S_n &= a_1 + a_1r + a_1r^2 + a_1r^3 + \cdots + a_1r^{n-2} + a_1r^{n-1} \\
    -\ r \cdot S_n &= a_1r + a_1r^2 + a_1r^3 + a_1r^4 + \cdots + a_1r^{n-1} + a_1r^n \\
    \hline
    S_n - r \cdot S_n &= a_1 - a_1r^n \qquad \rightarrow \text{Simplify} \\
    S_n(1-r) &= a_1(1-r^n) \qquad \rightarrow \text{Factor each side} \\
    S_n &= \frac{a_1(1-r^n)}{(1-r)} = a_1\left(\frac{1-r^n}{1-r}\right) \qquad \rightarrow \text{Divide both sides by } (1-r)
    \end{aligned}$$

2. Infinite Geometric Series

    Now, let's find the formula for the sum of an infinite geometric sequence. This only exists when $|r|<1$. If $|r|<1$, r^n approaches zero as n increases without bound. Let $r=\frac{1}{2}$ for example. Then $r^n = \left(\frac{1}{2}\right)^n = \left(\frac{1}{2}\right)^\infty = \frac{1}{2^\infty} = \frac{1}{\infty} \Rightarrow 0$.
    So, the formula for the sum of an infinite sequence is,

    $S_\infty = a_1 + a_2 + a_3 + \cdots + a_n + \cdots$, can be written as $S_\infty = a_1\left(\frac{1-r^\infty}{1-r}\right) = a_1\left(\frac{1-0}{1-r}\right) = \frac{a_1}{1-r}$.
    Remember that S_∞ exists only if when $|r|<1$.

Geometric Series

1. The sum of the first n terms (n^{th} partial sum) of a geometric sequence is
$$S_n = a_1 \left(\frac{1-r^n}{1-r} \right), \ r \neq 1$$

2. The sum of an infinite geometric sequence is
$$S_\infty = \frac{a_1}{1-r}, \ |r|<1 \rightarrow -1<r<1$$

Example 5

Find the sum of $1+2+4+8\cdots+128$.

Solution

$a_1=1$, $r=2$, $a_n=128$. We first need to find the number of terms n.
Since $a_n=a_1 r^{n-1}$, $128=(1)(2)^{n-1}$, $2^7=(2)^{n-1}$, $n=8$. There are 8 terms.

So the sum of 8 terms is $S_n = a_1 \left(\frac{1-r^n}{1-r} \right)$, $S_8 = 1 \left(\frac{1-(2)^8}{1-2} \right) = 255$

$$1+2+4+8\cdots+128=255$$

Check Point 5

Find the sum.

① $6+18+54+162+\cdots+13122$

② $1-\dfrac{2}{3}+\dfrac{4}{9}-\dfrac{8}{27}+\cdots-\dfrac{128}{2187}$

Example 6

Find the nth partial sum of the geometric sequence if

① $a_1=4$, $a_7=2916$; $n=7$

② $a_6=162$, $a_{16}=\dfrac{2}{729}$; $n=16$

Solution

① We first need to find the ratio r.
$a_n=a_1 r^{n-1}$, $a_7=a_1 r^{7-1}$, $2916=4r^6$, $r=3$
So the sum of 7 terms is $S_n=a_1\left(\dfrac{1-r^n}{1-r}\right)$, $S_7=4\left(\dfrac{1-(3)^7}{1-3}\right)=4372$

$S_7=4372$

② We first need to find the ratio r and first term a_1.
$a_n=a_k r^{n-1}$, $a_{16}=a_6 r^{16-6}$
$\dfrac{2}{729}=162 r^{10}$, $\left(\dfrac{1}{3}\right)^{10}=r^{10}$, $r=\dfrac{1}{3}$
$a_6=a_1 r^{6-1}$, $162=a_1\left(\dfrac{1}{3}\right)^5$, $a_1=39366$
So the sum of 16 terms is
$S_n=a_1\left(\dfrac{1-r^n}{1-r}\right)$, $S_{16}=39366\left(\dfrac{1-\left(\dfrac{1}{3}\right)^{16}}{1-\dfrac{1}{3}}\right)=\dfrac{43046720}{729}$

$S_{16}=\dfrac{43046720}{729}$

Check Point 6

Solutions_Page 162

Find the nth partial sum of the geometric sequence.

① $a_1=7$, $a_{10}=3584$; $n=10$

② $a_4=1$, $a_8=\dfrac{256}{81}$; $n=5$

Example 7

Find the infinite geometric series $27-9+3-1+\cdots$.

Solution

$a_1=27$, $r=-\dfrac{1}{3}$

$S_\infty = \dfrac{a_1}{1-r} = \dfrac{27}{1-\left(-\dfrac{1}{3}\right)} = \dfrac{81}{4}$

$27-9+3-1+\cdots = \dfrac{81}{4}$

Check Point 7

Find the infinite geometric series.

① $1+0.5+0.25+0.125+\cdots$

② $3-\dfrac{9}{4}+\dfrac{27}{16}-\dfrac{81}{64}+\cdots$

Review Exercise

01 Find $\sum_{k=1}^{30}(7-5k)$.

02 If the 6th term of an arithmetic sequence is 28 and 19th terms of the sequence is 119, what is the sum of the first 15 terms of the sequence?

03 The sum of the first five terms of an arithmetic sequence is 105 and the first term is 13.

(1) Find the 5th term.

(2) Find the 20th term.

(3) Find the sum of first 18 terms.

04 If the third term of a geometric sequence is $-\dfrac{3}{64}$ and eighth terms of the sequence is 48, what is the sum of the first 9 terms of the sequence?

05 In an arithmetic sequence, the first term is 25 and the common difference is 24. In a geometric sequence, the first term is 3 and the common ratio is 2. At what minimum number of terms will the sum of the terms in the geometric sequence be greater than the sum of the terms in the arithmetic sequence?

06 Determine the number of terms of the series.

(1) $-2-12-22-32-\cdots$, $S_n=-224$

(2) $7-21+63-189+\cdots$, $S_n=3829$

07 What is the sum of
$\frac{1}{2}+\left(\frac{1}{3^2}+\frac{1}{3^3}+\cdots+\frac{1}{3^n}+\cdots\right)$?

08 If a geometric series has a common ratio of 0.6 and a sum to infinity of 120, what is the first term?

09 Jason got a job in the company with a salary of $55,000 a year. If he is promised a $3,500 raise each subsequent year, what are his total earnings for a 20-year period?

10 A ball is dropped from a height of 150 ft above the ground. If the ball rebounds one-third the height from which it was dropped, find the total vertical distance the ball travels until it comes to rest?

11 Find the infinite geometric series $mk-mk^3+mk^5-mk^7+\cdots$ in terms of m and k. ($m\neq0$ and $|k|<1$)

3 Fundamental Counting Principles

01 Fundamental Counting Principle

Let S_1, S_2, and S_3 represent the three different shirts and P_1 and P_2 represent two different pairs of pants. The number of outfits consisting of a shirt and a pair of pants can be visualized as the tree diagram below.

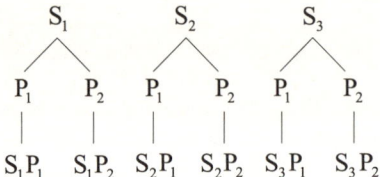

There are six possible outfits from which to choose. This is the best way to solve a counting problem. However, some events can occur in so many different ways so that it is almost impossible to write out the entire list. In such cases, we rely on the fundamental counting principle.

> Fundamental Counting Principle
> 1. Suppose one event can occur in r_1 different ways, and another event can occur in r_2 different ways. Then the number of ways in which these two events can occur is $r_1 \cdot r_2$.
> 2. If there are n number of events A_1, A_2, $\cdots$, A_n, and each event can occur in r_1, r_2, $\cdots$, r_n different ways respectively, then the number of ways in which the events can occur is $r_1 \cdot r_2 \cdots r_n$.

Example 1-1

There are three different shirts, four different pairs of jeans, and two different jackets. Determine the number of possible outfit arrangements with a shirt, a pair of jeans, and a jacket.

Solution

Outfit requires three separate decisions:

    Choosing a shirt   Choosing a jean   Choosing a jacket
      3 choices   4 choices   2 choices

For each choice of shirt, there are 4 choices of jeans ($3 \cdot 4 = 12$). And for each of these choices, there are 2 choices for jacket($12 \cdot 2 = 24$). So the number of possible outfit arrangement is simply $3 \cdot 4 \cdot 2 = 24$ different outfits.

24 outfits

Example 1-2

Suppose the Texas license plate consists of two upper-case letters followed by four numerical digits, zero through nine. How many different license plates are possible if
① There is no restriction on the letters or digits.
② No letter or digit can be repeated.

Solution

① The first and second selection each requires choosing a letter from 26 choices(A~Z) and third through sixth selection each requires choosing a digit from 10 choices(0~9). By the fundamental counting principle, we have
$\underline{26} \times \underline{26} \times \underline{10} \times \underline{10} \times \underline{10} \times \underline{10} = 676000$ possible ways.

6,760,000 ways

② The first selection requires choosing a letter from 26 choices. Then, since no letter can be repeated, the second selection requires choosing a letter from 25 choices. The same is true of third through sixth selection. By this principle, we have
$\underline{26} \times \underline{25} \times \underline{10} \times \underline{9} \times \underline{8} \times \underline{7} = 3276000$ possible ways.

3,276,000 ways

Check Point 1

Solutions_Page 164

① For the upcoming semester scheudle, David has 4 languages and 5 math classes to choose from. How many different schedules are possible if he chooses 1 language and 1 math class?

② How many distinct license plates can be issued consisting of three letters followed by four-digit number?

02 Permutation

One of the most important applications of the Fundamental Counting Principle is to count the number of ways that a set of objects can be arranged in order. Such ordering is called a permutation. In other words, a permutation of a set of objects is an arrangement of those objects into a particular order(order matters). The notation $_nP_r$ represents the number of ordered arrangements of r objects chosen from n distinct objects. Here is the formula for permutations.

Permutation

The number of permutations of n objects, taken r at a time is

$$_nP_r = \frac{n!}{(n-r)!}$$

Note:
1. $0! = 1$
2. $_nP_n = n!$

Proof

For the first selection, there are n choices; for the second selection, there are $n-1$ choices; for the third selection, there are $n-2$ choices; and so on. By the fundamental counting principle, we have

$$_nP_r = \underbrace{n}_{\text{1st selection}} \cdot \underbrace{(n-1)}_{\text{2nd selection}} \cdot \underbrace{(n-2)}_{\text{3nd selection}} \cdots \underbrace{(n-(r-1))}_{r\text{ th selection}}$$

$$= n \cdot (n-1) \cdot (n-2) \cdots (n-r+1)$$

420 Chapter 9. Discrete Mathematics

Now, in order to write in factorial notation, we will multiply the denominator and the numerator by $(n-r)\cdot(n-r-1)\cdots 1$.

$$_nP_r = n\cdot(n-1)\cdot(n-2)\cdots(n-r+1)\frac{(n-r)\cdot(n-r-1)\cdots 1}{(n-r)\cdot(n-r-1)\cdots 1} = \frac{n!}{(n-r)!}$$

Note:
1. $n! = n\cdot(n-1)\cdot(n-2)\cdots 1 = n\cdot(n-1)!$

   $\frac{n!}{n} = (n-1)!$

   If $n=1$, we have $\frac{1!}{1} = (1-1)!$, $1 = 0!$

2. $_nP_n = \frac{n!}{(n-n)!} = \frac{n!}{0!} = \frac{n!}{1} = n!$

Example 2

Evaluate $_4P_2$.

Solution

$_nP_r = \frac{n!}{(n-n)!}$, $_4P_2 = \frac{4!}{(4-2)!} = \frac{4!}{2!} = \frac{4\cdot 3\cdot 2\cdot 1}{2\cdot 1} = 4\cdot 3 = 12$

$_4P_2 = 12$

Check Point 2

Solutions_Page 164

Evaluate.

① $_8P_2$ 　　　　　　　　　　　　　　② $_{11}P_4$

Example 3-1

Determine the number of ways 5 people can line up for a photograph.

Chapter 9. Discrete Mathematics 421

> **Solution**

There are five people and five positions, 1st 2nd 3rd 4th 5th. Now, consider the following reason.

1st position has 5 choices	→ 5 __ __ __ __
2nd position has 4 choices	→ 5 4 __ __ __
3rd position has 3 choices	→ 5 4 3 __ __
4th position 2 choices	→ 5 4 3 2 __
5th position does not have any choice	→ 5 4 3 2 1

So, the total number of ways(permutations) is $\underline{5 \cdot 4 \cdot 3 \cdot 2 \cdot 1} = 5! = 120$.

Using the permutation formula: We have a permutation of 5 objects taken 5 at a time.

$$_5P_5 = \frac{5!}{(5-5)!} = \frac{5!}{0!} = \frac{5!}{1} = 5! = 120.$$

120 ways

Example 3-2

Mu Alpha Theta Club has 15 members, and they are electing a President, a Vice-President, and a Secretary from their members. Determine the number of possible combinations of people filling in these positions.

> **Solution**

There are three positions, President Vice-President Secretary. Since there are 15 members, there are 15 available choices for President(1st position), 14 available choices for Vice-President (2nd position), and 13 available choices for Secretary(3rd position).
So, $\underline{15 \cdot 14 \cdot 13} = 2730$ possible ways.

Using the permutation formula: We have a permutation of 13 objects taken 3 at a time.

$$_{15}P_3 = \frac{15!}{(15-3)!} = \frac{15!}{12!} = \frac{15 \cdot 14 \cdot 13 \cdot \cancel{12 \cdots 1}}{\cancel{12 \cdots 1}} = 15 \cdot 14 \cdot 13 = 2730.$$

2,730 ways

Check Point 3 Solutions_Page 164

① Seven students are in the cafeteria to have lunch together. In how many different ways can they line up?

② In how many ways can a president, a treasurer, and a secretary be chosen from among 10 candidates?

③ In how many different ways can four people sit in a seven-seat minivan?

03 Distinguishable Permutations

In this part of the section, we will consider a special case of permutations. The number of permutations of the letter A, B, C, D, E would be $5!=120$ because all the letters are different so that each permutation of letters would be all different. Suppose, however, we are asked to find the number of permutations of the letter "A, B, B, B, C". There are 5! permutations again, but many of them are same permutations as follows.

$AB_1B_2B_3C,\quad B_1AB_2B_3C,\quad B_1B_2AB_3C\ \cdots$
$AB_1B_3B_2C,\quad B_1AB_3B_2C,\quad B_1B_3AB_2C\ \cdots$
$AB_2B_1B_3C,\quad B_2AB_1B_3C,\quad B_2B_1AB_3C\ \cdots$
$AB_2B_3B_1C,\quad B_2AB_3B_1C,\quad B_2B_3AB_1C\ \cdots$
$AB_3B_1B_2C,\quad B_3AB_1B_2C,\quad B_3B_1AB_2C\ \cdots$
$AB_3B_2B_1C,\quad B_3AB_2B_1C,\quad B_3B_2AB_1C\ \cdots$

As we can see, each permutation has 3! identical permutations. So, actual number of permutations would be $\dfrac{5!}{3!}=\dfrac{5\cdot 4\cdot 3\cdot 2\cdot 1}{3\cdot 2\cdot 1}=5\cdot 4=20$.

Example 4

In how many distinguishable ways can the letters PINEAPPLE be arranged?

Solution

This word has 9 letters, but there are repeating letters: three P's and two E's.
So, the number of distinguishable ways to arrange these letters would be

$\dfrac{9!}{3!\cdot 2!}=\dfrac{9\cdot 8\cdot 7\cdots 1}{3\cdot 2\cdot 1\cdot 2\cdot 1}=30240$ ways.

30,240 ways

Check Point 4

Solutions_Page 165

In how many distinguishable ways can the following letters be arranged?

① CALCULUS   ② MISSISSIPPI

04 Combination

We just studied about the permutations of n objects, taken r at a time. In such cases, the order was important. However, a combination is a way of just selecting several things out of a larger group, where order does not matter. Assume there are four letters A, B, C, D, and three letters are selected.

1. If order matters, we have 24 permutations as follows.
   ABC, ABD, ACD, BCD
   ACB, ADB, ADC, BDC
   BAC, BAD, CAD, CBD
   BCA, BDA, CDA, CDB
   CAB, DAB, DAC, DBC
   CBA, DBA, DCA, DCB
    3!   3!   3!   3!

2. If order does not matter, we only have 4 combinations as follows.
   ABC, ABD, ACD, BCD

As we can observe, each column(3! permutations) is counted as 1 combination. So, the number of combinations of 4 objects taken 3 at a time is $\dfrac{_4P_3}{3!}=\dfrac{24}{6}=4$.
Here is the formula for combinations.

Combination

> The number of combinations of n objects, taken r at a time is
> $$_nC_r=\dfrac{_nP_r}{r!}=\dfrac{n!}{r!(n-r)!}$$
> Note:
> 1. $_nC_0=1,\ _nC_n=1,\ _nC_1=n$
> 2. $_nC_r={_nC_{n-r}}$

Proof

$$_nC_r = \frac{_nP_r}{r!} = \frac{\frac{n!}{(n-r)!}}{r!} = \frac{n!}{r!(n-r)!}$$

Note:

1. $_nC_0 = \frac{n!}{0!(n-0)!} = \frac{n!}{1 \cdot n!} = 1$; $\quad _nC_n = \frac{n!}{n!(n-n)!} = \frac{n!}{n!0!} = \frac{n!}{n! \cdot 1} = 1$

   $_nC_1 = \frac{n!}{1!(n-1)!} = \frac{n \cdot \cancel{(n-1) \cdot (n-2) \cdots 1}}{\cancel{(n-1) \cdot (n-2) \cdots 1}} = n$

2. $_nC_r = \frac{n!}{r!(n-r)!}$ and $_nC_{n-r} = \frac{n!}{(n-r)!(n-(n-r))!} = \frac{n!}{(n-r)!r!}$.

   Therefore, $_nC_r = {_nC_{n-r}}$.

Example 5

Evaluate $_8C_3$.

Solution

$_nC_r = \frac{n!}{r!(n-r)!}$, $\quad _8C_3 = \frac{8!}{3!(8-3)!} = \frac{8!}{3!5!} = \frac{8 \cdot 7 \cdot 6 \cdot \cancel{5 \cdots 1}}{3 \cdot 2 \cdot 1 \cdot \cancel{5 \cdots 1}} = 56$

$_8C_3 = 56$

Check Point 5

Evaluate.

① $_{12}C_2$

② $_9C_6$

Example 6

There are 7 girls and 8 boys in UT coed indoor soccer team.
① How many different teams of 5 can be formed?
② How many different teams of 5 can be formed if each person has a different position?
③ How many different teams of 2 girls and 3 boys can be formed?

Solution

① The order in which the team members are selected is not important. So, the selection is a combination of 5 people out of 15 people.

$$_{15}C_5 = \frac{15!}{5!(15-5)!} = \frac{15 \cdot 14 \cdot 13 \cdot 12 \cdot 11 \cdot \cancel{10 \cdots 1}}{5 \cdot 4 \cdot 3 \cdot 2 \cdot 1 \cdot \cancel{10 \cdots 1}} = 3003.$$

3,003 teams

② Since each member has a different position, the order is important in this case.

$$_{15}P_5 = \frac{15!}{(15-5)!} = \frac{15 \cdot 14 \cdot 13 \cdot 12 \cdot 11 \cdot \cancel{10 \cdots 1}}{\cancel{10 \cdots 1}} = 360360.$$

360,360 teams

③ Again, the order is not important in this case. Knowing that the events are independent, the number of combinations would be

$$\underbrace{_7C_2}_{\text{2 girls}} \cdot \underbrace{_8C_3}_{\text{3 boys}} = \frac{7!}{2!(7-2)!} \cdot \frac{8!}{3!(8-3)!} = \frac{7 \cdot 6 \cdot \cancel{5 \cdots 1}}{2 \cdot 1 \cdot \cancel{5 \cdots 1}} \cdot \frac{8 \cdot 7 \cdot 6 \cdot \cancel{5 \cdots 1}}{3 \cdot 2 \cdot 1 \cdot \cancel{5 \cdots 1}} = 1176.$$

1,176 teams

Check Point 6

Solutions_Page 165

① Suppose you have a survey with a total of 10 questions and you can only pick 7 of them to answer. In how many different ways can you pick those questions to answer?
② A five-member committee is to be formed having 2 professors and 3 engineers. How many different committees are possible if there are 6 professors and 12 engineers?

Review Exercise

01 Find n in the following.

(1) $7 \cdot {}_nP_3 = 6 \cdot {}_{n+1}P_3$

(2) ${}_nC_{n-2} = 10$

(3) $4 \cdot {}_nC_2 = {}_{n+2}C_3$

(4) ${}_nP_4 = 30 \cdot {}_nC_5$

02 A customer can choose one of three kinds of cheeses, one of four kinds of breads, and one of two kinds of meats for a sandwich. Determine the possible number of sandwiches.

03

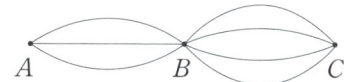

In Figure above, how many different routes are there from A to C through B?

04 Telephone numbers in Houston, TX currently have 10 digits. The first three are the area code and the next seven are the local telephone number. If their area code is either 281 or 832 and the first digit of the telephone number is NOT zero, how many different telephone numbers are possible in Houston, TX?

Review Exercise

05 How many four-digit numbers can be formed if
(1) There is no restriction?

(2) No digit can be repeated?

06 There are 25 seniors in Clear Lake high school and they want to select 3 board members, President, Vice-President, and Secretary. In how many different ways can these positions be filled?

07 There are five people and only two of them can drive. Determine the number of different ways these 5 people can sit in a five-passenger car.

08 Assume a poker game starts with 7 cards picked from a deck of 52. How many different poker hands are possible?

09 Mr. Smith has 12 students in his leadership training class.
(1) In how many ways can Mr. Smith select 3 students as representatives?

(2) In how many ways can Mr. Smith select 1 leader and 2 followers?

10 An indoor soccer team is made up of 3 strikers, 6 midfielders, 5 defenders, and 2 goal-keepers. A team can start a game with only 1 striker, 3 mid-fielders, 2 defenders, and 1 goal-keeper. How many different line-ups are possible?

11 ABC Company manufactured 20 LCD monitors, but 4 of them are defective. If a customer buys 5 monitors, how many different scenarios are possible where he will have

(1) All good monitors?

(2) Exactly 4 good monitors?

(3) At least 3 good monitors?

12 We are selecting 3 out of 8 men and 2 out of 6 women, respectively. Determine the number of ways 5 selected people can line up.

13 Find the number of diagonals of an octagon.

14

How many triangles can be formed by connecting three points in Figure above?

4 Probability

Probability is discussed in detail at AP Statistics. In this section, we will only cover very basic probabilities here.

01 Probability of an Event

If E is an event in a finite sample space of S of equally likely outcomes, the probability of event E is defined as follows.

$$P(E) = \frac{\text{the number of outcomes in } E}{\text{the number of outcomes in } S},$$

where the possible results of the experiments are outcomes. A set of all possible outcomes of an experiment is the sample space, and any subset of a sample space is an event.

The probability has following properties.
1. $0 \leq P(E) \leq 1$ for every outcome E.
2. The sum of the probabilities of all outcomes in S is equal to 1.
3. If $P(E) = 0$, event E cannot occur, and E is called an impossible event.
4. If $P(E) = 1$, event E must occur, and E is called a certain event.

Example 1

① What is the probability of drawing a king from a standard deck of playing cards?
② What is the probability of two coins landing tails up when they are tossed?
③ What is the probability of rolling a sum of 9 on a single roll of two six-sided dice?

Solution

① Since there are 52 cards in a standard deck of playing cards and four of them are kings, the probability of drawing a king is $P = \dfrac{4}{52} = \dfrac{1}{13}$.

② There are four equally likely outcomes: {TT, TH, HT, HH}. So, the probability of landing two tails up is $P = \dfrac{1}{4}$.

③ There are thirty-six equally likely outcomes: $\begin{Bmatrix} (1, 1), (1, 2), (1, 3), \cdots, (1, 6) \\ (2, 1), (2, 2), \cdots, (2, 6) \\ \vdots \vdots   \vdots \\ (6, 1), (6, 2), \cdots, (6, 6) \end{Bmatrix}$. Of these, four of the sample space {(3, 6), (4, 5), (5, 4), (6, 3)} yield a sum of 9. So, the probability is $P = \dfrac{4}{36} = \dfrac{1}{9}$.

Check Point 1-1

Solutions_Page 168

One card is selected from a deck of 52 cards. Find the probability of selecting
① A black card.
② A face card.
③ A "9" card.
④ A card that is 9 or higher.

Check Point 1-2

Solutions_Page 168

When two six-sided dices are tossed, what is the probability of getting a sum of 4 or 5?

02 Multiplication Principle of Probability

If events A and B are independent, the probability that both A and B occur is
$P(A \text{ and } B) = P(A) \cdot P(B)$

Example 2

Find the probability of having both even numbers when a six-sided die is tossed twice.

Solution

The probability of having an even number on the first toss is $\frac{3}{6} = \frac{1}{2}$. The probability of having an even number on the second toss is also $\frac{3}{6} = \frac{1}{2}$. So, the probability of having both even numbers is $P = \frac{1}{2} \cdot \frac{1}{2} = \frac{1}{4}$.

Check Point 2

A blue box has 8 items, of which 3 are made in U.S., and a red box has 9 items, of which 5 are made in U.S. If one item is drawn at random from each box, what is the probability that both items are made in U.S.?

Example 3

Find the probability of drawing two white marbles, without replacement, out of a bag containing three black, four blue, and two white marbles.

Solution

Total number of marbles in the bag is 9. The probability of drawing a white marble on the first draw is $\frac{2}{9}$. Now we have 8 marbles in the bag. The probability of drawing a white marble on the second draw is $\frac{1}{8}$. So, the probability of drawing a white marble on both draws is
$P = \frac{2}{9} \cdot \frac{1}{8} = \frac{1}{36}$

Check Point 3

Solutions_Page 168

In a box, there are 3 black, 2 blue, 2 yellow, and 4 green marbles.
① Without replacement, what is the probability of picking a blue marble first and then a green marble?
② What is the probability of picking a blue marble first, after returning a marble to the box, picking a green marble next?

03 Probability of Union of Events

If events A and B are in the same sample space, the probability of A or B occurring is

$$P(A \cup B) = P(A) + P(B) - P(A \cap B)$$

✔ Note that $P(A \cap B) = 0$ if A and B are mutually exclusive.

Example 4

A six-sided die is rolled. What is the probability that the number is either an even or multiple of 3?

Solution

The probability of rolling an even number (event A) is $P(A) = \frac{3}{6} = \frac{1}{2}$. From six-sided die, multiples of 3 are 3 and 6. So, the probability of rolling a multiple of 3 (event B) is $P(B) = \frac{2}{6} = \frac{1}{3}$.

Since 6 is both an even number and a multiple of 3, $P(A \cap B) = \frac{1}{6}$. Finally, the probability that the number is either an even or multiple of 3 is

$$P(A \cup B) = P(A) + P(B) - P(A \cap B) = \frac{1}{2} + \frac{1}{3} - \frac{1}{6} = \frac{2}{3}.$$

Check Point 4

Solutions_Page 168

One card is selected from a deck of 52 cards. What is the probability that the card is either black or face card?

Review Exercise

01 A six−sided die is tossed. What is the probability that a prime number is rolled?

02 When two six−sided dices are tossed, what is the probability of getting a sum of at least 10?

03 Two marbles are drawn at random from a bag containing 2 blue, 1 black, and 4 brown marbles. Without replacement, what is the probability of drawing,

(1) One blue and one black marble?

(2) Both brown marbles?

(3) Both non−brown marbles?

Review Exercise

04 A drawer contains 4 pairs of blue socks, 5 pairs of black socks, and 3 pairs of red socks. If 3 pairs of socks are randomly taken from the drawer one after the other without replacement, what is the probability that all of them are black?

05 The probability that it will snow tomorrow and the day after tomorrow is 25% and 20%, respectively. What is the probability of snowing tomorrow, but not snowing the day after tomorrow?

06 There are 52 students in Healing International High School and 75% of them are U.S. citizens. If we select 4 students at random from Healing International High School, what is the probability that all 4 students are U.S. citizens?

07 A company has 17 employees, 10 men and 7 women, and plans to form a committee of 5 people. What is the probability that the committee will consist of 3 men and 2 women?

08 There are 5 blue and 4 green marbles. If we draw 5 marbles at random, what is the probability of choosing 3 blue and 2 green marbles?

09 Two days before the Pre−Calculus final exam, a class is given a list of 25 review problems, from which 15 will be on the final exam. Frank only knows how to solve 16 problems of the review questions. Find the probability that Frank will be able to solve

(1) All 15 problems on the final exam.

(2) Exactly 14 problems on the final exam.

(3) At least 14 problems on the final exam.

10 The probability of correctly solving a certain math question for John, Chris, and Jenny is 60%, 75%, and 40%, respectively. What is the probability of at least two people solving the question correctly?

Chapter Test

01 Find the 10th term of the sequence.

(1) $\frac{2}{3}, 1, \frac{4}{3}, \frac{5}{3}, \cdots$

(2) $1, 0.1, 0.01, 0.001, \cdots$

02 The third term of an arithmetic sequence is -2, and the eleventh term is $-\frac{1}{6}$. What is the first term of this sequence?

03 The third term of a geometric sequence is $\frac{1}{32}$, and the eighth term is -1. What is the first term of this sequence?

04 $$a_n = \frac{1 - 5a_{n-1}}{2}$$

The sequence is defined recursively as above. If the first term is 1, what is the fourth term of the sequence?

05 Find $\sum_{k=2}^{20} \frac{1}{4} \cdot \left(\frac{2}{3}\right)^{k-1}$.

06 If the sixth term of an arithmetic sequence is 28 and the nineteenth term is 119, what is the sum of the first 35 terms?

07 If the third term of a geometric sequence is $-\frac{3}{64}$ and the eighth term is 48, what is the sum of first 9 terms?

Chapter Test

08 Determine the number of terms n in each series.

(1) $-50-49-48-47-\cdots$; $S_n=0$

(2) $1+4+16+64+\cdots$; $S_n=341$

09 What is the sum of $20-5+\dfrac{5}{4}-\dfrac{5}{16}+\cdots$?

10 Find the values of x and y for which the sequence

(1) $8, x, y, 27$ is geometric.

(2) $-2, x, y, 3$ is arithmetic.

11 In 2019, the town has a population of 45,000. The regions oil business is thriving and the population is expected to increase by 3% annually. Find the population in 2029.

12 What is the average of the first 320 positive integers?

13 The auditorium has 11 chairs in the first row, 15 in the second, 19 in the third, and so on. How many rows are there in the auditorium if there are 980 chairs in the auditorium?

14 In how many ways can 8 people be divided into two groups, one with 3 people and the other with 5 people?

Chapter Test

15 In a group of 10 employees at a restaurant, 5 are to be assigned as servers, 3 are to be assigned as hosts, and 2 are to be assigned as cashiers. In how many ways can the assignment be made?

16 In a soccer league, each team competes exactly twice against every other team during the season. If a total of 90 games are scheduled for the season, how many teams are in that soccer league?

17 A security code is created by 2 different letters followed by 3 different digits. If the letters are chosen from A or B and the digits are chosen from 1, 2, 3, 4, or 5, how many different security codes of this type can be created?

18 Jenny placed an order for a tablet PC and a speaker from Amazon on Tuesday. The probability that Jenny will receive the tablet PC on Wednesday is 0.7, and independently, the probability that she will receive the speaker on Wednesday is 0.8. What is the probability that Jenny will receive at least one of these shipments on Wednesday?

19 A six-sided dice is rolled twice. What is the probability of getting a prime number on the first roll and an odd number on the second roll?

Solutions Manual

Solutions Manual

Chapter 1: Working with Polynomials

1. Law of Exponents

Check Point 1

① $a^5 \times a^7 = a^{5+7} = a^{12}$
② $a^3 \times b^4 \times a^5 \times b^2 = (a^3 \times a^5) \times (b^4 \times b^2)$
$\qquad = a^{3+5} \times b^{4+2} = a^8 b^6$
③ $2^3 \times 5^3 \times 5^4 \times 2^5 \times 5^2 = (2^3 \times 2^5) \times (5^3 \times 5^4 \times 5^2)$
$\qquad = 2^{3+5} \times 5^{3+4+2} = 2^8 5^9$
④ $a^4 \times b^2 \times a^x \times b^y = (a^4 \times a^x) + (b^2 \times b^y)$
$\qquad = a^{4+x} b^{2+y}$

Check Point 2

① $(a^3)^7 = a^{3 \times 7} = a^{21}$
② $(b^5)^3 \times (b^2)^4 = b^{3 \times 5} \times b^{2 \times 4} = b^{15} \times b^8 = b^{15+8} = b^{23}$
③ $((a^2)^3)^2 \times (b^4)^2 = a^{2 \times 3 \times 2} \times b^{4 \times 2} = a^{12} b^8$
④ $(a^2)^x \times a^x \times (b^3)^y = a^{2 \times x} \times a^x \times b^{3 \times y} = a^{2x} \times a^x \times b^{3y}$
$\qquad = a^{2x+x} \times b^{3y} = a^{3x} b^{3y}$

Check Point 3

① $a^6 \div a^3 = a^{6-3} = a^3$
② $a^7 \div (a^2)^2 = a^7 \div a^4 = a^{7-4} = a^3$
③ $(b^6)^2 \div (b^4)^3 = b^{12} \div b^{12} = 1$
④ $b^5 \div (b^2)^2 \div (b^3)^4 = b^5 \div b^4 \div b^{12} = b^{5-4} \div b^{12}$
$\qquad = b \div b^{12} = \dfrac{1}{b^{12-1}} = \dfrac{1}{b^{11}}$

Check Point 4

① $(2a^5)^3 = 2^3 \times (a^5)^3 = 8a^{15}$
② $(a^3 b^2)^4 = (a^3)^4 \times (b^2)^4 = a^{12} b^8$
③ $\left(-\dfrac{2x^2}{y}\right)^5 = \dfrac{(-2)^5 (x^2)^5}{y^5} = \dfrac{-32x^{10}}{y^5} = -\dfrac{32x^{10}}{y^5}$
④ $\left(\dfrac{xy^3}{3z^2}\right)^2 = \dfrac{x^2(y^3)^2}{3^2(z^2)^2} = \dfrac{x^2 y^6}{9z^4}$

Review Exercises

01

(1) $(x^4)^5 \times (y^3)^4 \times y^2 = x^{20} \times y^{12} \times y^2$
$\qquad = x^{20} \times y^{12+2} = x^{20} y^{14}$
(2) $a^4 \times (b^2)^5 \times (a^2)^3 \times (b^3)^2 = a^4 \times b^{10} \times a^6 \times b^6$
$\qquad = a^{4+6} \times b^{10+6} = a^{10} b^{16}$
(3) $(-3)^2 \times (x^3)^5 \times x^2 = 9 \times x^{15} \times x^2$
$\qquad = 9 \times x^{15+2} = 9x^{17}$
(4) $(-2)^3 \times a^6 \times (a^3)^4 = -8 \times a^6 \times a^{12}$
$\qquad = -8 \times a^{6+12} = -8a^{18}$
(5) $4^2 \times (x^2)^4 \times x^6 \times (y^4)^2 \times y^3$
$\qquad = 16 \times x^8 \times x^6 \times y^8 \times y^3$
$\qquad = 16 \times x^{8+6} \times y^{8+3} = 16 x^{14} y^{11}$
(6) $(a^4)^x \times (b^2)^{3y} \times (a^{2x})^3 \times (b^4)^2$
$\qquad = a^{4x} \times b^{6y} \times a^{6x} \times b^8$
$\qquad = a^{4x+6x} \times b^{6y+8} = a^{10x} b^{6y+8}$

02

(1) $(a^2)^3 \div a^4 = a^6 \div a^4 = a^{6-4} = a^2$
(2) $(x^4)^5 \div x^4 \div (x^5)^2 = x^{20} \div x^4 \div x^{10}$
$\qquad = x^{20-4} = x^{16} \div x^{10}$
$\qquad = x^{16-10} = x^6$
(3) $2^{10} \div 2^5 \div (2^2)^4 = 2^{10} \div 2^5 \div 2^8$
$\qquad = 2^{10-5} \div 2^8 = 2^5 \div 2^8$
$\qquad = \dfrac{1}{2^{8-5}} = \dfrac{1}{2^3} = \dfrac{1}{8}$
(4) $a^{25} \div (a^4)^2 \div (a^3)^5 = a^{25} \div a^8 \div a^{15}$
$\qquad = a^{25-8} \div a^{15} = a^{17} \div a^{15}$
$\qquad = a^{17-15} = a^2$
(5) $(x^6)^5 \div (x^4)^4 \div (x^2)^6 = x^{30} \div x^{16} \div x^{12}$
$\qquad = x^{30-16} \div x^{12} = x^{14} \div x^{12}$

$$= x^{14-12} = x^2$$

(6) $a^{5x} \div a^x \div (a^{3x})^2 = a^{5x} \div a^x \div a^{6x}$
$$= a^{5x-x} \div a^{6x} = a^{4x} \div a^{6x}$$
$$= \frac{1}{a^{6x-4x}} = \frac{1}{a^{2x}}$$

03

(1) $(x^2y)^5 = (x^2)^5 \times (y)^5 = x^{10}y^5$

(2) $(-2x^6y^3)^2 = (-2)^2 \times (x^6)^2 \times (y^3)^2 = 4x^{12}y^6$

(3) $(3x^4y^5z^2)^3 = 3^3 \times (x^4)^3 \times (y^5)^3 \times (z^2)^3$
$$= 27x^{12}y^{15}z^6$$

(4) $\left(\dfrac{2a}{b^3}\right)^4 = \dfrac{2^4 a^4}{(b^3)^4} = \dfrac{16a^4}{b^{12}}$

(5) $\left(-\dfrac{3a^3c}{b^5}\right)^3 = \dfrac{(-3)^3(a^3)^3 c^3}{(b^5)^3} = -\dfrac{27a^9c^3}{b^{15}}$

(6) $\left(\dfrac{c^3}{ab^4}\right)^{4x} = \dfrac{(c^3)^{4x}}{a^{4x}(b^4)^{4x}} = \dfrac{c^{12x}}{a^{4x}b^{16x}}$

04

(1) $x^5 \times (y^{2b})^5 \times (x^a)^3 = x^{17}y^{20}$
$$x^5 \times y^{10b} \times x^{3a} = x^{17}y^{20}$$
$$x^{5+3a}y^{10b} = x^{17}y^{20}$$

Therefore,
$5+3a=17$ and $10b=20$
$a=4$ and $b=2$

(2) $\left(\dfrac{2x^{2a}}{y^{3b+1}}\right)^3 = \dfrac{8x^{12}}{y^{12}}$, $\dfrac{2^3(x^{2a})^3}{(y^{3b+1})^3} = \dfrac{8x^{12}}{y^{12}}$
$$\dfrac{8x^{6a}}{y^{9b+3}} = \dfrac{8x^{12}}{y^{12}}$$

Therefore,
$6a=12$ and $9b+3=12$
$a=2$ and $b=1$

(3) $(x^5)^{2a} \times (y^3)^{2b} \times y^{2b} = x^{10}y^{24}$
$$x^{10a} \times y^{6b} \times y^{2b} = x^{10}y^{24}$$
$$x^{10a}y^{6b+2b} = x^{10}y^{24}$$
$$x^{10a}y^{8b} = x^{10}y^{24}$$

Therefore,
$10a=10$ and $8b=24$
$a=1$ and $b=3$

(4) $\left(-\dfrac{3y^{b+1}}{x^{2a-1}}\right)^3 = -\dfrac{27y^{12}}{x^9}$

$\dfrac{(-3)^3(y^{b+1})^3}{(x^{2a-1})^3} = -\dfrac{27y^{12}}{x^9}$, $-\dfrac{27y^{3b+3}}{x^{6a-3}} = -\dfrac{27y^{12}}{x^9}$

Therefore,
$3b+3=12$ and $6a-3=9$
$b=3$ and $a=2$

05

(1) $2^x \times 16 = 4^x$
$16=2^4$ and $4^x=(2^2)^x=2^{2x}$
Therefore,
$2^x \times 2^4 = 2^{2x}$, $2^{x+4}=2^{2x}$
$x+4=2x$, $x=4$

(2) $27^4 \div 9^x = 9$
$27^4=(3^3)^4=3^{12}$, $9^x=(3^2)^x=3^{2x}$, and $9=3^2$
Therefore,
$3^{12} \div 3^{2x} = 3^2$, $3^{12-2x}=3^2$
$12-2x=2$, $x=5$

(3) $9^x \times (3^x)^4 = 27^{x-1}$
$9^x=(3^2)^x=3^{2x}$, $(3^x)^4=3^{4x}$, and
$27^{x-1}=(3^3)^{x-1}=3^{3x-3}$
Therefore,
$3^{2x} \times 3^{4x} = 3^{3x-3}$, $3^{2x+4x}=3^{3x-3}$
$3^{6x}=3^{3x-3}$, $6x=3x-3$
$3x=-3$, $x=-1$

(4) $32 \div 4^{x+1} \div 8 = \dfrac{1}{2}$
$32=2^5$, $4^{x+1}=(2^2)^{x+1}=2^{2x+2}$, $8=2^3$, and $\dfrac{1}{2}=2^{-1}$
Therefore,
$2^5 \div 2^{2x+2} \div 2^3 = 2^{-1}$, $2^{5-(2x+2)} \div 2^3 = 2^{-1}$
$2^{3-2x} \div 2^3 = 2^{-1}$, $2^{3-2x-3}=2^{-1}$
$2^{-2x}=2^{-1}$, $-2x=-1$, $x=\dfrac{1}{2}$

06

(1) $64=2^6=(2^3)^2=k^2$
(2) $2^{12}=(2^3)^4=k^4$
(3) $4^9=(2^2)^9=2^{18}=(2^3)^6=k^6$
(4) $8^5=(2^3)^5=k^5$

07

(1) Since 5^2 is added 5 times,
$5^2+5^2+5^2+5^2+5^2=5\times 5^2=5^3$

(2) Since 7^4 is added 7 times,
$7^4+7^4+7^4+7^4+7^4+7^4+7^4=7\times 7^4=7^5$

08

$m=3^{n+1}=3^n\times 3,\ 3^n=\dfrac{m}{3}$

$9^{n+2}=(3^2)^{n+2}=3^{2n+4}=3^{2n}\times 3^4$

$=(3^n)^2\times 3^4=\left(\dfrac{m}{3}\right)^2\times 3^4$

$=\dfrac{m^2}{3^2}\times 3^4=9m^2$

09

$a=2^{b-1}=\dfrac{2^b}{2},\ 2^b=2a$

$4^{2b}=(2^2)^{2b}=2^{4b}$
$=(2^b)^4=(2a)^4=16a^4$

10

$2^{x+2}+2^x=40$

$2^x\times 2^2+2^x=40,\ 2^x(2^2+1)=40$

$2^x\times 5=40,\ 2^x=8$

$2^x=2^3,\ x=3$

11

$m=2^{a+2}=2^a\times 2^2=2^a\times 4,\ 2^a=\dfrac{m}{4}$

$n=3^{1-a}=\dfrac{3}{3^a},\ 3^a=\dfrac{3}{n}$

$72^a=(2^3\times 3^2)^a=2^{3a}\times 3^{2a}=(2^a)^3\times (3^a)^2$

$=\left(\dfrac{m}{4}\right)^3\times \left(\dfrac{3}{n}\right)^2=\dfrac{m^3}{64}\times \dfrac{9}{n^2}=\dfrac{9m^3}{64n^2}$

2. Calculating Monomials

Check Point 1

① $2x^3\times 4x^6=(2\times 4)\times (x^3\times x^6)=8x^9$

② $-2xy^2\times 5x^2y^3=(-2\times 5)\times (xy^2\times x^2y^3)$
$=-10x^3y^5$

③ $(-2a^3b^5)\times \dfrac{1}{2}ab^2=\left(-2\times \dfrac{1}{2}\right)\times (a^3b^5\times ab^2)$
$=-a^4b^7$

④ $(-3a^2b^3)^3\times (2a^3b)^2=(-27a^6b^9)\times 4a^6b^2$
$=(-27\times 4)\times (a^6b^9\times a^6b^2)$
$=-108a^{12}b^{11}$

Check Point2

① $8x^5\div 6x^3=8x^5\times \dfrac{1}{6x^3}=\left(8\times \dfrac{1}{6}\right)\times \left(x^5\times \dfrac{1}{x^3}\right)$
$=\dfrac{4}{3}x^2$

② $(2a^2)^3\div 8a^6b^2=8a^6\div 8a^6b^2=8a^6\times \dfrac{1}{8a^6b^2}$
$=\left(8\times \dfrac{1}{8}\right)\times \left(a^6\times \dfrac{1}{a^6b^2}\right)$
$=1\times \dfrac{1}{b^2}=\dfrac{1}{b^2}$

③ $\dfrac{2}{3}x^3y^5\div (2x^2y^2)^2=\dfrac{2x^3y^5}{3}\div 4x^4y^4$
$=\dfrac{2x^3y^5}{3}\times \dfrac{1}{4x^4y^4}$
$=\left(\dfrac{2}{3}\times \dfrac{1}{4}\right)\times \left(x^3y^5\times \dfrac{1}{x^4y^4}\right)$
$=\dfrac{1}{6}\times \dfrac{y}{x}=\dfrac{y}{6x}$

④ $\left(-\dfrac{b^2}{2a}\right)^5\div \dfrac{4b^{10}}{a^2}\div \dfrac{1}{2b^2}=-\dfrac{b^{10}}{32a^5}\div \dfrac{4b^{10}}{a^2}\div \dfrac{1}{2b^2}$
$=-\dfrac{b^{10}}{32a^5}\times \dfrac{a^2}{4b^{10}}\times 2b^2$
$=\left(-\dfrac{1}{32}\times \dfrac{1}{4}\times 2\right)\times \left(\dfrac{b^{10}}{a^5}\times \dfrac{a^2}{b^{10}}\times b^2\right)$
$=-\dfrac{1}{64}\times \dfrac{b^2}{a^3}=-\dfrac{b^2}{64a^3}$

Check Point3

① $5y^2 \times 2x^4y \div (x^3y)^2 = 5y^2 \times 2x^4y \div x^6y^2$
$= 5y^2 \times 2x^4y \times \dfrac{1}{x^6y^2}$
$= (5 \times 2) \times \left(y^2 \times x^4y \times \dfrac{1}{x^6y^2}\right)$
$= 10 \times \dfrac{y}{x^2} = \dfrac{10y}{x^2}$

② $2x^3y \div (3xy^3)^2 \times 6y^5 = 2x^3y \div 9x^2y^6 \times 6y^5$
$= 2x^3y \times \dfrac{1}{9x^2y^6} \times 6y^5$
$= \left(2 \times \dfrac{1}{9} \times 6\right) \times \left(x^3y \times \dfrac{1}{x^2y^6} \times y^5\right)$
$= \dfrac{4}{3} \times x = \dfrac{4x}{3}$

③ $(-2ab)^3 \times \left(\dfrac{3a}{b^2}\right)^2 \div \dfrac{4a^3}{3b^5} = -8a^3b^3 \times \dfrac{9a^2}{b^4} \div \dfrac{4a^3}{3b^5}$
$= -8a^3b^3 \times \dfrac{9a^2}{b^4} \times \dfrac{3b^5}{4a^3}$
$= \left(-8 \times 9 \times \dfrac{3}{4}\right) \times \left(a^3b^3 \times \dfrac{a^2}{b^4} \times \dfrac{b^5}{a^3}\right)$
$= -54 \times a^2b^4 = -54a^2b^4$

④ $8a^2 \div (-3a^3b)^2 \times \left(-\dfrac{3}{2}b^2\right)^3$
$= 8a^2 \div 9a^6b^2 \times \left(-\dfrac{27}{8}b^6\right)$
$= 8a^2 \times \dfrac{1}{9a^6b^2} \times \left(-\dfrac{27}{8}b^6\right)$
$= \left(8 \times \dfrac{1}{9} \times \left(-\dfrac{27}{8}\right)\right) \times \left(a^2 \times \dfrac{1}{a^6b^2} \times b^6\right)$
$= -3 \times \dfrac{b^4}{a^4} = -\dfrac{3b^4}{a^4}$

Review Exercises

01

(1) $2x^3y \times 5x^2y^5 = (2 \times 5) \times (x^3y \times x^2y^5) = 10x^5y^6$
(2) $ab^3 \times a^2b^4c^3 = a^3b^7c^3$
(3) $4x^2 \times 2xy = (4 \times 2) \times (x^2 \times xy) = 8x^3y$
(4) $(2a^2)^2 \times 5a^2b^4 = 4a^4 \times 5a^2b^4$
$= (4 \times 5) \times (a^4 \times a^2b^4) = 20a^6b^4$
(5) $(4x^3)^2 \times 3x^3y^2 = 16x^6 \times 3x^3y^2$
$= (16 \times 3) \times (x^6 \times x^3y^2) = 48x^9y^2$
(6) $(-3x^4y)^2 \times (2x^2y^3)^3 = 9x^8y^2 \times 8x^6y^9$
$= (9 \times 8) \times (x^8y^2 \times x^6y^9)$
$= 72x^{14}y^{11}$

02

(1) $(a^2b)^3 \times ab^4 \times (a^3)^5 = a^6b^3 \times ab^4 \times a^{15} = a^{22}b^7$
(2) $3ab^2 \times (2a^4)^2 \times (3a^3b)^2 = 3ab^2 \times 4a^8 \times 9a^6b^2$
$= (3 \times 4 \times 9) \times (ab^2 \times a^8 \times a^6b^2)$
$= 108a^{15}b^4$
(3) $(-2a^2b)^3 \times (-ab^2)^4 \times \left(\dfrac{a^2b^3c}{2}\right)^2$
$= -8a^6b^3 \times a^4b^8 \times \dfrac{a^4b^6c^2}{4}$
$= \left(-8 \times \dfrac{1}{4}\right) \times (a^6b^3 \times a^4b^8 \times a^4b^6c^2) = -2a^{14}b^{17}c^2$
(4) $(a^2c)^2 \times \left(-\dfrac{b^3c^2}{4}\right)^3 \times (-4ab^2)^2$
$= a^4c^2 \times \left(-\dfrac{b^9c^6}{64}\right) \times 16a^2b^4$
$= \left(-\dfrac{1}{64} \times 16\right) \times (a^4c^2 \times b^9c^6 \times a^2b^4) = -\dfrac{a^6b^{13}c^8}{4}$

03

(1) $b^5 \div (ab^3)^2 = b^5 \div a^2b^6 = b^5 \times \dfrac{1}{a^2b^6} = \dfrac{1}{a^2b}$
(2) $2x^3y^2 \div 8x^5y = 2x^3y^2 \times \dfrac{1}{8x^5y}$
$= \left(2 \times \dfrac{1}{8}\right) \times \left(x^3y^2 \times \dfrac{1}{x^5y}\right) = \dfrac{y}{4x^2}$
(3) $(-2x^2y^3)^3 \div (4x^3y^4)^2 = -8x^6y^9 \div 16x^6y^8$
$= -8x^6y^9 \times \dfrac{1}{16x^6y^8}$
$= \left(-8 \times \dfrac{1}{16}\right) \times \left(x^6y^9 \times \dfrac{1}{x^6y^8}\right) = -\dfrac{y}{2}$
(4) $(x^2y^4)^2 \div (5x^3y)^2 = x^4y^8 \div 25x^6y^2$
$= x^4y^8 \times \dfrac{1}{25x^6y^2} = \dfrac{y^6}{25x^2}$

04

(1) $(-4x^3y)^3 \div (-2xy^2)^2 = -64x^9y^3 \div 4x^2y^4$
$= -64x^9y^3 \times \dfrac{1}{4x^2y^4}$
$= \left(-64 \times \dfrac{1}{4}\right) \times \left(x^9y^3 \times \dfrac{1}{x^2y^4}\right)$

Solutions Manual

$$= -\frac{16x^7}{y}$$

(2) $(4a^2bc^5)^3 \div (8b^3c^2)^2 = 64a^6b^3c^{15} \div 64b^6c^4$

$$= 64a^6b^3c^{15} \times \frac{1}{64b^6c^4}$$

$$= \left(64 \times \frac{1}{64}\right) \times \left(a^6b^3c^{15} \times \frac{1}{b^6c^4}\right)$$

$$= \frac{a^6c^{11}}{b^3}$$

(3) $(ab^2)^2 \div \left(-\frac{3b}{2a^3}\right) \div \left(-\frac{a^2}{3b^2}\right)^2$

$$= a^2b^4 \div \left(-\frac{3b}{2a^3}\right) \div \frac{a^4}{9b^4}$$

$$= a^2b^4 \times \left(-\frac{2a^3}{3b}\right) \times \frac{9b^4}{a^4}$$

$$= \left(-\frac{2}{3} \times 9\right) \times \left(a^2b^4 \times \frac{a^3}{b} \times \frac{b^4}{a^4}\right) = -6ab^7$$

(4) $(4ab^2)^3 \div (8a^2b^3)^2 \div 24ab^4$

$$= 64a^3b^6 \div 64a^4b^6 \div 24ab^4$$

$$= 64a^3b^6 \times \frac{1}{64a^4b^6} \times \frac{1}{24ab^4}$$

$$= \left(64 \times \frac{1}{64} \times \frac{1}{24}\right) \times \left(a^3b^6 \times \frac{1}{a^4b^6} \times \frac{1}{ab^4}\right)$$

$$= \frac{1}{24a^2b^4}$$

05

(1) $2^4 \times 5^3 \div (5^2)^3 \div (2^3)^4 = 2^4 \times 5^3 \div 5^6 \div 2^{12}$

$$= 2^4 \times 5^3 \times \frac{1}{5^6} \times \frac{1}{2^{12}}$$

$$= \frac{1}{2^8 \cdot 5^3}$$

(2) $(3^2)^2 \times 15^4 \div 15^5 \times 9^2$

$$= 3^4 \times (3 \times 5)^4 \div (3 \times 5)^5 \times (3^2)^2$$

$$= 3^4 \times 3^4 \times 5^4 \div (3^5 \times 5^5) \times 3^4$$

$$= 3^4 \times 3^4 \times 5^4 \times \frac{1}{3^5 \times 5^5} \times 3^4 = \frac{3^7}{5}$$

(3) $14^3 \div 49^2 \div (2^4)^2 \times (7^2)^2$

$$= (2 \times 7)^3 \div (7^2)^2 \div (2^4)^2 \times (7^2)^2$$

$$= 2^3 \times 7^3 \div 7^4 \div 2^8 \times 7^4$$

$$= 2^3 \times 7^3 \times \frac{1}{7^4} \times \frac{1}{2^8} \times 7^4 = \frac{7^3}{2^5}$$

(4) $2a^2b \times 6ab^4 \div 8a^3b^7 = 2a^2b \times 6ab^4 \times \frac{1}{8a^3b^7}$

$$= \left(2 \times 6 \times \frac{1}{8}\right) \times \left(a^2b \times ab^4 \times \frac{1}{a^3b^7}\right) = \frac{3}{2b^2}$$

(5) $3x^2y^3 \times 2x^2y \div 9xy^5 = 3x^2y^3 \times 2x^2y \times \frac{1}{9xy^5}$

$$= \left(3 \times 2 \times \frac{1}{9}\right) \times \left(x^2y^3 \times x^2y \times \frac{1}{9xy^5}\right) = \frac{2x^3}{3y}$$

(6) $(-5x^3)^2 \div \frac{5y^2}{4x^5} \times (2x^2y^3)^2 = 25x^6 \div \frac{5y^2}{4x^5} \times 4x^4y^6$

$$= 25x^6 \times \frac{4x^5}{5y^2} \times 4x^4y^6$$

$$= \left(25 \times \frac{4}{5} \times 4\right) \times \left(x^6 \times \frac{x^5}{y^2} \times x^4y^6\right) = 80x^{15}y^4$$

06

(1) $(2x^2y^4)^3 \div (4xy^2)^2 \times (5x^4y^3)^2$

$$= 8x^6y^{12} \div 16x^2y^4 \times 25x^8y^6$$

$$= 8x^6y^{12} \times \frac{1}{16x^2y^4} \times 25x^8y^6$$

$$= \left(8 \times \frac{1}{16} \times 25\right) \times \left(x^6y^{12} \times \frac{1}{x^2y^4} \times x^8y^6\right)$$

$$= \frac{25x^{12}y^{14}}{2}$$

(2) $4abc \div (ab^2)^2 \div 6a^4bc^2 \times (2a^3bc)^3$

$$= 4abc \div a^2b^4 \div 6a^4bc^2 \times 8a^9b^3c^3$$

$$= 4abc \times \frac{1}{a^2b^4} \times \frac{1}{6a^4bc^2} \times 8a^9b^3c^3$$

$$= \left(4 \times \frac{1}{6} \times 8\right) \times \left(abc \times \frac{1}{a^2b^4} \times \frac{1}{a^4bc^2} \times a^9b^3c^3\right)$$

$$= \frac{16a^4c^2}{3b}$$

(3) $3xy^3 \times 4x^3y^2 \div 8x^3y^5 \div 6x^5$

$$= 3xy^3 \times 4x^3y^2 \times \frac{1}{8x^3y^5} \times \frac{1}{6x^5}$$

$$= \left(3 \times 4 \times \frac{1}{8} \times \frac{1}{6}\right) \times \left(xy^3 \times x^3y^2 \times \frac{1}{x^3y^5} \times \frac{1}{x^5}\right)$$

$$= \frac{1}{4x^4}$$

(4) $12ab^2 \div (2b^3a^2)^3 \times 4a^3b^5 \div (6b^5)^2$

$$= 12ab^2 \div 8b^9a^6 \times 4a^3b^5 \div 36b^{10}$$

$$= 12ab^2 \times \frac{1}{8b^9a^6} \times 4a^3b^5 \times \frac{1}{36b^{10}}$$

$$= \left(12 \times \frac{1}{8} \times 4 \times \frac{1}{36}\right) \times \left(ab^2 \times \frac{1}{b^9a^6} \times a^3b^5 \times \frac{1}{b^{10}}\right)$$

$$= \frac{1}{6a^2b^{12}}$$

07

(1) $(-2x^2y)^4 \times \boxed{} \div (4x^3y^2)^3 = 8x^5y^4$

$16x^8y^4 \times \boxed{} \div 64x^9y^6 = 8x^5y^4$

$16x^8y^4 \times \boxed{} \times \dfrac{1}{64x^9y^6} = 8x^5y^4$

$\boxed{} \times \dfrac{1}{4xy^2} = 8x^5y^4$

$\boxed{} = 8x^5y^4 \times 4xy^2 = 32x^6y^6$

(2) $\boxed{} \div \dfrac{2a}{(b^2)^4} \times \dfrac{(a^3)^2}{6b^3} = \dfrac{a^4}{18b^5}$

$\boxed{} \div \dfrac{2a}{b^8} \times \dfrac{a^6}{6b^3} = \dfrac{a^4}{18b^5}$

$\boxed{} \times \dfrac{b^8}{2a} \times \dfrac{a^6}{6b^3} = \dfrac{a^4}{18b^5}$

$\boxed{} \times \dfrac{a^5b^5}{12} = \dfrac{a^4}{18b^5}$

$\boxed{} = \dfrac{a^4}{18b^5} \div \dfrac{a^5b^5}{12} = \dfrac{a^4}{18b^5} \times \dfrac{12}{a^5b^5} = \dfrac{2}{3ab^{10}}$

08

$x^2y^3 \times x^2y \div xy^5 = x^2y^3 \times x^2y \times \dfrac{1}{xy^5} = \dfrac{x^3}{y}$

By substituting $x=2$ and $y=4$,

$\dfrac{x^3}{y} = \dfrac{2^3}{4} = \dfrac{8}{4} = 2$

09

Since $a=1$, substitute $a=1$ and then simplify the expression.

$abc \div (ab^2)^2 \div a^4bc^2 \times (a^3bc)^3$

$= (1)bc \div ((1)b^2)^2 \div (1)^4bc^2 \times ((1)^3bc)^3$

$= bc \div (b^2)^2 \div bc^2 \times (bc)^3$

$= bc \times \dfrac{1}{b^4} \times \dfrac{1}{bc^2} \times b^3c^3 = \dfrac{c^2}{b}$

By substituting $b=2$ and $c=4$,

$\dfrac{c^2}{b} = \dfrac{4^2}{2} = \dfrac{16}{2} = 8$

3. Calculating Polynomials: Addition and Subtraction

Check Point 1

① $x^2 - 3x^4 + 2 = -3x^4 + x^2 + 2$

② $3x^4 - 5x - 2x^3 + 1 = 3x^4 - 2x^3 - 5x + 1$

③ $10 - 2x - x^2 + 3x^3 = 3x^3 - x^2 - 2x + 10$

④ $2y + 2 + 2y^3 + y^4 = y^4 + 2y^3 + 2y + 2$

Check Point 2

① $(3x-4) - (7x-2) = 3x - 4 - 7x + 2$
$= (3x - 7x) + (-4+2) = -4x - 2$

② $(1 - 2x + x^2) + (4x^2 - 5x + 1)$
$= 1 - 2x + x^2 + 4x^2 - 5x + 1$
$= (x^2 + 4x^2) + (-2x - 5x) + (1+1)$
$= 5x^2 - 7x + 2$

③ $2(5a - 3b) + 3(1 - 4b + 3a)$
$= 10a - 6b + 3 - 12b + 9a$
$= (10a + 9a) + (-6b - 12b) + 3$
$= 19a - 18b + 3$

④ $3(2x + 4y - 5) - 2(3x - 5y + 4)$
$= 6x + 12y - 15 - 6x + 10y - 8$
$= (6x - 6x) + (12y + 10y) + (-15 - 8)$
$= 22y - 23$

Check Point 3

① $\dfrac{2-4x}{3} + \dfrac{2x-5}{2} = \dfrac{2-4x}{3} \cdot \dfrac{2}{2} + \dfrac{2x-5}{2} \cdot \dfrac{3}{3}$

$= \dfrac{2(2-4x) + 3(2x-5)}{6}$

$= \dfrac{4 - 8x + 6x - 15}{6} = \dfrac{-2x - 11}{6} = -\dfrac{2x+11}{6}$

② $\dfrac{3y-1}{2} + 3 - 4y = \dfrac{3y-1}{2} + (3 - 4y) \cdot \dfrac{2}{2}$

$= \dfrac{3y - 1 + 2(3 - 4y)}{2} = \dfrac{3y - 1 + 6 - 8y}{2}$

$= \dfrac{-5y + 5}{2} = -\dfrac{5y - 5}{2}$

③ $\dfrac{a-b}{4} - \dfrac{b-a}{2} = \dfrac{a-b}{4} - \dfrac{b-a}{2} \cdot \dfrac{2}{2}$

Solutions Manual

$= \dfrac{(a-b)-2(b-a)}{4} = \dfrac{a-b-2b+2a}{4} = \dfrac{3a-3b}{4}$

④ $\dfrac{2a-b+1}{3} - \dfrac{b-3a}{4} + 1$

$= \dfrac{2a-b+1}{3} \cdot \dfrac{4}{4} - \dfrac{b-3a}{4} \cdot \dfrac{3}{3} + 1 \cdot \dfrac{12}{12}$

$= \dfrac{4(2a-b+1) - 3(b-3a) + 12}{12}$

$= \dfrac{8a-4b+4-3b+9a+12}{12} = \dfrac{17a-7b+16}{12}$

Review Exercises

01

(1) $(2x-7)+(5-4x) = 2x-7+5-4x = -2x-2$

(2) $(1-2x+x^2)-(4x^2-5x+1)$
$= 1-2x+x^2-4x^2+5x-1 = -3x^2+3x$

(3) $(4x^2-2+5x)+2(3x^2+3x-7)$
$= 4x^2-2+5x+6x^2+6x-14$
$= 10x^2+11x-16$

(4) $(2a^3-3a^2-3a+5)+(4a^3-6a^2+5a-1)$
$= 2a^3-3a^2-3a+5+4a^3-6a^2+5a-1$
$= 6a^3-9a^2+2a+4$

(5) $6(2a^3-a^2+4)-3(4a^3-3a^2-4a+2)$
$= 12a^3-6a^2+24-12a^3+9a^2+12a-6$
$= 3a^2+12a+18$

(6) $(a+2b-5)+(1-2a+3b)$
$= a+2b-5+1-2a+3b = -a+5b-4$

(7) $2(3x-y+2)-3(3y+2x+1)$
$= 6x-2y+4-9y-6x-3 = -11y+1$

(8) $(4-y-5y^2+2x)-2\left(-\dfrac{1}{2}x+y^2-5y-1\right)$
$= 4-y-5y^2+2x+x-2y^2+10y+2$
$= -7y^2+3x+9y+6$

(9) $4(3a-b+1)-2(b+3)-\dfrac{1}{2}(4a-8)$
$= 12a-4b+4-2b-6-2a+4$
$= 10a-6b+2$

(10) $4(a^2-3a-2)+5(a^2-1)-9(a^2-a+2)$
$= 4a^2-12a-8+5a^2-5-9a^2+9a-18$
$= -3a-31$

02

(1) $\dfrac{3x-1}{2} + \dfrac{x+2}{3} = \dfrac{3x-1}{2} \cdot \dfrac{3}{3} + \dfrac{x+2}{3} \cdot \dfrac{2}{2}$

$= \dfrac{3(3x-1)+2(x+2)}{6} = \dfrac{9x-3+2x+4}{6}$

$= \dfrac{11x+1}{6}$

(2) $\dfrac{4x+5}{2} - \dfrac{x-1}{4} = \dfrac{4x+5}{2} \cdot \dfrac{2}{2} - \dfrac{x-1}{4}$

$= \dfrac{2(4x+5)-(x-1)}{4}$

$= \dfrac{8x+10-x+1}{4} = \dfrac{7x+11}{4}$

(3) $x+3-\dfrac{3(2-x)}{5} = (x+3) \cdot \dfrac{5}{5} - \dfrac{3(2-x)}{5}$

$= \dfrac{5(x+3)-3(2-x)}{5} = \dfrac{5x+15-6+3x}{5}$

$= \dfrac{8x+9}{5}$

(4) $\dfrac{x+1}{4} - \dfrac{2(3-x)}{3} + \dfrac{3x-2}{2}$

$= \dfrac{x+1}{4} \cdot \dfrac{3}{3} - \dfrac{2(3-x)}{3} \cdot \dfrac{4}{4} + \dfrac{3x-2}{2} \cdot \dfrac{6}{6}$

$= \dfrac{3(x+1)-8(3-x)+6(3x-2)}{12}$

$= \dfrac{3x+3-24+8x+18x-12}{12} = \dfrac{29x-33}{12}$

(5) $\dfrac{2(3x-2y)}{5} + \dfrac{x-y+3}{4}$

$= \dfrac{2(3x-2y)}{5} \cdot \dfrac{4}{4} + \dfrac{x-y+3}{4} \cdot \dfrac{5}{5}$

$= \dfrac{8(3x-2y)+5(x-y+3)}{20}$

$= \dfrac{24x-16y+5x-5y+15}{20} = \dfrac{29x-21y+15}{20}$

(6) $\dfrac{3(2a+b-1)}{2} + \dfrac{3b-a+1}{6}$

$= \dfrac{3(2a+b-1)}{2} \cdot \dfrac{3}{3} + \dfrac{3b-a+1}{6}$

$= \dfrac{9(2a+b-1)+(3b-a+1)}{6}$

$= \dfrac{18a+9b-9+3b-a+1}{6} = \dfrac{17a+12b-8}{6}$

03

(1) $\dfrac{x-y}{2} - \dfrac{y-z}{3} - \dfrac{z-x}{6}$

$= \dfrac{x-y}{2} \cdot \dfrac{3}{3} - \dfrac{y-z}{3} \cdot \dfrac{2}{2} - \dfrac{z-x}{6}$

$= \dfrac{3(x-y) - 2(y-z) - (z-x)}{6}$

$= \dfrac{3x-3y-2y+2z-z+x}{6} = \dfrac{4x-5y+z}{6}$

(2) $\dfrac{a+b+c}{6} - \dfrac{a+b-c}{4} + \dfrac{a-b-c}{8}$

$= \dfrac{a+b+c}{6} \cdot \dfrac{4}{4} - \dfrac{a+b-c}{4} \cdot \dfrac{6}{6} + \dfrac{a-b-c}{8} \cdot \dfrac{3}{3}$

$= \dfrac{4(a+b+c) - 6(a+b-c) + 3(a-b-c)}{24}$

$= \dfrac{4a+4b+4c-6a-6b+6c+3a-3b-3c}{24}$

$= \dfrac{a-5b+7c}{24}$

04

(1) $4(2x+y-3) + \boxed{} = 4x-3y$

$\boxed{} = (4x-3y) - 4(2x+y-3)$

$= 4x-3y-8x-4y+12$

$= -4x-7y+12$

(2) $2(3a^2+a+4) - 2(a^2-3a+1) - \boxed{} = a^2-3$

$\boxed{} = 2(3a^2+a+4) - 2(a^2-3a+1) - (a^2-3)$

$= 6a^2+2a+8-2a^2+6a-2-a^2+3$

$= 3a^2+8a+9$

(3) $\dfrac{3x-4y}{2} + \boxed{} = \dfrac{x+2y+8}{4}$

$\boxed{} = \dfrac{x+2y+8}{4} - \dfrac{3x-4y}{2}$

$= \dfrac{x+2y+8}{4} - \dfrac{3x-4y}{2} \cdot \dfrac{2}{2}$

$= \dfrac{(x+2y+8) - 2(3x-4y)}{4}$

$= \dfrac{x+2y+8-6x+8y}{4} = \dfrac{-5x+10y+8}{4}$

(4) $\dfrac{a+2b}{3} - \boxed{} - \dfrac{a-2b}{6} = \dfrac{a+b}{6}$

$\boxed{} = \dfrac{a+2b}{3} - \dfrac{a-2b}{6} - \dfrac{a+b}{6}$

$= \dfrac{a+2b}{3} \cdot \dfrac{2}{2} - \dfrac{a-2b}{6} - \dfrac{a+b}{6}$

$= \dfrac{2a+4b-(a-2b)-(a+b)}{6}$

$= \dfrac{2a+4b-a+2b-a-b}{6} = \dfrac{5b}{6}$

05

Simplify in order from ( )→{ }→[ ].

(1) $3a - [4b-5a-\{4b+2(3b+3a)\}]$

$= 3a - [4b-5a-\{4b+6b+6a\}]$

$= 3a - [4b-5a-\{6a+10b\}]$

$= 3a - [4b-5a-6a-10b] = 3a - [-11a-6b]$

$= 3a+11a+6b = 14a+6b$

(2) $4x - [2x^2+3x-2\{3x-(5x^2-x)+2\}]$

$= 4x - [2x^2+3x-2\{3x-5x^2+x+2\}]$

$= 4x - [2x^2+3x-2\{-5x^2+4x+2\}]$

$= 4x - [2x^2+3x+10x^2-8x-4]$

$= 4x - [12x^2-5x-4]$

$= 4x-12x^2+5x+4 = -12x^2+9x+4$

06

$3b - 2[4b-3\{b-2(5b-2a)-a\}+2a]$

$= 3b - 2[4b-3\{b-10b+4a-a\}+2a]$

$= 3b - 2[4b-3\{3a-9b\}+2a]$

$= 3b - 2[4b-9a+27b+2a]$

$= 3b - 2[-7a+31b]$

$= 3b+14a-62b = 14a-59b$

Since $14a-59b = ma+nb$, $m=14$, $n=-59$,

and $m+n = 14+(-59) = -45$

07

$3x + [x-\{2x-(4x-\boxed{})+y\}+3y]$

$= 3x + [x-\{2x-4x+\boxed{}+y\}+3y]$

$= 3x + [x-\{-2x+\boxed{}+y\}+3y]$

$= 3x + [x+2x-\boxed{}-y+3y]$

$= 3x + [3x-\boxed{}+2y]$

$= 3x+3x-\boxed{}+2y = 6x-\boxed{}+2y$

Since $6x-\boxed{}+2y = 7x+8y$,

$\boxed{} = 6x+2y-7x-8y = -x-6y$

Solutions Manual

08

(1) $A-(a^2-3a-2)=4a^2+5a-4$
$A=4a^2+5a-4+(a^2-3a-2)$
$=4a^2+5a-4+a^2-3a-2=5a^2+2a-6$

(2) If we simplify correctly, the expression is
$A+(a^2-3a-2)=5a^2+2a-6+a^2-3a-2$
$=6a^2-a-8$

09

$\dfrac{x-2y}{3}-\dfrac{3x+2y}{4}=\dfrac{x-2y}{3}\cdot\dfrac{4}{4}-\dfrac{3x+2y}{4}\cdot\dfrac{3}{3}$

$=\dfrac{4(x-2y)-3(3x+2y)}{12}$

$=\dfrac{4x-8y-9x-6y}{12}$

$=\dfrac{-5x-14y}{12}=-\dfrac{5}{12}x-\dfrac{14}{12}y$

Since $-\dfrac{5}{12}x-\dfrac{14}{12}y=ax+by$, $a=-\dfrac{5}{12}$ and $b=-\dfrac{14}{12}$ Therefore,

$a+b=-\dfrac{5}{12}+\left(-\dfrac{14}{12}\right)=-\dfrac{19}{12}$

4. Calculating Polynomials: Multiplication, Part 1

Check Point 1

① $2(4x+1)=(2\times4x)+(2\times1)=8x+2$

② $4x(2x^2-5x+3)$
$=(4x\times2x^2)+(4x\times-5x)+(4x\times3)$
$=8x^3-20x^2+12x$

③ $5(3a-b)+4(2b-3a)$
$=(5\times3a)+(5\times-b)+(4\times2b)+(4\times-3a)$
$=15a-5b+8b-12a=3a+3b$

④ $\left(2a-\dfrac{1}{2}\right)4b-6b\left(-4+\dfrac{a}{3}\right)$
$=(2a\times4b)+\left(-\dfrac{1}{2}\times4b\right)$
$\qquad+(-6b\times-4)+\left(-6b\times\dfrac{a}{3}\right)$
$=8ab-2b+24b-2ab=6ab+22b$

Check Point 2

① $(4a+1)(a-2)$
$=(4a\times a)+(4a\times-2)+(1\times a)+(1\times-2)$
$=4a^2-8a+a-2=4a^2-7a-2$

② $(3x-y)(x+2)$
$=(3x\times x)+(3x\times2)+(-y\times x)+(-y\times2)$
$=3x^2+6x-xy-2y$

③ $(2x+y)(4x-3y)$
$=(2x\times4x)+(2x\times-3y)+(y\times4x)+(y\times-3y)$
$=8x^2-6xy+4xy-3y^2=8x^2-2xy-3y^2$

④ $(a^2-2)(4a^2+1)$
$=(a^2\times4a^2)+(a^2\times1)+(-2\times4a^2)+(-2\times1)$
$=4a^4+a^2-8a^2-2=4a^4-7a^2-2$

Check Point 3

① $(x-3)(x^2-x+1)$
$=(x\times x^2)+(x\times-x)+(x\times1)$
$\qquad+(-3\times x^2)+(-3\times-x)+(-3\times1)$
$=x^3-x^2+x-3x^2+3x-3=x^3-4x^2+4x-3$

② $(2x-4y+1)(3x+y)$
$=(2x\times3x)+(2x\times y)+(-4y\times3x)$
$\qquad+(-4y\times y)+(1\times3x)+(1\times y)$

$= 6x^2 + 2xy - 12xy - 4y^2 + 3x + y$
$= 6x^2 - 4y^2 - 10xy + 3x + y$

③ $(2a^2 - ab + b^2)(a - b)$
$= (2a^2 \times a) + (2a^2 \times -b) + (-ab \times a)$
$\quad + (-ab \times -b) + (b^2 \times a) + (b^2 \times -b)$
$= 2a^3 - 2a^2b - a^2b + ab^2 + ab^2 - b^3$
$= 2a^3 - 3a^2b + 2ab^2 - b^3$

Check Point 4

① $(x+2)^2 = x^2 + 2(x)(2) + 2^2 = x^2 + 4x + 4$

② $(2x - 5y)^2 = (2x)^2 - 2(2x)(5y) + (5y)^2$
$\qquad = 4x^2 - 20xy + 25y^2$

③ $\left(\dfrac{1}{4} + 3b\right)^2 = \left(\dfrac{1}{4}\right)^2 + 2\left(\dfrac{1}{4}\right)(3b) + (3b)^2$
$\qquad = \dfrac{1}{16} + \dfrac{3b}{2} + 9b^2$

④ $\left(-a - \dfrac{2b}{3}\right)^2 = \left(a + \dfrac{2b}{3}\right)^2$
$\qquad = a^2 + 2(a)\left(\dfrac{2b}{3}\right) + \left(\dfrac{2b}{3}\right)^2$
$\qquad = a^2 + \dfrac{4ab}{3} + \dfrac{4b^2}{9}$

Check Point 5

① $(x - 2y)(x + 2y) = x^2 - (2y)^2 = x^2 - 4y^2$

② $(2x - 5y)(-2x - 5y) = -(2x - 5y)(2x + 5y)$
$\qquad = -((2x)^2 - (5y)^2)$
$\qquad = -(4x^2 - 25y^2) = 25y^2 - 4x^2$

③ $\left(\dfrac{3a}{4} - \dfrac{b}{3}\right)\left(\dfrac{3a}{4} + \dfrac{b}{3}\right) = \left(\dfrac{3a}{4}\right)^2 - \left(\dfrac{b}{3}\right)^2$
$\qquad = \dfrac{9a^2}{16} - \dfrac{b^2}{9}$

④ $(a - 3)(a + 3)(a^2 + 9) = (a^2 - 3^2)(a^2 + 9)$
$\qquad = (a^2 - 9)(a^2 + 9)$
$\qquad = (a^2)^2 - 9^2 = a^4 - 81$

Review Exercises

01

(1) $3x(x^2 - y) = 3x^3 - 3xy$

(2) $\dfrac{2x}{5}\left(25xy - \dfrac{25}{2}x^2\right) = 10x^2y - 5x^3$

(3) $(a + 4b^2)(-2a) = -2a^2 - 8ab^2$

(4) $-4a(3a - b + 3) = -12a^2 + 4ab - 12a$

(5) $2a^2(2a - a^2) = 4a^3 - 2a^4$

(6) $\dfrac{1}{3}(6x^2 - 9x + 1) - \dfrac{2x}{5}(10x - 15)$
$= 2x^2 - 3x + \dfrac{1}{3} - 4x^2 + 6x = -2x^2 + 3x + \dfrac{1}{3}$

(7) $-2(x^2 + 2x - 5) - 2x(x - 1)$
$= -2x^2 - 4x + 10 - 2x^2 + 2x = -4x^2 - 2x + 10$

(8) $5(x^2 - 1) + 3(x^2 + x - 1) + 4$
$= 5x^2 - 5 + 3x^2 + 3x - 3 + 4 = 8x^2 + 3x - 4$

02

(1) $(x - 1)(2x + 3) = 2x^2 + 3x - 2x - 3$
$\qquad = 2x^2 + x - 3$

(2) $(3x - 1)(2x - 4) = 6x^2 - 12x - 2x + 4$
$\qquad = 6x^2 - 14x + 4$

(3) $(-2y + 3)(y - 1) = -2y^2 + 2y + 3y - 3$
$\qquad = -2y^2 + 5y - 3$

(4) $(1 - y)(-1 - 3y) = -1 - 3y + y + 3y^2$
$\qquad = 3y^2 - 2y - 1$

(5) $(x - y)(2x + 3y) = 2x^2 + 3xy - 2xy - 3y^2$
$\qquad = 2x^2 + xy - 3y^2$

(6) $(a^2 - 2)(4a + 1) = 4a^3 + a^2 - 8a - 2$

(7) $(2a + a^2)\left(-5 + \dfrac{1}{2}a\right) = -10a + a^2 - 5a^2 + \dfrac{1}{2}a^3$
$\qquad = \dfrac{1}{2}a^3 - 4a^2 - 10a$

(8) $(2m^2 - mn)(n^2 + 2mn)$
$= 2m^2n^2 + 4m^3n - mn^3 - 2m^2n^2$
$= 4m^3n - mn^3$

(9) $(-a + b + 4)(3a + 2b)$
$= -3a^2 - 2ab + 3ab + 2b^2 + 12a + 8b$
$= -3a^2 + 12a + ab + 8b + 2b^2$

(10) $(x + 2y)(-2x - 1 + 3y)$
$= -2x^2 - x + 3xy - 4xy - 2y + 6y^2$
$= -2x^2 - x - xy - 2y + 6y^2$

03

(1) $(x + 2)^2 = x^2 + 2(2)x + 2^2 = x^2 + 4x + 4$

(2) $(2x - 1)^2 = (2x)^2 - 2(2x)(1) + 1^2$
$\qquad = 4x^2 - 4x + 1$

(3) $(x + 5y)^2 = x^2 + 2x(5y) + (5y)^2$
$\qquad = x^2 + 10xy + 25y^2$

(4) $\left(\dfrac{2x}{3}-4y\right)^2=\left(\dfrac{2x}{3}\right)^2-2\left(\dfrac{2x}{3}\right)(4y)+(4y)^2$

$=\dfrac{4x^2}{9}-\dfrac{16xy}{3}+16y^2$

(5) $(-3a+4b)^2=(3a-4b)^2$

$=(3a)^2-2(3a)(4b)+(4b)^2$

$=9a^2-24ab+16b^2$

(6) $\left(-\dfrac{2a}{3}-\dfrac{b}{2}\right)^2=\left(\dfrac{2a}{3}+\dfrac{b}{2}\right)^2$

$=\left(\dfrac{2a}{3}\right)^2+2\left(\dfrac{2a}{3}\right)\left(\dfrac{b}{2}\right)+\left(\dfrac{b}{2}\right)^2$

$=\dfrac{4a^2}{9}+\dfrac{2ab}{3}+\dfrac{b^2}{4}$

(7) $(x-3)(x+3)=x^2-3^2=x^2-9$

(8) $\left(x+\dfrac{1}{2}\right)\left(x-\dfrac{1}{2}\right)=x^2-\left(\dfrac{1}{2}\right)^2=x^2-\dfrac{1}{4}$

(9) $(2a-3b)(2a+3b)=(2a)^2-(3b)^2=4a^2-9b^2$

(10) $\left(\dfrac{2b}{3}-\dfrac{a}{3}\right)\left(\dfrac{2b}{3}+\dfrac{a}{3}\right)=\left(\dfrac{2b}{3}\right)^2-\left(\dfrac{a}{3}\right)^2$

$=\dfrac{4b^2-a^2}{9}$

04

(1) $(4x+\boxed{A})^2=16x^2+16x+\boxed{B}$

$16x^2+8Ax+A^2=16x^2+16x+B$

$8A=16,\ A=2$

$A^2=B,\ 2^2=B,\ B=4$

(2) $(\boxed{A}x-4)^2=9x^2-\boxed{B}x+16$

$A^2x^2-8Ax+16=9x^2-Bx+16$

$A^2=9,\ A=\pm 3$. But, since $A>0,\ A=3$.

$8A=B,\ 8(3)=B,\ B=24$

(3) $(4a^2+3)(\boxed{A}a^2-3)=16a^4-\boxed{B}$

$4Aa^4-12a^2+3Aa^2-9=16a^4-B$

$4Aa^4-(12-3A)a^2-9=16a^4-B$

$4A=16,\ A=4$

$B=9$

(4) $(2a-3)(2a+3)(4a^2+9)$

$=(\boxed{A}a^2-9)(4a^2+9)=\boxed{B}a^4-\boxed{C}$

$(2a-3)(2a+3)(4a^2+9)=(4a^2-3^2)(4a^2+9)$

$=(4a^2-9)(4a^2+9)=(4a^2)^2-9^2=\underline{16}a^4-\underline{81}$

So $A=4,\ B=16$ and $C=81$

05

(1) $(x-a)(2x+3)=2x^2+3x-2ax-3a$

$=2x^2+(3-2a)x-3a$

Since $2x^2+(3-2a)x-3a=2x^2+bx-12$,

$3a=12,\ a=4$

$3-2a=b,\ 3-2(4)=b,\ b=-5$

(2) $(x-3)(5x+a)=5x^2+ax-15x-3a$

$=5x^2+(a-15)x-3a$

Since $5x^2+(a-15)x-3a=5x^2-11x+b$,

$a-15=-11,\ a=4$

$-3a=b,\ -3(4)=b,\ b=-12$

06

$(2x+ay)(bx-5y)=2bx^2-10xy+abxy-5ay^2$

$=2bx^2+(-10+ab)xy-5ay^2$

Since

$2bx^2+(-10+ab)xy-5ay^2=cx^2-4xy-10y^2$,

$5a=10,\ a=2$

$-10+ab=-4,\ -10+(2)b=-4,\ b=3$

$2b=c,\ 2(3)=c,\ c=6$. So $a+b+c=2+3+6=11$

07

Expand only the part of the xy term.

(1) $(x-4y+3)(3x+y-2)$

$xy+(-4y)(3x)=xy-12xy=-11xy$

So the coefficient of the xy term is -11.

(2) $(4-2x+3y)(5-2y+2x)$

$(-2x)(-2y)+(3y)(2x)=4xy+6xy=10xy$

So the coefficient of the xy term is 10.

08

Expand only the part of the xy terms.

$(3x+2y-4)(ax-3y+b)$

$\Rightarrow(3x)(-3y)+(2y)(ax)$

$=-9xy+2axy=(-9+2a)xy$

Since the coefficient of the xy term is 8,

$-9+2a=8,\ a=\dfrac{17}{2}$

09

$\left(\dfrac{3x}{4}-\dfrac{5y}{2}\right)\left(\dfrac{3x}{4}+\dfrac{5y}{2}\right)=\left(\dfrac{3x}{4}\right)^2-\left(\dfrac{5y}{2}\right)^2$

$=\dfrac{9x^2}{16}-\dfrac{25y^2}{4}=\dfrac{9(32)}{16}-\dfrac{25(20)}{4}=-107$

10

(1) $(4-1)(4+1)(4^2+1)(4^4+1)$
$=(4^2-1)(4^2+1)(4^4+1)=((4^2)^2-1^2)(4^4+1)$
$=(4^4-1)(4^4+1)=(4^4)^2-1^2=4^8-1$

(2) $(2^3-1)(2^3+1)(2^6+1)(2^{12}+1)$
$=((2^3)^2-1^2)(2^6+1)(2^{12}+1)$
$=(2^6-1)(2^6+1)(2^{12}+1)=((2^6)^2-1^2)(2^{12}+1)$
$=(2^{12}-1)(2^{12}+1)=((2^{12})^2-1^2)=2^{24}-1$

5. Calculating Polynomials: Multiplication, Part 2

Check Point 1

① $(x+y-z)^2$
$=x^2+y^2+(-z)^2+2xy+2y(-z)+2(-z)x$
$=x^2+y^2+z^2+2xy-2yz-2xz$

② $(2a-3b-c)^2$
$=(2a)^2+(-3b)^2+(-c)^2$
$\quad+2(2a)(-3b)+2(-3b)(-c)+2(-c)(2a)$
$=4a^2+9b^2+c^2-12ab+6bc-4ac$

③ $(3a+2)^3=(3a)^3+3(3a)^2(2)+3(3a)(2)^2+2^3$
$=27a^3+54a^2+36a+8$

④ $\left(2b-\dfrac{1}{2}\right)^3$
$=(2b)^3-3(2b)^2\left(\dfrac{1}{2}\right)+3(2b)\left(\dfrac{1}{2}\right)^2-\left(\dfrac{1}{2}\right)^3$
$=8b^3-6b^2+\dfrac{3}{2}b-\dfrac{1}{8}$

Check Point 2

① $(2x-y+4)(2x-y-4)$ → Let $2x-y=A$
$=(A+4)(A-4)=A^2-4^2$
$=(2x-y)^2-16=4x^2-4xy+y^2-16$

② $(a+3b-2)(3b+a+1)$ → Let $a+3b=A$
$=(A-2)(A+1)=A^2-A-2$
$=(a+3b)^2-(a+3b)-2$
$=a^2+6ab+9b^2-a-3b-2$

③ $(a^2-2a-1)(a^2+a-1)$
$=(a^2-1-2a)(a^2-1+a)$ → Let $a^2-1=A$
$=(A-2a)(A+a)=A^2-aA-2a^2$
$=(a^2-1)^2-a(a^2-1)-2a^2$
$=a^4-2a^2+1-a^3+a-2a^2$
$=a^4-a^3-4a^2+a+1$

④ $(a-1)(a+6)(a+2)(a+3)$
$=\{(a-1)(a+6)\}\{(a+2)(a+3)\}$
$=(a^2+5a-6)(a^2+5a+6)$ → Let $a^2+5a=A$
$=(A-6)(A+6)=A^2-6^2$
$=(a^2+5a)^2-36=a^4+10a^3+25a^2-36$

Solutions Manual

Check Point 3

① $98^2=(100-2)^2=100^2-2(100\times 2)+2^2$
$=10{,}000-400+4=9{,}604$

② $9.8\times 10.2=(10-0.2)(10+0.2)$
$=10^2-0.2^2=100-0.04=99.96$

③ $101\times 103=(100+1)(100+3)$
$=100^2+300+100+3=10{,}403$

Check Point 4

① $x^2+y^2=(x-y)^2+2xy$
$=(-5)^2+2(3)=25+6=31$

② $(x+y)^2=(x-y)^2+4xy$
$=(-5)^2+4(3)=25+12=37$

③ $\dfrac{x}{y}+\dfrac{y}{x}=\dfrac{x}{y}\cdot\dfrac{x}{x}+\dfrac{y}{x}\cdot\dfrac{y}{y}=\dfrac{x^2+y^2}{xy}=\dfrac{31}{3}$

Review Exercises

01

(1) $(2x+y-1)^2=(2x)^2+y^2+(-1)^2+2(2x)y$
$+2y(-1)+2(2x)(-1)$
$=4x^2+y^2+1+4xy-2y-4x$
$=4x^2+4xy+y^2-4x-2y+1$

(2) $\left(2-x+\dfrac{1}{2x}\right)^2=2^2+(-x)^2+\left(\dfrac{1}{2x}\right)^2$
$+2(2)(-x)+2(-x)\left(\dfrac{1}{2x}\right)+2(2)\left(\dfrac{1}{2x}\right)$
$=4+x^2+\dfrac{1}{4x^2}-4x-1+\dfrac{2}{x}$
$=x^2-4x+\dfrac{1}{4x^2}+\dfrac{2}{x}+3$

(3) $\left(\dfrac{a}{4}-4b+2\right)^2=\left(\dfrac{a}{4}\right)^2+(-4b)^2+2^2$
$+2\left(\dfrac{a}{4}\right)(-4b)+2(-4b)(2)+2\left(\dfrac{a}{4}\right)(2)$
$=\dfrac{a^2}{16}+16b^2+4-2ab-16b+a$
$=\dfrac{a^2}{16}-2ab+16b^2+a-16b+4$

(4) $\left(3a-5-\dfrac{3}{5a}\right)^2=(3a)^2+(-5)^2+\left(-\dfrac{3}{5a}\right)^2$
$+2(3a)(-5)+2(-5)\left(-\dfrac{3}{5a}\right)+2(3a)\left(-\dfrac{3}{5a}\right)$

$=9a^2+25+\dfrac{9}{25a^2}-30a+\dfrac{6}{a}-\dfrac{18}{5}$

$=9a^2-30a+\dfrac{9}{25a^2}+\dfrac{6}{a}+\dfrac{107}{5}$

(5) $(x+2)^3=x^3+3x^2(2)+3x(2)^2+(2)^3$
$=x^3+6x^2+12x+8$

(6) $(2x-1)^3=(2x)^3-3(2x)^2(1)+3(2x)(1)^2-1^3$
$=8x^3-12x^2+6x-1$

(7) $\left(2ab+\dfrac{1}{2}\right)^3$
$=(2ab)^3+3(2ab)^2\left(\dfrac{1}{2}\right)+3(2ab)\left(\dfrac{1}{2}\right)^2+\left(\dfrac{1}{2}\right)^3$
$=8a^3b^3+6a^2b^2+\dfrac{3ab}{2}+\dfrac{1}{8}$

(8) $(3a^2-b)^3$
$=(3a^2)^3-3(3a^2)^2(b)+3(3a^2)(b)^2-(b)^3$
$=27a^6-27a^4b+9a^2b^2-b^3$

02

(1) $(a-b+1)(a-b-1)$ → Let $a-b=A$
$=(A+1)(A-1)=A^2-1^2$
$=(a-b)^2-1=a^2-2ab+b^2-1$

(2) $(a^2-a-2)(a^2-a+2)$ → Let $a^2-a=A$
$=(A-2)(A+2)=A^2-2^2$
$=(a^2-a)^2-4=a^4-2a^3+a^2-4$

(3) $\left(a+2-\dfrac{1}{2b}\right)\left(a-3-\dfrac{1}{2b}\right)$
$=\left(a-\dfrac{1}{2b}+2\right)\left(a-\dfrac{1}{2b}-3\right)$ → Let $a-\dfrac{1}{2b}=A$
$=(A+2)(A-3)=A^2-A-6$
$=\left(a-\dfrac{1}{2b}\right)^2-\left(a-\dfrac{1}{2b}\right)-6$
$=a^2-\dfrac{a}{b}+\dfrac{1}{4b^2}-a+\dfrac{1}{2b}-6$

(4) $(x+2y+3z)(x+y+3z)$
$=(x+3z+2y)(x+3z+y)$ → Let $x+3z=A$
$=(A+2y)(A+y)=A^2+3Ay+2y^2$
$=(x+3z)^2+3(x+3z)y+2y^2$
$=x^2+6xz+9z^2+3xy+9yz+2y^2$

(5) $(2x+1)(2x+1-4y)$ → Let $2x+1=A$
$=A(A-4y)=A^2-4Ay$
$=(2x+1)^2-4(2x+1)y$
$=4x^2+4x+1-8xy-4y$
$=4x^2-8xy+4x-4y+1$

(6) $(x^2+x+1)(2x^2+2x-2)$
$=2(x^2+x+1)(x^2+x-1)$ → Let $x^2+x=A$
$=2(A+1)(A-1)=2(A^2-1^2)$
$=2((x^2+x)^2-1)=2(x^4+2x^3+x^2-1)$
$=2x^4+4x^3+2x^2-2$

(7) $(a-b)^2(a+b)^2$
$=(a^2-2ab+b^2)(a^2+2ab+b^2)$
$\quad\quad\quad\quad\quad\quad$ → Let $a^2+b^2=A$
$=(A-2ab)(A+2ab)$
$=A^2-(2ab)^2=(a^2+b^2)^2-4a^2b^2$
$=a^4+2a^2b^2+b^4-4a^2b^2$
$=a^4-2a^2b^2+b^4$

(8) $(a-2b+2)(a+2)^2$ → Let $a+2=A$
$=(A-2b)A^2=A^3-2bA^2$
$=(a+2)^3-2b(a+2)^2$
$=a^3+6a^2+12a+8-2b(a^2+4a+4)$
$=a^3+6a^2+12a+8-2a^2b-8ab-8b$
$=a^3-2a^2b+6a^2-8ab+12a-8b+8$

03

(1) $10.2^2=(10+0.2)^2$
$\quad\quad=10^2+2(10)(0.2)+(0.2)^2$
$\quad\quad=100+4+0.04=104.04$

(2) $299^2=(300-1)^2$
$\quad\quad=300^2-2(300)(1)+1^2$
$\quad\quad=90000-600+1=89,401$

(3) $50.2\times49.8=(50+0.2)(50-0.2)$
$\quad\quad\quad\quad=50^2-0.2^2$
$\quad\quad\quad\quad=2500-0.04=2,499.96$

(4) $101^2\times99^2=(100+1)^2\times(100-1)^2$
$=(100^2+200+1)\times(100^2-200+1)$
$\quad\quad\quad\quad\quad$ → Let $100^2+1=A$
$=(A+200)\times(A-200)=A^2-200^2$
$=(100^2+1)^2-200^2$
$=100^4+2\cdot100^2+1-200^2$
$=100000000+20000+1-40000$
$=99,980,001$

04

(1) $a^2+b^2=(a+b)^2-2ab$
$\quad\quad=8^2-2(6)=64-12=52$

(2) $(a-b)^2=(a+b)^2-4ab$
$\quad\quad=8^2-4(6)=64-24=40$

(3) $\dfrac{3}{a}+\dfrac{3}{b}=\dfrac{3}{a}\cdot\dfrac{b}{b}+\dfrac{3}{b}\cdot\dfrac{a}{a}=\dfrac{3b+3a}{ab}$
$\quad\quad=\dfrac{3(b+a)}{ab}=\dfrac{24}{6}=4$

05

(1) $x^2+\dfrac{1}{x^2}=\left(x+\dfrac{1}{x}\right)^2-2=4^2-2=14$

(2) $\left(x-\dfrac{1}{x}\right)^2=\left(x+\dfrac{1}{x}\right)^2-4=4^2-4=12$

(3) $x^4+\dfrac{1}{x^4}=\left(x^2+\dfrac{1}{x^2}\right)^2-2=14^2-2=194$

06

(1) Since $(x+y)^2=x^2+2xy+y^2$,
$3^2=8+2xy$, $xy=\dfrac{1}{2}$

(2) $\dfrac{x}{y}+\dfrac{y}{x}=\dfrac{x^2+y^2}{xy}=\dfrac{8}{\frac{1}{2}}=16$

07

Let $A=2019$ and $B=2018$.
$2020\times2018-2019\times2017$
$=(A+1)(A-1)-(B+1)(B-1)$
$=A^2-1-(B^2-1)$
$=A^2-B^2=(A-B)(A+B)$
$=(2019-2018)(2019+2018)$
$=1\cdot4037=4037$

08

Expand only the part of the xy term and x^2 term.
$(3x-4y+2)^2$
$\Rightarrow(3x)^2=9x^2$, $2(3x)(-4y)=-24xy$
So, the sum of the coefficients is
$9+(-24)=-15$

Solutions Manual

09

$x^2 - 7x + 1 = 0$

→ Divide both sides by $x\,(x \neq 0)$

$(x^2 - 7x + 1 = 0) \cdot \dfrac{1}{x}$

$x - 7 + \dfrac{1}{x} = 0,\ x + \dfrac{1}{x} = 7$

$x^2 + \dfrac{1}{x^2} = \left(x + \dfrac{1}{x}\right)^2 - 2 = 7^2 - 2 = 47$

10

$2x^2 - x + 2 = 0$

→ Divide both sides by $2x\,(x \neq 0)$

$(2x^2 - x + 2 = 0) \cdot \dfrac{1}{2x}$

$x - \dfrac{1}{2} + \dfrac{1}{x} = 0,\ x + \dfrac{1}{x} = \dfrac{1}{2}$

$x^2 + 1 + \dfrac{1}{x^2} = \left(x + \dfrac{1}{x}\right)^2 - 2 + 1$

$\qquad = \left(\dfrac{1}{2}\right)^2 - 1 = -\dfrac{3}{4}$

Chapter 1 Test Level 1

01

(A) $2^6 + 2^6 + 2^6 + 2^6 = 4 \times 2^6 = 2^2 \times 2^6 = 2^8$

(B) $2^2 \times 2^2 \times 2^2 \times 2^2 = 2^{2+2+2+2} = 2^8$

(C) $(4^2)^2 = 4^4 = (2^2)^4 = 2^8$

(D) $\dfrac{8^4}{2^3 + 2^3} = \dfrac{(2^3)^4}{2 \times 2^3} = \dfrac{2^{12}}{2^4} = 2^8$

(E) $4^8 \div 8^2 = (2^2)^8 \div (2^3)^2 = 2^{16} \div 2^6 = 2^{10}$

The answer is (E)

02

$\dfrac{6^4 + 6^4 + 6^4 + 6^4 + 6^4 + 6^4}{6^4 \times 6^4} = \dfrac{6 \times 6^4}{6^8} = \dfrac{6^5}{6^8} = \dfrac{1}{6^3}$

03

$\left(-\dfrac{3x^{a+1}y^2}{z^{4b-2}}\right)^3 = \dfrac{(-3)^3 x^{3a+3} y^6}{z^{12b-6}} = \dfrac{cx^9 y^6}{z^6}$

$(-3)^3 = c,\ 3a + 3 = 9,\ 12b - 6 = 6$

$c = -27,\ a = 2,\ b = 1$

So, $a + b + c = 2 + 1 + (-27) = -24$

04

$\dfrac{27^4}{81^5} = \dfrac{(3^3)^4}{(3^4)^5} = \dfrac{3^{12}}{3^{20}} = \dfrac{1}{3^8} = \dfrac{1}{(3^4)^2} = \dfrac{1}{m^2}$

The answer is (C)

05

$n = 2^{x+1} = 2^x \times 2 = 2 \cdot 2^x,\ 2^x = \dfrac{n}{2}$

$16^{x+1} = 16^x \times 16 = 16(2^4)^x$

$\qquad = 16(2^x)^4 = 16\left(\dfrac{n}{2}\right)^4$

$\qquad = 16 \cdot \dfrac{n^4}{16} = n^4$

The answer is (A)

06

$$\frac{4^{3x+1} \times 8^2}{16^{x-5}} = 32^{x-3}, \quad \frac{(2^2)^{3x+1} \times (2^3)^2}{(2^4)^{x-5}} = (2^5)^{x-3}$$

$$\frac{2^{6x+2} \times 2^6}{2^{4x-20}} = 2^{5x-15}, \quad 2^{6x+2+6-(4x-20)} = 2^{5x-15}$$

$$6x+2+6-(4x-20) = 5x-15$$

$$2x+28 = 5x-15, \quad 43 = 3x, \quad x = \frac{43}{3}$$

07

$(8a^3b^2)^2 \times \boxed{} \div (-4b^3)^3 = 2a^4b$

$64a^6b^4 \times \boxed{} \div (-64b^9) = 2a^4b$

$64a^6b^4 \times \boxed{} \times \dfrac{1}{(-64b^9)} = 2a^4b$

$\boxed{} \times \dfrac{a^6}{(-b^5)} = 2a^4b$

$\boxed{} = 2a^4b \times \dfrac{(-b^5)}{a^6} = -\dfrac{2b^6}{a^2}$

The answer is (D)

08

$3A - (B+2C) + 4C$
$= 3A - B - 2C + 4C = 3A - B + 2C$
$= 3(x^2-2x+3) - (3x^2-2) + 2(2x^2+x)$
$= 3x^2 - 6x + 9 - 3x^2 + 2 + 4x^2 + 2x$
$= 4x^2 - 4x + 11 \Rightarrow a=4, \; b=-4, \; c=11$

09

$5 - 2\left[3x - 4y + \dfrac{1}{2}\{5y - (4x-y) - 6\}\right]$

$= 5 - 2\left[3x - 4y + \dfrac{1}{2}\{5y - 4x + y - 6\}\right]$

$= 5 - 2\left[3x - 4y + \dfrac{1}{2}\{-4x + 6y - 6\}\right]$

$= 5 - 2[3x - 4y - 2x + 3y - 3] = 5 - 2[x - y - 3]$

$= 5 - 2x + 2y + 6 = -2x + 2y + 11$

10

$(4x-3)(4x+3) - 4(2x-1)^2$
$= (4x)^2 - 3^2 - 4(4x^2 - 4x + 1)$
$= 16x^2 - 9 - 16x^2 + 16x - 4$
$= 16x - 13$

The answer is (B)

11

(A) $(x-1)^2 = x^2 - 2x + 1 \Rightarrow A = 2$

(B) $(3x+By)^2 = 9x^2 + 6Bxy + B^2y^2$
$\Rightarrow 6B = 12, \; B = 2$

(C) $\left(\dfrac{a}{2}+4\right)\left(\dfrac{a}{2}-4\right) = \left(\dfrac{a}{2}\right)^2 - 4^2 = \dfrac{a^2}{4} - 16$
$\Rightarrow C = 4$

(D) $(a-5)(2a+8) = 2a^2 + 8a - 10a - 40$
$= 2a^2 - 2a - 40 \Rightarrow D = 2$

(E) $(x-y)(x-y-4) \rightarrow$ Let $x-y = X$
$(X)(X-4) = X^2 - 4X$
$= (x-y)^2 - 4(x-y)$
$= x^2 - 2xy + y^2 - 4x + 4y$
$= x^2 - 2xy - 4x + y^2 + 4y \Rightarrow E = 2$

So the answer is (C)

12

Let $\boxed{} = A$.

$5y - 4[2y - 2\{5y - (3x+A-4) + 3x - 2\}]$
$= 5y - 4[2y - 2\{5y - 3x - A + 4 + 3x - 2\}]$
$= 5y - 4[2y - 2\{5y - A + 2\}]$
$= 5y - 4[2y - 10y + 2A - 4]$
$= 5y - 4[-8y + 2A - 4]$
$= 5y + 32y - 8A + 16 = 37y - 8A + 16$

So, $37y - 8A + 16 = x + 2y + 4$

$-8A = x - 35y - 12, \quad A = -\dfrac{x - 35y - 12}{8}$

13

$$\frac{2020 \times 2022 + 1}{2021} = \frac{(2021-1) \times (2021+1) + 1}{2021}$$
$$= \frac{2021^2 - 1^2 + 1}{2021} = \frac{2021^2}{2021} = 2021$$

14

$x^2 - 4x + 1 = 0$

→ Divide both sides by $x (x \neq 0)$

$(x^2 - 4x + 1 = 0) \cdot \frac{1}{x}$

$x - 4 + \frac{1}{x} = 0, \quad x + \frac{1}{x} = 4$

$x^2 + x + \frac{1}{x} + \frac{1}{x^2} = \left(x^2 + \frac{1}{x^2}\right) + \left(x + \frac{1}{x}\right)$
$= \left(x + \frac{1}{x}\right)^2 - 2 + \left(x + \frac{1}{x}\right)$
$= 4^2 - 2 + 4 = 18$

15

$(5-1)(5+1)(5^2+1)(5^4+1)(5^8+1)$
$= (5^2-1)(5^2+1)(5^4+1)(5^8+1)$
$= (5^4-1)(5^4+1)(5^8+1)$
$= (5^8-1)(5^8+1) = 5^{16} - 1$

Chapter 1 Test Level 2

01

$16^{x+3} = (2^4)^{x+3} = 2^{4x+12}$
$4^{3x+1} = (2^2)^{3x+1} = 2^{6x+2}$
$\frac{8^4}{2^{y-2}} = \frac{(2^3)^4}{2^{y-2}} = \frac{2^{12}}{2^{y-2}} = 2^{12-(y-2)} = 2^{-y+14}$

Since $2^{4x+12} = 2^{6x+2}$, $4x + 12 = 6x + 2$, $x = 5$
Also, since $2^{6x+2} = 2^{-y+14}$,
$6x + 2 = -y + 14, \quad 6(5) + 2 = -y + 14$
$32 = -y + 14, \quad y = -18$
So, $x + y = 5 + (-18) = -13$

02

$(4^x \times 5^y)^z = (2^{2x} \times 5^y)^z = 2^{2xz} \times 5^{yz} = 2^{48} \times 5^{36}$
$2xz = 48, \quad xz = 24$ and $yz = 36$
Since the greatest common factor of 24 and 36 is 12, z is 12. Therefore, $x = 3$, $y = 2$, $z = 12$, and $x + y + z = 3 + 2 + 12 = 17$.

03

$(x+m)(x+n) = x^2 + (n+m)x + mn$
$\qquad\qquad\qquad = x^2 + kx + 40$
$n + m = k$ and $mn = 40$
Possible positive integers for m and n that satisfies $mn = 40$ are

m	n	n+m=k
1	40	41
2	20	22
4	10	14
5	8	13

So the answer is (B)

04

$\dfrac{2x^3y^2 - \boxed{A} + 8xy^4}{2xy^2} = (x - 2y)^2$

$2x^3y^2 - A + 8xy^4 = 2xy^2(x - 2y)^2$
$2x^3y^2 - A + 8xy^4 = 2xy^2(x^2 - 4xy + 4y^2)$
$2x^3y^2 - A + 8xy^4 = 2x^3y^2 - 8x^2y^3 + 8xy^4$
$\qquad\qquad A = 8x^2y^3$

The answer is (A)

05

Expand only the part of the x^2y^2 term.
$(x+2y^2)^3 \Rightarrow 3x^2(2y^2)=6x^2y^2$
$2x(x-y^2)^2 \Rightarrow 2x(-2xy^2)=-4x^2y^2$
So, the coefficients of the x^2y^2 term is
$6+(-4)=2$

06

$x^2+y^2=(x+y)^2-2xy=3^2-2\left(\dfrac{5}{2}\right)=4$

$\dfrac{1}{x^2}+\dfrac{1}{y^2}=\dfrac{1}{x^2}\cdot\dfrac{y^2}{y^2}+\dfrac{1}{y^2}\cdot\dfrac{x^2}{x^2}=\dfrac{y^2+x^2}{x^2y^2}$

$=\dfrac{x^2+y^2}{(xy)^2}=\dfrac{4}{\left(\dfrac{5}{2}\right)^2}=\dfrac{4}{\dfrac{25}{4}}=\dfrac{16}{25}$

07

$(a-4)(a-2)a^2(a+2)(a+4)$
$=a^2(a-2)(a+2)(a-4)(a+4)$
$=a^2(a^2-4)(a^2-16)$
$=16(16-4)(16-16)=0$

08

Multiply both sides by $(2-1)$.
$((2+1)(2^2+1)(2^4+1)(2^8+1)=2^a-b))(2-1)$
$(2-1)(2+1)(2^2+1)(2^4+1)(2^8+1)=2^a-b$
$(2^2-1)(2^2+1)(2^4+1)(2^8+1)=2^a-b$
$(2^4-1)(2^4+1)(2^8+1)=2^a-b$
$(2^8-1)(2^8+1)=2^a-b$
$2^{16}-1=2^a-b$, $a=16$ and $b=1$
So, $ab=(16)(1)=16$

Solutions Manual

Chapter 2
Factoring Polynomials

1. Factoring Binomials

Check Point 1

① $4a(a+4) = 1 \times 4 \times a \times (a+4)$
The factors are
1, 4, a, $(a+4)$, $4a$, $4(a+4)$,
$a(a+4)$, and $4a(a+4)$

② $x(2x+1)(x-4) = 1 \times x \times (2x+1) \times (x-4)$
The factors are
1, x, $(2x+1)$, $(x-4)$, $x(2x+1)$,
$x(x-4)$, $(2x+1)(x-4)$, and $x(2x+1)(x-4)$

Check Point 2

① $9x^2 - 36 = 9(x^2 - 4) = 9(x^2 - 2^2)$
$= 9(x-2)(x+2)$

② $4x^2 - \dfrac{y^2}{25} = (2x)^2 - \left(\dfrac{y}{5}\right)^2$
$= \left(2x - \dfrac{y}{5}\right)\left(2x + \dfrac{y}{5}\right)$

③ $32a^3b - 8ab^3 = 8ab(4a^2 - b^2)$
$= 8ab((2a)^2 - b^2)$
$= 8ab(2a-b)(2a+b)$

④ $(a^2-4)^2 - 5(a^2-4)$ → Let $a^2-4 = A$
$= A^2 - 5A = A(A-5)$
$= (a^2-4)(a^2-4-5)$
$= (a^2-4)(a^2-9) = (a^2-2^2)(a^2-3^2)$
$= (a-2)(a+2)(a-3)(a+3)$

⑤ $x^3 - 27y^3 = x^3 - (3y)^3$
$= (x-3y)(x^2 + x \cdot 3y + (3y)^2)$
$= (x-3y)(x^2 + 3xy + 9y^2)$

⑥ $\dfrac{x^3}{16} + \dfrac{125y^3}{2} = \dfrac{1}{2}\left(\dfrac{x^3}{8} + 125y^3\right)$
$= \dfrac{1}{2}\left(\left(\dfrac{x}{2}\right)^3 + (5y)^3\right)$
$= \dfrac{1}{2}\left(\dfrac{x}{2} + 5y\right)\left(\left(\dfrac{x}{2}\right)^2 - \dfrac{x}{2} \cdot 5y + (5y)^2\right)$
$= \dfrac{1}{2}\left(\dfrac{x}{2} + 5y\right)\left(\dfrac{x^2}{4} - \dfrac{5xy}{2} + 25y^2\right)$

⑦ $3ab^3 - 81a^4b^6 = 3ab^3(1 - 27a^3b^3)$
$= 3ab^3(1^3 - (3ab)^3)$
$= 3ab^3(1 - 3ab)(1^2 + 1 \cdot 3ab + (3ab)^2)$
$= 3ab^3(1 - 3ab)(1 + 3ab + 9a^2b^2)$

⑧ $a^4 - b^4 = (a^2)^2 - (b^2)^2 = (a^2 - b^2)(a^2 + b^2)$
$= (a-b)(a+b)(a^2 + b^2)$

Review Exercises

01

(1) $2ay + 4ax = 2a(y + 2x)$

(2) $10ab^2 - 15a^2b = 5ab(2b - 3a)$

(3) $xy^2 + x^2 - 2xy = x(y^2 + x - 2y)$

(4) $8ab^2 + 4ab - 6a^2b^2 = 2ab(4b + 2 - 3ab)$

(5) $x(a+b) - y(a+b)$ → Let $a+b = A$
$= xA - yA = A(x-y) = (a+b)(x-y)$

(6) $a(x-y) + b(y-x) = a(x-y) - b(x-y)$
→ Let $x-y = A$
$= aA - bA = A(a-b) = (x-y)(a-b)$

(7) $2x(2a+b^2) - 4y(2a+b^2)$ → Let $2a+b^2 = A$
$= 2xA - 4yA = A(2x - 4y)$
$= (2a+b^2)2(x - 2y)$

(8) $3a(4x-y) - 2b(y-4x)$
$= 3a(4x-y) + 2b(4x-y)$ → Let $4x-y = A$
$= 3aA + 2bA = A(3a + 2b)$
$= (4x-y)(3a + 2b)$

02

(1) $x^2 - 4 = x^2 - 2^2 = (x-2)(x+2)$

(2) $4x^2 - 100 = 4(x^2 - 25) = 4(x^2 - 5^2)$
$= 4(x-5)(x+5)$

(3) $16x^2 - 1 = (4x)^2 - 1^2 = (4x-1)(4x+1)$

(4) $4x^3-64x=4x(x^2-16)=4x(x^2-4^2)$
$\qquad =4x(x-4)(x+4)$
(5) $2x^2-8y^2=2(x^2-4y^2)=2(x^2-(2y)^2)$
$\qquad =2(x-2y)(x+2y)$
(6) $(x-5)^2-9y^4=(x-5)^2-(3y^2)^2$
$\qquad =((x-5)-3y^2)((x-5)+3y^2)$
$\qquad =-(3y^2-x+5)(3y^2+x-5)$
(7) $(2x+1)^2-(3x-2)^2$
$\qquad =((2x+1)-(3x-2))((2x+1)+(3x-2))$
$\qquad =(3-x)(5x-1)=-(x-3)(5x-1)$
(8) $4(x^2+6)^2-25(x^2+6)$ → Let $x^2+6=A$
$\qquad =4A^2-25A=A(4A-25)$
$\qquad =(x^2+6)(4(x^2+6)-25)$
$\qquad =(x^2+6)(4x^2-1)=(x^2+6)((2x)^2-1^2)$
$\qquad =(x^2+6)(2x-1)(2x+1)$

03

(1) $3(9a^2-4)+(9a^2-4)^2$ → Let $9a^2-4=A$
$\qquad =3A+A^2=A(3+A)$
$\qquad =(9a^2-4)(3+(9a^2-4))$
$\qquad =(9a^2-4)(9a^2-1)$
$\qquad =((3a)^2-2^2)((3a)^2-1^2)$
$\qquad =(3a-2)(3a+2)(3a-1)(3a+1)$
(2) $8a^3+1=(2a)^3+1^3=(2a+1)((2a)^2-2a\cdot 1+1^2)$
$\qquad =(2a+1)(4a^2-2a+1)$
(3) $3a^3+81b^3=3(a^3+27b^3)=3(a^3+(3b)^3)$
$\qquad =3(a+3b)(a^2-a\cdot 3b+(3b)^2)$
$\qquad =3(a+3b)(a^2-3ab+9b^2)$
(4) $16a^3-54b^6=2(8a^3-27b^6)$
$\qquad =2((2a)^3-(3b^2)^3)$
$\qquad =2(2a-3b^2)((2a)^2+(2a)(3b^2)+(3b^2)^2)$
$\qquad =2(2a-3b^2)(4a^2+6ab^2+9b^4)$
(5) $24a^3b+375b^4=3b(8a^3+125b^3)$
$\qquad =3b((2a)^3+(5b)^3)$
$\qquad =3b(2a+5b)((2a)^2-(2a)(5b)+(5b)^2)$
$\qquad =3b(2a+5b)(4a^2-10ab+25b^2)$
(6) $4a^6-\dfrac{b^3}{16}=\dfrac{1}{16}(64a^6-b^3)$
$\qquad =\dfrac{1}{16}((4a^2)^3-b^3)$
$\qquad =\dfrac{1}{16}(4a^2-b)((4a^2)^2+(4a^2)b+b^2)$
$\qquad =\dfrac{1}{16}(4a^2-b)(16a^4+4a^2b+b^2)$

04

$ab(a+b)(a-b)=a\times b\times (a+b)\times (a-b)$
The factors are
a, b, $(a+b)$, $(a-b)$, ab, $a(a+b)$, $a(a-b)$,
$b(a+b)$, $b(a-b)$, $(a+b)(a-b)$, and more.
Since $(a+b)(a-b)=a^2-b^2$,
The only answer choice that is not a factor is (D)

05

$2y(x-y)(x-2y)$
$x^2y-2xy^2=xy(x-2y)$
Since $y(x-2y)$ is one of the common factors, the answer is (C)

06

$6ab^2(a-3)+4ab(3-a)$
$=6ab^2(a-3)-4ab(a-3)$
$=(a-3)(6ab^2-4ab)$
$=2ab(a-3)(3b-2)=2ab(a-3)(xb+y)$
$\Rightarrow x=3,\ y=-2$
So, $xy=(3)(-2)=-6$

07

$9y^2-16x^4=(3y)^2-(4x^2)^2$
$\qquad =(3y-4x^2)(3y+4x^2)$
Since $3y-4x^2=-(4x^2-3y)=-2$,
$9y^2-16x^4=(3y-4x^2)(3y+4x^2)$
$\qquad -8=(-2)(3y+4x^2)$, $3y+4x^2=4$

08

$x^2(x-y)+y^2(y-x)=x^2(x-y)-y^2(x-y)$
$\qquad =(x-y)(x^2-y^2)$
$\qquad =(x-y)(x-y)(x+y)$
$\qquad =(x-y)^2(x+y)$
$\qquad =(-3)^2(4)=36$

09

First, rationalize a and b.

$a = \dfrac{\sqrt{5}+2}{\sqrt{5}-2} \cdot \dfrac{\sqrt{5}+2}{\sqrt{5}+2} = \dfrac{(\sqrt{5}+2)^2}{(\sqrt{5})^2-(2)^2} = \dfrac{5+4\sqrt{5}+4}{5-4}$

$\quad = 9+4\sqrt{5}$

$b = \dfrac{\sqrt{5}-2}{\sqrt{5}+2} \cdot \dfrac{\sqrt{5}-2}{\sqrt{5}-2} = \dfrac{(\sqrt{5}-2)^2}{(\sqrt{5})^2-(2)^2} = \dfrac{5-4\sqrt{5}+4}{5-4}$

$\quad = 9-4\sqrt{5}$

$a^2 - b^2 = (a-b)(a+b)$

$= ((9+4\sqrt{5})-(9-4\sqrt{5}))((9+4\sqrt{5})+(9-4\sqrt{5}))$

$= (8\sqrt{5})(18) = 144\sqrt{5}$

10

$8a^3 - 27b^3 = (2a)^3 - (3b)^3$

$\quad = (2a-3b)((2a)^2 + (2a)(3b) + (3b)^2)$

$\quad = (2a-3b)(4a^2 + 6ab + 9b^2)$

Therefore,

$\dfrac{8a^3 - 27b^3}{4a^2 + 6ab + 9b^2} = \dfrac{(2a-3b)(4a^2+6ab+9b^2)}{4a^2+6ab+9b^2}$

$\quad = 2a - 3b$

$\quad = 2(200) - 3(100) = 100$

11

(1) $2a^4 - 32b^4 = 2(a^4 - 16b^4)$

$= 2((a^2)^2 - (4b^2)^2)$

$= 2(a^2 - 4b^2)(a^2 + 4b^2)$

$= 2(a^2 - (2b)^2)(a^2 + 4b^2)$

$= 2(a-2b)(a+2b)(a^2 + 4b^2)$

(2) $a^6 - b^6 = (a^3)^2 - (b^3)^2$

$= (a^3 - b^3)(a^3 + b^3)$

$= (a-b)(a^2+ab+b^2)(a+b)(a^2-ab+b^2)$

2. Factoring Trinomials

Check Point 1

① $x^2 + 10x + 25 = x^2 + 2(x)(5) + 5^2 = (x+5)^2$

② $4x^2 - 12xy + 9y^2$
$= (2x)^2 - 2(2x)(3y) + (3y)^2 = (2x-3y)^2$

③ $25a^3b^2 - 20a^2b^3 + 4ab^4$
$= ab^2(25a^2 - 20ab + 4b^2)$
$= ab^2((5a)^2 - 2(5a)(2b) + (2b)^2)$
$= ab^2(5a-2b)^2$

④ $a^2 + \dfrac{ab}{2} + \dfrac{b^2}{16} = a^2 + 2(a)\left(\dfrac{b}{4}\right) + \left(\dfrac{b}{4}\right)^2 = \left(a+\dfrac{b}{4}\right)^2$

Check Point 2

① $x^2 - x - 12$

Since $-4 \times 3 = -12$ and $-4+3 = -1$,

$x^2 - x - 12 = (x-4)(x+3)$

② $x^2 + 3x - 10$

Since $-2 \times 5 = -10$ and $-2+5 = 3$,

$x^2 + 3x - 10 = (x-2)(x+5)$

③ $x^2 - xy - 30y^2$

Since $-6 \times 5 = -30$ and $-6+5 = -1$,

$x^2 - xy - 30y^2 = (x-6y)(x+5y)$

④ $3x^2y + 24xy^2 + 36y^3 = 3y(x^2 + 8xy + 12y^2)$

Since $2 \times 6 = 12$ and $2+6 = 8$,

$3y(x^2 + 8xy + 12y^2) = 3y(x+2y)(x+6y)$

Check Point 3

① $\underbrace{6x^2 - x - 2}_{6 \times -2 = -12} \rightarrow -12 = -4 \times 3 \Rightarrow -4+3 = -1$

$\begin{array}{l} 3x -2 \rightarrow -4x \\ 2x 1 \rightarrow \underline{(+)\ 3x} \\ -x \end{array}$

$6x^2 - x - 2 = (3x-2)(2x+1)$

② $\underbrace{3x^2 - 10x + 8}_{3 \times 8 = 24}$

$\rightarrow 24 = -4 \times -6 \Rightarrow -4 + (-6) = -10$

$$\begin{array}{r} 3x \quad\diagdown\quad -4 \to \quad -4x \\ x \quad\diagup\quad -2 \to \underline{(+)\ -6x} \\ -10x \end{array}$$

$3x^2-10x+8=(3x-4)(x-2)$

③ $\underline{12x^2-13x-35}$
$\quad {\scriptstyle 12\times-35=-420}$

$\to -420=15\times-28 \Rightarrow 15+(-28)=-13$

$$\begin{array}{r} 4x \quad\diagdown\quad 5 \to \quad 15x \\ 3x \quad\diagup\quad -7 \to \underline{(+)\ -28x} \\ -13x \end{array}$$

$12x^2-13x-35=(4x+5)(3x-7)$

④ $10x^2y+9xy^2-9y^3=y(10x^2+9xy-9y^2)$

$\underline{10x^2+9xy-9y^2}$
$\quad {\scriptstyle 10\times-9=-90}$

$\to -90=15\times-6 \Rightarrow 15+(-6)=9$

$$\begin{array}{r} 5x \quad\diagdown\quad -3y \to \quad -6xy \\ 2x \quad\diagup\quad 3y \to \underline{(+)\ 15xy} \\ 9xy \end{array}$$

$10x^2y+9xy^2-9y^3=y(5x-3y)(2x+3y)$

Review Exercises

01
(1) $x^2+8x+16=x^2+2(x)(4)+4^2=(x+4)^2$
(2) $x^2-12x+36=x^2-2(x)(6)+6^2=(x-6)^2$
(3) $4x^2+4x+1=(2x)^2+2(2x)(1)+1^2$
$\qquad =(2x+1)^2$
(4) $25x^2-30xy+9y^2$
$\qquad =(5x)^2-2(5x)(3y)+(3y)^2=(5x-3y)^2$
(5) $9x^2+3x+\dfrac{1}{4}=(3x)^2+2(3x)\left(\dfrac{1}{2}\right)+\left(\dfrac{1}{2}\right)^2$
$\qquad =\left(3x+\dfrac{1}{2}\right)^2$
(6) $2x^2-12x+18=2(x^2-6x+9)$
$\qquad =2(x^2-2(x)(3)+3^2)$
$\qquad =2(x-3)^2$
(7) $27x^2-36xy+12y^2=3(9x^2-12xy+4y^2)$
$\qquad =3((3x)^2-2(3x)(2y)+(2y)^2)$
$\qquad =3(3x-2y)^2$
(8) $20x^2+\dfrac{20xy}{3}+\dfrac{5y^2}{9}=5\left(4x^2+\dfrac{4}{3}xy+\dfrac{1}{9}y^2\right)$
$\qquad =5\left((2x)^2+2(2x)\left(\dfrac{1}{3}y\right)+\left(\dfrac{1}{3}y\right)^2\right)$
$\qquad =5\left(2x+\dfrac{1}{3}y\right)^2$

02
(1) x^2-8x+7
Since $-7\times-1=7$ and $-7+(-1)=-8$,
$x^2-8x+7=(x-1)(x-7)$
(2) $x^2+6x-16$
Since $-2\times 8=-16$ and $-2+8=6$,
$x^2+6x-16=(x-2)(x+8)$
(3) $\dfrac{x^2}{2}+8x+24=\dfrac{1}{2}(x^2+16x+48)$
Since $4\times 12=48$ and $4+12=16$,
$\dfrac{1}{2}(x^2+16x+48)=\dfrac{1}{2}(x+4)(x+12)$
(4) $18+3x-3x^2=-3(x^2-x-6)$
Since $-3\times 2=-6$ and $-3+2=-1$,
$-3(x^2-x-6)=-3(x-3)(x+2)$
(5) $3x^3y-9x^2y-30xy=3xy(x^2-3x-10)$
Since $-5\times 2=-10$ and $-5+2=-3$,
$3xy(x^2-3x-10)=3xy(x-5)(x+2)$
(6) $\dfrac{x^2}{4}-\dfrac{5xy}{2}+4y^2=\dfrac{1}{4}(x^2-10xy+16y^2)$
Since $-8\times-2=16$ and $-8+(-2)=-10$,
$\dfrac{1}{4}(x^2-10xy+16y^2)=\dfrac{1}{4}(x-8y)(x-2y)$

03
(1) $\underline{3x^2-7x-6} \to -18=-9\times 2 \Rightarrow -9+2=-7$
$\quad {\scriptstyle 3\times-6=-18}$

$$\begin{array}{r} 3x \quad\diagdown\quad 2 \to \quad 2x \\ x \quad\diagup\quad -3 \to \underline{(+)\ -9x} \\ -7x \end{array}$$

$3x^2-7x-6=(3x+2)(x-3)$

(2) $\underline{4x^2+7xy+3y^2} \to 12=3\times 4 \Rightarrow 3+4=7$
$\quad {\scriptstyle 4\times 3=12}$

$$\begin{array}{r} 4x \quad\diagdown\quad 3y \to \quad 3xy \\ x \quad\diagup\quad y \to \underline{(+)\ 4xy} \\ 7xy \end{array}$$

$4x^2+7xy+3y^2=(4x+3y)(x+y)$

(3) $5x^3y+4x^2y-xy=xy(5x^2+4x-1)$
$\underline{5x^2+4x-1} \to 5=-1\times 5 \Rightarrow -1+5=4$
$\quad {\scriptstyle 5\times-1=-5}$

$$\begin{array}{ccc} 5x & \diagdown & -1 \to -x \\ x & \diagup & 1 \to (+)\ 5x \\ & & \overline{\quad 4x\quad} \end{array}$$

$xy(5x^2+4x-1)=xy(5x-1)(x+1)$

(4) $6x^3y-13x^2y^2+6xy^3=xy(6x^2-13xy+6y^2)$

$\underbrace{6x^2-13xy+6y^2}_{6\times 6=36}$

→ $36=-9\times-4 \Rightarrow -9+(-4)=-13$

$$\begin{array}{ccc} 3x & \diagdown & -2y \to -4xy \\ 2x & \diagup & -3y \to (+)\ -9xy \\ & & \overline{\quad -13xy\quad} \end{array}$$

$xy(6x^2-13xy+6y^2)=xy(3x-2y)(2x-3y)$

(5) $2x^2-\dfrac{7xy}{3}-y^2=\dfrac{1}{3}(6x^2-7xy-3y^2)$

$\underbrace{6x^2-7xy-3y^2}_{6\times -3=-18}$

→ $-18=-9\times 2 \Rightarrow -9+2=-7$

$$\begin{array}{ccc} 3x & \diagdown & y \to 2xy \\ 2x & \diagup & -3y \to (+)\ -9xy \\ & & \overline{\quad -7xy\quad} \end{array}$$

$\dfrac{1}{3}(6x^2-7xy-3y^2)=\dfrac{1}{3}(3x+y)(2x-3y)$

(6) $2x^2-\dfrac{16xy}{3}+\dfrac{5y^2}{6}=\dfrac{1}{6}(12x^2-32xy+5y^2)$

$\underbrace{12x^2-32xy+5y^2}_{12\times 5=60}$

→ $60=-30\times-2 \Rightarrow -30+(-2)=-32$

$$\begin{array}{ccc} 6x & \diagdown & -y \to -2xy \\ 2x & \diagup & -5y \to (+)\ -30xy \\ & & \overline{\quad -32xy\quad} \end{array}$$

$\dfrac{1}{6}(12x^2-32xy+5y^2)=\dfrac{1}{6}(6x-y)(2x-5y)$

04

$x^2-x-12=(x-4)(x+3)$
$=(\sqrt{3}+4-4)(\sqrt{3}+4+3)$
$=\sqrt{3}\,(\sqrt{3}+7)=3+7\sqrt{3}$

05

First, rationalize a and b.

$a=\dfrac{\sqrt{5}+\sqrt{3}}{\sqrt{5}-\sqrt{3}}\cdot\dfrac{\sqrt{5}+\sqrt{3}}{\sqrt{5}+\sqrt{3}}=\dfrac{(\sqrt{5}+\sqrt{3})^2}{(\sqrt{5})^2-(\sqrt{3})^2}$

$=\dfrac{5+2\sqrt{15}+3}{5-3}=\dfrac{8+2\sqrt{15}}{2}=4+\sqrt{15}$

$b=\dfrac{\sqrt{5}-\sqrt{3}}{\sqrt{5}+\sqrt{3}}\cdot\dfrac{\sqrt{5}-\sqrt{3}}{\sqrt{5}-\sqrt{3}}=\dfrac{(\sqrt{5}-\sqrt{3})^2}{(\sqrt{5})^2-(\sqrt{3})^2}$

$=\dfrac{5-2\sqrt{15}+3}{5-3}=\dfrac{8-2\sqrt{15}}{2}=4-\sqrt{15}$

$4a^2+4b^2-8ab=4(a^2-2ab+b^2)$
$=4(a-b)^2$
$=4(4+\sqrt{15}-(4-\sqrt{15}))^2$
$=4(2\sqrt{15})^2=240$

06

Let $4x^2-5x+a=(x-2)(4x+k)$. Then,
$4x^2-5x+a=4x^2+kx-8x-2k$
$\qquad\qquad\quad =4x^2+(k-8)x-2k$
$-5x=(k-8)x,\ k=3$
$a=-2k=-2(3)=-6$

07

Let $\dfrac{6x^2+ax-10}{3x-2}=A$.

$\Rightarrow 6x^2+ax-10=(3x-2)A$
$\qquad\qquad\qquad\ =(3x-2)(2x+k)$
$\qquad\qquad\qquad\ =6x^2+3kx-4x-2k$
$\qquad\qquad\qquad\ =6x^2+(3k-4)x-2k$
$-10=-2k,\ k=5$
$ax=(3k-4)x$
$a=3k-4=3(5)-4=11$

08

Let $4x^2+11x+a=(x+3)(4x+m)$. Then,
$11x=mx+12x,\ 11x=(m+12)x,\ m=-1$
$a=3m=3(-1)=-3$
Also, let $2x^2+bx+3=(x+3)(2x+n)$. Then,
$3=3n,\ n=1$
$bx=nx+6x,\ bx=(n+6)x$
$bx=(1+6)x,\ b=7$
So, $a+b=-3+7=4$

09

$x^2+ax-12=(x+b)(x+c)$
$\qquad =x^2+(b+c)x+bc$

Find two integers b and c whose product $bc=-12$.

b	c	$a=b+c$
-1	12	11
1	-12	-11
-2	6	4
2	-6	-4
-3	4	1
3	-4	-1

So the answer is (B)

10

(1) $(x+5)(x+3)+a=x^2+3x+5x+15+a$
$\qquad\qquad\qquad\quad =x^2+8x+(15+a)$

Since $8x$ is equal to $2(x)(4)$,
$15+a=4^2$, $a=1$

(2) $5x^2+4x(x-a)+16=5x^2+4x^2-4ax+16$
$\qquad\qquad\qquad\quad =9x^2-4ax+16$
$\qquad\qquad\qquad\quad =(3x)^2-4ax+4^2$

Since $4ax$ must be equal to $2(3x)(4)$,
$4ax=2(3x)(4)$, $4ax=24x$, $a=6$

11

$16x^2+axy^2+\dfrac{9y^4}{4}=(4x)^2+axy^2+\left(\dfrac{3y^2}{2}\right)^2$

$axy^2=2(4x)\left(\dfrac{3y^2}{2}\right)$, $axy^2=12xy^2$, $a=12$

12

$x^4+4x^2y-12y^2=(x^2+ay)(x^2+by)$
$4x^2y=bx^2y+ax^2y$, $4x^2y=(b+a)x^2y$
$4=b+a \Rightarrow a+b=4$

13

$3x^2-\dfrac{9xy}{2}-\dfrac{27y^2}{2}=\dfrac{3}{2}(2x^2-3xy-9y^2)$
$\qquad\qquad\qquad\quad =\dfrac{3}{2}(2x+ay)(x+by)$

$\Rightarrow 2x^2-3xy-9y^2=(2x+ay)(x+by)$

$\underline{2x^2-3xy-9y^2}$
$\quad{}_{2\times -9=-18}$

$\rightarrow -18=-6\times 3 \Rightarrow -6+3=-3$

$2x \diagdown\!\!\!\!\diagup +3y \rightarrow \quad +3xy$
$x \diagup\!\!\!\!\diagdown -3y \rightarrow (+) \quad -6xy$
$\qquad\qquad\qquad\qquad\quad \overline{-3xy}$

$2x^2-3xy-9y^2=(2x+3y)(x-3y)$
$\qquad\qquad\qquad \Rightarrow a=3, \ b=-3$

3. Factoring by Grouping and Substitution

Check Point 1

① $xy-x-y+1 = (xy-x)-(y-1)$
$\quad = x(y-1)-(y-1)$
$\quad = (y-1)(x-1)$

② $xy-4x+3y-12 = (xy-4x)+(3y-12)$
$\quad\quad = x(y-4)+3(y-4)$
$\quad\quad = (y-4)(x+3)$

③ $1-2a-4b^2+8ab^2 = 8ab^2-2a-4b^2+1$
$\quad = 2a(4b^2-1)-(4b^2-1)$
$\quad = (4b^2-1)(2a-1)$
$\quad = (2b-1)(2b+1)(2a-1)$

④ $a^2+4b^2-4ab-9 = (a^2+4b^2-4ab)-(9)$
$\quad = (a-2b)^2-3^2$
$\quad = (a-2b-3)(a-2b+3)$

Check Point 2

① $(2x+3)^2-(2x+3)-12 \rightarrow$ Let $2x+3=A$
$= A^2-A-12 = (A-4)(A+3)$
$= ((2x+3)-4)((2x+3)+3)$
$= (2x-1)(2x+6) = 2(2x-1)(x+3)$

② $(x^2-1)^2-6(x^2-1)+9 \rightarrow$ Let $x^2-1=A$
$= A^2-6A+9 = (A-3)^2$
$= ((x^2-1)-3)^2 = (x^2-4)^2$
$= ((x-2)(x+2))^2 = (x-2)^2(x+2)^2$

③ $(a+b-2)(a+b+5)-8 \rightarrow$ Let $a+b=A$
$= (A-2)(A+5)-8$
$= A^2+3A-10-8 = A^2+3A-18$
$= (A+6)(A-3) = (a+b+6)(a+b-3)$

④ $2(a-2)^2+9(a-2)(a+1)+9(a+1)^2$
$\quad\quad \rightarrow$ Let $a-2=A$ and $a+1=B$
$= 2A^2+9AB+9B^2 = (2A+3B)(A+3B)$
$= (2(a-2)+3(a+1))((a-2)+3(a+1))$
$= (2a-4+3a+3)(a-2+3a+3)$
$= (5a-1)(4a+1)$

Check Point 3

① $12\times 157+12\times 43 = 12(157+43)$
$\quad\quad\quad\quad\quad\quad = 12\times 200 = 2{,}400$

② $37^2+23^2+2\times 37\times 23$
$= 37^2+2\times 37\times 23+23^2$
$= (37+23)^2 = 60^2 = 3{,}600$

③ $41^2-82+1 = 41^2-2\times 41\times 1+1^2$
$\quad\quad\quad\quad = (41-1)^2 = 40^2 = 1{,}600$

④ $50\times 54^2-50\times 46^2 = 50(54^2-46^2)$
$\quad\quad\quad\quad = 50(54-46)(54+46)$
$\quad\quad\quad\quad = 50\times 8\times 100 = 40{,}000$

Review Exercises

01

(1) $x^3-x^2+x-1 = x^2(x-1)+(x-1)$
$\quad\quad\quad\quad = (x-1)(x^2+1)$

(2) $ab-a-b+1 = a(b-1)-(b-1)$
$\quad\quad\quad\quad = (b-1)(a-1)$

(3) $2x^3+6x^2+5x+15$
$= 2x^2(x+3)+5(x+3)$
$= (x+3)(2x^2+5)$

(4) $3x^3y-x^2y+6x-2$
$= x^2y(3x-1)+2(3x-1)$
$= (3x-1)(x^2y+2)$

(5) $45-18a-5a^2+2a^3$
$= 9(5-2a)-a^2(5-2a)$
$= (5-2a)(9-a^2)$
$= (5-2a)(3-a)(3+a)$

(6) $a^3+5a^2b-4ab^2-20b^3$
$= a^2(a+5b)-4b^2(a+5b)$
$= (a+5b)(a^2-4b^2)$
$= (a+5b)(a-2b)(a+2b)$

(7) $32+16x^2-2x^4-x^6$
$= 16(2+x^2)-x^4(2+x^2)$
$= (2+x^2)(16-x^4) = (2+x^2)(4^2-(x^2)^2)$
$= (2+x^2)(4-x^2)(4+x^2)$
$= (2+x^2)(2-x)(2+x)(4+x^2)$

(8) $x^2-2x-16y^2+1 = (x^2-2x+1)-16y^2$
$\quad\quad\quad\quad = (x-1)^2-(4y)^2$

$=((x-1)-4y)((x-1)+4y)$
$=(x-4y-1)(x+4y-1)$
(9) $a^2+b^2-2ab-4=(a^2-2ab+b^2)-4$
$=(a-b)^2-2^2$
$=(a-b-2)(a-b+2)$
(10) $8a-9b^2+a^2+16=(a^2+8a+16)-9b^2$
$=(a+4)^2-(3b)^2$
$=((a+4)-3b)((a+4)+3b)$
$=(a-3b+4)(a+3b+4)$

02
(1) $(x-1)^2+9(x-1)+20$ → Let $x-1=A$
$=A^2+9A+20=(A+4)(A+5)$
$=((x-1)+4)((x-1)+5)=(x+3)(x+4)$
(2) $7(2x+3)^2-54(2x+3)-16$ → Let $2x+3=A$
$=7A^2-54A-16=(7A+2)(A-8)$
$=(7(2x+3)+2)((2x+3)-8)$
$=(14x+23)(2x-5)$
(3) $(a-2b)^2-3(a-2b)-4$ → Let $a-2b=A$
$=A^2-3A-4=(A-4)(A+1)$
$=(a-2b-4)(a-2b+1)$
(4) $(a+1)^2+(a+1)(2b-1)-12(2b-1)^2$
 → Let $a+1=A$ and $2b-1=B$
$=A^2+AB-12B^2=(A-3B)(A+4B)$
$=((a+1)-3(2b-1))((a+1)+4(2b-1))$
$=(a-6b+4)(a+8b-3)$
(5) $(x+3y-2)(x+3y+4)-27$ → Let $x+3y=A$
$=(A-2)(A+4)-27$
$=A^2+2A-8-27$
$=A^2+2A-35=(A-5)(A+7)$
$=(x+3y-5)(x+3y+7)$
(6) $(2a-5b)(2a-5b-3)-10$ → Let $2a-5b=A$
$=A(A-3)-10=A^2-3A-10$
$=(A-5)(A+2)$
$=(2a-5b-5)(2a-5b+2)$
(7) $5x^4-9x^2+4$ → Let $x^2=A$
$=5A^2-9A+4=(5A-4)(A-1)$
$=(5x^2-4)(x^2-1)$
$=(5x^2-4)(x-1)(x+1)$

(8) $2x^4-5x^2y^4-12y^8$ → Let $x^2=A$ and $y^4=B$
$=2A^2-5AB-12B^2$
$=(2A+3B)(A-4B)$
$=(2x^2+3y^4)(x^2-4y^4)$
$=(2x^2+3y^4)(x-2y^2)(x+2y^2)$
(9) $20-25(b-1)+8(b-1)^2-10(b-1)^3$
 → Let $b-1=A$
$=20-25A+8A^2-10A^3$
$=5(4-5A)+2A^2(4-5A)$
$=(4-5A)(5+2A^2)$
$=(4-5(b-1))(5+2(b-1)^2)$
$=(-5b+9)(2b^2-4b+7)$
$=-(5b-9)(2b^2-4b+7)$
(10) $3(a+1)^6-2(a+1)^4-8(a+1)^2$
 → Let $(a+1)^2=A$
$=3A^3-2A^2-8A$
$=A(3A^2-2A-8)$
$=A(3A+4)(A-2)$
$=(a+1)^2(3(a+1)^2+4)((a+1)^2-2)$
$=(a+1)^2(3a^2+6a+3+4)(a^2+2a+1-2)$
$=(a+1)^2(3a^2+6a+7)(a^2+2a-1)$

03
(1) $x^2+xy-2x-y+1$
$=(x^2-2x+1)+(xy-y)$
$=(x-1)^2+y(x-1)$
$=(x-1)((x-1)+y)$
$=(x-1)(x+y-1)$
(2) $x^2-y^2+4x+6y-5$
$=x^2+4x-y^2+6y-5$
$=(x^2+4x+4)-(y^2-6y+9)$
$=(x+2)^2-(y-3)^2$
$=((x+2)-(y-3))((x+2)+(y-3))$
$=(x-y+5)(x+y-1)$
(3) $x^2+2xy+4y+x-2$
$=(x^2+x-2)+(2xy+4y)$
$=(x+2)(x-1)+2y(x+2)$
$=(x+2)((x-1)+2y)$
$=(x+2)(x+2y-1)$

Solutions Manual

(4) $x^2-y^2+6x+2y+8$
$=x^2+6x-y^2+2y+8$
$=(x^2+6x+9)-(y^2-2y+1)$
$=(x+3)^2-(y-1)^2$
$=((x+3)-(y-1))((x+3)+(y-1))$
$=(x-y+4)(x+y+2)$

04

(1) $98^2-4=98^2-2^2=(98-2)(98+2)$
$=96\times 100=9{,}600$

(2) $25\times 77-25\times 75=25(77-75)$
$=25\times 2=50$

(3) $54^2-8\times 54+16=54^2-2\times 54\times 4+4^2$
$=(54-4)^2=50^2=2{,}500$

(4) $5.5^2\times 24.5-4.5^2\times 24.5$
$=24.5(5.5^2-4.5^2)$
$=24.5(5.5-4.5)(5.5+4.5)$
$=24.5\times 1\times 10=245$

(5) $9+6\times 27+27^2=3^2+2\times 3\times 27+27^2$
$=(3+27)^2=30^2=900$

(6) $\sqrt{6.5^2\times 12-5.5^2\times 12}$
$=\sqrt{12(6.5^2-5.5^2)}$
$=\sqrt{12(6.5-5.5)(6.5+5.5)}$
$=\sqrt{12\times 1\times 12}=12$

05

$10(x+2)^2-(x+2)-2=(ax+b)(2x+c)$
$\rightarrow$ Let $x+2=A$
$10A^2-A-2=(5A+2)(2A-1)$
$=(5(x+2)+2)(2(x+2)-1)$
$=(5x+12)(2x+3)$
$\Rightarrow a=5,\ b=12,\ \text{and } c=3$
So, $a+b+c=5+12+3=20$

06

$x^2-3xy+2x-6y=x(x-3y)+2(x-3y)$
$=(x-3y)(x+2)$
$2x^2-6xy-x+3y=2x(x-3y)-(x-3y)$
$=(x-3y)(2x-1)$
The common factor is $(x-3y)$.

So the answer is (C)

07

x^2-y^2-4x+4
$=(x^2-4x+4)-y^2=(x-2)^2-y^2$
$=(x-2-y)(x-2+y)=(x-y-2)(x+y-2)$
$=(\sqrt{2}-2)(2+\sqrt{2}-2)=2-2\sqrt{2}$

08

$(x-y)^2=(x+y)^2-4xy=7^2-4(9)=13$
$x-y=\pm\sqrt{13} \Rightarrow x-y=\sqrt{13}$ because $x>y$.
x^2-y^2+x-y
$=(x-y)(x+y)+(x-y)$
$=(x-y)(x+y+1)$
$=\sqrt{13}\ (7+1)=8\sqrt{13}$

09

(1) $x^2-y^2-2x+4y-3$
$=x^2-2x-(y^2-4y+3)$
$=x^2-2x-(y-1)(y-3)$

$x \quad -(y-1) \rightarrow \quad -(y-1)x$
$x \quad (y-3) \rightarrow (+)\ (y-3)x$
$\qquad\qquad\qquad\qquad\qquad -2x$

$=(x-(y-1))(x+(y-3))$
$=(x-y+1)(x+y-3)$

(2) $x^2-y^2+8x+2y+15$
$=x^2+8x-(y^2-2y-15)$
$=x^2+8x-(y-5)(y+3)$

$x \quad -(y-5) \rightarrow \quad -(y-5)x$
$x \quad (y+3) \rightarrow (+)\ (y+3)x$
$\qquad\qquad\qquad\qquad\qquad 8x$

$=(x-(y-5))(x+(y+3))$
$=(x-y+5)(x+y+3)$

(3) $(x-3)(x-2)(x+1)(x+2)+3$
$=\{(x-3)(x+2)\}\{(x-2)(x+1)\}+3$
$=(x^2-x-6)(x^2-x-2)+3 \rightarrow$ Let $x^2-x=A$
$=(A-6)(A-2)+3$
$=A^2-8A+12+3=A^2-8A+15$
$=(A-3)(A-5)$
$=(x^2-x-3)(x^2-x-5)$

(4) $(a+1)(a+2)^2(a+3)-6$
$=\{(a+1)(a+3)\}(a+2)^2-6$
$=(a^2+4a+3)(a^2+4a+4)-6$
→ Let $a^2+4a=A$
$=(A+3)(A+4)-6$
$=A^2+7A+12-6=A^2+7A+6$
$=(A+1)(A+6)$
$=(a^2+4a+1)(a^2+4a+6)$

Chapter 2 Test Level 1

01

$4xy-12xy^2=4xy(1-3y)$
$4xy^2$ is not a factor. So the answer is (B)

02

(D) $(2x-y)(2x-y-3)-4$ → Let $2x-y=A$
$=A(A-3)-4=A^2-3A-4$
$=(A-4)(A+1)$
$=(2x-y-4)(2x-y+1)$
(E) $4xy-2x+10y-5=2x(2y-1)+5(2y-1)$
$=(2x+5)(2y-1)$
So the answer is (E)

03

(1) $4(x-1)(x+7)+k$
$=4(x^2+7x-x-7)+k=4(x^2+6x-7)+k$
$=4x^2+24x-28+k$
$=(2x)^2+24x+(-28+k)$
Since $24x$ is equal to $2(2x)(6)$,
$-28+k=6^2$, $k=36+28=64$
(2) $4x^2-(4k-1)xy+y^2$
$=(2x)^2-(4k-1)xy+y^2$
Since $(4k-1)xy$ must be equal to $2(2x)y$,
$(4k-1)xy=2(2x)y$
$4k-1=4$, $k=\dfrac{5}{4}$

04

$x+y=(1-\sqrt{2})+(1+\sqrt{2})=2$
$x-y=(1-\sqrt{2})-(1+\sqrt{2})=-2\sqrt{2}$
$xy=(1-\sqrt{2})(1+\sqrt{2})=1^2-(\sqrt{2})^2=-1$
(1) $x^2-y^2=(x-y)(x+y)=-2\sqrt{2}\times 2=-4\sqrt{2}$
(2) $x^2+y^2=(x+y)^2-2xy=2^2-2(-1)=6$
(3) $x^2-2xy+y^2=(x-y)^2=(-2\sqrt{2})^2=8$
(4) $x^3+y^3=(x+y)(x^2-xy+y^2)$
$=(x+y)(x^2+y^2-xy)$
$=2(6-(-1))=14$

05

(A) $x^2-6xy+9y^2=x^2-2x(3y)+(3y)^2$
$=(x-3y)^2$
(B) $4x^2-x+\dfrac{1}{16}=(2x)^2-2(2x)\left(\dfrac{1}{4}\right)+\left(\dfrac{1}{4}\right)^2$
$=\left(2x-\dfrac{1}{4}\right)^2$
(C) $1-2a+a^2=1^2-2(1)(a)+a^2=(1-a)^2$
(D) $9a^2+12ab+4b^2=(3a)^2+2(3a)(2b)+(2b)^2$
$=(3a+2b)^2$
(E) $25y^2-\dfrac{10}{3}y+\dfrac{4}{9}\neq(5y)^2-2(5y)\left(\dfrac{2}{3}\right)+\left(\dfrac{2}{3}\right)^2$
So the answer is (E)

06

$ax^2+(2b-1)x-12=(3x+4)(5x+c)$
$=15x^2+3cx+20x+4c$
$=15x^2+(3c+20)x+4c$
⇒ $a=15$
$-12=4c$, $c=-3$
$2b-1=3c+20$, $2b-1=3(-3)+20$, $b=6$
So, $a+b+c=15+6+(-3)=18$

07

$ax^2-c=(2x+a)(x+b)$
$=2x^2+2bx+ax+ab$
$=2x^2+(2b+a)x+ab$
⇒ $a=2$
$0=2b+a$, $0=2b+2$, $b=-1$
$-c=ab=(2)(-1)$, $c=2$
So, $a+b+c=2+(-1)+2=3$

08

$6x^2y-8xy-8y=2y(3x^2-4x-4)$
$\qquad\qquad\qquad\quad =2y(3x+2)(x-2)$
$12x^3y-4x^2y-8xy=4xy(3x^2-x-2)$
$\qquad\qquad\qquad\qquad\;\;=4xy(3x+2)(x-1)$
Since $y(3x+2)$ is one of the common factors, the answer is (A)

09

Let $4x^2+kx-5=(2x-1)(2x+a)$. Then,
$4x^2+kx-5=4x^2+2ax-2x-a$
$\qquad\qquad\quad=4x^2+(2a-2)x-a$
$\Rightarrow a=5$
$k=2a-2=2(5)-2=8$

10

$-a^2(2b-a)-4b^2(a-2b)$
$=a^2(a-2b)-4b^2(a-2b)$
$=(a-2b)(a^2-4b^2)$
$=(a-2b)(a-2b)(a+2b)$
$=(a-2b)^2(a+2b)=2^2\times 5=20$

11

(1) $15.5^2-15.5+0.5^2$
$=15.5^2-2\times 15.5\times 0.5+0.5^2$
$=(15.5-0.5)^2=15^2=225$

(2) $\dfrac{92\times 184+92\times 16}{96^2-16}=\dfrac{92(184+16)}{96^2-4^2}$
$\qquad\qquad\qquad\qquad\;\;=\dfrac{92\times 200}{(96-4)(96+4)}$
$\qquad\qquad\qquad\qquad\;\;=\dfrac{92\times 200}{92\times 100}=2$

12

$2x^2-2y^2-4x+4y=2(x^2-y^2)-4(x-y)$
$\qquad\qquad\qquad\qquad\;\;=2(x-y)(x+y)-4(x-y)$
$\qquad\qquad\qquad\qquad\;\;=(x-y)(2(x+y)-4)$
$\qquad\qquad\qquad\qquad\;\;=(-3)(2(4)-4)=-12$

Chapter 2 Test Level 2

01

(1) $(x+2y-1)^2-(3x-2y)^2$
$=((x+2y-1)-(3x-2y))((x+2y-1)+(3x-2y))$
$=(-2x+4y-1)(4x-1)$
$=-(4x-1)(2x-4y+1)$

(2) $24x^3y+1029y^4=3y(8x^3+343y^3)$
$=3y((2x)^3+(7y)^3)$
$=3y(2x+7y)((2x)^2-(2x)(7y)+(7y)^2)$
$=3y(2x+7y)(4x^2-14xy+49y^2)$

(3) $4x^3y-32x^2y^2+64xy^3$
$=4xy(x^2-8xy+16y^2)$
$=4xy(x^2-2(x)(4y)+(4y)^2)$
$=4xy(x-4y)^2$

(4) $64-\dfrac{81}{4}x^4=8^2-\left(\dfrac{9}{2}x^2\right)^2$
$=\left(8-\dfrac{9}{2}x^2\right)\left(8+\dfrac{9}{2}x^2\right)$
$=\dfrac{1}{2}(16-9x^2)\left(8+\dfrac{9}{2}x^2\right)$
$=\dfrac{1}{2}(4-3x)(4+3x)\left(8+\dfrac{9}{2}x^2\right)$

(5) $(x+y)^3-(x-y)^3$
$=((x+y)-(x-y))((x+y)^2+(x+y)(x-y)+(x-y)^2)$
$=2y(x^2+2xy+y^2+x^2-y^2+x^2-2xy+y^2)$
$=2y(3x^2+y^2)$

(6) $(2x^2+3x)^2-(2x^2+3x+3)-3$
$\qquad\qquad\qquad\qquad\;\;\to$ Let $2x^2+3x=A$
$=A^2-(A+3)-3=A^2-A-6$
$=(A-3)(A+2)$
$=(2x^2+3x-3)(2x^2+3x+2)$

(7) $2(x-2)^2-3(x-2)(x+3)-20(x+3)^2$
$\qquad\qquad\qquad\qquad\;\;\to$ Let $x-2=A$ and $x+3=B$
$=2A^2-3AB-20B^2$
$=(2A+5B)(A-4B)$

$$= (2(x-2)+5(x+3))((x-2)-4(x+3))$$
$$= (7x+11)(-3x-14) = -(7x+11)(3x+14)$$

(8) $x^2+4y^2-4xy-2x+4y$
$$= (x^2-4xy+4y^2)-2x+4y$$
$$= (x-2y)^2-2(x-2y)$$
$$= (x-2y)((x-2y)-2)$$
$$= (x-2y)(x-2y-2)$$

02

$16a^3-2b^3 = 2(8a^3-b^3)$
$\qquad = 2(2a-b)(4a^2+2ab+b^2)$
$6 = 2\left(\dfrac{1}{2}\right)(4a^2+2ab+b^2)$
$\Rightarrow\ 4a^2+2ab+b^2 = 6$

03

$x^2+y^2 = (x+y)^2-2xy$
$\qquad = (\sqrt{5})^2-2(2) = 5-4 = 1$
$x^3+x^2y+xy^2+y^3 = x^2(x+y)+y^2(x+y)$
$\qquad = (x+y)(x^2+y^2)$
$\qquad = \sqrt{5}\times 1 = \sqrt{5}$

04

$\dfrac{1}{16}x^2-\dfrac{1}{4}xy+ky^2$
$= \left(\dfrac{1}{4}x\right)^2-2\left(\dfrac{1}{4}x\right)(\sqrt{k}y)+(\sqrt{k}y)^2$
$\Rightarrow\ \dfrac{1}{4}xy = 2\left(\dfrac{1}{4}x\right)(\sqrt{k}y)$
$\qquad \dfrac{1}{4}xy = \dfrac{\sqrt{k}}{2}xy,\ 1 = 2\sqrt{k},\ k = \dfrac{1}{4}$

05

Let $3x^2-7x+a = (3x+2)(x+m)$. Then,
$-7x = 3mx+2x,\ -7x = (3m+2)x,\ m = -3$
$a = 2m = 2(-3) = -6$
Let $6x^2+bx-2 = (3x+2)(2x+n)$. Then,
$-2 = 2n,\ n = -1$
$bx = 3nx+4x,\ bx = (3n+4)x,$
$bx = (3(-1)+4)x,\ b = 1$
So, $a+b = (-6)+1 = -5$

06

$x^2+ax+16 = (x+b)(x+c)$
$\qquad\qquad = x^2+(b+c)x+bc$
Find two integers b and c whose product $bc=16$.

b	c	$a=b+c$
1	16	17
-1	-16	-17
2	8	10
-2	-8	-10
4	4	8
-4	-4	-8

So the answer is (D)

07

$98\times 98+98\times 101-98\times 99-102\times 102$
$= 98^2-102^2+98\times 101-98\times 99$
$= (98-102)(98+102)+98(101-99)$
$= (-4)(200)+98(2)$
$= -800+196 = -604$

08

$x^2-y^2+9x+y+20$
$= x^2+9x-(y^2-y-20)$
$= x^2+9x-(y-5)(y+4)$

$x \qquad\quad -(y-5)\ \rightarrow\ -(y-5)x$
$x \qquad\quad\ \ (y+4)\ \rightarrow\ \underline{(+)\ (y+4)x}$
$\qquad\qquad\qquad\qquad\qquad\quad\ 9x$

$= (x-(y-5))(x+(y+4))$
$= (x-y+5)(x+y+4)$
So the answer is (A)

Solutions Manual

Chapter 3 — Rational Expression

1. Introduction to Rational Expression

Check Point 1

① $\dfrac{18ab^3}{72a^3b^2c} = \dfrac{18ab^2 \cdot b}{4 \cdot 18ab^2 \cdot a^2 c} = \dfrac{b}{4a^2 c}$

② $\dfrac{x^2-x-2}{x^2+x-6} = \dfrac{(x-2)(x+1)}{(x-2)(x+3)} = \dfrac{x+1}{x+3}$

③ $\dfrac{3x^2+x-4}{5x^2-3x-2} = \dfrac{(3x+4)(x-1)}{(5x+2)(x-1)} = \dfrac{3x+4}{5x+2}$

④ $\dfrac{2x^3+11x^2+12x}{3x^2+11x-4} = \dfrac{x(2x^2+11x+12)}{3x^2+11x-4}$
$= \dfrac{x(2x+3)(x+4)}{(3x-1)(x+4)}$
$= \dfrac{x(2x+3)}{3x-1}$

⑤ $\dfrac{(a^3+b^3)(a^2-b^2)}{a^4-b^4}$
$= \dfrac{(a+b)(a^2-ab+b^2)(a^2-b^2)}{(a^2-b^2)(a^2+b^2)}$
$= \dfrac{(a+b)(a^2-ab+b^2)}{a^2+b^2}$

⑥ $\dfrac{(a^3-b^3)(a^4-b^4)}{(a-b)(a^6-b^6)}$
$= \dfrac{(a^3-b^3)(a^2-b^2)(a^2+b^2)}{(a-b)(a^3-b^3)(a^3+b^3)}$
$= \dfrac{(a^2-b^2)(a^2+b^2)}{(a-b)(a^3+b^3)}$
$= \dfrac{(a-b)(a+b)(a^2+b^2)}{(a-b)(a+b)(a^2-ab+b^2)} = \dfrac{a^2+b^2}{a^2-ab+b^2}$

Check Point 2

① $\dfrac{2x^2 y}{6xy^4} \times \dfrac{8x^3}{10x^2} = \dfrac{2xy \cdot x}{2xy \cdot 3y^3} \times \dfrac{2x^2 \cdot 4x}{2x^2 \cdot 5} = \dfrac{4x^2}{15y^3}$

② $\dfrac{x-3}{x-4} \times \dfrac{x^2-16}{5x-15} = \dfrac{x-3}{x-4} \times \dfrac{(x-4)(x+4)}{5(x-3)}$
$= \dfrac{x+4}{5}$

③ $\dfrac{x^2+8x+16}{x+2} \times \dfrac{x^2-4}{x^2+6x+8}$
$= \dfrac{(x+4)^2}{x+2} \times \dfrac{(x-2)(x+2)}{(x+2)(x+4)} = \dfrac{(x+4)(x-2)}{x+2}$

④ $\dfrac{x^2-1}{2x^2+x-1} \times (8x^3-1) = \dfrac{x^2-1}{2x^2+x-1} \times \dfrac{(2x)^3-1^3}{1}$
$= \dfrac{(x-1)(x+1)}{(2x-1)(x+1)} \times \dfrac{(2x-1)(4x^2+2x+1)}{1}$
$= (x-1)(4x^2+2x+1)$

Check Point 3

① $\dfrac{9xy^2 z}{x^3 z^2} \div \dfrac{18x^2 y^3}{x^3 y^4} = \dfrac{9xy^2 z}{x^3 z^2} \times \dfrac{x^3 y^4}{18x^2 y^3}$
$= \dfrac{xz \cdot 9y^2}{xz \cdot x^2 z} \times \dfrac{x^2 y^3 \cdot xy}{18 \cdot x^2 y^3}$
$= \dfrac{9x \cdot y^3}{9x \cdot 2xz} = \dfrac{y^3}{2xz}$

② $\dfrac{x^2+6x-7}{3x^2} \div \dfrac{2x+14}{3x} = \dfrac{x^2+6x-7}{3x^2} \times \dfrac{3x}{2x+14}$
$= \dfrac{(x-1)(x+7)}{3x \cdot x} \times \dfrac{3x}{2(x+7)}$
$= \dfrac{x-1}{2x}$

③ $\dfrac{a^3-a^2-a+1}{(a+1)^2} \div \dfrac{a^2-1}{a^3+1} = \dfrac{a^3-a^2-a+1}{(a+1)^2} \times \dfrac{a^3+1}{a^2-1}$
$= \dfrac{a^2(a-1)-(a-1)}{(a+1)^2} \times \dfrac{a^3+1^3}{(a-1)(a+1)}$
$= \dfrac{(a-1)(a^2-1)}{(a+1)^2} \times \dfrac{(a+1)(a^2-a+1)}{(a-1)(a+1)}$
$= \dfrac{(a-1)(a-1)(a+1)}{(a+1)^2} \times \dfrac{(a+1)(a^2-a+1)}{(a-1)(a+1)}$
$= \dfrac{(a-1)(a^2-a+1)}{a+1}$

④ $\dfrac{2x-12}{x^2-4} \div \dfrac{x^2-2x+4}{3x-6} \div \dfrac{1}{x^3+8}$
$= \dfrac{2x-12}{x^2-4} \times \dfrac{3x-6}{x^2-2x+4} \times \dfrac{x^3+8}{1}$

$$= \frac{2(x-6)}{(x-2)(x+2)} \times \frac{3(x-2)}{x^2-2x+4}$$
$$\times \frac{(x+2)(x^2-2x+4)}{1}$$
$$= 6(x-6)$$

Review Exercises

01

(1) $\dfrac{75x^3y^6}{(5y^5)^2} = \dfrac{3 \cdot 5^2 x^3 y^6}{5^2 y^{10}} = \dfrac{3x^3}{y^4}$

(2) $\dfrac{27a^2b^3c}{(3bc^2)^3} = \dfrac{3^3 a^2 b^3 c}{3^3 b^3 c^6} = \dfrac{a^2}{c^5}$

(3) $\dfrac{6y^4-15y}{9y^2} = \dfrac{3y(2y^3-5)}{9y^2} = \dfrac{2y^3-5}{3y}$

(4) $\dfrac{2y^3+4y^2}{y+y^2-2} = \dfrac{2y^2(y+2)}{(y+2)(y-1)} = \dfrac{2y^2}{y-1}$

(5) $\dfrac{(a-b)^2}{a^2-b^2} = \dfrac{(a-b)^2}{(a-b)(a+b)} = \dfrac{a-b}{a+b}$

(6) $\dfrac{a^2-5a+6}{a^2-7a+12} = \dfrac{(a-2)(a-3)}{(a-3)(a-4)} = \dfrac{a-2}{a-4}$

(7) $\dfrac{6a^2-5a+1}{12a^2+2a-2} = \dfrac{(2a-1)(3a-1)}{2(2a+1)(3a-1)}$
$$= \dfrac{2a-1}{2(2a+1)}$$

02

(1) $\dfrac{x^3+27}{x^2-9} = \dfrac{(x+3)(x^2-3x+9)}{(x-3)(x+3)} = \dfrac{x^2-3x+9}{x-3}$

(2) $\dfrac{x^4-x^2}{x^4-1} = \dfrac{x^2(x^2-1)}{(x^2-1)(x^2+1)} = \dfrac{x^2}{x^2+1}$

(3) $\dfrac{a^3+a^2-a-1}{a^3-a^2-a+1} = \dfrac{a^2(a+1)-(a+1)}{a^2(a-1)-(a-1)}$
$$= \dfrac{(a^2-1)(a+1)}{(a^2-1)(a-1)} = \dfrac{a+1}{a-1}$$

(4) $\dfrac{-b^3+2b^2-b+2}{8+2b-3b^2} = \dfrac{b^3-2b^2+b-2}{3b^2-2b-8}$
$$= \dfrac{b^2(b-2)+(b-2)}{(b-2)(3b+4)}$$
$$= \dfrac{(b^2+1)(b-2)}{(b-2)(3b+4)}$$
$$= \dfrac{b^2+1}{3b+4}$$

(5) $\dfrac{b^3+2b^2-2b-4}{b^3+8} = \dfrac{b^2(b+2)-2(b+2)}{(b+2)(b^2-2b+4)}$
$$= \dfrac{(b^2-2)(b+2)}{(b+2)(b^2-2b+4)}$$
$$= \dfrac{b^2-2}{b^2-2b+4}$$

(6) $\dfrac{a^4-2a^2b^2+b^4}{a^4-b^4} = \dfrac{(a^2-b^2)^2}{(a^2-b^2)(a^2+b^2)}$
$$= \dfrac{a^2-b^2}{a^2+b^2} = \dfrac{(a-b)(a+b)}{a^2+b^2}$$

(7) $\dfrac{a^4-b^4}{a^4+a^3b-ab^3-b^4} = \dfrac{(a^2-b^2)(a^2+b^2)}{a^3(a+b)-b^3(a+b)}$
$$= \dfrac{(a^2-b^2)(a^2+b^2)}{(a^3-b^3)(a+b)}$$
$$= \dfrac{(a-b)(a+b)(a^2+b^2)}{(a-b)(a^2+ab+b^2)(a+b)}$$
$$= \dfrac{a^2+b^2}{a^2+ab+b^2}$$

03

(1) $\left(-\dfrac{4x^3}{12}\right) \times \left(-\dfrac{18}{x^2}\right) = \dfrac{x^3}{3} \times \dfrac{18}{x^2} = 6x$

(2) $\left(\dfrac{1}{x}\right)^3 \times \left(\dfrac{x^2}{2}\right)^2 = \dfrac{1}{x^3} \times \dfrac{x^4}{4} = \dfrac{x}{4}$

(3) $\dfrac{(-2x^2y)^2}{x^2y^5} \times \dfrac{4xy^2}{(2y^3)^3} = \dfrac{2^2 x^4 y^2}{x^2 y^5} \times \dfrac{2^2 xy^2}{2^3 y^9}$
$$= \dfrac{2^2 x^2}{y^3} \times \dfrac{x}{2y^7} = \dfrac{2x^3}{y^{10}}$$

(4) $\left(\dfrac{a^2}{b}\right)^3 \times \left(\dfrac{a}{b^3}\right)^2 \times (ab^2)^{-2} = \dfrac{a^6}{b^3} \times \dfrac{a^2}{b^6} \times \dfrac{1}{(ab^2)^2}$
$$= \dfrac{a^6}{b^3} \times \dfrac{a^2}{b^6} \times \dfrac{1}{a^2b^4} = \dfrac{a^6}{b^{13}}$$

(5) $\dfrac{x^2-9}{x^2+5x+6} \times \dfrac{3-x}{x+2}$
$$= \dfrac{(x-3)(x+3)}{(x+2)(x+3)} \times \dfrac{-(x-3)}{x+2} = -\dfrac{(x-3)^2}{(x+2)^2}$$

(6) $\dfrac{x^2-7x+12}{2x^2-32} \times (x^2-5x+6)$
$$= \dfrac{(x-3)(x-4)}{2(x^2-16)} \times (x-2)(x-3)$$
$$= \dfrac{(x-3)(x-4)}{2(x-4)(x+4)} \times (x-2)(x-3)$$
$$= \dfrac{(x-3)^2(x-2)}{2(x+4)}$$

Solutions Manual

04

(1) $\dfrac{6a^2-a-2}{2a^2-5a-3} \times \dfrac{2a^2-18}{3a^2+7a-6}$

$= \dfrac{(2a+1)(3a-2)}{(a-3)(2a+1)} \times \dfrac{2(a^2-9)}{(a+3)(3a-2)}$

$= \dfrac{(2a+1)(3a-2)}{(a-3)(2a+1)} \times \dfrac{2(a-3)(a+3)}{(a+3)(3a-2)} = 2$

(2) $\dfrac{a^2b-b^3}{4ab-8b^2} \times \dfrac{a^2-ab-2b^2}{a^4-2a^3b+a^2b^2}$

$= \dfrac{b(a^2-b^2)}{4b(a-2b)} \times \dfrac{(a+b)(a-2b)}{a^2(a^2-2ab+b^2)}$

$= \dfrac{(a-b)(a+b)}{4(a-2b)} \times \dfrac{(a+b)(a-2b)}{a^2(a-b)^2}$

$= \dfrac{(a+b)^2}{4a^2(a-b)}$

05

(1) $\dfrac{4y^2}{y^3} \div \left(-\dfrac{6y^3}{y^4}\right) = \dfrac{4y^2}{y^3} \times \left(-\dfrac{y^4}{6y^3}\right)$

$= \dfrac{2^2}{y} \times \left(-\dfrac{y}{2\cdot 3}\right) = -\dfrac{2}{3}$

(2) $(-2a^3b^{-1})^3 \div \left(-\dfrac{3ab^2}{2b^2a^3}\right)^2 = -8a^9b^{-3} \div \dfrac{9}{4a^4}$

$= -\dfrac{8a^9}{b^3} \times \dfrac{4a^4}{9}$

$= -\dfrac{32a^{13}}{9b^3}$

(3) $\dfrac{15y^2}{4x} \times \dfrac{7x^2}{9y} \div \dfrac{35}{6xy} = \dfrac{15y^2}{4x} \times \dfrac{7x^2}{9y} \times \dfrac{6xy}{35}$

$= \dfrac{3\cdot 5y^2}{2^2 x} \times \dfrac{7x^2}{3^2 y} \times \dfrac{2\cdot 3xy}{5\cdot 7}$

$= \dfrac{x^2 y^2}{2}$

(4) $\dfrac{x^2-5x-14}{x^2-3x+2} \div \dfrac{x^2-14x+49}{x^2-4}$

$= \dfrac{x^2-5x-14}{x^2-3x+2} \times \dfrac{x^2-4}{x^2-14x+49}$

$= \dfrac{(x-7)(x+2)}{(x-1)(x-2)} \times \dfrac{(x-2)(x+2)}{(x-7)^2}$

$= \dfrac{(x+2)^2}{(x-1)(x-7)}$

06

(1) $\dfrac{a^2-1}{a^2-4} \div \dfrac{2a-1}{a-2} \times \dfrac{a+2}{2a^2+a}$

$= \dfrac{a^2-1}{a^2-4} \times \dfrac{a-2}{2a-1} \times \dfrac{a+2}{2a^2+a}$

$= \dfrac{(a-1)(a+1)}{(a-2)(a+2)} \times \dfrac{a-2}{2a-1} \times \dfrac{a+2}{a(2a+1)}$

$= \dfrac{(a-1)(a+1)}{a(2a-1)(2a+1)}$

(2) $\dfrac{4x^2-1}{2x^2-3x-2} \times \dfrac{2x-1}{x^2-4} \div \dfrac{2x-1}{x+2}$

$= \dfrac{4x^2-1}{2x^2-3x-2} \times \dfrac{2x-1}{x^2-4} \times \dfrac{x+2}{2x-1}$

$= \dfrac{(2x-1)(2x+1)}{(2x+1)(x-2)} \times \dfrac{2x-1}{(x-2)(x+2)} \times \dfrac{x+2}{2x-1}$

$= \dfrac{2x-1}{(x-2)^2}$

(3) $\dfrac{x^2-4}{x+11} \times (3x^3+6x^2) \div \dfrac{2x-4}{x^2+11x}$

$= \dfrac{x^2-4}{x+11} \times \dfrac{3x^3+6x^2}{1} \times \dfrac{x^2+11x}{2x-4}$

$= \dfrac{(x-2)(x+2)}{x+11} \times \dfrac{3x^2(x+2)}{1} \times \dfrac{x(x+11)}{2(x-2)}$

$= \dfrac{3x^3(x+2)^2}{2}$

(4) $(2x-10) \div \dfrac{x^2-9x+20}{4x^2-9} \div \dfrac{6x^3-9x^2}{x^3-4x^2}$

$= (2x-10) \times \dfrac{4x^2-9}{x^2-9x+20} \times \dfrac{x^3-4x^2}{6x^3-9x^2}$

$= \dfrac{2(x-5)}{1} \times \dfrac{(2x-3)(2x+3)}{(x-5)(x-4)} \times \dfrac{x^2(x-4)}{3x^2(2x-3)}$

$= \dfrac{2(2x+3)}{3}$

(5) $(x-y) \div (x^4-y^4) \times (x^4+2x^2y^2+y^4)$

$= (x-y) \times \dfrac{1}{x^4-y^4} \times (x^4+2x^2y^2+y^4)$

$= (x-y) \times \dfrac{1}{(x^2-y^2)(x^2+y^2)} \times (x^2+y^2)^2$

$= \dfrac{(x-y)(x^2+y^2)}{(x-y)(x+y)(x^2+y^2)} = \dfrac{x^2+y^2}{x+y}$

2. Addition, Subtraction, and Complex Fraction

Check Point 1

① $\dfrac{2x-4}{x+3} - \dfrac{x+1}{3x-1}$

$= \dfrac{(2x-4)(3x-1)}{(x+3)(3x-1)} - \dfrac{(x+1)(x+3)}{(3x-1)(x+3)}$

$= \dfrac{6x^2-14x+4}{(x+3)(3x-1)} - \dfrac{x^2+4x+3}{(x+3)(3x-1)}$

$= \dfrac{5x^2-18x+1}{(x+3)(3x-1)}$

② $\dfrac{x-4}{x} + \dfrac{x+3}{x+2} = \dfrac{(x-4)(x+2)}{x(x+2)} + \dfrac{(x+3)x}{(x+2)x}$

$= \dfrac{x^2-2x-8}{x(x+2)} + \dfrac{x^2+3x}{x(x+2)}$

$= \dfrac{2x^2+x-8}{x(x+2)}$

③ $\dfrac{x+4}{x^2-x-2} - \dfrac{x+2}{x^2-1}$

$= \dfrac{x+4}{(x+1)(x-2)} - \dfrac{x+2}{(x-1)(x+1)}$

$= \dfrac{(x+4)(x-1)}{(x+1)(x-2)(x-1)} - \dfrac{(x+2)(x-2)}{(x-1)(x+1)(x-2)}$

$= \dfrac{x^2+3x-4}{(x-1)(x+1)(x-2)} - \dfrac{x^2-4}{(x-1)(x+1)(x-2)}$

$= \dfrac{3x}{(x-1)(x+1)(x-2)}$

④ $\dfrac{2}{x} - \dfrac{x}{x+1} + \dfrac{x+1}{x+2}$

$= \dfrac{2(x+1)(x+2)}{x(x+1)(x+2)} - \dfrac{x \cdot x(x+2)}{(x+1)x(x+2)}$

$\qquad + \dfrac{(x+1)x(x+1)}{(x+2)x(x+1)}$

$= \dfrac{2x^2+6x+4}{x(x+1)(x+2)} - \dfrac{x^3+2x^2}{x(x+1)(x+2)}$

$\qquad + \dfrac{x^3+2x^2+x}{x(x+1)(x+2)}$

$= \dfrac{2x^2+7x+4}{x(x+1)(x+2)}$

Check Point 2

① $\dfrac{\tfrac{x}{3}-7}{9+\tfrac{1}{x}} = \dfrac{\left(\tfrac{x}{3}-7\right)\cdot 3x}{\left(9+\tfrac{1}{x}\right)\cdot 3x} = \dfrac{x^2-21x}{27x+3} = \dfrac{x(x-21)}{3(9x+1)}$

② $\dfrac{\tfrac{10}{x-1}}{\tfrac{1}{5}-\tfrac{2}{x-1}} = \dfrac{\left(\tfrac{10}{x-1}\right)\cdot 5(x-1)}{\left(\tfrac{1}{5}-\tfrac{2}{x-1}\right)\cdot 5(x-1)}$

$= \dfrac{50}{(x-1)-10} = \dfrac{50}{x-11}$

③ $\dfrac{xy^{-1}-1}{x^2-y^{-2}} = \dfrac{\tfrac{x}{y}-1}{x^2-\tfrac{1}{y^2}} = \dfrac{\left(\tfrac{x}{y}-1\right)\cdot y^2}{\left(x^2-\tfrac{1}{y^2}\right)\cdot y^2}$

$= \dfrac{xy-y^2}{x^2y^2-1} = \dfrac{y(x-y)}{(xy-1)(xy+1)}$

④ $\dfrac{\tfrac{1}{1-a}-\tfrac{1}{1+a}}{\tfrac{1}{1-a}+\tfrac{1}{1+a}} = \dfrac{\left(\tfrac{1}{1-a}-\tfrac{1}{1+a}\right)(1-a)(1+a)}{\left(\tfrac{1}{1-a}+\tfrac{1}{1+a}\right)(1-a)(1+a)}$

$= \dfrac{(1+a)-(1-a)}{(1+a)+(1-a)} = \dfrac{2a}{2} = a$

Check Point 3

① $\dfrac{2}{(x+1)(x+3)} + \dfrac{2}{(x+3)(x+5)}$

$= \dfrac{2}{(x+3)-(x+1)}\left(\dfrac{1}{x+1}-\dfrac{1}{x+3}\right)$

$\qquad + \dfrac{2}{(x+5)-(x+3)}\left(\dfrac{1}{x+3}-\dfrac{1}{x+5}\right)$

$= \left(\dfrac{1}{x+1}-\dfrac{1}{x+3}\right)+\left(\dfrac{1}{x+3}-\dfrac{1}{x+5}\right)$

$= \dfrac{1}{x+1}-\dfrac{1}{x+5} = \dfrac{x+5-(x+1)}{(x+1)(x+5)}$

$= \dfrac{4}{(x+1)(x+5)}$

② $\dfrac{1}{x(x+2)} + \dfrac{1}{(x+2)(x+4)} + \dfrac{1}{(x+4)(x+6)}$

$= \dfrac{1}{(x+2)-x}\left(\dfrac{1}{x}-\dfrac{1}{x+2}\right)$

$\quad + \dfrac{1}{(x+4)-(x+2)}\left(\dfrac{1}{x+2}-\dfrac{1}{x+4}\right)$

$\quad + \dfrac{1}{(x+6)-(x+4)}\left(\dfrac{1}{x+4}-\dfrac{1}{x+6}\right)$

Solutions Manual

$$= \frac{1}{2}\left\{\left(\frac{1}{x}-\frac{1}{x+2}\right)+\left(\frac{1}{x+2}-\frac{1}{x+4}\right) \\ +\left(\frac{1}{x+4}-\frac{1}{x+6}\right)\right\}$$

$$=\frac{1}{2}\left(\frac{1}{x}-\frac{1}{x+6}\right)=\frac{1}{2}\left(\frac{x+6-x}{x(x+6)}\right)=\frac{3}{x(x+6)}$$

Review Exercises

01

(1) $\dfrac{x+2}{3}+\dfrac{x-4}{6}=\dfrac{2(x+2)+x-4}{6}=\dfrac{3x}{6}=\dfrac{x}{2}$

(2) $\dfrac{5}{2x+2}+\dfrac{2x-3}{2x+2}=\dfrac{5+2x-3}{2x+2}=\dfrac{2x+2}{2x+2}=1$

(3) $1-\dfrac{x-4}{x^2-1}=\dfrac{x^2-1}{x^2-1}-\dfrac{x-4}{x^2-1}=\dfrac{x^2-x+3}{x^2-1}$

(4) $\dfrac{-1}{2x^2+2x}+\dfrac{1}{2}=\dfrac{-1}{2x(x+1)}+\dfrac{x(x+1)}{2x(x+1)}$

$$=\dfrac{x^2+x-1}{2x(x+1)}$$

(5) $\dfrac{3}{x+5}+\dfrac{5x}{2x-1}$

$$=\dfrac{3(2x-1)}{(x+5)(2x-1)}+\dfrac{5x(x+5)}{(2x-1)(x+5)}$$

$$=\dfrac{6x-3}{(x+5)(2x-1)}+\dfrac{5x^2+25x}{(2x-1)(x+5)}$$

$$=\dfrac{5x^2+31x-3}{(2x-1)(x+5)}$$

(6) $\dfrac{x}{2x^2+8x}-\dfrac{7}{2x}=\dfrac{x}{2x(x+4)}-\dfrac{7}{2x}$

$$=\dfrac{x}{2x(x+4)}-\dfrac{7(x+4)}{2x(x+4)}$$

$$=\dfrac{-6x-28}{2x(x+4)}=-\dfrac{3x+14}{x(x+4)}$$

(7) $\dfrac{3}{x-6}+\dfrac{1}{x+2}$

$$=\dfrac{3(x+2)}{(x-6)(x+2)}+\dfrac{(x-6)}{(x+2)(x-6)}$$

$$=\dfrac{4x}{(x-6)(x+2)}$$

(8) $\dfrac{1}{(x-1)^2}-\dfrac{1}{x^2-1}$

$$=\dfrac{1}{(x-1)^2}-\dfrac{1}{(x-1)(x+1)}$$

$$=\dfrac{x+1}{(x-1)^2(x+1)}-\dfrac{x-1}{(x-1)(x+1)(x-1)}$$

$$=\dfrac{2}{(x-1)^2(x+1)}$$

02

(1) $\dfrac{x^2+2x}{x^2-2x}-\dfrac{x}{2x^2-8}$

$$=\dfrac{x(x+2)}{x(x-2)}-\dfrac{x}{2(x-2)(x+2)}$$

$$=\dfrac{(x+2)(x+2)\cdot 2}{(x-2)(x+2)\cdot 2}-\dfrac{x}{2(x-2)(x+2)}$$

$$=\dfrac{2(x+2)^2-x}{2(x-2)(x+2)}=\dfrac{2x^2+7x+8}{2(x-2)(x+2)}$$

(2) $\dfrac{3x-1}{x^2+4x+4}-\dfrac{2}{x^2-4}$

$$=\dfrac{3x-1}{(x+2)^2}-\dfrac{2}{(x+2)(x-2)}$$

$$=\dfrac{(3x-1)(x-2)}{(x+2)^2(x-2)}-\dfrac{2(x+2)}{(x+2)(x-2)(x+2)}$$

$$=\dfrac{3x^2-7x+2}{(x+2)^2(x-2)}-\dfrac{2x+4}{(x+2)^2(x-2)}$$

$$=\dfrac{3x^2-9x-2}{(x+2)^2(x-2)}$$

(3) $\dfrac{1}{4x^2-y^2}+\dfrac{1}{2x^2-3xy+y^2}$

$$=\dfrac{1}{(2x-y)(2x+y)}+\dfrac{1}{(x-y)(2x-y)}$$

$$=\dfrac{x-y}{(2x-y)(2x+y)(x-y)}+\dfrac{2x+y}{(x-y)(2x-y)(2x+y)}$$

$$=\dfrac{3x}{(2x-y)(2x+y)(x-y)}$$

(4) $\dfrac{1}{x-y}+\dfrac{x}{x+y}-\dfrac{y}{x^2-y^2}$

$$=\dfrac{x+y}{(x-y)(x+y)}+\dfrac{x(x-y)}{(x+y)(x-y)}-\dfrac{y}{(x+y)(x-y)}$$

$$=\dfrac{x+y+x^2-xy-y}{(x-y)(x+y)}=\dfrac{x^2-xy+x}{(x-y)(x+y)}$$

03

(1) $\dfrac{\dfrac{1}{x}-x}{\dfrac{1}{x}-1}=\dfrac{\left(\dfrac{1}{x}-x\right)\cdot x}{\left(\dfrac{1}{x}-1\right)\cdot x}=\dfrac{1-x^2}{1-x}$

$$=\dfrac{(1-x)(1+x)}{1-x}=x+1$$

(2) $\dfrac{\dfrac{10}{x-1}}{\dfrac{1}{5}-\dfrac{2}{x-1}} = \dfrac{\left(\dfrac{10}{x-1}\right)\cdot 5(x-1)}{\left(\dfrac{1}{5}-\dfrac{2}{x-1}\right)\cdot 5(x-1)}$

$= \dfrac{50}{(x-1)-10} = \dfrac{50}{x-11}$

(3) $\dfrac{\dfrac{1+x}{x^3}}{\dfrac{1}{x^2}-\dfrac{1}{x(x+1)}} = \dfrac{\left(\dfrac{1+x}{x^3}\right)\cdot x^3(x+1)}{\left(\dfrac{1}{x^2}-\dfrac{1}{x(x+1)}\right)\cdot x^3(x+1)}$

$= \dfrac{(1+x)(x+1)}{x(x+1)-x^2} = \dfrac{(x+1)^2}{x}$

(4) $\dfrac{x-y}{\dfrac{1}{x}-\dfrac{1}{y^2}} = \dfrac{(x-y)\cdot xy^2}{\left(\dfrac{1}{x}-\dfrac{1}{y^2}\right)\cdot xy^2} = \dfrac{xy^2(x-y)}{y^2-x}$

(5) $\dfrac{1-\dfrac{1}{xy}}{\dfrac{1}{x}-\dfrac{1}{y}} = \dfrac{\left(1-\dfrac{1}{xy}\right)\cdot xy}{\left(\dfrac{1}{x}-\dfrac{1}{y}\right)\cdot xy} = \dfrac{xy-1}{y-x}$

(6) $\dfrac{\dfrac{1}{x-1}-\dfrac{1}{x+1}}{\dfrac{1}{x+1}+\dfrac{1}{x-1}} = \dfrac{\left(\dfrac{1}{x-1}-\dfrac{1}{x+1}\right)\cdot (x-1)(x+1)}{\left(\dfrac{1}{x+1}+\dfrac{1}{x-1}\right)\cdot (x-1)(x+1)}$

$= \dfrac{(x+1)-(x-1)}{(x-1)+(x+1)} = \dfrac{2}{2x} = \dfrac{1}{x}$

04

(1) $\dfrac{\dfrac{1}{x}-\dfrac{1}{y}}{\dfrac{1}{x^2}-\dfrac{1}{xy}+\dfrac{1}{y^2}} = \dfrac{\left(\dfrac{1}{x}-\dfrac{1}{y}\right)\cdot x^2y^2}{\left(\dfrac{1}{x^2}-\dfrac{1}{xy}+\dfrac{1}{y^2}\right)\cdot x^2y^2}$

$= \dfrac{xy^2-x^2y}{y^2-xy+x^2} = \dfrac{xy(y-x)}{x^2-xy+y^2}$

(2) $\dfrac{1-\dfrac{1}{x-2}}{x+1-\dfrac{2}{x+1}} = \dfrac{\left(1-\dfrac{1}{x-2}\right)\cdot (x-2)(x+1)}{\left(x+1-\dfrac{2}{x+1}\right)\cdot (x-2)(x+1)}$

$= \dfrac{(x-2)(x+1)-(x+1)}{(x-2)(x+1)^2-2(x-2)}$

$= \dfrac{(x+1)((x-2)-1)}{(x-2)((x+1)^2-2)}$

$= \dfrac{(x+1)(x-3)}{(x-2)(x^2+2x+1-2)}$

$= \dfrac{(x+1)(x-3)}{(x-2)(x^2+2x-1)}$

(3) $\dfrac{1+\dfrac{x}{x-y}}{\dfrac{y}{x+y}-2} = \dfrac{\left(1+\dfrac{x}{x-y}\right)\cdot (x-y)(x+y)}{\left(\dfrac{y}{x+y}-2\right)\cdot (x-y)(x+y)}$

$= \dfrac{(x-y)(x+y)+x(x+y)}{y(x-y)-2(x-y)(x+y)}$

$= \dfrac{(x+y)((x-y)+x)}{(x-y)(y-2(x+y))}$

$= \dfrac{(x+y)(2x-y)}{(x-y)(-2x-y)}$

$= -\dfrac{(x+y)(2x-y)}{(x-y)(2x+y)}$

(4) $\dfrac{\dfrac{x+y}{x-y}-\dfrac{x-y}{x+y}}{\dfrac{x+y}{x-y}+\dfrac{x-y}{x+y}}$

$= \dfrac{\left(\dfrac{x+y}{x-y}-\dfrac{x-y}{x+y}\right)\cdot (x-y)(x+y)}{\left(\dfrac{x+y}{x-y}+\dfrac{x-y}{x+y}\right)\cdot (x-y)(x+y)}$

$= \dfrac{(x+y)^2-(x-y)^2}{(x+y)^2+(x-y)^2}$

$= \dfrac{x^2+2xy+y^2-(x^2-2xy+y^2)}{x^2+2xy+y^2+x^2-2xy+y^2}$

$= \dfrac{4xy}{2x^2+2y^2} = \dfrac{2xy}{x^2+y^2}$

05

Simplify the right side of a given equation.

(1) $\dfrac{a}{x-2}+\dfrac{b}{x+2} = \dfrac{a(x+2)+b(x-2)}{(x-2)(x+2)}$

$= \dfrac{(a+b)x+2a-2b}{x^2-4}$

So the equation is

$\dfrac{12}{x^2-4} = \dfrac{(a+b)x+2a-2b}{x^2-4}$

$12 = (a+b)x+2a-2b$

$\Rightarrow a+b=0,\ 2a-2b=12$

Solving the system of equations, we have $a=3$ and $b=-3$. Therefore, $ab=3(-3)=-9$

(2) $\dfrac{a}{2x-1}+\dfrac{b}{x+2} = \dfrac{a(x+2)+b(2x-1)}{(2x-1)(x+2)}$

$= \dfrac{(a+2b)x+2a-b}{(2x-1)(x+2)}$

Solutions Manual

So the equation is
$$\frac{10}{(2x-1)(x+2)}=\frac{(a+2b)x+2a-b}{(2x-1)(x+2)}$$
$$10=(a+2b)x+2a-b$$
$$\Rightarrow a+2b=0,\ 2a-b=10$$
Solving the system of equations, we have $a=4$ and $b=-2$. Therefore,
$$ab=4(-2)=-8$$

06

$$\frac{2}{1-x}+\frac{2}{1+x}+\frac{4}{1+x^2}+\frac{8}{1+x^4}$$
$$=\frac{2(1+x)+2(1-x)}{(1-x)(1+x)}+\frac{4}{1+x^2}+\frac{8}{1+x^4}$$
$$=\frac{4}{1-x^2}+\frac{4}{1+x^2}+\frac{8}{1+x^4}$$
$$=\frac{4(1+x^2)+4(1-x^2)}{(1-x^2)(1+x^2)}+\frac{8}{1+x^4}$$
$$=\frac{8}{1-x^4}+\frac{8}{1+x^4}$$
$$=\frac{8(1+x^4)+8(1-x^4)}{(1-x^4)(1+x^4)}=\frac{16}{1-x^8}$$

07

Use the decomposition of partial fractions.

(1) $\dfrac{2}{x(x+2)}+\dfrac{2}{(x+2)(x+4)}-\dfrac{4}{x(x+4)}$

$=\dfrac{2}{(x+2)-x}\left(\dfrac{1}{x}-\dfrac{1}{x+2}\right)$
$+\dfrac{2}{(x+4)-(x+2)}\left(\dfrac{1}{x+2}-\dfrac{1}{x+4}\right)$
$-\dfrac{4}{(x+4)-x}\left(\dfrac{1}{x}-\dfrac{1}{x+4}\right)$
$=\left(\dfrac{1}{x}-\dfrac{1}{x+2}\right)+\left(\dfrac{1}{x+2}-\dfrac{1}{x+4}\right)$
$-\left(\dfrac{1}{x}-\dfrac{1}{x+4}\right)$
$=\dfrac{1}{x}-\dfrac{1}{x+2}+\dfrac{1}{x+2}-\dfrac{1}{x+4}-\dfrac{1}{x}+\dfrac{1}{x+4}=0$

(2) $\dfrac{y}{x(x+y)}+\dfrac{z}{(x+y)(x+y+z)}$
$+\dfrac{1}{(x+y+z)(x+y+z+1)}$

$=\dfrac{y}{(x+y)-x}\left(\dfrac{1}{x}-\dfrac{1}{x+y}\right)$
$+\dfrac{z}{(x+y+z)-(x+y)}\left(\dfrac{1}{x+y}-\dfrac{1}{x+y+z}\right)$
$+\dfrac{1}{(x+y+z+1)-(x+y+z)}$
$\quad\left(\dfrac{1}{x+y+z}-\dfrac{1}{x+y+z+1}\right)$
$=\left(\dfrac{1}{x}-\dfrac{1}{x+y}\right)+\left(\dfrac{1}{x+y}-\dfrac{1}{x+y+z}\right)$
$+\left(\dfrac{1}{x+y+z}-\dfrac{1}{x+y+z+1}\right)$
$=\dfrac{1}{x}-\dfrac{1}{x+y+z+1}$
$=\dfrac{x+y+z+1-x}{x(x+y+z+1)}=\dfrac{y+z+1}{x(x+y+z+1)}$

08

$\dfrac{1}{2\times 4}+\dfrac{1}{4\times 6}+\dfrac{1}{6\times 8}+\dfrac{1}{8\times 10}$
$=\dfrac{1}{4-2}\left(\dfrac{1}{2}-\dfrac{1}{4}\right)+\dfrac{1}{6-4}\left(\dfrac{1}{4}-\dfrac{1}{6}\right)$
$+\dfrac{1}{8-6}\left(\dfrac{1}{6}-\dfrac{1}{8}\right)+\dfrac{1}{10-8}\left(\dfrac{1}{8}-\dfrac{1}{10}\right)$
$=\dfrac{1}{2}\left\{\left(\dfrac{1}{2}-\dfrac{1}{4}\right)+\left(\dfrac{1}{4}-\dfrac{1}{6}\right)+\left(\dfrac{1}{6}-\dfrac{1}{8}\right)+\left(\dfrac{1}{8}-\dfrac{1}{10}\right)\right\}$
$=\dfrac{1}{2}\left(\dfrac{1}{2}-\dfrac{1}{10}\right)=\dfrac{1}{2}\times\dfrac{2}{5}=\dfrac{1}{5}$

09

$x-4+\dfrac{1}{x}=0,\ x+\dfrac{1}{x}=4$

(1) $x^2+\dfrac{1}{x^2}=\left(x+\dfrac{1}{x}\right)^2-2=4^2-2=14$

(2) $\left(x-\dfrac{1}{x}\right)^2=\left(x+\dfrac{1}{x}\right)^2-4=4^2-4=12$
$x-\dfrac{1}{x}=\pm\sqrt{12}=\pm 2\sqrt{3}$

(3) $x^2-\dfrac{1}{x^2}=\left(x-\dfrac{1}{x}\right)\left(x+\dfrac{1}{x}\right)$
$=(\pm 2\sqrt{3})(4)=\pm 8\sqrt{3}$

(4) $x^3+\dfrac{1}{x^3}=\left(x+\dfrac{1}{x}\right)\left(x^2-x\cdot\dfrac{1}{x}+\left(\dfrac{1}{x}\right)^2\right)$
$=\left(x+\dfrac{1}{x}\right)\left(x^2+\dfrac{1}{x^2}-1\right)$
$=4(14-1)=52$

10

Simplify the left side of a given equation.

(1) $1-\dfrac{1}{1-\dfrac{1}{1-\dfrac{1}{x}}} = 1-\dfrac{1}{1-\dfrac{1}{\dfrac{x-1}{x}}}$

$=1-\dfrac{1}{1-\dfrac{x}{x-1}} = 1-\dfrac{1}{\dfrac{x-1-x}{x-1}}$

$=1+\dfrac{1}{\dfrac{1}{x-1}} = 1+x-1 = x$

So the equation is
$x = ax+b \Rightarrow a=1,\ b=0$

(2) $2-\dfrac{2}{2-\dfrac{2}{2-\dfrac{2}{x-2}}} = 2-\dfrac{2}{2-\dfrac{2}{\dfrac{2(x-2)-2}{x-2}}}$

$=2-\dfrac{2}{2-\dfrac{2}{\dfrac{2x-6}{x-2}}} = 2-\dfrac{2}{2-\dfrac{2(x-2)}{2x-6}}$

$=2-\dfrac{2}{2-\dfrac{x-2}{x-3}} = 2-\dfrac{2}{\dfrac{2(x-3)-(x-2)}{x-3}}$

$=2-\dfrac{2}{\dfrac{x-4}{x-3}} = 2-\dfrac{2(x-3)}{x-4}$

$=\dfrac{2(x-4)-2(x-3)}{x-4} = \dfrac{-2}{x-4}$

So the equation is

$-\dfrac{2}{x-4} = -\dfrac{2}{ax+b} \Rightarrow a=1,\ b=-4$

11

$\left(x+\dfrac{1}{x}\right)^2 = x^2 + 2(x)\left(\dfrac{1}{x}\right) + \left(\dfrac{1}{x}\right)^2$

$= x^2 + \dfrac{1}{x^2} + 2 = 14 + 2 = 16$

$x + \dfrac{1}{x} = \pm 4 \Rightarrow x + \dfrac{1}{x} = 4$

3. Rational Equations

Check Point 1

① $2 + \dfrac{12}{5x} = \dfrac{2}{x}$

$\left(2 + \dfrac{12}{5x}\right) \cdot 5x = \left(\dfrac{2}{x}\right) \cdot 5x$

$10x + 12 = 10$

$10x = -2,\ x = -\dfrac{1}{5}$

Check the solution: $2 + \dfrac{12}{5\left(-\dfrac{1}{5}\right) \neq 0} = \dfrac{2}{-\dfrac{1}{5} \neq 0}$

$x = -\dfrac{1}{5}$

② $\dfrac{1}{x} + \dfrac{1}{x^2} = \dfrac{1}{2x^2}$

$\left(\dfrac{1}{x} + \dfrac{1}{x^2}\right) \cdot 2x^2 = \left(\dfrac{1}{2x^2}\right) \cdot 2x^2$

$2x + 2 = 1$

$2x = -1,\ x = -\dfrac{1}{2}$

Check the solution:

$\dfrac{1}{-\dfrac{1}{2} \neq 0} + \dfrac{1}{\left(-\dfrac{1}{2}\right)^2 \neq 0} = \dfrac{1}{2\left(-\dfrac{1}{2}\right)^2 \neq 0}$

$x = -\dfrac{1}{2}$

③ $\dfrac{5}{x^2-2x} + \dfrac{2}{x} = \dfrac{5}{x^2-2x}$

$\left(\dfrac{5}{x(x-2)} + \dfrac{2}{x}\right)x(x-2) = \left(\dfrac{5}{x(x-2)}\right)x(x-2)$

$5 + 2(x-2) = 5,\ 5 + 2x - 4 = 5$

$2x = 4,\ x = 2$

Check the solution:

$\dfrac{5}{2^2-2(2)=0} + \dfrac{2}{2 \neq 0} \neq \dfrac{5}{2(2)-4=0}$

$x=2$ is the extraneous solution. There is NO solution to the equation.

No Solution

④ $\dfrac{30}{x+2} + \dfrac{x}{x-2} = 9$

$\left(\dfrac{30}{x+2} + \dfrac{x}{x-2}\right)(x+2)(x-2) = 9(x+2)(x-2)$

$30(x-2) + x(x+2) = 9(x^2-4)$

Solutions Manual

$30x-60+x^2+2x=9x^2-36$
$8x^2-32x+24=0$
$x^2-4x+3=0,$
$(x-3)(x-1)=0, \ x=3 \text{ or } x=1$
Check the solution:
$\dfrac{30}{3+2\neq 0}+\dfrac{30}{3-2\neq 0}=9$ and
$\dfrac{30}{1+2\neq 0}+\dfrac{1}{1-2\neq 0}=9$

$$x=3 \text{ or } x=1$$

Check Point 2

Let $x=2k$ and $y=5k$ from $x:y=2:5$

① $\dfrac{5x+y}{x-5y}=\dfrac{5(2k)+5k}{2k-5(5k)}=\dfrac{15k}{-23k}=-\dfrac{15}{23}$

② $\dfrac{x^2-y^2}{2x^2+xy}=\dfrac{(x-y)(x+y)}{x(2x+y)}$

$=\dfrac{(2k-5k)(2k+5k)}{2k(2(2k)+5k)}$

$=\dfrac{(-3k)(7k)}{2k(9k)}=\dfrac{-21k^2}{18k^2}=-\dfrac{7}{6}$

Check Point 3

$\dfrac{a-2b}{4}=\dfrac{a}{3}=\dfrac{4b+2c}{5}$

$\Rightarrow \dfrac{a-2b}{4}=\dfrac{a}{3}\cdot\dfrac{2}{2}=\dfrac{4b+2c}{5}$

Using $\dfrac{a}{b}=\dfrac{c}{d}=\dfrac{e}{f}=\dfrac{a+c+e}{b+d+f}$,

$\dfrac{a-2b+2a+4b+2c}{4+3\cdot 2+5}=\dfrac{3a+2b+2c}{15}$

$=\dfrac{3a+2b+2c}{k}$

Therefore, $k=15$

Review Exercises

01

(1) $\dfrac{6}{x^2}=\dfrac{1}{x^2}+\dfrac{1}{x}$

$\dfrac{6}{x^2}\cdot x^2=\left(\dfrac{1}{x^2}+\dfrac{1}{x}\right)\cdot x^2$

$6=1+x, \ x=5$
Check the solution:
$\dfrac{6}{5^2\neq 0}=\dfrac{1}{5^2\neq 0}+\dfrac{1}{5\neq 0}$

$$x=5$$

(2) $\dfrac{1}{x}-\dfrac{1}{3x^2}=-\dfrac{1}{6x^2}$

$\left(\dfrac{1}{x}-\dfrac{1}{3x^2}\right)\cdot 6x^2=-\dfrac{1}{6x^2}\cdot 6x^2$

$6x-2=-1, \ x=\dfrac{1}{6}$
Check the solution:
$\dfrac{1}{\frac{1}{6}\neq 0}-\dfrac{1}{3\left(\frac{1}{6}\right)^2\neq 0}=\dfrac{1}{6\left(\frac{1}{6}\right)^2\neq 0}$

$$x=\dfrac{1}{6}$$

(3) $\dfrac{x-6}{3x}-1=\dfrac{x^2-5x-24}{3x}$

$\left(\dfrac{x-6}{3x}-1\right)\cdot 3x=\dfrac{x^2-5x-24}{3x}\cdot 3x$

$(x-6)-3x=x^2-5x-24$
$x^2-3x-18=0$
$(x+3)(x-6)=0, \ x=-3 \text{ or } x=6$
Check the solution:
$\dfrac{-3-6}{3(-3)\neq 0}-1=\dfrac{(-3)^2-5(-3)-24}{3(-3)\neq 0}$ and

$\dfrac{6-6}{3\cdot 6\neq 0}-1=\dfrac{6^2-5\cdot 6-24}{3\cdot 6\neq 0}$

$$x=-3 \text{ or } x=6$$

(4) $\dfrac{1}{x}+\dfrac{3x+12}{x^2-5x}=\dfrac{7x-56}{x^2-5x}$

$\left(\dfrac{1}{x}+\dfrac{3x+12}{x(x-5)}\right)x(x-5)=\left(\dfrac{7x-56}{x(x-5)}\right)x(x-5)$

$(x-5)+(3x+12)=7x-56$
$4x+7=7x-56, \ x=21$
Check the solution:
$\dfrac{1}{21\neq 0}+\dfrac{3\cdot 21+12}{21^2-5\cdot 21\neq 0}=\dfrac{7\cdot 21-56}{21^2-5\cdot 21\neq 0}$

$$x=21$$

(5) $\dfrac{1}{x-2}+\dfrac{1}{x^2-7x+10}=\dfrac{6}{x-2}$

$\dfrac{1}{x-2}+\dfrac{1}{(x-2)(x-5)}=\dfrac{6}{x-2}$

$\left(\dfrac{1}{x-2}+\dfrac{1}{(x-2)(x-5)}\right)(x-2)(x-5)$

$$=\frac{6}{x-2}\cdot(x-2)(x-5)$$
$(x-5)+1=6(x-5)$
$x-4=6x-30,\ x=\frac{26}{5}$

Check the solution:
$$\frac{1}{\frac{26}{5}-2\ne0}-\frac{1}{\left(\frac{26}{5}\right)^2-7\left(\frac{26}{5}\right)+10\ne0}=\frac{1}{\frac{26}{5}-2\ne0}$$
$$x=\frac{26}{5}$$

(6) $1-\dfrac{1}{x^2+2x}=\dfrac{x-1}{x}$

$\left(1-\dfrac{1}{x(x+2)}\right)x(x+2)=\dfrac{x-1}{x}\cdot x(x+2)$

$x(x+2)-1=(x-1)(x+2)$

$x^2+2x-1=x^2+x-2,\ x=-1$

Check the solution:
$$1-\frac{1}{(-1)^2+2(-1)\ne0}=\frac{-1-1}{-1\ne0}$$
$$x=-1$$

02

(1) $\dfrac{x-2}{x+3}-\dfrac{3}{x+2}=1$

$\left(\dfrac{x-2}{x+3}-\dfrac{3}{x+2}\right)(x+3)(x+2)=1\cdot(x+3)(x+2)$

$(x-2)(x+2)-3(x+3)=(x+3)(x+2)$

$x^2-4-3x-9=x^2+5x+6$

$-19=8x,\ x=-\dfrac{19}{8}$

Check the solution:
$$\frac{-\frac{19}{8}-2}{-\frac{19}{8}+3\ne0}-\frac{3}{-\frac{19}{8}+2\ne0}=1$$
$$x=-\frac{19}{8}$$

(2) $\dfrac{4}{x+5}+\dfrac{1}{x^2}=\dfrac{5}{x^3+5x^2}$

$\dfrac{4}{x+5}+\dfrac{1}{x^2}=\dfrac{5}{x^2(x+5)}$

$\left(\dfrac{4}{x+5}+\dfrac{1}{x^2}\right)x^2(x+5)=\dfrac{5}{x^2(x+5)}\cdot x^2(x+5)$

$4x^2+(x+5)=5,\ 4x^2+x=0$

$x(4x+1)=0,\ x=0$ or $x=-\dfrac{1}{4}$

Check the solution:
$$\frac{4}{0+5\ne0}+\frac{1}{0^2=0}\ne\frac{5}{0^3+5\cdot0^2=0}\ \rightarrow\ x=0\text{ is}$$
an extraneous solution.
$$\frac{4}{-\frac{1}{4}+5\ne0}-\frac{1}{\left(-\frac{1}{4}\right)^2\ne0}=\frac{5}{\left(-\frac{1}{4}\right)^3+5\left(-\frac{1}{4}\right)^2\ne0}$$
$$x=-\frac{1}{4}$$

(3) $\dfrac{x+5}{x^2+x}=\dfrac{1}{x^2+x}-\dfrac{x-6}{x+1}$

$\dfrac{x+5}{x(x+1)}\cdot x(x+1)=\left(\dfrac{1}{x(x+1)}-\dfrac{x-6}{x+1}\right)x(x+1)$

$x+5=1-x(x-6),\ x+5=-x^2+6x+1$

$x^2-5x+4=0$

$(x-1)(x-4),\ x=1$ or $x=4$

Check the solution:
$$\frac{1+5}{1^2+1\ne0}=\frac{1}{1^2+1\ne0}-\frac{1-6}{1+1\ne0}\text{ and}$$
$$\frac{4+5}{4^2+4\ne0}=\frac{1}{4^2+4\ne0}-\frac{4-6}{4+4\ne0}$$
$$x=1\text{ or }x=4$$

(4) $\dfrac{x}{x-1}-\dfrac{1}{x+2}=\dfrac{3}{x^2+x-2}$

$\dfrac{x}{x-1}-\dfrac{1}{x+2}=\dfrac{3}{(x-1)(x+2)}$

$\left(\dfrac{x}{x-1}-\dfrac{1}{x+2}\right)(x-1)(x+2)$

$=\dfrac{3}{(x-1)(x+2)}\cdot(x-1)(x+2)$

$x(x+2)-(x-1)=3,\ x^2+x-2=0$

$(x+2)(x-1)=0,\ x=-2$ or $x=1$

Check the solution:
$$\frac{-2}{-2-1\ne0}-\frac{1}{-2+2=0}\ne\frac{3}{(-2)^2+-2-2=0}$$
$\rightarrow\ x=-2$ is an extraneous solution.
$$\frac{1}{1-1=0}\quad\frac{1}{1+2\ne0}\ne\frac{3}{1^2+1-2=0}\ \rightarrow\ x-1$$
is also an extraneous solution.

No Solution

Solutions Manual

03

(1) $\dfrac{2}{2x^2-7x-4} = \dfrac{a}{x-4} - \dfrac{bx}{(x-4)(2x+1)}$

$\dfrac{2}{(x-4)(2x+1)} \cdot (x-4)(2x+1)$

$= \left(\dfrac{a}{x-4} - \dfrac{bx}{(x-4)(2x+1)}\right)(x-4)(2x+1)$

$2 = a(2x+1) - bx$

$2 = 2ax + a - bx,\ 2 = (2a-b)x + a$

$\Rightarrow 2 = a$

$2a - b = 0,\ 2(2) - b = 0,\ b = 4$

Therefore, $a+b = 2+4 = 6$

(2) $\dfrac{3x-5}{3x^2-11x+6} = \dfrac{a}{x-3} - \dfrac{x}{(x-3)(3x-2)} + \dfrac{b}{3x-2}$

$\dfrac{3x-5}{(x-3)(3x-2)} \cdot (x-3)(3x-2)$

$= \left(\dfrac{a}{x-3} - \dfrac{x}{(x-3)(3x-2)} + \dfrac{b}{3x-2}\right)(x-3)(3x-2)$

$3x-5 = a(3x-2) - x + b(x-3)$

$3x-5 = 3ax - 2a - x + bx - 3b$

$3x-5 = (3a-1+b)x - (2a+3b)$

$\Rightarrow 3 = 3a - 1 + b,\ 3a + b = 4 \qquad (1)$

$\qquad 2a + 3b = 5 \qquad (2)$

Solving the system of equations (1) and (2), we have $a=1$ and $b=1$.

Therefore, $a+b = 1+1 = 2$

04

Let $a=4k$ and $b=5k$ from $a:b=4:5$.

(1) $\dfrac{a^2+b^2}{2ab} = \dfrac{(4k)^2+(5k)^2}{2(4k)(5k)} = \dfrac{41k^2}{40k^2} = \dfrac{41}{40}$

(2) $\dfrac{ab+b^2}{a^2-ab} = \dfrac{b(a+b)}{a(a-b)} = \dfrac{5k(4k+5k)}{4k(4k-5k)} = \dfrac{5k(9k)}{4k(-k)}$

$= \dfrac{45k^2}{-4k^2} = -\dfrac{45}{4}$

05

Let $x=k$, $y=2k$ and $z=3k$ from $x:y:z=1:2:3$.

(1) $\dfrac{2x-y+2z}{x+y+z} = \dfrac{2k-2k+2(3k)}{k+2k+3k} = \dfrac{6k}{6k} = 1$

(2) $\dfrac{xy-xz+yz}{x^2+z^2} = \dfrac{k(2k)-k(3k)+2k(3k)}{k^2+(3k)^2}$

$= \dfrac{2k^2-3k^2+6k^2}{10k^2}$

$= \dfrac{5k^2}{10k^2} = \dfrac{1}{2}$

06

Since $x=2y$ and $3y=4z \Rightarrow z=\dfrac{3y}{4}$, we have $x:y:z = 2y:y:\dfrac{3}{4}y = 8:4:3$.

If we let $x=8k$, $y=4k$ and $z=3k$,

$\dfrac{4x+2y+3z}{x+y+z} = \dfrac{4(8k)+2(4k)+3(3k)}{8k+4k+3k}$

$= \dfrac{4(8k)+2(4k)+3(3k)}{15k}$

$= \dfrac{49k}{15k} = \dfrac{49}{15}$

07

Using the property $\dfrac{a}{b} = \dfrac{c}{d} = \dfrac{e}{f} = \dfrac{a+c+e}{b+d+f}$,

$k = \dfrac{4a+3c}{7a+9b+10c} = \dfrac{b+3c}{5a-2c} = \dfrac{2a+5b}{3b+4c}$

$= \dfrac{4a+3c+b+3c+2a+5b}{7a+9b+10c+5a-2c+3b+4c}$

$= \dfrac{6(a+b+c)}{12(a+b+c)} = \dfrac{1}{2}$

Therefore, $k = \dfrac{1}{2}$

08

$\dfrac{2a+4b}{2} = \dfrac{b+3c}{3} = \dfrac{2c-a}{4}$

$\Rightarrow \dfrac{2a+4b}{2} \cdot \dfrac{3}{3} = \dfrac{b+3c}{3} \cdot \dfrac{2}{2} = \dfrac{2c-a}{4}$

Using the property $\dfrac{a}{b} = \dfrac{c}{d} = \dfrac{e}{f} = \dfrac{a+c+e}{b+d+f}$,

$\dfrac{3(2a+4b)+2(b+3c)+2c-a}{6+6+4} = \dfrac{5a+14b+8c}{16}$

$= \dfrac{5a+14b+8c}{k}$

Therefore, $k = 16$

42 Solutions Manual

09

If we let $\dfrac{a+b}{3}=\dfrac{b+c}{4}=\dfrac{a+c}{5}=k$, then $a+b=3k$ (1), $b+c=4k$ (2), and

$a+c=5k$ (3). By adding (1), (2), and (3),
$a+b+b+c+a+c=3k+4k+5k$
$2(a+b+c)=12k$
$a+b+c=6k$ (4)

By subtracting each of (1), (2), and (3) from (4), we have $c=3k$, $a=2k$, and $b=k$. Therefore, $a:b:c=2k:k:3k=2:1:3$

4. Application of Rational Equations

Check Point 1

① Let two positive numbers be x and y, and $x>y$. Then we have $\begin{cases} x-y=8 \\ \dfrac{1}{y}-\dfrac{1}{x}=\dfrac{1}{6} \end{cases}$. Since $x-y=8 \;\to\; x=y+8$, we have

$\dfrac{1}{y}-\dfrac{1}{x}=\dfrac{1}{6}$

$\dfrac{1}{y}-\dfrac{1}{y+8}=\dfrac{1}{6}$

$\left(\dfrac{1}{y}-\dfrac{1}{y+8}\right)6y(y+8)=\dfrac{1}{6}\cdot 6y(y+8)$

$6(y+8)-6y=y(y+8)$

$y^2+8y-48=0$

$(y+12)(y-4)=0$, $y=-12$ or $y=4$

Since y is a positive number, $y=4$ and $x=y+8=4+8=12$.

       Two positive numbers are 4 and 12

② Let two integers be x and y, and $x>y$. Then we have $\begin{cases} x-y=5 \\ 2\cdot\dfrac{1}{x}+\dfrac{1}{y}=\dfrac{23}{66} \end{cases}$. Since $x-y=5 \;\to\; x=y+5$, we have

$2\cdot\dfrac{1}{x}+\dfrac{1}{y}=\dfrac{23}{66}$

$\dfrac{2}{y+5}+\dfrac{1}{y}=\dfrac{23}{66}$

$\left(\dfrac{2}{y+5}+\dfrac{1}{y}\right)66y(y+5)=\dfrac{23}{66}\cdot 66y(y+5)$

$132y+66(y+5)=23y(y+5)$

$23y^2-83y-330=0$

$(23y+55)(y-6)=0$, $y=-\dfrac{55}{23}$ or $y=6$

Since y is an integer, $y=6$ and $x=y+5=6+5=11$.

       Two integers are 6 and 11

Check Point 2

① Let x be the rate of Josh's car when it is rainy.

	Rainy	Not Rainy
Rate	x	$x+10$
Distance	75	30
Time	$\dfrac{75}{x}$	$\dfrac{30}{x+10}$

Since Jose drove for 10 hours in total, we have

$\dfrac{75}{x}+\dfrac{30}{x+10}=2$

$\left(\dfrac{75}{x}+\dfrac{30}{x+10}\right)x(x+10)=2\cdot x(x+10)$

$75(x+10)+30x=2x^2+20x$

$105x+750=2x^2+20x$

$2x^2-85x-750=0,\ 2x^2-85x-750=0$

$(2x+15)(x-50)=0,\ x=-\dfrac{15}{2}$ or $x=50$

Since the rate cannot be negative, the value of x must be 50.

Josh was driving with 50 mph while raining

② Let be x and t be the speed and time of roller skate, respectively.

	Roller Skate	Bicycle
Speed	x	$2x$
Distance	24	24
Time	t	$t-2$

Since $r=\dfrac{d}{t}$, we have $x=\dfrac{24}{t}$ and $2x=\dfrac{24}{t-2}$

$2\left(\dfrac{24}{t}\right)=\dfrac{24}{t-2}$

$\dfrac{48}{t}=\dfrac{24}{t-2}$

$\dfrac{48}{t}\cdot t(t-2)=\dfrac{24}{t-2}\cdot t(t-2)$

$48(t-2)=24t$

$24t=96,\ t=4$

Now, the average speed is

$\dfrac{24+24}{t+(t-2)}=\dfrac{48}{4+(4-2)}=\dfrac{48}{6}=8.$

The average speed is 8 miles per hour

Check Point 3

① Let t be the number of hours for Nick to paint the room. Then, since Joseph can paint twice as fast as Nick, it only takes him $\dfrac{t}{2}$ hours to paint the room. Assume that the total amount of work done is W.

Nick paints $\dfrac{W}{t}$ in one hour.

Joseph paints $\dfrac{W}{\frac{t}{2}}=\dfrac{2W}{t}$ in one hour.

Together, they paint $\dfrac{W}{t}+\dfrac{2W}{t}$ in one hour.

Therefore, we have

$\left(\dfrac{W}{t}+\dfrac{2W}{t}\right)\times 5=W,\ \left(\dfrac{3W}{t}\right)\times 5=W$

$\dfrac{15W}{t}=W,\ t=15$

Nick can paint the room in 15 hours by Himself

② Let t be the number of hours needed to fill the tank when both pumps work together and assume that the total amount of work done is W.

Pump A can fill $\dfrac{W}{30}$ in one hour.

Pump A can fill $\dfrac{W}{24}$ in one hour.

If both pumps are used together, we have

$\left(\dfrac{W}{30}+\dfrac{W}{24}\right)t=W$

$\left(\dfrac{Wt}{30}+\dfrac{Wt}{24}\right)\cdot\dfrac{30\cdot 24}{W}=W\cdot\dfrac{30\cdot 24}{W}$

$24t+30t=720$

$54t=720,\ t=\dfrac{40}{3}$

It takes $\dfrac{40}{3}$ hours

Review Exercises

01

Let two positive integers be x and y, and $x > y$. Then we have $\begin{cases} x = y+4 \\ \dfrac{1}{x} + \dfrac{1}{y} = \dfrac{14}{45} \end{cases}$.

Solving by substituting the first expression into the second expression, we have

$\dfrac{1}{y+4} + \dfrac{1}{y} = \dfrac{14}{45}$

$\left(\dfrac{1}{y+4} + \dfrac{1}{y}\right) \cdot 45y(y+4) = \dfrac{14}{45} \cdot 45y(y+4)$

$45y + 45(y+4) = 14y(y+4)$

$90y + 180 = 14y^2 + 56y$

$14y^2 - 34y - 180 = 0$

$7y^2 - 17y - 90 = 0$

$(y-5)(7y+18) = 0$, $y = 5$ or $y = -\dfrac{18}{7}$

Since y is a positive number, $y = 5$ and $x = y + 4 = 5 + 4 = 9$.

Two positive integers are 5 and 9

02

Let two positive integers be x and y, and $x > y$. Then we have $\begin{cases} x = y+5 \\ \dfrac{1}{y} - \dfrac{1}{x} = \dfrac{5}{14} \end{cases}$. Solving by substituting the first expression into the second expression, we have

$\dfrac{1}{y} - \dfrac{1}{y+5} = \dfrac{5}{14}$

$\left(\dfrac{1}{y} - \dfrac{1}{y+5}\right) \cdot 14y(y+5) = \dfrac{5}{14} \cdot 14y(y+5)$

$14(y+5) - 14y = 5y(y+5)$

$14y + 70 - 14y = 5y^2 + 25y$

$5y^2 + 25y - 70 = 0$

$y^2 + 5y - 14 = 0$

$(y-2)(y+7) = 0$, $y = 2$ or $y = -7$

Since y is a positive number, $y = 2$ and $x = y + 5 = 2 + 5 = 7$.

Two positive integers are 2 and 7

03

Let two consecutive positive odd integers be x and $x+2$. Then, we have

$\dfrac{1}{x} - \dfrac{1}{x+2} = \dfrac{2}{15}$

$\left(\dfrac{1}{x} - \dfrac{1}{x+2}\right) \cdot 15x(x+2) = \dfrac{2}{15} \cdot 15x(x+2)$

$15(x+2) - 15x = 2x(x+2)$

$15x + 30 - 15x = 2x^2 + 4x$

$2x^2 + 4x - 30 = 0$

$x^2 + 2x - 15 = 0$

$(x-3)(x+5) = 0$, $x = 3$ or $x = -5$

Since x is a positive odd integer, $x = 3$.

Two consecutive positive odd integers are 3 and 5

04

Let d and t be the distance and time the boat went upstream.

	Upstream	Downstream
Rate	12	18
Distance	d	d
Time	$\dfrac{d}{12}$	$\dfrac{d}{18}$

Since the total time for the trip was 5 hours, we have

$\dfrac{d}{12} + \dfrac{d}{18} = 5$

$\dfrac{5d}{36} = 5$, $d = 36$

The boat traveled upstream 36 km

05

Let x be the speed of the current.

	Upstream	Downstream
Rate	$8-x$	$8+x$
Distance	15	15
Time	$\dfrac{15}{8-x}$	$\dfrac{15}{8+x}$

Since the total time for the trip was 4 hours, we have

$\dfrac{15}{8-x} + \dfrac{15}{8+x} = 4$

Solutions Manual 45

Solutions Manual

$\left(\dfrac{15}{8-x}+\dfrac{15}{8+x}\right)(8-x)(8+x)=4(8-x)(8+x)$

$15(8+x)+15(8-x)=4(64-x^2)$

$120+15x+120-15x=256-4x^2$

$4x^2=16,\ x=\pm 2$

Since the speed of the current is positive,

$x=2$.

The speed of the current is 2 miles per hour

06

Let x be the speed of motorcycle.

	With Winds	Against winds
Speed	$x+3$	$x-3$
Distance	60	30
Time	$\dfrac{60}{x+3}$	$\dfrac{30}{x-3}$

Since it took same amount of time for Min against the wind and with the wind, we have $\dfrac{60}{x+3}=\dfrac{30}{x-3}$

$\dfrac{60}{x+3}\cdot(x+3)(x-3)=\dfrac{30}{x-3}\cdot(x+3)(x-3)$

$60(x-3)=30(x+3)$

$60x-180=30x+90,\ x=9$

The speed of Min's motorcycle with wind is $x+3=9+3=12$ mph

07

Let x be the speed of the bicycle from city K to city L.

	K to L	L to K
Speed	x	$x+2$
Distance	12	12
Time	$\dfrac{12}{x}$	$\dfrac{12}{x+2}$

Since the total time for the trip was 5 hours, we have

$\dfrac{12}{x}+\dfrac{12}{x+2}=5$

$\left(\dfrac{12}{x}+\dfrac{12}{x+2}\right)\cdot x(x+2)=5\cdot x(x+2)$

$12(x+2)+12x=5x^2+10x$

$24x+24=5x^2+10x$

$5x^2-14x-24=0$

$(x-4)(5x+6)=0,\ x=4$ or $x=-\dfrac{6}{5}$

Since the speed of the bicycle is positive,

$x=4$.

Vincent rode bicycle at 4 miles per hour from city K to L

08

Let t be the time needed to fill the pool when both hoses work together and assume that the total amount of work done is W.

Tom's gardent hose can fill $\dfrac{W}{12}$ in 1 hour.

Neighbor's hose can fill $\dfrac{W}{15}$ in 1 hour.

If both hoses are used together, we have

$\left(\dfrac{W}{12}+\dfrac{W}{15}\right)t=W$

$\left(\dfrac{Wt}{12}+\dfrac{Wt}{15}\right)\cdot\dfrac{12\cdot 15}{W}=W\cdot\dfrac{12\cdot 15}{W}$

$15t+12t=180$

$27t=180,\ t=\dfrac{20}{3}$

It takes $\dfrac{20}{3}$ hours

09

Let t the time needed for Eric's son to finish the job and assume that the total amount of work done is W.

Eric can complete $\dfrac{W}{3}$ in 1 hour.

Eric's son can complete $\dfrac{W}{t}$ in 1 hour.

Because working together can get them done in 2 hours, we have

$\left(\dfrac{W}{3}+\dfrac{W}{t}\right)2=W$

$\left(\dfrac{2W}{3}+\dfrac{2W}{t}\right)\cdot\dfrac{3t}{W}=W\cdot\dfrac{3t}{W}$

$2t+6=3t,\ t=6$

It takes 6 hours

10

Let t be the time needed to mow the lawn when Jason and his brother work together and assume that the total amount of work done is W.

Jason can mow $\dfrac{W}{80}$ in 1 minute.

Jason's brother can mow $\dfrac{W}{60}$ in 1 minute.

If they mow the lawn together, we have

$\left(\dfrac{W}{80}+\dfrac{W}{60}\right)t=W$

$\left(\dfrac{Wt}{80}+\dfrac{Wt}{60}\right)\cdot\dfrac{80\cdot 60}{W}=W\cdot\dfrac{80\cdot 60}{W}$

$60t+80t=4800$

$140t=4800,\ t=\dfrac{240}{7}$

It takes $\dfrac{240}{7}$ (approximately 34) minutes

Chapter 3 Test Level 1

01

(1) $\dfrac{16x^2-1}{8x-2}=\dfrac{(4x-1)(4x+1)}{2(4x-1)}=\dfrac{4x+1}{2}$

(2) $\dfrac{6x^2-5x-6}{3x^2+14x+8}=\dfrac{(2x-3)(3x+2)}{(x+4)(3x+2)}=\dfrac{2x-3}{x+4}$

02

(1) $\dfrac{4a+8}{a^2+a-2}\times\dfrac{a^2-1}{4a^3+4a^2}$

$=\dfrac{4(a+2)}{(a-1)(a+2)}\times\dfrac{(a-1)(a+1)}{4a^2(a+1)}=\dfrac{1}{a^2}$

(2) $\dfrac{x^2+2x+1}{x^2+3x+2}\div\dfrac{1}{x^2+2x}$

$=\dfrac{x^2+2x+1}{x^2+3x+2}\times(x^2+2x)$

$=\dfrac{(x+1)^2}{(x+1)(x+2)}\times x(x+2)=x(x+1)$

03

(1) $\dfrac{1-4x}{2x+1}+\dfrac{2x}{x-4}=\dfrac{(1-4x)(x-4)+2x(2x+1)}{(2x+1)(x-4)}$

$=\dfrac{-4x^2+17x-4+4x^2+2x}{(2x+1)(x-4)}$

$=\dfrac{19x-4}{(2x+1)(x-4)}$

(2) $\dfrac{x+2}{x^2-6x+8}-\dfrac{2}{x-2}=\dfrac{x+2}{(x-2)(x-4)}-\dfrac{2}{x-2}$

$=\dfrac{x+2-2(x-4)}{(x-2)(x-4)}$

$=\dfrac{-x+10}{(x-2)(x-4)}$

04

(1) $\dfrac{2-\dfrac{2}{x+2}}{\dfrac{2}{x+2}+2} = \dfrac{\left(2-\dfrac{2}{x+2}\right)\cdot(x+2)}{\left(\dfrac{2}{x+2}+2\right)\cdot(x+2)}$

$= \dfrac{2(x+2)-2}{2+2(x+2)}$

$= \dfrac{2x+2}{2x+6} = \dfrac{x+1}{x+3}$

(2) $4 - \dfrac{1}{3-\dfrac{1}{1-\dfrac{1}{x}}} = 4 - \dfrac{1}{3-\dfrac{1}{\dfrac{x-1}{x}}}$

$= 4 - \dfrac{1}{3-\dfrac{x}{x-1}} = 4 - \dfrac{1}{\dfrac{3(x-1)-x}{x-1}}$

$= 4 - \dfrac{x-1}{2x-3} = \dfrac{4(2x-3)-(x-1)}{2x-3}$

$= \dfrac{7x-11}{2x-3}$

05

(1) $\dfrac{6}{x+3} + \dfrac{2}{x-2} = 3$

$\left(\dfrac{6}{x+3} + \dfrac{2}{x-2}\right)(x+3)(x-2) = 3(x+3)(x-2)$

$6(x-2) + 2(x+3) = 3(x+3)(x-2)$

$8x - 6 = 3x^2 + 3x - 18$

$3x^2 - 5x - 12 = 0$

$(3x+4)(x-3) = 0$, $x = -\dfrac{4}{3}$ or $x = 3$

Check the solution:

$\dfrac{6}{-4/3+3 \neq 0} + \dfrac{2}{-4/3-2 \neq 0} = 3$ and

$\dfrac{6}{3+3 \neq 0} + \dfrac{2}{3-2 \neq 0} = 3$

$x = -\dfrac{4}{3}$ or $x = 3$

(2) $\dfrac{x-4}{x^2-x-12} + \dfrac{1}{x+3} = 1$

$\dfrac{x-4}{(x-4)(x+3)} + \dfrac{1}{x+3} = 1$

$\dfrac{1}{x+3} + \dfrac{1}{x+3} = 1$, $\dfrac{2}{x+3} = 1$

$x+3 = 2$, $x = -1$

Check the solution:

$\dfrac{-1-4}{(-1)^2-(-1)-12 \neq 0} + \dfrac{1}{-1+3 \neq 0} = 1$

$x = -1$

06

(1) $\dfrac{10x+1}{x^2-x-2} = \dfrac{ax+b}{x-2} - \dfrac{cx}{x+1}$

$\dfrac{10x+1}{(x+1)(x-2)} = \dfrac{ax+b}{x-2} - \dfrac{cx}{x+1}$

$\dfrac{10x+1}{(x+1)(x-2)} \cdot (x+1)(x-2)$

$= \left(\dfrac{ax+b}{x-2} - \dfrac{cx}{x+1}\right)(x+1)(x-2)$

$10x+1 = (ax+b)(x+1) - cx(x-2)$

$10x+1 = ax^2 + ax + bx + b - cx^2 + 2cx$

$10x+1 = (a-c)x^2 + (a+b+2c)x + b$

$\Rightarrow b = 1$

$a + 1 + 2c = 10$, $a + 2c = 9$ → (1)

$a - c = 0$ → (2)

Solving the system of equations (1) and (2), we have $a=3$ and $c=3$. Therefore, $a+b+c = 3+1+3 = 7$

(2) $\dfrac{9x^2+2x-5}{3x^2-5x-2} = \dfrac{a}{3x+1} + \dfrac{bx+c}{x-2}$

$\dfrac{9x^2+2x-5}{(3x+1)(x-2)} \cdot (3x+1)(x-2)$

$= \left(\dfrac{a}{3x+1} + \dfrac{bx+c}{x-2}\right)(3x+1)(x-2)$

$9x^2 + 2x - 5 = a(x-2) + (bx+c)(3x+1)$

$9x^2 + 2x - 5 = ax - 2a + 3bx^2 + bx + 3cx + c$

$9x^2 + 2x - 5 = 3bx^2 + (a+b+3c)x + (c-2a)$

$\Rightarrow 3b = 9$, $b = 3$

$a + 3 + 3c = 2$, $a + 3c = -1$ → (1)

$c - 2a = -5$, $2a - c = 5$ → (2)

Solving the system of equations (1) and (2), we have $a=2$ and $c=-1$. Therefore, $a+b+c = 2+3+(-1) = 4$

48 Solutions Manual

07

$$\frac{C}{AB}=\frac{C}{B-A}\left(\frac{1}{A}-\frac{1}{B}\right)$$

(1) $\dfrac{1}{x(x-1)}+\dfrac{1}{(x-1)(x-2)}$

$=\dfrac{1}{(x-1)-x}\left(\dfrac{1}{x}-\dfrac{1}{x-1}\right)$

$\quad +\dfrac{1}{(x-2)-(x-1)}\left(\dfrac{1}{x-1}-\dfrac{1}{x-2}\right)$

$=-\left(\dfrac{1}{x}-\dfrac{1}{x-1}\right)-\left(\dfrac{1}{x-1}-\dfrac{1}{x-2}\right)$

$=\dfrac{1}{x-2}-\dfrac{1}{x}=\dfrac{x-(x-2)}{x(x-2)}=\dfrac{2}{x(x-2)}$

(2) $\dfrac{1}{(x-2)x}+\dfrac{1}{x(x+2)}+\dfrac{1}{(x+2)(x+4)}$

$=\dfrac{1}{x-(x-2)}\left(\dfrac{1}{x-2}-\dfrac{1}{x}\right)$

$\quad +\dfrac{1}{(x+2)-x}\left(\dfrac{1}{x}-\dfrac{1}{x+2}\right)$

$\quad +\dfrac{1}{(x+4)-(x+2)}\left(\dfrac{1}{x+2}-\dfrac{1}{x+4}\right)$

$=\dfrac{1}{2}\left(\dfrac{1}{x-2}-\dfrac{1}{x}+\dfrac{1}{x}-\dfrac{1}{x+2}+\dfrac{1}{x+2}-\dfrac{1}{x+4}\right)$

$=\dfrac{1}{2}\left(\dfrac{1}{x-2}-\dfrac{1}{x+4}\right)=\dfrac{1}{2}\left(\dfrac{x+4-(x-2)}{(x-2)(x+4)}\right)$

$=\dfrac{3}{(x-2)(x+4)}$

08

$\dfrac{1}{1\cdot 2}+\dfrac{1}{2\cdot 3}+\dfrac{1}{3\cdot 4}+\cdots+\dfrac{1}{9\cdot 10}$

$=\dfrac{1}{2-1}\left(\dfrac{1}{1}-\dfrac{1}{2}\right)+\dfrac{1}{3-2}\left(\dfrac{1}{2}-\dfrac{1}{3}\right)$

$\quad +\dfrac{1}{4-3}\left(\dfrac{1}{3}-\dfrac{1}{4}\right)+\cdots+\dfrac{1}{10-9}\left(\dfrac{1}{9}-\dfrac{1}{10}\right)$

$=1-\dfrac{1}{2}+\dfrac{1}{2}-\dfrac{1}{3}+\dfrac{1}{3}-\dfrac{1}{4}+\cdots+\dfrac{1}{9}-\dfrac{1}{10}$

$=1-\dfrac{1}{10}=\dfrac{9}{10}$

09

Let $x=2k$ and $y=3k$ from $x:y=2:3$.

(1) $\dfrac{3x+2y}{4x-2y}=\dfrac{3(2k)+2(3k)}{4(2k)-2(3k)}=\dfrac{12k}{2k}=6$

(2) $\dfrac{x^2+y^2}{xy}=\dfrac{(2k)^2+(3k)^2}{(2k)(3k)}=\dfrac{13k^2}{6k^2}=\dfrac{13}{6}$

10

Using the property $\dfrac{a}{b}=\dfrac{c}{d}=\dfrac{e}{f}=\dfrac{a+c+e}{b+d+f}$,

$k=\dfrac{a+2b}{2a+3b}=\dfrac{b+2c}{3b+4c}=\dfrac{c+2a}{2c+4a}$

$=\dfrac{a+2b+b+2c+c+2a}{2a+3b+3b+4c+2c+4a}$

$=\dfrac{3(a+b+c)}{6(a+b+c)}=\dfrac{1}{2}$

11

Let two positive integers be x and y, and $x>y$. Then we have $\begin{cases} x=y+2 \\ \dfrac{1}{y}-\dfrac{1}{x}=\dfrac{1}{4} \end{cases}$. Solving by substituting the first expression into the second expression, we have

$\dfrac{1}{y}-\dfrac{1}{y+2}=\dfrac{1}{4}$

$\left(\dfrac{1}{y}-\dfrac{1}{y+2}\right)\cdot 4y(y+2)=\dfrac{1}{4}\cdot 4y(y+2)$

$4(y+2)-4y=y(y+2)$

$4y+8-4y=y^2+2y$

$y^2+2y-8=0$

$(y+4)(y-2)=0$, $y=-4$ or $y=2$

Since y is a positive number, $y=2$ and $x=y+2=2+2=4$.

    Two positive integers are 2 and 4

12

Let x be the speed of the car from home to work.

	Going	Returning
Speed	x	$x+10$
Distance	50	50
Time	$\dfrac{50}{x}$	$\dfrac{50}{x+10}$

Since 10 minutes is equal to $\dfrac{1}{6}$ hour, we have

$$\dfrac{50}{x} - \dfrac{50}{x+10} = \dfrac{1}{6}$$

$$\left(\dfrac{50}{x} - \dfrac{50}{x+10}\right)\cdot 6x(x+10) = \dfrac{1}{6}\cdot 6x(x+10)$$

$$300(x+10) - 300x = x^2 + 10x$$

$$3000 = x^2 + 10x$$

$$x^2 + 10x - 3000 = 0$$

$$(x-50)(x+60) = 0, \; x=50 \text{ or } x=-60$$

Since the speed of the car is positive, $x=50$.

Andy drove at 50 miles per hour from home to work.

Chapter 3 Test Level 2

01

(1) $\dfrac{(a^3+b^3)(a^2+ab+b^2)}{a^6-b^6}$

$= \dfrac{(a^3+b^3)(a^2+ab+b^2)}{(a^3-b^3)(a^3+b^3)}$

$= \dfrac{a^2+ab+b^2}{(a-b)(a^2+ab+b^2)} = \dfrac{1}{a-b}$

(2) $\dfrac{(x^4-y^4)(x^2+xy+y^2)}{(x^3-y^3)(x+y)}$

$= \dfrac{(x^2-y^2)(x^2+y^2)(x^2+xy+y^2)}{(x-y)(x^2+xy+y^2)(x+y)}$

$= \dfrac{(x-y)(x+y)(x^2+y^2)}{(x-y)(x+y)} = x^2+y^2$

02

(1) $\dfrac{2x+y}{x^3-y^3} \times \dfrac{x^2-y^2}{2x^2+3xy+y^2}$

$= \dfrac{2x+y}{(x-y)(x^2+xy+y^2)} \times \dfrac{(x-y)(x+y)}{(2x+y)(x+y)}$

$= \dfrac{1}{x^2+xy+y^2}$

(2) $\dfrac{x+2}{x^2-x-2} \div \dfrac{x^2-1}{x^3-8} \div \dfrac{x^2+4x+4}{x-1}$

$= \dfrac{x+2}{x^2-x-2} \times \dfrac{x^3-8}{x^2-1} \times \dfrac{x-1}{x^2+4x+4}$

$= \dfrac{x+2}{(x-2)(x+1)} \times \dfrac{(x-2)(x^2+2x+4)}{(x-1)(x+1)} \times \dfrac{x-1}{(x+2)^2}$

$= \dfrac{x^2+2x+4}{(x+1)^2(x+2)}$

03

(1) $\dfrac{x-2}{2x^2-5x-3} + \dfrac{2}{2x+1} - \dfrac{3}{x-3}$

$= \dfrac{x-2}{(2x+1)(x-3)} + \dfrac{2}{2x+1} - \dfrac{3}{x-3}$

$= \dfrac{x-2+2(x-3)-3(2x+1)}{(2x+1)(x-3)}$

$= \dfrac{x-2+2x-6-6x-3}{(2x+1)(x-3)}$

$= \dfrac{-3x-11}{(2x+1)(x-3)} = -\dfrac{3x+11}{(2x+1)(x-3)}$

(2) $\dfrac{3}{x^2-x-12} - \dfrac{2}{x^2-16} + \dfrac{1}{x+4}$

$= \dfrac{3}{(x-4)(x+3)} - \dfrac{2}{(x-4)(x+4)} + \dfrac{1}{x+4}$

$= \dfrac{3(x+4)-2(x+3)+(x-4)(x+3)}{(x-4)(x+3)(x+4)}$

$= \dfrac{3x+12-2x-6+x^2-x-12}{(x-4)(x+3)(x+4)}$

$= \dfrac{x^2-6}{(x-4)(x+3)(x+4)}$

04

$$2-\cfrac{1}{2-\cfrac{1}{2-\cfrac{1}{2-x}}} = 2-\cfrac{1}{2-\cfrac{1}{\frac{2(2-x)-1}{2-x}}}$$

$$=2-\cfrac{1}{2-\cfrac{2-x}{3-2x}} = 2-\cfrac{1}{\frac{2(3-2x)-(2-x)}{3-2x}}$$

$$=2-\cfrac{3-2x}{4-3x} = \cfrac{2(4-3x)-(3-2x)}{4-3x}$$

$$=\cfrac{5-4x}{4-3x} = \cfrac{4x-5}{3x-4}$$

So the equation is $\dfrac{4x-5}{3x-4}=\dfrac{ax-b}{cx-d}$

$\Rightarrow a=4$, $b=5$, $c=3$, $d=4$. Therefore, $a+b+c+d=4+5+3+4=16$

05

(1) $\dfrac{43}{30}=1+\dfrac{13}{30}=1+\cfrac{1}{\frac{30}{13}}$

$=1+\cfrac{1}{2+\frac{4}{13}}=1+\cfrac{1}{2+\cfrac{1}{\frac{13}{4}}}$

$=1+\cfrac{1}{2+\cfrac{1}{3+\frac{1}{4}}}$

$\Rightarrow a=2$, $b=3$, $c=4$

Therefore, $a+b+c=2+3+4=9$

(2) $\dfrac{20}{69}=\cfrac{1}{\frac{69}{20}}=\cfrac{1}{3+\frac{9}{20}}$

$=\cfrac{1}{3+\cfrac{1}{\frac{20}{9}}}=\cfrac{1}{3+\cfrac{1}{2+\frac{2}{9}}}$

$=\cfrac{1}{3+\cfrac{1}{2+\cfrac{1}{\frac{9}{2}}}}=\cfrac{1}{3+\cfrac{1}{2+\cfrac{1}{4+\frac{1}{2}}}}$

$\Rightarrow a=3$, $b=2$, $c=4$

Therefore, $a+b+c=3+2+4=9$

06

(1) $\dfrac{x+1}{x}+\dfrac{x+2}{x+1}-\dfrac{x+3}{x+2}-\dfrac{x+4}{x+3}$

$=\dfrac{x+1}{x}+\dfrac{(x+1)+1}{x+1}-\dfrac{(x+2)+1}{x+2}-\dfrac{(x+3)+1}{x+3}$

$=\left(1+\dfrac{1}{x}\right)+\left(1+\dfrac{1}{x+1}\right)-\left(1+\dfrac{1}{x+2}\right)-\left(1+\dfrac{1}{x+3}\right)$

$=\left(\dfrac{1}{x}-\dfrac{1}{x+2}\right)+\left(\dfrac{1}{x+1}-\dfrac{1}{x+3}\right)$

$=\dfrac{x+2-x}{x(x+2)}+\dfrac{x+3-(x+1)}{(x+1)(x+3)}$

$=\dfrac{2}{x(x+2)}+\dfrac{2}{(x+1)(x+3)}$

$=\dfrac{2(x+1)(x+3)+2x(x+2)}{x(x+2)(x+1)(x+3)}$

$=\dfrac{2(2x^2+6x+3)}{x(x+2)(x+1)(x+3)}$

(2) $\dfrac{x^2+2x+2}{x+2}-\dfrac{x^2-2x+2}{x-2}$

$=\dfrac{x(x+2)+2}{x+2}-\dfrac{x(x-2)+2}{x-2}$

$=x+\dfrac{2}{x+2}-\left(x+\dfrac{2}{x-2}\right)$

$=\dfrac{2}{x+2}-\dfrac{2}{x-2}=\dfrac{2(x-2)-2(x+2)}{(x+2)(x-2)}$

$=-\dfrac{8}{(x+2)(x-2)}$

07

$\dfrac{C}{AB}=\dfrac{C}{(B-A)}\left(\dfrac{1}{A}-\dfrac{1}{B}\right)$

(1) $\dfrac{1}{(x-4)(x-2)}+\dfrac{1}{(x-2)x}+\dfrac{1}{x(x+2)}$

$\qquad\qquad\qquad\qquad+\dfrac{1}{(x+2)(x+4)}$

$=\dfrac{1}{(x-2)-(x-4)}\left(\dfrac{1}{x-4}-\dfrac{1}{x-2}\right)$

$+\dfrac{1}{x-(x-2)}\left(\dfrac{1}{x-2}-\dfrac{1}{x}\right)$

$+\dfrac{1}{(x+2)-x}\left(\dfrac{1}{x}-\dfrac{1}{x-2}\right)$

$+\dfrac{1}{(x+4)-(x+2)}\left(\dfrac{1}{x+2}-\dfrac{1}{x+4}\right)$

Solutions Manual

$$=\frac{1}{2}\left(\begin{array}{c}\frac{1}{x-4}-\frac{1}{x-2}+\frac{1}{x-2}-\frac{1}{x}\\+\frac{1}{x}-\frac{1}{x+2}+\frac{1}{x+2}-\frac{1}{x+4}\end{array}\right)$$

$$=\frac{1}{2}\left(\frac{1}{x-4}-\frac{1}{x+4}\right)=\frac{1}{2}\left(\frac{x+4-(x-4)}{(x-4)(x+4)}\right)$$

$$=\frac{4}{(x-4)(x+4)}$$

(2) $\dfrac{2}{x^2+2x}+\dfrac{1}{x^2+5x+6}+\dfrac{2}{x^2+8x+15}-\dfrac{5}{x^2+5x}$

$$=\frac{2}{x(x+2)}+\frac{1}{(x+2)(x+3)}+\frac{2}{(x+3)(x+5)}$$
$$-\frac{5}{x(x+5)}$$

$$=\frac{2}{(x+2)-x}\left(\frac{1}{x}-\frac{1}{x+2}\right)$$
$$+\frac{1}{(x+3)-(x+2)}\left(\frac{1}{x+2}-\frac{1}{x-3}\right)$$
$$+\frac{2}{(x+5)-(x+3)}\left(\frac{1}{x+3}-\frac{1}{x+5}\right)$$
$$-\frac{5}{(x+5)-x}\left(\frac{1}{x}-\frac{1}{x+5}\right)$$

$$=\frac{1}{x}-\frac{1}{x+2}+\frac{1}{x+2}-\frac{1}{x-3}$$
$$+\frac{1}{x+3}-\frac{1}{x+5}-\left(\frac{1}{x}-\frac{1}{x+5}\right)=0$$

08

$$\frac{y}{x(x+y)}+\frac{z}{(x+y)(x+y+z)}$$
$$+\frac{k}{(x+y+z)(x+y+z+k)}$$

$$=\frac{y}{(x+y)-x}\left(\frac{1}{x}-\frac{1}{x+y}\right)$$
$$+\frac{z}{(x+y+z)-(x+y)}\left(\frac{1}{x+y}-\frac{1}{x+y+z}\right)$$
$$+\frac{k}{(x+y+z+k)-(x+y+z)}$$
$$\left(\frac{1}{x+y+z}-\frac{1}{x+y+z+k}\right)$$

$$=\frac{1}{x}-\frac{1}{x+y}+\frac{1}{x+y}-\frac{1}{x+y+z}+\frac{1}{x+y+z}$$
$$-\frac{1}{x+y+z+k}$$

$$=\frac{1}{x}-\frac{1}{x+y+z+k}=\frac{x+y+z+k-x}{x(x+y+z+k)}$$

$$=\frac{y+z+k}{x(x+y+z+k)}$$

09

$$(x^2-3x+1=0)\cdot\frac{1}{x}$$
$$x-3+\frac{1}{x}=0,\ x+\frac{1}{x}=3$$

(1) $\left(x+\dfrac{1}{x}\right)^3=x^3+3x+\dfrac{3}{x}+\dfrac{1}{x^3}$

$$=x^3+\frac{1}{x^3}+3\left(x+\frac{1}{x}\right)$$

$$3^3=x^3+\frac{1}{x^3}+3(3)$$

$$\Rightarrow x^3+\frac{1}{x^3}=27-9=18$$

(2) $x^2+\dfrac{1}{x^2}=\left(x+\dfrac{1}{x}\right)^2-2=3^2-2=7$

$$x^4+\frac{1}{x^4}=\left(x^2+\frac{1}{x^2}\right)^2-2=7^2-2=47$$

(3) $\left(x^2+\dfrac{1}{x^2}\right)\left(x^3+\dfrac{1}{x^3}\right)=x^5+\dfrac{1}{x}+x+\dfrac{1}{x^5}$

$$=\left(x^5+\frac{1}{x^5}\right)+\left(x+\frac{1}{x}\right)$$

$$(7)(18)=x^5+\frac{1}{x^5}+3$$

$$\Rightarrow x^5+\frac{1}{x^5}=123$$

10

Method 1

Let $\dfrac{3a}{4}=\dfrac{3a-b}{2}=\dfrac{2b-c}{3}=\dfrac{3a+b-2c}{k}=m$.

Then

$3a=4m,\ 3a-b=2m,\ 2b-c=3m$

$\Rightarrow a=\dfrac{4}{3}m$

$3\left(\dfrac{4}{3}m\right)-b=2m,\ b=2m$

$2(2m)-c=3m,\ c=m$

Since $\dfrac{3a+b-2c}{k}=m$,

$$\frac{3\left(\frac{4}{3}m\right)+2m-2m}{k}=m,\ 4m=mk,\ k=4$$

Method 2

$$\frac{3a}{4}\cdot\frac{-2}{-2}=\frac{3a-b}{2}\cdot\frac{3}{3}=\frac{2b-c}{3}\cdot\frac{2}{2}=\frac{3a+b-2c}{k}$$

Using the property $\frac{a}{b}=\frac{c}{d}=\frac{e}{f}=\frac{a+c+e}{b+d+f}$,

$$\frac{-6a+9a-3b+4b-2c}{-8+6+6}=\frac{3a+b-2c}{4}$$
$$=\frac{3a+b-2c}{k}$$

Therefore, $k=4$

Solutions Manual

Chapter 4

Quadratic Equations

1. Solving Basic Quadratic Equations

Check Point 1

(A) $3x+1=4(x-2)$
$3x+1=4x-8$
$x-9=0$ → Linear equation

(B) $x^3-3x+1=2(x^2+1)$
$x^3-3x+1=2x^2+2$
$x^3-2x^2-3x-1=0$ → Cubic equation

(C) $(2x+1)^2-4x^2=0$
$4x^2+4x+1-4x^2=0$
$4x+1=0$ → Linear equation

(D) $(x-2)(x+2)-(2x-1)(2x+1)+3=0$
$x^2-4-(4x^2-1)+3=0$
$3x^2=0$ → Quadratic equation

(E) $(x-4)(4+x)+(x+1)(1-x)=x$
$x^2-16+(1-x^2)=x$
$x+15=0$ → Linear equation

The answer is (D)

Check Point 2

① $6x^2+5=59$
$6x^2=54$
$x^2=9,\ x=\pm\sqrt{9}$
$x=3$ or $x=-3$

② $4x^2-3=2-x^2$
$5x^2=5$
$x^2=1,\ x=\pm\sqrt{1}$
$x=1$ or $x=-1$

③ $(2x-1)^2=25$
$2x-1=\pm\sqrt{25},\ 2x-1=\pm5$
$2x=6$ or $2x=-4$
$x=3$ or $x=-2$

④ $2(2x-3)^2-4=10$
$2(2x-3)^2=14,\ (2x-3)^2=7$
$2x-3=\pm\sqrt{7},\ 2x=3\pm\sqrt{7}$
$x=\dfrac{3+\sqrt{7}}{2}$ or $x=\dfrac{3-\sqrt{7}}{2}$

Check Point 3

① $2x^2+3x-2=0$
$(2x-1)(x+2)=0$
$2x-1=0$ or $x+2=0$
$x=\dfrac{1}{2}$ or $x=-2$

② $3x^2-2x=2x^2+24$
$x^2-2x-24=0$
$(x-6)(x+4)=0$
$x-6=0$ or $x+4=0$
$x=6$ or $x=-4$

③ $2(x-3)^2=8x,\ (x-3)^2=4x$
$x^2-6x+9=4x,\ x^2-10x+9=0$
$(x-1)(x-9)=0$
$x-1=0$ or $x-9=0$
$x=1$ or $x=9$

④ $(x+2)(x-2)=3x(x-1)-(x+2)$
$x^2-4=3x^2-3x-x-2$
$-2x^2+4x-2=0$
$x^2-2x+1=0,\ (x-1)^2=0$

54 Solutions Manual

$x-1=0$, $x=1$

Review Exercises

01

(1) $x^2+4=8$
$x^2=4$, $x=\pm 2$

(2) $x^2-4=32$
$x^2=36$, $x=\pm 6$

(3) $9x^2-12=60$
$9x^2=72$
$x^2=8$, $x=\pm 2\sqrt{2}$

(4) $10+5x^2=330$
$5x^2=320$
$x^2=64$, $x=\pm 8$

(5) $8x^2+8=31$
$8x^2=23$, $x^2=\dfrac{23}{8}$
$x=\pm\sqrt{\dfrac{23}{8}}=\pm\dfrac{\sqrt{46}}{4}$

(6) $(2x-5)^2=81$
$2x-5=9$ or $2x-5=-9$
$x=7$ or $x=-2$

(7) $4(3x+1)^2=36$
$(3x+1)^2=9$
$3x+1=3$ or $3x+1=-3$
$x=\dfrac{2}{3}$ or $x=-\dfrac{4}{3}$

(8) $\dfrac{5x^2}{2}-x^2=216$
$\dfrac{3x^2}{2}=216$
$x^2=144$, $x=\pm 12$

02

(1) $x^2+4x+4=0$
$(x+2)^2=0$
$x+2=0$, $x=-2$

(2) $x^2-15x-100=0$
$(x-20)(x+5)=0$
$x-20=0$ or $x+5=0$

$x=20$ or $x=-5$

(3) $8x^2+4x=0$
$4x(2x+1)=0$
$4x=0$ or $2x+1=0$
$x=0$ or $x=-\dfrac{1}{2}$

(4) $3x^2-33x+72=0$
$x^2-11x+24=0$
$(x-8)(x-3)=0$
$x-8=0$ or $x-3=0$
$x=8$ or $x=3$

(5) $7x^2+35x-42=0$
$x^2+5x-6=0$
$(x-1)(x+6)=0$
$x-1=0$ or $x+6=0$
$x=1$ or $x=-6$

(6) $6x^2+15x+9=0$
$2x^2+5x+3=0$
$(x+1)(2x+3)=0$
$x+1=0$ or $2x+3=0$
$x=-1$ or $x=-\dfrac{3}{2}$

(7) $7x^2+32=7-40x$
$7x^2+40x+25=0$
$(x+5)(7x+5)=0$
$x+5=0$ or $7x+5=0$
$x=-5$ or $x=-\dfrac{5}{7}$

(8) $x(x-2)=3(x-2)$
$x^2-2x=3x-6$
$x^2-5x+6=0$
$(x-3)(x-2)=0$
$x-3=0$ or $x-2=0$
$x=3$ or $x=2$

03

(1) $(x+6)^2+x^2=3(x+12)$
$x^2+12x+36+x^2=3x+36$
$2x^2+9x=0$, $x(2x+9)=0$
$x=0$ or $2x+9=0$
$x=0$ or $x=-\dfrac{9}{2}$

(2) $\dfrac{(3x+1)(2x-3)}{2}=x^2-3$

$(3x+1)(2x-3)=2(x^2-3)$

$6x^2-7x-3=2x^2-6$

$4x^2-7x+3=0$

$(x-1)(4x-3)=0$

$x-1=0$ or $4x-3=0$

$x=1$ or $x=\dfrac{3}{4}$

(3) $2x^2+12=3(x-2)^2$

$2x^2+12=3x^2-12x+12$

$x^2-12x=0$, $x(x-12)=0$

$x=0$ or $x-12=0$

$x=0$ or $x=12$

(4) $x^2-5x=\dfrac{3}{4}(x-4)(x+2)$

$4(x^2-5x)=3(x-4)(x+2)$

$4x^2-20x=3x^2-6x-24$

$x^2-14x+24=0$

$(x-2)(x-12)=0$

$x-2=0$ or $x-12=0$

$x=2$ or $x=12$

04

$4(x+3)(x-4)=\dfrac{1}{2}(2x+1)(x-2)+\dfrac{3}{2}x$

$4(x^2-x-12)=\dfrac{1}{2}(2x^2-3x-2)+\dfrac{3}{2}x$

$4x^2-4x-48=x^2-\dfrac{3}{2}x-1+\dfrac{3}{2}x$

$3x^2-4x-47=0$

$\Rightarrow a=3,\ b=-4,\ c=-47$

Therefore, $a+b+c=3+(-4)+(-47)=-48$

05

$(x+3)^2+x^2=ax^2-4x+1$

$x^2+6x+9+x^2=ax^2-4x+1$

$ax^2-2x^2-10x-8=0$

$(a-2)x^2-10x-8=0$

Since the coefficient of the quadratic term cannot be zero,

$a-2\neq 0,\ a\neq 2$

06

(A) $3x^2-x=0$

$x(3x-1)=0,\ x=0$ or $x=\dfrac{1}{3}$

(B) $3x^2+8x-3=0$

$(3x-1)(x+3)=0,\ x=\dfrac{1}{3}$ or $x=-3$

(C) $(x-3)^2-1=0,\ (x-3)^2=1$

$x-3=\pm 1,\ x=4$ or $x=2$

(D) $(x+3)(x-4)+2x=0$

$x^2-x-12+2x=0$

$x^2+x-12=0$

$(x+4)(x-3)=0,\ x=-4$ or $x=3$

(E) $\dfrac{(x+1)^2}{2}=2,\ (x+1)^2=4$

$x+1=\pm 2,\ x=-3$ or $x=1$

So the answer is (D)

07

Substitute the solution $x=4$ into the equation.

$\dfrac{1}{2}(4)^2+2k(4)-5=0$

$8+8k-5=0$

$8k=-3,\ k=-\dfrac{3}{8}$

08

Substitute the solution $x=m$ into the equation. Then, we have $2m^2-m+2=0$.

(1) Since $2m^2-m=-2$,

$2m^2-m+12=-2+12=10$

(2) $(2m^2-m+2=0)\cdot\dfrac{1}{2m}$

$m-\dfrac{1}{2}+\dfrac{1}{m}=0,\ m+\dfrac{1}{m}=\dfrac{1}{2}$

Therefore,

$m^2+\dfrac{1}{m^2}=\left(m+\dfrac{1}{m}\right)^2-2=\left(\dfrac{1}{2}\right)^2-2=-\dfrac{7}{4}$

09

$(x-2)(x+3)=2(x-2)(2x+1)$

$x^2+x-6=2(2x^2-3x-2)$

$x^2+x-6=4x^2-6x-4$

$3x^2-7x+2=0$
$(3x-1)(x-2)=0$, $x=\dfrac{1}{3}$ or $x=2$

10
$x^2+5x-14=0$
$(x+7)(x-2)=0$, $x=-7$ or $x=2$
So $x=2$ is the solution to the equation $5x^2-2x-k=0$. Therefore,
$5(2)^2-2(2)-k=0$
$20-4-k=0$, $k=16$

2. Complex Number

Check Point 1

① $3a-b(2-i)=4$
$3a-2b+bi=4$
$(3a-2b)+bi=4$
$3a-2b=4$ and $b=0$
$a=\dfrac{4}{3}$ and $b=0$

② $a(1-i)+(1+2i)b=6+3i$
$a-ai+b+2bi=6+3i$
$(a+b)+(-a+2b)i=6+3i$
$a+b=6$ and $-a+2b=3$
$a=3$, $b=3$

③ $(1+i)a-(1-i)b+2-3i=0$
$a+ai-b+bi=-2+3i$
$(a-b)+(a+b)i=-2+3i$
$a-b=-2$ and $a+b=3$
$a=\dfrac{1}{2}$, $b=\dfrac{5}{2}$

Check Point 2

① $(2-3i)+(5-i)=2-3i+5-i$
$=(2+5)+(-3-1)i=7-4i$

② $(3-4i)-(4-9i)=3-4i-4+9i$
$=(3-4)+(-4+9)i=-1+5i$

③ $2\sqrt{-121}+(4+\sqrt{-25})$
$=2\sqrt{121}i+4+\sqrt{25}i$
$=2\cdot 11i+4+5i=22i+4+5i$
$=4+(22+5)i=4+27i$

④ $(7+\sqrt{-16})+(2-\sqrt{-49})-2\sqrt{-9}$
$=(7+\sqrt{16}i)+(2-\sqrt{49}i)-2\sqrt{9}i$
$=7+4i+2-7i-2\cdot 3i$
$=(7+2)+(4-7-6)i=9-9i$

Solutions Manual

Check Point 3

① $\sqrt{-4}(4-\sqrt{-9})=2i(4-3i)=8i-6i^2=6+8i$

② $(-2-i)(4+i)=-8-2i-4i-i^2$
$\qquad =-8-6i+1=-7-6i$

③ $(2-\sqrt{-25})^2=(2-5i)^2=4-20i+25i^2$
$\qquad =4-20i-25=-21-20i$

④ $\dfrac{3-2i}{3+2i}=\dfrac{(3-2i)(3-2i)}{(3+2i)(3-2i)}=\dfrac{9-12i+4i^2}{9-4i^2}$
$\qquad =\dfrac{9-12i-4}{9+4}=\dfrac{5-12i}{13}$

Review Exercises

01

(1) $a(2-i)+b(3+i)=10$
$2a-ai+3b+bi=10$
$(2a+3b)+(-a+b)i=10$
$2a+3b=10$ and $-a+b=0$
$a=2$, $b=2$

(2) $(i-4)a-(2+3i)b=-2(2i-1)$
$ai-4a-2b-3bi=-4i+2$
$(-4a-2b)+(a-3b)i=2-4i$
$-4a-2b=2$ and $a-3b=-4$
$a=-1$, $b=1$

(3) $(2a+1)(3+2i)+8=bi$
$6a+4ai+3+2i+8=bi$
$(6a+3+8)+(4a+2)i=bi$
$6a+11=0$ and $4a+2=b$
$a=-\dfrac{11}{6}$, $b=-\dfrac{16}{3}$

(4) $\dfrac{a}{1+i}+\dfrac{b}{1-i}=2-3i$
$\left(\dfrac{a}{1+i}+\dfrac{b}{1-i}\right)(1+i)(1-i)$
$\quad =(2-3i)(1+i)(1-i)$
$a(1-i)+b(1+i)=(2-3i)(1-i^2)$
$a-ai+b+bi=(2-3i)\cdot 2$
$(a+b)+(-a+b)i=4-6i$
$a+b=4$ and $-a+b=-6$
$a=5$, $b=-1$

02

(1) $(2+i)+6i=2+7i$

(2) $\sqrt{-16}+\sqrt{-4}=4i+2i=6i$

(3) $(2+3i)-(4-6i)=2+3i-4+6i$
$\qquad =(2-4)+(3+6)i=-2+9i$

(4) $(3+\sqrt{-1})-\sqrt{-27}=(3+i)-3\sqrt{3}i$
$\qquad =3+(1-3\sqrt{3})i$

(5) $-3\sqrt{-75}+\sqrt{-9}=-3\cdot 5\sqrt{3}i+3i$
$\qquad =-15\sqrt{3}i+3i=(3-15\sqrt{3})i$

(6) $3(-1-\sqrt{-4})+(-\sqrt{-9}+7)$
$=3(-1-2i)+(-3i+7)=-3-6i-3i+7$
$=(-3+7)+(-6-3)i=4-9i$

(7) $(21-2i)-2(-3i+12)-(1+9i)$
$=21-2i+6i-24-1-9i$
$=(21-24-1)+(-2+6-9)i=-4-5i$

(8) $\left(\dfrac{3}{2}+\dfrac{5}{8}i\right)+\left(-\dfrac{1}{4}+\dfrac{1}{4}i\right)$
$=\dfrac{3}{2}+\dfrac{5}{8}i-\dfrac{1}{4}+\dfrac{1}{4}i$
$=\left(\dfrac{3}{2}-\dfrac{1}{4}\right)+\left(\dfrac{5}{8}+\dfrac{1}{4}\right)i$
$=\dfrac{5}{4}+\dfrac{7}{8}i$

03

(1) $-i(2-i)=-2i+i^2=-1-2i$

(2) $(7-6i)(3i-8)=21i-56-18i^2+48i$
$\qquad =-56+18+69i=-38+69i$

(3) $(1+\sqrt{-1})(2-\sqrt{-4})=(1+i)(2-2i)$
$\qquad =2(1+i)(1-i)$
$\qquad =2(1-i^2)=2(1+1)=4$

(4) $(\sqrt{-36}-8)(4+\sqrt{-16})=(6i-8)(4+4i)$
$=2(3i-4)4(1+i)=8(3i+3i^2-4-4i)$
$=8(-3-4-i)=8(-7-i)=-56-8i$

(5) $-i(3i+7)(-1-2i)=(-3i^2-7i)(-1-2i)$
$=(3-7i)(-1-2i)=-3-6i+7i+14i^2$
$=-3+i-14=-17+i$

(6) $(1+i)(4+3i)(7+8i)$
$=(4+3i+4i+3i^2)(7+8i)$
$=(4+7i-3)(7+8i)=(1+7i)(7+8i)$
$=7+8i+49i+56i^2=7+57i-56$

$= -49 + 57i$

(7) $(1-i)^3 = 1 - 3i + 3i^2 - i^3$
$= 1 - 3i - 3 + i = -2 - 2i$

(8) $(3+2i)^2(3-2i)^2$
$= (9 + 12i + 4i^2)(9 - 12i + 4i^2)$
$= (9 + 12i - 4)(9 - 12i - 4)$
$= (5 + 12i)(5 - 12i) = 25 - 144i^2$
$= 25 + 144 = 169$

04

(1) $\dfrac{8i-1}{i} = \dfrac{8i-1}{i} \cdot \dfrac{i}{i} = \dfrac{8i^2 - i}{i^2} = \dfrac{-8-i}{-1} = 8 + i$

(2) $\dfrac{8}{1-i} = \dfrac{8}{(1-i)} \cdot \dfrac{(1+i)}{(1+i)} = \dfrac{8+8i}{1-i^2}$
$= \dfrac{8+8i}{1+1} = 4 + 4i$

(3) $\dfrac{\sqrt{-1}}{\sqrt{-9}-1} = \dfrac{i}{3i-1} = \dfrac{i}{3i-1} \cdot \dfrac{(3i+1)}{(3i+1)}$
$= \dfrac{3i^2 + i}{9i^2 - 1} = \dfrac{-3+i}{-9-1} = \dfrac{3-i}{10}$

(4) $\dfrac{1+\sqrt{-1}}{1-\sqrt{-1}} = \dfrac{1+i}{1-i} = \dfrac{(1+i)}{(1-i)} \cdot \dfrac{(1+i)}{(1+i)}$
$= \dfrac{1+2i+i^2}{1-i^2} = \dfrac{1+2i-1}{1+1} = \dfrac{2i}{2} = i$

(5) $\dfrac{3i+5}{10i-7} = \dfrac{(3i+5)}{(10i-7)} \cdot \dfrac{(10i+7)}{(10i+7)}$
$= \dfrac{30i^2 + 71i + 35}{100i^2 - 49}$
$= \dfrac{-30 + 71i + 35}{-100 - 49} = -\dfrac{5 + 71i}{149}$

(6) $\dfrac{5i+10}{6-6i} = \dfrac{5(i+2)}{6(1-i)} = \dfrac{5(i+2)}{6(1-i)} \cdot \dfrac{(1+i)}{(1+i)}$
$= \dfrac{5(2+3i+i^2)}{6(1-i^2)} = \dfrac{5(2+3i-1)}{6(1+1)}$
$= \dfrac{5+15i}{12}$

05

(1) $i^{18} = (i^4)^4 \cdot i^2 = 1^4(-1) = -1$

(2) $(1+i)^2 = 1 + 2i + i^2 = 1 + 2i - 1 = 2i$

(3) $(1-3i)^2 = 1 - 6i + 9i^2$
$= 1 - 6i - 9 = -8 - 6i$

(4) $(1+i)^4 = ((1+i)^2)^2 = (2i)^2 = 4i^2 = -4$

06

(1) $x^2 - 5x + 6 = (x-2)(x-3)$
$= (2-i-2)(2-i-3)$
$= -i(-1-i) = i + i^2 = -1 + i$

(2) $x^3 - x^2 + 1 = (2-i)^3 - (2-i)^2 + 1$
$= 8 - 3(2)^2 i + 3(2)i^2 - i^3 - (4 - 4i + i^2) + 1$
$= 8 - 12i - 6 + i - (4 - 4i - 1) + 1$
$= -7i$

07

$A^2 B + AB^2 = AB(A+B)$
$= (4-3i)(4+3i)(4-3i+4+3i)$
$= (16 - 9i^2)(8)$
$= (16 + 9)(8) = 200$

$a = 200$ and $b = 0$. So, $a + b = 200 + 0 = 200$

08

(1) $(1+i)^{10} = ((1+i)^2)^5 = (2i)^5$
$= 32i^5 = 32 \cdot i^4 \cdot i = 32i$

(2) $\dfrac{1+i}{1-i} = \dfrac{1+i}{1-i} \cdot \dfrac{1+i}{1+i} = \dfrac{1+2i+i^2}{1-i^2}$
$= \dfrac{1+2i-1}{1+1} = i$

$\left(\dfrac{1+i}{1+i}\right)^{16} = i^{16} = (i^4)^4 = 1$

(3) $i + i^2 + i^3 + i^4 = i - 1 - i + 1 = 0$
$i + i^2 + i^3 + i^4 + \cdots + i^{20}$
$= (i + i^2 + i^3 + i^4) + i^4(i + i^2 + i^3 + i^4)$
$\quad + \cdots + i^{16}(i + i^2 + i^3 + i^4)$
$= 0 + i^4(0) + \cdots + i^{16}(0) = 0$

(4) $i+2i^2+3i^3+4i^4+\cdots+20i^{20}$
$=i+2i^2+3i^3+4i^4+5i^5+6i^6+7i^7+8i^8$
$\quad+\cdots+20i^{20}$
$=(i-2-3i+4)+(5i-6-7i+8)$
$\quad+(9i-10-11i+12)$
$\quad+\cdots+(17i-18-19i+20)$
$=(2-2i)+(2-2i)+(2-2i)+\cdots+(2-2i)$
$=5(2-2i)=10-10i$

09

Since $0<k<1$, $1-k>0$ and $k-1<0$.

$\sqrt{-k}\times\sqrt{k}-\dfrac{\sqrt{k-1}}{\sqrt{1-k}}\times\sqrt{\dfrac{k-1}{1-k}}$

$=\sqrt{-k}\times\sqrt{k}-\dfrac{\sqrt{-(1-k)}}{\sqrt{1-k}}\times\sqrt{\dfrac{-(1-k)}{1-k}}$

$=\sqrt{k}i\times\sqrt{k}-\dfrac{\sqrt{1-k}i}{\sqrt{1-k}}\times\sqrt{-1}$

$=ki-i\times i=ki-i^2=ki+1$

The answer is (B)

10

$\dfrac{1}{i}=\dfrac{1}{i}\cdot\dfrac{i}{i}=\dfrac{i}{i^2}=-i,\ \dfrac{1}{i^2}=\dfrac{1}{-1}=-1$

$\dfrac{1}{i^3}=-\dfrac{1}{i}=-(-i)=i,\ \dfrac{1}{i^4}=1$

$\dfrac{1}{i}+\dfrac{1}{i^2}+\dfrac{1}{i^3}+\dfrac{1}{i^4}+\cdots+\dfrac{1}{i^{100}}$

$=\left(\dfrac{1}{i}+\dfrac{1}{i^2}+\dfrac{1}{i^3}+\dfrac{1}{i^4}\right)+\dfrac{1}{i^4}\left(\dfrac{1}{i}+\dfrac{1}{i^2}+\dfrac{1}{i^3}+\dfrac{1}{i^4}\right)$

$\quad+\dfrac{1}{i^8}\left(\dfrac{1}{i}+\dfrac{1}{i^2}+\dfrac{1}{i^3}+\dfrac{1}{i^4}\right)$

$\quad+\cdots+\dfrac{1}{i^{96}}\left(\dfrac{1}{i}+\dfrac{1}{i^2}+\dfrac{1}{i^3}+\dfrac{1}{i^4}\right)$

$=(-i-1+i+1)+\dfrac{1}{i^4}(-i-1+i+1)$

$\quad+\dfrac{1}{i^8}(-i-1+i+1)+\cdots+\dfrac{1}{i^{96}}(-i-1+i+1)$

$=0+\cdots+0=0$

3. Completing the Square and the Quadratic Formula

Check Point 1

① $x^2-8x+6=0$
$x^2-8x=-6$
$x^2-8x+(4)^2=-6+(4)^2$
$(x-4)^2=10$
$x-4=\pm\sqrt{10},\ x=4\pm\sqrt{10}$

② $(4x^2+12x-5=0)\cdot\dfrac{1}{4},\ x^2+3x-\dfrac{5}{4}=0$

$x^2+3x=\dfrac{5}{4}$

$x^2+3x+\left(\dfrac{3}{2}\right)^2=\dfrac{5}{4}+\left(\dfrac{3}{2}\right)^2$

$\left(x+\dfrac{3}{2}\right)^2=\dfrac{14}{4}$

$x+\dfrac{3}{2}=\pm\sqrt{\dfrac{14}{4}},\ x=-\dfrac{3}{2}\pm\dfrac{\sqrt{14}}{2}$

③ $4x^2-1=(x+3)(x-2),\ 4x^2-1=x^2+x-6$

$(3x^2-x+5=0)\cdot\dfrac{1}{3},\ x^2-\dfrac{1}{3}x+\dfrac{5}{3}=0$

$x^2-\dfrac{1}{3}x=-\dfrac{5}{3}$

$x^2-\dfrac{1}{3}x+\left(\dfrac{1}{6}\right)^2=-\dfrac{5}{3}+\left(\dfrac{1}{6}\right)^2$

$\left(x-\dfrac{1}{6}\right)^2=-\dfrac{59}{36}$

$x-\dfrac{1}{6}=\pm\sqrt{-\dfrac{59}{36}},\ x=\dfrac{1}{6}\pm\dfrac{\sqrt{59}}{6}i$

④ $\left(\dfrac{1}{2}x^2+8x-\dfrac{3}{2}=0\right)\cdot 2,\ x^2+16x-3=0$

$x^2+16x=3$

$x^2+16x+(8)^2=3+(8)^2$

$(x+8)^2=67$

$x+8=\pm\sqrt{67},\ x=-8\pm\sqrt{67}$

Check Point 2

① $x^2-4x-5=0 \rightarrow a=1, b=-4, c=-5$

$$x=\frac{-(-4)\pm\sqrt{(-4)^2-4(1)(-5)}}{2(1)}$$

$$=\frac{4\pm\sqrt{16+20}}{2}=\frac{4\pm\sqrt{36}}{2}=\frac{4\pm 6}{2}$$

$x=\frac{4+6}{2}=5$ or $x=\frac{4-6}{2}=-1$

② $2x^2-3x-3=0 \rightarrow a=2, b=-3, c=-3$

$$x=\frac{-(-3)\pm\sqrt{(-3)^2-4(2)(-3)}}{2(2)}$$

$$=\frac{3\pm\sqrt{9+24}}{4}=\frac{3\pm\sqrt{33}}{4}$$

③ $(0.3x^2+0.5x-1.1=0)\cdot 10$

$3x^2+5x-11=0 \rightarrow a=3, b=5, c=-11$

$$x=\frac{-5\pm\sqrt{(5)^2-4(3)(-11)}}{2(3)}$$

$$=\frac{-5\pm\sqrt{25+132}}{6}=\frac{-5\pm\sqrt{157}}{4}$$

Review Exercises

01

(1) $x^2-4x-12=0$

$x^2-4x+(2)^2=12+(2)^2$

$(x-2)^2=16$

$x-2=\pm 4, x=6$ or $x=-2$

(2) $x^2-2x-35=0$

$x^2-2x+(1)^2=35+(1)^2$

$(x-1)^2=36$

$x-1=\pm 6, x=7$ or $x=-5$

(3) $x^2=-10x+3$

$x^2+10x+(5)^2=3+(5)^2$

$(x+5)^2=28$

$x+5=\pm 2\sqrt{7}, x=-5\pm 2\sqrt{7}$

(4) $9x^2-18x+5=0, 9x^2-18x=-5$

$x^2-2x=-\frac{5}{9}$

$x^2-2x+(1)^2=-\frac{5}{9}+(1)^2$

$(x-1)^2=\frac{4}{9}$

$x-1=\pm\frac{2}{3}, x=\frac{5}{3}$ or $x=\frac{1}{3}$

(5) $4x^2+8x+31=0, 4x^2+8x=-31$

$x^2+2x=-\frac{31}{4}$

$x^2+2x+(1)^2=-\frac{31}{4}+(1)^2$

$(x+1)^2=-\frac{27}{4}$

$x+1=\pm\frac{3\sqrt{3}}{2}i, x=-1\pm\frac{3\sqrt{3}}{2}i$

(6) $5x^2-2x=16$

$x^2-\frac{2}{5}x=\frac{16}{5}$

$x^2-\frac{2}{5}x+\left(\frac{1}{5}\right)^2=\frac{16}{5}+\left(\frac{1}{5}\right)^2$

$\left(x-\frac{1}{5}\right)^2=\frac{81}{25}$

$x-\frac{1}{5}=\pm\frac{9}{5}, x=2$ or $x=-\frac{8}{5}$

02

(1) $\frac{1}{3}x^2-3x-\frac{1}{2}=0, \frac{1}{3}x^2-3x=\frac{1}{2}$

$x^2-9x=\frac{3}{2}$

$x^2-9x+\left(\frac{9}{2}\right)^2=\frac{3}{2}+\left(\frac{9}{2}\right)^2$

$\left(x-\frac{9}{2}\right)^2=\frac{87}{4}$

$x-\frac{9}{2}=\pm\frac{\sqrt{87}}{2}, x=\frac{9}{2}\pm\frac{\sqrt{87}}{2}$

(2) $\frac{1}{2}x^2-4x=-3$

$x^2-8x=-6$

$x^2-8x+(4)^2=-6+(4)^2$

$(x-4)^2=10$

$x-4=\pm\sqrt{10}, x=4\pm\sqrt{10}$

(3) $0.5x^2-x+0.2=0, 0.5x^2-x=-0.2$

$x^2-2x=-0.4$

$x^2-2x+(1)^2=-0.4+(1)^2$

$(x-1)^2=0.6$

$x-1=\pm\sqrt{0.6}, x=1\pm\sqrt{0.6}$

(4) $(x+2)^2=3(x-4)$

$x^2+4x+4=3x-12$

$x^2+x=-16$

$x^2+x+\left(\frac{1}{2}\right)^2=-16+\left(\frac{1}{2}\right)^2$

$\left(x+\dfrac{1}{2}\right)^2=-\dfrac{63}{4}$

$x+\dfrac{1}{2}=\pm\dfrac{3\sqrt{7}}{2}i,\ x=-\dfrac{1}{2}\pm\dfrac{3\sqrt{7}}{2}i$

(5) $(x-1)(x+1)-4x=(2x-1)(2x+1)$

$x^2-1-4x=4x^2-1,\ 3x^2+4x=0$

$x^2+\dfrac{4}{3}x=0$

$x^2+\dfrac{4}{3}x+\left(\dfrac{2}{3}\right)^2=\left(\dfrac{2}{3}\right)^2$

$\left(x+\dfrac{2}{3}\right)^2=\left(\dfrac{2}{3}\right)^2$

$x+\dfrac{2}{3}=\pm\dfrac{2}{3},\ x=0\ \text{or}\ x=-\dfrac{4}{3}$

(6) $ax^2+bx+c=0,\ x^2+\dfrac{b}{a}x+\dfrac{c}{a}=0$

$x^2+\dfrac{b}{a}x=-\dfrac{c}{a}$

$x^2+\dfrac{b}{a}x+\left(\dfrac{b}{2a}\right)^2=-\dfrac{c}{a}+\left(\dfrac{b}{2a}\right)^2$

$\left(x+\dfrac{b}{2a}\right)^2=\dfrac{-4ac+b^2}{4a^2}$

$x+\dfrac{b}{2a}=\pm\dfrac{\sqrt{b^2-4ac}}{2a},$

$x=-\dfrac{b}{2a}\pm\dfrac{\sqrt{b^2-4ac}}{2a}$

03

(1) $x^2-x-12=0\ \rightarrow\ a=1,\ b=-1,\ c=-12$

$x=\dfrac{-(-1)\pm\sqrt{(-1)^2-4(1)(-12)}}{2(1)}$

$=\dfrac{1\pm\sqrt{1+48}}{2}=\dfrac{1\pm\sqrt{49}}{2}=\dfrac{1\pm7}{2}$

$x=-3\ \text{or}\ x=4$

(2) $x^2+5x-6=0\ \rightarrow\ a=1,\ b=5,\ c=-6$

$x=\dfrac{-(5)\pm\sqrt{(5)^2-4(1)(-6)}}{2(1)}$

$=\dfrac{-5\pm\sqrt{25+24}}{2}$

$=\dfrac{-5\pm\sqrt{49}}{2}=\dfrac{-5\pm7}{2}$

$x=-6\ \text{or}\ x=1$

(3) $2x^2-x-6=0\ \rightarrow\ a=2,\ b=-1,\ c=-6$

$x=\dfrac{-(-1)\pm\sqrt{(-1)^2-4(2)(-6)}}{2(2)}$

$=\dfrac{1\pm\sqrt{1+48}}{4}=\dfrac{1\pm\sqrt{49}}{4}=\dfrac{1\pm7}{4}$

$x=-\dfrac{3}{2}\ \text{or}\ x=2$

(4) $x^2-3x+1=0\ \rightarrow\ a=1,\ b=-3,\ c=1$

$x=\dfrac{-(-3)\pm\sqrt{(-3)^2-4(1)(1)}}{2(1)}$

$=\dfrac{3\pm\sqrt{9-4}}{2}=\dfrac{3\pm\sqrt{5}}{2}$

(5) $-8x^2=6x+5$

$8x^2+6x+5=0\rightarrow\ a=8,\ b=6,\ c=5$

$x=\dfrac{-(6)\pm\sqrt{(6)^2-4(8)(5)}}{2(8)}$

$=\dfrac{-6\pm\sqrt{36-160}}{16}=\dfrac{-6\pm\sqrt{-124}}{16}$

$=\dfrac{-6\pm2\sqrt{31}i}{16}=\dfrac{-3\pm\sqrt{31}i}{8}$

(6) $3x^2-x=-2$

$3x^2-x+2=0\ \rightarrow\ a=3,\ b=-1,\ c=2$

$x=\dfrac{-(-1)\pm\sqrt{(-1)^2-4(3)(2)}}{2(3)}$

$=\dfrac{1\pm\sqrt{1-24}}{6}=\dfrac{1\pm\sqrt{-23}}{6}=\dfrac{1\pm\sqrt{23}i}{6}$

04

(1) $\left(\dfrac{3}{4}x^2-\dfrac{1}{2}x-\dfrac{5}{6}=0\right)\cdot12$

$9x^2-6x-10=0\ \rightarrow\ a=9,\ b=-6,\ c=-10$

$x=\dfrac{-(-6)\pm\sqrt{(-6)^2-4(9)(-10)}}{2(9)}$

$=\dfrac{6\pm\sqrt{36+360}}{18}=\dfrac{6\pm\sqrt{396}}{18}$

$=\dfrac{6\pm6\sqrt{11}}{18}=\dfrac{1\pm\sqrt{11}}{3}$

(2) $0.4x^2-x-0.1=0$
$4x^2-10x-1=0 \rightarrow a=4, b=-10, c=-1$
$x=\dfrac{-(-10)\pm\sqrt{(-10)^2-4(4)(-1)}}{2(4)}$
$=\dfrac{10\pm\sqrt{100+16}}{8}=\dfrac{10\pm\sqrt{116}}{8}$
$=\dfrac{10\pm 2\sqrt{29}}{8}=\dfrac{5\pm\sqrt{29}}{4}$

(3) $x^2-\dfrac{5}{3}x=0.6,\ x^2-\dfrac{5}{3}x-0.6=0$
$\left(x^2-\dfrac{5}{3}x-\dfrac{3}{5}=0\right)\cdot 15$
$15x^2-25x-9=0 \rightarrow a=15, b=-25, c=-9$
$x=\dfrac{-(-25)\pm\sqrt{(-25)^2-4(15)(-9)}}{2(15)}$
$=\dfrac{25\pm\sqrt{625+540}}{30}=\dfrac{25\pm\sqrt{1165}}{30}$

(4) $(0.5x+2)\left(x-\dfrac{1}{2}\right)=x-1$
$0.5x^2+\dfrac{7}{4}x-1=x-1$
$\left(\dfrac{1}{2}x^2+\dfrac{3}{4}x=0\right)\cdot 4$
$2x^2+3x=0 \rightarrow a=2, b=3, c=0$
$x=\dfrac{-(3)\pm\sqrt{(3)^2-4(2)(0)}}{2(2)}$
$=\dfrac{-3\pm\sqrt{9-0}}{4}=\dfrac{-3\pm 3}{4},\ x=0$ or $x=-\dfrac{3}{2}$

05

$x^2-2x+a=0,\ x^2-2x=-a$
$x^2-2x+1^2=-a+1^2$
$(x-1)^2=1-a,\ x-1=\pm\sqrt{1-a}$
$x=1\pm\sqrt{1-a}$
$\Rightarrow 1-a=7,\ a=-6$

06

$\left(\dfrac{1}{2}x^2-x-\dfrac{1}{4}=0\right)\cdot 4$
$2x^2-4x-1=0 \rightarrow a=2, b=-4, c=-1$
$x=\dfrac{-(-4)\pm\sqrt{(-4)^2-4(2)(-1)}}{2(2)}$

$=\dfrac{4\pm\sqrt{24}}{4}=\dfrac{4\pm 2\sqrt{6}}{4}=1\pm\dfrac{\sqrt{6}}{2}$
$\Rightarrow a=1, b=6, c=2$
Therefore, $abc=(1)(6)(2)=12$

07

$2x^2+\dfrac{1}{4}x+a=2\left(x+\dfrac{1}{b}\right)^2$
$2x^2+\dfrac{1}{4}x+a=2\left(x^2+\dfrac{2}{b}x+\dfrac{1}{b^2}\right)$
$2x^2+\dfrac{1}{4}x+a=2x^2+\dfrac{4}{b}x+\dfrac{2}{b^2}$
$\Rightarrow \dfrac{1}{4}=\dfrac{4}{b},\ b=16$ and $a=\dfrac{2}{b^2}=\dfrac{2}{16^2}$
Therefore, $ab=\dfrac{2}{16^2}\times 16=\dfrac{1}{8}$

08

If the quadratic equation has only one real solution, it means that $b^2-4ac=0$ in the quadratic formula $x=\dfrac{-b\pm\sqrt{b^2-4ac}}{2a}$.
$x^2-10x+2m=5$
$x^2-10x+2m-5=0$
$\rightarrow a=1, b=-10, c=2m-5$
$b^2-4ac=(-10)^2-4(1)(2m-5)$
$\quad\quad\quad =100-8m+20$
$\quad\quad\quad =120-8m=0$
$\Rightarrow m=15$

09

$(5x^2+4x+1=0)\cdot\dfrac{1}{5}$
$x^2+\dfrac{4}{5}x+\dfrac{1}{5}=0$
$x^2+\dfrac{4}{5}x+\left(\dfrac{2}{5}\right)^2=-\dfrac{1}{5}+\left(\dfrac{2}{5}\right)^2$
$\left(x+\dfrac{2}{5}\right)^2=-\dfrac{1}{25} \Rightarrow h=\dfrac{2}{5},\ k=-\dfrac{1}{25}$
Therefore, $\dfrac{h}{k}=\dfrac{\dfrac{2}{5}}{-\dfrac{1}{25}}=-10$

Solutions Manual

4. More Complicated Quadratic Equations

Check Point 1

① $(2a-5)^2-7(2a-5)+10=0$
Substitute k for $2a-5$
$k^2-7k+10=0$
$(k-2)(k-5)=0$
$k-2=0$ or $k-5=0$
$(2a-5)-2=0$ or $(2a-5)-5=0$
$a=\dfrac{7}{2}$ or $a=5$

② $2x^4+5x^2-12=0$, $2(x^2)^2+5x^2-12=0$
Substitute k for x^2
$2k^2+5k-12=0$
$(2k-3)(k+4)=0$
$2k-3=0$ or $k+4=0$
$2x^2-3=0$ or $x^2+4=0$
$x=\pm\sqrt{\dfrac{3}{2}}=\pm\dfrac{\sqrt{6}}{2}$ or $x=\pm\sqrt{-4}=\pm 2i$

③ $y^{-2}-y^{-1}-12=0$, $(y^{-1})^2-(y^{-1})-12=0$
Substitute k for y^{-1}
$k^2-k-12=0$
$(k-4)(k+3)=0$
$k-4=0$ or $k+3=0$
$y^{-1}-4=0$ or $y^{-1}+3=0$
$y=\dfrac{1}{4}$ or $y=-\dfrac{1}{3}$

④ $5\left(\dfrac{3x-1}{2}\right)^2-3\left(\dfrac{3x-1}{2}\right)-2=0$
Substitute k for $\dfrac{3x-1}{2}$
$5k^2-3k-2=0$
$(5k+2)(k-1)=0$
$5k+2=0$ or $k-1=0$
$5\left(\dfrac{3x-1}{2}\right)+2=0$ or $\dfrac{3x-1}{2}-1=0$
$x=\dfrac{1}{15}$ or $x=1$

Review Exercises

01

(1) $(x+3)^2-5(x+3)+4=0$
Substitute k for $x+3$
$k^2-5k+4=0$, $(k-1)(k-4)=0$
$(x+3-1)(x+3-4)=0$
$(x+2)(x-1)=0$
$x+2=0$ or $x-1=0$
$x=-2$ or $x=1$

(2) $(2y-5)^2-(2y-5)-2=0$
Substitute k for $2y-5$
$k^2-k-2=0$, $(k-2)(k+1)=0$
$((2y-5)-2)((2y-5)+1)=0$
$(2y-7)(2y-4)=0$
$2y-7=0$ or $2y-4=0$
$y=\dfrac{7}{2}$ or $y=2$

(3) $(x^2-4)^2-2(x^2-4)-15=0$
Substitute k for x^2-4
$k^2-2k-15=0$, $(k-5)(k+3)=0$
$((x^2-4)-5)((x^2-4)+3)=0$
$(x^2-9)(x^2-1)=0$
$x^2-9=0$ or $x^2-1=1$
$x=\pm 3$ or $x=\pm 1$

(4) $(2y^2-1)^2-10(2y^2-1)+24=0$
Substitute k for $2y^2-1$
$k^2-10k+24=0$, $(k-4)(k-6)=0$
$((2y^2-1)-4)((2y^2-1)-6)=0$
$(2y^2-5)(2y^2-7)=0$
$2y^2-5=0$ or $2y^2-7=0$
$y=\pm\sqrt{\dfrac{5}{2}}=\pm\dfrac{\sqrt{10}}{2}$ or $y=\pm\sqrt{\dfrac{7}{2}}=\pm\dfrac{\sqrt{14}}{2}$

(5) $\left(\dfrac{2x-5}{3}\right)^2-5\left(\dfrac{2x-5}{3}\right)+6=0$
Substitute k for $\dfrac{2x-5}{3}$
$k^2-5k+6=0$, $(k-2)(k-3)=0$
$\left(\dfrac{2x-5}{3}-2\right)\left(\dfrac{2x-5}{3}-3\right)=0$
$\dfrac{2x-5}{3}-2=0$ or $\dfrac{2x-5}{3}-3=0$

$x=\dfrac{11}{2}$ or $x=7$

(6) $2\left(\dfrac{1}{x}\right)^2+5\left(\dfrac{1}{x}\right)-3=0$

Substitute k for $\dfrac{1}{x}$

$2k^2+5k-3=0$, $(2k-1)(k+3)=0$

$\left(\dfrac{2}{x}-1\right)\left(\dfrac{1}{x}+3\right)=0$

$\dfrac{2}{x}-1=0$ or $\dfrac{1}{x}+3=0$

$x=2$ or $x=-\dfrac{1}{3}$

02

(1) $a^{-2}-a^{-1}=20$, $\dfrac{1}{a^2}-\dfrac{1}{a}-20=0$

Substitute k for $\dfrac{1}{a}$

$k^2-k-20=0$, $(k-5)(k+4)=0$

$\left(\dfrac{1}{a}-5\right)\left(\dfrac{1}{a}+4\right)=0$

$\dfrac{1}{a}-5=0$ or $\dfrac{1}{a}+4=0$

$a=\dfrac{1}{5}$ or $a=-\dfrac{1}{4}$

(2) $3a^{-2}-8a^{-1}+4=0$, $\dfrac{3}{a^2}-\dfrac{8}{a}+4=0$

Substitute k for $\dfrac{1}{a}$

$3k^2-8k+4=0$, $(3k-2)(k-2)=0$

$\left(\dfrac{3}{a}-2\right)\left(\dfrac{1}{a}-2\right)=0$

$\dfrac{3}{a}-2=0$ or $\dfrac{1}{a}-2=0$

$a=\dfrac{3}{2}$ or $a=\dfrac{1}{2}$

(3) $x^4-6x^2+8=0$

Substitute k for x^2

$k^2-6k+8=0$, $(k-4)(k-2)=0$

$(x^2-4)(x^2-2)=0$

$x^2-4=0$ or $x^2-2=0$

$x=\pm 2$ or $x=\pm\sqrt{2}$

(4) $2h^4+5h^2-12=0$

Substitute k for h^2

$2k^2+5k-12=0$, $(k+4)(2k-3)=0$

$(h^2+4)(2h^2-3)=0$

$h^2+4=0$ or $2h^2-3=0$

$h=\pm 2i$ or $h=\pm\dfrac{\sqrt{6}}{2}$

03

(1) $y^6-8y^3+15=0$

Substitute k for y^3

$k^2-8k+15=0$, $(k-3)(k-5)=0$

$(y^3-3)(y^3-5)=0$

$y^3-3=0$ or $y^3-5=0$

$y=3^{\frac{1}{3}}$ or $y=5^{\frac{1}{3}}$

(2) $\left(\dfrac{3}{2}(2x-3)^2-8(2x-3)=-\dfrac{5}{2}\right)\cdot 2$

$3(2x-3)^2-16(2x-3)+5=0$

Substitute k for $2x-3$

$3k^2-16k+5=0$, $(k-5)(3k-1)=0$

$((2x-3)-5)(3(2x-3)-1)=0$

$(2x-8)(6x-10)=0$

$2x-8=0$ or $6x-10=0$

$x=4$ or $x=\dfrac{5}{3}$

(3) $\left(\dfrac{1}{4}(x-2)^2-\dfrac{3}{20}(x-2)-\dfrac{1}{10}=0\right)\cdot 20$

$5(x-2)^2-3(x-2)-2=0$

Substitute k for $x-2$

$5k^2-3k-2=0$, $(k-1)(5k+2)=0$

$((x-2)-1)(5(x-2)+2)=0$

$(x-3)(5x-8)=0$

$x-3=0$ or $5x-8=0$

$x=3$ or $x=\dfrac{8}{5}$

(4) $\left(\dfrac{3}{2}\left(\dfrac{1}{3x}+2\right)^2-\left(\dfrac{1}{3x}+2\right)=\dfrac{1}{2}\right)\cdot 2$

$3\left(\dfrac{1}{3x}+2\right)^2-2\left(\dfrac{1}{3x}+2\right)=1$

Substitute k for $\dfrac{1}{3x}+2$

$3k^2-2k-1=0$, $(k-1)(3k+1)=0$

$\left(\left(\dfrac{1}{3x}+2\right)-1\right)\left(3\left(\dfrac{1}{3x}+2\right)+1\right)=0$

$\left(\dfrac{1}{3x}+1\right)\left(\dfrac{1}{x}+7\right)=0$

$\dfrac{1}{3x}+1=0$ or $\dfrac{1}{x}+7=0$

$x=-\dfrac{1}{3}$ or $x=-\dfrac{1}{7}$

04

$(x-2y)(x-2y-4)=5$

Substitute k for $x-2y$

$k(k-4)=5$

$k^2-4k-5=0$

$(k+1)(k-5)=0$, $k=-1$ or $k=5$

$\Rightarrow x-2y=-1$ or $x-2y=5$

Therefore, $4x-8y=4(x-2y)$
$\qquad\qquad\qquad =4(-1)=-4$

or $4x-8y=4(x-2y)$
$\qquad\qquad\quad =4(5)=20$

5. Solutions and Coefficients of the Quadratic Equations

Check Point 1

① $3x^2+5x-1=0 \rightarrow a=3$, $b=5$, and $c=-1$

$D=b^2-4ac=5^2-4(3)(-1)=37>0$

There are two real solutions

② $\frac{1}{2}x^2-5x+\frac{25}{2}=0$

$\rightarrow a=\frac{1}{2}$, $b=-5$, and $c=\frac{25}{2}$

$D=b^2-4ac=(-5)^2-4\left(\frac{1}{2}\right)\left(\frac{25}{2}\right)=0$

There is one real solution

③ $2x^2-4x+6=0 \rightarrow a=2$, $b=-4$, and $c=6$

$D=b^2-4ac=(-4)^2-4(2)(6)=-32<0$

There is no real solution, but two imaginary solutions

④ $(x-4)^2-7=2x(x-4)$

$x^2-8x+16-7=2x^2-8x$

$x^2-9=0$

$\rightarrow a=1$, $b=0$, and $c=-9$

$D=b^2-4ac=0^2-4(1)(-9)=36>0$

There are two real solutions

Check Point 2

$3x^2-6x-k=0 \rightarrow a=3$, $b=-6$, and $c=-k$

① $D=(-6)^2-4(3)(-k)>0$

$36+12k>0 \rightarrow k>-3$

② $D=(-6)^2-4(3)(-k)=0$

$36+12k=0 \rightarrow k=-3$

③ $D=(-6)^2-4(3)(-k)<0$

$36+12k<0 \rightarrow k<-3$

Check Point 3

① $2x^2+5x-7=0 \ \rightarrow \ a=2, \ b=5, \text{ and } c=-7$

The Sum of solutions: $-\dfrac{b}{a}=-\dfrac{5}{2}$

The Product of solutions: $\dfrac{c}{a}=\dfrac{-7}{2}=-\dfrac{7}{2}$

② $\dfrac{1}{5}x^2-x=0.7, \ \left(\dfrac{1}{5}x^2-x=0.7\right)\cdot 10$

$2x^2-10x=7$

$2x^2-10x-7=0$

$\rightarrow \ a=2, \ b=-10, \text{ and } c=-7$

The Sum of solutions: $-\dfrac{b}{a}=-\dfrac{-10}{2}=5$

The Product of solutions: $\dfrac{c}{a}=\dfrac{-7}{2}=-\dfrac{7}{2}$

③ $(x-4)^2=2x(x+3)$

$x^2-8x+16=2x^2+6x$

$x^2+14x-16=0$

$\rightarrow \ a=1, \ b=14, \text{ and } c=-16$

The Sum of solutions: $-\dfrac{b}{a}=-\dfrac{14}{1}=-14$

The Product of solutions: $\dfrac{c}{a}=\dfrac{-16}{1}=-16$

Check Point 4

$5x^2+4x-8=0 \ \rightarrow \ a=5, \ b=4, \text{ and } c=-8$

$\alpha+\beta=-\dfrac{b}{a}=-\dfrac{4}{5}$ and $\alpha\beta=\dfrac{c}{a}=-\dfrac{8}{5}$

① $\dfrac{1}{\alpha}+\dfrac{1}{\beta}=\dfrac{\beta+\alpha}{\alpha\beta}=\dfrac{\left(-\dfrac{4}{5}\right)}{\left(-\dfrac{8}{5}\right)}=\dfrac{1}{2}$

② $\alpha^2+\beta^2=(\alpha+\beta)^2-2\alpha\beta$

$=\left(-\dfrac{4}{5}\right)^2-2\left(-\dfrac{8}{5}\right)=\dfrac{96}{25}$

Check Point 5

① $2(x-6)^2=0$

$2(x^2-2(6)x+6^2)$

$2(x^2-12x+36)=0$

$2x^2-24x+72=0$

② $4\left(x+\dfrac{3}{2}\right)(x-3)=0$

$4\left(x^2-\left(-\dfrac{3}{2}+3\right)x+\left(-\dfrac{3}{2}\right)(3)\right)=0$

$4\left(x^2-\dfrac{3}{2}x-\dfrac{9}{2}\right)=0$

$4x^2-6x-18=0$

③ $(x-(1-2\sqrt{2}))(x-(1+2\sqrt{2}))=0$

$x^2-((1-2\sqrt{2})+(1+2\sqrt{2}))x$

$+((1-2\sqrt{2})(1+2\sqrt{2}))=0$

$x^2-2x+(1-8)=0$

$x^2-2x-7=0$

④ $8\left(x-\dfrac{3-i}{2}\right)\left(x-\dfrac{3+i}{2}\right)=0$

$8\left(x^2-\left(\dfrac{3-i}{2}+\dfrac{3+i}{2}\right)x+\left(\dfrac{3-i}{2}\right)\left(\dfrac{3+i}{2}\right)\right)=0$

$8\left(x^2-\left(\dfrac{6}{2}\right)x+\dfrac{3^2-i^2}{4}\right)=0$

$8\left(x^2-3x+\dfrac{10}{4}\right)=0$

$8x^2-24x+20=0$

Review Exercises

01

(1) $x^2-x+3=0 \ \rightarrow \ a=1, \ b=-1, \text{ and } c=3$

$D=b^2-4ac=(-1)^2-4(1)(3)=-11<0$

There is no real solution, but two imaginary solutions

(2) $2x^2+3x-1=0 \ \rightarrow \ a=2, \ b=3, \text{ and } c=-1$

$D=b^2-4ac=(3)^2-4(2)(-1)=17>0$

There are two real solutions

(3) $4x^2-8x+4=0 \ \rightarrow \ a=4, \ b=-8, \text{ and } c=4$

$D=b^2-4ac=(-8)^2-4(4)(4)=0$

There is one real solution

(4) $10x^2+2x=x(x-2)$

$10x^2+2x=x^2-2x$

$9x^2+4x=0 \ \rightarrow \ a=9, \ b=4, \text{ and } c=0$

$D=b^2-4ac=4^2-4(9)(0)=16>0$

There are two real solutions

(5) $2x^2+2x+3=0 \ \rightarrow \ a=2, \ b=2, \text{ and } c=3$

$D=b^2-4ac=(2)^2-4(2)(3)=-20<0$

Solutions Manual

There is no real solution, but two imaginary solutions

(6) $3x^2-5x-2=-8x$
$3x^2+3x-2=0 \to a=3, b=3,$ and $c=-2$
$D=b^2-4ac=(3)^2-4(3)(-2)=33>0$

There are two real solutions

02

(1) $x^2-4x-2k=0 \to a=1, b=-4,$ and $c=-2k$
(A) $D=(-4)^2-4(1)(-2k)>0$
$16+8k>0 \to k>-2$
(B) $D=(-4)^2-4(1)(-2k)=0$
$16+8k=0 \to k=-2$
(C) $D=(-4)^2-4(1)(-2k)<0$
$16+8k<0 \to k<-2$

(2) $k^2x^2-8x+4=0 \to a=k^2, b=-8,$ and $c=4$
(A) $D=(-8)^2-4(k^2)(4)>0$
$64-16k^2>0$
$k^2<4 \to -2<k<2$
(B) $D=(-8)^2-4(k^2)(4)=0$
$64-16k^2=0$
$k^2=4 \to k=\pm 2$
(C) $D=(-8)^2-4(k^2)(4)<0$
$64-16k^2<0$
$k^2>4 \to k>2$ or $k<-2$

03

(1) $x^2+7x-9=0 \to a=1, b=7,$ and $c=-9$
The Sum of solutions: $-\dfrac{b}{a}=-\dfrac{7}{1}=-7$
The Product of solutions: $\dfrac{c}{a}=\dfrac{-9}{1}=-9$

(2) $7x^2+2x-6=0 \to a=7, b=2,$ and $c=-6$
The Sum of solutions: $-\dfrac{b}{a}=-\dfrac{2}{7}$
The Product of solutions: $\dfrac{c}{a}=-\dfrac{6}{7}$

(3) $2x^2+3x=1$
$2x^2+3x-1=0 \to a=2, b=3,$ and $c=-1$
The Sum of solutions: $-\dfrac{b}{a}=-\dfrac{3}{2}$
The Product of solutions: $\dfrac{c}{a}=-\dfrac{1}{2}$

(4) $x^2-4x=4x^2+5$
$3x^2+4x+5=0 \to a=3, b=4,$ and $c=5$
The Sum of solutions: $-\dfrac{b}{a}=-\dfrac{4}{3}$
The Product of solutions: $\dfrac{c}{a}=\dfrac{5}{3}$

(5) $\left(\dfrac{1}{3}x^2-\dfrac{2}{5}x=4-x\right)\cdot 15$
$5x^2-6x=60-15x$
$5x^2+9x-60=0 \to a=5, b=9,$ and $c=-60$
The Sum of solutions: $-\dfrac{b}{a}=-\dfrac{9}{5}$
The Product of solutions: $\dfrac{c}{a}=\dfrac{-60}{5}=-12$

(6) $x(2-x)=5x-2(2x-1)$
$2x-x^2=5x-4x+2$
$x^2-x+2 \to a=1, b=-1,$ and $c=2$
The Sum of solutions: $-\dfrac{b}{a}=-\dfrac{-1}{1}=1$
The Product of solutions: $\dfrac{c}{a}=\dfrac{2}{1}=2$

04

(1) $4x^2-4x+3=0 \to a=4, b=-4,$ and $c=3$
$\alpha+\beta=-\dfrac{b}{a}=-\dfrac{-4}{4}=1$ and $\alpha\beta=\dfrac{c}{a}=\dfrac{3}{4}$
(A) $\dfrac{1}{\alpha}+\dfrac{1}{\beta}=\dfrac{\beta+\alpha}{\alpha\beta}=\dfrac{1}{\frac{3}{4}}=\dfrac{4}{3}$
(B) $\alpha^2+\beta^2=(\alpha+\beta)^2-2\alpha\beta$
$=(1)^2-2\left(\dfrac{3}{4}\right)=-\dfrac{1}{2}$

(2) $\left(\dfrac{1}{2}x^2+2x+1=0\right)\cdot 2$
$x^2+4x+2=0 \to a=1, b=4,$ and $c=2$
$\alpha+\beta=-\dfrac{b}{a}=-\dfrac{4}{1}=-4$ and $\alpha\beta=\dfrac{c}{a}=\dfrac{2}{1}=2$
(A) $\dfrac{1}{\alpha}+\dfrac{1}{\beta}=\dfrac{\beta+\alpha}{\alpha\beta}=\dfrac{-4}{2}=-2$
(B) $\alpha^2+\beta^2=(\alpha+\beta)^2-2\alpha\beta=(-4)^2-2(2)=12$

05

(1) $(x+2)(x-1)=0$
$x^2-(-2+1)x+(-2)(1)=0$
$x^2+x-2=0$

(2) $5(x+4)^2=0$
$5(x^2+8x+16)=0$
$5x^2+40x+80=0$

(3) $(x-\sqrt{3})(x+\sqrt{3})=0$
$x^2-(-\sqrt{3}+\sqrt{3})x+(\sqrt{3})^2=0$
$x^2-3=0$

Alternative Solution
Using $(a-b)(a+b)=a^2-b^2$,
$(x-\sqrt{3})(x+\sqrt{3})=0$
$x^2-(\sqrt{3})^2=0$, $x^2-3=0$

(4) $3(x-(1-\sqrt{2}))(x-(1+\sqrt{2}))=0$
$3(x^2-((1-\sqrt{2})+(1+\sqrt{2}))x+(1-\sqrt{2})(1+\sqrt{2}))$
$=0$
$3(x^2-2x+(1-2))=0$
$3(x^2-2x-1)=0$, $3x^2-6x-3=0$

(5) $2(x-(3-i))(x-(3+i))=0$
$2(x^2-((3-i)+(3+i))x+(3-i)(3+i))=0$
$2(x^2-6x+(9-i^2))=0$
$2(x^2-6x+10)=0$, $2x^2-12x+20=0$

(6) $4\left(x-\dfrac{1+3i\sqrt{5}}{2}\right)\left(x-\dfrac{1-3i\sqrt{5}}{2}\right)=0$
$4\left(\begin{array}{c}x^2-\left(\dfrac{1+3i\sqrt{5}}{2}+\dfrac{1-3i\sqrt{5}}{2}\right)\\+\dfrac{1+3i\sqrt{5}}{2}\cdot\dfrac{1-3i\sqrt{5}}{2}\end{array}\right)=0$
$4\left(x^2-x+\dfrac{1-45i^2}{4}\right)=0$
$4\left(x^2-x+\dfrac{46}{4}\right)=0$, $4x^2-4x+46=0$

06

Two solutions are $\dfrac{2}{3}$ and $-\dfrac{1}{2}$, and the coefficient of the quadratic term is 6.
$6\left(x-\dfrac{2}{3}\right)\left(x+\dfrac{1}{2}\right)=0$
$6\left(x^2-\dfrac{1}{6}x-\dfrac{1}{3}\right)=0$
$6x^2-x-2=0 \rightarrow m=-1$ and $n=-2$
Therefore, $mn=(-1)(-2)=2$

07

$4x^2-8x+3=0$
The sum of solutions: $m=-\dfrac{b}{a}=-\dfrac{-8}{4}=2$
The product of solutions: $n=\dfrac{c}{a}=\dfrac{3}{4}$
Two solutions are $m=2$ and $n=\dfrac{3}{4}$, and the coefficient of the quadratic term is 2.
Therefore, the quadratic equation is
$2(x-2)\left(x-\dfrac{3}{4}\right)=0$
$2\left(x^2-\dfrac{11}{4}x+\dfrac{3}{2}\right)=0$
$2x^2-\dfrac{11}{2}x+3=0$

08

The sum of solutions of $2x^2-6x+9=0$ is
$-\dfrac{b}{a}=-\dfrac{-6}{2}=3$. Since 3 is one of the solution of $5x^2+(k-2)x-3=0$,
we have
$5(3)^2+(k-2)(3)-3=0$
$45+3k-6-3=0$
$3k=-36$, $k=-12$

09

$a(3x+1)+2x^2=-\dfrac{1}{8}$
$2x^2+3ax+a+\dfrac{1}{8}=0$
Using the discriminant,
$D=(3a)^2-4(2)\left(a+\dfrac{1}{8}\right)=0$

$9a^2-8\left(a+\dfrac{1}{8}\right)=0$

$9a^2-8a-1=0$

$(9a+1)(a-1)=0$

$a=-\dfrac{1}{9}$ or $a=1$

10

Let two solutions of the equation $x^2-6x+m=0$ be α and $\alpha+2$.
Use the sum and product of the solutions.
The sum of solutions:
$\alpha+(\alpha+2)=-\dfrac{-6}{1}$, $2\alpha+2=6$, $\alpha=2$
The product of solutions:
$\alpha(\alpha+2)=\dfrac{m}{1}$, $2(2+2)=m$, $m=8$

11

Let two solutions of the equation $x^2+10x+n+4=0$ be 2α and 3α. Use the sum and product of the solutions.
The sum of solutions:
$2\alpha+3\alpha=-\dfrac{10}{1}$, $5\alpha=-10$, $\alpha=-2$
The product of solutions:
$2\alpha\times 3\alpha=\dfrac{n+4}{1}$, $6\alpha^2=n+4$
$6(-2)^2=n+4$, $n=20$

6. Word Problems

Check Point 1

① Let x and $x+2$ be two consecutive positive odd integers. Then we have
$x(x+2)=255$
$x^2+2x-255=0$
$(x+17)(x-15)=0$
$x=-17$ or $x=15$
Since $x>0$, $x=15$.
Two integers are 15 and 17

② Let x be the number. Then we have
$x+\dfrac{1}{x}=\dfrac{10}{3}$
$\left(x+\dfrac{1}{x}\right)\cdot 3x=\dfrac{10}{3}\cdot 3x$
$3x^2-10x+3=0$
$(3x-1)(x-3)=0$, $x=\dfrac{1}{3}$ or $x=3$
The number is either $\dfrac{1}{3}$ or 3

Check Point 2

①

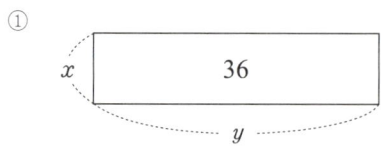

The area is $A=xy=36$ and the perimeter is $P=2x+2y=30 \rightarrow y=15-x$.
Now substitute $15-x$ for y. Then we have
$x(15-x)=36$
$15x-x^2=36$
$x^2-15x+36=0$
$(x-12)(x-3)=0$, $x=12$ or $x=3$
Since the length is longer side of the rectangle while width is the shorter side, $x=3$ and $xy=(3)y=36$, $y=12$.
The dimensions of the rectangle are 3 cm by 12 cm.

②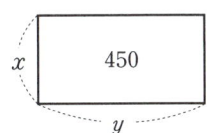

The area is $A=xy=450$. Since $y=2x$, we have
$x(2x)=450$
$x^2=225$, $x=\pm 15$
Since $x>0$, $x=15$ and then length is
$y=2x=2(15)=30$.

The dimensions of the rectangle
are 15 meters by 30 meters

Check Point 3

① Let x be the speed of the bus A. Then, the speed of the bus B is $x+1$.

	Bus A	Bus B
Speed	x	$x+1$
Time	2	2
Distance	$2x$	$2(x+1)$

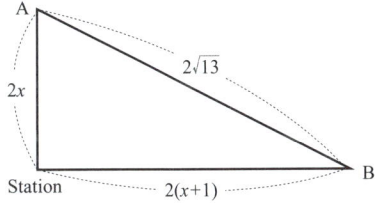

By the Pythagorean Theorem, we have
$(2x)^2+(2(x+1))^2=(2\sqrt{13})^2$
$4x^2+4x^2+8x+4=52$
$8x^2+8x-48=0$
$x^2+x-6=0$
$(x+3)(x-2)=0$, $x=-3$ or $x=2$
Since $x>0$, $x=2$.

The speed of the bus A and B is 2 miles per hour and 3 miles per hour, respectively.

② Let x be the distance traveled by the bicycle heading east. Then the distance between the bicycles is $2x+3$.

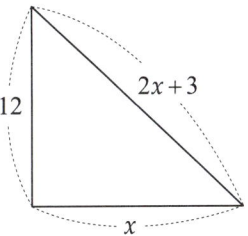

By the Pythagorean Theorem, we have
$12^2+x^2=(2x+3)^2$
$144+x^2=4x^2+12x+9$
$3x^2+12x-135=0$
$x^2+4x-45=0$
$(x+9)(x-5)=0$, $x=-9$ or $x=5$
Since $x>0$, $x=5$.

So the distance between two bicycles
is $2x+3=2\cdot 5+3=13$ miles.

Solutions Manual

Review Exercises

01

Let x and $x+2$ be two consecutive positive even integers. Then we have
$x(x+2)=80$
$x^2+2x-80=0$
$(x+10)(x-8)=0$
$x=-10$ or $x=8$
Since $x>0$, $x=8$.

Two integers are 8 and 10.

02

Let x and $x+1$ be two consecutive negative integers. Then we have
$x^2+(x+1)^2=113$
$x^2+x^2+2x+1=113$
$2x^2+2x-112=0$
$x^2+x-56=0$
$(x-7)(x+8)=0$, $x=7$ or $x=-8$
Since $x<0$, $x=-8$.

Two integers are -8 and -7.

03

Let x and $x+2$ be two consecutive odd integers. Then we have
$\frac{1}{x}+\frac{1}{x+2}=\frac{8}{15}$
$\left(\frac{1}{x}+\frac{1}{x+2}\right)\cdot 15x(x+2)=\frac{8}{15}\cdot 15x(x+2)$
$15(x+2)+15x=8x(x+2)$
$15x+30+15x=8x^2+16x$
$8x^2-14x-30=0$, $4x^2-7x-15=0$
$(x-3)(4x+5)=0$, $x=3$ or $x=-\frac{5}{4}$
Since x is a integer, $x=3$.

Two integers are 3 and 5.

04

Let $9x$ and $4x$ be the length and width of the rectangle. Then we have
$9x \times 4x=144$
$36x^2=144$
$x^2=4$, $x=\pm 2$
Since $x>0$, $x=2$.

So the dimensions of the rectangle are $9x=9(2)=18$ inches by $4x=4(2)=8$ inches.

05

Let x and $2x+1$ be two legs of the right triangle, respectively.

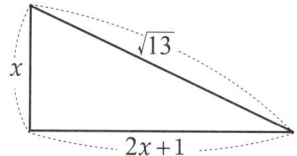

By the Pythagorean Theorem, we have
$x^2+(2x+1)^2=(\sqrt{13})^2$
$x^2+4x^2+4x+1=13$
$5x^2+4x-12=0$
$(5x-6)(x+2)=0$, $x=\frac{6}{5}$ or $x=-2$
Since $x>0$, $x=\frac{6}{5}$ and the longer leg is
$2x+1=2\left(\frac{6}{5}\right)+1=\frac{17}{5}$.

The lengths of the two legs are $\frac{6}{5}$ inches and $\frac{17}{5}$ inches.

06

Let x be the length of the side of the square.

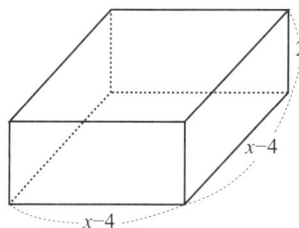

Since the volume of the box is
V=Base×Height, we have
$(x-4)(x-4)\cdot 2=128$
$(x-4)^2=64$
$x-4=\pm 8$, $x=-4$ or $x=12$
Since $x>0$, $x=12$.

The length of one side of the square is 12 inches

07

Let x be the length of one side of the original square. Then we have
$(x+1)(x-2)=70$
$x^2-x-2=70$
$x^2-x-72=0$
$(x+8)(x-9)=0$, $x=-8$ or $x=9$
Since $x>0$, $x=9$.

The length of one side of the original square is 9 inches

08

(1) When the ball hits the ground, the height of the ball is 0. So we have
$-16x^2+28x=0$
$-4x(4x-7)=0$, $x=0$ or $x=\frac{7}{4}$
Since $x>0$, $x=\frac{7}{4}$.

The ball hits the ground after $x=\frac{7}{4}$ seconds.

(2) If the ball reaches 12 feet above the ground, we have
$-16x^2+28x=12$
$16x^2-28x+12=0$
$4x^2-7x+3=0$
$(4x-3)(x-1)=0$, $x=\frac{3}{4}$ or $x=1$

The ball reaches 9 feet above the ground aftet $x=\frac{3}{4}$ (on the way up) and $x=1$ (on the way down) seconds.

09

x is the width of the flower garden.

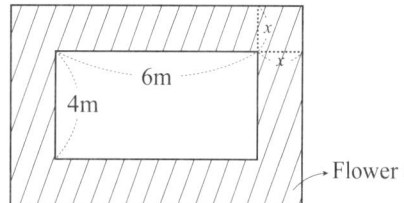

Flower Garden

Since the area of flower garden is 144 square meters, we have
$(6+2x)(4+2x)-6\cdot 4=144$
$24+20x+4x^2-24=144$
$4x^2+20x-144=0$
$x^2+5x-36=0$
$(x+9)(x-4)=0$, $x=-9$ or $x=4$
Since $x>0$, $x=4$.

The width of the flower garden is 4 meters

10

Let x be the speed of the car in still air.

	To Austin	Back to Houston
Speed	$x+4$	$x-4$
Distance	200	200
Time	$\dfrac{200}{x+4}$	$\dfrac{200}{x-4}$

Since it took a total of 6 hours to complete a round trip, we have

$\dfrac{200}{x+4}+\dfrac{200}{x-4}=6$

$\left(\dfrac{200}{x+4}+\dfrac{200}{x-4}\right)(x+4)(x-4)=6(x+4)(x-4)$

$200(x-4)+200(x+4)=6(x+4)(x-4)$
$200x-800+200x+800=6x^2-96$
$6x^2-400x-96=0$
$3x^2-200x-48=0$

Using the quadratic formula, we have

$x=\dfrac{-(-200)\pm\sqrt{(-200)^2-4(3)(-48)}}{2(3)}$

$x=-0.239$ or $x=66.906$
Since $x>0$, $x=66.906$

The speed of the car in still air is approximately 66.906 miles per hour

Chapter 4 Test Level 1

01

(A) $2x^3-5x^2+1=0$ → Cubic equation
(B) $(x+1)(x+2)-(x+3)(x+4)=0$
    $x^2+3x+2-(x^2+7x+12)=0$
    $-4x-10=0$ → Linear equation
(C) $x(2x^2+x-1)-2x(x^2-x+1)=0$
    $2x^3+x^2-x-2x^3+2x^2-2x=0$
    $3x^2-3x=0$ → Quadratic equation
(D) $4x^2+3x-2=4(1-x)(1+x)$
    $4x^2+3x-2=4(1-x^2)$
    $4x^2+3x-2=4-4x^2$
    $8x^2+3x-6=0$ → Quadratic equation
(E) $(1-2x)(1+2x)+4x^2=x$
    $1-4x^2+4x^2=x$
    $x-1=0$ → Linear equation

So the answer are (C) and (D).

02

(A) $x^2+4x+4=0$
    $(x+2)^2=0$, $x=-2$
(B) $x^2+2x=0$
    $x(x+2)=0$, $x=0$ or $x=-2$
(C) $2x^2+5x+2=0$
    $(2x+1)(x+2)=0$, $x=-\dfrac{1}{2}$ or $x=-2$
(D) $2x^2-5x+2=0$
    $(2x-1)(x-2)=0$, $x=\dfrac{1}{2}$ or $x=2$
(E) $3x^2+4x-4=0$
    $(3x-2)(x+2)=0$, $x=\dfrac{2}{3}$ or $x=-2$

Only (D) does NOT have $x=-2$ as the solution. The answer is (D).

03

Substitute $x=3$ into two equations
$x^2-4x+m=0$ and $2x^2+nx-7=0$.
$3^2-4(3)+m=0$, $m=3$
$2(3)^2+n(3)-7=0$, $3n=-11$, $n=-\dfrac{11}{3}$

Therefore, $m+n=3+\left(-\dfrac{11}{3}\right)=-\dfrac{2}{3}$

04

Substitute $x=a$ into $x^2+6x-4=0$.
$a^2+6a-4=0$, $a^2+6a=4$
Therefore,
$2a^2+12a+7=2(a^2+6a)+7$
$\qquad = 2(4)+7=15$

05

$x^2+\dfrac{4}{3}x=\dfrac{5}{9}$

$x^2+\dfrac{4}{3}x+\left(\dfrac{2}{3}\right)^2=\dfrac{5}{9}+\left(\dfrac{2}{3}\right)^2$

$\left(x+\dfrac{2}{3}\right)^2=1$, $x+\dfrac{2}{3}=\pm 1$

$x=-\dfrac{2}{3}\pm 1$, $x=-\dfrac{5}{3}$ or $x=\dfrac{1}{3}$

$\Rightarrow A=\left(\dfrac{2}{3}\right)^2=\dfrac{4}{9}$, $B=\dfrac{2}{3}$, $C=1$,

$\qquad D=-\dfrac{5}{3}$ and $E=\dfrac{1}{3}$

06

Solve the equation $2x^2+12x-9=0$ by completing the square.

$(2x^2+12x-9=0)\cdot \dfrac{1}{2}$

$x^2+6x-\dfrac{9}{2}=0$, $x^2+6x=\dfrac{9}{2}$

$x^2+6x+(3)^2=\dfrac{9}{2}+(3)^2$

$(x+3)^2=\dfrac{27}{2}$ $\Rightarrow h=3$ and $k=\dfrac{27}{2}$

Therefore, $h+k=3+\dfrac{27}{2}=\dfrac{33}{2}$

07

Method 1
Solve the equation $2x^2+mx-4=0$ by using quadratic formula.

$x=\dfrac{-m\pm\sqrt{m^2-4(2)(-4)}}{2(2)}=\dfrac{-m\pm\sqrt{m^2+32}}{4}$

Since $x=\dfrac{1\pm\sqrt{n}}{2}\cdot\dfrac{2}{2}=\dfrac{2\pm 2\sqrt{n}}{4}$,

$-m=2$, $m=-2$
$2\sqrt{n}=\sqrt{m^2+32}$, $\sqrt{4n}=\sqrt{m^2+32}$
$4n=m^2+32$, $4n=(-2)^2+32$, $n=9$

Method 2
Write a quadratic equation $ax^2+bx+c=0$ with coefficient 2 and solutions

$x=\dfrac{1\pm\sqrt{n}}{2}$.

$2\left(x^2-\left(\dfrac{1+\sqrt{n}}{2}+\dfrac{1-\sqrt{n}}{2}\right)x+\left(\dfrac{1+\sqrt{n}}{2}\cdot\dfrac{1-\sqrt{n}}{2}\right)\right)$
$\qquad\qquad\qquad\qquad\qquad\qquad\qquad =0$

$2\left(x^2-x+\dfrac{1-n}{4}\right)=0$

$2x^2-2x+\dfrac{1-n}{2}=0$

$\Rightarrow m=-2$, $\dfrac{1-n}{2}=-4$, $n=9$

Therefore, $m+n=-2+9=7$.

08

Since $x=2$ is the solution of the equation $(k^2-4)x^2+(k+2)x=0$, substitute $x=2$ into the equation.
$(k^2-4)\cdot 2^2+(k+2)\cdot 2=0$
$4k^2-16+2k+4=0$
$4k^2+2k-12=0$
$2k^2+k-6=0$
$(k+2)(2k-3)=0$, $k=-2$ or $k=\dfrac{3}{2}$

Solutions Manual

09

$(a+b)(a+b-3)=10$
Substitute k for $a+b$.
$k(k-3)=10$
$k^2-3k-10=0$
$(k-5)(k+2)=0$
$k=5$ or $k=-2 \Rightarrow a+b=5$ or $a+b=-2$
Since $a+b>0$, $a+b=5$.

10

$mn=(1-2i)(2+2i)=2-2i-4i^2$
$\quad =2-2i+4=6-2i$
$m+n=(1-2i)+(2+2i)=3$
$m^2n+mn^2=mn(m+n)=(6-2i)(3)$
$=18-6i \Rightarrow a=18$ and $b=-6$
Therefore, $a+b=18+(-6)=12$.

11

$\dfrac{a}{1+i}+\dfrac{b}{1-i}$
$=\dfrac{a(1-i)+b(1+i)}{(1+i)(1-i)}$
$=\dfrac{a+b-ai+bi}{1-i^2}=\dfrac{a+b+(-a+b)i}{1+1}$
$=\dfrac{1}{2}(a+b)+\dfrac{1}{2}(-a+b)i$
Since $\dfrac{1}{2}(a+b)+\dfrac{1}{2}(-a+b)i=2+i$,
$\dfrac{1}{2}(a+b)=2$, $a+b=4$
$\dfrac{1}{2}(-a+b)=1$, $-a+b=2$

Solving the system of equations above, we have $a=1$ and $b=3$. Therefore, $ab=3$.

12

$\alpha+\beta=-\dfrac{-6}{2}=3$ and $\alpha\beta=\dfrac{1}{2}$

(1) $\alpha^2+\beta^2=(\alpha+\beta)^2-2\alpha\beta$
$\qquad =(3)^2-2\left(\dfrac{1}{2}\right)=9-1=8$

(2) $(\alpha-\beta)^2=\alpha^2+\beta^2-2\alpha\beta$
$\qquad =8-2\left(\dfrac{1}{2}\right)=7$

(3) $\dfrac{1}{\alpha^2}+\dfrac{1}{\beta^2}=\dfrac{\beta^2+\alpha^2}{\alpha^2\beta^2}=\dfrac{\alpha^2+\beta^2}{(\alpha\beta)^2}$
$\qquad =\dfrac{8}{\left(\dfrac{1}{2}\right)^2}=\dfrac{8}{\dfrac{1}{4}}=32$

(4) $\dfrac{1}{\alpha+1}+\dfrac{1}{\beta+1}=\dfrac{\beta+1+\alpha+1}{(\alpha+1)(\beta+1)}$
$\qquad =\dfrac{(\alpha+\beta)+2}{\alpha\beta+(\alpha+\beta)+1}$
$\qquad =\dfrac{3+2}{\dfrac{1}{2}+3+1}=\dfrac{5}{\dfrac{9}{2}}=\dfrac{10}{9}$

13

Let two solutions of the equation be α and $\alpha+2$. Use the sum and product of the solutions.
The product of solutions: $\alpha(\alpha+2)=24$
$\alpha^2+2\alpha-24=0$
$(\alpha+6)(\alpha-4)=0$, $\alpha=-6$ or $\alpha=4$
The sum of solutions:
$\alpha+(\alpha+2)=-\dfrac{-(2k+1)}{1}$
$2\alpha+2=2k+1$, $2k-2\alpha=1$
If $\alpha=-6$, then $2k-2(-6)=1$, $k=-\dfrac{11}{2}$
If $\alpha=4$, then $2k-2(4)=1$, $k=\dfrac{9}{2}$
The possible values of k are $k=-\dfrac{11}{2}$ and $k=\dfrac{9}{2}$.

14

Let x be the number of students. Then, $x-5$ is the number of marbles each student receives. Since there are 300 marbles in total,
$x(x-5)=300$
$x^2-5x-300=0$
$(x+15)(x-20)=0$, $x=-15$ or $x=20$
Since $x>0$, $x=20$.

There are 20 students.

15

Let x be the length of one side of the small square. Then, $x+2$ is length of one side of the large square. Since the sum of the areas of the two squares is 100 square inches, we have,
$x^2+(x+2)^2=100$
$x^2+x^2+4x+4=100$
$2x^2+4x-96=0$
$x^2+2x-48=0$
$(x+8)(x-6)=0$, $x=-8$ or $x=6$
Since $x>0$, $x=6$.

The length of one side of the small square 6 inches.

Chapter 4 Test Level 2

01
$k(2x-1)+x^2=-2$
$x^2+2kx+(-k+2)=0$
Using the discriminant,
$D=b^2-4ac=(2k)^2-4(1)(-k+2)=0$
$4k^2+4k-8=0$
$k^2+k-2=0$
$(k+2)(k-1)=0$, $k=-2$ or $k=1$
Since $k<0$, $k=-2$.

02
$A:\ \dfrac{9}{4}x^2-3x+1=0,\ \dfrac{1}{4}(9x^2-12x+4)=0$
$(3x-2)^2=0,\ x=\dfrac{2}{3}$

Substitute $x=\dfrac{2}{3}$ into the equation B.
$6\left(\dfrac{2}{3}\right)^2-k\left(\dfrac{2}{3}\right)+2=0$
$\dfrac{8}{3}-\dfrac{2}{3}k+2=0,\ k=7$
So the equation of B is $6x^2-7x+2=0$.
$6x^2-7x+2=0$
$(2x-1)(3x-2)=0,\ x=\dfrac{1}{2}$ or $x=\dfrac{2}{3}$

The other solution is $x=\dfrac{1}{2}$.

03
$x^2-8x+(m^2+3m+6)=0$
$\to a=1,\ b=-8,\ c=m^2+3m+6$
Using the discriminant,
$D=b^2-4ac$
$=(-8)^2-4(1)(m^2+3m+6)=0$
$64-4m^2-12m-24=0$
$m^2+3m-10=0$
$(m+5)(m-2)=0,\ m=-5$ or $m=2$
Since $m>0$, $m=2$.

Solutions Manual

04

Let a and $4a$ be the solutions respectively. Then, the sum of solutions of the equation $2x^2-5x+m=0$ is
$a+4a=-\dfrac{-5}{2}$, $5a=\dfrac{5}{2}$, $a=\dfrac{1}{2}$

The product of the solutions is
$a \times 4a = \dfrac{m}{2}$, $4 \cdot \left(\dfrac{1}{2}\right)^2 = \dfrac{m}{2}$, $m=2$

05

Since $x=3$ is the solution of the equation A, it is also the solution of the equation B. Because A and B are equal. Substituting $x=3$ into the equation B,
$2(3)^2+n(3)+3=0$
$18+3n+3=0$, $n=-7$
Now the equation B is
$2x^2-7x+3=0$, $(2x-1)(x-3)=0$
Therefore, $m=1$ and $m+n=1+(-7)=-6$.

06

$x = \dfrac{2+i}{1+2i} = \dfrac{2+i}{1+2i} \cdot \dfrac{1-2i}{1-2i}$
$= \dfrac{2-3i-2i^2}{1-4i^2} = \dfrac{2-3i+2}{1+4} = \dfrac{4-3i}{5}$

$25x^2-5x+1 = 5x(5x-1)+1$
$= 5\left(\dfrac{4-3i}{5}\right)\left(5\left(\dfrac{4-3i}{5}\right)-1\right)+1$
$= (4-3i)(4-3i-1)+1$
$= (4-3i)(3-3i)+1$
$= 12-21i+9i^2+1$
$= 13-21i-9 = 4-21i$
$\Rightarrow a=4$ and $b=-21$
Therefore, $a+b=4+(-21)=-17$.

07

Use the sum and product of the solutions.
$\alpha+\beta=-\dfrac{1}{2}$, $\alpha\beta=\dfrac{-4}{2}=-2$

In the quadratic equation with solutions $\alpha-2$ and $\beta-2$,
$(\alpha-2)+(\beta-2)=\alpha+\beta-4=-\dfrac{1}{2}-4=-\dfrac{9}{2}$
$(\alpha-2)(\beta-2)=\alpha\beta-2(\alpha+\beta)+4$
$\qquad = -2-2\left(-\dfrac{1}{2}\right)+4=3$

Therefore, since the coefficient of x^2 is 2, the quadratic equation is
$2(x^2-((\alpha-2)+(\beta-2))x+(\alpha-2)(\beta-2))=0$
$2\left(x^2-\left(-\dfrac{9}{2}\right)x+3\right)=0$
$2x^2+9x+6=0$

08

$6x^2+7xy-3y^2=0$
$(3x-y)(2x+3y)=0$, $x=\dfrac{y}{3}$ or $x=-\dfrac{3y}{2}$
Since $xy>0$, $x=\dfrac{y}{3}$. Therefore,

$\dfrac{3x^2+y^2}{4xy} = \dfrac{3\left(\dfrac{y}{3}\right)^2+y^2}{4\left(\dfrac{y}{3}\right)y} = \dfrac{\dfrac{y^2}{3}+y^2}{\dfrac{4y^2}{3}} \cdot \dfrac{3}{3}$

$= \dfrac{y^2+3y^2}{4y^2} = \dfrac{4y^2}{4y^2} = 1$

09

$2x^2+(a-2)x+a(a+4)=0$
The product of the two solutions is
$\dfrac{a(a+4)}{2}=6$, $a(a+4)=12$
$a^2+4a-12=0$
$(a+6)(a-2)=0$, $a=-6$ or $a=2$
Since $a<0$, $a=-6$. So the equation is
$2x^2+(-6-2)x+(-6)(-6+4)=0$
$2x^2-8x+12=0$
Now, the sum of the two solutions is
$-\dfrac{-8}{2}=4$.

10

(1) Since α is the solutions of $x^2-8x+9=0$,
$\alpha^2-8\alpha+9=0$, $\alpha^2-8\alpha=-9$
$2(\alpha^2-8\alpha=-9)$
$2\alpha^2-16\alpha=-18$

(2) Since $\alpha+\beta=-\dfrac{-8}{1}=8$ and $\alpha\beta=\dfrac{9}{1}=9$,

$(\sqrt{\alpha}+\sqrt{\beta})^2 = \alpha+2\sqrt{\alpha}\sqrt{\beta}+\beta$
$\qquad = \alpha+\beta+2\sqrt{\alpha\beta}$
$\qquad = 8+2\sqrt{9}=14$

$\sqrt{\alpha}+\sqrt{\beta}=\pm\sqrt{14}$

Because α and β are positive real solutions, $\sqrt{\alpha}>0$ and $\sqrt{\beta}>0$.

Therefore, $\sqrt{\alpha}+\sqrt{\beta}=\sqrt{14}$.

11

When I opened the algebra book, the number of pages are two consecutive positive integers. So let x and $x+1$ be the number of two pages. Then, we have
$x(x+1)=210$
$x^2+x-210=0$
$(x+15)(x-14)=0$, $x=-15$ or $x=14$
Since $x>0$, $x=14$.

The number of pages on each page are 14 and 15

12

Let x be the amount of time it takes for the new area to be equal to the first one. Then, the length and width is $16-x$ and $10+2x$, respectively. Therefore, we have
$(16-x)(10+2x)=16\times 10$
$160+22x-2x^2=160$
$-2x^2+22x=0$, $x^2-11x=0$
$x(x-11)=0$, $x=0$ or $x=11$
Since $x>0$, $x=11$.

It takes 11 seconds

Solutions Manual

Chapter 5
Quadratic Functions, Part 1

1. The Graph of $y=ax^2$

Check Point 1

(A) $y=-x(x+4)=-x^2-4x$
  → Quadratic function
(B) $y=4+x-x^2$ → Quadratic function
(C) $y=2(x^2-1)-(1-2x^2)=2x^2-2-1+2x^2$
  $=4x^2-3$ → Quadratic function
(D) $y=4x^2-2(2+x^2)=4x^2-4-2x^2$
  $=2x^2-4$ → Quadratic function
(E) $y=3x(2+3x)-(3x+1)^2$
  $=6x+9x^2-9x^2-6x-1$
  $=-1$ → Constant function

The answer is (E).

Check Point 2

Since $\left|\dfrac{1}{2}\right|<|-1|<|-4|<|5|$, $y=5x^2$ has narrowest parabola and $y=\dfrac{1}{2}x^2$ has widest parabola.
① B
② D
In $y=ax^2$, the graph opens upward if $a>0$ and downward if $a<0$.
③ B and D
④ A and C

Check Point 3

Substitute m for x and 6 for y.
$y=\dfrac{3}{4}x^2$
$6=\dfrac{3}{4}m^2$, $m^2=8$, $m=\pm 2\sqrt{2}$

Review Exercises

01
(A) $y=2x^2-2(x+1)^2=2x^2-2(x^2+2x+1)$
  $=2x^2-2x^2-4x-2=-4x-2$
  → Linear function
(B) $y=x^2(x+2)-2x^2$
  $=x^3+2x^2-2x^2=x^3$
  → Cubic function
(C) $y=2x(x-1)-(2x+1)^2$
  $=2x^2-2x-(4x^2+4x+1)$
  $=-2x^2-6x-1$
  → Quadratic function
(D) $y=(2x-1)(2x+1)-(2x^2-1)$
  $=4x^2-1-2x^2+1=2x^2$
  → Quadratic function
(E) $y=x^2(x-2)-2x^2(x-2)$
  $=x^3-2x^2-2x^3+4x^2=-x^3+2x^2$
  → Cubic function

The answers are (C) and (D).

02
(1) In $y=ax^2$, the graph opens upward if $a>0$. Thus, the graphs of B, E, and F open upward. Since $\left|\dfrac{1}{2}\right|<\left|\dfrac{3}{2}\right|<|2|$, the graph of B has narrowest parabola.
(2) In $y=ax^2$, the graph opens downward if $a<0$. Thus, the graphs of A, C, and D open downward.
Since $\left|-\dfrac{1}{4}\right|<\left|-\dfrac{3}{2}\right|<|-4|$, the graph of A has widest parabola.

03

Substitute a for x and 72 for y.

$y = \dfrac{9}{2}x^2$

$72 = \dfrac{9}{2}a^2$, $a^2 = 16$, $a^2 = \pm 4$

04

Substitute -2 for x and 32 for y to find a.

$y = ax^2$

$32 = a(-2)^2$, $32 = 4a$, $a = 8$

Now, substitute $\dfrac{1}{2}$ for x and b for y to find b.

$y = 8x^2$

$b = 8 \cdot \left(\dfrac{1}{2}\right)^2$, $b = 2$

Therefore, $a + b = 8 + 2 = 10$.

05

Substitute 3 for x and -6 for y to find a.

$y = ax^2$

$-6 = a(3)^2$, $-6 = 9a$, $a = -\dfrac{2}{3}$

So the function is $y = -\dfrac{2}{3}x^2$.

(A) $y(1) = -\dfrac{2}{3}(1)^2 = -\dfrac{2}{3}$

$\rightarrow \left(1, -\dfrac{2}{3}\right)$ is on the graph

(B) $y(2) = -\dfrac{2}{3}(2)^2 = -\dfrac{8}{3}$

$\rightarrow \left(2, \dfrac{8}{3}\right)$ is NOT on the graph

(C) $y(-3) = -\dfrac{2}{3}(-3)^2 = -6$

$\rightarrow (-3, -8)$ is NOT on the graph

(D) $y(-4) = -\dfrac{2}{3}(-4)^2 = -\dfrac{32}{3}$

$\rightarrow (-4, 10)$ is NOT on the graph

(E) $y(-2) = -\dfrac{2}{3}(-2)^2 = -\dfrac{8}{3}$

$\rightarrow \left(-2, -\dfrac{8}{3}\right)$ is on the graph

So the answer is (A) and (E)

06

Since the graph passes through $(-2, 6)$, substitute -2 for x and 6 for y to find a.

$y = ax^2$

$6 = a(-2)^2$, $6 = 4a$, $a = \dfrac{3}{2}$

Now, substitute 4 for x and m for y to find m.

$y = \dfrac{3}{2}x^2$, $m = \dfrac{3}{2} \cdot (4)^2 = 24$

2. Translation of the Graph

Check Point 1

① To graph $y = x^2 - 2$, sketch the graph of $y = x^2$ first and then shift 2 units down.

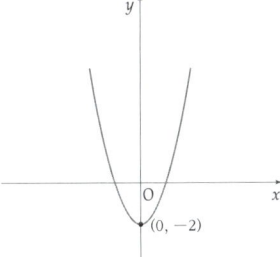

Axis of Symmetry: $x = 0$

Vertex: $(0, -2)$

y-intercepts: $y = 0^2 - 2 = -2$

② To graph $y = -2x^2 + 3$, sketch the graph of $y = -2x^2$ first and then shift 3 units up.

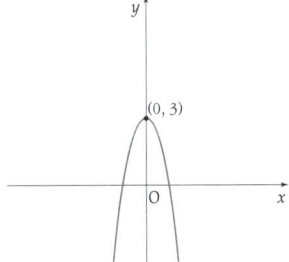

Axis of Symmetry: $x=0$
Vertex: $(0, 3)$
y-intercepts: $y=-2\cdot 0^2+3=3$

③ To graph $y=\dfrac{1}{2}x^2+1$, sketch the graph of $y=\dfrac{1}{2}x^2$ first and then shift 1 unit up.

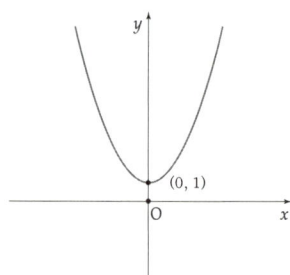

Axis of Symmetry: $x=0$
Vertex: $(0, 1)$
y-intercepts: $y=\dfrac{1}{2}\cdot 0^2+1=1$

④ To graph $y=-\dfrac{1}{3}x^2-2$, sketch the graph of $y=-\dfrac{1}{3}x^2$ first and then shift 2 units down.

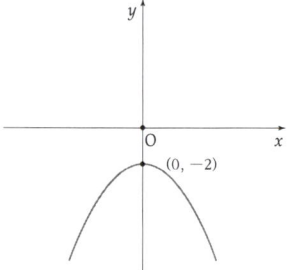

Axis of Symmetry: $x=0$
Vertex: $(0, -2)$
y-intercepts: $y=-\dfrac{1}{3}\cdot 0^2-2=-2$

Check Point 2

① To graph $y=(x+1)^2$, sketch the graph of $y=x^2$ first and then shift 1 unit to the left.

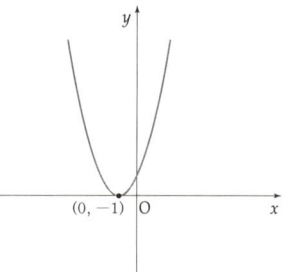

Axis of Symmetry: $x=-1$
Vertex: $(-1, 0)$
y-intercepts: $y=(0+1)^2=1$

② To graph $y=-(x-2)^2$, sketch the graph of $y=-x^2$ first and then shift 2 units to the right.

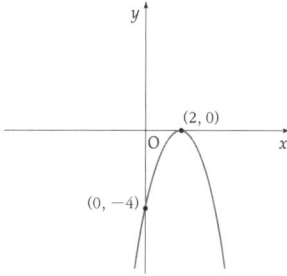

Axis of Symmetry: $x=2$
Vertex: $(2, 0)$
y-intercepts: $y=-(0-2)^2=-4$

③ To graph $y=\dfrac{1}{2}(x-2)^2$, sketch the graph of $y=\dfrac{1}{2}x^2$ first and then shift 2 units to the right.

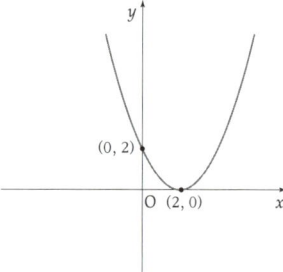

Axis of Symmetry: $x=2$

Vertex: (2, 0)

y-intercepts: $y=\frac{1}{2}(0-2)^2=2$

④ To graph $y=-2(x+3)^2$, sketch the graph of $y=-2x^2$ first and then shift 3 units to the left.

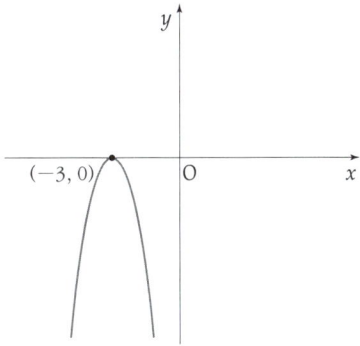

Axis of Symmetry: $x=-3$
Vertex: $(-3, 0)$
y-intercepts: $y=-2(0+3)^2=-18$

Check Point 3

① To graph $y=(x-2)^2+1$, sketch the graph of $y=x^2$ first and then shift 2 units to the right and 1 unit up.

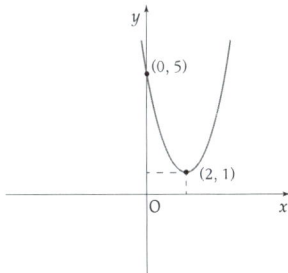

Axis of Symmetry: $x=2$
Vertex: $(2, 1)$
y-intercepts: $y=(0-2)^2+1=5$

② To graph $y=2(x-1)^2-1$, sketch the graph of $y=2x^2$ first and then shift 1 unit to the right and 1 unit down.

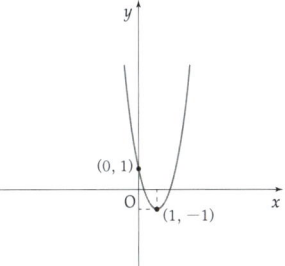

Axis of Symmetry: $x=1$
Vertex: $(1, -1)$
y-intercepts: $y=2(0-1)^2-1=1$

③ To graph $y=-\frac{1}{3}(x+3)^2+2$, sketch the graph of $y=-\frac{1}{3}x^2$ first and then shift 3 units to the left and 2 units up.

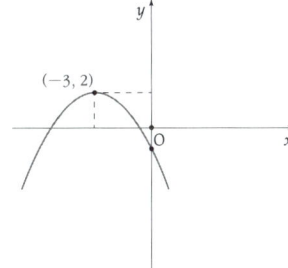

Axis of Symmetry: $x=-3$
Vertex: $(-3, 2)$
y-intercepts: $y=-\frac{1}{3}(0+3)^2+2=-1$

④ To graph $y=-\frac{1}{2}(x-2)^2-3$, sketch the graph of $y=-\frac{1}{2}x^2$ first and then shift 2 units to the right and 3 units down.

Solutions Manual

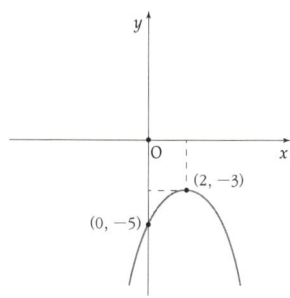

Axis of Symmetry: $x=2$
Vertex: $(2, -3)$
y-intercepts: $y=-\dfrac{1}{2}(0-2)^2-3=-5$

Review Exercises

01

(1) To graph $y=x^2+3$, sketch the graph of $y=x^2$ first and then shift 3 units up.

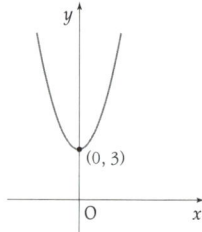

Axis of Symmetry: $x=0$
Vertex: $(0, 3)$
y-intercepts: $y=(0)^2+3=3$

(2) To graph $y=-2x^2-2$, sketch the graph of $y=-2x^2$ first and then shift 2 units down.

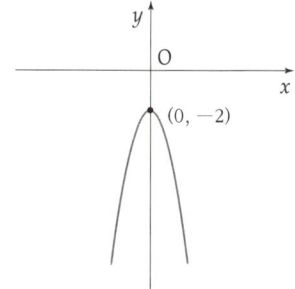

Axis of Symmetry: $x=0$
Vertex: $(0, -2)$
y-intercepts: $y=-2(0)^2-2=-2$

(3) To graph $y=(x-2)^2$, sketch the graph of $y=x^2$ first and then shift 2 units to the right.

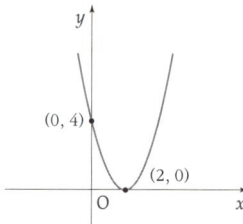

Axis of Symmetry: $x=2$
Vertex: $(2, 0)$
y-intercepts: $y(0)=(0-2)^2=4$

(4) To graph $y=-\dfrac{1}{3}(x+3)^2$, sketch the graph of $y=-\dfrac{1}{3}x^2$ first and then shift 3 units to the left.

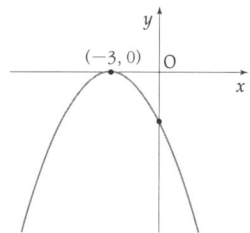

Axis of Symmetry: $x=-3$
Vertex: $(-3, 0)$
y-intercepts: $y(0)=-\dfrac{1}{3}(0+3)^2=-3$

02

(1) To graph $y=(x-2)^2-2$, sketch the graph of $y=x^2$ first and then shift 2 units to the right and 2 units down.

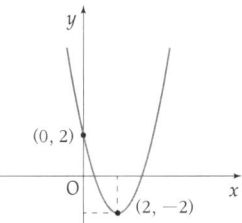

Axis of Symmetry: $x=2$
Vertex: $(2, -2)$
y-intercepts: $y(0)=(0-2)^2-2=2$

(2) To graph $y=-2(x+1)^2+1$, sketch the graph of $y=-2x^2$ first and then shift 1 unit to the left and 1 unit up.

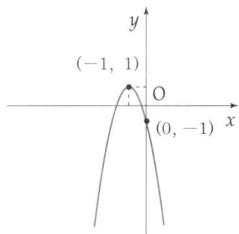

Axis of Symmetry: $x=-1$
Vertex: $(-1, 1)$
y-intercepts: $y(0)=-2(0+1)^2+1=-1$

(3) To graph $y=4(x-1)^2+3$, sketch the graph of $y=4x^2$ first and then shift 1 unit to the right and 3 units up.

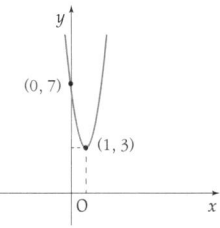

Axis of Symmetry: $x=1$
Vertex: $(1, 3)$

y-intercepts: $y(0)=4(0-1)^2+3=7$

(4) To graph $y=-\frac{1}{2}(x+3)^2-2$, sketch the graph of $y=-\frac{1}{2}x^2$ first and then shift 3 units to the left and 2 units down.

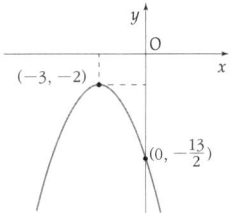

Axis of Symmetry: $x=-3$
Vertex: $(-3, -2)$
y-intercepts: $y(0)=-\frac{1}{2}(0+3)^2-2=-\frac{13}{2}$

03

The shifted equation is $y=2(x-3)^2$.
By substituting $(a, 8)$, we have
$y=2(x-3)^2$
$8=2(a-3)^2$, $4=(a-3)^2$
$a-3=\pm 2$, $a=5$ or $a=1$

04

The shifted equation is $y=-4(x+1)^2+2$.
By substituting $(-2, b)$, we have
$y=-4(x+1)^2+2$
$b=-4(-2+1)^2+2=-4+2=-2$
$b=-2$

05

The shifted equation is $y=-\frac{1}{2}(x-1)^2+k$.
By substituting $(3, 4)$, we have
$y=-\frac{1}{2}(x-1)^2+k$
$4=-\frac{1}{2}(3-1)^2+k$, $4=-\frac{1}{2}\cdot 4+k$
$4=-2+k$, $k=6$

06

The vertex of the function $y=3x^2-2$ is $(0, -2)$. So, if the graph is shifted 4 unit to the right and 2 units up, the coordinate of the vertex of the new function is $(0+4, -2+2) \Rightarrow (4, 0)$.

07

(A) True because $a=2>0$
(B) True
(C) True
(D) False because the graph is shifted 2 units to the right, NOT to the left.
(E) True because
$y(1)=2(1-2)^2-5=2-5=-3$
Therefore, the answer is (D).

08

Since the graph of $y=2(x-h)^2+k$ has an axis of symmetry at $x=-2$, $h=-2$ and we have $y=2(x+2)^2+k$.
Now, by substituting $(-1, 9)$, we have
$9=2(-1+2)^2+k$
$9=2+k$, $k=7$
Therefore, $h+k=-2+7=5$.

09

(1) Since the vertex of the graph is $(3, 0)$, we have $y=a(x-3)^2$. The graph passes through the point $(0, 2)$. By substituting the point, we have
$y=a(x-3)^2$
$2=a(0-3)^2$, $2=9a$, $a=\frac{2}{9}$
Therefore, the equation of the function is
$y=\frac{2}{9}(x-3)^2$.

(2) Since the vertex of the graph is $(-2, 1)$, we have $y=a(x+2)^2+1$. The graph passes through the point $(0, -3)$. By substituting the point, we have
$y=a(x+2)^2+1$
$-3=a(0+2)^2+1$, $-3=4a+1$, $a=-1$
Therefore, the equation of the function is
$y=-(x+2)^2+1$.

10

If the vertex of the graph is $\left(-2, \frac{3}{2}\right)$,
$y=a(x+2)^2+\frac{3}{2}$.
Since the graph passes through the point $\left(1, \frac{9}{2}\right)$, we have
$\frac{9}{2}=a(1+2)^2+\frac{3}{2}$
$3=9a$, $a=\frac{1}{3}$
$\Rightarrow y=\frac{1}{3}(x+2)^2+\frac{3}{2}$
The coordinate of the y-intercept is
$y(0)=\frac{1}{3}(0+2)^2+\frac{3}{2}=\frac{4}{3}+\frac{3}{2}=\frac{17}{6}$
$\Rightarrow \left(0, \frac{17}{6}\right)$

3. Application of Quadratic Functions

Check Point 1

Substitute $x+4$ for x and $y+2$ for y.
$$y=\frac{1}{2}(x-4)^2-1 \rightarrow y+2=\frac{1}{2}(x+4-4)^2-1$$
$$y=\frac{1}{2}x^2-3$$

Check Point 2

① Substitute $-y$ for y.
$$y=\frac{3}{2}x^2+2 \rightarrow -y=\frac{3}{2}x^2+2$$
$$y=-\frac{3}{2}x^2-2$$

② Substitute $-x$ for x.
$$y=\frac{3}{2}x^2+2 \rightarrow y=\frac{3}{2}(-x)^2+2$$
$$y=\frac{3}{2}x^2+2$$

Check Point 3

The graph opens upward: $a>0$
The vertex is in quadrant IV: $h>0$, $k<0$

Review Exercises

01

(1) Substitute $x+3$ for x and $y+2$ for y.
$$y=\frac{2}{3}(x-3)^2-2 \rightarrow y+2=\frac{2}{3}(x+3-3)^2-2$$
$$y=\frac{2}{3}x^2-4$$

(2) Substitute $x-2$ for x and $y-3$ for y.
$$y=\frac{2}{3}(x-3)^2-2 \rightarrow y-3=\frac{2}{3}(x-2-3)^2-2$$
$$y=\frac{2}{3}(x-5)^2+1$$

02

(1) Substitute $-y$ for y.
$$y=\frac{2}{3}(x-3)^2-2 \rightarrow -y=\frac{2}{3}(x-3)^2-2$$
$$y=-\frac{2}{3}(x-3)^2+2$$

(2) Substitute $-x$ for x.
$$y=\frac{2}{3}(x-3)^2-2 \rightarrow y=\frac{2}{3}(-x-3)^2-2$$
$$y=\frac{2}{3}(x+3)^2-2$$

(3) Substitute $-y$ for y and $-x$ for x.
$$y=\frac{2}{3}(x-3)^2-2 \rightarrow -y=\frac{2}{3}(-x-3)^2-2$$
$$y=-\frac{2}{3}(x+3)^2+2$$

03

The graph opens downward: $a<0$
The vertex is in quadrant II: $h<0$, $k>0$
The answer is (D)

04

The graph opens upward: $a>0$
The vertex is in quadrant III: $h<0$, $k<0$
The answers are (B) and (E)

05

$a<0$ → The graph opens downward.
$h>0$, $k<0$ → The vertex is in quadrant IV.
The answer is (E)

06

Substitute $x-h$ for x and $y-k$ for y.
$$y=5(x+2)^2-1$$
$$\Rightarrow y-k=5(x-h+2)^2-1$$
$$y=5(x-h+2)^2-1+k$$

The shifted function is the same as the function $y=5(x-1)^2-4$. So we have
$x-h+2=x-1$, $h=3$
$-1+k=-4$, $k=-3$
Therefore, $h+k=3+(-3)=0$.

07

If the graph is reflected both about the x−axis and y−axis, substitute $-y$ for y and $-x$ for x.

$y=-(x+2)^2+3 \rightarrow -y=-(-x+2)^2+3$
$ y=(x-2)^2-3$

Since the graph passes through the point $(a, 6)$, we have

$6=(a-2)^2-3, \ (a-2)^2=9$
$a-2=\pm 3, \ a=5 \text{ or } a=-1$

08

Given quadratic function has $(2, 3)$, as vertex. So we have $y=a(x-2)^2+3$. Now, since the graph passes through the point $(0, 2)$, we have

$2=a(0-2)^2+3$
$-1=4a, \ a=-\dfrac{1}{4}$
$\Rightarrow y=-\dfrac{1}{4}(x-2)^2+3$

Because the graph is shifted 3 units to the left and 1 unit up, substitute $x+3$ for x and $y-1$ for y.

$y-1=-\dfrac{1}{4}(x+3-2)^2+3$
$y=-\dfrac{1}{4}(x+1)^2+4$

Finally, substitute $-y$ for y since the graph is reflected about the x−axis.

$-y=-\dfrac{1}{4}(x+1)^2+4$
$y=\dfrac{1}{4}(x+1)^2-4$

Chapter 5 Test Level 1

01

(A) $y=(2x-1)^2-4x^2=4x^2-4x+1-4x^2$
$=-4x+1 \quad \rightarrow$ Linear function

(B) $y=x(2x+1)-x^2=2x^2+x-x^2$
$=x^2+x \quad \rightarrow$ Quadratic function

(C) $y=x(x-1)(x+1)-x^2+1$
$=x(x^2-1)-x^2+1=x^3-x-x^2+1$
$=x^3-x^2-x+1 \quad \rightarrow$ Cubic function

(D) $y=2(3-x)(2x-1)=2(6x-3-2x^2+x)$
$=-4x^2+14x-6 \rightarrow$ Quadratic function

(E) $y=4x^2(x+2)-2x^2(2x+1)$
$=4x^3+8x^2-4x^3-2x^2=6x^2$
$ \rightarrow$ Quadratic function

The answers are (A) and (C).

02

In $y=ax^2$, the graph opens upward if $a>0$ and opens downward if $a<0$. So, the graph of (B), (D), and (E) opens downward.

Since $\left|-\dfrac{1}{2}\right|<|-3|<|-4|$, the graph of (D) has narrowest parabola. Therefore, the answer is (D).

03

$y=2x^2-3$

(A) $-3=2(0)^2-3, \ -3=-3$
(B) $-1=2(1)^2-3, \ -1=-1$
(C) $5=2(2)^2-3, \ 5=5$
(D) $1=2(-1)^2-3, \ 1 \neq -1$
(E) $5=2(-2)^2-3, \ 5=5$

The answer is (D).

04

$f(x)=a(x+3)^2-4$ and $f(-1)=8$
$8=a(-1+3)^2-4$
$12=4a,\ a=3$
So, we have
$f(x)=3(x+3)^2-4$
$f(-4)=3(-4+3)^2-4=-1$

05

Since the quadratic function that has vertex $(-3,\ -2)$, the function is $y=a(x+3)-2$. Now, by substituting $(0,\ 2)$, we have
$2=a(0+3)^2-2$
$4=9a,\ a=\dfrac{4}{9}$

Therefore, the quadratic function is
$y=\dfrac{4}{9}(x+3)^2-2$

06

To be the graph of $y=-3(x+2)^2-1$ by shifting, the coefficient of x^2 term must be -3. So, the answer is (B).

07

If the graph of $y=\dfrac{1}{2}(x-2)^2$ is shifted 3 units to the right and 4 units down, we have
$y+4=\dfrac{1}{2}(x-3-2)^2$
$y=\dfrac{1}{2}(x-5)^2-4$

Since the graph passes through the point $(3,\ n)$, we have
$n=\dfrac{1}{2}(3-5)^2-4=2-4=-2$

08

(A) True because $a=-\dfrac{1}{2}<0$
(B) True
(C) False. Since the graph opens downward, y decreases as x increases when $x>1$.
(D) True
(E) True because
$y(0)=-\dfrac{1}{2}(0-1)^2-2=-2.5$

The answer is (C).

09

If the graph of $y=2-4x^2$ is shifted 1 unit to the left and 2 units down, we have
$y+2=2-4(x+1)^2$
$y=-4(x+1)^2$

Since the graph passes through the point $(a,-6)$, we have
$-6=-4(a+1)^2,\ \dfrac{3}{2}=(a+1)^2$
$a+1=\pm\sqrt{\dfrac{3}{2}},\ a=-1\pm\sqrt{\dfrac{3}{2}}=-1\pm\dfrac{\sqrt{6}}{2}$

The possible values of a are $-1+\dfrac{\sqrt{6}}{2}$ and $-1-\dfrac{\sqrt{6}}{2}$.

10

If the vertex of the graph is $\left(\dfrac{1}{2},\ -2\right)$,
$y=a\left(x-\dfrac{1}{2}\right)^2-2$.

Since the graph passes through the point $\left(-\dfrac{3}{2},\ 6\right)$, we have
$6=a\left(-\dfrac{3}{2}-\dfrac{1}{2}\right)^2-2$
$8=4a,\ a=2$

11

Substitute $x-h$ for x and $y-k$ for y.
$$y=-2(x-4)^2+2$$
$$y-k=-2(x-h-4)^2+2$$
$$y=-2(x-h-4)^2+2+k$$
The shifted function is the same as the function $y=-2x^2-5$. So we have
$$x-h-4=x,\ h=-4$$
$$2+k=-5,\ k=-7$$
Therefore, $h+k=-4+(-7)=-11$.

12

(1) Since the vertex of the graph is $(-4, -4)$, we have $y=a(x+4)^2-4$.
The graph passes through the point $(0, 0)$. By substituting the point, we have
$$0=a(0+4)^2-4$$
$$4=16a,\ a=\frac{1}{4}$$
Therefore, the equation of the function is
$$y=\frac{1}{4}(x+4)^2-4$$

(2) Since the vertex of the graph is $(2, 8)$, we have $y=a(x-2)^2+8$. The graph passes through the point $(-3, 0)$. By substituting the point, we have
$$0=a(-3-2)^2+8$$
$$-8=25a,\ a=-\frac{8}{25}$$
Therefore, the equation of the function is
$$y=-\frac{8}{25}(x-2)^2+8$$

13

The graph opens downward: $a<0$
The vertex is in quadrant II: $h<0,\ k>0$
The answer is (C).

14

$a>0\ \to$ The graph opens upward.
$h<0,\ k<0\ \to$ The vertex is in quadrant III.
The answer is (D).

Chapter 5 Test Level 2

01

Substitute $x+2$ for x and then $-x$ for x.
$$y=a(x+3)^2-1$$
$$\Rightarrow y=a(x+2+3)^2-1,\ y=a(x+5)^2-1$$
$$\Rightarrow y=a(-x+5)^2-1,\ y=a(x-5)^2-1$$
Since the graph passes through the point $(1, 4)$, we have
$$4=a(1-5)^2-1$$
$$5=16a,\ a=\frac{5}{16}$$

02

If the function has an axis of symmetry $x=2$ and y-coordinate of the vertex is 5, then we have
$$y=a(x-h)^2+k,\ y=a(x-2)^2+5$$
Since the y-intercept of the graph is 2,
$$2=a(0-2)^2+5$$
$$-3=4a,\ a=-\frac{3}{4}$$
Therefore, $ahk=\left(-\frac{3}{4}\right)(2)(5)=-\frac{15}{2}$.

03

If the function has an axis of symmetry $x=-4$, then we have $y=a(x+4)^2+k$.
Since the graph passes through two points $(-5, 3)$ and $(-1, 0)$, we have
$$3=a(-5+4)^2+k,\ 3=a+k\ \to\ (1)$$
$$0=a(-1+4)^2+k,\ 0=9a+k\ \to\ (2)$$
Solving the system of equations (1) and

(2), We have $a=-\dfrac{3}{8}$ and $k=\dfrac{27}{8}$.
Therefore, the function is
$y=-\dfrac{3}{8}(x+4)^2+\dfrac{27}{8}$.

04

The graph of $y=\dfrac{1}{3}(x+2)^2-1$ has the vertex at $(-2,\ -1)$ and its y-intercept is $y(0)=\dfrac{1}{3}(0+2)^2-1=\dfrac{1}{3}$, as shown below.

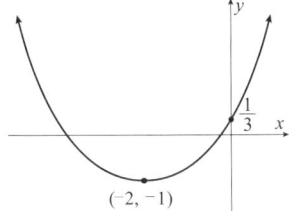

Therefore, the graph does NOT pass through quadrant IV. The answer is (C).

05

Substitute $-y$ for y first. Then we have
$-y=3(x-1)^2-2$
$y=-3(x-1)^2+2$
Now, substitute $x+2$ for x and $y-4$ for y.
$y-4=-3(x+2-1)^2+2$
$y=-3(x+1)^2+6$
Since the graph passes through the point $(-2,\ m)$, we have
$m=3(-2+1)^2+6=-3+6=3$.

06

If the graph of $y=-(x+2)^2$ is shifted m units horizontally and $m+2$ units vertically, we have
$y-(m+2)=-(x-m+2)^2$
$y=-(x-(m-2))^2+m+2$
The vertex of this function is $(m-2,\ m+2)$. Since this vertex is on the line $y=2x+1$,
$m+2=2(m-2)+1$
$m+2=2m-3,\ m=5$

07

$\overline{EB}=4$ because $\overline{AB}=8$. The point B is on the graph of $y=\dfrac{3}{4}x^2-6$. If we let $(4,\ y)$ be the coordinate of the point B, we have
$y=\dfrac{3}{4}(4)^2-6=12-6=6$
So you can see that the coordinate of B is $(4,\ 6)$ and the length of $\overline{OE}=6$.
Also, since two points C and D are the x-intercept of the function $y=\dfrac{3}{4}x^2-6$, we have
$0=\dfrac{3}{4}x^2-6,\ 6=\dfrac{3}{4}x^2$
$x^2=8,\ x=\pm 2\sqrt{2}$
$C(2\sqrt{2},\ 0),\ D(-2\sqrt{2},\ 0)$ and $\overline{CD}=4\sqrt{2}$
Finally, the area of the trapezoid ABCD is
$\dfrac{1}{2}(\overline{AB}+\overline{CD})\cdot\overline{OE}=\dfrac{1}{2}(8+4\sqrt{2})\cdot 6$
$=24+12\sqrt{2}$

08

$y=a(x-h)^2+k$
(1) The graph opens upward: $a>0$
(2) The vertex is in quadrant IV:
$h>0,\ k<0$

$y=k(x-a)^2+h$
(1) $k<0\ \rightarrow$ The graph opens downward.
(2) $a>0,\ h>0$
$\rightarrow$ The vertex is in quadrant I.
The answer is (B).

Solutions Manual

Chapter 6
Quadratic Functions, Part 2

1. The Graph of $y = ax^2 + bx + c$

Check Point 1-1

① $y = 3x^2 - 6x - 1$
$y = 3(x^2 - 2x) - 1$
$y = 3(x^2 - 2x + (1)^2 - (1)^2) - 1$
$y = 3(x-1)^2 - 1 - 3$
$y = 3(x-1)^2 - 4$
Vertex: $(1, -4)$
Axis of Symmetry: $x = 1$
y-intercept: $(0, -1)$

② $y = \frac{1}{2}x^2 + 3x - \frac{3}{2}$
$y = \frac{1}{2}(x^2 + 6x) - \frac{3}{2}$
$y = \frac{1}{2}(x^2 + 6x + (3)^2 - (3)^2) - \frac{3}{2}$
$y = \frac{1}{2}(x+3)^2 - \frac{3}{2} - \frac{9}{2}$
$y = \frac{1}{2}(x+3)^2 - 6$
Vertex: $(-3, -6)$
Axis of Symmetry: $x = -3$
y-intercept: $\left(0, -\frac{3}{2}\right)$

Check Point 1-2

① Axis of Symmetry: $x = -\frac{b}{2a} = -\frac{-6}{2 \cdot 3} = 1$

Since $y(1) = 3 \cdot 1^2 - 6 \cdot 1 - 1 = -4$, its vertex is $(1, -4)$.
y-intercept: $(0, -1)$

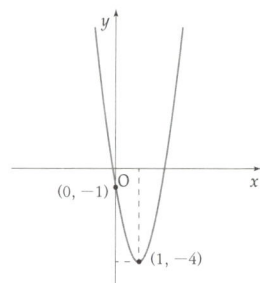

② Axis of Symmetry: $x = -\frac{b}{2a} = -\frac{3}{2 \cdot \frac{1}{2}} = -3$

Since $y(-3) = \frac{1}{2}(-3)^2 + 3(-3) - \frac{3}{2} = -6$,

its vertex is $(-3, -6)$.
y-intercept: $\left(0, -\frac{3}{2}\right)$

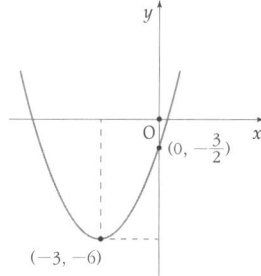

Check Point 2

The graph opens downward: $a < 0$
The axis is to the right of the y-axis: a and b have the different signs. So, $b > 0$
The y-intercept is below the x-axis: $c < 0$

Check Point 3

① $y=2x^2-5x-3$
$0=2x^2-5x-3$
$0=(2x+1)(x-3)$, $x=-\dfrac{1}{2}$ or $x=3$

② $y=-3x^2+\dfrac{1}{2}x+\dfrac{5}{2}$
$\left(0=-3x^2+\dfrac{1}{2}x+\dfrac{5}{2}\right)(-2)$
$0=6x^2-x-5$
$0=(6x+5)(x-1)$, $x=-\dfrac{5}{6}$ or $x=1$

③ $y=x^2-5x-1$
$0=x^2-5x-1$
$x=\dfrac{-b\pm\sqrt{b^2-4ac}}{2a}$
$=\dfrac{-(-5)\pm\sqrt{(-5)^2-4\cdot 1\cdot(-1)}}{2\cdot 1}$
$=\dfrac{5\pm\sqrt{29}}{2}$

④ $y=-\dfrac{1}{4}x^2+x-2$
$\left(0=-\dfrac{1}{4}x^2+x-2\right)(-4)$
$0=x^2-4x+8$
$x=\dfrac{-b\pm\sqrt{b^2-4ac}}{2a}$
$=\dfrac{-(-4)\pm\sqrt{(-4)^2-4\cdot 1\cdot 8}}{2\cdot 1}$
$=\dfrac{4\pm\sqrt{-16}}{2}=\dfrac{4\pm 4i}{2}=2\pm 2i$

Check Point 4

① $y=x^2+4x+3$
$D=b^2-4ac$
$=4^2-4\cdot 1\cdot 3=4>0$
Since $D>0$, there are two zeros.

② $y=-2x^2+5x-7$
$D=b^2-4ac$
$=5^2-4(-2)(-7)=-31<0$
Since $D<0$, there is no zero.

③ $y=-3x^2+\dfrac{1}{2}x+1$
$D=b^2-4ac$
$=\left(\dfrac{1}{2}\right)^2-4(-3)\cdot 1=\dfrac{49}{4}>0$
Since $D>0$, there are two zeros.

④ $y=\dfrac{1}{4}x^2-\dfrac{3}{2}x+\dfrac{9}{4}$
$D=b^2-4ac$
$=\left(-\dfrac{3}{2}\right)^2-4\cdot\dfrac{1}{4}\cdot\dfrac{9}{4}=0$
Since $D=0$, there is one zero.

Review Exercises

01

(1) $y=x^2-4x-5$
$y=x^2-4x+2^2-2^2-5$
$y=(x-2)^2-9$
Vertex: $(2, -9)$
Axis of Symmetry: $x=2$
y-intercept: $(0, -5)$

(2) $y=-x^2-4x$
$y=-(x^2+4x)$
$y=-(x^2+4x+2^2-2^2)$
$y=-(x+2)^2+4$
Vertex: $(-2, 4)$
Axis of Symmetry: $x=-2$
y-intercept: $(0, 0)$

(3) $y=x^2-7x-10$
$y=x^2-7x+\left(\dfrac{7}{2}\right)^2-\left(\dfrac{7}{2}\right)^2-10$
$y=\left(x-\dfrac{7}{2}\right)^2-\dfrac{89}{4}$
Vertex: $\left(\dfrac{7}{2}, -\dfrac{89}{4}\right)$
Axis of Symmetry: $x=\dfrac{7}{2}$
y-intercept: $(0, -10)$

(4) $y=2x^2+12x-9$
$y=2(x^2+6x)-9$
$y=2(x^2+6x+3^2-3^2)-9$
$y=2(x+3)^2-27$
Vertex: $(-3, -27)$

Axis of Symmetry: $x=-3$
y-intercept: $(0, -9)$

02

(1) $y=\dfrac{1}{4}x^2+3x-4$

$x=-\dfrac{b}{2a}=-\dfrac{3}{2\left(\dfrac{1}{4}\right)}=-6$

$y(-6)=\dfrac{1}{4}(-6)^2+3(-6)-4=-13$

Vertex: $(-6, -13)$
Axis of Symmetry: $x=-6$
y-intercept: $(0, -4)$

(2) $y=5x^2-8x+10$

$x=-\dfrac{b}{2a}=-\dfrac{-8}{2(5)}=\dfrac{4}{5}$

$y\left(\dfrac{4}{5}\right)=5\left(\dfrac{4}{5}\right)^2-8\left(\dfrac{4}{5}\right)+10=\dfrac{34}{5}$

Vertex: $\left(\dfrac{4}{5}, \dfrac{34}{5}\right)$

Axis of Symmetry: $x=\dfrac{4}{5}$

y-intercept: $(0, 10)$

(3) $y=-2x^2-7x-3$

$x=-\dfrac{b}{2a}=-\dfrac{-7}{2(-2)}=-\dfrac{7}{4}$

$y\left(-\dfrac{7}{4}\right)=-2\left(-\dfrac{7}{4}\right)^2-7\left(-\dfrac{7}{4}\right)-3=\dfrac{25}{8}$

Vertex: $\left(-\dfrac{7}{4}, \dfrac{25}{8}\right)$

Axis of Symmetry: $x=-\dfrac{7}{4}$

y-intercept: $(0, -3)$

(4) $y=\dfrac{1}{3}x^2-\dfrac{10}{3}x+\dfrac{13}{3}$

$x=-\dfrac{b}{2a}=-\dfrac{-\dfrac{10}{3}}{2\left(\dfrac{1}{3}\right)}=5$

$y(5)=\dfrac{1}{3}(5)^2-\dfrac{10}{3}(5)+\dfrac{13}{3}=-4$

Vertex: $(5, -4)$
Axis of Symmetry: $x=5$

y-intercept: $\left(0, \dfrac{13}{3}\right)$

03

Since the axis symmetry is $x=4$,

$x=-\dfrac{b}{2a}$

$4=-\dfrac{-2m}{2\left(\dfrac{3}{2}\right)}$, $12=2m$, $m=6$

Since the y-intercept is $(0, 9)$,

$3n=9$, $n=3$

So, $m+n=6+3=9$

04

Since the graph of $y=ax^2+5x-2$ passes through $(-1, -3)$, we have

$-3=a(-1)^2+5(-1)-2$

$-3=a-5-2$, $a=4$

So the function is $y=4x^2+5x-2$ and its axis of symmetry is

$x=-\dfrac{b}{2a}=-\dfrac{5}{2(4)}=-\dfrac{5}{8}$

05

(A) Since $a=2>0$, the graph opens upward

(B) $x=-\dfrac{b}{2a}=-\dfrac{4}{2(2)}=-1$ and

$y(-1)=2(-1)^2+4(-1)-\dfrac{3}{4}=-\dfrac{11}{4}$

So the vertex is $\left(-1, -\dfrac{11}{4}\right)$

(C) Since the vertex is $\left(-1, -\dfrac{11}{4}\right)$, the graph of $y=2x^2$ is sifted 1 unit to the left and $\dfrac{11}{4}$ units down

(D) Since the graph opens upward and the vertex is $\left(-1, -\dfrac{11}{4}\right)$, y increases as x increases when $x>-1$

(E) The y-intercept of the graph is $\left(0, -\dfrac{3}{4}\right)$

The answers are (B) and (D).

06

(1) The graph opens upward: $a>0$
The axis is to the left of the y−axis:
a and b have the same signs. So, $b>0$
The y−intercept is above the x−axis: $c>0$

(2) The graph opens downward: $a<0$
The axis is to the right of the y−axis:
a and b have the different signs. So, $b>0$
The y−intercept is on the x−axis: $c=0$

(3) The graph opens upward: $a>0$
The axis is to the right of the y−axis:
a and b have the different signs. So, $b<0$
The y−intercept is above the x−axis: $c>0$

(4) The graph opens downward: $a<0$
The axis is to the left of the y−axis:
a and b have the same signs. So, $b<0$
The y−intercept is below the x−axis: $c<0$

07

(1) $y=3x^2-27$
$(0=3x^2-27)\cdot\frac{1}{3}$
$0=x^2-9$
$0=(x-3)(x+3)$, $x=\pm 3$

(2) $y=x^2+4x+4$
$0=x^2+4x+4$
$0=(x+2)^2$, $x=-2$

(3) $y=\frac{1}{2}x^2+3x-\frac{7}{2}$
$0=\left(\frac{1}{2}x^2+3x-\frac{7}{2}\right)\cdot 2$
$0=x^2+6x-7$
$0=(x-1)(x+7)$, $x=1$ or $x=-7$

(4) $y=0.6x^2+1.1x-0.9$
$(0=0.6x^2+1.1x-0.9)\cdot 10$
$0=6x^2+11x-9$
$x=\frac{-(11)\pm\sqrt{(11)^2-4(6)(-9)}}{2(6)}$
$=\frac{-11\pm\sqrt{337}}{12}$

08

Substitute $\left(\frac{3}{2},\ 0\right)$ into $y=4x^2+kx-15$.
$0=4\left(\frac{3}{2}\right)^2+k\left(\frac{3}{2}\right)-15$
$0=9+\frac{3}{2}k-15,\ 6=\frac{3}{2}k,\ k=4$

So we have $y=4x^2+4x-15$. Now, find another x−intercept.
$0=4x^2+4x-15$
$0=(2x-3)(2x+5)$, $x=\frac{3}{2}$ or $x=-\frac{5}{2}$

Therefore, the coordinate of the other point is $\left(-\frac{5}{2},\ 0\right)$.

09

(1) $y=x^2-2x-10$
$D=b^2-4ac$
$=(-2)^2-4(1)(-10)=44>0$
Since $D>0$, there are two zeros.

(2) $y=\frac{1}{2}x^2-2x-8$
$D=b^2-4ac$
$=(-2)^2-4\left(\frac{1}{2}\right)(-8)=20>0$
Since $D>0$, there are two zeros.

(3) $y=5x^2-8x+10$
$D=b^2-4ac$
$=(-8)^2-4(5)(10)=-136<0$
Since $D<0$, there is no zero.

(4) $y=\frac{1}{4}x^2+\frac{3}{2}x-5$
$D=b^2-4ac$
$=\left(\frac{3}{2}\right)^2-4\left(\frac{1}{4}\right)(-5)=\frac{29}{4}>0$
Since $D>0$, there are two zeros.

10

If the graph intersects the x-axis at one point, the function has one zero. Using the discriminant,
$b^2-4ac=0$
$(-m)^2-4(4)(3)=0$
$m^2=48,\ m=\pm 4\sqrt{3}$

11

If the graph does not intersect the, the function has no zero. Using the discriminant,
$b^2-4ac<0$
$(-4)^2-4(a)(-5)<0$
$20a<-16,\ a<-\dfrac{4}{5}$

2. Writing Quadratic Functions

Check Point 1

① $y=a(x-h)^2+k$
Since the vertex is $(3,\ -3)$,
we have $y=a(x-3)^2-3$.
Now, substitute $(5,\ 2)$ to find a.
$2=a(5-3)^2-3,\ a=\dfrac{5}{4}$
Thus, $y=\dfrac{5}{4}(x-3)^2-3$

② $y=a(x-h)^2+k$
Since the vertex is $\left(\dfrac{1}{2},\ 0\right)$,
we have $y=a\left(x-\dfrac{1}{2}\right)^2$.
Now, substitute $(1,\ -1)$ to find a.
$-1=a\left(1-\dfrac{1}{2}\right)^2,\ a=-4$
Thus, $y=-4\left(x-\dfrac{1}{2}\right)^2$

Check Point 2

① $y=a(x-h)^2+k$
Since the axis of symmetry is $x=-3$
we have $y=a(x+3)^2+k$. Now, substitute $(-2,\ 4)$ and $(0,\ -4)$ to find a and k.
$\begin{cases} 4=a(-2+3)^2+k \\ -4=a(0+3)^2+k \end{cases} = \begin{cases} a+k=4 \\ 9a+k=-4 \end{cases}$
By solving the system of equations above, we have $a=-1$ and $k=5$.
Thus, $y=-(x+3)^2+5$

② $y=a(x-h)^2+k$
Since the axis of symmetry is $x=\dfrac{1}{2}$
we have $y=a\left(x-\dfrac{1}{2}\right)^2+k$.
Now, substitute $\left(\dfrac{3}{2},\ 1\right)$ and

$\left(-\dfrac{3}{2},\ 7\right)$ to find a and k.

$\begin{cases} 1=a\left(\dfrac{3}{2}-\dfrac{1}{2}\right)^2+k \\ 7=a\left(-\dfrac{3}{2}-\dfrac{1}{2}\right)^2+k \end{cases} = \begin{cases} a+k=1 \\ 4a+k=7 \end{cases}$

By solving the system of equations above, we have $a=2$ and $k=-1$.

Thus, $y=2\left(x-\dfrac{1}{2}\right)^2-1$

Check Point 3

(1) $y=ax^2+bx+c$

Substitute all three points and solve the system.

$\begin{cases} 6=a(0)^2+b(0)+c \\ 4=a(-1)^2+b(-1)+6 \\ -2=a(-2)^2+b(-2)+6 \end{cases} \Rightarrow \begin{cases} c=6 \\ a-b=-2 \\ 4a-2b=-8 \end{cases}$

$a=-2$, $b=0$, and $c=6$.

Thus, $y=-2x^2+6$

(2) $y=ax^2+bx+c$

Substitute all three points and solve the system.

$\begin{cases} -4=a(0)^2+b(0)+c \\ 1=a(2)^2+b(2)-4 \\ \dfrac{5}{2}=a\left(\dfrac{1}{2}\right)^2+b\left(\dfrac{1}{2}\right)-4 \end{cases} \Rightarrow \begin{cases} c=-4 \\ 4a+2b=5 \\ \dfrac{1}{4}a+\dfrac{1}{2}b=\dfrac{13}{2} \end{cases}$

$a=-7$, $b=\dfrac{33}{2}$, and $c=-4$.

Thus, $y=-7x^2+\dfrac{33}{2}x-4$

Check Point 4

① $y=a(x-m)(x-n)$

Since the graph has the x-intercepts $(2,\ 0)$ and $(5,\ 0)$, we have $y=a(x-2)(x-5)$. Now, substitute $(3,\ 4)$ to find a.

$4=a(3-2)(3-5)$, $a=-2$.

Thus, $y=-2(x-2)(x-5)$

② $y=a(x-m)(x-n)$

Since the graph has the x-intercepts $\left(\dfrac{1}{4},\ 0\right)$ and $(-1,\ 0)$,

we have $y=a\left(x-\dfrac{1}{4}\right)(x+1)$.

Now, substitute $\left(-\dfrac{1}{2},\ -\dfrac{5}{2}\right)$ to find a.

$-\dfrac{5}{2}=a\left(-\dfrac{1}{2}-\dfrac{1}{4}\right)\left(-\dfrac{1}{2}+1\right)$, $a=\dfrac{20}{3}$

Thus, $y=\dfrac{20}{3}\left(x-\dfrac{1}{4}\right)(x+1)$

Review Exercises

01

(1) $y=a(x-h)^2+k$

Since the vertex is $(0,\ 0)$,

$y=a(x-0)^2+0$, $y=ax^2$

Now substitute $(2,\ 3)$ to find a.

$3=a(2)^2$, $a=\dfrac{3}{4}$

Thus, $y=\dfrac{3}{4}x^2$

(2) $y=a(x-h)^2+k$

Since the vertex is $(0,\ -2)$,

$y=a(x-0)^2-2$, $y=ax^2-2$

Now substitute $(2,\ 0)$ to find a.

$0=a(2)^2-2$, $a=\dfrac{1}{2}$

Thus, $y=\dfrac{1}{2}x^2-2$

# Solutions Manual

(3) $y=a(x-h)^2+k$
Since the vertex is $(-2, -5)$,
$y=a(x+2)^2-5$
Now substitute $(3, 7)$ to find a.
$7=a(3+2)^2-5$, $a=\dfrac{12}{25}$
Thus, $y=\dfrac{12}{25}(x+2)^2-5$

(4) $y=a(x-h)^2+k$
Since the vertex is $\left(\dfrac{1}{3}, 2\right)$,
$y=a\left(x-\dfrac{1}{3}\right)^2+2$
Now substitute $\left(-\dfrac{2}{3}, 1\right)$ to find a.
$1=a\left(-\dfrac{2}{3}-\dfrac{1}{3}\right)^2+2$, $a=-1$
Thus, $y=-\left(x-\dfrac{1}{3}\right)^2+2$

02

(1) $y=a(x-h)^2+k$
Since the axis of symmetry is $x=0$,
$y=a(x-0)^2+k$, $y=ax^2+k$
Now substitute $(-1, -2)$ and $(2, -4)$ to find a and k.
$\begin{cases} -2=a(-1)^2+k \\ -4=a(2)^2+k \end{cases} = \begin{cases} a+k=-2 \\ 4a+k=-4 \end{cases}$
$a=-\dfrac{2}{3}$ and $k=-\dfrac{4}{3}$
Thus, $y=-\dfrac{2}{3}x^2-\dfrac{4}{3}$

(2) $y=a(x-h)^2+k$
Since the axis of symmetry is $x=3$,
$y=a(x-3)^2+k$
Now substitute $(1, 4)$ and $(4, 7)$ to find a and k.
$\begin{cases} 4=a(1-3)^2+k \\ 7=a(4-3)^2+k \end{cases} = \begin{cases} 4a+k=4 \\ a+k=7 \end{cases}$
$a=-1$ and $k=8$
Thus, $y=-(x-3)^2+8$

(3) $y=a(x-h)^2+k$
Since the axis of symmetry is $x=-1$,
$y=a(x+1)^2+k$
Now substitute $(0, 2)$ and $(-3, 6)$ to find a and k.
$\begin{cases} 2=a(0+1)^2+k \\ 6=a(-3+1)^2+k \end{cases} = \begin{cases} a+k=2 \\ 4a+k=6 \end{cases}$
$a=\dfrac{4}{3}$ and $k=\dfrac{2}{3}$
Thus, $y=\dfrac{4}{3}(x+1)^2+\dfrac{2}{3}$

(4) $y=a(x-h)^2+k$
Since the axis of symmetry is $x=-\dfrac{3}{5}$,
$y=a\left(x+\dfrac{3}{5}\right)^2+k$
Now substitute $(0, 0)$ and $(2, 3)$ to find a and k.
$\begin{cases} 0=a\left(0+\dfrac{3}{5}\right)^2+k \\ 3=a\left(2+\dfrac{3}{5}\right)^2+k \end{cases} = \begin{cases} \dfrac{9}{25}a+k=0 \\ \dfrac{169}{25}a+k=3 \end{cases}$
$a=\dfrac{15}{32}$ and $k=-\dfrac{27}{160}$
Thus, $y=\dfrac{15}{32}\left(x+\dfrac{3}{5}\right)^2-\dfrac{27}{160}$

03

(1) $y=ax^2+bx+c$
Substitute all three points and solve the system.
$\begin{cases} 0=a(0)^2+b(0)+c \\ 1=a(-1)^2+b(-1)+0 \\ 1=a(1)^2+b(1)+0 \end{cases} \Rightarrow \begin{cases} c=0 \\ a-b=1 \\ a+b=1 \end{cases}$
$a=1$, $b=0$, and $c=0$
Thus, $y=x^2$

(2) $y=ax^2+bx+c$
Substitute all three points and solve the system.

$\begin{cases} 4=a(0)^2+b(0)+c \\ 0=a(2)^2+b(2)+4 \\ 2=a(3)^2+b(3)+4 \end{cases} \Rightarrow \begin{cases} c=4 \\ 4a+2b=-4 \\ 9a+3b=-2 \end{cases}$

$a=\frac{4}{3}$, $b=-\frac{14}{3}$, and $c=4$

Thus, $y=\frac{4}{3}x^2-\frac{14}{3}x+4$

(3) $y=ax^2+bx+c$

Substitute all three points and solve the system.

$\begin{cases} 3=a(0)^2+b(0)+c \\ -1=a(-2)^2+b(-2)+3 \\ -2=a(1)^2+b(1)+3 \end{cases} \Rightarrow \begin{cases} c=3 \\ 4a-2b=-4 \\ a+b=-5 \end{cases}$

$a=-\frac{7}{3}$, $b=-\frac{8}{3}$, and $c=3$

Thus, $y=-\frac{7}{3}x^2-\frac{8}{3}x+3$

(4) $y=ax^2+bx+c$

Substitute all three points and solve the system.

$\begin{cases} \frac{7}{2}=a(0)^2+b(0)+c \\ \frac{7}{2}=a(3)^2+b(3)+\frac{7}{2} \\ -\frac{3}{2}=a\left(\frac{1}{2}\right)^2+b\left(\frac{1}{2}\right)+\frac{7}{2} \end{cases} \Rightarrow \begin{cases} c=\frac{7}{2} \\ 9a+3b=0 \\ \frac{1}{4}a+\frac{1}{2}b=-5 \end{cases}$

$a=4$, $b=-12$, and $c=\frac{7}{2}$

Thus, $y=4x^2-12x+\frac{7}{2}$

04

(1) $y=a(x-m)(x-n)$

Since the graph has the x-intercepts $(1, 0)$, and $(-1, 0)$, $y=a(x-1)(x+1)$.
Now substitute $(0, 1)$ to find a.
$1=a(0-1)(0+1)$, $a=-1$
Thus, $y=-(x-1)(x+1)$

(2) $y=a(x-m)(x-n)$

Since the graph has the x-intercepts $(0, 0)$, and $(6, 0)$, $y=ax(x-6)$.
Now substitute $(4, 2)$ to find a.

$2=a(4)(4-6)$, $a=-\frac{1}{4}$

Thus, $y=-\frac{1}{4}x(x-6)$

(3) $y=a(x-m)(x-n)$

Since the graph has the x-intercepts $(-4, 0)$, and $(2,0)$, $y=a(x+4)(x-2)$.
Now substitute $(0, -6)$ to find a.

$-6=a(0+4)(0-2)$, $a=\frac{3}{4}$

Thus, $y=\frac{3}{4}(x+4)(x-2)$

(4) $y=a(x-m)(x-n)$

Since the graph has the x-intercepts $\left(\frac{3}{4}, 0\right)$, and $\left(-\frac{5}{4}, 0\right)$,

$y=a\left(x-\frac{3}{4}\right)\left(x+\frac{5}{4}\right)$.

Now substitute $\left(1, -\frac{1}{2}\right)$ to find a.

$-\frac{1}{2}=a\left(1-\frac{3}{4}\right)\left(1+\frac{5}{4}\right)$, $a=-\frac{8}{9}$

Thus, $y=-\frac{8}{9}\left(x-\frac{3}{4}\right)\left(x+\frac{5}{4}\right)$

05

(1) The graph has the vertex $(2, 3)$ and passes through $(0, 2)$. So, start with the function $y=a(x-2)^2+3$. Now substitute $(0, 2)$ to find a.

$2=a(0-2)^2+3$, $a=-\frac{1}{4}$

Thus, $y=-\frac{1}{4}(x-2)^2+3$

(2) The graph has 2 x-intercepts $(-5, 0)$ and $(-1, 0)$, and passes through $\left(0, \frac{3}{2}\right)$.
So, start with the function $y=a(x+5)(x+1)$. Now substitute $\left(0, \frac{3}{2}\right)$ to find a.

$\frac{3}{2}=a(0+5)(0+1)$, $a=\frac{3}{10}$

Thus, $y=\frac{3}{10}(x+5)(x+1)$

Solutions Manual

(3) The graph has the axis of symmetry at $x=3$ and passes through $(0, -4)$ and $(8, -8)$. So, start with the function $y=a(x-3)^2+k$. Now substitute two points to find a and k.

$$\begin{cases} -4=a(0-3)^2+k \\ -8=a(8-3)^2+k \end{cases} = \begin{cases} 9a+k=-4 \\ 25a+k=-8 \end{cases}$$

$a=-\dfrac{1}{4}$ and $k=-\dfrac{7}{4}$

Thus, $y=-\dfrac{1}{4}(x-3)^2-\dfrac{7}{4}$

(4) The graph has the vertex $(-3, 0)$ and passes through $(0, 4)$. So, start with the function $y=a(x+3)^2+0$. Now substitute $(0, 4)$ to find a.

$$4=a(0+3)^2, \ a=\dfrac{4}{9}$$

Thus, $y=\dfrac{4}{9}(x+3)^2$

06

The quadratic function with $\left(4, \dfrac{3}{2}\right)$ is $y=a(x-4)^2+\dfrac{3}{2}$. Since this function has y-intercept -2, we have

$$-2=a(0-4)^2+\dfrac{3}{2}$$

$$-\dfrac{7}{2}=16a, \ a=-\dfrac{7}{32}$$

Therefore, the quadratic function is

$$y=-\dfrac{7}{32}(x-4)^2+\dfrac{3}{2}$$

3. The Minimum and Maximum

Check Point 1

① $y=x^2-6x+8$

$a=1>0$: It has the minimum value.

Axis of symmetry: $x=-\dfrac{b}{2a}=-\dfrac{-6}{2\cdot 1}=3$

Minimum value: $y(3)=(3)^2-6(3)+8=-1$

② $y=-2x^2-5x$

$a=-2<0$: It has the maximum value.

Axis of symmetry:

$$x=-\dfrac{b}{2a}=-\dfrac{-5}{2(-2)}=-\dfrac{5}{4}$$

Maximum value:

$$y\left(-\dfrac{5}{4}\right)=-2\left(-\dfrac{5}{4}\right)^2-5\left(-\dfrac{5}{4}\right)=\dfrac{25}{8}$$

③ $y=\dfrac{1}{3}x^2-3$

$a=\dfrac{1}{3}>0$: It has the minimum value.

Axis of symmetry: $x=-\dfrac{b}{2a}=-\dfrac{0}{2\cdot\dfrac{1}{3}}=0$

Minimum value: $y(0)=\dfrac{1}{3}(0)^2-3=-3$

Check Point 2

① The axis of symmetry is $x=\dfrac{-5+5}{2}=0$, so the vertex is $(0, -4)$. Using the vertex, we have $y=a(x-0)^2-4$, By Substituting one of the zeros $(5, 0)$, we have

$$0=a(5)^2-4, \ a=\dfrac{4}{25}$$

Thus, the function is $y=\dfrac{4}{25}x^2-4$

② Since the vertex is $(-1, -8)$, we have $y=a(x+1)^2-8$. Now, by Substituting one of the zeros $(-5, 0)$, we have

$$0=a(-5+1)^2-8, \ a=\dfrac{1}{2}$$

Thus, the function is $y=\frac{1}{2}(x+1)^2-8$

Check Point 3

Let x be one of two numbers. Then, the other number is $x+6$. Also, let y be the product of these two numbers. Then, we have

Method 1
$y=x(x+6)$
$=x^2+6x$
$=x^2+6x+3^2-3^2$
$=(x+3)^2-9$

Method 2
Since $y=x(x+6)$ has two zeros $x=0$ and $x=-6$, the axis of symmetry is
$x=\frac{0+(-6)}{2}=-3$ and
$y(-3)=-3(-3+6)=-9$.

So, y is minimum when $x=-3$ and the minimum value is -9. Therefore, two numbers are $x=-3$ and $x+6=-3+6=3$.
-3 and 3

Check Point 4

Let x be the length of the garden. Then, the width of the garden is $\frac{28-x}{2}$, as shown in Figure below.

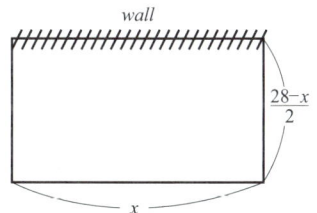

Method 1
$y=x\left(\frac{28-x}{2}\right)=-\frac{1}{2}x^2+14x$
$=-\frac{1}{2}(x^2-28x+14^2-14^2)$
$=-\frac{1}{2}(x-14)^2+98$

Method 2
Since $y=x\left(\frac{28-x}{2}\right)=\frac{1}{2}x(28-x)$ has two zeros $x=0$ and $x=28$, the axis of symmetry is
$x=\frac{0+28}{2}=14$ and
$y(14)=14\left(\frac{28-14}{2}\right)=98$.

So, y is maximum when $x=14$ and the maximum value is 98.
The maximum area of the garden is 98 square meters.

Check Point 5

Using the axis of symmetry
$t=-\frac{b}{2a}=-\frac{19.6}{2(-4.9)}=2$,
the maximum height of the ball is
$h(2)=-4.9(2)^2+19.6(2)=19.6$
The ball reaches its maximum height of 19.6 meters.

Solutions Manual

Review Exercises

01

(1) $y = -x^2 + 2x + 8$

$a = -1 < 0$: It has the maximum value.

Axis of symmetry: $x = -\dfrac{b}{2a} = -\dfrac{2}{2(-1)} = 1$

Maximum value: $y(1) = -(1)^2 + 2(1) + 8 = 9$

(2) $y = -2x^2 - 2x + 4$

$a = -2 < 0$: It has the maximum value.

Axis of symmetry:

$x = -\dfrac{b}{2a} = -\dfrac{-2}{2(-2)} = -\dfrac{1}{2}$

Maximum value:

$y\left(-\dfrac{1}{2}\right) = -2\left(-\dfrac{1}{2}\right)^2 - 2\left(-\dfrac{1}{2}\right) + 4 = \dfrac{9}{2}$

(3) $y = \dfrac{1}{2}x^2 + 3x - \dfrac{9}{2}$

$a = \dfrac{1}{2} > 0$: It has the minimum value.

Axis of symmetry:

$x = -\dfrac{b}{2a} = -\dfrac{3}{2\left(\dfrac{1}{2}\right)} = -3$

Minimum value:

$y(-3) = \dfrac{1}{2}(-3)^2 + 3(-3) - \dfrac{9}{2} = -9$

(4) $y = x^2 - \dfrac{5}{3}x$

$a = 1 > 0$: It has the minimum value.

Axis of symmetry:

$x = -\dfrac{b}{2a} = -\dfrac{-\dfrac{5}{3}}{(2 \cdot 1)} = \dfrac{5}{6}$

Minimum value:

$y\left(\dfrac{5}{6}\right) = \left(\dfrac{5}{6}\right)^2 - \dfrac{5}{3}\left(\dfrac{5}{6}\right) = -\dfrac{25}{36}$

(5) $y = 4x^2 - 3x - 1$

$a = 4 > 0$: It has the minimum value.

Axis of symmetry: $x = -\dfrac{b}{2a} = -\dfrac{-3}{2 \cdot 4} = \dfrac{3}{8}$

Minimum value:

$y\left(\dfrac{3}{8}\right) = 4\left(\dfrac{3}{8}\right)^2 - 3\left(\dfrac{3}{8}\right) - 1 = -\dfrac{25}{16}$

(6) $y = -2x^2 + 6x - \dfrac{3}{2}$

$a = -2 < 0$: It has the maximum value.

Axis of symmetry: $x = -\dfrac{b}{2a} = -\dfrac{6}{2(-2)} = \dfrac{3}{2}$

Maximum value:

$y\left(\dfrac{3}{2}\right) = -2\left(\dfrac{3}{2}\right)^2 + 6\left(\dfrac{3}{2}\right) - \dfrac{3}{2} = 3$

02

The axis of symmetry is

$x = -\dfrac{b}{2a} = -\dfrac{-4}{2 \cdot 1} = 2$, $n = 2$.

Since the minimum value of the function occurs at $x = 2$,

$y(2) = (2)^2 - 4(2) + 3m - 2 = 4$

$4 - 8 + 3m - 2 = 4$, $m = \dfrac{10}{3}$

So, $m + n = \dfrac{10}{3} + 2 = \dfrac{16}{3}$

03

Since the maximum value of the function occurs at $x = -\dfrac{1}{2}$, the axis of symmetry is

$x = -\dfrac{b}{2a}$

$-\dfrac{1}{2} = -\dfrac{m}{2(-4)}$, $m = -4$

Now, since the maximum value is equal to 1, we have

$y = -4x^2 + (-4)x - 5n + 1$

$y\left(-\dfrac{1}{2}\right) = -4\left(-\dfrac{1}{2}\right)^2 - 4\left(-\dfrac{1}{2}\right) - 5n + 1 = 1$

$-1 + 2 - 5n + 1 = 1$, $n = \dfrac{1}{5}$

So, $mn = (-4)\left(\dfrac{1}{5}\right) = -\dfrac{4}{5}$

04

The function $y = 2mx^2 - 6x + 3$ has the axis of symmetry at $x = -\dfrac{b}{2a} = -\dfrac{-6}{2(2m)} = \dfrac{3}{2m}$.

So the maximum value is

$y\left(\dfrac{3}{2m}\right) = 2m\left(\dfrac{3}{2m}\right)^2 - 6\left(\dfrac{3}{2m}\right) + 3$

$= -\dfrac{9}{2m} + 3$.

The function $y=\frac{1}{2}x^2+x-6$ has the axis of symmetry at $x=-\frac{b}{2a}=-\frac{1}{2\left(\frac{1}{2}\right)}=-1$.

So the minimum value is
$y(-1)=\frac{1}{2}(-1)^2+(-1)-6=-\frac{13}{2}$

Therefore, we have
$-\frac{9}{2m}+3=-\frac{13}{2}$, $\frac{9}{2m}=\frac{19}{2}$, $m=\frac{9}{19}$

05

Let x be the width of the henhouse. Then, the length is $52-2x$, as shown in Figure below.

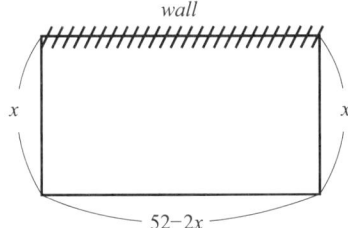

If we let y be the area of the henhouse, then we have
$y=x(52-2x)$
$=-2x^2+52x$
$=-2(x^2-26x+13^2-13^2)$
$=-2(x-13)^2+338$

So the maximum area of the henhouse is 338 square inches.

06

The length and width of the new rectangle is $10-x$ and $6+x$, respectively. If we let y be the area of the new rectangle, then we have
$y=(10-x)(6+x)$
$=-x^2+4x+60$
$=-(x^2-4x+2^2-2^2)+60$
$=-(x-2)^2+64$

So the maximum area of the new rectangle is 64.

07

Using the axis of symmetry
$t=-\frac{b}{2a}=-\frac{16}{2(-16)}=\frac{1}{2}$, the ball reaches the maximum height after $\frac{1}{2}$ seconds and the maximum height of the soccer ball is
$h\left(\frac{1}{2}\right)=-16\left(\frac{1}{2}\right)^2+16\left(\frac{1}{2}\right)+12=16$

So the soccer ball reaches its maximum height of 16 feet after $\frac{1}{2}$ second.

08

Let $y=-\frac{x^2}{2}+12x-40$. Using the axis of symmetry $x=-\frac{b}{2a}=-\frac{12}{2\left(-\frac{1}{2}\right)}=12$,

the maximum profit for the factory per day is
$y(12)=-\frac{12^2}{2}+12(12)-40=32$.

So, when producing 12 products in the factory, the maximum daily profit is $3,200.

09

Let $h=xy$. Since $x+2y=12$, we have
$2y=12-x$, $y=6-\frac{x}{2}$

By substituting $y=6-\frac{x}{2}$ into $h=xy$, we have
$h=xy=x\left(6-\frac{x}{2}\right)$
$=-\frac{1}{2}x^2+6x$
$=-\frac{1}{2}(x^2-12x+6^2-6^2)$
$=-\frac{1}{2}(x-6)^2+18$

So the maximum value of xy is 18.

10

Let x and h be the base and height of the triangle, respectively. Also, let y be the area of the triangle Then, we have $x+h=16$, $h=16-x$ and
$$y=\frac{1}{2}xh=\frac{1}{2}x(16-x)$$
$$=-\frac{1}{2}x^2+8x$$
$$=-\frac{1}{2}(x^2-16x+8^2-8^2)$$
$$=-\frac{1}{2}(x-8)^2+32$$

So the maximum area of the triangle is 32.

11

If you raise the price of cake by $\$x$ per piece, the price of a piece of cake is $5+x$, and the number of pieces sold is $30-2x$. If y is profit, then we have
$$y=(5+x)(30-2x)$$
$$=-2x^2+20x+150$$
$$=-2(x^2-10x+5^2-5^2)+150$$
$$=-2(x-5)^2+50+150$$
$$=-2(x-5)^2+200$$

y is maximum when x is 5.
So the profit is maximized when the price of a piece of cake is $5+x=5+5=\$10$.

Chapter 6 Test Level 1

01

Find the vertex and y-intercept of $y=2x^2-8x+11$.
$$x=-\frac{b}{2a}=-\frac{-8}{2(2)}=2$$
$$y(2)=2(2)^2-8(2)+11=3$$

The vertex is $(2, 3)$ and y-intercept is 11. Therefore, the graph does NOT pass through III and IV quadrants as shown below.

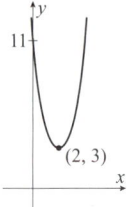

The answer is (E).

02

(A) $x=-\dfrac{b}{2a}=-\dfrac{6}{2(-3)}=1$
$y(1)=-3(1)^2+6(1)-5=-2$
The vertex is $(1, -2)$
(B) The axis of symmetry is $x=1$
(C) Since the graph opens downward, y decreases as x increases when $x>1$
(D) Since the function $y=-3x^2$ has the vertex $(0, 0)$, the graph of $y=-3x^2+6x-5$ is shifted 1 unit to the right and 2 units down
(E) The y-intercept is $y(0)=-5$
The answer is (D).

03

Since the axis symmetry is $x=-3$,
$$x=-\frac{b}{2a}$$
$-3=-\frac{5a+1}{2(2)}$, $12=5a+1$, $a=\frac{11}{5}$

Since the y-intercept is 4,
$3b-1=4$, $b=\frac{5}{3}$

Therefore, $ab=\left(\frac{11}{5}\right)\left(\frac{5}{3}\right)=\frac{11}{3}$

04

Substitute $(4, 0)$ into $y=3x^2-(2a+5)x-8$.
$$0=3(4)^2-(2a+5)(4)-8$$
$$0=48-8a-20-8$$
$$8a=20, \ a=\frac{5}{2}$$

So we have
$$y=3x^2-\left(2\cdot\frac{5}{2}+5\right)x-8$$
$$y=3x^2-10x-8$$

Now, find another x-intercept.
$$0=3x^2-10x-8$$
$$0=(x-4)(3x+2), \ x=4 \text{ or } x=-\frac{2}{3}$$

Therefore, the coordinate of the other point is $\left(-\frac{2}{3}, 0\right)$.

05

Find the vertices of both functions.
$y=2x^2-6x+m$
$=2\left(x^2-3x+\left(\frac{3}{2}\right)^2-\left(\frac{3}{2}\right)^2\right)+m$
$=2\left(x-\frac{3}{2}\right)^2+m-\frac{9}{2}$

The vertex is $\left(\frac{3}{2}, \ m-\frac{9}{2}\right)$.

$y=-3x^2+9x-2m+1$
$=-3\left(x^2-3x+\left(\frac{3}{2}\right)^2-\left(\frac{3}{2}\right)^2\right)-2m+1$
$=-3\left(x-\frac{3}{2}\right)^2-2m+1+\frac{27}{4}$
$=-3\left(x-\frac{3}{2}\right)^2-2m+\frac{31}{4}$

The vertex is $\left(\frac{3}{2}, \ -2m+\frac{31}{4}\right)$.

Since these two functions have the same vertex, we have
$$m-\frac{9}{2}=-2m+\frac{31}{4}$$
$$3m=\frac{49}{4}, \ m=\frac{49}{12}$$

06

Substitute $x-2$ for x and $y-3$ for y.
$$y-3=3(x-2)^2-6(x-2)+5$$
$$y=3(x^2-4x+4)-6x+12+8$$
$$y=3x^2-12x+12-6x+20$$
$$y=3x^2-18x+32$$

Therefore, $a+b+c=3+(-18)+32=17$.

07

Since the graph opens downward and the axis is to the left of the y-axis, $a<0$ and $b<0$. Also, $c>0$ because the y-intercept is above the x-axis. The answer is (A).

08

Since the graph of $y=ax^2+bx+c$ opens upward and the axis is to the right of the y-axis, $a>0$ and $b<0$. Also, $c>0$ because the y-intercept is above the x-axis.

Now, since $a>0$, $b<0$, $c>0$, the graph of $y=cx^2+ax+b$ opens upward and its axis of symmetry is to the left side of the y-axis. Also, the y-intercept is below the x-axis. Therefore, the graph could be (B).

Solutions Manual

09
The function $y=-3x^2-6x+m+1$ has the axis of symmetry at
$$x=-\frac{b}{2a}=-\frac{-6}{2(-3)}=-1.$$
The maximum value is $y(-1)$ and we have
$$y(-1)=-3(-1)^2-6(-1)+m+1$$
$$12=-3+6+m+1,\ m=8$$

10
(1) Since the function has the maximum value of 4 when $x=2$, we have
$$y=a(x-2)^2+4$$
Also, since the graph passes through the point $(4, -1)$, we have
$$-1=a(4-2)^2+4$$
$$-5=4a,\ a=-\frac{5}{4}$$
Therefore,
$$y=-\frac{5}{4}(x-2)^2+4$$
$$=-\frac{5}{4}(x^2-4x+4)+4$$
$$=-\frac{5}{4}x^2+5x-1$$

(2) Since the function has the minimum value of 0 when $x=-3$, we have
$$y=a(x+3)^2$$
Also, since the graph passes through the point $(-6, 6)$, we have
$$6=a(-6+3)^2$$
$$6=9a,\ a=\frac{2}{3}$$
Therefore,
$$y=\frac{2}{3}(x+3)^2=\frac{2}{3}(x^2+6x+9)$$
$$=\frac{2}{3}x^2+4x+6$$

(3) Since the function has two zeros $(-3, 0)$ and $(5, 0)$, we have
$$y=a(x+3)(x-5)$$

The axis of symmetry of function is at the midpoint of two zeros: $x=\frac{-3+5}{2}=1$.
Since the maximum of the function is at the axis of symmetry, the graph passes through the point $(1, 8)$. So we have
$$8=a(1+3)(1-5)$$
$$8=-16a,\ a=-\frac{1}{2}$$
Therefore,
$$y=-\frac{1}{2}(x+3)(x-5)$$
$$=-\frac{1}{2}(x^2-2x-15)$$
$$=-\frac{1}{2}x^2+x+\frac{15}{2}$$

11
Two zeros of the function $y=4x-x^2$ are
$$0=4x-x^2$$
$$0=x(4-x),\ x=0 \text{ or } x=4$$
$$\Rightarrow A(0, 0) \text{ and } C(4, 0)$$
The axis of symmetry of function is at the midpoint of two zeros: $x=\frac{0+4}{2}=2$.
So the maximum is
$$y(2)=4(2)-(2)^2=4$$
$$\Rightarrow B(2, 4)$$
Therefore, the area of triangle ABC is
$$\frac{1}{2}\times 4\times 4=8$$

12
(1) Using the axis of symmetry
$$t=-\frac{b}{2a}=-\frac{30}{2(-5)}=3,$$
the baseball reaches its maximum height after 3 seconds.

(2) The maximum height of the baseball is
$$h(3)=-5(3)^2+30(3)+2=47$$
Therefore, the baseball reaches its maximum height of 47 meters.

13

Let x be the length of the radius of the sector y be the area of the sector. Then, the arc length $\overset{\frown}{AB}=40-2x$ and we have

$$y=\frac{1}{2}x(40-2x)=\frac{1}{2}\cdot-2(x^2-20x)$$
$$=-(x^2-20x+10^2-10^2)$$
$$=-(x-10)^2+100$$

The maximum value of y is 100 when $x=10$.

This means that the area of the section is maximized when the radius is 10 inches.

Chapter 6 Test Level 2

01

If the graph intersects the x-axis at one point, the function has one zero. Using the discriminant,
$$b^2-4ac=0$$
$$(-6)^2-4(4)(b)=0$$
$$16b=36, \ b=\frac{9}{4}$$

02

If the function has the axis of symmetry at $x=1$, we have $y=a(x-1)^2+k$.
Since the graph passes through two points $(0, -2)$ and $(3, -4)$, we have
$$-2=a(0-1)^2+k, \ a+k=-2 \rightarrow (1)$$
$$-4=a(3-1)^2+k, \ 4a+k=-4 \rightarrow (2)$$
Solving the system of equations (1) and (2), $a=-\frac{2}{3}$ and $k=-\frac{4}{3}$
and then
$$y=-\frac{2}{3}(x-1)^2-\frac{4}{3}$$
$$=-\frac{2}{3}(x^2-2x+1)-\frac{4}{3}$$
$$=-\frac{2}{3}x^2+\frac{4}{3}x-2$$
Therefore, $a+b+c=-\frac{2}{3}+\frac{4}{3}+(-2)=-\frac{4}{3}$

03

$$y=-x^2+kx-2k+2$$
$$=-\left(x^2-kx+\left(\frac{k}{2}\right)^2-\left(\frac{k}{2}\right)^2\right)-2k+2$$
$$=-\left(x-\frac{k}{2}\right)^2+\frac{k^2}{4}-2k+2$$

The vertex is $\left(\frac{k}{2}, \ \frac{k^2}{4}-2k+2\right)$ and this is on the line $y=2x-2$. So, we have
$$\frac{k^2}{4}-2k+2=2\left(\frac{k}{2}\right)-2$$

Solutions Manual

$$\frac{k^2}{4} - 3k + 4 = 0$$

$$k^2 - 12k + 16 = 0, \quad k = 6 \pm 2\sqrt{5}$$

04

The axis of symmetry of $y = -\frac{1}{2}x^2 - 6x + k$ is

$$x = -\frac{b}{2a} = -\frac{-6}{2\left(-\frac{1}{2}\right)} = -6$$

Since the axis of symmetry is the midpoint of two zeros, the graph passes through $(-2, 0)$ and $(-10, 0)$ as shown below.

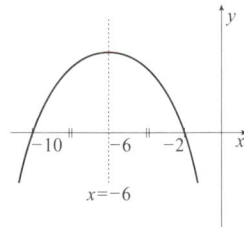

Now, by substituting $(-2, 0)$ into the function, we have

$$0 = -\frac{1}{2}(-2)^2 - 6(-2) + k$$

$$0 = -2 + 12 + k, \quad k = -10$$

05

The axis of symmetry of $y = 2x^2 - 12x + b$ is

$$x = -\frac{b}{2a} = -\frac{-12}{2(2)} = 3$$

Since the axis of symmetry is the midpoint of two zeros A and C, we have $A(2, 0)$ and $C(4, 0)$ as shown below.

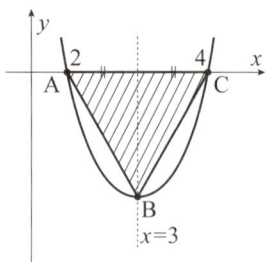

Now, by substituting $(2, 0)$ into the function, we have

$$0 = 2(2)^2 - 12(2) + b$$

$$b = 16$$

So, $y = 2x^2 - 12x + 16$ and

$$y(3) = 2(3)^2 - 12(3) + 16 = -2$$

$$\Rightarrow B(3, -2)$$

Therefore, the area of triangle ABC is

$$\frac{1}{2} \times 2 \times 2 = 2$$

06

$y = kx^2 - 5kx + 2x - 3 = kx^2 - (5k-2)x - 3$

The x-coordinate of the vertex is 2.
So using the axis of symmetry,

$$x = -\frac{b}{2a} = -\frac{-(5k-2)}{2k}$$

$$2 = \frac{5k-2}{2k}, \quad 4k = 5k - 2, \quad k = 2$$

Now, by substituting $k = 2$ into the function, we have

$$y = 2x^2 - (5(2) - 2)x - 3$$
$$= 2x^2 - 8x - 3$$

and the y-coordinate of the vertex is

$$y(2) = 2(2)^2 - 8(2) - 3 = -11$$

$$\Rightarrow m = -11$$

Therefore, $k + m = 2 + (-11) = -9$

07

Let x be the larger of the two numbers
Then, the other number is $x-6$. If y is the product of these two numbers, we have
$$y=x(x-6)=x^2-6x+3^2-3^2$$
$$=(x-3)^2-9$$
y is minimum when $x=3$.
Therefore, the larger number is 3.

08

Let $h=2xy$. Since $2x-y=4$,
we have $y=2x-4$.
By substituting $y=2x-4$ into $h=2xy$,
we have
$$h=2xy=2x(2x-4)$$
$$=4(x^2-2x)$$
$$=4(x^2-2x+1^2-1^2)$$
$$=4(x-1)^2-4$$
So the minimum value of $2xy$ is -4.

09

If Jason drops the price by $\$x$ per product, the price of the product is $8-x$, and the number of products sold each day is $12+2x$. If y is profit, then we have
$$y=(8-x)(12+2x)$$
$$=-2x^2+4x+96$$
$$=-2(x^2-2x+1^2-1^2)+96$$
$$=-2(x-1)^2+2+96$$
$$=-2(x-1)^2+98$$
y is maximum when x is 1.
So the profit is maximized when the price of the product is $8-x=8-1=\$7$.

Solutions Manual

Chapter 7: Roots and Radicals

1. The Square Roots

Check Point 1

① $6^2=36$ and $(-6)^2=36$
  ⇒ The square roots of 36 are ± 6
② $\left(\dfrac{3}{4}\right)^2=\dfrac{9}{16}$ and $\left(-\dfrac{3}{4}\right)^2=\dfrac{9}{16}$
  ⇒ The square roots of $\dfrac{9}{16}$ are $\pm\dfrac{3}{4}$
③ $(0.9)^2=0.81$ and $(-0.9)^2=0.81$
  ⇒ The square roots of 0.81 are ± 0.9
④ $(-5)^2=25$.
  $5^2=25$ and $(-5)^2=25$
  ⇒ The square roots of 25 are ± 5

Check Point 2

① $\sqrt{0.04}=\sqrt{(0.2)^2}=0.2$
② $-\sqrt{121}=-\sqrt{11^2}=-11$
③ $\sqrt{\left(-\dfrac{1}{2}\right)^2}-\sqrt{\dfrac{1}{9}}+(-\sqrt{2})^2=\dfrac{1}{2}-\sqrt{\left(\dfrac{1}{3}\right)^2}+2$
  $=\dfrac{1}{2}-\dfrac{1}{3}+2=\dfrac{13}{6}$
④ $\sqrt{25}-\sqrt{\left(\dfrac{5}{2}\right)^2}+\left(-\sqrt{\dfrac{1}{4}}\right)^2=5-\dfrac{5}{2}+\dfrac{1}{4}=\dfrac{11}{4}$

Check Point 3

① Since $x+3\geq 0$ when $x\geq -3$,
  $\sqrt{(x+3)^2}=x+3$
② Since $x+3<0$ when $x<-3$,
  $\sqrt{(x+3)^2}=-(x+3)=-x-3$
③ Since $x-y\geq 0$ when $x\geq y$,
  $\sqrt{(x-y)^2}=x-y$
④ Since $x-y<0$ when $x<y$,
  $\sqrt{(x-y)^2}=-(x-y)=-x+y$

Check Point 4

3 negative numbers: $-\sqrt{5}$, -2, $-\sqrt{9}$
$-\sqrt{9}<-\sqrt{5}<-2(=-\sqrt{4})$
3 positive numbers: $\sqrt{8}$, 3, $\sqrt{10}$
$\sqrt{8}<3(=\sqrt{9})<\sqrt{10}$
Therefore,
$-\sqrt{9}<-\sqrt{5}<-2<0<\sqrt{8}<3<\sqrt{10}$

Check Point 5

① $3<\sqrt{x-1}<4$
  $3^2<(\sqrt{x-1})^2<4^2$, $9<x-1<16$
  $10<x<17$
  So the solutions for x are 11, 12, 13, 14, 15 and 16.
② $-3<-\sqrt{2x-1}<-1$.
  $3>\sqrt{2x-1}>1$, $1<\sqrt{2x-1}<3$
  $1^2<(\sqrt{2x-1})^2<3^2$, $1<2x-1<9$
  $2<2x<10$, $1<x<5$
  The solutions for x are 2, 3, and 4.
  So there are 3 positive integers.

Review Exercises

01
(1) $5^2=25$ and $(-5)^2=25$
  $\Rightarrow$ The square roots of 25 are ± 5
(2) $12^2=144$ and $(-12)^2=144$
  $\Rightarrow$ The square roots of 144 are ± 12
(3) $\left(\dfrac{1}{2}\right)^2=\dfrac{1}{4}$ and $\left(-\dfrac{1}{2}\right)^2=\dfrac{1}{4}$
  $\Rightarrow$ The square roots of $\dfrac{1}{4}$ are $\pm\dfrac{1}{2}$
(4) $0.4^2=0.16$ and $(-0.4)^2=0.16$
  $\Rightarrow$ The square roots of 0.16 are ± 0.4
(5) $(-7)^2=49$.
  $7^2=49$ and $(-7)^2=49$
  $\Rightarrow$ The square roots of 49 are ± 7
(6) $\left(-\dfrac{2}{3}\right)^2=\dfrac{4}{9}$
  $\left(\dfrac{2}{3}\right)^2=\dfrac{4}{9}$ and $\left(-\dfrac{2}{3}\right)^2=\dfrac{4}{9}$
  $\Rightarrow$ The square roots of $\dfrac{4}{9}$ are $\pm\dfrac{2}{3}$

02
(1) $\sqrt{196}=\sqrt{(14)^2}=14$
(2) $\sqrt{0.25}=\sqrt{(0.5)^2}=0.5$
(3) $-\sqrt{\dfrac{9}{100}}=-\sqrt{\left(\dfrac{3}{10}\right)^2}=-\dfrac{3}{10}$
(4) $\sqrt{36}-(\sqrt{5})^2=\sqrt{(6)^2}-5=6-5=1$
(5) $(-\sqrt{6})^2+\sqrt{(-5)^2}-\sqrt{16}$
  $=6+5-\sqrt{(4)^2}=6+5-4=7$
(6) $\sqrt{\left(\dfrac{1}{3}\right)^2}+\sqrt{\left(-\dfrac{1}{9}\right)^2}-\left(-\sqrt{\dfrac{1}{4}}\right)^2$
  $=\dfrac{1}{3}+\dfrac{1}{9}-\dfrac{1}{4}=\dfrac{7}{36}$
(7) $\sqrt{2.25}-\sqrt{(-5)^2}=\sqrt{(1.5)^2}-5$
  $=1.5-5=-3.5$
(8) $\sqrt{\left(-\dfrac{1}{2}\right)^2}-\sqrt{0.16}-\sqrt{25}$
  $=\dfrac{1}{2}-\sqrt{(0.4)^2}-\sqrt{(5)^2}$
  $=\dfrac{1}{2}-0.4-5=-\dfrac{49}{10}$

03
$\sqrt{81}=\sqrt{(9)^2}=9$ and $(-3)^2=9$.
The positive square root of 9 is $m=3$ and the negative square root of 9 is $n=-3$.
So, $m+n=3+(-3)=0$

04
(1) $\left(-\sqrt{\dfrac{9}{4}}\right)^2=\dfrac{9}{4}$ and $\sqrt{(-4)^2}=4$.
The positive square root of $\dfrac{9}{4}$ is $a=\dfrac{3}{2}$ and the negative square root of 4 is $b=-2$. So,
$2a-b=2\left(\dfrac{3}{2}\right)-(-2)=5$

05
By the properties of the square root, (A), (B), and (C) are all 4.
(D) $-(-\sqrt{4^2})=-(-4)=4$
(E) $-\sqrt{(-4)^2}=-4$
So the answer is (E)

06
(1) $\sqrt{a^2}=a$ if $a>0$ and $\sqrt{b^2}=-b$ if $b<0$.
Thus, $\sqrt{a^2}-\sqrt{b^2}=a-(-b)=a+b$
(2) If $-1<a<3$, $a-3<0$ and $a+1>0$. Thus,
$\sqrt{(a-3)^2}+\sqrt{(a+1)^2}=-(a-3)+(a+1)$
$=4$
(3) If $x<2$, $x-2<0$ and if $y>\dfrac{1}{2}$, $2y-1>0$.
Thus,
$\sqrt{(x-2)^2}+\sqrt{(2y-1)^2}=-(x-2)+(2y-1)$
$=-x+2y+1$
(4) $\sqrt{x^2}=x$ if $x>0$ and $\sqrt{y^2}=-y$ if $y<0$.
Also, $y-x<0$ if $x>0$, $y<0$. Thus,
$\sqrt{x^2}+\sqrt{y^2}-2\sqrt{(y-x)^2}$
$=x-y-2(-(y-x))$
$=x-y+2(y-x)=-x+y$

Solutions Manual

07

$\sqrt{20x} = \sqrt{2^2 \times 5 \times x}$

x must be 5, and

$\sqrt{20 \times 5} = \sqrt{100} = \sqrt{10^2} = 10$

08

$4 < \sqrt{3x+1} < 5$

$4^2 < (\sqrt{3x+1})^2 < 5^2$

$16 < 3x+1 < 25$

$15 < 3x < 24, \quad 5 < x < 8$

The solutions for x are 6 and 7. So there are 2 positive integers.

2. n^{th} Roots and Rational Exponents

Check Point 1

① Since n is even and $a > 0$, a has two real square roots: $\pm\sqrt{36} = \pm 6$

② Since n is odd, a has one real cube root: $\sqrt[3]{-125} = -5$

③ Since n is even and $a < 0$, a has NO real fourth root.

④ Since n is odd, a has one real fifth root: $\sqrt[5]{\dfrac{1}{32}} = \dfrac{1}{2}$

Check Point 2

① Since $(-2)^3 = -8$, $\sqrt[3]{-8} = -2$

② Since $5^4 = 625$, $\sqrt[4]{625} = 5$

③ Since $\left(\dfrac{2}{3}\right)^4 = \dfrac{16}{81}$, $\sqrt[4]{\dfrac{16}{81}} = \dfrac{2}{3}$

④ Since $(-0.1)^3 = -0.001$, $\sqrt[3]{-0.001} = -0.1$

Check Point 3

① $\sqrt[3]{4} = \sqrt[3]{2^2} = (2^2)^{\frac{1}{3}} = 2^{\frac{2}{3}}$

② $\sqrt[4]{36} = \sqrt[4]{2^2 \cdot 3^2} = (2^2 \cdot 3^2)^{\frac{1}{4}} = 2^{\frac{1}{2}} \cdot 3^{\frac{1}{2}}$

③ $-(\sqrt[4]{20})^7 = -(\sqrt[4]{2^2 \cdot 5})^7 = -\left((2^2 \cdot 5)^{\frac{1}{4}}\right)^7$

$= -\left(2^{\frac{1}{2}} \cdot 5^{\frac{1}{4}}\right)^7 = -2^{\frac{7}{2}} \cdot 5^{\frac{7}{4}}$

④ $\sqrt[3]{-\dfrac{4}{9}} = \sqrt[3]{-\left(\dfrac{2}{3}\right)^2} = \left(-\left(\dfrac{2}{3}\right)^2\right)^{\frac{1}{3}} = -\left(\dfrac{2}{3}\right)^{\frac{2}{3}}$

Check Point 4

① $3^{\frac{4}{3}} = \sqrt[3]{3^4} = \sqrt[3]{81}$

② $2 \cdot 5^{\frac{1}{4}} = 2^{\frac{4}{4}} \cdot 5^{\frac{1}{4}} = \sqrt[4]{2^4 \cdot 5} = \sqrt[4]{80}$

③ $\left(\dfrac{1}{2}\right)^{-\frac{1}{3}} = (2^{-1})^{-\frac{1}{3}} = 2^{\frac{1}{3}} = \sqrt[3]{2}$

④ $\left(\dfrac{4}{25}\right)^{\frac{3}{2}} = \left(\left(\dfrac{2}{5}\right)^2\right)^{\frac{3}{2}} = \left(\dfrac{2}{5}\right)^3 = \dfrac{8}{125}$

Review Exercises

01

(1) Since n is even and $a > 0$, a has two real square roots: $\pm\sqrt{49} = \pm 7$

(2) Since n is odd, a has one real cube root
$\sqrt[3]{-64} = -4$

(3) Since n is odd, a has one real cube root
$\sqrt[3]{-\dfrac{8}{27}} = -\dfrac{2}{3}$

(4) Since n is even and $a > 0$, a has two real square roots: $\pm\sqrt[4]{0.0081} = \pm 0.3$

02

(1) Since $(-3)^3 = -27$, $\sqrt[3]{-27} = -3$

(2) Since $\left(\dfrac{1}{2}\right)^4 = \dfrac{1}{16}$, $\sqrt[4]{\dfrac{1}{16}} = \dfrac{1}{2}$

(3) Using the property of radical,
$(\sqrt{9})^2 = (\sqrt[2]{9})^2 = |9| = 9$

(4) Using the property of radical,
$(\sqrt[5]{-3})^5 = -3$

(5) Since $0.5^4 = 0.0625$, $\sqrt[4]{0.0625} = 0.5$

(6) Since $(-0.01)^3 = -0.000001$,
$\sqrt[3]{-0.000001} = -0.01$

03

(1) $\sqrt[3]{9} = \sqrt[3]{3^2} = (3^2)^{\frac{1}{3}} = 3^{\frac{2}{3}}$

(2) $\sqrt[4]{121} = \sqrt[4]{11^2} = (11^2)^{\frac{1}{4}} = 11^{\frac{1}{2}}$

(3) $\sqrt{\dfrac{27}{4}} = \sqrt{\dfrac{3^3}{2^2}} = \left(\dfrac{3^3}{2^2}\right)^{\frac{1}{2}} = \dfrac{3^{\frac{3}{2}}}{2}$

(4) $\sqrt[5]{\sqrt{\left(\dfrac{1}{64}\right)^2}} = \sqrt[5]{\sqrt{\left(\dfrac{1}{2^6}\right)^2}} = \sqrt[5]{\dfrac{1}{2^{12}}} = \left(\dfrac{1}{2^{12}}\right)^{\frac{1}{5}} = \dfrac{1}{2^{\frac{12}{5}}}$

(5) $\sqrt{0.0025} = \sqrt{0.05^2} = (0.05^2)^{\frac{1}{2}} = 0.05$

(6) $\sqrt[3]{(0.36)^2} = \sqrt[3]{(0.6)^2} = (0.6^2)^{\frac{1}{3}} = 0.6^{\frac{2}{3}}$

04

(1) $3^{\frac{2}{3}} = \sqrt[3]{3^2} = \sqrt[3]{9}$

(2) $2 \cdot 5^{\frac{1}{2}} = 2^{\frac{2}{2}} \cdot 5^{\frac{1}{2}} = \sqrt{2^2 \cdot 5} = \sqrt{20}$

(3) $3^{\frac{3}{4}} = \sqrt[4]{3^3} = \sqrt[4]{27}$

(4) $27^{\frac{4}{5}} = (3^3)^{\frac{4}{5}} = 3^{\frac{12}{5}} = \sqrt[5]{3^{12}}$

(5) $\left(\dfrac{3}{2}\right)^{\frac{3}{2}} = \sqrt{\left(\dfrac{3}{2}\right)^3} = \sqrt{\dfrac{27}{8}}$

(6) $5^{-\frac{1}{4}} = \dfrac{1}{5^{\frac{1}{4}}} = \dfrac{1}{\sqrt[4]{5}}$

05

Using the properties of nth roots,
$a = \sqrt[4]{16} = \sqrt[4]{2^4} = |2| = 2$
$b = \sqrt[3]{(-3)^3} = -3$
$a + b = 2 + (-3) = -1$

06

By the properties of nth roots, $\sqrt[n]{a^n} = a$ if n is odd.

I. $\sqrt[3]{3^3} = 3$

II. $-\sqrt[3]{3^3} = -3$

III. $\sqrt[3]{(-3)^3} = -3$

IV. $-\sqrt[3]{(-3)^3} = -(-3) = 3$

The answer is (B)

07

By the properties of nth roots, $\sqrt[n]{a^n} = |a|$ if n is even.

(A) $\sqrt[4]{5^4} = |5| = 5$

(B) $\sqrt[4]{(-5)^4} = |-5| = 5$

(C) $(-\sqrt[4]{5})^4 = (-1)^4 (\sqrt[4]{5})^4 = 5$

(D) $-(-\sqrt[4]{5^4}) = \sqrt[4]{5^4} = |5| = 5$

(E) $-\sqrt[4]{(-5)^4} = -|-5| = -5$

The answer is (E)

08

Use the properties of nth roots.

(1) $\sqrt[3]{a^3} - \sqrt[3]{b^3} = a - b$

(2) If $2 < a < 4$, $a - 2 > 0$ and $a - 4 < 0$.
Therefore,
$$\sqrt[4]{(a-2)^4} - \sqrt[4]{(a-4)^4} = |a-2| - |a-4|$$
$$= (a-2) - (-(a-4))$$
$$= a - 2 + a - 4 = 2a - 6$$

(3) If $x > -\dfrac{1}{2}$, $2x + 1 > 0$ and if $y < 3$,
$y - 3 < 0$. Therefore,
$$\sqrt[4]{(2x+1)^4} + \sqrt[4]{(y-3)^4} = |2x+1| + |y-3|$$
$$= (2x+1) - (y-3)$$
$$= 2x - y + 4$$

3. Properties of Radicals, Part 1

Check Point 1

① $3\sqrt[4]{162} = 3\sqrt[4]{3^4 \times 2} = 3(3\sqrt[4]{2}) = 9\sqrt[4]{2}$

② $\sqrt[3]{\dfrac{16}{27}} = \sqrt[3]{\dfrac{2^3 \times 2}{3^3}} = \dfrac{2\sqrt[3]{2}}{3}$

③ $\sqrt{4a^2 b} = \sqrt{2^2 \times a^2 \times b} = 2|a|\sqrt{b}$

④ $\sqrt[3]{54x^5 y^3} = \sqrt[3]{3^3 \times 2 \times x^3 \times x^2 \times y^3} = 3xy\sqrt[3]{2x^2}$

⑤ $\dfrac{\sqrt[4]{48x^4 y^6}}{2} = \dfrac{\sqrt[4]{2^4 \times 3 \times x^4 \times y^4 \times y^2}}{2} = \dfrac{2|xy|\sqrt[4]{3y^2}}{2}$
$= |xy|\sqrt[4]{3y^2}$

⑥ $\sqrt[5]{\dfrac{64a^5 b^{10}}{243}} = \sqrt[5]{\dfrac{2^5 \times 2 \times a^5 \times (b^2)^5}{3^5}} = \dfrac{2ab^2 \sqrt[5]{2}}{3}$

Check Point 2

① $\sqrt{2a} \times \sqrt{5a} \times \sqrt{10} = \sqrt{2a \times 5a \times 10} = \sqrt{2^2 \times 5^2 \times a^2}$
$= 2 \times 5 \times a = 10a$

② $3\sqrt[3]{x^2 y} \times \sqrt[3]{4xy^2} \times \sqrt[3]{6x} = 3\sqrt[3]{x^2 y \times 4xy^2 \times 6x}$
$= 3\sqrt[3]{2^3 \times 3 \times x^3 \times x \times y^3}$
$= 6xy\sqrt[3]{3x}$

③ $2\sqrt[4]{32x^5 y^2} \div 4\sqrt[4]{2xy^3} = \dfrac{2\sqrt[4]{32x^5 y^2}}{4\sqrt[4]{2xy^3}} = \dfrac{1}{2}\sqrt[4]{\dfrac{32x^5 y^2}{2xy^3}}$
$= \dfrac{1}{2}\sqrt[4]{\dfrac{16x^4}{y}} = \dfrac{1}{2}\sqrt[4]{\dfrac{2^4 \times x^4}{y}}$
$= \dfrac{2x}{2}\sqrt[4]{\dfrac{1}{y}} = x\sqrt[4]{\dfrac{1}{y}}$
$= x \cdot \dfrac{1}{\sqrt[4]{y}} = \dfrac{x}{\sqrt[4]{y}}$

④ $4\sqrt{9a} \div \sqrt{3b} \div 6\sqrt{b} = \dfrac{4\sqrt{9a}}{\sqrt{3b} \times 6\sqrt{b}} = \dfrac{4}{6}\sqrt{\dfrac{9a}{3b^2}}$
$= \dfrac{2}{3}\sqrt{\dfrac{3a}{b^2}} = \dfrac{2}{3b}\sqrt{3a} = \dfrac{2\sqrt{3a}}{3b}$

Review Exercises

01
(1) $\sqrt{125}=\sqrt{5^2\times 5}=5\sqrt{5}$
(2) $\sqrt[3]{64}=\sqrt[3]{4^3}=4$
(3) $\sqrt[4]{162}=\sqrt[4]{3^4\times 2}=3\sqrt[4]{2}$
(4) $\sqrt[3]{\dfrac{36}{1500}}=\sqrt[3]{\dfrac{3}{125}}=\dfrac{\sqrt[3]{3}}{\sqrt[3]{5^3}}=\dfrac{\sqrt[3]{3}}{5}$

02
(1) $\sqrt{512x^2}=\sqrt{(2^4)^2\times 2\times x^2}$
$=2^4|x|\sqrt{2}=16|x|\sqrt{2}$
(2) $\sqrt[4]{x^7y^7}=\sqrt[4]{x^4\times x^3\times y^4\times y^3}=|xy|\sqrt[4]{x^3y^3}$
(3) $\sqrt[3]{27x^{-7}y^{12}}=\sqrt[3]{\dfrac{27y^{12}}{x^7}}=\dfrac{\sqrt[3]{3^3\times(y^4)^3}}{\sqrt[3]{(x^2)^3\times x}}=\dfrac{3y^4}{x^2\sqrt[3]{x}}$
(4) $\sqrt[3]{-16x^3y^8}=\sqrt[3]{(-2)^3\times 2\times x^3\times(y^2)^3\times y^2}$
$=-2xy^2\sqrt[3]{2y^2}$
(5) $\sqrt{\dfrac{9x^5}{8y^3}}=\sqrt{\dfrac{3^2\times(x^2)^2\times x}{2^2\times 2\times y^2\times y}}=\dfrac{3x^2}{2|y|}\sqrt{\dfrac{x}{2y}}$
(6) $\sqrt[3]{-\dfrac{5x^{13}y^4}{54z^6}}=\sqrt[3]{\dfrac{(-1)^3\times 5\times(x^4)^3\times x\times y^3\times y}{2\times 3^3\times(z^2)^3}}$
$=-\dfrac{x^4y}{3z^2}\sqrt[3]{\dfrac{5xy}{2}}$

03
(1) $\sqrt{12}\times\sqrt{24}\times\sqrt{6}=\sqrt{12\times 24\times 6}$
$=\sqrt{(2^3)^2\times 3^2\times 3}$
$=2^3\cdot 3\sqrt{3}=24\sqrt{3}$
(2) $\sqrt[3]{4}\times\sqrt[3]{40}\times\sqrt[3]{2}=\sqrt[3]{4\times 40\times 2}=\sqrt[3]{(2^2)^3\times 5}$
$=2^2\sqrt[3]{5}=4\sqrt[3]{5}$
(3) $\sqrt{6x}\times\sqrt{3}\times\sqrt{8x^3}=\sqrt{6x\times 3\times 8x^3}$
$=\sqrt{(2^2)^2\times 3^2\times(x^2)^2}$
$=2^2\cdot 3x^2=12x^2$
(4) $2\sqrt[3]{4x^5}\times 3\sqrt[3]{6xy^4}=6\sqrt[3]{4x^5\times 6xy^4}$
$=6\sqrt[3]{2^3\times 3\times(x^2)^3\times y^3\times y}$
$=6\cdot 2x^2y\sqrt[3]{3y}=12x^2y\sqrt[3]{3y}$

04
(1) $\sqrt[3]{48x^3y^4}\div\sqrt[3]{3y^2}=\sqrt[3]{\dfrac{48x^3y^4}{3y^2}}=\sqrt[3]{16x^3y^2}$
$=\sqrt[3]{2^3\times 2\times x^3\times y^2}$
$=2x\sqrt[3]{2y^2}$
(2) $3\sqrt[4]{54x^2y}\times 4\sqrt[4]{6x^7y^3}=12\sqrt[4]{54x^2y\times 6x^7y^3}$
$=12\sqrt[4]{2^2\times 3^4\times(x^2)^4\times x\times y^4}$
$=36x^2y\sqrt[4]{4x}$
(3) $15\sqrt[4]{2x^5y}\div 30\sqrt[4]{32x^3}\times 4\sqrt[4]{x^2y^3}$
$=\dfrac{15\times 4}{30}\cdot\dfrac{\sqrt[4]{2x^5y}\times\sqrt[4]{x^2y^3}}{\sqrt[4]{32x^3}}$
$=2\sqrt[4]{\dfrac{2x^7y^4}{32x^3}}=2\sqrt[4]{\dfrac{x^4y^4}{16}}=2\sqrt[4]{\dfrac{x^4\times y^4}{2^4}}$
$=2\cdot\dfrac{xy}{2}=xy$
(4) $6\sqrt{y}\div 18\sqrt{4x^3}\div\sqrt{xy^3}$
$=\dfrac{6\sqrt{y}}{18\sqrt{4x^3}\times\sqrt{xy^3}}=\dfrac{6}{18}\cdot\dfrac{\sqrt{y}}{\sqrt{4x^4y^3}}$
$=\dfrac{1}{3}\sqrt{\dfrac{y}{4x^4y^3}}=\dfrac{1}{3}\cdot\sqrt{\dfrac{1}{2^2\times(x^2)^2\times y^2}}$
$=\dfrac{1}{3}\cdot\dfrac{1}{2x^2y}=\dfrac{1}{6x^2y}$

05
$2\sqrt{5}=\sqrt{2^2\times 5}=\sqrt{20}\quad\to\ a=20$
$\sqrt[3]{0.024}=\sqrt[3]{\dfrac{24}{1000}}=\sqrt[3]{\dfrac{2^3\times 3}{10^3}}=\dfrac{2}{10}\sqrt[3]{3}=\dfrac{1}{5}\sqrt[3]{3}$
$\to\ b=\dfrac{1}{5}$ and $c=3$
So, $abc=20\cdot\dfrac{1}{5}\cdot 3=12$

06
$\sqrt{360}=\sqrt{2^3\times 3^2\times 5}=\sqrt{2^3}\times\sqrt{3^2}\times\sqrt{5}$
$=(\sqrt{2})^3\times(\sqrt{3})^2\times\sqrt{5}$
$=a^3\times b^2\times c=a^3b^2c$

07
$\sqrt[3]{720}=\sqrt[3]{2^4\times 3^2\times 5}=\sqrt[3]{2^4}\times\sqrt[3]{3^2}\times\sqrt[3]{5}$
$=(\sqrt[3]{2})^4\times(\sqrt[3]{3})^2\times\sqrt[3]{5}$
$=a^4\times b^2\times c=a^4b^2c$

08

(1) $\sqrt{ab^2}=b\sqrt{a}=4m\sqrt{2m}$

(2) $\sqrt{ab}\times\sqrt{2a^2b^3}=\sqrt{2a^3b^4}=ab^2\sqrt{2a}$
$=(2m)(4m)^2\sqrt{2(2m)}$
$=32m^3\cdot 2\sqrt{m}$
$=64m^3\sqrt{m}$

(3) $\sqrt[3]{4a^2b}=\sqrt[3]{4\times(2m)^2\times 4m}$
$=\sqrt[3]{(2^2)^3\times m^3}=2^2m=4m$

(4) $\sqrt[4]{6b}\times\sqrt[4]{9a^3b}=\sqrt[4]{6b\times 9a^3b}=\sqrt[4]{54a^3b^2}$
$=\sqrt[4]{54\times(2m)^3\times(4m)^2}$
$=\sqrt[4]{(2^2)^4\times 3^3\times m^4\times m}$
$=2^2m\sqrt[4]{3^3\times m}=4m\sqrt[4]{27m}$

4. Properties of Radicals, Part 2

Check Point 1

① $-4\sqrt{5}-3\sqrt{5}+5\sqrt{5}=(-4-3+5)\sqrt{5}=-2\sqrt{5}$

② $\sqrt[3]{81}-2\sqrt[3]{24}-2\sqrt[3]{3}=\sqrt[3]{3^3\times 3}-2\sqrt[3]{2^3\times 3}-2\sqrt[3]{3}$
$=3\sqrt[3]{3}-4\sqrt[3]{3}-2\sqrt[3]{3}$
$=(3-4-2)\sqrt[3]{3}=-3\sqrt[3]{3}$

③ $\sqrt{4ab^3}+3\sqrt{a^3b}=\sqrt{2^2\times a\times b^2\times b}+3\sqrt{a^2\times a\times b}$
$=2b\sqrt{ab}+3a\sqrt{ab}$
$=(2b+3a)\sqrt{ab}$

④ $\sqrt[4]{32x^6y}-\sqrt[4]{2x^6y}$
$=\sqrt[4]{2^4\times 2\times x^4\times x^2\times y}-\sqrt[4]{2\times x^4\times x^2\times y}$
$=2x\sqrt[4]{2x^2y}-x\sqrt[4]{2x^2y}$
$=(2-1)x\sqrt[4]{2x^2y}=x\sqrt[4]{2x^2y}$

Check Point 2

① $(\sqrt{2}-\sqrt{3})(\sqrt{2}+\sqrt{3})=(\sqrt{2})^2-(\sqrt{3})^2$
$=2-3=-1$

② $(\sqrt{6}+x\sqrt{2})^2=(\sqrt{6})^2+2(\sqrt{6}\times x\sqrt{2})+(x\sqrt{2})^2$
$=6+2x\sqrt{6\times 2}+2x^2$
$=6+2x\sqrt{2^2\times 3}+2x^2$
$=2x^2+4x\sqrt{3}+6$

③ $\sqrt{x}(2\sqrt{x^2y}+4x\sqrt{9y})$
$=\sqrt{x}(2\sqrt{x^2\times y}+4x\sqrt{3^2\times y})$
$=\sqrt{x}(2x\sqrt{y}+12x\sqrt{y})$
$=\sqrt{x}(14x\sqrt{y})=14x\sqrt{xy}$

④ $(\sqrt{2a}+\sqrt{6b})(2\sqrt{3b}-3\sqrt{a})$
$=(\sqrt{2a}\times 2\sqrt{3b})+(\sqrt{2a}\times(-3\sqrt{a}))$
$+(\sqrt{6b}\times 2\sqrt{3b})+(\sqrt{6b}\times(-3\sqrt{a}))$
$=2\sqrt{6ab}-3\sqrt{2\times a^2}+2\sqrt{3^2\times 2\times b^2}-3\sqrt{6ab}$
$=2\sqrt{6ab}-3a\sqrt{2}+6b\sqrt{2}-3\sqrt{6ab}$
$=-\sqrt{6ab}-3a\sqrt{2}+6b\sqrt{2}$

Check Point 3

① $5\sqrt{\dfrac{3}{5}} = \dfrac{5\sqrt{3}}{\sqrt{5}} = \dfrac{5\sqrt{3}}{\sqrt{5}} \cdot \dfrac{\sqrt{5}}{\sqrt{5}} = \dfrac{5\sqrt{15}}{5} = \sqrt{15}$

② $\dfrac{\sqrt{2}}{\sqrt{3}-2} = \dfrac{\sqrt{2}}{\sqrt{3}-2} \cdot \dfrac{\sqrt{3}+2}{\sqrt{3}+2} = \dfrac{\sqrt{2}(\sqrt{3}+2)}{(\sqrt{3})^2-(2)^2}$
$= \dfrac{\sqrt{6}+2\sqrt{2}}{3-4} = -\sqrt{6}-2\sqrt{2}$

③ $\dfrac{1}{\sqrt{2}+\sqrt{5}} = \dfrac{1}{\sqrt{2}+\sqrt{5}} \cdot \dfrac{\sqrt{2}-\sqrt{5}}{\sqrt{2}-\sqrt{5}}$
$= \dfrac{\sqrt{2}-\sqrt{5}}{(\sqrt{2})^2-(\sqrt{5})^2} = \dfrac{\sqrt{2}-\sqrt{5}}{2-5}$
$= \dfrac{\sqrt{5}-\sqrt{2}}{3}$

Review Exercises

01

(1) $7\sqrt{7}-2\sqrt{7}+3\sqrt{7} = (7-2+3)\sqrt{7} = 8\sqrt{7}$

(2) $\sqrt{98}+\sqrt{8}+\sqrt{18} = \sqrt{7^2 \times 2}+\sqrt{2^2 \times 2}+\sqrt{3^2 \times 2}$
$= 7\sqrt{2}+2\sqrt{2}+3\sqrt{2}$
$= (7+2+3)\sqrt{2} = 12\sqrt{2}$

(3) $2\sqrt[3]{16}-3\sqrt[3]{54}+\sqrt[3]{40}$
$= 2\sqrt[3]{2^3 \times 2}-3\sqrt[3]{3^3 \times 2}+\sqrt[3]{2^3 \times 5}$
$= 4\sqrt[3]{2}-9\sqrt[3]{2}+2\sqrt[3]{5}$
$= 2\sqrt[3]{5}+(4-9)\sqrt[3]{2} = 2\sqrt[3]{5}-5\sqrt[3]{2}$

(4) $2\sqrt[3]{135}+2\sqrt[3]{16}-4\sqrt[3]{5}-\sqrt[3]{320}$
$= 2\sqrt[3]{3^3 \times 5}+2\sqrt[3]{2^3 \times 2}-4\sqrt[3]{5}-\sqrt[3]{(2^2)^3 \times 5}$
$= 6\sqrt[3]{5}+4\sqrt[3]{2}-4\sqrt[3]{5}-4\sqrt[3]{5}$
$= 4\sqrt[3]{2}+(6-4-4)\sqrt[3]{5} = 4\sqrt[3]{2}-2\sqrt[3]{5}$

(5) $2\sqrt[4]{48}+3\sqrt[4]{3}+\sqrt[4]{80}-4\sqrt[4]{5}$
$= 2\sqrt[4]{2^4 \times 3}+3\sqrt[4]{3}+\sqrt[4]{2^4 \times 5}-4\sqrt[4]{5}$
$= 4\sqrt[4]{3}+3\sqrt[4]{3}+2\sqrt[4]{5}-4\sqrt[4]{5}$
$= (4+3)\sqrt[4]{3}+(2-4)\sqrt[4]{5}$
$= 7\sqrt[4]{3}-2\sqrt[4]{5}$

(6) $5\sqrt{72x}-4\sqrt{50x}$
$= 5\sqrt{2^2 \times 2 \times 3^2 \times x}-4\sqrt{5^2 \times 2 \times x}$
$= 30\sqrt{2x}-20\sqrt{2x}$
$= (30-20)\sqrt{2x} = 10\sqrt{2x}$

(7) $3\sqrt{x^5 y}+4\sqrt{xy^5}$
$= 3\sqrt{(x^2)^2 \times x \times y}+4\sqrt{x \times (y^2)^2 \times y}$
$= 3x^2\sqrt{xy}+4y^2\sqrt{xy}$
$= (3x^2+4y^2)\sqrt{xy}$

(8) $x\sqrt[3]{2x^3 y^6}+y\sqrt[3]{16x^6 y^3}-2\sqrt[3]{2x^6 y^6}$
$= x\sqrt[3]{2 \times x^3 \times (y^2)^3}+y\sqrt[3]{2^3 \times 2 \times (x^2)^3 \times y^3}$
$\quad -2\sqrt[3]{2 \times (x^2)^3 \times (y^2)^3}$
$= x^2 y^2 \sqrt[3]{2}+2x^2 y^2 \sqrt[3]{2}-2x^2 y^2 \sqrt[3]{2}$
$= (1+2-2)x^2 y^2 \sqrt[3]{2} = x^2 y^2 \sqrt[3]{2}$

02

(1) $(\sqrt{5}-1)(\sqrt{5}+1) = (\sqrt{5})^2-1^2 = 4$

(2) $\sqrt{2}(4\sqrt{6}-\sqrt{10}) = 4\sqrt{2^2 \times 3}-\sqrt{2^2 \times 5}$
$= 8\sqrt{3}-2\sqrt{5}$

(3) $(2\sqrt{5}-\sqrt{3})^2 = (2\sqrt{5})^2-2(2\sqrt{5} \times \sqrt{3})+(\sqrt{3})^2$
$= 20-4\sqrt{15}+3 = 23-4\sqrt{15}$

(4) $\sqrt{3x}(\sqrt{6x}+x\sqrt{2x}) = \sqrt{3x \times 6x}+x\sqrt{2x \times 3x}$
$= \sqrt{3^2 \times 2 \times x^2}+x\sqrt{6 \times x^2}$
$= 3x\sqrt{2}+x^2\sqrt{6}$

(5) $(4+\sqrt{3x})(\sqrt{3x}-7)$
$= 4\sqrt{3x}-28+3x-7\sqrt{3x} = 3x-3\sqrt{3x}-28$

(6) $(\sqrt{a}-\sqrt{b})(2\sqrt{a}-2\sqrt{b})$
$= 2a-2\sqrt{ab}-2\sqrt{ab}+2b = 2a-4\sqrt{ab}+2b$

(7) $(\sqrt{xy^3}+1)(\sqrt{x}-\sqrt{y})$
$= \sqrt{x^2 y^3}-\sqrt{xy^4}+\sqrt{x}-\sqrt{y}$
$= \sqrt{x^2 \times y^2 \times y}-\sqrt{x \times (y^2)^2}+\sqrt{x}-\sqrt{y}$
$= xy\sqrt{y}-y^2\sqrt{x}+\sqrt{x}-\sqrt{y}$

(8) $(\sqrt{x}-\sqrt{y})^2(\sqrt{x}+y)^2$
$= (x-2\sqrt{xy}+y)(x+y)$
$= x^2+xy-2x\sqrt{xy}-2y\sqrt{xy}+xy+y^2$
$= x^2-2\sqrt{xy}(x+y)+2xy+y^2$

03

(1) $\dfrac{2}{\sqrt{3}} = \dfrac{2}{\sqrt{3}} \cdot \dfrac{\sqrt{3}}{\sqrt{3}} = \dfrac{2\sqrt{3}}{\sqrt{3}}$

(2) $\dfrac{15\sqrt{2}}{\sqrt{5}} = \dfrac{15\sqrt{2}}{\sqrt{5}} \cdot \dfrac{\sqrt{5}}{\sqrt{5}} = \dfrac{15\sqrt{10}}{5} = 3\sqrt{10}$

(3) $\dfrac{1-\sqrt{3}}{1+\sqrt{3}} = \dfrac{(1-\sqrt{3})}{(1+\sqrt{3})} \cdot \dfrac{(1-\sqrt{3})}{(1-\sqrt{3})} = \dfrac{1-2\sqrt{3}+3}{1-3}$
$= -\dfrac{4-2\sqrt{3}}{2} = \sqrt{3}-2$

(4) $\dfrac{4+3\sqrt{2}}{3+\sqrt{2}} = \dfrac{4+3\sqrt{2}}{3+\sqrt{2}} \cdot \dfrac{3-\sqrt{2}}{3-\sqrt{2}}$

$$=\frac{12-4\sqrt{2}+9\sqrt{2}-6}{9-2}=\frac{6+5\sqrt{2}}{7}$$

(5) $\dfrac{\sqrt{2}}{3-\sqrt{x}}=\dfrac{\sqrt{2}}{3-\sqrt{x}}\cdot\dfrac{3+\sqrt{x}}{3+\sqrt{x}}=\dfrac{3\sqrt{2}+\sqrt{2x}}{9-x}$

(6) $\dfrac{\sqrt{x}}{4-2\sqrt{x}}=\dfrac{\sqrt{x}}{4-2\sqrt{x}}\cdot\dfrac{4+2\sqrt{x}}{4+2\sqrt{x}}=\dfrac{\sqrt{x}(4+2\sqrt{x})}{16-4x}$

$$=\frac{4\sqrt{x}+2x}{16-4x}=\frac{2\sqrt{x}+x}{8-2x}$$

04

(1) $ab=(\sqrt{5}+\sqrt{3})(\sqrt{5}-\sqrt{3})$
$=5-3=2$

(2) $a\sqrt{3}+b\sqrt{5}$
$=(\sqrt{5}+\sqrt{3})\sqrt{3}+(\sqrt{5}-\sqrt{3})\sqrt{5}$
$=\sqrt{15}+3+5-\sqrt{15}=8$

(3) $a\sqrt{5}-2b\sqrt{3}$
$=(\sqrt{5}+\sqrt{3})\sqrt{5}-2(\sqrt{5}-\sqrt{3})\sqrt{3}$
$=5+\sqrt{15}-2\sqrt{15}+6$
$=11-\sqrt{15}$

(4) $ab\sqrt{3}+ab^2=ab(\sqrt{3}+b)$
$=2(\sqrt{3}+\sqrt{5}-\sqrt{3})=2\sqrt{5}$

05

$\dfrac{\sqrt{2}}{\sqrt{3}}+\dfrac{2}{\sqrt{6}}+\dfrac{\sqrt{3}}{\sqrt{2}}$

$=\dfrac{\sqrt{2}}{\sqrt{3}}\cdot\dfrac{\sqrt{3}}{\sqrt{3}}+\dfrac{2}{\sqrt{6}}\cdot\dfrac{\sqrt{6}}{\sqrt{6}}+\dfrac{\sqrt{3}}{\sqrt{2}}\cdot\dfrac{\sqrt{2}}{\sqrt{2}}$

$=\dfrac{\sqrt{6}}{3}+\dfrac{2\sqrt{6}}{6}+\dfrac{\sqrt{6}}{2}$

$=\dfrac{\sqrt{6}}{3}\cdot\dfrac{2}{2}+\dfrac{2\sqrt{6}}{6}+\dfrac{\sqrt{6}}{2}\cdot\dfrac{3}{3}$

$=\dfrac{2\sqrt{6}}{6}+\dfrac{2\sqrt{6}}{6}+\dfrac{3\sqrt{6}}{6}=\dfrac{7\sqrt{6}}{6}=\dfrac{7}{6}\sqrt{6}$

$\Rightarrow a=\dfrac{7}{6}$ and $b=6$

Therefore, $ab=\dfrac{7}{6}\cdot 6=7$

06

(1) $2k\sqrt{3}-4k+3-4\sqrt{3}=-4k+3+(2k-4)\sqrt{3}$

In order for the expression above to be rational, $2k-4$ must be zero. So,
$$2k-4=0,\ k=2$$

(2) $(2-5\sqrt{2})(3k+2\sqrt{2})$
$=6k+4\sqrt{2}-15k\sqrt{2}-20$
$=6k-20+(4-15k)\sqrt{2}$

In order for the expression above to be rational, $4-15k$ must be zero. So,
$$4-15k=0,\ k=\frac{4}{15}$$

(3) $\sqrt{2}(\sqrt{2}-1)-\dfrac{k(3\sqrt{2}-1)}{3\sqrt{2}}$

$=2-\sqrt{2}-\dfrac{3k\sqrt{2}-k}{3\sqrt{2}}\cdot\dfrac{\sqrt{2}}{\sqrt{2}}$

$=2-\sqrt{2}-\dfrac{6k-k\sqrt{2}}{6}$

$=2-\sqrt{2}-k+\dfrac{k\sqrt{2}}{6}$

$=2-k+\left(-1+\dfrac{k}{6}\right)\sqrt{2}$

In order for the expression above to be rational, $-1+\dfrac{k}{6}$ must be zero. So,
$$-1+\frac{k}{6}=0,\ k=6$$

07

$x=\dfrac{2}{\sqrt{6}-2}\cdot\dfrac{\sqrt{6}+2}{\sqrt{6}+2}=\dfrac{2\sqrt{6}+4}{6-4}$

$=\dfrac{2\sqrt{6}+4}{2}=\sqrt{6}+2$

(1) $x^2-4x+4=(x-2)^2=(\sqrt{6}+2-2)^2$
$=(\sqrt{6})^2=6$

(2) x^3-6x^2+8x
$=x(x^2-6x+8)=x(x-2)(x-4)$
$=(\sqrt{6}+2)(\sqrt{6}+2-2)(\sqrt{6}+2-4)$
$=\sqrt{6}(\sqrt{6}+2)(\sqrt{6}-2)$
$=\sqrt{6}(6-4)=2\sqrt{6}$

08

$x = \dfrac{4}{3-\sqrt{5}} \cdot \dfrac{3+\sqrt{5}}{3+\sqrt{5}} = \dfrac{4(3+\sqrt{5})}{9-5}$

$= \dfrac{4(3+\sqrt{5})}{4} = 3+\sqrt{5}$

$y = \dfrac{4}{3+\sqrt{5}} \cdot \dfrac{3-\sqrt{5}}{3-\sqrt{5}} = \dfrac{4(3-\sqrt{5})}{9-5}$

$= \dfrac{4(3-\sqrt{5})}{4} = 3-\sqrt{5}$

(1) $x^2 - y^2 = (x-y)(x+y)$
Since $x-y = (3+\sqrt{5}) - (3-\sqrt{5}) = 2\sqrt{5}$ and
$x+y = (3+\sqrt{5}) + (3-\sqrt{5}) = 6$,
$x^2 - y^2 = (x-y)(x+y)$
$= (2\sqrt{5})(6) = 12\sqrt{5}$

(2) $\dfrac{x}{y} - 2 + \dfrac{y}{x} = \dfrac{x}{y} \cdot \dfrac{x}{x} - 2 \cdot \dfrac{xy}{xy} + \dfrac{y}{x} \cdot \dfrac{y}{y}$

$= \dfrac{x^2 - 2xy + y^2}{xy} = \dfrac{(x-y)^2}{xy}$

Since $x-y = (3+\sqrt{5}) - (3-\sqrt{5}) = 2\sqrt{5}$ and
$xy = (3+\sqrt{5})(3-\sqrt{5}) = 9-5 = 4$,

$\dfrac{x}{y} - 2 + \dfrac{y}{x} = \dfrac{(x-y)^2}{xy} = \dfrac{(2\sqrt{5})^2}{4}$

$= \dfrac{20}{4} = 5$

5. Radical Equations

Check Point 1

① $\sqrt{6x-5} - 7 = 0$
$\sqrt{6x-5} = 7$
$(\sqrt{6x-5})^2 = (7)^2$
$6x - 5 = 49,\ x = 9$

✔ Check $x=9$ in the original equation.
$\sqrt{6(9)-5} - 7 = 0$
$\sqrt{49} - 7 = 0$
$7 - 7 = 0,\ 0 = 0 \rightarrow$ Solution checks

The solution is $x = 9$

② $2\sqrt{-3x+6} + 1 = 5$
$2\sqrt{-3x+6} = 4$
$\sqrt{-3x+6} = 2$
$(\sqrt{-3x+6})^2 = (2)^2$
$-3x + 6 = 4,\ x = \dfrac{2}{3}$

✔ Check $x = \dfrac{2}{3}$ in the original equation.

$2\sqrt{-3\left(\dfrac{2}{3}\right)+6} + 1 = 5$

$2\sqrt{-2+6} + 1 = 5$
$2\sqrt{4} + 1 = 5$
$4 + 1 = 5,\ 5 = 5 \rightarrow$ Solution checks

The solution is $x = \dfrac{2}{3}$

③ $\sqrt{x} - \sqrt{x-5} = 2$
$\sqrt{x} - 2 = \sqrt{x-5}$
$(\sqrt{x} - 2)^2 = (\sqrt{x-5})^2$
$x - 4\sqrt{x} + 4 = x - 5$
$-4\sqrt{x} = -9,\ \sqrt{x} = \dfrac{9}{4}$

$(\sqrt{x})^2 = \left(\dfrac{9}{4}\right)^2,\ x = \dfrac{81}{16}$

✔ Check $x = \dfrac{81}{16}$ in the original equation.

$\sqrt{\dfrac{81}{16}} - \sqrt{\dfrac{81}{16} - 5} = 2$

$\dfrac{9}{4} - \sqrt{\dfrac{1}{16}} = 2$

Solutions Manual 119

Solutions Manual

$\frac{9}{4} - \frac{1}{4} = 2$, $2=2$ → Solution checks

The solution is $x = \frac{81}{16}$

④ $3(\sqrt{x-3}-x)+15=0$
$3(\sqrt{x-3}-x)=-15$
$\sqrt{x-3}-x=-5$
$\sqrt{x-3}=x-5$
$(\sqrt{x-3})^2=(x-5)^2$
$x-3=x^2-10x+25$
$0=x^2-11x+28$
$0=(x-7)(x-4)$, $x=7$ or $x=4$

✔ Check $x=7$ in the original equation.
$3(\sqrt{7-3}-7)+15=0$
$3(\sqrt{4}-7+15=0$
$3(-5)+15=0$, $0=0$ → Solution checks

✔ Check $x=4$ in the original equation.
$3(\sqrt{4-3}-4)+15=0$
$3(\sqrt{1}-4)+15=0$
$-9+15=0$, $6 \neq 0$ → Extraneous solution

The solution is $x=7$

Check Point 2

① $\sqrt[3]{4x-1}=3$
$(\sqrt[3]{4x-1})^3=3^3$
$4x-1=27$
$4x=28$, $x=7$

The solution is $x=7$

② $\frac{1}{2}\sqrt[3]{(x-2)^2}-\frac{25}{2}=0$
$\frac{1}{2}\sqrt[3]{(x-2)^2}=\frac{25}{2}$, $\sqrt[3]{(x-2)^2}=25$
$(\sqrt[3]{(x-2)^2})^3=(25)^3$, $(x-2)^2=5^6$
$|x-2|=125$, $x-2=\pm 125$
$x=127$ or $x=-123$

The solution is $x=127$ or $x=-123$

Review Exercises

01

(1) $\sqrt{3x+1}=7$
$(\sqrt{3x+1})^2=(7)^2$
$3x+1=49$, $x=16$

✔ Check $x=16$ in the original equation.
$\sqrt{3(16)+1}=7$
$\sqrt{49}=7$, $7=7$ → Solution checks

The solution is $x=16$

(2) $8\sqrt{2x-5}-7=3$
$\sqrt{2x-5}=\frac{5}{4}$
$(\sqrt{2x-5})^2=\left(\frac{5}{4}\right)^2$
$2x-5=\frac{25}{16}$, $x=\frac{105}{32}$

✔ Check $x=\frac{105}{32}$ in the original equation.
$8\sqrt{2\left(\frac{105}{32}\right)-5}-7=3$
$8\sqrt{\frac{25}{16}}-7=3$
$8\left(\frac{5}{4}\right)-7=3$, $3=3$ → Solution checks

The solution is $x=\frac{105}{32}$

(3) $\sqrt{x-2}+x=4$
$\sqrt{x-2}=4-x$
$(\sqrt{x-2})^2=(4-x)^2$
$x-2=16-8x+x^2$
$x^2-9x+18=0$
$(x-3)(x-6)=0$, $x=3$ or $x=6$

✔ Check $x=3$ in the original equation.
$\sqrt{3-2}+3=4$
$\sqrt{1}+3=4$, $4=4$ → Solution checks

✔ Check $x=6$ in the original equation.
$\sqrt{6-2}+6=4$
$\sqrt{4}+6=4$, $8 \neq 4$ → Extraneous solution

The solution is $x=3$

(4) $\sqrt{3x+10}=4+x$
$(\sqrt{3x+10})^2=(4+x)^2$
$3x+10=16+8x+x^2$
$x^2+5x+6=0$
$(x+3)(x+2)=0$, $x=-3$ or $x=-2$
✔ Check $x=-3$ in the original equation.
$\sqrt{3(-3)+10}=4+(-3)$
$\sqrt{1}=1$, $1=1$ → Solution checks
✔ Check $x=-2$ in the original equation.
$\sqrt{3(-2)+10}=4+(-2)$
$\sqrt{4}=2$, $2=2$ → Solution checks
　　　　The solutions are $x=-3$ and $x=-2$

02

(1) $\sqrt{3x-2}-\sqrt{10-x}=2$
$\sqrt{3x-2}=\sqrt{10-x}+2$
$(\sqrt{3x-2})^2=(\sqrt{10-x}+2)^2$
$3x-2=(10-x)+4\sqrt{10-x}+4$
$4x-16=4\sqrt{10-x}$, $x-4=\sqrt{10-x}$
$(x-4)^2=(\sqrt{10-x})^2$
$x^2-8x+16=10-x$
$x^2-7x+6=0$, $(x-1)(x-6)=0$
$x=1$ or $x=6$
✔ Check $x=1$ in the original equation.
$\sqrt{3(1)-2}-\sqrt{10-(1)}=2$
$\sqrt{1}-\sqrt{9}=2$
$1-3=2$, $-2\ne2$ → Extraneous solution
✔ Check $x=6$ in the original equation.
$\sqrt{3(6)-2}-\sqrt{10-(6)}=2$
$\sqrt{16}-\sqrt{4}=2$
$4-2=2$, $2=2$ → Solution checks
　　　　The solution is $x=6$

(2) $\sqrt{x+3}-3=\sqrt{2-x}$
$(\sqrt{x+3}-3)^2=(\sqrt{2-x})^2$
$(x+3)-6\sqrt{x+3}+9=2-x$
$6\sqrt{x+3}=2x+10$, $3\sqrt{x+3}=x+5$
$(3\sqrt{x+3})^2=(x+5)^2$
$9(x+3)=x^2+10x+25$
$x^2+x-2=0$, $(x+2)(x-1)=0$
$x=-2$ or $x=1$

✔ Check $x=-2$ in the original equation.
$\sqrt{(-2)+3}-3=\sqrt{2-(-2)}$
$\sqrt{1}-3=\sqrt{4}$
$-2\ne2$ → Extraneous solution
✔ Check $x=1$ in the original equation.
$\sqrt{(1)+3}-3=\sqrt{2-(1)}$
$\sqrt{4}-3=\sqrt{1}$
$-1\ne1$ → Extraneous solution
　　　　There is NO solution

(3) $\sqrt{x}+\sqrt{x+5}=5$
$\sqrt{x+5}=5-\sqrt{x}$
$(\sqrt{x+5})^2=(5-\sqrt{x})^2$
$x+5=25-10\sqrt{x}+x$
$10\sqrt{x}=20$, $\sqrt{x}=2$
$(\sqrt{x})^2=2^2$, $x=4$
✔ Check $x=4$ in the original equation.
$\sqrt{4}+\sqrt{4+5}=5$
$2+\sqrt{9}=5$, $5=5$ → Solution checks
　　　　The solution is $x=4$

03

(1) $\sqrt[3]{3x-1}=8$
$(\sqrt[3]{3x-1})^3=(8)^3$
$3x-1=512$, $x=171$
　　　　The solution is $x=171$

(2) $2\sqrt[3]{2x-5}-1=5$
$\sqrt[3]{2x-5}=3$
$(\sqrt[3]{2x-5})^3=(3)^3$
$2x-5=27$, $x=16$
　　　　The solution is $x=16$

(3) $\dfrac{\sqrt[3]{x}}{4}=\dfrac{\sqrt[3]{x-7}}{2}$, $\sqrt[3]{x}=2\sqrt[3]{x-7}$
$(\sqrt[3]{x})^3=(2\sqrt[3]{x-7})^3$
$x=8(x-7)$
$-7x=-56$, $x=8$
　　　　The solution is $x=8$

(4) $2\sqrt[3]{(x-2)^2}-17=1$, $\sqrt[3]{(x-2)^2}=9$
$(\sqrt[3]{(x-2)^2})^3=(9)^3$, $(x-2)^2=729$
$|x-2|=27$, $x-2=\pm27$
$x=-25$ or $x=29$

The solutions are $x=-25$ and $x=29$

04
(1) $\sqrt{1+\sqrt{x}}=\sqrt{x+1}$
$(\sqrt{1+\sqrt{x}})^2=(\sqrt{x+1})^2$
$1+\sqrt{x}=x+1$ $\sqrt{x}=x$
$(\sqrt{x})^2=(x)^2$, $x=x^2$
$x^2-x=0$, $x(x-1)=0$
$x=0$ or $x=1$

✔ Check $x=0$ in the original equation.
$\sqrt{1+\sqrt{0}}=\sqrt{(0)+1}$
$\sqrt{1}=\sqrt{1}$, $1=1$ → Solution checks

✔ Check $x=1$ in the original equation.
$\sqrt{1+\sqrt{1}}=\sqrt{(1)+1}$
$\sqrt{2}=\sqrt{2}$ → Solution checks

The solutions are $x=0$ and $x=1$

(2) $\sqrt{4-\sqrt{x+4}}=\sqrt{x+6}$
$(\sqrt{4-\sqrt{x+4}})^2=(\sqrt{x+6})^2$
$4-\sqrt{x+4}=x+6$
$-x-2=\sqrt{x+4}$
$(-x-2)^2=(\sqrt{x+4})^2$
$x^2+4x+4=x+4$
$x^2+3x=0$, $x(x+3)=0$
$x=0$ or $x=-3$

✔ Check $x=0$ in the original equation.
$\sqrt{4-\sqrt{(0)+4}}=\sqrt{(0)+6}$
$\sqrt{4-2}=\sqrt{6}$
$\sqrt{2}\neq\sqrt{6}$ → Extraneous solution

✔ Check $x=-3$ in the original equation.
$\sqrt{4-\sqrt{(-3)+4}}=\sqrt{(-3)+6}$
$\sqrt{4-1}=\sqrt{3}$
$\sqrt{3}=\sqrt{3}$ → Solution checks

The solution is $x=-3$

6. Graphing Radical Functions

Check Point 1

① $y=2\sqrt{x}$, $y=2\sqrt{-x}$

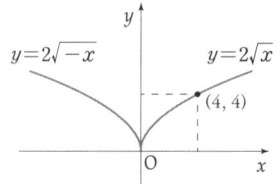

Symmetric about the y-axis

② $y=\sqrt{4x}$, $y=-\sqrt{4x}$

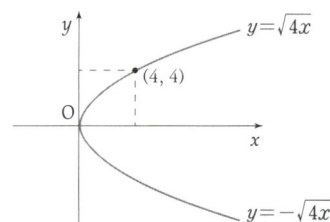

Symmetric about the x-axis

③ $y=\dfrac{1}{2}\sqrt{3x}$, $y=-\dfrac{1}{2}\sqrt{-3x}$

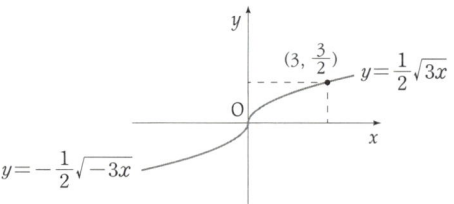

Symmetric about the origin

Check Point 2

① $y=\sqrt{2x-4} \Rightarrow y=\sqrt{2(x-2)}$

Graph $y=\sqrt{2x}$ first and then shift the graph 2 units to the right.

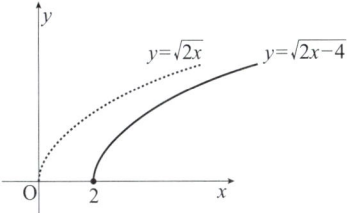

Domain: $\{x\,|\,x\geq 2\}$
Range: $\{y\,|\,y\geq 0\}$

② $y=\sqrt{-\dfrac{1}{2}x}-1$

Graph $y=\sqrt{-\dfrac{1}{2}x}$ first and then shift the graph 1 unit down.

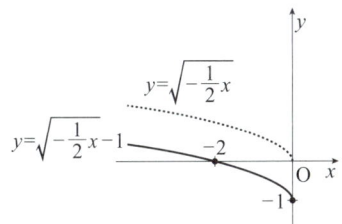

Domain: $\{x\,|\,x\leq 0\}$
Range: $\{y\,|\,y\geq -1\}$

③ $y=-\dfrac{1}{2}\sqrt{x+1}+2$

Graph $y=-\dfrac{1}{2}\sqrt{x}$ first and then shift the graph 1 unit to the left and 2 units up.

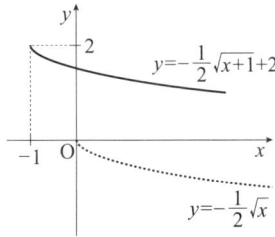

Domain: $\{x\,|\,x\geq -1\}$
Range: $\{y\,|\,y\leq 2\}$

④ $y=-2\sqrt{-2x-5}-4$

$\Rightarrow y=-2\sqrt{-2\left(x+\dfrac{5}{2}\right)}-4$

Graph $f(x)=-2\sqrt{-2x}$ first and then shift the graph $\dfrac{5}{2}$ units to the left and 4 units down.

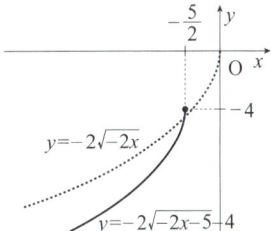

Domain: $\left\{x\,\Big|\,x\leq -\dfrac{5}{2}\right\}$
Range: $\{y\,|\,y\leq -4\}$

Check Point 3

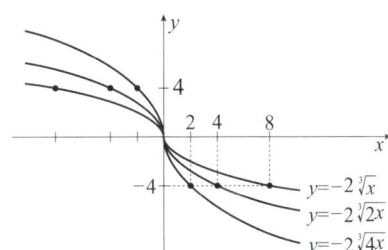

Check Point 4

① $y=\sqrt[3]{2x}-2$

Graph $y=\sqrt[3]{2x}$ first and then shift the graph 2 units down.

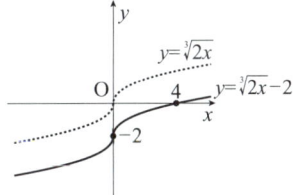

Solutions Manual

② $y=2\sqrt[3]{\dfrac{1}{2}x+1} \Rightarrow y=2\sqrt[3]{\dfrac{1}{2}(x+2)}$

Graph $y=2\sqrt[3]{\dfrac{1}{2}x}$ first and then shift the graph 2 units to the left.

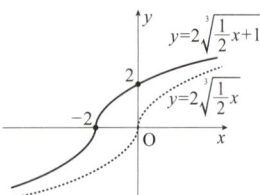

③ $y=\sqrt[3]{-x+3}-1 \Rightarrow y=\sqrt[3]{-(x-3)}-1$

Graph $y=\sqrt[3]{-x}$ first and then shift the graph 3 units to the right and 1 unit down.

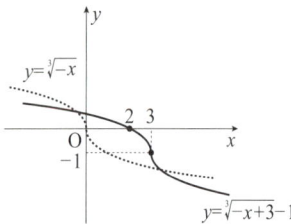

④ $y=-3\sqrt[3]{\dfrac{1}{3}x-\dfrac{1}{2}}+2$

$\Rightarrow y=-3\sqrt[3]{\dfrac{1}{3}\left(x-\dfrac{3}{2}\right)}+2$

Graph $y=-3\sqrt[3]{\dfrac{1}{3}x}$ first and then shift the graph $\dfrac{3}{2}$ units to the right and 2 units up.

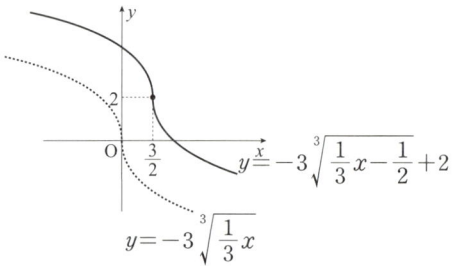

Review Exercises

01

(1) $y=\sqrt{x-2},\ y=-\sqrt{x-2}$

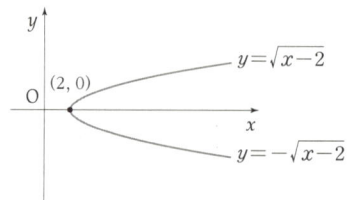

Symmetric about the x-axis

(2) $y=\sqrt{2x+3},\ y=\sqrt{-(2x+3)}$

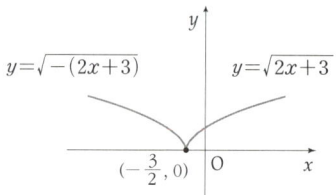

Symmetric about the line $x=-\dfrac{3}{2}$

(3) $y=\sqrt{\dfrac{1}{2}x-1},\ y=-\sqrt{-\left(\dfrac{1}{2}x-1\right)}$

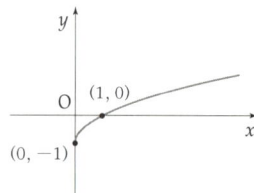

Symmetric about the x-axis and then about the line $x=2$

02

(1) $y=\sqrt{x}-1$

Domain: $\{x \mid x \geq 0\}$

Range: $\{y \mid y \geq -1\}$

(2) $y=\sqrt{-x-2} \Rightarrow y=\sqrt{-(x+2)}$

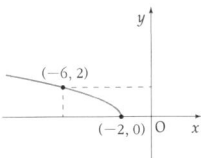

Domain: $\{x \mid x \leq -2\}$

Range: $\{y \mid y \geq 0\}$

(3) $y=\frac{1}{2}\sqrt{3x+4} \Rightarrow y=\frac{1}{2}\sqrt{3\left(x+\frac{4}{3}\right)}$

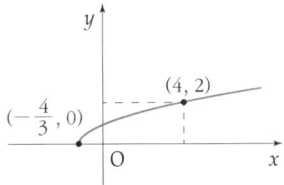

Domain: $\left\{x \mid x \geq -\frac{3}{4}\right\}$

Range: $\{y \mid y \geq 0\}$

(4) $y=-\sqrt{x+1}+1$

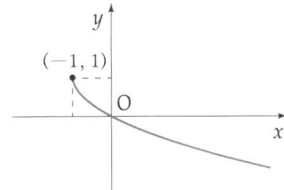

Domain: $\{x \mid x \geq -1\}$

Range: $\{y \mid y \leq 1\}$

(5) $y=3\sqrt{2x-5}+3$

$\Rightarrow y=3\sqrt{2\left(x-\frac{5}{2}\right)}+3$

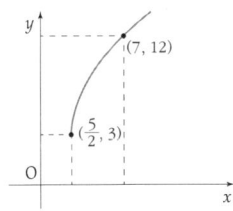

Domain: $\left\{x \mid x \geq \frac{5}{2}\right\}$

Range: $\{y \mid y \geq 3\}$

(6) $y=-\frac{1}{2}\sqrt{\frac{1}{3}x-\frac{1}{2}}-2$

$\Rightarrow y=-\frac{1}{2}\sqrt{\frac{1}{3}\left(x-\frac{3}{2}\right)}-2$

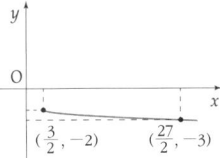

Domain: $\left\{x \mid x \geq \frac{3}{2}\right\}$

Range: $\{y \mid y \leq -2\}$

03

(1) The graph is shifted 1 unit to the right from the graph of $y=\sqrt{ax}$. So we have
$$y=\sqrt{a(x-1)}$$
Since the graph passes through the point (5, 2), we have
$$2=\sqrt{a(5-1)}, \ 2=\sqrt{4a}$$
$$4=4a, \ a=1$$
Therefore, the function is $y=\sqrt{x-1}$

(2) The graph is shifted 3 units to the right and 2 units down from the graph of $y=-\sqrt{ax}$. So we have
$$y=\sqrt{a(x-3)}-2$$
Since the graph passes through the point $(-1, -4)$, we have
$$-4=-\sqrt{a(-1-3)}-2, \ -2=-\sqrt{-4a}$$
$$2=\sqrt{-4a}, \ a=-1$$
Therefore, the function is
$$y=-\sqrt{-(x-3)}-2$$
$$y=-\sqrt{-x+3}-2$$

(3) The graph is shifted 2 units to the left and 3 units up from the graph of $y=-\sqrt{ax}$. So we have

$y=-\sqrt{a(x+2)}+3$

Since the graph passes through the point (7, 2), we have
$2=-\sqrt{a(7+2)}+3, \ -1=-\sqrt{9a}$
$1=\sqrt{9a}, \ 1=9a, \ a=\dfrac{1}{9}$

Therefore, the function is
$y=-\sqrt{\dfrac{1}{9}(x+2)}+3$
$y=-\sqrt{\dfrac{x}{9}+\dfrac{2}{9}}+3$

04
(1) $y=\sqrt[3]{x+2}$

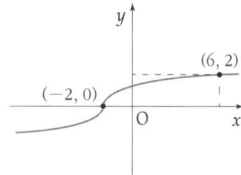

(2) $y=-3+\sqrt[3]{x} \ \Rightarrow \ y=\sqrt[3]{x}-3$

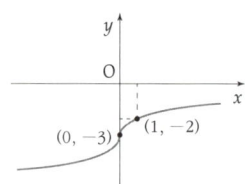

(3) $y=\sqrt[3]{2x-3}+5 \ \Rightarrow \ y=\sqrt[3]{2\left(x-\dfrac{3}{2}\right)}+5$

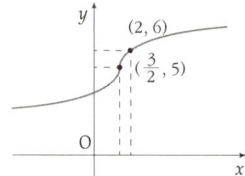

(4) $y=-\sqrt[3]{x-1}+1$

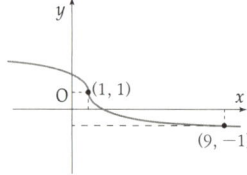

05
(1) The graph is shifted 1 unit to the left and 1 unit down from the graph of $y=\sqrt[3]{ax}$. So we have
$y=\sqrt[3]{a(x+1)}-1$

Since the graph passes through the point (0, 0), we have
$0=\sqrt[3]{a(0+1)}-1, \ 0=\sqrt[3]{a}-1$
$1=\sqrt[3]{a}, \ a=1$

Therefore, the function is $y=\sqrt[3]{x+1}-1$

(2) The graph is shifted $\dfrac{3}{2}$ units to the left and 2 units down from the graph of $y=-\sqrt[3]{ax}$. So we have
$y=-\sqrt[3]{a\left(x+\dfrac{3}{2}\right)}-2$

Since the graph passes through the point $\left(\dfrac{5}{2}, \ -6\right)$, we have
$-6=-\sqrt[3]{a\left(\dfrac{5}{2}+\dfrac{3}{2}\right)}-2, \ -4=-\sqrt[3]{4a}$
$4=\sqrt[3]{4a}, \ 64=4a, \ a=16$

Therefore, the function is
$y=-\sqrt[3]{16\left(x+\dfrac{3}{2}\right)}-2$
$y=-\sqrt[3]{16x+24}-2$

06
The domain of the function $y=\sqrt{ax-2}+b$ is
$ax-2\geq 0, \ x\geq\dfrac{2}{a} \ \Rightarrow \ \left\{x\,|\,x\geq\dfrac{2}{a}\right\}$.

So, $\dfrac{2}{a}=-1, \ a=-2$. Now we have the function $y=\sqrt{-2x-2}+b$ and since $\sqrt{-2x-2}\geq 0$, the range is
$\{y\,|\,y\geq b\}, \ b=3$.

Therefore, $a+b=-2+3=1$.

07
The domain of the function $y=\sqrt{-ax+b}+c$ is
$-ax+b\geq 0, \ b\geq ax$
$x\leq\dfrac{b}{a} \ \Rightarrow \ \left\{x\,|\,x\leq\dfrac{b}{a}\right\}$.

So, $\dfrac{b}{a}=4, \ b=4a$. Since $\sqrt{-ax+b}\geq 0$,

the range is
$$\{y|y\geq c\},\ c=-4.$$
Now, we have the function
$$y=\sqrt{-ax+b}+c,\ y=\sqrt{-ax+4a}-4$$

Since the function passes through the point $(1,\ -2)$, we have
$$y=\sqrt{-ax+4a}-4$$
$$-2=\sqrt{-a(1)+4a}-4$$
$$2=\sqrt{3a},\ 4=3a,\ a=\frac{4}{3}$$
Therefore,
$$a+b+c=a+4a+c=5a+c$$
$$=5\left(\frac{4}{3}\right)-4=\frac{8}{3}$$

08

$$y=\sqrt[3]{8x-1}+4=\sqrt[3]{8\left(x-\frac{1}{8}\right)}+4$$
$$=2\sqrt[3]{x-\frac{1}{8}}+4$$

The graph of $y=\sqrt[3]{8x-1}+4$ is the result of the graph $y=2\sqrt[3]{x}$ by shifting $\frac{1}{8}$ unit to the right and 4 units up. Therefore,
$$m=\frac{1}{8},\ n=4,\ \text{and}\ mn=\frac{1}{8}\cdot4=\frac{1}{2}$$

09

Since the graph starts at the point $(1,\ 0)$, the function is
$$y=-\sqrt{a(x-1)}\ \Rightarrow\ h=1,\ k=0$$
Also, since the graph passes through the point $(-2,\ -1)$, we have
$$-1=-\sqrt{a(-2-1)},\ 1=\sqrt{-3a}$$
$$1=-3a,\ a=-\frac{1}{3}$$
Therefore, $a+h+k=-\frac{1}{3}+1+0=\frac{2}{3}$.

10

(A) The domain is
$$-x-4\geq0,\ x\leq-4\ \Rightarrow\ \{x|x\leq-4\}$$

(B) Since $-2\sqrt{-x-4}\leq0$, the range is
$$y\leq-1\ \Rightarrow\ \{y|y\leq-1\}$$

(C) $y=-2\sqrt{-x-4}-1,\ y=-2\sqrt{-(x+4)}-1$
The graph of $y=-2\sqrt{(-x)}$ is shifted 4 units to the left and 1 unit down.

(D)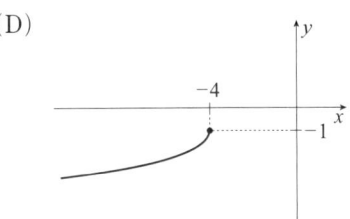

Since the graph is drawn as above, it passes through the points in quadrant III only

(E) By substituting $x=-8$, we have
$$y(-8)=-2\sqrt{-(-8)-4}-1$$
$$=-2\sqrt{4}-1=-5$$
So the graph passes through $(-8,\ -5)$
Therefore, the answer is (C).

Solutions Manual

Chapter 7 Test Level 1

01

(A) $\sqrt{(-a)^2}=\sqrt{a^2}=a$
(B) $(-\sqrt{a})^2=(\sqrt{a})^2=a$
(C) $\sqrt[3]{(-a)^3}=\sqrt[3]{-a^3}=-a$
(D) $-\sqrt[3]{(-a)^3}=-\sqrt[3]{-a^3}=-(-a)=a$
(E) $-(-\sqrt{a^2})=-(-a)=a$

The answer is (C).

02

If $a<0$ and $ab<0$, then $a<0$ and $b>0$.
$\sqrt{(-b)^2}-\sqrt{4a^2}+\sqrt{16a^2b^2}$
$=\sqrt{b^2}-\sqrt{(2a)^2}+\sqrt{(4ab)^2}$
$=b-(-2a)+(-4ab)$
$=2a+b-4ab$

The answer is (A).

03

If $-2<a<4$, then $a+2>0$, $-a-2<0$, and $4-a>0$.
$\sqrt{(a+2)^2}-\sqrt{(-a-2)^2}-2\sqrt{(4-a)^2}$
$=(a+2)-(-(-a-2))-2(4-a)$
$=a+2-(a+2)-8+2a$
$=a+2-a-2-8+2a=-8+2a$

The answer is (B).

04

If $0<x<2$, then $-2+x<0$.
$\sqrt[3]{(x-2)^3}+\sqrt[3]{(2-x)^3}-\sqrt[4]{(-2+x)^4}$
$=(x-2)+(2-x)-(-(-2+x))$
$=-2+x=x-2$

The answer is (A).

05

$\sqrt{6}<x<\sqrt{40}$
$\sqrt{6}<\sqrt{x^2}<\sqrt{40}$
$6<x^2<40$
Since x is positive integer,
$x^2=9$, 16, 25, or 36
$x=3$, 4, 5 or 6
So there are 4 positive integers.

06

$\dfrac{4xy}{\sqrt{75}}\times(-\sqrt{120x^3})\div\dfrac{\sqrt{80x}}{5y^2}$
$=\dfrac{4xy}{5\sqrt{3}}\times(-2x\sqrt{30x})\times\dfrac{5y^2}{4\sqrt{5x}}$
$=\dfrac{4\times(-2)\times 5}{5\times 4}\cdot xy\times x\times y^2\cdot\dfrac{\sqrt{30x}}{\sqrt{3}\times\sqrt{5x}}$
$=-2x^2y^3\sqrt{\dfrac{30x}{15x}}=-2x^2y^3\sqrt{2}$
$\Rightarrow a\sqrt{2}=-2x^2y^3\sqrt{2}$, $a=-2x^2y^3$

The answer is (D).

07

$(1+\sqrt{2}-\sqrt{3})(1-\sqrt{2}+\sqrt{3})$
$=(1+(\sqrt{2}-\sqrt{3}))(1-(\sqrt{2}-\sqrt{3}))$
$=1^2-(\sqrt{2}-\sqrt{3})^2$
$=1-(2-2\sqrt{6}+3)=-4+2\sqrt{6}$

08

$\dfrac{\sqrt{32}-4}{\sqrt{2}}-\dfrac{\sqrt{12}+\sqrt{48}}{\sqrt{3}}$
$=\dfrac{4\sqrt{2}-4}{\sqrt{2}}\cdot\dfrac{\sqrt{2}}{\sqrt{2}}-\dfrac{2\sqrt{3}+4\sqrt{3}}{\sqrt{3}}\cdot\dfrac{\sqrt{3}}{\sqrt{3}}$
$=\dfrac{8-4\sqrt{2}}{2}-\dfrac{6+12}{3}$
$=4-2\sqrt{2}-6=-2-2\sqrt{2}\Rightarrow a+b\sqrt{c}=-2-2\sqrt{2}$
$a=-2$, $b=-2$, and $c=2$
Therefore, $abc=(-2)\cdot(-2)\cdot 2=8$

09

$(\sqrt{12}-2)(\sqrt{27}-a+2)$
$=(2\sqrt{3}-2)(3\sqrt{3}-a+2)$
$=18-2a\sqrt{3}+4\sqrt{3}-6\sqrt{3}+2a-4$
$=14+2a-2a\sqrt{3}-2\sqrt{3}$
$=14+2a-(2a+2)\sqrt{3}$

In order for the expression above to be rational, $2a+2$ must be zero. Therefore, $2a+2=0$, $a=-1$

10

$x=\dfrac{1}{3\sqrt{2}-4}=\dfrac{1}{3\sqrt{2}-4}\cdot\dfrac{3\sqrt{2}+4}{3\sqrt{2}+4}=\dfrac{3\sqrt{2}+4}{(3\sqrt{2})^2-4^2}$
$=\dfrac{3\sqrt{2}+4}{18-16}=\dfrac{3\sqrt{2}+4}{2}=\dfrac{3\sqrt{2}}{2}+2$

So, the value of x^2+2x-8 is
$x^2+2x-8=(x-2)(x+4)$
$=\left(\dfrac{3\sqrt{2}}{2}+2-2\right)\left(\dfrac{3\sqrt{2}}{2}+2+4\right)$
$=\dfrac{3\sqrt{2}}{2}\cdot\left(\dfrac{3\sqrt{2}}{2}+6\right)=\dfrac{9}{2}+9\sqrt{2}$

11

$a+b=\dfrac{\sqrt{3}-\sqrt{2}}{4}+\dfrac{\sqrt{3}+\sqrt{2}}{4}=\dfrac{2\sqrt{3}}{4}=\dfrac{\sqrt{3}}{2}$
$a-b=\dfrac{\sqrt{3}-\sqrt{2}}{4}-\dfrac{\sqrt{3}+\sqrt{2}}{4}=-\dfrac{2\sqrt{2}}{4}=-\dfrac{\sqrt{2}}{2}$
$(a+b)^2(a-b)^2=\left(\dfrac{\sqrt{3}}{2}\right)^2\left(-\dfrac{\sqrt{2}}{2}\right)^2$
$\qquad\qquad\qquad=\dfrac{3}{4}\times\dfrac{2}{4}=\dfrac{3}{8}$

12

(1) $2\sqrt{2x+1}+4x=-2$
$2\sqrt{2x+1}=-4x-2$, $\sqrt{2x+1}=-2x-1$
$(\sqrt{2x+1})^2=(-2x-1)^2$
$2x+1=4x^2+4x+1$
$4x^2+2x=0$, $2x(2x+1)=0$
$x=0$ or $x=-\dfrac{1}{2}$

✔ Check $x=0$ in the original equation.
$2\sqrt{2(0)+1}+4(0)=-2$
$2\sqrt{1}+0=-2$
$2\neq-2$ → Extraneous solution

✔ Check $x=-\dfrac{1}{2}$ in the original equation.
$2\sqrt{2\left(-\dfrac{1}{2}\right)+1}+4\left(-\dfrac{1}{2}\right)=-2$
$2\sqrt{0}-2=-2$
$-2=-2$ → Solution checks

The solution is $x=-\dfrac{1}{2}$

(2) $\sqrt{2x+9}-x=3$
$\sqrt{2x+9}=x+3$
$(\sqrt{2x+9})^2=(x+3)^2$
$2x+9=x^2+6x+9$
$x^2+4x=0$
$x(x+4)=0$, $x=0$ or $x=-4$

✔ Check $x=0$ in the original equation.
$\sqrt{2(0)+9}-(0)=3$
$\sqrt{9}=3$, $3=3$ → Solution checks

✔ Check $x=-4$ in the original equation.
$\sqrt{2(-4)+9}-(-4)=3$
$\sqrt{1}+4=3$, $5\neq3$ → Extraneous solution

The solution is $x=0$

(3) $\sqrt{x}-\sqrt{x+3}=\sqrt{3}$
$\sqrt{x}=\sqrt{x+3}+\sqrt{3}$
$(\sqrt{x})^2=(\sqrt{x+3}+\sqrt{3})^2$
$x=(x+3)+2\sqrt{3x+9}+3$
$2\sqrt{3x+9}=-6$, $\sqrt{3x+9}=-3$
$(\sqrt{3x+9})^2=(-3)^2$
$3x+9=9$, $x=0$

✔ Check $x=0$ in the original equation.
$\sqrt{0}-\sqrt{0+3}=\sqrt{3}$
$-\sqrt{3}\neq\sqrt{3}$ → Extraneous solution

There is NO solution

13

$y = -\frac{1}{2}\sqrt{4x+8} - 2 = -\frac{1}{2}\sqrt{4(x+2)} - 2$
$= -\frac{1}{2} \cdot 2\sqrt{x+2} - 2 = -\sqrt{x+2} - 2$

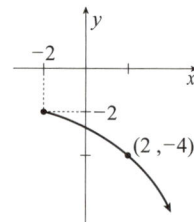

Domain: $\{x \mid x \geq -2\}$
Range: $\{y \mid y \leq -2\}$

14

$y = 3\sqrt[3]{\frac{1}{2}x - 1} + 1 = 3\sqrt[3]{\frac{1}{2}(x-2)} + 1$

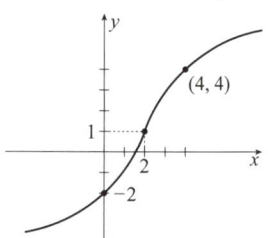

15

The domain of $y = \sqrt{-4x+3} + 1 - 2b$ is
$-4x + 3 \geq 0$, $3 \geq 4x$, $x \leq \frac{3}{4}$
$\Rightarrow a = \frac{3}{4}$
Since $\sqrt{-4x+3} \geq 0$ and $\{y \mid y \geq 7\}$,
$1 - 2b = 7$, $b = -3$
Therefore, $a + b = \frac{3}{4} + (-3) = -\frac{9}{4}$.

16

Since the graph starts at the point $(-2, -1)$, the function is
$y = a\sqrt{2(x+2)} - 1$.
Also, since the graph passes through the point $(0, 1)$, we have
$1 = a\sqrt{2(0+2)} - 1$, $2 = a\sqrt{4}$
$2 = 2a$, $a = 1$
Therefore, $a + h + k = 1 + (-2) + (-1) = -2$.

Chapter 7 Test Level 2

01

(1) $\sqrt{(-4)^2}+(-3\sqrt{2})^2-\sqrt{125}\left(\sqrt{20}-\sqrt{\dfrac{1}{5}}\right)$

$=4+18-5\sqrt{5}\left(2\sqrt{5}-\dfrac{1}{\sqrt{5}}\right)$

$=22-50+5=-23$

(2) $\dfrac{4\sqrt{12}}{\sqrt{3}}+\sqrt{6}(\sqrt{24}-2\sqrt{3})-\dfrac{4-2\sqrt{2}}{\sqrt{8}}$

$=4\sqrt{4}+\sqrt{6}(2\sqrt{6}-2\sqrt{3})-\dfrac{4-2\sqrt{2}}{2\sqrt{2}}$

$=8+12-2\sqrt{18}-\dfrac{2}{\sqrt{2}}+1$

$=21-6\sqrt{2}-\sqrt{2}=21-7\sqrt{2}$

02

$a=\dfrac{1+\sqrt{2}}{1-\sqrt{2}}=\dfrac{1+\sqrt{2}}{1-\sqrt{2}}\cdot\dfrac{1+\sqrt{2}}{1+\sqrt{2}}$

$=\dfrac{1+2\sqrt{2}+2}{1-2}=-3-2\sqrt{2}$

$b=\dfrac{1-\sqrt{2}}{1+\sqrt{2}}=\dfrac{1-\sqrt{2}}{1+\sqrt{2}}\cdot\dfrac{1-\sqrt{2}}{1-\sqrt{2}}$

$=\dfrac{1-2\sqrt{2}+2}{1-2}=-3+2\sqrt{2}$

$a+b=(-3-2\sqrt{2})+(-3+2\sqrt{2})=-6$

$a-b=(-3-2\sqrt{2})-(-3+2\sqrt{2})=-4\sqrt{2}$

$ab=(-3-2\sqrt{2})(-3+2\sqrt{2})=9-8=1$

Therefore,

$\dfrac{\sqrt{a}-\sqrt{b}}{\sqrt{a}+\sqrt{b}}=\dfrac{\sqrt{a}-\sqrt{b}}{\sqrt{a}+\sqrt{b}}\cdot\dfrac{\sqrt{a}-\sqrt{b}}{\sqrt{a}-\sqrt{b}}$

$=\dfrac{a-2\sqrt{ab}+b}{a-b}=\dfrac{-6-2\sqrt{1}}{-4\sqrt{2}}$

$=\dfrac{2}{\sqrt{2}}=\dfrac{2}{\sqrt{2}}\cdot\dfrac{\sqrt{2}}{\sqrt{2}}=\dfrac{2\sqrt{2}}{2}=\sqrt{2}$

03

$\dfrac{a}{2\sqrt{3}}(\sqrt{54}-4\sqrt{6})+2(2a\sqrt[3]{27}+2\sqrt{2})$

$=\dfrac{a}{2\sqrt{3}}(3\sqrt{6}-4\sqrt{6})+2(2a(3)+2\sqrt{2})$

$=\dfrac{a}{2\sqrt{3}}(-\sqrt{6})+2(6a+2\sqrt{2})$

$=-\dfrac{a\sqrt{2}}{2}+12a+4\sqrt{2}=12a+\left(-\dfrac{a}{2}+4\right)\sqrt{2}$

In order for the expression above to be rational, $-\dfrac{a}{2}+4$ must be zero. Therefore,

$-\dfrac{a}{2}+4=0,\ a=8$

04

$\dfrac{a}{\sqrt{10}-3}-\dfrac{b}{\sqrt{10}+3}$

$=\dfrac{a(\sqrt{10}+3)-b(\sqrt{10}-3)}{(\sqrt{10}-3)(\sqrt{10}+3)}$

$=\dfrac{a\sqrt{10}+3a-b\sqrt{10}+3b}{10-9}$

$=(3a+3b)+(a-b)\sqrt{10}$

Since $(3a+3b)+(a-b)\sqrt{10}=6+4\sqrt{10}$,

$3a+3b=6,\ a+b=2$

and $a-b=4$

Therefore, $a^2-b^2=(a-b)(a+b)=4\cdot 2=8$

05

$x\sqrt{\dfrac{2y}{x}}-\dfrac{4}{y}\sqrt{\dfrac{y}{2x}}+x\sqrt[3]{y^2}\times y\sqrt[3]{x^2}$

$=\sqrt{x^2\times\dfrac{2y}{x}}-\sqrt{\dfrac{16}{y^2}\times\dfrac{y}{2x}}+xy\sqrt[3]{x^2y^2}$

$=\sqrt{2xy}-\sqrt{\dfrac{8}{xy}}+xy\sqrt[3]{(xy)^2}$

$=\sqrt{2(8)}-\sqrt{\dfrac{8}{8}}+8\sqrt[3]{64}$

$=4-1+32=35$

06

$\dfrac{1}{\sqrt{2}+\sqrt{1}}+\dfrac{1}{\sqrt{3}+\sqrt{2}}+\cdots+\dfrac{1}{\sqrt{100}+\sqrt{99}}$

$=\dfrac{1}{\sqrt{1}+\sqrt{2}}+\dfrac{1}{\sqrt{2}+\sqrt{3}}+\cdots+\dfrac{1}{\sqrt{99}+\sqrt{100}}$

If we rationalize each term,

Solutions Manual

$\dfrac{1}{\sqrt{1}+\sqrt{2}} \cdot \dfrac{\sqrt{1}-\sqrt{2}}{\sqrt{1}-\sqrt{2}} = \dfrac{\sqrt{1}-\sqrt{2}}{1-2} = -1+\sqrt{2}$,

$= \dfrac{1}{\sqrt{2}+\sqrt{3}} \cdot \dfrac{\sqrt{2}-\sqrt{3}}{\sqrt{2}-\sqrt{3}} = \dfrac{\sqrt{2}-\sqrt{3}}{2-3} = -\sqrt{2}+\sqrt{3}$,

and so on. Therefore,

$\dfrac{1}{\sqrt{2}+\sqrt{1}} + \dfrac{1}{\sqrt{3}+\sqrt{2}} + \cdots + \dfrac{1}{\sqrt{100}+\sqrt{99}}$
$= -1+\sqrt{2}-\sqrt{2}+\sqrt{3}-\cdots-\sqrt{99}+\sqrt{100}$
$= -1+\sqrt{100} = -1+10 = 9$

07

(1) $\sqrt{\sqrt{3x+1}} = \sqrt{2x-6}$

$(\sqrt{\sqrt{3x+1}})^2 = (\sqrt{2x-6})^2$

$\sqrt{3x+1} = 2x-6$, $(\sqrt{3x+1})^2 = (2x-6)^2$

$3x+1 = 4x^2-24x+36$

$4x^2-27x+35 = 0$, $(x-5)(4x-7) = 0$

$x=5$ or $x=\dfrac{7}{4}$

✔ Check $x=5$ in the original equation.

$\sqrt{\sqrt{3(5)+1}} = \sqrt{2(5)-6}$

$\sqrt{\sqrt{16}} = \sqrt{4}$, $\sqrt{4}=2$

$2=2$ → Solution checks

✔ Check $x=\dfrac{7}{4}$ in the original equation.

$\sqrt{\sqrt{3\left(\dfrac{7}{4}\right)+1}} = \sqrt{2\left(\dfrac{7}{4}\right)-6}$

$\sqrt{\sqrt{\dfrac{25}{4}}} = \sqrt{-\dfrac{5}{2}}$

$\sqrt{\dfrac{5}{2}} \ne \sqrt{-\dfrac{5}{2}}$ → Extraneous solution

The solution is $x=5$

(2) $\sqrt{\sqrt{2x-1}-\sqrt{x-1}} = 1$

$(\sqrt{\sqrt{2x-1}-\sqrt{x-1}})^2 = (1)^2$

$\sqrt{2x-1}-\sqrt{x-1} = 1$

$\sqrt{2x-1} = 1+\sqrt{x-1}$

$(\sqrt{2x-1})^2 = (1+\sqrt{x-1})^2$

$2x-1 = 1+2\sqrt{x-1}+(x-1)$

$x-1 = 2\sqrt{x-1}$, $(x-1)^2 = (2\sqrt{x-1})^2$

$x^2-2x+1 = 4(x-1)$

$x^2-6x+5 = 0$

$(x-1)(x-5) = 0$

$x=1$ or $x=5$

✔ Check $x=1$ in the original equation.

$\sqrt{\sqrt{2(1)-1}-\sqrt{(1)-1}} = 1$

$\sqrt{\sqrt{1}-\sqrt{0}} = 1$

$\sqrt{1}=1$, $1=1$ → Solution checks

✔ Check $x=5$ in the original equation.

$\sqrt{\sqrt{2(5)-1}-\sqrt{5-1}} = 1$

$\sqrt{\sqrt{9}-\sqrt{4}} = 1$

$\sqrt{3-2}=1$, $1=1$ → Solution checks

The solution is $x=5$ and $x=1$

08

$y = \sqrt{ax+b}+c = \sqrt{a\left(x+\dfrac{b}{a}\right)}+c$

Since the graph starts at the point $(1, -2)$,

$\dfrac{b}{a} = -1$, $b=-a$

$c=-2$

So, we have

$y = \sqrt{ax+b}+c$, $y = \sqrt{ax-a}-2$

Since the graph passes through the point $(-2, 0)$, we have

$0 = \sqrt{a(-2)-a}-2$, $2 = \sqrt{-3a}$

$4 = -3a$, $a = -\dfrac{4}{3}$

Therefore,

$abc = a(-a)c = \left(-\dfrac{4}{3}\right)\left(\dfrac{4}{3}\right)(-2) = \dfrac{32}{9}$

09

The domain of $y = -\sqrt{ax+b}+c$ is

$ax+b \ge 0$, $ax \ge -b$

$x \ge -\dfrac{b}{a}$ ⇒ $\left\{x \mid x \ge -\dfrac{b}{a}\right\}$

So, $-\dfrac{b}{a} = -\dfrac{3}{2}$, $b = \dfrac{3}{2}a$.

Since $-\sqrt{ax+b} \le 0$, the range is

$\{y \mid y \le c\}$, $c=3$

Now, we have the function

$y = -\sqrt{ax+b}+c$, $y = -\sqrt{ax+\dfrac{3}{2}a}+3$

Since the function passes through the point $(2, -4)$, we have
$$y = -\sqrt{ax + \frac{3}{2}a} + 3$$
$$-4 = -\sqrt{a(2) + \frac{3}{2}a} + 3$$
$$-7 = -\sqrt{\frac{7}{2}a}, \quad 49 = \frac{7}{2}a, \quad a = 14$$

Therefore,
$$a + b + c = a + \frac{3}{2}a + c = \frac{5}{2}a + c$$
$$= \frac{5}{2}(14) + 3 = 38$$

10

$$y = \frac{1}{3}\sqrt{9x - 18} - 3 = \frac{1}{3}\sqrt{9(x-2)} - 3$$
$$= \frac{1}{3} \cdot 3\sqrt{x-2} - 3 = \sqrt{x-2} - 3$$

The graph of $y = \sqrt{x-2} - 3$ starts at the point $(2, -3)$ and the graph of $y = \sqrt{x+1} + 2$ starts at the point $(-1, 2)$, as shown below.

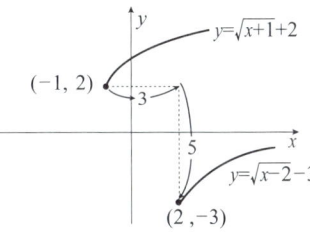

So, the graph of $y = \sqrt{x-2} - 3$ is the result of the graph $y = \sqrt{x+1} + 2$ by shifting 3 units to the right and 5 units down. Therefore,
$h = 3$, $k = 5$, and $h + k = 8$

Solutions Manual

Chapter 8

Special Functions

1. Absolute Value Functions

Check Point 1

① $y=2|x| \Rightarrow y=\begin{cases} 2x, & \text{if } x\geq 0 \\ -2x, & \text{if } x<0 \end{cases}$

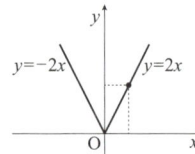

② $y=2|x+5|$

$y=\begin{cases} 2(x+5), & \text{if } x\geq 5 \\ -2(x+5), & \text{if } x<-5 \end{cases}$

$=\begin{cases} 2x+10, & \text{if } x\geq -5 \\ -2x-10, & \text{if } x<-5 \end{cases}$

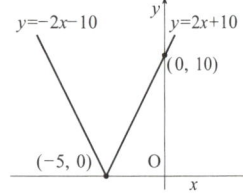

③ $y=|3x+6|-2=3|x+2|-2$

$y=\begin{cases} 3(x+2)-2, & \text{if } x\geq -2 \\ -3(x+2)-2, & \text{if } x<-5 \end{cases}$

$=\begin{cases} 3x+4, & \text{if } x\geq -2 \\ -3x-8, & \text{if } x<-2 \end{cases}$

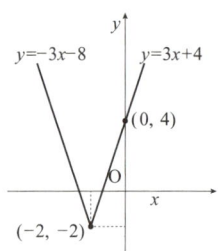

Check Point 2

① $y=2|x|$

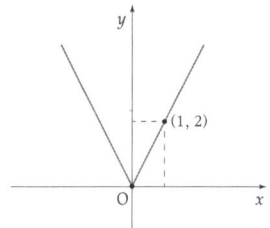

② $y=-4|x|$

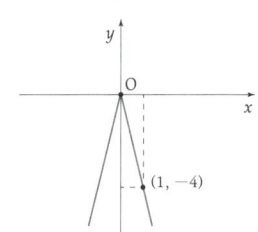

③ $y=\dfrac{1}{4}|-2x|=\dfrac{1}{4}|2x|=\dfrac{1}{2}|x|$

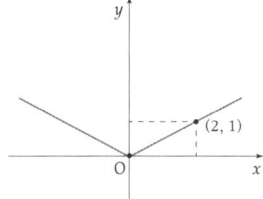

④ $y=-\dfrac{1}{2}|-4x|=-\dfrac{1}{2}|4x|=-2|x|$

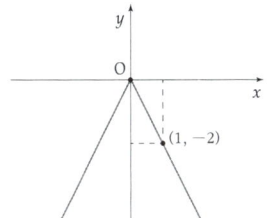

Check Point 3

① $y=2|x-1|$

Graph $y=2|x|$ first and then shift the graph 1 unit to the right.

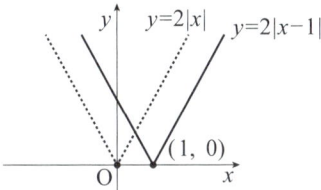

② $y=-|3x|+2=-3|x|+2$

Graph $y=-3|x|$ first and then shift the graph 2 units up.

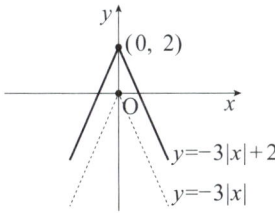

③ $y=2|-x+3|+1=2|-(x-3)|+1$
  $=2|x-3|+1$

Graph $y=2|x|$ first and then shift the graph 3 units to the right and 1 unit up

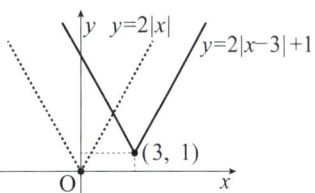

④ $y=-\left|-\dfrac{1}{2}x-2\right|-4=-\left|-\dfrac{1}{2}(x+4)\right|-4$
  $=-\left|\dfrac{1}{2}(x+4)\right|-4=-\dfrac{1}{2}|x+4|-4$

Graph $y=-\dfrac{1}{2}|x|$ first and then shift the graph 4 units to the left and 4 units down

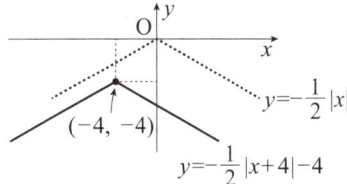

Check Point 4

① $y=2|x-1|+|x+1|$

$x-1$	$-$	$-$	$+$
$x+1$	$-$	$+$	$+$
	-1	1	x

$y=\begin{cases} 2(x-1)+(x+1), & \text{if } x\geq 1 \\ -2(x-1)+(x+1), & \text{if } -1\leq x<1 \\ -2(x-1)-(x+1), & \text{if } x<-1 \end{cases}$

$=\begin{cases} 3x-1, & \text{if } x\geq 1 \\ -x+3, & \text{if } -1\leq x<1 \\ -3x+1, & \text{if } x<-1 \end{cases}$

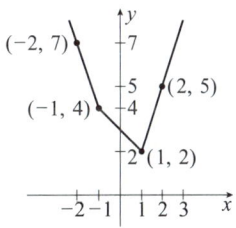

Solutions Manual 135

Solutions Manual

② $y=\left|\dfrac{1}{2}x+1\right|-|x-2|$

| $\dfrac{1}{2}x+1$ | $-$ | $+$ | $+$ |
| $x-2$ | $-$ | $-$ | $+$ |

$\qquad\qquad -2 \qquad 2 \qquad x$

$y=\begin{cases}\left(\dfrac{1}{2}x+1\right)-(x-2),\text{ if }x\geq 2\\ \left(\dfrac{1}{2}x+1\right)+(x-2),\text{ if }-2\leq x<2\\ -\left(\dfrac{1}{2}x+1\right)+(x-2),\text{ if }x<-2\end{cases}$

$=\begin{cases}-\dfrac{1}{2}x+3,\text{ if }x\geq 2\\ \dfrac{3}{2}x-1,\text{ if }-2\leq x<2\\ \dfrac{1}{2}x-3,\text{ if }x<-2\end{cases}$

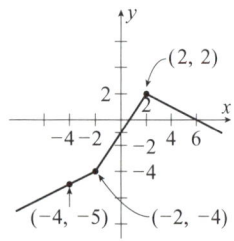

Review Exercises

01

(1) $y=-|3x|=-3|x|$

$y=\begin{cases}-3x,\text{ if }x\geq 0\\ -(-3x),\text{ if }x<0\end{cases},$

$y=\begin{cases}-3x,\text{ if }x\geq 0\\ 3x,\text{ if }x<0\end{cases},$

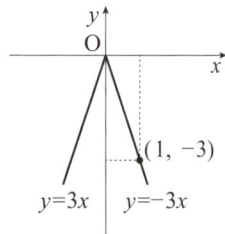

(2) $y=-\left|\dfrac{1}{2}x\right|-4=-\dfrac{1}{2}|x|-4$

$y=\begin{cases}-\dfrac{1}{2}x-4,\text{ if }x\geq 0\\ -\dfrac{1}{2}(-x)-4,\text{ if }x<0\end{cases}$

$=\begin{cases}-\dfrac{1}{2}x-4,\text{ if }x\geq 0\\ \dfrac{1}{2}x-4,\text{ if }x<0\end{cases}$

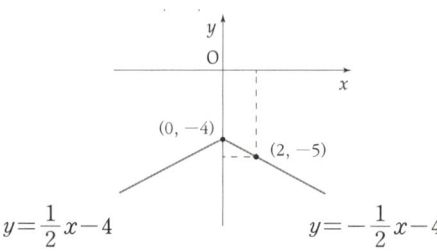

(3) $y=|x-2|-1$

$y=\begin{cases}(x-2)-1,\text{ if }x\geq 2\\ -(x-2)-1,\text{ if }x<2\end{cases}$

$=\begin{cases}x-3,\text{ if }x\geq 2\\ -x+1,\text{ if }x<2\end{cases}$

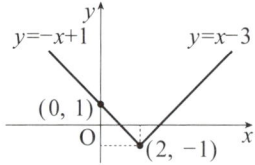

(4) $y=-\dfrac{1}{2}|4x+12|-3=-\dfrac{1}{2}|4(x+3)|-3$

$=-2|x+3|-3$

$y=\begin{cases}-2(x+3)-3,\text{ if }x\geq -3\\ -2\cdot-(x+3)-3,\text{ if }x<-3\end{cases}$

$=\begin{cases}-2x-9,\text{ if }x\geq -3\\ 2x+3,\text{ if }x<-3\end{cases}$

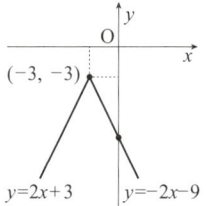

02

(1) $y=-2\left|-\dfrac{3}{2}x\right|=-2\left|\dfrac{3}{2}x\right|$
$=-3|x|$

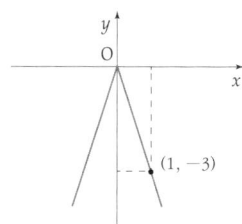

(2) $y=|x|+1$

Graph $y=|x|$ and then shift 1 unit up.

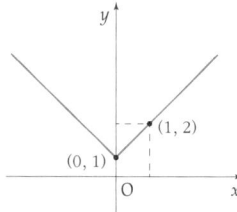

(3) $y=2|-2x+2|-4=2|-2(x-1)|-4$
$=2|2(x-1)|-4=4|x-1|-4$

Graph $y=4|x|$ and then shift 1 unit to the right and 4 units down

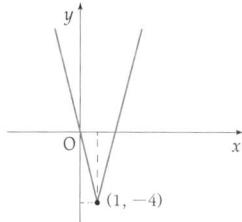

(4) $y=-4\left|-\dfrac{2}{3}x+1\right|+1$
$=-4\left|-\dfrac{2}{3}\left(x-\dfrac{3}{2}\right)\right|+1$
$=-4\left|\dfrac{2}{3}\left(x-\dfrac{3}{2}\right)\right|+1$
$=-\dfrac{8}{3}\left|x-\dfrac{3}{2}\right|+1$

Graph $y=-\dfrac{8}{3}|x|$ and then shift $\dfrac{3}{2}$ units to the right and 1 unit up

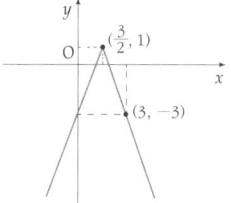

03

All functions, including absolute value functions, can be shifted like quadratic functions.

(1) Shifted 2 units to the right
⇒ Substitute $x-2$ for x
$y=2|(x-2)-4|+2$, $y=2|x-6|+2$

(2) Shifted 3 units down
⇒ Substitute $y+3$ for y
$y+3=2|x-4|+2$, $y=2|x-4|-1$

(3) Shifted 3 units to the left and 4 units up
⇒ Substitute $x+3$ for x and $y-4$ for y
$y-4=2|(x+3)-4|+2$
$y=2|x-1|+6$

(4) Shifted 1 unit to the right and $\dfrac{1}{2}$ unit down
⇒ Substitute $x-1$ for x and $y+\dfrac{1}{2}$ for y
$y+\dfrac{1}{2}=2|(x-1)-4|+2$
$y=2|x-5|+\dfrac{3}{2}$

(5) Shifted 5 units to the right
⇒ Substitute $x-5$ for x
$y=2|(x-5)-4|+2=2|x-9|+2$
and reflected over x-axis
⇒ Substitute $-y$ for y
$-y=2|x-9|+2$, $y=-2|x-9|-2$

(6) Shifted 2 units to the left and $\dfrac{5}{3}$ units down
⇒ Substitute $x+2$ for x and $y+\dfrac{5}{3}$ for y
$y+\dfrac{5}{3}=2|(x+2)-4|+2$

Solutions Manual

$y=2|x-2|+\frac{1}{3}$

Then reflected over x-axis

$\Rightarrow$ Substitute $-y$ for y

$-y=2|x-2|+\frac{1}{3}$, $y=-2|x-2|-\frac{1}{3}$

04

(1) The vertex of the graph is $(-2, -1)$.

So we have

$y=a|x+2|-1 \Rightarrow b=2$ and $c=-1$

Since the graph passes through the point $(0, 3)$, we have

$3=a|0+2|-1$, $3=2a-1$

$4=2a$, $a=2$

Therefore, the value

$a+b+c=2+2+(-1)=3$

(2) The vertex of the graph is $(4, 2)$.

So we have

$y=a|x-4|+2 \Rightarrow b=-4$ and $c=2$

Since the graph passes through the point $(0, 0)$, we have

$0=a|0-4|+2$, $0=4a+2$

$4a=-2$, $a=-\frac{1}{2}$

Therefore, the value

$a+b+c=-\frac{1}{2}+(-4)+2=-\frac{5}{2}$

05

(1) $y=|2x-3|-2|x+2|+x$

$2x-3$	$-$	$-$	$+$
$x+2$	$-$	$+$	$+$
	-2	$\frac{3}{2}$	x

$y=\begin{cases} (2x-3)-2(x+2)+x, & \text{if } x\geq\frac{3}{2} \\ -(2x-3)-2(x+2)+x, & \text{if } -2\leq x<\frac{3}{2} \\ -(2x-3)+2(x+2)+x, & \text{if } x<-2 \end{cases}$

$=\begin{cases} x-7, & \text{if } x\geq\frac{3}{2} \\ -3x-1, & \text{if } -2\leq x<\frac{3}{2} \\ x+7, & \text{if } x<-2 \end{cases}$

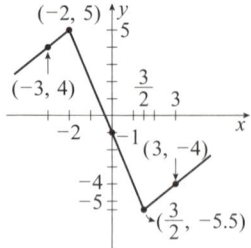

(2) $y=|x+1|+|x|-|x-1|$

$x+1$	$-$	$+$	$+$	$+$
x	$-$	$-$	$+$	$+$
$x-1$	$-$	$-$	$-$	$+$
	-1	0	1	

$y=\begin{cases} (x+1)+x-(x-1), & \text{if } x\geq 1 \\ (x+1)+x+(x-1), & \text{if } 0\leq x<1 \\ (x+1)-x+(x-1), & \text{if } -1\leq x<0 \\ -(x+1)-x+(x-1), & \text{if } x<-1 \end{cases}$

$=\begin{cases} x+2, & \text{if } x\geq 1 \\ 3x, & \text{if } 0\leq x<1 \\ x, & \text{if } -1\leq x<0 \\ -x-2, & \text{if } x<-1 \end{cases}$

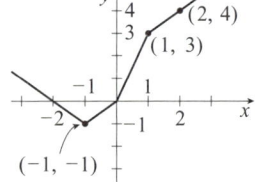

06

$y=|x-2|+x$ and $|x|\leq 3 \Rightarrow -3\leq x\leq 3$

$x-2$	$-$	$+$
	-3	$2 \quad 3$

$y=\begin{cases} (x-2)+x, & \text{if } 2\leq x\leq 3 \\ -(x-2)+x, & \text{if } -3\leq x<2 \end{cases}$

$=\begin{cases} 2x-2, & \text{if } -3\leq x<2 \\ 2, & \text{if } -3\leq x<2 \end{cases}$

138 Solutions Manual

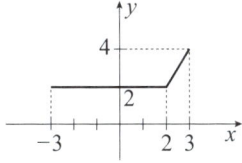

The minimum value is 2 and the maximum value is 4.

07

$y = x^2 - 2|x| - 8$

$\Rightarrow y = \begin{cases} x^2 - 2x - 8, & \text{if } x \geq 0 \\ x^2 + 2x - 8, & \text{if } x < 0 \end{cases}$

(i) If $x \geq 0$, $y = (x+2)(x-4)$

(ii) If $x < 0$, $y = (x-2)(x+4)$

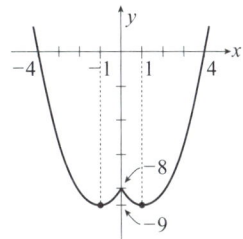

2. Greatest Integer Functions and Piecewise Functions

Check Point 1

① $2[-4.1] = 2(-5) = -10$

② $2[1.8] + [0.8] = 2(1) + 0 = 2$

③ $3[-5.6] - \dfrac{1}{2}[1.98] = 3(-6) - \dfrac{1}{2}(1) = -\dfrac{37}{2}$

④ $\dfrac{[-6.9998] \cdot [-1.0001]}{2[-0.001]} = \dfrac{(-7)(-2)}{2(-1)} = -7$

Check Point 2

① $y = \dfrac{1}{2}[x]$

x	$\dfrac{1}{2}[x]$
$-2 \leq x < -1$	-1
$-1 \leq x < 0$	-0.5
$0 \leq x < 1$	0
$1 \leq x < 2$	0.5
$2 \leq x < 3$	1

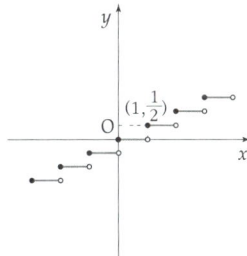

② $y = \left[\dfrac{1}{2}x\right]$

x	$\left[\dfrac{1}{2}x\right]$
$-4 \leq x < -2$	-2
$-2 \leq x < 0$	-1
$0 \leq x < 2$	0
$2 \leq x < 4$	1
$4 \leq x < 6$	2

Solutions Manual

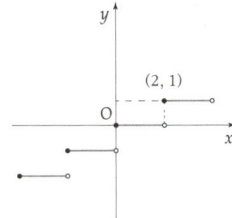
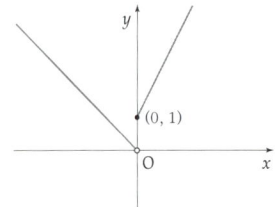

Check Point 3

① $y=[x]+1$

x	$[x]$	$[x]+1$
$-2 \leq x < -1$	-2	-1
$-1 \leq x < 0$	-1	0
$0 \leq x < 1$	0	1
$1 \leq x < 2$	1	2
$2 \leq x < 3$	2	3
$3 \leq x < 4$	3	4

Check Point 4

① Since $4 \geq 1$, $y(4) = \sqrt{4}+4=6$
② Since $-1<1$, $y(-1)=2(-1)^2-1=1$
③ Since $1 \geq 1$, $y(1)=\sqrt{1}+4=5$
④ Since $a+1<1$, $y(a+1)=2(a+1)^2-1$

Check Point 5

① Graph $y=2x+1$ for $x \geq 0$ and graph $y=-x$ for $x<0$.

The range of $y=2x+1$, $x \geq 0$ is $\{y|y \geq 1\}$ and the range of $y=-x$, $x<0$ is $\{y|y>0\}$. So, the union of the range of these two functions is $\{y|y>0\}$.

② $y=[x-2]-1$

x	$[x]$	x	$[x-2]-1$
$-3 \leq x < -2$	-3	$-1 \leq x < 0$	-4
$-2 \leq x < -1$	-2	$0 \leq x < 1$	-3
$-1 \leq x < 0$	-1	$1 \leq x < 2$	-2
$0 \leq x < 1$	0	$2 \leq x < 3$	-1
$1 \leq x < 2$	1	$3 \leq x < 4$	0
$2 \leq x < 3$	2	$4 \leq x < 5$	1

② Graph $y=\sqrt{x}$ for $x>0$ and graph $y=x-2$ for $x\leq 0$.

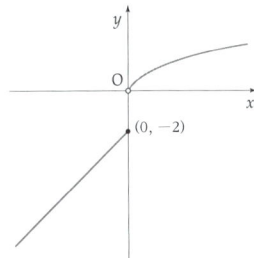

The range of $y=\sqrt{x}$, $x>0$ is $\{y|y>0\}$ and the range of $y=x-2$, $x\leq 0$ is $\{y|y\leq -2\}$. So, the union of the range of these two functions is $\{y|y\leq -2 \text{ or } y>0\}$.

③ Graph $y=2x+1$ for $x>1$ and graph $y=x^2-1$ for $x\leq 1$.

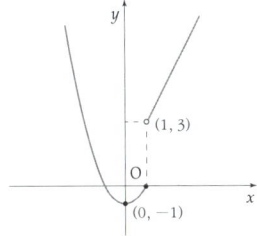

The range of $y=2x+1$, $x>1$ is $\{y|y>3\}$ and the range of $y=x^2-1$, $x\leq 1$ is $\{y|y\geq -1\}$. So, the union of the range of these two functions is $\{y|y\geq -1\}$.

Review Exercises

01

(1) $[3.91]=3$
(2) $[3(1.2)-4]=[-0.4]=-1$
(3) $4\left[\dfrac{1}{2}-\dfrac{1}{3}\right]=4\left[\dfrac{1}{6}\right]=4(0)=0$
(4) $\dfrac{2}{3}\left[-1-\dfrac{3}{2}\right]+3=\dfrac{2}{3}\left[-\dfrac{5}{2}\right]+3$
$\qquad =\dfrac{2}{3}(-3)+3=1$

02

(1) $y=[x-2]$

x	$[x]$	x	$[x-2]$
$-3\leq x<-2$	-3	$-1\leq x<0$	-3
$-2\leq x<-1$	-2	$0\leq x<1$	-2
$-1\leq x<0$	-1	$1\leq x<2$	-1
$0\leq x<1$	0	$2\leq x<3$	0
$1\leq x<2$	1	$3\leq x<4$	1

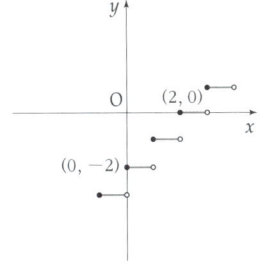

(2) $y=[2x+3]$, $y=\left[2\left(x+\dfrac{3}{2}\right)\right]$

x	$[2x]$	x	$[2x+3]$
$-1\leq x<-0.5$	-2	$-2.5\leq x<-2$	-2
$-0.5\leq x<0$	-1	$-2\leq x<-1.5$	-1
$0\leq x<0.5$	0	$-1.5\leq x<-1$	0
$0.5\leq x<1$	1	$-1<x<-0.5$	1
$1\leq x<1.5$	2	$-0.5\leq x<0$	2
$1.5\leq x<2$	3	$0\leq x<0.5$	3

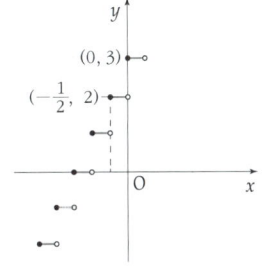

(3) $y=-[x]+2$

x	$-[x]$	$-[x]+2$
$-1\leq x<0$	1	3
$0\leq x<1$	0	2
$1\leq x<2$	-1	1
$2\leq x<3$	-2	0
$3\leq x<4$	-3	-1

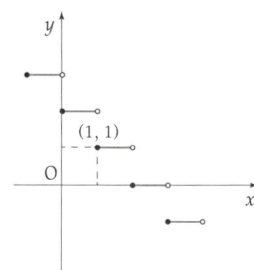

(4) $y=[x+1]-1$

x	$[x]$	x	$[x+1]-1$
$-1\leq x<0$	-1	$-2\leq x<-1$	-2
$0\leq x<1$	0	$-1\leq x<0$	-1
$1\leq x<2$	1	$0\leq x<1$	0
$2\leq x<3$	2	$1\leq x<2$	1
$3\leq x<4$	3	$2\leq x<3$	2

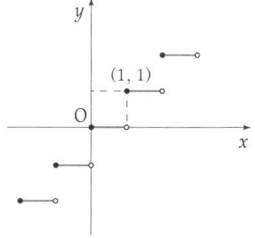

03

(1) Since $0\leq 1<2$, $f(1)=4\sqrt{(1)-1}=0$
(2) Since $2\geq 2$, $f(2)=\frac{1}{2}(2)+3=4$
(3) Since $-2<0$, $f(-2)=(-2)^3-2=-10$
(4) Since $0\leq \frac{5}{4}<2$, $f\left(\frac{5}{4}\right)=4\sqrt{\frac{5}{4}-1}=2$
(5) Since $a+2\geq 2$, $f(a+2)=\frac{1}{2}(a+2)+3$
(6) Since $2b-1<0$, $f(2b-1)=(2b-1)^3-2$

04

(1) Graph $y=x-2$ for $x>2$ and graph $y=\frac{1}{2}x$ for $x\leq 2$.

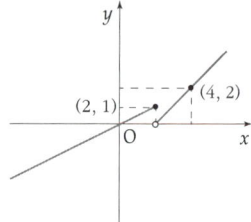

Range of each function
$y=x-2$, $x>2$: $\{y|y>0\}$
$y=\frac{1}{2}x$, $x\leq 2$: $\{y|y\leq 1\}$
$y=\begin{cases} x-2, \text{ if } x>2 \\ \frac{1}{2}x, \text{ if } x\leq 2 \end{cases}$: All real numbers

(2) Graph $y=3-2x$ for $x\geq 1$ and graph $y=x^2+2$ for $x<1$.

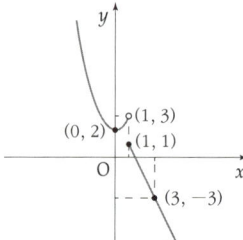

Range of each function
$y=3-2x$, $x\geq 1$: $\{y|y\leq 1\}$
$y=x^2+2$, $x<1$: $\{y|y\geq 2\}$
$y=\begin{cases} 3-2x, \text{ if } x\geq 1 \\ x^2+2, \text{ if } x<1 \end{cases}$: $\{y|y\leq 1 \text{ or } y\geq 2\}$

(3) Graph $y=(x-1)^2+1$ for $x\geq 0$ and graph $y=|x+2|$ for $x<0$.

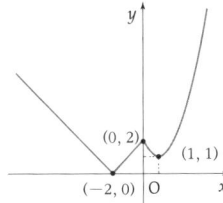

Range of each function
$y=(x-1)^2+1$, $x\geq 0$: $\{y|y\geq 1\}$
$y=|x+2|$, $x<0$: $\{y|y\geq 0\}$
$y=\begin{cases}(x-1)^2+1, \text{ if } x\geq 0\\|x+2|, \text{ if } x<0\end{cases}$: $\{y|y\geq 0\}$

05

$[x]=n \Rightarrow n\leq x<n+1$ (n is integer)
(1) $[x-2]=5$
$5\leq x-2<6$, $7\leq x<8$
(2) $2[2x+1]+1=7$
$2[2x+1]=6$, $[2x+1]=3$
$3\leq 2x+1<4$, $2\leq 2x<3$
$1\leq x<\dfrac{3}{2}$
(3) $[-x+1]=-2$
$-2\leq -x+1<-1$, $-3\leq -x<-2$
$3\geq x>2$, $2<x\leq 3$

06

$[\sqrt{1}]+[\sqrt{2}]+[\sqrt{3}]+\cdots+[\sqrt{9}]$
First, since $1\leq \sqrt{1}, \sqrt{2}, \sqrt{3}<2$,
$[\sqrt{1}]=[\sqrt{2}]=[\sqrt{3}]=1$.
Also, since $2\leq \sqrt{4}, \sqrt{5}, \cdots \sqrt{8}<3$,
$[\sqrt{4}]=[\sqrt{5}]=\cdots=[\sqrt{8}]=2$.
Lastly, $[\sqrt{9}]=[3]=3$. Therefore,
$[\sqrt{1}]+[\sqrt{2}]+[\sqrt{3}]+\cdots+[\sqrt{9}]$
$=1+1+1+2+2+\cdots+2+3$
$=1(3)+2(5)+3=16$

07

Create a table for the function $y=[x]$ and $y=x-[x]$.

x	$y=[x]$	$y=x-[x]$
$-3\leq x<-2$	-3	$y=x+3$
$-2\leq x<-1$	-2	$y=x+2$
$-1\leq x<0$	-1	$y=x+1$
$0\leq x<1$	0	$y=x$
$1\leq x<2$	1	$y=x-1$
$2\leq x<3$	2	$y=x-2$

Now, graph each linear function in the given domain.

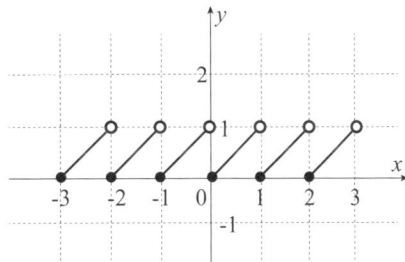

Solutions Manual

3. Operation of Functions

Check Point 1

① $(f+g)(x) = \left(1 - \frac{1}{x+2}\right) + (x+1)$

$= x - \frac{1}{x+2} + 2$

② $(f-g)(x) = \left(1 - \frac{1}{x+2}\right) - (x+1)$

$= -x - \frac{1}{x+2}$

③ $(fg)(x) = \left(1 - \frac{1}{x+2}\right) \cdot (x+1)$

$= x + 1 - \frac{x+1}{x+2}$

④ $\left(\frac{f}{g}\right)(x) = \frac{1 - \frac{1}{x+2}}{x+1} = \frac{1 - \frac{1}{x+2}}{x+1} \cdot \frac{x+2}{x+2}$

$= \frac{x+2-1}{(x+1)(x+2)} = \frac{x+1}{(x+1)(x+2)}$

$= \frac{1}{x+2}$

Domain of f: All real numbers except $x = -2$

Domain of g: All real numbers

Domain of $f+g$, $f-g$, and fg: All real numbers except $x = -2$

Domain of $\frac{f}{g}$: All real numbers except $x = -2$ and $x = -1$

Check Point 2

① $f \circ g = f(g(x)) = f(2x)$

$= \frac{1}{2}(2x)^2 - 2 = 2x^2 - 2$

② $g \circ f = g(f(x)) = g\left(\frac{1}{2}x^2 - 2\right)$

$= 2\left(\frac{1}{2}x^2 - 2\right) = x^2 - 4$

③ $(f \circ g)(2) = f(g(2)) = f(2(2))$

$= f(4) = \frac{1}{2}(4)^2 - 2 = 6$

④ $(g \circ g \circ f)(-1) = g(g(f(-1)))$

$= g\left(g\left(\frac{1}{2}(-1)^2 - 2\right)\right) = g\left(g\left(-\frac{3}{2}\right)\right)$

$= g\left(2\left(-\frac{3}{2}\right)\right) = g(-3) = 2(-3) = -6$

Check Point 3

Domain of $f(x) = \frac{2}{x}$: All real numbers except for $x = 0$

Domain of $g(x) = 2x + 5$: All real numbers

① $f \circ g = f(g(x)) = f(2x+5) = \frac{2}{2x+5}$

Domain of $f \circ g \Rightarrow y = \frac{2}{2x+5}$:

All real numbers except for $x = -\frac{5}{2}$

$g(x) = 2x+5$
⟶ x

$y = \frac{2}{2x+5}$
$-\frac{5}{2}$ ⟶ x

Domain of $f \circ g$: All real numbers except for $x = -\frac{5}{2}$

② $g \circ f = g\left(\frac{2}{x}\right) = 2\left(\frac{2}{x}\right) + 5 = \frac{4}{x} + 5$

Domain of $g \circ f \Rightarrow y = \frac{4}{x} + 5$:

All real numbers except for $x = 0$

$f(x) = \frac{1}{x}$
0 ⟶ x

$y = \frac{4}{x} + 5$
0 ⟶ x

Domain of $g \circ f$: All real numbers except for $x = 0$

③ $f \circ f = f\left(\dfrac{2}{x}\right) = \dfrac{2}{\left(\dfrac{2}{x}\right)} = x$

Domain of $f \circ f \Rightarrow y = x$: All real numbers

$f(x) = \dfrac{2}{x}$

$y = x$

Domain of $f \circ f$: All real numbers except for $x = 0$

Review Exercises

01

(1) $(f+g)(x) = (2x^2 + x - 2) + \left(\dfrac{x}{2} + 3\right)$

$= 2x^2 + \dfrac{3x}{2} + 1$

(2) $(f-g)(x) = (2x^2 + x - 2) - \left(\dfrac{x}{2} + 3\right)$

$= 2x^2 + \dfrac{x}{2} - 5$

(3) $f(x) \cdot g(x) = (2x^2 + x - 2) \cdot \left(\dfrac{x}{2} + 3\right)$

$= x^3 + \dfrac{x^2}{2} - x + 6x^2 + 3x - 6$

$= x^3 + \dfrac{13x^2}{2} + 2x - 6$

(4) $\left(\dfrac{f}{g}\right)(x) = \dfrac{2x^2 + x - 2}{\dfrac{x}{2} + 3} = \dfrac{2(2x^2 + x - 2)}{x + 6}$

$= \dfrac{4x^2 + 2x - 4}{x + 6}$

Domain of f: All real numbers
Domain of g: All real numbers
Domain of $f+g$, $f-g$, and fg: All real numbers
Domain of $\dfrac{f}{g}$: All real numbers except $x = -6$

02

(1) $(f+g)(x) = \dfrac{x}{x-2} + \dfrac{x-2}{x-1}$

$= \dfrac{x(x-1)}{(x-2)(x-1)} + \dfrac{(x-2)^2}{(x-2)(x-1)}$

$= \dfrac{2x^2 - 5x + 4}{(x-2)(x-1)}$

(2) $(f-g)(x) = \dfrac{x}{x-2} - \dfrac{x-2}{x-1}$

$= \dfrac{x(x-1)}{(x-2)(x-1)} - \dfrac{(x-2)^2}{(x-2)(x-1)}$

$= \dfrac{3x - 4}{(x-2)(x-1)}$

(3) $f(x) \cdot g(x) = \dfrac{x}{x-2} \cdot \dfrac{x-2}{x-1} = \dfrac{x}{x-1}$

(4) $\left(\dfrac{f}{g}\right)(x) = \dfrac{\dfrac{x}{x-2}}{\dfrac{x-2}{x-1}} = \dfrac{x(x-1)}{(x-2)^2}$

Domain of f: All real numbers except $x = 2$
Domain of g: All real numbers except $x = 1$
Domain of $f+g$, $f-g$, and fg: All real numbers except $x = 1$ and $x = 2$
Domain of $\dfrac{f}{g}$: All real numbers except $x = 1$ and $x = 2$

03

(1) $(f \circ g)(-4) = f(g(-4)) = f\left(\dfrac{1}{(-4) - 1}\right)$

$= 2\left(-\dfrac{1}{5}\right) - 1 = -\dfrac{7}{5}$

(2) $(g \circ h)\left(\dfrac{2}{3}\right) = g\left(h\left(\dfrac{2}{3}\right)\right) = g\left(\sqrt{3\left(\dfrac{2}{3}\right) + 2}\right)$

$= g(2) = \dfrac{1}{2 - 1} = 1$

(3) $(f \circ g \circ h)(2) = f(g(h(2)))$

$= f(g(\sqrt{3(2) + 2})) = f(g(\sqrt{8}))$

$= f\left(\dfrac{1}{\sqrt{8} - 1}\right) = 2\left(\dfrac{1}{\sqrt{8} - 1}\right) - 1$

Solutions Manual

(4) $(g \circ g \circ g)(3) = g(g(g(3))) = g\left(g\left(\dfrac{1}{3-1}\right)\right)$

$= g\left(g\left(\dfrac{1}{2}\right)\right) = g\left(\dfrac{1}{\frac{1}{2}-1}\right)$

$= g(-2) = \dfrac{1}{-2-1} = -\dfrac{1}{3}$

(5) $g \circ f = g(f(x)) = g(2x-1)$

$= \dfrac{1}{(2x-1)-1} = \dfrac{1}{2x-2}$

Domain of f: All real numbers

Domain of $g \circ f \Rightarrow y = \dfrac{1}{2x-2}$:

All real numbers except for $x=1$

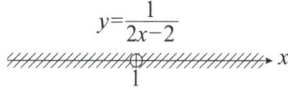

Domain of $g \circ f$: All real numbers except for $x=1$

(6) $g \circ h = g(h(x)) = g(\sqrt{3x+2})$

$= \dfrac{1}{\sqrt{3x+2}-1}$

Domain of h: $\{x \mid x \geq -\dfrac{2}{3}\}$

Domain of $g \circ h \Rightarrow y = \dfrac{1}{\sqrt{3x+2}-1}$:

$\sqrt{3x+2}-1 \neq 0$, $\sqrt{3x+2} \neq 1$

$3x+2 \neq 1$, $x \neq -\dfrac{1}{3}$

All real numbers except for $x = -\dfrac{1}{3}$

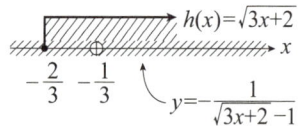

Domain of $g \circ h$: $\{x \mid x \geq -\dfrac{2}{3},$ but $x \neq -\dfrac{1}{3}\}$

04

(1) $(f \circ g)(2) = f(g(2)) = f(-2(2)+5)$

$= f(1) = 4(1) - a = 4 - a$

Since $(f \circ g)(2) = 4$,

$4 - a = 4$, $a = 0$

(2) $(g \circ g \circ g)(b) = g(g(g(b)))$

$= g(g(-2b+5))$

$= g(-2(-2b+5)+5) = g(4b-5)$

$= -2(4b-5)+5 = -8b+15$

Since $(g \circ g \circ g)(b) = -11$,

$-8b+15 = -11$, $b = \dfrac{13}{4}$

05

From $f(1-4x) = \dfrac{3x-2}{4}$, let $1-4x = u$.

Then, $-4x = u-1$, $x = \dfrac{1-u}{4}$.

Rewriting f as a function of u,
we have

$f(u) = \dfrac{3\left(\dfrac{1-u}{4}\right) - 2}{4} = \dfrac{\dfrac{3-3u}{4} - 2}{4}$

$= \dfrac{\dfrac{-3u-5}{4}}{4} = -\dfrac{3u+5}{16}$

(1) By substituting x for u,

$f(x) = -\dfrac{3x+5}{16}$

(2) By substituting $4a-1$ for u,

$f(4a-1) = -\dfrac{3(4a-1)+5}{16} = -\dfrac{12a+2}{16}$

$= -\dfrac{6a+1}{8}$

06

From $f\left(\dfrac{3x+1}{2}\right) = 2x+5$, let $\dfrac{3x+1}{2} = u$.

Then, $3x+1 = 2u$, $x = \dfrac{2u-1}{3}$.

Rewriting f as a function of u, we have

$f(u) = 2\left(\dfrac{2u-1}{3}\right) + 5 = \dfrac{4u-2}{3} + 5$

$= \dfrac{4u+13}{3}$

Therefore,
$f(2)+f(5)=\dfrac{4(2)+13}{3}+\dfrac{4(5)+13}{3}$
$=\dfrac{21}{3}+\dfrac{33}{3}=7+11=18$

07

$f \circ g = f(g(x)) = f(kx+2)$
$= 3(kx+2)-2 = 3kx+4$
$g \circ f = g(f(x)) = f(3x-2)$
$= k(3x-2)+2 = 3kx-2k+2$
Since $f \circ g = g \circ f$,
$3kx+4 = 3kx-2k+2$
$4 = -2k+2, \; k=-1$

08

(1) Since $f \circ h = f(h(x)) = g$,
$-3h(x)+4 = 4x-1$
$-3h(x) = 4x-5, \; h(x) = -\dfrac{4}{3}x+\dfrac{5}{3}$

(2) Since $h \circ g = h(g(x)) = f$,
$h(4x-1) = -3x+4$.
If we let $4x-1=u$, then $x=\dfrac{u+1}{4}$ and
we have $h(u) = -3\left(\dfrac{u+1}{4}\right)+4$. If we
rewrite this function as a function of x,
$h(x) = -3\left(\dfrac{x+1}{4}\right)+4$

09

(1) $(f \circ g)(0) = f(g(0)) = f(-1) = 0$
(2) $(g \circ f)(2) = g(f(2)) = g(-2) = -1$
(3) $(f \circ f \circ f)(1) = f(f(f(1))) = f(f(-2))$
$= f(2) = -2$
(4) $(g \circ f \circ g)(-1) = g(f(g(-1))) = g(f(-1))$
$= g(0) = -1$

4. Inverse Functions

Check Point 1

① $g(5) = 2\sqrt{5-1}+1 = 2(2)+1 = 5$
② $5 = 2\sqrt{x-1}+1, \; 4 = 2\sqrt{x-1}$
$\sqrt{x-1} = 2, \; x-1 = 4$
$x = 5, \; g^{-1}(5) = 5$
③ $a = 2\sqrt{x-1}+1, \; a-1 = 2\sqrt{x-1}$
$\dfrac{a-1}{2} = \sqrt{x-1}, \; x-1 = \dfrac{(a-1)^2}{4}$
$x = \dfrac{(a-1)^2}{4}+1$
$g^{-1}(a) = \dfrac{(a-1)^2}{4}+1$ where $a \geq 1$

Check Point 2

① $f(3) = c$
② $f^{-1}(b) = 4$
③ $f^{-1}(d) = 1$
④ $(f^{-1})^{-1}(4) = f(4) = b$
⑤ $(f^{-1} \circ f)(4) = 4$
⑥ $(f \circ f^{-1})(a) = a$

Check Point 3

If g is inverse of f, $(f \circ g)(x) = x$ and
$(g \circ f)(x) = x$.
$(f \circ g)(x) = f(g(x)) = f\left(\dfrac{1-2x}{4}\right)$
$= -2\left(\dfrac{1-2x}{4}\right)+\dfrac{1}{2}$
$= \dfrac{-1+2x}{2}+\dfrac{1}{2} = x$
$(g \circ f)(x) = g(f(x)) = g\left(-2x+\dfrac{1}{2}\right)$
$= \dfrac{1-2\left(-2x+\dfrac{1}{2}\right)}{4}$
$= \dfrac{1+4x-1}{4} = x$

Solutions Manual

Check Point 4

① $f(x)=\sqrt{x-3}+1$, $y=\sqrt{x-3}+1$
$x=\sqrt{y-3}+1$, $x-1=\sqrt{y-3}$
$(x-1)^2=(\sqrt{y-3})^2$, $(x-1)^2=y-3$
$(x-1)^2+3=y$
$f^{-1}(x)=(x-1)^2+3$, where $x\geq 1$
f^{-1} is a function because f is a one-to-one.

② $f(x)=\sqrt[3]{x}+1$, $y=\sqrt[3]{x}+1$
$x=\sqrt[3]{y}+1$, $x-1=\sqrt[3]{y}$
$(x-1)^3=y$
$f^{-1}(x)=(x-1)^3$
f^{-1} is a function because f is a one-to-one.

Check Point 5

① $f(x)=-4x-3$, $y=-4x-3$
$x=-4y-3$, $x+3=-4y$
$y=-\dfrac{x+3}{4}$
$f^{-1}(x)=-\dfrac{x+3}{4}$

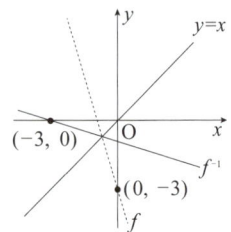

② $f(x)=\dfrac{2-3x}{3}$, $y=\dfrac{2-3x}{3}$
$x=\dfrac{2-3y}{3}$, $3x=2-3y$
$3y=2-3x$, $y=\dfrac{2-3x}{3}$
$f^{-1}(x)=\dfrac{2-3x}{3}$

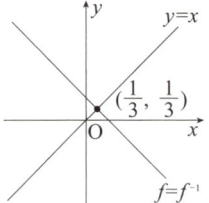

③ $f(x)=x^2-3$, $x\geq 0$
$y=x^2-3$
$x=y^2-3$, $x+3=y^2$
$y=\sqrt{x+3}$
$f^{-1}(x)=\sqrt{x+3}$, $x\geq -3$

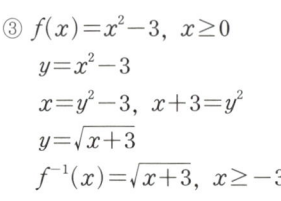

④ $f(x)=\sqrt{x-2}$, $y=\sqrt{x-2}$
$x=\sqrt{y-2}$, $x^2=y-2$
$x^2+2=y$
$f^{-1}(x)=x^2+2$, $x\geq 0$

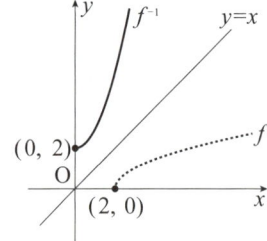

148 Solutions Manual

Review Exercises

01

(A)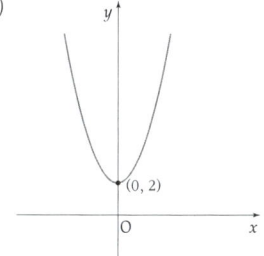

(B)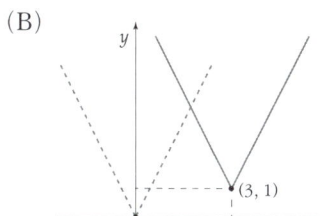

(C)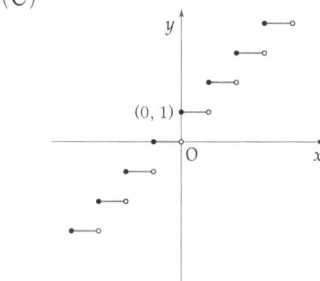

(D)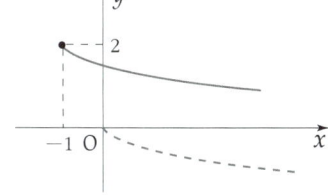

(E)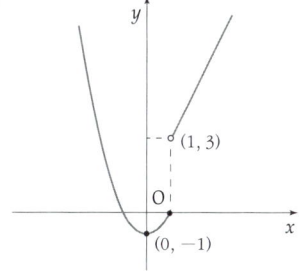

The function has an inverse function only if it is a one-to-one function. Since (D) is a one-to-one function that always decreases, the answer is (D)

02

(1) $f(3) = \dfrac{1+(3)}{(3)-2} = 4$

(2) $3 = \dfrac{1+x}{x-2}$, $3(x-2) = 1+x$
$3x - 6 = 1 + x$, $2x = 7$
$x = \dfrac{7}{2}$, $f^{-1}(3) = \dfrac{7}{2}$

(3) $k = \dfrac{1+x}{x-2}$, $k(x-2) = 1+x$
$kx - 2k = 1 + x$, $kx - x = 1 + 2k$
$x(k-1) = 1 + 2k$, $x = \dfrac{1+2k}{k-1}$
$f^{-1}(k) = \dfrac{1+2k}{k-1}$

(4) $\dfrac{m}{2} = \dfrac{1+x}{x-2}$, $m(x-2) = 2(1+x)$
$mx - 2m = 2 + 2x$, $mx - 2x = 2m + 2$
$x(m-2) = 2m + 2$, $x = \dfrac{2m+2}{m-2}$
$f^{-1}\left(\dfrac{m}{2}\right) = \dfrac{2m+2}{m-2}$

03

If g is inverse of f, $(f \circ g)(x) = x$ and $(g \circ f)(x) = x$.

(1) $f(x) = 2x - 1$, $g(x) = \dfrac{x+1}{2}$

Solutions Manual

$(f \circ g)(x) = f(g(x)) = f\left(\dfrac{x+1}{2}\right)$

$\qquad = 2\left(\dfrac{x+1}{2}\right) - 1$

$\qquad = x + 1 - 1 = x$

$(g \circ f)(x) = g(f(x)) = g(2x-1)$

$\qquad = \dfrac{(2x-1)+1}{2} = \dfrac{2x}{2} = x$

(2) $f(x) = \sqrt{x-4}$, $g(x) = x^2 + 4$ where $x \geq 0$

$(f \circ g)(x) = f(g(x)) = f(x^2 + 4)$

$\qquad = \sqrt{(x^2+4) - 4} = \sqrt{x^2} = x$

$(g \circ f)(x) = g(f(x)) = g(\sqrt{x-4})$

$\qquad = (\sqrt{x-4})^2 + 4 = x - 4 + 4 = x$

(3) $f(x) = \dfrac{x-1}{x+5}$, $g(x) = -\dfrac{5x+1}{x-1}$

$(f \circ g)(x) = f(g(x)) = f\left(-\dfrac{5x+1}{x-1}\right)$

$\qquad = \dfrac{\left(-\dfrac{5x+1}{x-1}\right) - 1}{\left(-\dfrac{5x+1}{x-1}\right) + 5} \cdot \dfrac{x-1}{x-1}$

$\qquad = \dfrac{5x+1+(x-1)}{5x+1-5(x-1)} = \dfrac{6x}{6} = x$

$(g \circ f)(x) = g(f(x)) = g\left(\dfrac{x-1}{x+5}\right)$

$\qquad = -\dfrac{5\left(\dfrac{x-1}{x+5}\right) + 1}{\left(\dfrac{x-1}{x+5}\right) - 1} \cdot \dfrac{x+5}{x+5}$

$\qquad = -\dfrac{5(x-1)+(x+5)}{x-1-(x+5)} = -\dfrac{6x}{-6} = x$

(4) $f(x) = x^3 - 1$, $g(x) = \sqrt[3]{x+1}$

$(f \circ g)(x) = f(g(x)) = f(\sqrt[3]{x+1})$

$\qquad = (\sqrt[3]{x+1})^3 - 1 = x + 1 - 1 = x$

$(g \circ f)(x) = g(f(x)) = g(x^3 - 1)$

$\qquad = \sqrt[3]{(x^3-1)+1} = \sqrt[3]{x^3} = x$

04

(1) $f(x) = 2x - 4$, $y = 2x - 4$

$x = 2y - 4$, $x + 4 = 2y$

$y = \dfrac{x+4}{2}$, $f^{-1}(x) = \dfrac{x+4}{2}$

f^{-1} is a function because f is a one-to-one.

(2) $f(x) = \dfrac{2x+1}{x-2}$, $y = \dfrac{2x+1}{x-2}$

$x = \dfrac{2y+1}{y-2}$, $x(y-2) = 2y+1$

$xy - 2x = 2y + 1$

$xy - 2y = 2x + 1$

$y(x-2) = 2x + 1$

$y = \dfrac{2x+1}{x-2}$, $f^{-1}(x) = \dfrac{2x+1}{x-2}$

f^{-1} is a function because f is a one-to-one.

(3) $f(x) = \dfrac{1}{2}x^2 + 2$, $y = \dfrac{1}{2}x^2 + 2$

$x = \dfrac{1}{2}y^2 + 2$, $x - 2 = \dfrac{1}{2}y^2$

$2(x-2) = y^2$

$y = \pm\sqrt{2(x-2)}$, $f^{-1}(x) = \pm\sqrt{2(x-2)}$

f^{-1} is NOT a function because f is NOT a one-to-one.

(4) $f(x) = \sqrt{x-2} + 3$, $y = \sqrt{x-2} + 3$

$x = \sqrt{y-2} + 3$, $x - 3 = \sqrt{y-2}$

$(x-3)^2 = y - 2$, $y = (x-3)^2 + 2$

$f^{-1}(x) = (x-3)^2 + 2$ where $x \geq 3$

f^{-1} is a function because f is a one-to-one.

05

(1) $f(x) = 4 - x^2$, $x \geq 0$

$y = 4 - x^2$, $x = 4 - y^2$

$x - 4 = -y^2$, $4 - x = y^2$

$y = \sqrt{4-x}$, $f^{-1}(x) = \sqrt{4-x}$

(2) $f(x)=\dfrac{2}{x}$, $y=\dfrac{2}{x}$

$x=\dfrac{2}{y}$, $y=\dfrac{2}{x}$, $f^{-1}(x)=\dfrac{2}{x}$

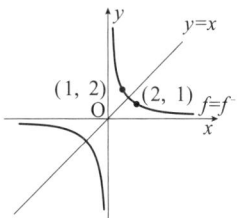

(3) $f(x)=2\sqrt[3]{x-2}-2$, $y=2\sqrt[3]{x-2}-2$

$x=2\sqrt[3]{y-2}-2$, $x+2=2\sqrt[3]{y-2}$

$\dfrac{x+2}{2}=\sqrt[3]{y-2}$, $\left(\dfrac{x+2}{2}\right)^3=y-2$

$y=\dfrac{(x+2)^3}{8}+2$, $f^{-1}(x)=\dfrac{(x+2)^3}{8}+2$

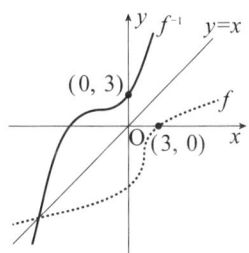

06

If $f^{-1}(a)=4$, then $a=f(4)$.

$a=f(4)=5(4)+2=22$

07

If $f^{-1}(2)=1$, then $2=f(1)$.

$f(1)=3\sqrt{b(1)-2}+1=2$

$3\sqrt{b-2}=1$, $\sqrt{b-2}=\dfrac{1}{3}$

$b-2=\dfrac{1}{9}$, $b=\dfrac{19}{9}$

08

Since the graph of f^{-1} passes through two points $(2, -3)$ and $(10, 1)$,

$f^{-1}(2)=-3$ $\qquad$ $f^{-1}(10)=1$

$2=f(-3)$ $\qquad$ $10=f(1)$

$2=-3a+b$ $\qquad$ $10=a+b$

Solving the system, we have

$a=2$ and $b=8$.

Therefore, $a+b=2+8=10$

09

(1) $(f^{-1}\circ g)(2)=f^{-1}(g(2))$
$=f^{-1}(2^3)=f^{-1}(8)$

$8=\dfrac{1}{4}x-1$, $x=36 \rightarrow f^{-1}(8)=36$

Therefore, $(f^{-1}\circ g)(2)=f^{-1}(g(2))=36$

(2) $(f\circ g^{-1})(8)=f(g^{-1}(8))$

$8=x^3$, $x=2 \rightarrow g^{-1}(8)=2$

$f(g^{-1}(8))=f(2)=\dfrac{1}{4}(2)-1=-\dfrac{1}{2}$

(3) $(f^{-1}\circ g^{-1})(1)=f^{-1}(g^{-1}(1))$

$1=x^3$, $x=1 \rightarrow g^{-1}(1)=1$

$f^{-1}(g^{-1}(1))=f^{-1}(1)$

$1=\dfrac{1}{4}x-1$, $x=8 \rightarrow f^{-1}(1)=8$

Therefore,

$(f^{-1}\circ g^{-1})(1)=f^{-1}(g^{-1}(1))=8$

(4) $(g^{-1}\circ f^{-1})(-3)=g^{-1}(f^{-1}(-3))$

$-3=\dfrac{1}{4}x-1$, $x=-8 \rightarrow f^{-1}(-3)=-8$

$g^{-1}(f^{-1}(-3))=g^{-1}(-8)$

$-8=x^3$, $x=-2 \rightarrow g^{-1}(-8)=-2$

Therefore,

$(g^{-1}\circ f^{-1})(-3)=g^{-1}(f^{-1}(-3))=-2$

(5) $(f^{-1}\circ f^{-1})(0)=f^{-1}(f^{-1}(0))$

$0=\dfrac{1}{4}x-1$, $x=4 \rightarrow f^{-1}(0)=4$

$f^{-1}(f^{-1}(0))=f^{-1}(4)$

$4=\dfrac{1}{4}x-1$, $x=20 \rightarrow f^{-1}(4)=20$

Therefore,

$(f^{-1}\circ f^{-1})(0)=f^{-1}(f^{-1}(0))=20$

(6) $(f^{-1}\circ g)(a)=f^{-1}(g(a))=f^{-1}(a^3)$

$a^3=\dfrac{1}{4}x-1$, $a^3+1=\dfrac{1}{4}x$

$x=4(a^3+1) \rightarrow f^{-1}(a^3)=4(a^3+1)$

Therefore,

$(f^{-1}\circ g)(a)=f^{-1}(g(a))=4(a^3+1)$

(7) $(g^{-1} \circ f^{-1})(a+3) = g^{-1}(f^{-1}(a+3))$

$a+3 = \frac{1}{4}x - 1$, $a+4 = \frac{1}{4}x$

$x = 4a+16 \rightarrow f^{-1}(a+3) = 4a+16$

$g^{-1}(f^{-1}(a+3)) = g^{-1}(4a+16)$

$4a+16 = x^3$

$x = \sqrt[3]{4a+16} \rightarrow g^{-1}(4a+16) = \sqrt[3]{4a+16}$

Therefore,

$(g^{-1} \circ f^{-1})(a+3) = g^{-1}(f^{-1}(a+3)) = \sqrt[3]{4a+16}$

(8) $(f \circ g)^{-1}(b) \rightarrow$ Let $h = f \circ g = f(g(x))$.

$h(x) = f(g(x)) = f(x^3) = \frac{1}{4}x^3 - 1$

$(f \circ g)^{-1}(b) = h^{-1}(b)$

$b = \frac{1}{4}x^3 - 1$, $4(b+1) = x^3$

$x = \sqrt[3]{4(b+1)} \rightarrow h^{-1}(b) = \sqrt[3]{4(b+1)}$

Therefore, $(f \circ g)^{-1}(b) = \sqrt[3]{4(b+1)}$

Chapter 8 Test Level 1

01

(1) Substitute $x+4$ for x and $y+1$ for y

$y+1 = \frac{1}{2}|(x+4)+1| - 2$

$y = \frac{1}{2}|x+5| - 3$

(2) First, substitute $y-2$ for y

$y-2 = \frac{1}{2}|x+1| - 2$

$y = \frac{1}{2}|x+1|$

Then, substitute $-x$ for x

$y = \frac{1}{2}|-x+1| = \frac{1}{2}|-(x-1)|$

$= \frac{1}{2}|x-1|$

(3) First, substitute $-y$ for y

$-y = \frac{1}{2}|x+1| - 2$

$y = -\frac{1}{2}|x+1| + 2$

Then, substitute $x-3$ for x and $y - \frac{5}{2}$ for y

$y - \frac{5}{2} = -\frac{1}{2}|(x-3)+1| + 2$

$y = -\frac{1}{2}|x-2| + \frac{9}{2}$

02

$x + \frac{1}{2}$	$-$	$+$	$+$
$x - \frac{1}{4}$	$-$	$-$	$+$
	$-\frac{1}{2}$	$\frac{1}{4}$	x

$y = \begin{cases} 2\left(x+\frac{1}{2}\right) - 4\left(x-\frac{1}{4}\right), & \text{if } x \geq \frac{1}{4} \\ 2\left(x+\frac{1}{2}\right) + 4\left(x-\frac{1}{4}\right), & \text{if } -\frac{1}{2} \leq x < \frac{1}{4} \\ -2\left(x+\frac{1}{2}\right) + 4\left(x-\frac{1}{4}\right), & \text{if } x < -\frac{1}{2} \end{cases}$

$= \begin{cases} -2x+2, & \text{if } x \geq \frac{1}{4} \\ 6x, & \text{if } -\frac{1}{2} \leq x < \frac{1}{4} \\ 2x-2, & \text{if } x < -\frac{1}{2} \end{cases}$

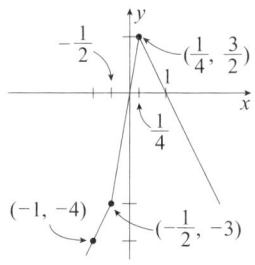

03

(1) $-[2.78]+[-2.78]=-(2)+(-3)=-5$

(2) $5\left[\dfrac{7}{2}\left(\dfrac{1}{2}-1\right)\right]-2[-3.25]=5\left[-\dfrac{7}{4}\right]-2(-4)$
$\qquad =5(-2)+8=-2$

04

(1) $y=[2x]-1$

x	$[2x]$	$[2x]-1$
$-0.5\leq x<0$	-1	-2
$0\leq x<0.5$	0	-1
$0.5\leq x<1$	1	0
$1\leq x<1.5$	2	1
$1.5\leq x<2$	3	2
$2\leq x<2.5$	4	3

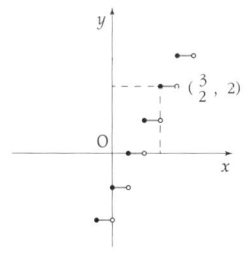

(2) $y=-[x-1]-\dfrac{1}{2}$

x	$-[x]$	x	$-[x-1]-\dfrac{1}{2}$
$-4\leq x<-3$	4	$-3\leq x<-2$	3.5
$-3\leq x<-2$	3	$-2\leq x<-1$	2.5
$-2\leq x<-1$	2	$-1\leq x<0$	1.5
$-1\leq x<0$	1	$0\leq x<1$	0.5
$0\leq x<1$	0	$1\leq x<2$	-0.5
$1\leq x<2$	-1	$2\leq x<3$	-1.5

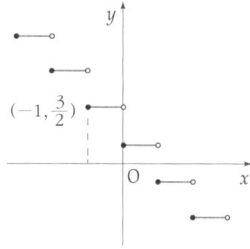

05

(1) Since $-1\leq -1$, $f(-1)=5-4(-1)=9$
(2) Since $-1<0<3$, $f(0)=|3(0)-2|-1=1$
(3) Since $-1<2<3$, $f(2)=|3(2)-2|-1=3$
(4) Since $3\geq 3$, $f(3)=2(3)^2-3=15$
(5) Since $-1<a<3$,
$f(a)=|3(a)-2|-1$
$\qquad =-(3a-2)-1=-3a+1$
(6) Since $b+3\geq 3$, $f(b+3)=2(b+3)^2-3$

06

Graph $y=-x-1$ for $x>2$, $y=x$ for $0\leq x<2$, and $y=-x^2+2$ for $x<0$.

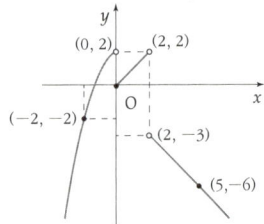

Range of each function
$y=-x-1$, $x>2$: $\{y|y<-3\}$
$y=x$, $0\leq x<2$: $\{y|0\leq y<2\}$
$y=-x^2+2$, $x<0$: $\{y|y<2\}$

$$y=\begin{cases}-x-1, & \text{if } x>2 \\ x, & \text{if } 0\leq x<2 \\ -x^2+2, & \text{if } x<0\end{cases}: \{y|y<2\}$$

07

(1) $(f\circ g)(2)=f(g(2))=f(4(2)-1)$
$$=f(7)=\frac{2}{7-2}=\frac{2}{5}$$

(2) $(g\circ h)(0)=g(h(0))=g(\sqrt{2(0)+1}+3)$
$$=g(4)=4(4)-1=15$$

(3) $(f\circ g\circ h)(4)=f(g(h(4)))$
$$=f(g(\sqrt{2(4)+1}+3))$$
$$=f(g(6))=f(4(6)-1)$$
$$=f(23)=\frac{2}{23-2}=\frac{2}{21}$$

(4) $(f\circ f\circ f)(4)=f(f(f(4)))$
$$=f\left(f\left(\frac{2}{4-2}\right)\right)$$
$$=f(f(1))=f\left(\frac{2}{1-2}\right)$$
$$=f(-2)=\frac{2}{-2-2}=-\frac{1}{2}$$

(5) $g\circ f=g(f(x))=g\left(\frac{2}{x-2}\right)$
$$=4\left(\frac{2}{x-2}\right)-1=\frac{8}{x-2}-1$$

Domain of f: All real numbers except for $x=2$
Domain of $g\circ f \Rightarrow y=\frac{8}{x-2}-1$:

All real numbers except for $x=2$
Domain of $g\circ f$: All real numbers except for $x=2$

(6) $h\circ f=h(f(x))=h\left(\frac{2}{x-2}\right)$
$$=\sqrt{2\left(\frac{2}{x-2}\right)+1}+3=\sqrt{\frac{4}{x-2}+1}+3$$

Domain of f: All real numbers except for $x=2$

Domain of $h\circ f \Rightarrow y=\sqrt{\frac{4}{x-2}+1}+3$:

$\frac{4}{x-2}+1\geq 0$, $1\geq -\frac{4}{x-2}$
$x-2\geq -4$, $x\geq -2$

Domain of $h\circ f$: $\{x|x\geq -2, \text{ but } x\neq 2\}$

08

(1) $(f\circ g)(0)=f(g(0))=f(-1)=2$
(2) $(g\circ f)(-1)=g(f(-1))=g(2)=2$
(3) $(g\circ f\circ g)(4)=g(f(g(4)))$
$$=g(f(0))=g(-2)=-2$$
(4) $(f\circ g\circ g)(-3)=f(g(g(-3)))$
$$=f(g(-1))=f\left(-\frac{3}{2}\right)=\frac{5}{2}$$

09

(1) $(g\circ f)(-4)=g(f(-4))=g\left(-\frac{1}{2}(-4)+3\right)$
$$=g(5)=3(5)+k=15+k$$
Since $(g\circ f)(-4)=-2$,
$15+k=-2$, $k=-17$

(2) $(f\circ g\circ g)(1)=f(g(g(1)))$
$$=f(g(3(1)+k))=f(g(3+k))$$
$$=f(3(3+k)+k)=f(9+4k)$$
$$=-\frac{1}{2}(9+4k)+3=-2k-\frac{3}{2}$$
Since $(f\circ g\circ g)(1)=6$,
$-2k-\frac{3}{2}=6$, $-2k=\frac{15}{2}$, $k=-\frac{15}{4}$

10

Find the inverse of g.
$g(x)=x+3k-1$, $y=x+3k-1$
$x=y+3k-1$, $y=x-3k+1$
$g^{-1}(x)=x-3k+1$
Since $g=g^{-1}$, we have
$x+3k-1=x-3k+1$
$6k=2$, $k=\dfrac{1}{3}$

11

Find the inverse of f.
$f(x)=\dfrac{ax+b}{x-c}$, $y=\dfrac{ax+b}{x-c}$
$x=\dfrac{ay+b}{y-c}$, $x(y-c)=ay+b$
$xy-cx=ay+b$, $xy-ay=cx+b$
$y(x-a)=cx+b$, $y=\dfrac{cx+b}{x-a}$
$f^{-1}(x)=\dfrac{cx+b}{x-a}$
$\Rightarrow a=3$, $b=1$, $c=5$
Therefore, $a+b+c=3+1+5=9$

12

Since the graph of h^{-1} passes through two points $(-4, 6)$ and $(8, 3)$,
$f^{-1}(-4)=6$, $f^{-1}(8)=3$
$-4=f(6)$, $8=f(3)$
$-4=6a+b$, $8=3a+b$
Solving the system, we have
$a=-4$ and $b=20$.
Therefore, $a+b=-4+20=16$

13

(1) $(f^{-1}\circ g)(2)=f^{-1}(g(2))$
$\qquad =f^{-1}(-2^2+4)=f^{-1}(0)$
$0=2x+6$, $x=-3 \to f^{-1}(0)=-3$
Therefore, $(f^{-1}\circ g)(2)=f^{-1}(g(2))=-3$

(2) $(f\circ g^{-1})(-5)=f(g^{-1}(-5))$
$-5=-x^2+4$, $x^2=9$
$x=3 \to g^{-1}(-5)=3$

$f(g^{-1}(-5))=f(3)=2(3)+6=12$

(3) $(f^{-1}\circ g^{-1})(2)=f^{-1}(g^{-1}(2))$
$2=-x^2+4$, $x^2=2$
$x=\sqrt{2} \to g^{-1}(2)=\sqrt{2}$
$f^{-1}(g^{-1}(2))=f^{-1}(\sqrt{2})$
$\sqrt{2}=2x+6$, $x=\dfrac{\sqrt{2}-6}{2}$
$\to f^{-1}(\sqrt{2})=\dfrac{\sqrt{2}-6}{2}$
Therefore,
$(f^{-1}\circ g^{-1})(2)=f^{-1}(g^{-1}(2))=\dfrac{\sqrt{2}-6}{2}$

(4) $(f^{-1}\circ f^{-1})(4)=f^{-1}(f^{-1}(4))$
$4=2x+6$, $x=-1 \to f^{-1}(4)=-1$
$f^{-1}(f^{-1}(4))=f^{-1}(-1)$
$-1=2x+6$, $x=-\dfrac{7}{2} \to f^{-1}(-1)=-\dfrac{7}{2}$
Therefore,
$(f^{-1}\circ f^{-1})(4)=f^{-1}(f^{-1}(4))=-\dfrac{7}{2}$

Chapter 8 Test Level 2

01

(1) $y=2|x|+3|x+2|+|x-1|$

x	−	−	+	+
$x+2$	−	+	+	+
$x-1$	−	−	−	+

       -2 0 1 x

$y=\begin{cases} 2x+3(x+2)+(x-1), & \text{if } x\geq 1 \\ 2x+3(x+2)-(x-1), & \text{if } 0\leq x<1 \\ -2x+3(x+2)-(x-1), & \text{if } -2\leq x<0 \\ -2x-3(x+2)-(x-1), & \text{if } x<-2 \end{cases}$

$=\begin{cases} 6x+5, & \text{if } x\geq 1 \\ 4x+7, & \text{if } 0\leq x<1 \\ 7, & \text{if } -2\leq x<0 \\ -6x-5, & \text{if } x<-2 \end{cases}$

Solutions Manual

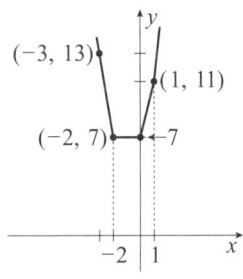

(2) $y=|(|x+2|-|x-1|)|$

From $y=|x+2|-|x-1|$, we have

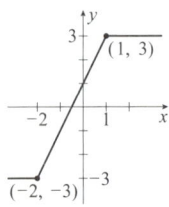

$$y=\begin{cases}(x+2)-(x-1), & \text{if } x\geq 1\\ (x+2)+(x-1), & \text{if } -2\leq x<1\\ -(x+2)+(x-1), & \text{if } x<-2\end{cases}$$

$$=\begin{cases}3, & \text{if } x\geq 1\\ 2x+1, & \text{if } -2\leq x<1\\ -3, & \text{if } x<-2\end{cases}$$

So the graph of $y=|x+2|-|x-1|$ is

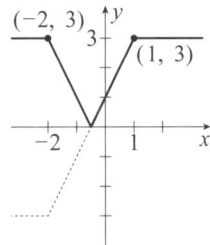

Therefore, the graph of
$y=|(|x+2|-|x-1|)|$ is

02

$|x|\leq 2 \Rightarrow -2\leq x\leq 2$

The graph of $y=2|x-1|+|x+1|$ is

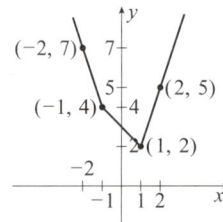

The maximum value is 7 when $x=-2$, and the minimum value is 2 when $x=1$. So the difference between them is $7-2=5$.

03

$[3x-4]-2=-7$
$[3x-4]=-5$
$-5\leq 3x-4<-4,\ -1\leq 3x<0$
$-\dfrac{1}{3}\leq x<0$

04

From $f\left(\dfrac{4-2x}{3}\right)=\dfrac{2x+1}{5}$, let $\dfrac{4-2x}{3}=u$.

Then we have
$3u=4-2x,\ 2x=4-3u,\ x=2-\dfrac{3u}{2}$ and

$f(u)=\dfrac{2\left(2-\dfrac{3u}{2}\right)+1}{5}=\dfrac{4-3u+1}{5}=1-\dfrac{3u}{5}$

Therefore, $f(x)=1-\dfrac{3x}{5}$ and

$f(5x+4)=1-\dfrac{3(5x+4)}{5}$

$=1-\dfrac{15x+12}{5}=-3x-\dfrac{7}{5}$

05

(1) Since $f\circ h=f(h(x))=g$, we have
$2h(x)-3=3x+2$
$2h(x)=3x+5,\ h(x)=\dfrac{3x+5}{2}$

(2) $h\circ g\circ f=h(g(f(x)))=h(g(2x-3))$
$=h(3(2x-3)+2)=h(6x-7)$

Since $h \circ g \circ f = f$, we have
$h(6x-7) = 2x-3$
Let $6x-7 = u$. Then,
$6x = u+7$, $x = \dfrac{u+7}{6}$
and $h(u) = 2\left(\dfrac{u+7}{6}\right) - 3 = \dfrac{u+7}{3} - 3$
Therefore, $h(x) = \dfrac{x+7}{3} - 3$

06
$f \circ g = f(g(x)) = f(bx-3)$
$\quad = 2 - 5(bx-3) = -5bx + 17$
$g \circ f = g(f(x)) = g(2-5x)$
$\quad = b(2-5x) - 3 = -5bx + 2b - 3$
Since $f \circ g = g \circ f$,
$-5bx + 17 = -5bx + 2b - 3$
$17 = 2b - 3$, $b = 10$

07
$(f \circ f \circ f)(m) = f(f(f(m))) = 2$
$\Rightarrow f(f(m)) = 0 \Rightarrow f(m) = 2$
$\Rightarrow m = 0$

08
Find the inverse of f.
$f(x) = 5x+2$, $y = 5x+2$
$x = 5y+2$, $x-2 = 5y$
$y = \dfrac{x-2}{5}$, $f^{-1}(x) = \dfrac{x-2}{5}$
Now, find the intersection point of f and f^{-1}.
$5x+2 = \dfrac{x-2}{5}$
$25x + 10 = x - 2$
$24x = -12$, $x = -\dfrac{1}{2}$
$f\left(-\dfrac{1}{2}\right) = 5\left(-\dfrac{1}{2}\right) + 2 = -\dfrac{1}{2}$
Therefore, $a = -\dfrac{1}{2}$ and $b = -\dfrac{1}{2}$.

09
Find the inverse of f.
$f(x) = \dfrac{2}{x+k} - 3$, $y = \dfrac{2}{x+k} - 3$
$x = \dfrac{2}{y+k} - 3$, $x+3 = \dfrac{2}{y+k}$
$\dfrac{1}{x+3} = \dfrac{y+k}{2}$, $y+k = \dfrac{2}{x+3}$
$y = \dfrac{2}{x+3} - k$, $f^{-1}(x) = \dfrac{2}{x+3} - k$
Since $f = f^{-1}$,
$\dfrac{2}{x+k} - 3 = \dfrac{2}{x+3} - k \Rightarrow k = 3$

Solutions Manual

Chapter 9: Discrete Mathematics

1. Introduction to Sequences

Check Point 1

① $a_n = n^2 - n + 3$, $a_1 = 1^2 - 1 + 3 = 3$
$a_2 = 2^2 - 2 + 3 = 5$, $a_3 = 3^2 - 3 + 3 = 9$
$a_{(n+1)} = (n+1)^2 - (n+1) + 3$
$= n^2 + 2n + 1 - n - 1 + 3 = n^2 + n + 3$

② $a_n = \dfrac{n^3}{(2n-1)^2}$, $a_1 = \dfrac{1^3}{(2(1)-1)^2} = \dfrac{1}{1^2} = 1$

$a_2 = \dfrac{2^3}{(2(2)-1)^2} = \dfrac{8}{3^2} = \dfrac{8}{9}$

$a_3 = \dfrac{3^3}{(2(3)-1)^2} = \dfrac{27}{5^2} = \dfrac{27}{25}$

$a_{(n+1)} = \dfrac{(n+1)^3}{(2(n+1)-1)^2} = \dfrac{(n+1)^3}{(2n+1)^2}$

Check Point 2

① 2, 5, 8, 11, ⋯ → $a_1 = 2$ and $d = 3$
$a_n = a_1 + (n-1)d$
$a_n = 2 + (n-1)(3)$, $a_n = 3n - 1$
$a_{10} = 3(10) - 1 = 29$

② 4, 1, −2, −5, ⋯ → $a_1 = 4$ and $d = -3$
$a_n = a_1 + (n-1)d$
$a_n = 4 + (n-1)(-3)$, $a_n = -3n + 7$
$a_{10} = -3(10) + 7 = -23$

Check Point 3

① $a_{12} = 38$, $d = 4$
$a_n = a_1 + (n-1)d$
$38 = a_1 + (12-1)(4)$, $a_1 = -6$
$a_n = -6 + (n-1)(4) = 4n - 10$, $a_n = 4n - 10$

② $a_{12} = 10$, $a_4 = -38$
$a_n = a_1 + (n-1)d$ → $\begin{array}{r} 10 = a_1 + (12-1)d \\ -\underline{\;-38 = a_1 + (4-1)d\;} \\ 48 = 8d \to d = 6 \end{array}$

$10 = a_1 + (12-1)(6)$, $a_1 = -56$
$a_n = a_1 + (n-1)d = -56 + (n-1) \cdot 6 = 6n - 62$
$a_n = 6n - 62$

Alternative solution:
$a_n = a_k + (n-k)d$
$a_{12} = a_4 + (12-4)d$, $10 = -38 + 8d$, $d = 6$
$a_n = a_1 + (n-1)d$, $a_4 = a_1 + (4-1)d$
$-38 = a_1 + 3 \cdot 6$, $a_1 = -56$
$a_n = a_1 + (n-1)d = -56 + (n-1) \cdot 6 = 6n - 62$
$a_n = 6n - 62$

Check Point 4

① 3, 9, 27, 81, ⋯ $a_1 = 3$ and $r = 3$
$a_n = a_1 r^{n-1}$, $a_n = 3 \cdot 3^{n-1}$
$a_{10} = 3 \cdot 3^{10-1} = 3^{10}$, $a_{10} = 3^{10}$

② −5, 10, −20, 40, ⋯ $a_1 = -5$ and $r = -2$
$a_n = a_1 r^{n-1}$
$a_n = (-5) \cdot (-2)^{n-1} = (-1 \cdot 5) \cdot (-1 \cdot 2)^{n-1}$
$= (-1) \cdot 5 \cdot (-1)^{n-1} \cdot 2^{n-1} = (-1)^n \cdot 5 \cdot 2^{n-1}$
$a_n = (-1)^n \cdot 5 \cdot 2^{n-1}$
$a_{10} = (-1)^{10} \cdot 5 \cdot 2^{10-1} = 5 \cdot 2^9$, $a_{10} = 5 \cdot 2^9$

Check Point 5

① $a_2 = 3$, $r = -2$
$a_n = a_1 r^{n-1}$, $3 = a_1(-2)^{2-1}$, $a_1 = -\dfrac{3}{2}$
$a_n = \left(-\dfrac{3}{2}\right) \cdot (-2)^{n-1}$

② $a_3 = 10$, $a_6 = 1250$
$a_n = a_1 r^{n-1}$

$\begin{cases} a_6 = a_1 r^{6-1} \\ a_3 = a_1 r^{3-1} \end{cases} \rightarrow \begin{cases} 1250 = a_1 r^5 \\ 10 = a_1 r^2 \end{cases}$

$\dfrac{a_1 r^5}{a_1 r^2} = \dfrac{1250}{10}$, $r^3 = 125$, $r = 5$

$a_3 = a_1 r^{3-1}$, $10 = a_1 \cdot 5^2$, $a_1 = \dfrac{10}{25} = \dfrac{2}{5}$

$a_n = a_1 r^{n-1} = \dfrac{2}{5} \cdot 5^{n-1}$, $a_n = \dfrac{2}{5} \cdot 5^{n-1}$

Alternative solution:

$a_n = a_k r^{n-k}$, $a_6 = a_3 r^{6-3}$

$1250 = 10 \cdot r^3$, $r^3 = 125$, $r = 5$

$a_n = a_1 r^{n-1}$

$a_3 = a_1 r^{3-1}$, $10 = a_1 \cdot 5^2$, $a_1 = \dfrac{2}{5}$

$a_n = a_1 r^{n-1} = \dfrac{2}{5} \cdot 5^{n-1}$, $a_n = \dfrac{2}{5} \cdot 5^{n-1}$

Check Point 6

① $a_1 = 6$, $a_2 = -2$, $a_n = a_{n-1} - a_{n-2}$

$a_3 = a_2 - a_1 = -2 - 6 = -8$

$a_4 = a_3 - a_2 = -8 - (-2) = -6$

$a_5 = a_4 - a_3 = -6 - (-8) = 2$

So the first 5 terms are 6, −2, −8, −6, 2

② $a_1 = 6$, $a_2 = 4$, $a_n = \dfrac{a_{n-1} - n}{2} + \dfrac{3 a_{n-2}}{4}$

$a_3 = \dfrac{a_2 - 3}{2} + \dfrac{3 a_1}{4} = \dfrac{4-3}{2} + \dfrac{3(6)}{4} = \dfrac{1}{2} + \dfrac{9}{2} = 5$

$a_4 = \dfrac{a_3 - 4}{2} + \dfrac{3 a_2}{4} = \dfrac{5-4}{2} + \dfrac{3(4)}{4} = \dfrac{1}{2} + 3 = \dfrac{7}{2}$

$a_5 = \dfrac{a_4 - 5}{2} + \dfrac{3 a_3}{4} = \dfrac{\tfrac{7}{2} - 5}{2} + \dfrac{3(5)}{4} = -\dfrac{3}{4} + \dfrac{15}{4} = 3$

So the first 5 terms are 6, 4, 5, $\dfrac{7}{2}$, 3

Review Exercises

01

15, 9, 3, −3, ⋯ is an arithmetic sequence with $a_1 = 15$ and $d = -6$.

$a_n = a_1 + (n-1)d$

$a_n = 15 + (n-1)(-6) = -6n + 21$

$a_{10} = -6(10) + 21 = -39$

02

$a_4 = 24$, $a_8 = 8$

$a_n = a_1 + (n-1)d \rightarrow \begin{cases} 24 = a_1 + (4-1)d \\ 8 = a_1 + (8-1)d \end{cases}$

$\begin{array}{r} 24 = a_1 + 3d \\ -\underline{ 8 = a_1 + 7d} \\ 16 = -4d \end{array} \rightarrow d = -4$

$a_n = a_1 + (n-1)d$, $a_8 = a_1 + (8-1)(-4)$

$8 = a_1 - 28$, $a_1 = 36$

Alternative solution:

$a_n = a_k + (n-k)d$, $a_8 = a_4 + (8-4)d$

$8 = 24 + 4d$, $d = -4$

$a_n = a_1 + (n-1)d$, $a_8 = a_1 + (8-1)(-4)$

$8 = a_1 - 28$, $a_1 = 36$

03

200, 100, 50, 25, ⋯ is a geometric sequence with $a_1 = 200$ and $r = \dfrac{1}{2}$.

$a_n = a_1 r^{n-1}$, $a_n = 200 \left(\dfrac{1}{2} \right)^{n-1}$

$a_8 = 200 \left(\dfrac{1}{2} \right)^{8-1} = 200 \times \dfrac{1}{2^7} = \dfrac{25}{16}$, $a_8 = \dfrac{25}{16}$

04

$a_3 = 5$, $a_6 = 625$

$a_n = a_1 r^{n-1} \rightarrow \begin{cases} a_6 = a_1 r^{6-1} \\ a_3 = a_1 r^{3-1} \end{cases}$

$\begin{cases} 625 = a_1 r^5 \\ 5 = a_1 r^2 \end{cases} \rightarrow \dfrac{a_1 r^5}{a_1 r^2} = \dfrac{625}{5}$, $r^3 = 125$, $r = 5$

$a_n = a_1 r^{n-1}$

$a_3 = a_1 r^{3-1}$, $5 = a_1 (5)^2$, $a_1 = \dfrac{1}{5}$

Alternative solution:

$a_n = a_k r^{n-k}$, $a_6 = a_3 r^{6-3}$

$625 = 5 \cdot r^3$, $r^3 = 125$, $r = 5$

$a_n = a_1 r^{n-1}$, $a_3 = a_1 r^{3-1}$

$5 = a_1 (5)^2$, $a_1 = \dfrac{1}{5}$

05

The sequence is defined recursively.

$a_1 = 10$, $a_n = a_{n-1} - 4n - 1$

$a_2 = a_1 - 4(2) - 1 = 10 - 8 - 1 = 1$
$a_3 = a_2 - 4(3) - 1 = 1 - 12 - 1 = -12$
$a_4 = a_3 - 4(4) - 1 = -12 - 16 - 1 = -29$

06

When 2 is added to each of the terms, the resulting numbers form a geometric sequence with ratio $r = 3$.
$\{-1, 1, 7, 25\}$
$\{-1+2, 1+2, 7+2, 25+2\} = \{1, 3, 9, 27\}$
$r = \dfrac{a_n}{a_{n-1}}$, $r = \dfrac{27}{9} = \dfrac{9}{3} = \dfrac{3}{1} = 3$
So the answer is (C).

07

$a_1 = 2$, $a_5 = 14$, $a_n = a_1 + (n-1)d$
$a_5 = a_1 + (5-1)d$, $14 = 2 + 4d$, $d = 3$
So we have an arithmetic sequence 2, 5, 8, 11, $\cdots$. Since we are looking for the first term of the sequence to exceed 600,
$a_n = a_1 + (n-1)d > 600$
$2 + (n-1) \cdot 3 > 600$
$3n - 1 > 600$
The minimum value of n satisfying the above inequality is 201. Therefore,
$a_{201} = 2 + (201 - 1) \cdot 3 = 602$.
The value of the first term to exceed 600 is 602.

08

Since 2 additional squares are added for each new row, this is an arithmetic sequence with
$a_1 = 1$ and $d = 2$. In 100th row, we have
$a_n = a_1 + (n-1)d$
$a_{100} = 1 + (100 - 1) \cdot 2 = 199$
There are 199 squares.

09

The sequence is defined recursively and $a_1 = 2$.
$n = 1 (a_1$ is even$)$; $a_2 = a_1 + 3 = 2 + 3 = 5$
$n = 2 (a_2$ is odd$)$; $a_3 = 2a_2 - 2 = 2 \cdot 5 - 2 = 8$
$n = 3 (a_3$ is even$)$; $a_4 = a_3 + 3 = 8 + 3 = 11$
$n = 4 (a_4$ is odd$)$; $a_5 = 2a_4 - 2 = 2 \cdot 11 - 2 = 20$
The sum of the first five terms is
$a_1 + a_2 + a_3 + a_4 + a_5 = 2 + 5 + 8 + 11 + 20 = 46$

10

Every time the ball bounces, the height of the ball rebounded is $\dfrac{2}{3}$ times the previous height. If we let the height of the ball after the first bounce be $a_1 = 243 \times \dfrac{2}{3} = 162$, this is a geometric sequence with $a_1 = 162$ and $r = \dfrac{2}{3}$. Then the height of the ball after fifth bounce (a_5) is
$a_n = a_1 r^{n-1}$, $a_5 = 162 \cdot \left(\dfrac{2}{3}\right)^4 = 32$ ft.
The height of the ball is 32 ft.

2. Introduction to Series

Check Point 1

① $\sum_{k=1}^{4}(5k-1)$
$=(5 \cdot 1-1)+(5 \cdot 2-1)+(5 \cdot 3-1)+(5 \cdot 4-1)$
$=4+9+14+19=46$

② $\sum_{k=1}^{3}\frac{1}{2} \cdot (-3)^k$
$=\frac{1}{2} \cdot (-3)^1 + \frac{1}{2} \cdot (-3)^2 + \frac{1}{2} \cdot (-3)^3$
$=-\frac{3}{2}+\frac{9}{2}-\frac{27}{2}=-\frac{21}{2}$

Check Point 2

① $1+3+5+7+\cdots+179 \rightarrow a_1=1, d=2, a_n=179$
$a_n=a_1+(n-1)d$
$a_n=1+(n-1) \cdot 2, a_n=2n-1$
The number of terms is
$179=2n-1, n=90$. So we have
$1+3+5+7+\cdots+179 = \sum_{k=1}^{90}(2k-1)$

② $8-4+2-1+\cdots+\frac{1}{32}$
$\rightarrow a_1=8, r=-\frac{1}{2}, a_n=\frac{1}{32}$
$a_n=a_1 r^{n-1}, a_n=8\left(-\frac{1}{2}\right)^{n-1}$
The number of terms is
$\frac{1}{32}=8\left(-\frac{1}{2}\right)^{n-1}, \frac{1}{256}=\left(-\frac{1}{2}\right)^{n-1}$
$\left(-\frac{1}{2}\right)^8 = \left(-\frac{1}{2}\right)^{n-1}$
$8=n-1, n=9$. So we have
$8-4+2-1+\cdots+\frac{1}{32} = \sum_{k=1}^{9} 8\left(-\frac{1}{2}\right)^{k-1}$

Check Point 3

① $5+7+9+11+\cdots+135 \rightarrow a_1=5, d=2, a_n=135$
$a_n=a_1+(n-1)d$
$135=5+(n-1) \cdot 2, 135=2n+3, n=66$
There are 66 terms. So the sum is
$S_n=\frac{n}{2}(a_1+a_n), S_{66}=\frac{66}{2}(5+135)=4,620$

② $10+4-2-8-\cdots-110$
$\rightarrow a_1=10, d=-6, a_n=-110$
$a_n=a_1+(n-1)d$
$-110=10+(n-1)(-6)$
$-110=-6n+16, n=21$
There are 21 terms. So the sum is
$S_n=\frac{n}{2}(a_1+a_n)$
$S_{21}=\frac{21}{2}(10+(-110))=-1,050$

Check Point 4

① $a_1=3, a_{15}=59; n=34$
$a_n=a_1+(n-1)d$
$a_{15}=a_1+(15-1)d, 59=3+14d, d=4$
So the sum of 34 terms is
$S_n=\frac{n}{2}(2a_1+(n-1)d)$
$S_{34}=\frac{34}{2}(2 \cdot 3+(34-1) \cdot 4)=2,346$

② $a_8=9, a_{29}=-33; n=29$
$a_n=a_k+(n-k)d$
$a_{29}=a_8+(29-8)d, -33=9+21d, d=-2$
$a_n=a_1+(n-1)d$
$a_8=a_1+(8-1)d, 9=a_1+7(-2), a_1=23$
So the sum of 29 terms is
$S_n=\frac{n}{2}(a_1+a_n)$
$S_{29}=\frac{29}{2}(23+(-33))=-145$

Check Point 5

① $6+18+54+162+\cdots+13122$
$\rightarrow a_1=6, r=3, a_n=13122$
$a_n=a_1 r^{n-1}$
$13122=6 \cdot 3^{n-1}, 2187=3^{n-1}$
$3^7=3^{n-1}, n-1=7, n=8$
There are 8 terms. So the sum is
$S_n=a_1\left(\frac{1-r^n}{1-r}\right), S_8=6 \cdot \left(\frac{1-3^8}{1-3}\right)=19,680$

② $1-\frac{2}{3}+\frac{4}{9}-\frac{8}{27}+\cdots-\frac{128}{2187}$

Solutions Manual

→ $a_1=1$, $r=-\dfrac{2}{3}$, $a_n=-\dfrac{128}{2187}$

$a_n=a_1r^{n-1}$

$-\dfrac{128}{2187}=1\cdot\left(-\dfrac{2}{3}\right)^{n-1}$, $\left(-\dfrac{2}{3}\right)^7=\left(-\dfrac{2}{3}\right)^{n-1}$

$n-1=7$, $n=8$

There are 8 terms. So the sum is

$S_n=a_1\left(\dfrac{1-r^n}{1-r}\right)$, $S_8=1\cdot\left(\dfrac{1-\left(-\dfrac{2}{3}\right)^8}{1-\left(-\dfrac{2}{3}\right)}\right)=\dfrac{1,261}{2,187}$

Check Point 6

① $a_1=7$, $a_{10}=3584$; $n=10$

$a_n=a_1r^{n-1}$, $a_{10}=a_1r^{10-1}$

$3584=7r^9$, $512=r^9$, $r=2$

So the sum of 10 terms is

$S_n=a_1\left(\dfrac{1-r^n}{1-r}\right)$, $S_{10}=7\left(\dfrac{1-2^{10}}{1-2}\right)=7,161$

② $a_4=1$, $a_8=\dfrac{256}{81}$; $n=5$

$a_n=a_kr^{n-k}$, $a_8=a_4r^{8-4}$

$\dfrac{256}{81}=1\cdot r^4$, $r=\dfrac{4}{3}$

$a_n=a_1r^{n-1}$, $a_4=a_1r^{4-1}$

$1=a_1\cdot\left(\dfrac{4}{3}\right)^3$, $a_1=\dfrac{27}{64}$

So the sum of 5 terms is

$S_n=a_1\left(\dfrac{1-r^n}{1-r}\right)$, $S_5=\dfrac{27}{64}\cdot\left(\dfrac{1-\left(\dfrac{4}{3}\right)^5}{1-\left(\dfrac{4}{3}\right)}\right)=\dfrac{781}{192}$

Check Point 7

① $1+0.5+0.25+0.125+\cdots \to a_1=1$, $r=0.5=\dfrac{1}{2}$

$S_\infty=\dfrac{a_1}{1-r}=\dfrac{1}{1-\dfrac{1}{2}}=2$

② $3-\dfrac{9}{4}+\dfrac{27}{16}-\dfrac{81}{64}+\cdots \to a_1=3$, $r=-\dfrac{3}{4}$

$S_\infty=\dfrac{a}{1-r}=\dfrac{3}{1-\left(-\dfrac{3}{4}\right)}=\dfrac{12}{7}$

Review Exercises

01

$\sum_{n=1}^{30}(7-5k)$

$=(7-5\cdot1)+(7-5\cdot2)+\cdots+(7-5\cdot30)$

$=2-3-\cdots-143$

This is an arithmetic series with

$a_1=2$, $a_{30}=-143$, $d=-5$, and $n=30$.

So the sum of 30 terms is

$S_n=\dfrac{n}{2}(a_1+a_n)$

$S_{30}=\dfrac{30}{2}(2+(-143))=-2,115$

02

$a_6=28$, $a_{19}=119$

$a_n=a_k+(n-k)d$, $a_{19}=a_6+(19-6)d$

$119=28+13\cdot d$, $91=13d$, $d=7$

$a_n=a_1+(n-1)d$, $a_6=a_1+(6-1)\cdot7$

$28=a_1+35$, $a_1=-7$

So the sum of the first 15 terms is

$S_n=\dfrac{n}{2}(2a_1+(n-1)d)$

$S_{15}=\dfrac{15}{2}(2(-7)+(15-1)\cdot7)=630$

03

(1) $S_5=105$, $a_1=13$

$S_n=\dfrac{n}{2}(a_1+a_n)$, $S_5=\dfrac{5}{2}(a_1+a_5)$

$105=\dfrac{5}{2}(13+a_5)$, $42=13+a_5$, $a_5=29$

(2) $a_n=a_1+(n-1)d$

$a_5=a_1+(5-1)d$, $29=13+4d$, $d=4$

$a_{20}=a_1+(20-1)d$, $a_{20}=13+19\cdot4=89$

(3) $S_n=\dfrac{n}{2}(2a_1+(n-1)d)$

$S_{18}=\dfrac{18}{2}(2\cdot13+(18-1)\cdot4)=846$

04

$a_3=-\dfrac{3}{64}$, $a_8=48$

$a_n=a_kr^{n-k}$, $a_8=a_3r^{8-3}$

$48=\left(-\dfrac{3}{64}\right)\cdot r^5$, $-1024=r^5$, $r=-4$

$a_n=a_1r^{n-1}$, $a_3=a_1r^{3-1}$

$-\dfrac{3}{64}=a_1(-4)^2$, $a_1=-\dfrac{3}{1024}$

So the sum of the first 9 terms is

$S_n=a_1\left(\dfrac{1-r^n}{1-r}\right)$

$S_9=\left(-\dfrac{3}{1024}\right)\cdot\left(\dfrac{1-(-4)^9}{1-(-4)}\right)=-\dfrac{157,287}{1,024}$

05

Arithmetic sequence → $a_1=25$, $d=24$
Geometric sequence → $a_1=3$, $r=2$

$a_1\left(\dfrac{1-r^n}{1-r}\right)>\dfrac{n}{2}(2a_1+(n-1)d)$

$3\left(\dfrac{1-2^n}{1-2}\right)>\dfrac{n}{2}(50+(n-1)\cdot 24)$

$3(2^n-1)>\dfrac{n}{2}(24n+26)$

$3\cdot 2^n-3>12n^2+13n$

By trial and error, when $n=9$,

$3\cdot 2^9-3>12\cdot 9^2+13\cdot 9$

$1533>1089$

Therefore, the minimum number of terms is 9.

06

(1) $-2-12-22-32\cdots$; $S_n=-224$

This is an arithmetic series with
$a_1=-2$, $d=-10$.

$S_n=\dfrac{n}{2}(2a_1+(n-1)d)$

$-224=\dfrac{n}{2}(2(-2)+(n-1)(-10))$

$-224=\dfrac{n}{2}(-10n+6)$, $10n^2-6n-448=0$

$2(n-7)(5n+32)=0$, $n=7$ or $n=-\dfrac{32}{5}$

Since the number of terms must be positive integer, $n=7$.

(2) $7-21+63-189+\cdots$; $S_n=3829$

This is a geometric series with
$a_1=7$, $r=-3$.

$S_n=a_1\left(\dfrac{1-r^n}{1-r}\right)$, $3829=7\cdot\left(\dfrac{1-(-3)^n}{1-(-3)}\right)$,

$547=\dfrac{1-(-3)^n}{1-(-3)}$, $(-3)^n=-2187$, $n=7$

07

$\dfrac{1}{3^2}+\dfrac{1}{3^3}+\cdots+\dfrac{1}{3^n}+\cdots$ is an infinite

geometric series with $a_1=\dfrac{1}{3^2}$ and $r=\dfrac{1}{3}$.

So $\dfrac{1}{2}+\left(\dfrac{1}{3^2}+\dfrac{1}{3^3}+\cdots+\dfrac{1}{3^n}+\cdots\right)$

$=\dfrac{1}{2}+\dfrac{a_1}{1-r}=\dfrac{1}{2}+\dfrac{\dfrac{1}{3^2}}{1-\dfrac{1}{3}}=\dfrac{1}{2}+\dfrac{1}{6}=\dfrac{2}{3}$

08

$r=0.6$, $S_\infty=120$

The sum of the infinite series with $|r|<1$
is $S_\infty=\dfrac{a_1}{1-r}$. So we have

$S_\infty=\dfrac{a_1}{1-r}$, $120=\dfrac{a_1}{1-0.6}$, $a_1=48$

09

The salary of Jason increases as follows:
$a_1=55000$, $a_2=55000+3500$,
$a_3=55000+3500(2)$, $\cdots$

This is an arithmetic series with $a_1=55000$
and $d=3500$, and we need to find S_{20}.

$S_n=\dfrac{n}{2}(2a_1+(n-1)d)$

$S_{20}=\dfrac{20}{2}(2\cdot 55000+(20-1)\cdot 3500)$

$=\$1,765,000$

10

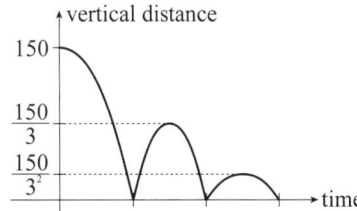

The vertical distance on the way down:

$a_1=150$, $a_2=\dfrac{150}{3}$, $a_3=\dfrac{150}{3^2}$, $\cdots$

This is an infinite geometric series with
$a_1=150$ and $r=\dfrac{1}{3}$.

Solutions Manual

$$150+\frac{150}{3}+\frac{150}{3^2}\cdots=\frac{a_1}{1-r}=\frac{150}{1-\frac{1}{3}}=225$$

The vertical distance on the way up.

$$a_1=\frac{150}{3},\ a_2=\frac{150}{3^2},\ a_3=\frac{150}{3^3},\cdots$$

This is an infinite geometric seires with $a_1=\frac{150}{3}$ and $r=\frac{1}{3}$.

$$\frac{150}{3}+\frac{150}{3^2}+\frac{150}{3^3}\cdots=\frac{a_1}{1-r}=\frac{\frac{150}{3}}{1-\frac{1}{3}}=75$$

Therefore, the total vertical distance the ball travels is $225+75=300\ ft$.

11

$mk-mk^3+mk^5-mk^7+\cdots \rightarrow a_1=mk,\ r=-k^2$

$$S_\infty=\frac{a_1}{1-r}=\frac{mk}{1-(-k^2)}=\frac{mk}{1+k^2}$$

3. Fundamental Counting Principles

Check Point 1

① For each choice of language class, there are 5 choices of math classes. So we have
$$\underbrace{4}_{language}\cdot\underbrace{5}_{math}=20\text{ different schedules.}$$

② There are 26 letters(A~Z) and 10 digits (0~9). So we have
$$\underbrace{26\cdot 26\cdot 26}_{Letters}\cdot\underbrace{10\cdot 10\cdot 10\cdot 10}_{Digits}=26^3\cdot 10^4$$
$=175{,}760{,}000$ license plates.

Check Point 2

① $_8P_2=\dfrac{8!}{(8-2)!}=\dfrac{8!}{6!}=\dfrac{8\cdot 7\cdot \cancel{6\cdot 5\cdots 1}}{\cancel{6\cdot 5\cdots 1}}=8\cdot 7=56$

② $_{11}P_4=\dfrac{11!}{(11-4)!}=\dfrac{11!}{7!}=\dfrac{11\cdot 10\cdot 9\cdot 8\cdot \cancel{7\cdot 6\cdots 1}}{\cancel{7\cdot 6\cdots 1}}$
$=11\cdot 10\cdot 9\cdot 8=7{,}920$

Check Point 3

① There are seven students and seven positions.
$$\underline{1st}\ \underline{2nd}\ \underline{3rd}\ \cdots\ \underline{7th}$$
$$=\underbrace{7}_{1st\ place}\cdot\underbrace{6}_{2nd\ place}\cdot\underbrace{5}_{3rd\ place}\cdots\underbrace{1}_{7th\ place}$$
$=7!=5{,}040$ ways.

Using the permutation formula,
$$_7P_7=\frac{7!}{(7-7)!}=\frac{7!}{1}=7!=5{,}040\text{ ways.}$$

② There are 10 candidates and three positions.
$$=\underbrace{10}_{President}\cdot\underbrace{9}_{Treasurer}\cdot\underbrace{8}_{Secretary}=720\text{ ways.}$$

Using the permutation formula,
$$_{10}P_3=\frac{10!}{(10-3)!}=\frac{10!}{7!}=\frac{10\cdot 9\cdot 8\cdot 7\cdot 6\cdots 1}{7\cdot 6\cdots 1}$$
$=10\cdot 9\cdot 8=720$ ways.

③ This is a permutation problem in

which four people choose a seat from 7 possible seats.

$$\underbrace{7}_{1st\ person} \cdot \underbrace{6}_{2nd\ person} \cdot \underbrace{5}_{3rd\ person} \cdot \underbrace{4}_{4th\ person} = 840 \text{ ways.}$$

Using the permutation formula,

$$_7P_4 = \frac{7!}{(7-4)!} = \frac{7!}{3!} = \frac{7 \cdot 6 \cdot 5 \cdot 4 \cdot 3 \cdot 2 \cdot 1}{3 \cdot 2 \cdot 1}$$
$$= 7 \cdot 6 \cdot 5 \cdot 4 = 840 \text{ ways.}$$

Check Point 4

① This word has 8 letters, but there are repeating letters: 2 C's, 2 L's, and 2 U's. So we have
$$\frac{8!}{2!2!2!} = \frac{8 \cdot 7 \cdots 1}{2 \cdot 1 \cdot 2 \cdot 1 \cdot 2 \cdot 1} = 5{,}040 \text{ ways.}$$

② This word has 11 letters, but there are repeating letters: 4 I's, 4 S's, and 2 P's. So we have
$$\frac{11!}{4!4!2!} = \frac{11 \cdot 10 \cdots 1}{4 \cdots 1 \cdot 4 \cdots 1 \cdot 2 \cdot 1} = 34{,}650 \text{ ways.}$$

Check Point 5

① $_{12}C_2 = \frac{12!}{2!(12-2)!} = \frac{12!}{2!10!} = \frac{12 \cdot 11 \cdot 10 \cdots 1}{2 \cdot 1 \cdot 10 \cdots 1} = 66$

② $_9C_6 = \frac{9!}{6!(9-6)!} = \frac{9!}{6!3!} = \frac{9 \cdot 8 \cdot 7 \cdot 6 \cdots 1}{6 \cdots 1 \cdot 3 \cdot 2 \cdot 1} = 84$

Check Point 6

① The order of choosing questions is not important. So the selection is a combination of 7 questions out of 10 questions.
$$_{10}C_7 = \frac{10!}{7!(10-7)!} = \frac{10!}{7!3!} = \frac{10 \cdot 9 \cdot 8 \cdot 7 \cdots 1}{7 \cdots 1 \cdot 3 \cdot 2 \cdot 1}$$
$$= 120 \text{ ways.}$$

② The order of choosing professors and engineers is not important. Since the events are independent, the number of combinations would be

$$\underbrace{_6C_2}_{Professors} \cdot \underbrace{_{12}C_3}_{Engineers} = \frac{6!}{2!(6-2)!} \cdot \frac{12!}{3!(12-3)!}$$
$$= \frac{6!}{2!4!} \cdot \frac{12!}{3!9!} = \frac{6 \cdot 5 \cdot 4 \cdots 1}{2 \cdot 1 \cdot 4 \cdots 1} \cdot \frac{12 \cdot 11 \cdot 10 \cdot 9 \cdots 1}{3 \cdot 2 \cdot 1 \cdot 9 \cdots 1}$$
$$= 15 \cdot 220 = 3{,}300 \text{ ways.}$$

Review Exercises

01

(1) $7 \cdot {_nP_3} = 6 \cdot {_{n+1}P_3}$

$$7 \cdot \frac{n!}{(n-3)!} = 6 \cdot \frac{(n+1)!}{(n+1-3)!}$$

$$7 \cdot \frac{n!}{(n-3)!} = 6 \cdot \frac{(n+1)!}{(n-2)!},$$

$$\frac{7(n-2)!}{(n-3)!} = \frac{6(n+1)!}{n!}$$

$$\frac{7(n-2)(n-3)\cdots 1}{(n-3)\cdots 1} = \frac{6(n+1) \cdot n \cdot (n-1) \cdots 1}{n \cdot (n-1) \cdots 1}$$

$7(n-2) = 6(n+1)$, $7n - 14 = 6n + 6$, $n = 20$

(2) $_nC_{n-2} = 10$

$$\frac{n!}{(n-2)!(n-(n-2))!} = 10, \quad \frac{n!}{(n-2)!2!} = 10$$

$$\frac{n \cdot (n-1) \cdot (n-2) \cdots 1}{(n-2) \cdots 1 \cdot 2 \cdot 1} = 10$$

$n(n-1) = 20$, $n^2 - n - 20 = 0$
$(n-5)(n+4) = 0$, $n = 5$ or $n = -4$
Since n is the number of objects, $n > 0$. So $n = 5$.

(3) $4 \cdot {_nC_2} = {_{n+2}C_3}$

$$\frac{4n!}{2!(n-2)!} = \frac{(n+2)!}{3!((n+2)-3)!}$$

$$\frac{4 \cdot n!}{2(n-2)!} = \frac{(n+2)!}{6(n-1)!}, \quad \frac{12(n-1)!}{(n-2)!} = \frac{(n+2)!}{n!}$$

$$\frac{12(n-1)(n-2)\cdots 1}{(n-2)\cdots 1} = \frac{(n+2)(n+1) \cdot n \cdots 1}{n \cdots 1}$$

$12(n-1) = (n+2)(n+1)$, $n^2 - 9n + 14 = 0$
$(n-2)(n-7) = 0$, $n = 2$ or $n = 7$

(4) $_nP_4 = 30 \cdot {_nC_5}$

$$\frac{n!}{(n-4)!} = 30 \cdot \frac{n!}{5!(n-5)!}$$

$$1 = \frac{30(n-4)!}{120(n-5)!}, \quad 1 = \frac{(n-4)(n-5)\cdots 1}{4(n-5)\cdots 1}$$

$4 = n - 4$, $n = 8$

Solutions Manual

02

For each choice of cheese, there are 4 choices of breads($3 \cdot 4 = 12$). And for each of these choices, there are 2 choices for meats($12 \cdot 2 = 24$). So the number of possible sandwiches is simply

$$\underbrace{3}_{Cheeses} \cdot \underbrace{4}_{Breads} \cdot \underbrace{2}_{Meats} = 24 \text{ sandwiches.}$$

03

For each choice from A to B, there are 4 choices from B to C($3 \cdot 4 = 12$). So the number of possible routes from A to C through B is

$$\underbrace{3}_{From\ A\ to\ B} \cdot \underbrace{4}_{From\ B\ to\ C} = 12 \text{ routes.}$$

04

There are 2 choices for area codes(281 or 832), 9 choices for the first digit($1\sim9$), and 10 choices($0\sim9$) for the rest of the digits. By the fundamental counting principle, we have

$$\underbrace{2}_{Area\ code} \cdot \underbrace{9}_{First\ digit} \cdot \underbrace{10 \cdot 10 \cdot 10 \cdot 10 \cdot 10 \cdot 10}_{Last\ 6\ digits}$$
$$= 2 \cdot 9 \cdot 10^6 = 18{,}000{,}000 \text{ telephone numbers.}$$

05

(1) Notice that first digit cannot be 0. So there are 9 choices for the first digit ($1\sim9$), and 10 choices ($0\sim9$) for the rest of the digits. By the fundamental counting principle, we have
$9 \cdot 10 \cdot 10 \cdot 10 = 9 \cdot 10^3 = 9{,}000$ numbers.

(2) There are 9 choices for the first digit ($1\sim9$). The next digit cannot be repeated, so the number we can select for the next digit reduces by one. Since we can select 0 from the second digit, we have
$9 \cdot 9 \cdot 8 \cdot 7 = 4{,}536$ numbers.

06

There are 25 seniors and three positions,
$$\underbrace{President}_{} \underbrace{Vice\ President}_{} \underbrace{Secretary}_{}$$
$$= \underbrace{25}_{President} \cdot \underbrace{24}_{Vice\ President} \cdot \underbrace{23}_{Secretary}$$

Using the permutation formula,
$${}_{25}P_3 = \frac{25!}{(25-3)!} = \frac{25!}{22!} = \frac{25 \cdot 24 \cdot 23 \cdot \cancel{22 \cdots 1}}{\cancel{22 \cdots 1}}$$
$$= 25 \cdot 24 \cdot 23 = 13{,}800 \text{ ways.}$$

07

Notice that, in the driver's seat, one of the two people who can drive must sit. So we have
$$\underbrace{2}_{Driver's\ seat} \cdot \underbrace{4 \cdot 3 \cdot 2 \cdot 1}_{Other\ 4\ seats} = 48 \text{ ways.}$$

08

The order of choosing cards is not important. So the selection is a combination of 7 cards out of 52 cards.
$${}_{52}C_7 = \frac{52!}{7!(52-7)!} = \frac{52!}{7!45!}$$
$$= \frac{52 \cdot 51 \cdots 46 \cdot \cancel{45 \cdot 44 \cdots 1}}{7 \cdot 6 \cdots 1 \cdot \cancel{45 \cdot 44 \cdots 1}}$$
$$= 133{,}784{,}560 \text{ poker hands.}$$

09

(1) The order of choosing students is not important. So the selection is a combination of 3 students out of 12 students.
$${}_{12}C_3 = \frac{12!}{3!(12-3)!} = \frac{12!}{3!9!} = \frac{12 \cdot 11 \cdot 10 \cdot \cancel{9 \cdots 1}}{3 \cdot 2 \cdot 1 \cdot \cancel{9 \cdots 1}}$$
$$= \frac{12 \cdot 11 \cdot 10}{6}$$
$$= 220 \text{ ways.}$$

(2) The order of choosing a leader and 2 followers is not important. For the leader, the selection is a combination of 1 student out of 12 students. So we have ${}_{12}C_1$. For the followers, the selection is a combination of 2 student out of the remaining 11

students. So we have $_{11}C_2$. Since two events are independent, the number of combinations would be

$$\underbrace{_{12}C_1}_{Leader} \cdot \underbrace{_{11}C_2}_{Followers} = 12 \cdot \frac{11!}{2!(11-2)!} = 12 \cdot \frac{11!}{2!9!}$$

$$= 12 \cdot \frac{11 \cdot 10 \cdot 9 \cdots 1}{2 \cdot 1 \cdot 9 \cdots 1} = 660 \text{ ways.}$$

10

The order of choosing players for each position is not important. Since events are independent, the number of combinations would be

$$\underbrace{_3C_1}_{Striker} \cdot \underbrace{_6C_3}_{Mid-fielders} \cdot \underbrace{_5C_2}_{Defenders} \cdot \underbrace{_2C_1}_{Goal-keeper}$$

$$= 3 \cdot \frac{6!}{3!(6-3)!} \cdot \frac{5!}{2!(5-2)!} \cdot 2 = 6 \cdot \frac{6!}{3!3!} \cdot \frac{5!}{2!3!}$$

$$= 6 \cdot \frac{6 \cdot 5 \cdot 4 \cdot 3 \cdots 1}{3 \cdots 1 \cdot 3 \cdots 1} \cdot \frac{5 \cdot 4 \cdot 3 \cdots 1}{2 \cdot 1 \cdot 3 \cdots 1} = 1,200 \text{ line-ups.}$$

11

There are 16 good monitors and 4 defective monitors.

The order of choosing LCD monitors is not important. Since events are independent, the number of combinations would be

(1) $_{16}C_5 = \frac{16!}{5!(16-5)!} = \frac{16!}{5!11!}$

$= \frac{16 \cdot 15 \cdots 12 \cdot 11 \cdots 1}{5 \cdot 4 \cdots 1 \cdot 11 \cdots 1} = 4,368$ scenarios.

(2) $\underbrace{_{16}C_4}_{Good} \cdot \underbrace{_4C_1}_{Defective} = \frac{16!}{4!(16-4)!} \cdot 4 = \frac{16!}{4!12!} \cdot 4$

$= \frac{16 \cdot 15 \cdot 14 \cdot 13 \cdot 12 \cdots 1}{4 \cdot 3 \cdot 2 \cdot 1 \cdot 12 \cdots 1} \cdot 4 = 7,280$ scenarios.

(3) Having at least 3 monitors means having 3, 4, or 5 monitors. So we have to determine

$\underbrace{_{16}C_5}_{5 \text{ good}} + \underbrace{_{16}C_4 \cdot _4C_1}_{4 \text{ good, 1 defective}} + \underbrace{_{16}C_3 \cdot _4C_2}_{3 \text{ good, 2 defective}}$

$_{16}C_3 \cdot _4C_2 = \frac{16!}{3!(16-3)!} \cdot \frac{4!}{2!(4-2)!} = \frac{16!}{3!13!} \cdot \frac{4!}{2!2!}$

$= \frac{16 \cdot 15 \cdot 14 \cdot 13 \cdots 1}{3 \cdot 2 \cdot 1 \cdot 13 \cdots 1} \cdot \frac{4 \cdot 3 \cdot 2 \cdot 1}{2 \cdot 1 \cdot 2 \cdot 1}$

$= \frac{16 \cdot 15 \cdot 14}{6} \cdot \frac{4 \cdot 3}{2} = 3,360$

$_{16}C_5 + _{16}C_4 \cdot _4C_1 + _{16}C_3 \cdot _4C_2$
$= 4,368 + 7,280 + 3,360 = 15,008$ scenarios.

12

The order of choosing men and women is not important. Since the events are independent, the number of combinations would be

$$\underbrace{_8C_3}_{Men} \cdot \underbrace{_6C_2}_{Women} = \frac{8!}{3!(8-3)!} \frac{6!}{2!(6-2)!} = \frac{8!}{3!5!} \frac{6!}{2!4!}$$

The number of ways in which five selected people are lined up is 5!. Therefore, we have

$$\frac{8!}{3!5!} \cdot \frac{6!}{2!4!} \cdot 5! = \frac{8 \cdots 1}{3 \cdots 1} \cdot \frac{6 \cdot 5 \cdot 4 \cdots 1}{2 \cdot 1 \cdot 4 \cdots 1} = 100,800 \text{ ways.}$$

13

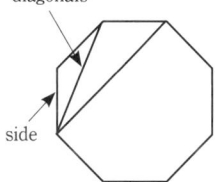

diagonals

side

Notice each 2 vertices form a side. So, # of diagonals

$= _8C_2 - \text{\# of sides} = \frac{8!}{2!(8-2)!} - 8$

$= \frac{8!}{2!6!} - 8 = \frac{8 \cdot 7 \cdot 6 \cdots 1}{2 \cdot 1 \cdot 6 \cdots 1} - 8$

$= \frac{8 \cdot 7}{2} - 8 = 20$ diagonals.

14

The triangle is formed by connecting 3 points, so the number of combination is $_7C_3$. However, three points from bottom segment cannot be a triangle, which the number of combination is $_4C_3$. Therefore, the number of triangle is

$_7C_3 - _4C_3 = \frac{7!}{3!(7-3)!} - \frac{4!}{3!(4-3)!} = \frac{7!}{3!4!} - \frac{4!}{3!1!}$

$= \frac{7 \cdot 6 \cdot 5 \cdot 4 \cdots 1}{3 \cdot 2 \cdot 1 \cdot 4 \cdots 1} - \frac{4 \cdot 3 \cdots 1}{3 \cdots 1}$

$= 31$ triangles.

Solutions Manual

4. Probability

Check Point 1-1

① There are 26 black cards.
$P = \frac{26}{52} = \frac{1}{2}$
② There are 12 face cards.
$P = \frac{12}{52} = \frac{3}{13}$
③ There are 4 "9" cards.
$P = \frac{4}{52} = \frac{1}{13}$
④ There are 20 of "9 or higher" cards.
$P = \frac{20}{52} = \frac{5}{13}$

Check Point 1-2

There are thirty-six(6×6) equally likely outcomes. Of these,
Sum of 4: (1,3),(2,2),(3,1)
Sum of 5: (1,4),(2,3),(3,2),(4,1)
There are 7 events in total. So the probability is $P = \frac{7}{36}$

Check Point 2

The probability of having an item made in U.S. from a blue box is $\frac{3}{8}$.
The probability of having an item made in U.S. from a red box is $\frac{5}{9}$.
So, the probability of having both items made in U.S. is
$P = \underbrace{\frac{3}{8}}_{Blue\ box} \cdot \underbrace{\frac{5}{9}}_{Red\ box} = \frac{15}{72} = \frac{5}{24}$

Check Point 3

① There are 11 marbles in total.
The probability of picking a blue marble on the first draw is $\frac{2}{11}$. Now we have 10 marbles in a box. So the probability of picking a green marble on the second draw is $\frac{4}{10}$. Now, the probability of picking a blue marble first and then a green marble is
$P = \underbrace{\frac{2}{11}}_{Blue} \cdot \underbrace{\frac{4}{10}}_{Green} = \frac{4}{55}$

② If the marble is returned to the box after the first draw, then there will be 11 marbles at the second draw.
So the probability is
$P = \underbrace{\frac{2}{11}}_{Blue} \cdot \underbrace{\frac{4}{11}}_{Green} = \frac{8}{121}$

Check Point 4

There are 26 black cards and 12 face cards. Of these, 6 cards are both black and face cards. So the probability is
$P = \underbrace{\frac{26}{52}}_{Black} + \underbrace{\frac{12}{52}}_{Face} - \underbrace{\frac{6}{52}}_{Both} = \frac{32}{52} = \frac{8}{13}$

Review Exercises

01

Prime numbers from 1~6 are 2, 3 and 5. There are 3 prime numbers. So the probability is $P = \frac{3}{6} = \frac{1}{2}$

02

There are thirty-six(6×6) equally likely outcomes. Of these,
Sum of 10: (4, 6), (5, 5), (6, 4)
Sum of 11: (5, 6), (6, 5); Sum of 12: (6, 6)
There are 6 events. So the probability is
$P = \frac{6}{36} = \frac{1}{6}$

03

There are 7 marbles in total. Without replacement,

(1) $P = \underbrace{\frac{2}{7}}_{Blue} \cdot \underbrace{\frac{1}{6}}_{Black} = \frac{1}{21}$

(2) $P = \underbrace{\frac{4}{7}}_{Brown} \cdot \underbrace{\frac{3}{6}}_{Brown} = \frac{2}{7}$

(3) Non-brown marbles are either blue or black marble. So the probability is

$P = \underbrace{\frac{3}{7}}_{Non-brown} \cdot \underbrace{\frac{2}{6}}_{Non-brown} = \frac{1}{7}$

04

There are 12 marbles in total. Without replacement,

$P = \underbrace{\frac{5}{12}}_{Black} \cdot \underbrace{\frac{4}{11}}_{Black} \cdot \underbrace{\frac{3}{10}}_{Black} = \frac{1}{22}$

05

A: Probability of snowing tomorrow: $\frac{25}{100}$

B: Probability of not snowing the day after tomorrow: $1 - \frac{20}{100} = \frac{80}{100}$

Since events A and B are independent,

$P = \frac{25}{100} \cdot \frac{80}{100} = \frac{1}{4} \cdot \frac{4}{5} = \frac{1}{5}$

06

$52 \times \frac{75}{100} = 39$ students are U.S. citizens.

The probability of selecting 1st U.S. citizen: $\frac{39}{52}$

The probability of selecting 2nd U.S. citizen: $\frac{38}{51}$

The probability of selecting 3rd U.S. citizen: $\frac{37}{50}$

The probability of selecting 4th U.S. citizen: $\frac{36}{49}$

So the probability that all 4 students are U.S. citizens is

$P = \frac{39}{52} \cdot \frac{38}{51} \cdot \frac{37}{50} \cdot \frac{36}{49} = \frac{6327}{20825} = 0.304$.

07

Since we are choosing 5 people out of 17 people, the number of combinations is

$_{17}C_5 = \frac{17!}{5!(17-5)!} = \frac{17!}{5!12!} = \frac{17 \cdot 16 \cdot 15 \cdot 14 \cdot 13}{5!} = 6,188$.

Of the 10 men, the number of the 3 men combination is

$_{10}C_3 = \frac{10!}{3!(10-3)!} = \frac{10!}{3!7!} = \frac{10 \cdot 9 \cdot 8}{3!} = 120$.

Of the 7 women, the number of the 2 women combination is

$_7C_2 = \frac{7!}{2!(7-2)!} = \frac{7!}{2!5!} = \frac{7 \cdot 6}{2!} = 21$.

So the probability is

$P = \frac{_{10}C_3 \cdot _7C_2}{_{17}C_5} = \frac{120 \cdot 21}{6188} = \frac{90}{221}$

08

Since we are choosing 5 marbles out of 9 marbles, the number of combinations is

$_9C_5 = \frac{9!}{2!(9-5)!} = \frac{9!}{5!4!} = \frac{9 \cdot 8 \cdot 7 \cdot 6}{4!} = 126$.

Of the 5 blue marbles, the number of the 3 blue marble combination is

$_5C_3 = \frac{4!}{2!(4-2)!} = \frac{4!}{2!2!} = 10$.

Of the 4 green marbles, the number of the 2 green marble combination is

$_4C_2 = \frac{5!}{3!(5-3)!} = \frac{5!}{3!2!} = 6$.

So the probability is

$P = \frac{_5C_3 \cdot _4C_2}{_9C_5} = \frac{10 \cdot 6}{126} = \frac{10}{21}$

09

Since Frank is having 15 problems out of 25 problems, the number of combinations is

$_{25}C_{15} = \frac{25!}{15!(25-15)!} = \frac{25!}{15!10!} = 3,268,760$.

(1) Of the 16 problems Frank knows, the number of the 15 problem combination is

$$_{16}C_{15} = \frac{16!}{15!(16-15)!} = \frac{16!}{15!1!} = 16.$$

So the probability is

$$P = \frac{_{16}C_{15}}{_{25}C_{15}} = \frac{16}{3,268,760} = \frac{2}{408,595}$$

(2) Of the 16 problems Frank knows, the number of the 14 problem combination is

$$_{16}C_{14} = \frac{16!}{14!(16-14)!} = \frac{16!}{14!2!} = 120.$$

Of the 9 problems Frank does not know, the number of the 1 problem combination is

$$_9C_1 = \frac{9!}{1!(9-1)!} = \frac{9!}{1!8!} = 9.$$

So the probability is

$$P = \frac{_{16}C_{14} \cdot _9C_1}{_{25}C_{15}} = \frac{120 \cdot 9}{3,268,760} = \frac{27}{81,719}$$

(3) At least 14 means 14 or 15 problems. So the probability is

$$P = \underbrace{\frac{_{16}C_{14} \cdot _9C_1}{_{25}C_{15}}}_{14 \ Problems} + \underbrace{\frac{_{16}C_{15}}{_{25}C_{15}}}_{15 \ Problems}$$

$$= \frac{27}{81,719} + \frac{2}{408,595} = \frac{137}{408,595}$$

10

The probability that John and Chris are correct and Jenny is wrong:

$$P = \frac{60}{100} \cdot \frac{75}{100} \cdot \frac{100-40}{100} = \frac{27}{10}.$$

The probability that John and Jenny are correct and Chris is wrong:

$$P = \frac{60}{100} \cdot \frac{100-75}{100} \cdot \frac{40}{100} = \frac{3}{50}.$$

The probability that Chris and Jenny are correct and John is wrong:

$$P = \frac{100-60}{10} \cdot \frac{75}{100} \cdot \frac{40}{100} = \frac{3}{25}.$$

The probability that all three of them are correct:

$$P = \frac{60}{100} \cdot \frac{75}{100} \cdot \frac{40}{100} = \frac{9}{50}.$$

So the probability of at least two people solving the question correctly is

$$P = \underbrace{\frac{27}{100} + \frac{3}{50} + \frac{3}{25}}_{exactly \ 2 \ are \ corrrect} + \underbrace{\frac{9}{50}}_{all \ 3 \ are \ correct} = \frac{63}{100}$$

Chapter 9 Test

01

(1) $\frac{2}{3}$, 1, $\frac{4}{3}$, $\frac{5}{3}$, $\cdots$ is an arithmetic sequence with $a_1=\frac{2}{3}$ and $d=\frac{1}{3}$.

$a_n=a_1+(n-1)d$, $a_n=\frac{2}{3}+(n-1)\left(\frac{1}{3}\right)$

$=\frac{1}{3}n+\frac{1}{3}$

$a_{10}=\frac{1}{3}\cdot 10+\frac{1}{3}=\frac{11}{3}$

(2) 1, 0.1, 0.01, 0.001, $\cdots$ is a geometric sequence with $a_1=1$ and $r=0.1$.

$a_n=ar^{n-1}$, $a_n=1\cdot(0.1)^{n-1}$

$a_{10}=1\cdot(0.1)^{10-1}=0.1^9$

02

$a_3=-2$, $a_{11}=-\frac{1}{6}$

$a_n=a_k+(n-k)d$

$a_{11}=a_3+(11-3)d$, $-\frac{1}{6}=-2+8d$, $d=\frac{11}{48}$

$a_n=a_1+(n-1)d$

$a_3=a_1+(3-1)d$, $-2=a_1+2\cdot\frac{11}{48}$, $a_1=-\frac{59}{24}$

03

$a_3=\frac{1}{32}$, $a_8=-1$

$a_n=a_k r^{n-k}$

$a_8=a_3 r^{8-3}$, $-1=\frac{1}{32}\cdot r^5$, $r=-2$

$a_n=a_1 r^{n-1}$

$a_3=a_1 r^{3-1}$, $\frac{1}{32}=a_1\cdot(-2)^2$, $a_1=\frac{1}{128}$

04

$a_n=\frac{1-5a_{n-1}}{2}$ and $a_1=1$

$a_2=\frac{1-5\cdot 1}{2}=-2$, $a_3=\frac{1-5(-2)}{2}=\frac{11}{2}$,

$a_4=\frac{1-5\cdot\frac{11}{2}}{2}=-\frac{53}{4}$

05

$\sum_{k=2}^{20}\frac{1}{4}\cdot\left(\frac{2}{3}\right)^{k-1}=\frac{1}{6}+\frac{1}{9}+\cdots+\frac{1}{4}\cdot\left(\frac{2}{3}\right)^{19}$

This is a geometric series with

$a_1=\frac{1}{6}$, $a_{19}=\frac{1}{4}\left(\frac{2}{3}\right)^{19}$, $r=\frac{2}{3}$ and $n=19$.

So the sum of 19 terms is

$S_n=a_1\left(\frac{1-r^n}{1-r}\right)$, $S_{19}=\frac{1}{6}\cdot\left(\frac{1-\left(\frac{2}{3}\right)^{19}}{1-\frac{2}{3}}\right)$

06

$a_6=28$, $a_{19}=119$; $n=35$

$a_n=a_k+(n-k)d$

$a_{19}=a_6+(19-6)d$, $119=28+13d$, $d=7$

$a_n=a_1+(n-1)d$

$a_6=a_1+(6-1)d$, $28=a_1+5(7)$, $a_1=-7$

So the sum of first 35 terms is

$S_n=\frac{n}{2}(2a_1+(n-1)d)$

$S_{35}=\frac{35}{2}(2(-7)+(35-1)(7))=3{,}920$

07

$a_3=-\frac{3}{64}$, $a_8=48$; $n=9$

$a_n=a_k r^{n-k}$

$a_8=a_3 r^{8-3}$, $48=\left(-\frac{3}{64}\right)\cdot r^5$, $r=-4$

$a_n=a_1 r^{n-1}$

$a_3=a_1 r^{3-1}$, $-\frac{3}{64}=a_1(-4)^2$, $a_1=-\frac{3}{1024}$

So the sum of first 9 terms is

$S_n=a_1\left(\frac{1-r^n}{1-r}\right)$, $S_9=\left(-\frac{3}{1024}\right)\left(\frac{1-(-4)^9}{1-(-4)}\right)$

08

(1) -50 -49 -48 -47 $\cdots$; $S_n=0$

This is an arithmetic series with $a_1=-50$, $d=1$.

$S_n=\frac{n}{2}(2a_1+(n-1)d)$

$0=\frac{n}{2}(2(-50)+(n-1)(1))$,

$0=n(-100+n-1)$

$n(n-101)=0$, $n=0$ or $n=101$

Solutions Manual

Since the number of terms must be positive integer, $n=101$.

(2) $1+4+16+64+\cdots$; $S_n=341$

This is a geometric series with $a_1=1$, $d=4$.

$S_n=a_1\left(\dfrac{1-r^n}{1-r}\right)$, $341=1\cdot\left(\dfrac{1-4^n}{1-4}\right)$

$-1023=1-4^n$, $4^n=1024$, $n=5$

09

$20-5+\dfrac{5}{4}-\dfrac{5}{16}+\cdots$ is an infinite geometric series with $a_1=20$ and $r=-\dfrac{1}{4}$. So

$20-5+\dfrac{5}{4}-\dfrac{5}{16}+\cdots=\dfrac{a_1}{1-r}=\dfrac{20}{1-\left(-\dfrac{1}{4}\right)}$

$=\dfrac{20}{\dfrac{5}{4}}=16$

10

(1) Let $a_1=8$ and $a_4=27$. If $8, x, y, 27$ is a geometric sequence, $a_4=a_1\cdot r^3$. So we have

$a_4=a_1\cdot r^3$

$27=8\cdot r^3$, $r^3=\dfrac{27}{8}$, $r=\dfrac{3}{2}$

Therefore, $x=8\cdot\dfrac{3}{2}=12$ and $y=12\cdot\dfrac{3}{2}=18$.

(2) Let $a_1=-2$ and $a_4=3$. If $-2, x, y, 3$ is an arithmetic sequence, $a_4=a_1+(4-1)d$.

So we have

$a_4=a_1+(4-1)d$

$3=-2+3d$, $3d=5$, $d=\dfrac{5}{3}$

Therefore,

$x=-2+\dfrac{5}{3}=-\dfrac{1}{3}$ and $y=-\dfrac{1}{3}+\dfrac{5}{3}=\dfrac{4}{3}$.

11

From 2019, the population will increase every year as follows:

Year 2019: $a_1=45000$

Year 2020: $a_2=45000(1.03)$

Year 2021: $a_3=45000(1.03)^2$

$\vdots$

Year 2029: $a_{11}=45000(1.03)^{10}=60476.2$

There will be approximately 60,476 people by 2029.

12

The average of first 320 positive integers is

$\dfrac{1+2+3+\cdots+320}{320}$.

Notice that $1+2+3+\cdots+320$ is an arithmetic series with $a_1=1$, $a_{320}=320$, and $n=320$. So the average is

$\dfrac{1+2+3+\cdots+320}{320}=\dfrac{\dfrac{n}{2}(a_1+a_{320})}{320}$

$=\dfrac{\dfrac{320}{2}(1+320)}{320}=160.5$

13

$a_1=11$, $a_2=15$, $a_3=19$ → This is an arithmetic series with $d=4$ and $S_n=980$.

$S_n=\dfrac{n}{2}(2a_1+(n-1)d)$

$980=\dfrac{n}{2}(2\cdot 11+(n-1)\cdot 4)$

$980=\dfrac{n}{2}(4n+18)$, $2n^2+9n-980=0$

$(n-20)(2n+49)=0$, $n=20$ or $n=-\dfrac{49}{2}$

Since the number of rows must be positive integer, $n=20$. There are 20 rows.

14

The order of choosing people to have two groups is not important. So, dividing 8 people into two groups of 3 people and 5 people can be thought of as a combination of $_8C_3$ or $_8C_5$.

$_8C_5={_8C_3}=\dfrac{8!}{3!(8-3)!}=\dfrac{8!}{3!5!}=\dfrac{8\cdot 7\cdot 6\cdot \cancel{5}\cdot \cancel{1}}{3\cdot 2\cdot 1\cdot \cancel{5}\cdot \cancel{1}}$

$=56$ ways.

15

The order of choosing employees for each position is not important. The combination of 5 servers from 10 employees is $_{10}C_5$.

Also, the combination of 3 hosts from the remaining 5 employees is $_5C_3$. Finally, the combination of 2 cashiers from the remaining 2 employees is $_2C_2$. Since all three events are independent, we have

$$_{10}C_5 \cdot {}_5C_3 \cdot {}_2C_2 = \frac{10!}{5!(10-5)!} \cdot \frac{5!}{3!(5-3)!} \cdot 1$$

$$= \frac{10!}{5!5!} \cdot \frac{5!}{3!2!}$$

$$= 252 \cdot 10 = 2,520 \text{ ways}$$

16

Let n be the number of teams. Since the two teams play 2 games during the season, the total number of games can be expressed in terms of the following combinations.

$2 \cdot {}_nC_2 = 90, \quad {}_nC_2 = 45$

$\dfrac{n!}{2!(n-2)!} = 45, \quad \dfrac{n(n-1)\cancel{(n-2)\cdots 1}}{2 \cdot 1 \cdot \cancel{(n-2)\cdots 1}} = 45$

$n(n-1) = 90, \quad n^2 - n - 90 = 0$

$(n+9)(n-10) = 0, \quad n = -9 \text{ or } n = 10$

Since the number of teams must be positive integer, $n = 10$. There are 10 teams.

17

The first selection requires choosing a letter from 2 choices, A or B. Then, since no letter can be repeated, the second selection requires choosing a letter from 1 choice. The same is true of third through fifth selection. By this principle, we have

$\underbrace{2 \cdot 1}_{2 \text{ letter}} \cdot \underbrace{5 \cdot 4 \cdot 3}_{3 \text{ dights}} = 120$ security codes.

18

The probability that Jenny will receive at least one of these shipments on Wednesday is equal to 1 minus the probability of not getting both the PC and the speaker on Wednesday. So we have

$P = 1 - (1 - 0.7) \cdot (1 - 0.8)$
$= 1 - (0.3)(0.7) = 0.79$

19

In the 6-sided dice, the primes are 2, 3, 5, and the odd numbers are 1, 3, 5. So, the probability of getting a prime number on the first roll and an odd number on the second roll is

$$P = \frac{3}{6} \cdot \frac{3}{6} = \frac{1}{2} \cdot \frac{1}{2} = \frac{1}{4}$$

memo

A well-structured workbook plays a critical role in students' learning experience!

CONCEPT & EXAMPLE ▸ **CHECK POINT** ▸ **REVIEW EXERCISE** ▸ **CHAPTER TEST**

Online Math Courses and Books
www.jmeducation.net

▶ YouTube Channel: "Math-Up PLUS"
https://youtube.com/@math-upplus

53410

9791197067068
ISBN 979-11-970670-6-8

JMEDU